The Presidency
and the Political System

The Presidency
and the Political System

NINTH EDITION

Michael Nelson, *Editor*
Rhodes College

A Division of SAGE
Washington, D.C.

CQ Press
2300 N Street, NW, Suite 800
Washington, DC 20037

Phone: 202-729-1900; toll-free, 1-866-4CQ-PRESS (1-866-427-7737)

Web: www.cqpress.com

Cover design: Paula Goldstein, Blue Bungalow Design
Composition: C&M Digitals (P) Ltd.

∞ The paper used in this publication exceeds the requirements of the American National Standard for Information Sciences—Permanence of Paper for Printed Library Materials, ANSI Z39.48–1992.

Printed and bound in the United States of America

13   12   11   10   09   1   2   3   4   5

Library of Congress Cataloging-in-Publication Data

The presidency and the political system / Michael Nelson, editor.—9th ed.
    p. cm.
  Includes index.
  ISBN 978-0-87289-964-3 (alk. paper)
1. Presidents—United States. I. Nelson, Michael

  JK516.P639 2009
  352.230973—dc22

                                                    2009023329

To my beloved wife, Linda.

She opens her mouth with wisdom,
and the teaching of kindness is on her tongue. . . .
Her children rise up and call her blessed;
her husband also, and he praises her.

PROVERBS 31:26, 28

Contents

Preface   ix

Contributors   xi

PART I   **APPROACHES TO THE PRESIDENCY**

✓   1   The Two Constitutional Presidencies   1   *57*
Jeffrey K. Tulis

2   Studying the Presidency: Why Presidents Need Political
Scientists   34
Lyn Ragsdale

PART II   **ELEMENTS OF PRESIDENTIAL POWER**

(✓)   3   The Presidency in the Eye of the Storm   68
Marc Landy and Sidney M. Milkis

✓   4   Presidential Competence   108   *136*
Paul J. Quirk

✓   5   The Psychological Presidency   142   *170*
Michael Nelson

PART III   **PRESIDENTIAL SELECTION**

✓   6   The Presidency and the Nominating Process: *195*
Politics and Power   167
Richard M. Pious

(✓)   7   The Faulty Premises of the Electoral College   192
George C. Edwards III

PART IV   **PRESIDENTS AND POLITICS**

✓   8   The Presidential Spectacle   210   *255*
Bruce Miroff

✓ 9 The Presidency and the Press: The Paradox of the White House Communications War 236 *283*
Lawrence R. Jacobs

10 The Presidency and Interest Groups: Allies, Adversaries, and Policy Leadership 264 *311*
Daniel J. Tichenor

11 The Presidency and Political Parties 295 *341*
Sidney M. Milkis

PART V PRESIDENTS AND GOVERNMENT

12 The Institutional Presidency 341 *383*
John P. Burke

13 The Presidency and the Bureaucracy: The Levers of Presidential Control 367 *(410)*
David E. Lewis and Terry M. Moe

14 The President and Congress 401 *455*
Matthew J. Dickinson

15 The Presidency and the Judiciary 435 *481*
David A. Yalof

16 The Presidency and Unilateral Power: A Taxonomy 463
Andrew Rudalevige

17 The Presidency at War: Unchecked Power, Uncertain Leadership 489 *557*
Andrew J. Polsky

18 The Vice Presidency: Dick Cheney, Joe Biden, and the New Vice Presidency 509
Joseph A. Pika

Index 535

Preface

Twenty-five years have passed since the first edition of this book was published. The book's goal then and ever since has been to match the most important topics concerning the presidency with the best contemporary scholarship in ways that are accessible and interesting to every student of the office. Apparently this goal has been achieved: in a 2007 Hauenstein Center for Presidential Studies survey of books used in courses on the American presidency, *The Presidency and the Political System* ranked first.

The passage of time affects this book in another way. Every syllabus for a college course notes the term and year the course is offered, usually at the top of the first page. In many academic disciplines, this is simply a clerical entry: it really doesn't matter all that much whether you take Spanish or calculus in fall 2010 or spring 2012. Time matters immensely, however, in a course on the American presidency. Indeed, what makes political science so interesting is that its subject (succinctly described by political scientist Harold D. Lasswell as "who gets what, when, and how") refuses to stand still. This observation applies especially to the presidency, in which the nature of the institution is so closely intertwined with that of the person who, at any given moment, occupies it.

Consider the most important developments in the three years since this book's eighth edition was published: the end of the George W. Bush presidency, the historic election of 2008 between Sen. Barack Obama of Illinois and Sen. John McCain of Arizona, and the early months of the Obama presidency. All of these political developments and more, along with the new contributions to the flourishing scholarly literature on the presidency and the political system they have inspired, are treated fully in this ninth edition. The book's eighteen chapters are organized into five parts: Approaches to the Presidency, Elements of Presidential Power, Presidential Selection, Presidents and Politics, and Presidents and Government.

To note that the authors have taken recent developments into account is not to say that this is merely a "current events" book—far from it. The presidency is an office with deep roots in history, shaped by decisions that were made at the Constitutional Convention of 1787 and by more than two centuries of change in the American political system since its founding. The presidency also is shaped by the history and current functioning of the myriad parts of the political system, such as Congress, the courts, the bureaucracy, interest groups, the media, public opinion, the electoral process, and the party system. This broader understanding of the presidency underlies all of the analyses of more recent events that the writers present.

The most noteworthy addition to the ninth edition is the roster of new contributors: George C. Edwards III, Marc Landy, Terry Moe, Joseph Pika, and Lyn Ragsdale. Topically, this edition devotes greater attention to unilateral presidential powers, the vice presidency, and what presidents can learn from political scientists.

I do not agree with everything that every author has to say in this book; nor will any reader. But together the contributors constitute an all-star team of presidential scholars, and the intellectual substance of the chapters is fully matched by their readability. Through eight previous editions, this book has been widely assigned in courses and extensively cited and reviewed in scholarly books and articles. Students may be assured of receiving the most comprehensive understanding of the presidency, and scholars will continue to find the essays valuable in conducting their research.

I am deeply grateful to those who helped in the preparation of the ninth edition, the authors first and foremost and also Jason McMann, Amy Marks, and Lorna Notsch of CQ Press. Susan Sullivan and Jean Woy, formerly of Congressional Quarterly, and Erwin C. Hargrove of Vanderbilt University helped me to think through the themes and organization of the first edition, and Barbara de Boinville served as a helpful editor. Joanne Daniels, Nola Healy Lynch, and Tracy White contributed mightily to the second edition, as did Nancy Lammers, Kristen Carpenter Stoever, and Ann O'Malley to the third. Every edition since then has enjoyed the gentle guiding hands of Brenda Carter and Charisse Kiino. The fourth and fifth editions also benefited from the work of Joanne Ainsworth and Talia Greenberg, as did the sixth edition from the contributions of Gwenda Larsen, Belinda Josey, and Debbie K. Hardin, and the seventh edition, from the contributions of Carolyn Goldinger, Elizabeth Jones, and Belinda Josey. Nancy Geltman, Anna Socrates, and Colleen Ganey contributed skillfully to the eighth edition. Finally, I appreciate the helpful insights of the seven reviewers whose judgments we sought in preparing the ninth edition: William Adler, Hunter College, City University of New York; Bruce Altschuler, State University of New York at Oswego; Napp Nazworth, Southern Charleston University; Steven Schier, Carleton College; Keith Smith, University of California, Davis; Margaret Thompson, Syracuse University; and Heather Trela, University at Albany, SUNY.

Michael Nelson

Contributors

JOHN P. BURKE is professor of political science at the University of Vermont. His most recent book is *Honest Broker? The National Security Advisor and Presidential Decision Making* (2009). He is also author of *Becoming President: The Bush Transition 2000–2003* (2004), *The Institutional Presidency: Organizing and Managing the White House from FDR to Bill Clinton* (2000), *Presidential Transitions: From Politics to Practice* (2000), *The Institutional Presidency* (1992), and *Bureaucratic Responsibility* (1986). He is coauthor of *Advising Ike: The Memoirs of Attorney General Herbert Brownell* (1993) and *How Presidents Test Reality: Decisions on Vietnam 1954 and 1965* (1989), which won the 1990 Richard E. Neustadt Award from the American Political Science Association for the best book on the presidency.

MATTHEW J. DICKINSON is professor of political science at Middlebury College. His blog on presidential power can be found at http://blogs.middle bury.edu/presidentialpower. He is author of *Bitter Harvest: FDR, Presidential Power, and the Growth of the Presidential Branch* (1999) and has published numerous articles on the presidency, presidential decision making, and presidential advisers. His current book manuscript, titled *The President and the White House Staff: People, Positions and Processes, 1945–2008*, examines the growth of presidential staff in the post–World War II era.

GEORGE C. EDWARDS III is Distinguished Professor of Political Science at Texas A&M University and holds the Jordan Chair in Presidential Studies. A leading scholar of the presidency, he has written or edited twenty-three books on American politics. He is also editor of *Presidential Studies Quarterly* and general editor of the Oxford Handbook of American Politics series. Among his latest books, *On Deaf Ears: The Limits of the Bully Pulpit* (2003) examines the effectiveness of presidential leadership on public opinion; *Why the Electoral College Is Bad for America* (2005) evaluates the consequences of the method of electing the president; *Governing by Campaigning* (2007) analyzes the politics of the George W. Bush presidency; and *The Strategic President* (2009) offers a new formulation for understanding presidential leadership. Professor Edwards has served as president of the Presidency Research Group of the American Political Science Association, which has named its annual Dissertation Prize in his honor and awarded him its Career Service Award.

LAWRENCE R. JACOBS is the Walter F. and Joan Mondale Chair for Political Studies and Director of the Center for the Study of Politics and Governance in the Hubert H. Humphrey Institute and Department of Political Science at the University of Minnesota. In addition to engaging in a wide range of public activities, Jacobs coedits the Chicago Series in American Politics for the University of Chicago Press and has published five scholarly books, including *Healthy, Wealthy, and Fair* (with James Morone, 2005); *Inequality and American Democracy* (with Theda Skocpol, 2005); and *Politicians Don't Pander: Political Manipulation and the Loss of Democratic Responsiveness* (with Robert Y. Shapiro, 2000). He has also authored numerous articles in *American Political Science Review, World Politics, Comparative Politics, Journal of Politics, Public Opinion Quarterly, Presidential Studies Quarterly,* and other scholarly outlets.

MARC LANDY is professor of political science at Boston College. He and Sidney M. Milkis wrote *Presidential Greatness* (2000) and *American Government: Balancing Democracy and Rights* (2008). His essay "Great Presidents Are Agents of Democratic Change" was published in Richard Ellis and Michael Nelson's edited volume *Debating the Presidency* (2006). In addition to writing about the presidency, he also writes about federalism, public policy, and the environment. His article "Mega-Disasters and Federalism" was published in *Public Administration Review* (October 2008). He is coauthor of *The Environmental Protection Agency: Asking the Right Questions: From Nixon to Clinton* (1994) and coeditor of *Creating Competitive Markets: The Politics of Regulatory Reform* (2007), *Seeking the Center: Politics and Policymaking at the New Century* (2001), and *The New Politics of Public Policy* (1995).

DAVID E. LEWIS is professor of political science and law (by courtesy) at Vanderbilt University. His research interests include the presidency, executive branch politics, and public administration. He is author of *Presidents and the Politics of Agency Design* (2003) and numerous articles on American politics, public administration, and public management. His new book, *The Politics of Presidential Appointments: Political Control and Bureaucratic Performance* (2008), analyzes the causes and consequences of presidential politicization of the executive branch. Current projects explore the political views of government agencies and their employees, the politics of presidential appointments, and various aspects of public sector management performance.

SIDNEY M. MILKIS is the White Burkett Miller Professor of the Department of Politics and assistant director for academic programs at the Miller Center of Public Affairs at the University of Virginia. His books include *The President and Parties: The Transformation of the American Party System Since the New Deal* (1993); *Political Parties and Constitutional Government: Remaking American Democracy* (1999); *Presidential Greatness* (with coauthor Marc Landy, 2000); *The American Presidency: Origins and Development, 1776–2007* (with coauthor Michael Nelson, 2007); and *Theodore Roosevelt, the Progressive Party, and the Transformation of American Democracy* (2009). He is coeditor, with Jerome Mileur, of three volumes on twentieth-century political reform: *Progressivism and the New Democracy* (1999), *The New Deal and the Triumph of Liberalism* (2002), and *The Great Society and the High Tide of Liberalism* (2005).

BRUCE MIROFF is professor of political science and a Collins Fellow at SUNY Albany. He has published numerous articles and books on the presidency, political leadership, American political development, and American political theory. His most recent book is *The Liberals' Moment: The McGovern Insurgency and the Identity Crisis of the Democratic Party* (2007).

TERRY M. MOE is the William Bennett Monroe Professor of Political Science and a senior fellow at the Hoover Institution. He has written extensively on polit-ical institutions, public bureaucracy, and the presidency. His work includes "The New Economics of Organization," "The Politicized Presidency," "The Politics of Bureaucratic Structure," "Presidents, Institutions, and Theory," "The Presidential Power of Unilateral Action" (with William Howell), and "Power and Political Institutions." He has also done influential work on the politics, institutions, and performance of public education, including *Politics, Markets, and America's Schools* (1990) and *Liberating Learning: Technology, Politics, and the Future of American Education* (2009), both with John E. Chubb.

MICHAEL NELSON is the Fulmer Professor of Political Science at Rhodes College and a senior fellow of the Miller Center of Public Affairs at the University of Virginia. More than fifty of his articles have been anthologized in works of political science, history, sociology, and English composition, and he has won national writing awards for articles on music and baseball. His recent books include *The Elections of 2008*; *The American Presidency: Origins and Development, 1776–2007* (with Sidney M. Milkis); and *How the South Joined the Gambling Nation: The Politics of State Policy Innovation* (with John Mason), which won the Southern Political Science Association's V. O. Key Award for the

Outstanding Book on Southern Politics. He edits the American Presidential Elections book series for the University Press of Kansas and is currently working on books about the 1968 election and West Point.

JOSEPH A. PIKA is the James R. Soles Professor of Political Science and International Relations at the University of Delaware. His research concentrates on the American presidency, Delaware politics, and education policy. He has published *Politics of the Presidency*, 7th ed. (with John Maltese, 2008) and *Confrontation and Compromise: Presidential and Congressional Leadership, 2001–2006* (with Jason Mycoff, 2007). He is currently working on a coauthored American government textbook to be published by McGraw-Hill in 2010 (with John Maltese and Phil Shively). His extensive public service has included eight years on the Delaware State Board of Education, with a term as president.

RICHARD M. PIOUS is the Adolph and Effie Ochs Professor at Barnard College and professor at the Graduate School of Arts and Sciences at Columbia University. His scholarly books include *The American Presidency* (1979); *The President, Congress and the Constitution* (1984); *Why Presidents Fail* (2008); and a book of cases and materials, *The War on Terrorism and the Rule of Law* (2006). He edited a ten-volume series of classic editions in public, comparative, and international law and has published articles in many anthologies, as well as in *Political Science Quarterly, The Wisconsin Law Review, Journal of International Affairs, Journal of Armed Forces and Society*, and *Presidential Studies Quarterly*. He has coauthored a widely used print and online reference work, *The Oxford Guide to American Government*. Pious has lectured on war powers at the U.S. Military Academy at West Point, at universities in the United States and Canada, and at seminars in the Far East organized by the government of Taiwan; he has lectured on presidential power and the war on terrorism at Oxford University and the British Library. He has served as a senior consultant to the Foreign Ministry of the Government of Japan since 1994. Pious is on the editorial advisory board of *Presidential Studies Quarterly* and served on the foreign experts panel of the *Journal des Élections*.

ANDREW J. POLSKY is professor of political science at Hunter College and the Graduate Center, CUNY, and editor of *Polity*. He is author of *The Rise of the Therapeutic State* (1991). A scholar of American political development, Polsky's current research focuses on partisan coalitions in American politics, wartime presidential leadership, and relations among political institutions during military conflicts. His articles have appeared in such journals as *Studies in American Political Development, American Politics Research, Journal of Theoretical Politics, Polity,* and *Political Science Quarterly.* He has also written a piece on publishing in political science journals that has been reprinted in the American Political Science Association's *Publishing Political Science: APSA Guide to Writing and Publishing* (2008).

PAUL J. QUIRK holds the Phil Lind Chair in U.S. Politics and Representation at the University of British Columbia. He has held faculty appointments at several American universities. He has published widely on the presidency, Congress, public opinion, and public policymaking. Among his many awards, he received the Aaron Wildavsky Enduring Contribution Award of the Public Policy Section of the American Political Science Association and the Brownlow Book Award of the National Academy of Public Administration. He serves on the editorial boards of several scholarly journals, including *American Political Science Review.* Among recent works, he coedited *Institutions of American Democracy: The Legislative Branch* (2005) and coauthored *Deliberative Choices: Debating Public Policy in Congress* (2006). He is working on a book-length study of the presidency and Congress as policymaking institutions.

LYN RAGSDALE is dean of Social Sciences at Rice University—the first woman to hold this position at the institution. She is also the Radoslav Tsanoff Professor of Public Affairs and professor of political science. Previously she was the head of the Political Science Department at the University of Illinois at Chicago from 2001 to 2006, after having been on the faculty of the University of Arizona for twenty years. She is a past president of the Western Political Science Association and has served as editor of *Political Research Quarterly.* She has written four books and numerous articles on the American presidency and electoral behavior. Her most recent book, *Vital Statistics on the Presidency,* was published in its third edition this year. Her current research is about the major decisions of American presidents and American nonvoters.

ANDREW RUDALEVIGE is associate professor of political science at Dickinson College. His books as author and editor include *The George W. Bush Legacy* (2008), *The New Imperial Presidency: Renewing Presidential Power after Watergate* (2005), and *Managing the President's Program* (2002), the last of which won the American Political Science Association's Richard E. Neustadt Award as that year's best book on the presidency. In 2008–2009, he directed Dickinson's program in the United Kingdom as visiting professor in the School of American Studies at the University of East Anglia in Norwich, England.

DANIEL J. TICHENOR is the Phillip H. Knight Professor of Social Science and Senior Faculty Fellow at the Wayne Morse Center for Law and Politics at the University of Oregon. He is editor of *A History of the American Political System: Ideas, Interests and Institutions* (2009) and *The Oxford Handbook on International Migration* (forthcoming). He is author of *Dividing Lines: The Politics of Immigration Control in America* (2002), which won the American Political Science Association's Gladys M. Kammerer Award for the best book in American public policy. He also received the Jack Walter Prize and the Mary Parker Follett Award for publications on interest groups and social movements in American political development. His forthcoming works include *Faustian Bargains: The Origins and Development of America's Illegal Immigration Dilemma* and *Abiding Interests: The Washington Lobbying Community*. He has been a Faculty Scholar at the Center for the Study of Democratic Politics at Princeton University, a Research Fellow at the Brookings Institution, and the Abba Schwartz Fellow at the John F. Kennedy Presidential Library. He is completing a book on liberty, democracy, and the prerogative presidency during the Civil War, World War I, World War II, the Cold War, and the war on terror.

JEFFREY K. TULIS teaches American politics and political theory at the University of Texas at Austin. He recently published *The Constitutional Presidency*, coedited with Joseph M. Bessette (2009). He is currently completing *The Limits of Constitutional Democracy*, coedited with Stephen Macedo; *Legacies of Loss in American Politics*, coauthored with Nicole Mellow; and a book on congressional abdication, *The Politics of Deference*. A special retrospective issue of the journal *Critical Review* (Spring 2008) offers articles by seventeen scholars on his book *The Rhetorical Presidency*.

DAVID A. YALOF is associate professor of political science at the University of Connecticut. His first book, *Pursuit of Justices: Presidential Politics and the Selection of Supreme Court Nominees*, won the 1999 Richard E. Neustadt Award as the best book on the presidency from the American Political Science Association's Presidency Research Group. He is coauthor of *The First Amendment and the Media in the Court of Public Opinion* (2002) and *The Future of the First Amendment* (2008). His articles on connections between the branches of government have appeared in, among other publications, *Political Research Quarterly*, *Judicature*, and *Constitutional Commentary*. He is currently completing a book examining how and why the Supreme Court overrules its own precedents.

The Presidency
and the Political System

1 The Two Constitutional Presidencies

Jeffrey K. Tulis

The formal design of the presidency can be found in Article II of the Constitution. Yet, according to Jeffrey K. Tulis, two constitutional presidencies exist. One is the enduring, capital C version that the Framers invented at the Constitutional Convention of 1787, the formal provisions of which remain substantially unaltered. The other is the adapted, lowercase c constitution that Woodrow Wilson devised and that most presidents during the past century have followed. Sometimes the fit between the formal and informal constitutional presidencies is close—for example, in the months following the September 11, 2001, terrorist attacks on the United States. But, Tulis argues, the two constitutional presidencies usually are in tension. Both constitutions value "energy" in the presidency, but the exercise of popular rhetorical leadership that is proscribed by the Framers' Constitution is prescribed by Wilson's. As a result, Tulis concludes, "many of the dilemmas and frustrations of the modern presidency may be traced to the president's ambiguous constitutional station, a vantage place composed of conflicting elements."

The modern presidency is buffeted by two "constitutions." Presidential action continues to be constrained, and presidential behavior shaped, by the institutions created by the original Constitution. The core structures established in 1789 and debated during the founding era remain essentially unchanged. For the most part, later amendments to the Constitution have left intact the basic features of the executive, legislative, and judicial branches of government. Great questions, such as the merits of unity or plurality in the executive, have not been seriously reopened. Because most of the structure persists, it seems plausible that the theory on which the presidency was constructed remains relevant to its current functioning.[1]

Presidential and public understanding of the constitutional system, and of the president's place in it, has changed, however. This new understanding is the "second constitution" under which presidents attempt to govern. Central to this second constitution is a view of statecraft that is in tension with the original Constitution—indeed it is opposed to the Founders' understanding of the presidency's place in the political system. The second constitution, which puts a premium on active and continuous presidential leadership of popular opinion, is buttressed by several institutional, albeit extraconstitutional, developments. These include the proliferation of presidential primaries as a mode of selection and the emergence of the mass media as a pervasive force.[2]

Many of the dilemmas and frustrations of the modern presidency may be traced to the president's ambiguous constitutional station, a vantage place composed of conflicting elements. This chapter lays bare the theoretical core of each of the two constitutions to highlight those elements that are in tension between them.

To uncover the principles that underlie the original Constitution, I rely heavily on *The Federalist*. A set of papers justifying the Constitution, the text was written by three of the Constitution's most articulate proponents, Alexander Hamilton, James Madison, and John Jay. The purpose of this journey back to the Founders is not to point to their authority or to lament change; nor do I mean to imply that all the supporters of the Constitution agreed with each of their arguments. *The Federalist* does represent, however, the most coherent articulation of the implications of, and interconnections among, the principles and practices that were generally accepted when the Constitution was ratified.[3]

I explore the political thought of Woodrow Wilson to outline the principles of the second constitution. Wilson self-consciously attacked *The Federalist* in his writings; as president he tried to act according to the dictates of his reinterpretation of the American political system. Presidents have continued to follow his example, and presidential scholars tend to repeat his arguments. Most presidents have not thought through the issues Wilson discussed—they are too busy for that. But if pushed and questioned, modern presidents would probably (and occasionally do) justify their behavior with arguments that echo Wilson's. Just as *The Federalist* represents the deepest and most coherent articulation of understandings of the presidency held through the nineteenth century, Wilson offers the most comprehensive theory in support of contemporary impulses and practices.

The Founding Perspective

Perhaps the most striking feature of the founding perspective, particularly in comparison with contemporary political analyses, is its synoptic character. The

Founders' task was to create a whole government, one in which the executive would play an important part, but only a part. By contrast, contemporary scholars of American politics often study institutions individually and therefore tend to be partisans of "their institution" in its contests with other actors in American politics.[4] Presidency scholars often restrict their inquiries to the strategic concerns of presidents as they quest for power. Recovering the founding perspective provides a way to think about the systemic legitimacy and utility of presidential power as well. To uncover such a synoptic vision, one must range widely in search of the principles that guided or justified the Founders' view of the executive. Some of these principles are discussed most thoroughly in *The Federalist* in the context of other institutions, such as Congress or the judiciary.

The Founders' general and far-reaching institutional analysis was preceded by a more fundamental decision of enormous import. Federalists and Anti-Federalists alike sought a government devoted to limited ends. In contrast to polities that attempt to shape the souls of their citizenry and foster certain excellences or moral qualities by penetrating deeply into the "private" sphere, the Founders wanted their government to be limited to establishing and securing such a sphere. Politics would extend only to the tasks of protecting individual rights and fostering liberty for the exercise of those rights. Civic virtue would still be necessary, but it would be elicited from the people rather than imposed on them.

Proponents and critics of the Constitution agreed about the proper ends of government, but they disagreed over the best institutional means to secure them.[5] Some critics of the Constitution worried that its institutions would undermine its limited liberal ends. Although these kinds of arguments were settled politically by the Federalist victory, *The Federalist* concedes that they were not resolved fundamentally because they continued as problems built into the structure of American politics.

Is a vigorous executive consistent with the genius of republican government? Hasty readers of *The Federalist* think yes, unequivocally. Closer reading of *The Federalist* reveals a deeper ambivalence regarding the compatibility of executive power and republican freedom.[6]

Demagoguery

The Founders worried especially about the danger that a powerful executive might pose to the system if power were derived from the role of popular leader.[7] For most Federalists, "demagogue" and "popular leader" were synonyms, and nearly all references to popular leaders in their writings are pejorative. Demagoguery, combined with majority tyranny, was regarded as the peculiar vice to which democracies were susceptible. Although much historical evidence supported this insight, the Founders were made more acutely aware of the problem by the presence in their own midst of popular leaders such as Daniel Shays, who led an insurrection in Massachusetts. The Founders' preoccupation with demagoguery may appear today as quaint, yet it may be that we do not fear it today because the Founders were so successful in institutionally proscribing some forms of it.

The original Greek meaning of *demagogue* was simply "leader of the people," and the term was applied in premodern times to champions of the people's claim to rule as against that of aristocrats and monarchs. As James Ceaser pointed out, the term has been more characteristically applied to a certain quality of leadership—that which attempts to sway popular passions. Because most speech contains a mix of rational and passionate appeals, it is difficult to specify demagoguery with precision. But as Ceaser argued, one cannot ignore the phenomenon because it is difficult to define, suggesting that it possesses at least enough intuitive clarity that few would label Dwight Eisenhower, for example, a demagogue, whereas most would not hesitate to so label Joseph McCarthy. The main characteristic of demagoguery seems to be an excess of passionate appeals. Ceaser categorized demagogues according to the kinds of passions that are summoned, dividing these into "soft" and "hard" types.

The soft demagogue tends to flatter constituents "by claiming that they know what is best, and makes a point of claiming his closeness (to them) by manner or gesture."[8] Hard demagogues attempt to create or encourage divisions among the people to build and maintain their constituency. Typically this sort of appeal uses extremist rhetoric that panders to fear. James Madison worried about the possibility of class appeals that would pit the poor against the wealthy. But the hard demagogue might appeal to a very different passion. "Excessive encouragement of morality and hope" might be employed to create a division between those alleged to be compassionate, moral, or progressive, and those thought insensitive, selfish, or backward. Hard demagogues may be of the right or the left.[9]

Demagogues can also be classified by their object, in which case the issue becomes more complicated. Demagoguery might be good if it were a means to a good end, such as preservation of a decent nation or successful prosecution of a just war. The difficulty is to ensure by institutional means that demagoguery would be used only for good ends and not simply to satisfy the overweening ambition of an immoral leader or potential tyrant. How are political structures created that permit demagoguery when appeals to passion are needed but proscribe it for normal politics?

The Founders did not have a straightforward answer to this problem, perhaps because there is no unproblematic institutional solution. Instead, they addressed it indirectly in two ways: they attempted both to narrow the range of acceptable demagogic appeals through the architectonic act of founding itself and to mitigate the effects of such appeals in the day-to-day conduct of governance through the particular institutions they created. The Founders did not choose to make provision for the institutional encouragement of demagoguery in time of crisis, refusing to adopt, for example, the Roman model of constitutional dictatorship for emergencies.[10] Behind their indirect approach may have been the thought that excessive ambition needs no institutional support and the faith that in extraordinary circumstances popular rhetoric, even forceful demagoguery, would gain legitimacy through the pressure of necessity.

Many references in *The Federalist* and in the ratification debates over the Constitution warn of demagogues of the hard variety who through divisive appeals would aim at tyranny. *The Federalist* literally begins and ends with this issue. In the final paper Hamilton offered "a lesson of moderation to all sincere lovers of the Union [that] ought to put them on their guard against hazarding anarchy, civil war, a perpetual alienation of the states from each other, and perhaps the military despotism of a victorious demagogue."[11] The Founders' concern with hard demagoguery was not merely a rhetorical device designed to facilitate passage of the Constitution. It also reveals a concern to address the kinds of divisions and issues exploited by hard demagoguery. From this perspective, the founding can be understood as an attempt to settle the large issue of whether the one, few, or many ruled (in favor of the many "through" a constitution); to reconfirm the limited purposes of government (security, prosperity, and the protection of rights); and, thereby, to give effect to the distinction between public and private life. At the founding these large questions were still matters of political dispute. Hamilton argued that adopting the Constitution would settle these perennially divisive questions for Americans, replacing those questions with smaller, less-contentious issues. Hamilton called this new American politics a politics of "administration," distinguishing it from the traditional politics of disputed ends. If politics was transformed and narrowed in this way, thought Hamilton, demagogues would be deprived of part of their once-powerful arsenal of rhetorical weapons because certain topics would be rendered illegitimate for public discussion. By constituting an American understanding of politics, the founding would also reconstitute the problem of demagoguery.[12]

If the overriding concern about demagoguery in the extraordinary period before the ratification of the Constitution was to prevent social disruption, division, and possibly tyranny, the concerns expressed through the Constitution for normal times were broader: to create institutions that would be most likely to generate and execute good policy and resist bad policy. Underlying the institutional structures and powers the Constitution created are three principles designed to address this broad concern: representation, independence of the executive, and separation of powers.

Representation

As the Founders realized, the problem with any simple distinction between good and bad law is that it is difficult to provide clear criteria to distinguish the two in any particular instance. It will not do to suggest that in a democracy good legislation reflects the majority will. A majority may tyrannize a minority, violating its rights; and even a nontyrannical majority may be a foolish one, preferring policies that do not further its interests. These considerations lay behind the Founders' distrust of "direct" or "pure" democracy.[13]

Yet an alternative understanding—that legislation is good if it objectively furthers the limited ends of the polity—is also problematic. It is perhaps impossible to assess the "interests" of a nation without giving significant attention to what the citizenry considers its interests to be. This concern lay behind the Founders' animus toward monarchy and aristocracy.[14] Identifying and embodying the proper weight to be given popular opinion and its appropriate institutional reflections constitute one of the characteristic problems of democratic constitutionalism. The Founders' understanding of republicanism as representative government reveals this problem and the Constitution's attempted solution.

Practically, the Founders attempted to accommodate these two requisites of good government by four devices. First, they established popular election as the fundamental basis of the Constitution and of the government's legitimacy. They modified that requirement by allowing "indirect" selection for some institutions (for example, the Senate, Supreme Court, and presidency)—that is, selection by others who were themselves chosen by the people. With respect to the president, the Founders wanted to elicit the "sense of the people," but they feared an inability to do so if the people acted in a "collective capacity." They worried that the dynamics of mass politics would at best produce poorly qualified presidents and at worst open the door to demagoguery and regime instability. At the same time, the Founders wanted to give popular opinion a greater role in presidential selection than it would have if Congress chose the executive. The institutional solution to these concerns was the Electoral College, originally designed as a semiautonomous locus of decision for presidential selection and chosen by state legislatures at each election.[15]

Second, the Founders established differing lengths of tenure for officeholders in the major national institutions, which corresponded to the institutions' varying "proximity" to the people. House members were to face reelection every two years, making them more responsive to constituent pressure than members of the other national institutions. The president was given a four-year term, sufficient time, it was thought, to "contribute to the firmness of the executive" without justifying "any alarm for the public liberty."[16]

Third, the Founders derived the authority and formal power of the institutions and their officers ultimately from the people but immediately from the Constitution. The effect would be to insulate officials from day-to-day currents of public opinion, while allowing assertion of deeply felt and widely shared public opinion through constitutional amendment.

Fourth, the Founders envisioned that the extent of the nation itself would insulate governing officials from sudden shifts of public opinion. In his well-known arguments for an extended republic, Madison reasoned that large size would improve democracy by making the formation of majority factions difficult. But again, argued Madison, the extent of the territory and diversity of factions would not prevent the formation of a majority if the issue was an important one.[17]

The brakes on public opinion, not the provision for its influence, are what cause skepticism today.[18] Because popular leadership is so central to modern theories of the presidency, the rationale behind the Founders' distrust of "direct democracy" should be noted specifically. This issue was raised dramatically in *The Federalist* no. 49, in which Madison addressed Jefferson's suggestion that "whenever two of the three branches of government shall concur in [the] opinion . . . that a convention is necessary for altering the Constitution, *or correcting breaches of it,* a convention shall be called for the purpose." Madison recounted Jefferson's reasoning: because the Constitution was formed by the people, it rightfully ought to be modified by them. Madison admitted "that a constitutional road to the decision of the people ought to be marked out and kept open for great and extraordinary occasions." But he objected to bringing directly to the people disputes among the branches about the extent of their authority. In the normal course of governance, such disputes could be expected to arise fairly often. In our day they would include, for example, the war powers controversy, the impoundment controversy, and the issue of executive privilege.

Madison objected to recourse to "the people" on three basic grounds. First, popular appeals would imply "some defect" in the government: "Frequent appeals would, in great measure, deprive the government of that veneration which time bestows on everything, and without which perhaps the wisest and freest governments would not possess the requisite stability." *The Federalist* pointed to the institutional benefits of popular veneration—stability of government and the enhanced authority of its constitutional officers. Second, the tranquility of the society as a whole might be disturbed. Madison expressed the fear that an enterprising demagogue might reopen disputes over "great national questions" in a political context less favorable to their resolution than the Constitutional Convention.

Third, Madison voiced "the greatest objection of all" to frequent appeals to the people: "The decisions which would probably result from such appeals would not answer the purpose of maintaining the constitutional equilibrium of government." Chief executives might face political difficulties if frequent appeals to the people were permitted because other features of the office (its singularity, independence, and executive powers) would leave presidents at a rhetorical disadvantage in contests with the legislature. Presidents will be "generally the objects of jealousy and their administrations . . . liable to be discolored and rendered unpopular," Madison argued. "The Members of the legislatures on the other hand are numerous. . . . Their connections of blood, of friendship, and of acquaintance embrace a great proportion of the most influential part of society. The nature of their public trust implies a personal influence among the people."[19]

Madison realized that there may be circumstances "less adverse to the executive and judiciary departments." If the executive power were "in the hands of a peculiar favorite of the people . . . the public decision might be less swayed in favor of the [legislature]. But still it could never be expected to turn on the true merits of the question." The ultimate reason for the rejection of "frequent popular appeals" is that they would undermine *deliberation* and result in bad public policy:

The *passions,* therefore, not the *reason,* of the public would sit in judgment. But it is the reason, alone, of the public, that ought to control and regulate the government. The passions ought to be controlled and regulated by the government.[20]

There are two frequent misunderstandings of the Founders' opinion on the deliberative function of representation. The first is that they naively believed that deliberation constituted the whole of legislative politics—that there would be no bargaining, logrolling, or nondeliberative rhetorical appeals. The discussions of Congress in *The Federalist* nos. 52 to 68 and in the Constitutional Convention debates reveal quite clearly that the Founders understood that the legislative process would involve a mixture of these elements. The founding task was to create an institutional context that made deliberation most likely, not to assume that it would occur "naturally" or, even in the best of legislatures, predominantly.[21]

The second common error, prevalent in leading historical accounts of the period, is to interpret the deliberative elements of the Founders' design as an attempt to rid the legislative councils of "common men" and replace them with "better sorts"—more educated and, above all, more propertied individuals.[22] Deliberation, in this view, is the by-product of the kind of person elected to office. The public's opinions are "refined and enlarged" because refined individuals do the governing. Although this view finds some support in *The Federalist* and was a worry of several Anti-Federalists, the Founders' Constitution placed much greater emphasis on the formal structures of the national institutions than on the background of officeholders.[23] Indeed, good character and high intelligence, they reasoned, would be of little help to the government if it resembled a direct democracy: "In all very numerous assemblies, of whatever characters composed, passion never fails to wrest the sceptre from reason. Had every Athenian citizen been a Socrates, every Athenian assembly would still have been a mob."[24]

The presidency was thus intended to be representative of the people, but not merely responsive to popular will. Drawn from the people through an election (albeit an indirect one), presidents were to be free enough from the daily shifts in public opinion that they could refine it and, paradoxically, better serve popular interests. Hamilton expressed well this element of the theory in a passage in which he linked the problem of representation to that of demagoguery:

There are those who would be inclined to regard the servile pliancy of the executive to a prevailing current, either in the community or in the legislature, as its best recommendation. But such men entertain very crude notions, as well of the purposes for which government was instituted, as of the true means by which public happiness may be promoted. The republican principle demands that the deliberative sense of the community should govern the conduct of those to whom they intrust the management of their affairs; but it does not require an unqualified complaisance . . . to every transient impulse which the people may receive from the arts of men, who flatter their prejudices to betray their interests. . . . When occasions present themselves in which the interests of the people are at variance with their inclinations, it is the duty of the persons whom they have appointed to be the guardians of those interests to withstand the temporary delusion, in order to give them time and opportunity for more cool and sedate reflection.[25]

Independence of the Executive

To "withstand the temporary delusion" of popular opinion, the executive was made independent. The office would draw its authority from the Constitution rather than from another government branch. The Framers were led to this decision from their knowledge of the states. According to John Marshall, the state governments (with the exception of New York's) lacked any structure "which could resist the wild projects of the moment, give the people an opportunity to reflect and allow the good sense of the nation time for exertion." As Madison stated at the convention, "Experience had proved a tendency in our governments to throw all power into the legislative vortex. The executives of the states are in general little more than Cyphers; the legislatures omnipotent."[26]

Independence from Congress was the immediate practical need, yet the need was based on the close connection between legislatures and popular opinion. Because insufficient independence from public opinion was the source of the concern about the legislatures, the Founders rejected James Wilson's arguments on behalf of popular election as a means of making the president independent of Congress.

Executive independence created the conditions under which presidents would be most likely to adopt a different perspective from Congress on matters of public policy. Congress would be dominated by local factions that, according to plan, would give great weight to constituent opinion. The president, as Thomas Jefferson was to argue, was the only national officer "who commanded a view of the whole ground." Metaphorically, independence gave presidents their own space within, and their own angle of vision on, the polity. According to the founding theory, these constituent features of discretion are required by the twin activities of executing the will of the legislature and leading a legislature to construct good laws to be executed, laws that would be responsive to the long-term needs of the nation.[27]

Separation of Powers

The constitutional role of the president in lawmaking raises the question of the meaning and purpose of separation of powers. What is the meaning of separation of power if power is shared among the branches of government? Clearly, legalists are wrong if they assume that the Founders wished to distinguish so carefully among executive, legislative, and judicial powers as to make each the exclusive preserve of a particular branch. However, such an error gives rise to another one.

Political scientists, following Richard Neustadt, have assumed that because powers were not divided according to the principle of "one branch, one function," the Founders made no principled distinction among kinds of power. Instead, according to Neustadt, they created "separate institutions sharing power."[28] The premise of that claim is that power is an entity that can be divided up to prevent any one branch from having enough to rule another. In this view, the sole purpose of separation of powers is to preserve liberty by preventing the arbitrary rule of any one center of power.

The Neustadt perspective finds some support both in the Founders' deliberations and in the Constitution. Much attention was given to making each branch "weighty" enough to resist encroachment by the others. Yet this "checks and balances" view of separation of powers can be understood better in tandem with an alternative understanding of the concept: powers were separated, and *Tulis* structures of each branch differentiated, to equip each branch to perform dif- *functional* ferent tasks. Each branch would be superior (although not the sole power) in its own sphere and in its own way. The purpose of separation of powers was to make effective governance more likely.[29] *Separation = empowering*

Ensuring the protection of liberty and individual rights was one element of effective governance as the Founders conceived it, but it was not the only one. Government also needed to ensure the security of the nation and to craft policies that reflected popular will.[30] These governmental objectives may conflict, for example, if popular opinion favors policies that violate rights. Separation of powers was thought to be an institutional way of accommodating the tensions among governmental objectives.

Table 1.1 presents a simplified view of the purposes behind the separation of powers. Note that the three objectives of government—popular will, individual rights, and self-preservation—are mixed twice in the Constitution. They are mixed among the branches and within each branch so that each objective is

Table 1.1 Separation of Powers

Objectives (in order of priority)	Special qualities and functions (to be aimed at)	Structures and means
CONGRESS		
1. Popular will	Deliberation	a. Plurality
2. Popular rights		b. Proximity (frequent House elections)
3. Self-preservation		c. Bicameralism
		d. Competent powers
PRESIDENT		
1. Self-preservation	Energy and "steady administration of law"	a. Unity
2. Popular rights		b. Four-year term and reeligibility
3. Popular will		c. Competent powers
COURTS		
1. Popular rights	"Judgment, not will"	a. Small collegial body
		b. Life tenure
		c. Power linked to argument

given priority in one branch. Congress and the president were to concern themselves with all three, but the priority of their concern differs, with self-preservation, or national security, of utmost concern to the president.

The term *separation of powers* has perhaps obstructed understanding of the extent to which different structures were designed to give each branch the special quality needed to secure its governmental objectives. Thus, although the Founders were not so naive as to expect that Congress would be simply "deliberative," they hoped its plural membership and bicameral structure would provide necessary, if not sufficient, conditions for deliberation to emerge. Similarly, the president's "energy," it was hoped, would be enhanced by unity, the prospect of reelection, and substantial discretion. As we all know, the Supreme Court does not simply "judge" dispassionately; it also makes policies and exercises will. But the Founders believed it made no sense to have a Court if it were intended to be just like a Congress. The judiciary was structured to make the dispassionate protection of rights more likely, if by no means certain.

The Founders differentiated powers as well as structures in the original design. These powers ("the executive power" vested in the president in Article II and "all legislative power herein granted" given to Congress in Article I) overlap and sometimes conflict. Yet both the legalists' view of power as "parchment distinction" and the political scientists' view of "separate institutions sharing power" provide inadequate guides to what happens and what the Founders thought *ought* to happen when powers collide. The Founders urged that "line drawing" among spheres of authority be the product of political conflict among the branches, not the result of dispassionate legal analysis. Contrary to more contemporary views, they did not believe that such conflict would lead to deadlock or stalemate.[31]

Consider the disputes that sometimes arise from claims of "executive privilege."[32] Presidents occasionally refuse to provide Congress with information that its members deem necessary to carry out their special functions. They usually justify assertions of executive privilege on the grounds of either national security or the need to maintain the conditions necessary for sound execution, including the unfettered canvassing of opinions.

Both Congress and the president have legitimate constitutional prerogatives at stake: Congress has a right to know, and the president has a need for secrecy. How does one discover whether in any particular instance the president's claim is more or less weighty than Congress's? The answer depends on the circumstances—for example, the importance of the particular piece of legislation in the congressional agenda versus the importance of the particular secret to the executive. There is no formula independent of political circumstance with which to weigh such competing institutional claims. The most knowledgeable observers of those political conflicts are the parties themselves: Congress and the president.

Each branch has weapons at its disposal to use against the other. Congress can threaten to hold up legislation or appointments important to presidents. Ultimately, it could impeach and convict them. For their part, presidents may continue to "stonewall"; they may veto bills or fail to support legislation of interest to their legislative opponents; they may delay political appointments; and they may put the issue to public test, even submitting to an impeachment inquiry for their own advantage. The lengths to which presidents and Congresses are willing to go were thought to be a rough measure of the importance of their respective constitutional claims. Nearly always, executive-legislative disputes are resolved at a relatively low stage of potential conflict. In 1981, for example, President Ronald Reagan ordered Interior Secretary James Watt to release information to a Senate committee after the committee had agreed to maintain confidentiality. The compromise was reached after public debate and "contempt of Congress" hearings were held.

This political process is dynamic. Viewed at particular moments, the system may appear deadlocked. Looked at over time, considerable movement becomes apparent. Similar scenarios could be constructed for the other issues over which congressional and presidential claims to authority conflict, such as the use of executive agreements in place of treaties, the deployment of military force, or the executive impoundment of appropriated monies.[33]

Although conflict may continue to be institutionally fostered or constrained in ways that were intended by the Founders, one still may wonder whether their broad objectives have been secured and whether their priorities should be ours. At the beginning of the twentieth century, Woodrow Wilson mounted an attack on the Founders' design, convinced that it had not achieved its objectives. More important, his attack resulted in a reordering of those objectives in the understandings that presidents have of their roles. His theory underlies the second constitution that buffets the presidency.

The Modern Perspective

Woodrow Wilson's influential critique of *The Federalist* contains another synoptic vision. Yet his comprehensive reinterpretation of the constitutional order appears, at first glance, to be internally inconsistent. Between writing his classic dissertation, *Congressional Government,* in 1884 and publishing his well-known series of lectures, *Constitutional Government in the United States,* in

1908, Wilson shifted his position on important structural features of the constitutional system.

Early in his career Wilson depicted the House of Representatives as the potential motive force in American politics and urged reforms to make it more unified and energetic. He paid little attention to the presidency or judiciary. In later years he focused his attention on the presidency. In his early writings Wilson urged a plethora of constitutional amendments that were designed to emulate the British parliamentary system, including proposals to synchronize the terms of representatives and senators with that of the president and to require presidents to choose leaders of the majority party as cabinet secretaries. Wilson later abandoned formal amendment as a strategy, urging instead that the existing Constitution be reinterpreted to encompass his parliamentary views.

Wilson also altered his views at a deeper theoretical level. According to Christopher Wolfe, although the early Wilson held a traditional view of the Constitution, as a document whose meaning persists over time, the later Wilson adopted a historicist understanding, claiming that the meaning of the Constitution changed as a reflection of the prevailing thought of successive generations.[34]

As interesting as these shifts in Wilson's thought are, they all rest on an underlying critique of the American polity that Wilson maintained consistently throughout his career. Wilson's altered constitutional proposals—indeed, his altered understanding of constitutionalism itself—ought to be viewed as a series of strategic moves designed to remedy the same alleged systemic defects. Our task is to review Wilson's understanding of those defects and to outline the doctrine he developed to contend with them—a doctrine whose centerpiece would ultimately be the rhetorical presidency.

Wilson's doctrine counterpoises the Founders' understandings of demagoguery, representation, independence of the executive, and separation of powers. For clarity, I examine these principles in a slightly different order from before: separation of powers, representation, independence of the executive, and demagoguery.

Separation of Powers

For Wilson, separation of powers was the central defect of American politics. He was the first and most sophisticated proponent of the now conventional argument that "separation of powers" is a synonym for "checks and balances"—that is, the negation of power by one branch over another. Yet Wilson's view was more sophisticated than its progeny because his ultimate indictment of the Founders' conception was a functionalist one. Wilson claimed that under the auspices of the Founders' view, formal and informal political institutions failed to promote true deliberation in the legislature and impeded energy in the executive.

Wilson characterized the Founders' understanding as "Newtonian," a yearning for equipoise and balance in a machinelike system:

The admirable positions of the *Federalist* read like thoughtful applications of Montesquieu to the political needs and circumstances of America. They are full of the theory of checks and balances. The President is balanced off against Congress, Congress against the President, and each against the Court.... Politics is turned into mechanics under [Montesquieu's] touch. The theory of gravitation is supreme.[35]

The accuracy of Wilson's portrayal of the Founders may be questioned. He reasoned backward from the malfunctioning system as he found it to how they must have intended it. Wilson's depiction of the system, rather than his interpretation of the Founders' intentions, however, is of present concern.

Rather than equipoise and balance, Wilson found a system dominated by Congress, with several attendant functional infirmities: major legislation frustrated by narrow-minded committees, lack of coordination and direction of policies, a general breakdown of deliberation, and an absence of leadership. Extraconstitutional institutions—boss-led political parties chief among them—had sprung up to assume the functions not performed by Congress or the president, but they had not performed them well. Wilson also acknowledged that the formal institutions had not always performed badly, that some prior Congresses (those of Webster and Clay) and some presidencies (those of Washington, Adams, Jefferson, Jackson, Lincoln, Roosevelt, and, surprisingly, Madison) had been examples of forceful leadership.[36]

These two strands of thought—the growth of extraconstitutional institutions and the periodic excellence of the constitutional structures—led Wilson to conclude that the Founders had mischaracterized their own system. The Founders' rhetoric was "Newtonian," but their constitutional structure, like all government, was actually "Darwinian." Wilson explained:

The trouble with the Newtonian theory is that government is not a machine but a living thing. It falls, not under the theory of the universe, but under the theory of organic life. It is accountable to Darwin, not to Newton. It is modified by its environment, necessitated by its tasks, shaped to its functions by the sheer pressure of life.[37]

The Founders' doctrine had affected the working of the structure to the extent that the power of the political branches was interpreted mechanically and many of the structural features reflected the Newtonian yearning. A tension arose between the "organic" core of the system and the "mechanical" understanding of it by politicians and citizens. Thus "the constitutional structure of the government has hampered and limited [the president's] actions but it has not prevented [them.]" Wilson tried to resolve the tension between the understanding of American politics as Newtonian and its actual Darwinian character to make the evolution self-conscious and thereby more rational and effective.[38]

Wilson attacked the Founders for relying on mere "parchment barriers" to effectuate a separation of powers. This claim is an obvious distortion of founding views. In *Federalist* nos. 47 and 48, the argument is precisely that the federal Constitution, unlike earlier state constitutions, would not rely primarily on parchment distinctions of power but on differentiation of institutional structures.[39] Through Wilson's discussion of parchment barriers, however, an important difference between his and the Founders' views of the same problem becomes visible. Both worried over the tendency of legislatures to dominate in republican systems.

To mitigate the danger posed by legislatures, the Founders had relied primarily on an independent president with an office structured to give its occupant the personal incentive and means to stand up to Congress when it exceeded its authority. These structural features included a nonlegislative mode of election, constitutionally fixed salary, qualified veto, four-year term, and indefinite reeligibility. Although the parchment powers of Congress and the president overlapped (contrary to Wilson's depiction of them), the demarcation of powers proper to each branch would result primarily from political interplay and conflict between the political branches rather than from a theoretical drawing of lines by the judiciary.[40]

Wilson offered a quite different view. First, he claimed that because of the inadequacy of mere parchment barriers, Congress, in the latter half of the nineteenth century, had encroached uncontested on the executive sphere. Second, he contended that when the president's institutional check was used, it took the form of a "negative"—prevention of a bad outcome rather than provision for a good one. In this view, separation of powers hindered efficient, coordinated, well-led policy.[41]

Wilson did not wish to bolster structures to thwart the legislature. He preferred that the president and Congress be fully integrated into, and implicated in, each other's activities. Rather than merely assail Congress, Wilson would tame or, as it were, domesticate it. Separation would be replaced by institutionally structured cooperation. Cooperation was especially necessary because presidents lacked the energy they needed, energy that could be provided only by policy backed by Congress and its majority. Although Congress had failed as a deliberative body, it could now be restored to its true function by presidential leadership that raised and defended crucial policies.

Cooperation needed because
1) Presidents lacked "energy"
2) Congress had failed as a deliberative body, but could be restored as a policy-making body

These latter two claims represent the major purposes of the Wilsonian theory: leadership and deliberation. Unlike the Founders, who saw these two functions in conflict, Wilson regarded them as dependent on each other. In "Leaderless Government" he stated,

I take it for granted that when one is speaking of a representative legislature he means by an "efficient organization" an organization which provides for deliberate, and deliberative, action and which enables the nation to affix responsibility for what is done and what is not done. The Senate is deliberate enough; but it is hardly deliberative after its ancient and better manner. . . . The House of Representatives is neither deliberate nor deliberative. We have not forgotten that one of the most energetic of its recent Speakers thanked God, in his frankness, that the House was not a deliberative body. It has not the time for the leadership of argument. . . . For debate and leadership of that sort the House must have a party organization and discipline such as it has never had.[42]

It appears that the Founders and Wilson differed on the means to common ends. Both wanted "deliberation" and an "energetic" executive, but each proposed different constitutional arrangements to achieve those objectives. In fact, their differences went much deeper, for each theory defined deliberation and energy differently. These differences, hinted at in the previous quotation, will become clearer as we examine Wilson's reinterpretation of representation and independence of the executive.

Representation

In the discussion of the founding perspective, the competing requirements of popular consent and insulation from public opinion as a requisite of impartial judgment were canvassed. Woodrow Wilson gave much greater weight to the role of public opinion in the ordinary conduct of representative government than did the Founders. Some scholars have suggested that Wilson's rhetoric and the institutional practices he established (especially regarding the nomination of presidential candidates) are the major sources of contemporary efforts to create a more "participatory" democracy. However, Wilson's understanding of representation, like his views on separation of powers, was more sophisticated than that of his followers.[43]

Wilson categorically rejected the Burkean view that legislators are elected for their quality of judgment and position on a few issues and then left free to exercise that judgment:

It used to be thought that legislation was an affair to be conducted by the few who were instructed for the benefit of the many who were uninstructed: that statesmanship was a function of origination for which only trained and instructed men were fit. Those who actually conducted legislation and conducted affairs were rather whimsically chosen by Fortune to illustrate this theory, but such was the ruling thought in politics. The Sovereignty of the People, however . . . has created a very different practice. . . . It is a dignified proposition with us—is it not?—that as is the majority, so ought the government to be.[44]

Wilson did not think his view was equivalent to "direct democracy" or to subservience to public opinion (understood, as it often is today, as response to public opinion polls). He favored an interplay between representative and constituent that would, in fact, educate the constituent. This process differed, at least in theory, from the older attempts to "form" public opinion: it did not begin in the minds of the elite but in the hearts of the masses. Wilson called the process of fathoming the people's desires (often only vaguely known to the people until instructed) "interpretation." Interpretation was the core of leadership for him.[45] Before we explore its meaning further, it is useful to dwell on Wilson's notion of the desired interplay between the "leader-interpreter" and the people so that we may see how his understanding of deliberation differed from that of the Founders.

For the Founders, deliberation meant reasoning on the merits of policy. The character and content of deliberation would thus vary with the character of the policy at issue. In "normal" times, there would be squabbles among competing interests. Deliberation would occur to the extent that such interests were compelled to offer arguments and respond to those made by others. The arguments might be relatively crude, specialized, and technical, or they might involve matters of legal or constitutional propriety. But in none of these instances would they resemble the great debates over fundamental principles—for example, over the question of whether to promote interests in the first place. Great questions were the stuff of crisis politics, and the Founders placed much hope in securing the distinction between crisis and normal political life.

Wilson effaced the distinction between "crisis" and "normal" political argument:

Crises give birth and a new growth to statesmanship because they are peculiarly periods of action . . . [and] also of unusual opportunity for gaining leadership and a controlling and guiding influence. . . . And we thus come upon the principle . . . that governmental forms will call to the work of the administration able minds and strong hearts constantly or infrequently, according as they do or do not afford at all times an opportunity of gaining and retaining a commanding authority and an undisputed leadership in the nation's councils.[46]

Wilson's lament that little deliberation took place in Congress was not that the merits of policies were left unexplored but rather that, because the discussions were not elevated to the level of major contests of principle, the public generally did not interest itself. True deliberation, he urged, would rivet the attention of press and public, whereas what substituted for it in his day were virtually secret contests of interest-based factions. Wilson rested this view on three observations. First, the congressional workload was parceled out to specialized standing committees, whose decisions usually were ratified by the respective houses without any general debate. Second, the arguments that did take place in committee were technical and structured by the "special pleadings" of interest groups, whose advocates adopted the model of legal litigation as their mode of discussion. As Wilson characterized committee debates,

They have about them none of the searching, critical, illuminating character of the higher order of parliamentary debate, in which men are pitted against each other as equals, and urged to sharp contest and masterful strife by the inspiration of political principle and personal ambition, through the rivalry of parties and the competition of policies. They represent a joust between antagonistic interests, not a contest of principles.[47]

Finally, because debates were hidden away in committee, technical, and interest based, the public cared little about them. "The ordinary citizen cannot be induced to pay much heed to the details, or even the main principles of lawmaking," Wilson wrote, "unless something more interesting than the law itself be involved in the pending decision of the lawmaker." For the Founders this would not have been disturbing, but for Wilson the very heart of representative government was the principle of publicity: "The informing function of Congress should be preferred even to its legislative function." The informing function was to be preferred both as an end in itself and because the accountability of public officials required policies that were connected with one another and explained to the people. Argument from "principle" would connect policy and present constellations of policies as coherent wholes to be approved or disapproved by the people. "Principles, as statesmen conceive them, are threads to the labyrinth of circumstances."[48]

Wilson attacked separation of powers in an effort to improve leadership for the purpose of fostering deliberation. "Congress cannot, under our present system . . . be effective for the instruction of public opinion, or the cleansing of political action." As mentioned at the outset of this section, Wilson first looked to Congress itself, specifically to its Speaker, for such leadership. Several years after the publication of *Congressional Government,* Wilson turned his attention to the president. "There is no trouble now about getting the president's speeches printed and read, every word," he wrote at the turn of the century.[49]

Independence of the Executive

The attempt to bring the president into more intimate contact with Congress and the people raises the question of the president's "independence." Wilson altered the meaning of this notion, which originally had been that the president's special authority came independently from the Constitution, not from Congress or the people. For the Founders, presidents' constitutional station afforded them the possibility and responsibility of taking a perspective on policy different from that of either Congress or the people. Wilson urged us to consider presidents as receiving their authority independently through a mandate from the people. For Wilson, presidents remained "special" because they were the only government officers with a national mandate.[50]

Political scientists today have difficulty finding mandates in election years, let alone between them, because of the great number of issues and the lack of public consensus on them. Wilson understood this problem and urged the leader to sift through the multifarious currents of opinion to find a core of issues that he believed reflected majority will even if the majority was not yet fully aware of it.

The leader's rhetoric could translate the people's felt desires into public policy. Wilson cited Daniel Webster as an example of such an interpreter of the public will:

The nation lay as it were unconscious of its unity and purpose, and he called it into full consciousness. It could never again be anything less than what he said it was. It is at such moments and in the mouths of such interpreters that nations spring from age to age in their development.[51]

"Interpretation" involves two skills. First, the leader must understand the true majority sentiment underneath the contradictory positions of factions and the discordant views of the masses. Second, the leader must explain the people's true desires to them in a way that is easily comprehended and convincing.

Wilson's desire to raise politics to the level of rational disputation and his professed aim to have leaders educate the masses are contradictory. He acknowledged candidly that the power to command would require simplification of the arguments to accommodate the masses: "The arguments which induce popular action must always be broad and obvious arguments; only a very gross substance of concrete conception can make any impression on the minds of the masses."[52] Not only is argument simplified, but disseminating "information"—a common concern of contemporary democratic theory—is not the function of a deliberative leader, in Wilson's view:

Men are not led by being told what they don't know. Persuasion is a force, but not information; and persuasion is accomplished by creeping into the confidence of those you would lead. . . . Mark the simplicity and directness of the arguments and ideas of true leaders. The motives which they urge are elemental; the morality which they seek to enforce is large and obvious; the policy they emphasize, purged of all subtlety.[53]

Demagoguery

Wilson's understanding of leadership raises again the problem of demagoguery. What distinguishes a leader-interpreter from a demagogue? Who is to make this distinction? The Founders feared there was no institutionally effective way to exclude the demagogue if popular oratory during "normal" times was encouraged. Indeed, the term *leader,* which appears a dozen times in *The Federalist,* is used disparagingly in all but one instance, and that one is a reference to leaders of the Revolution.[54]

Wilson was sensitive to this problem. "The most despotic of governments under the control of wise statesmen is preferable to the freest ruled by demagogues," he wrote. Wilson relied on two criteria to distinguish the demagogue from the leader, one based on the nature of the appeal, the other on the character of the leader. The demagogue appeals to "the momentary and whimsical popular mood, the transitory or popular passion," whereas the leader appeals to "true" and durable majority sentiment. The demagogue is motivated by the desire to augment personal power, and the leader is more interested in fostering the permanent interests of the community. "The one [trims] to the inclinations of the moment, the other [is] obedient to the permanent purposes of the public mind."[55]

Theoretically these distinctions present a number of difficulties. If popular opinion is the source of the leader's rhetoric, what basis apart from popular opinion is there to distinguish the "permanent" from the "transient"? If popular opinion is constantly evolving, what sense is there to the notion of "the permanent purposes of the public mind"? Yet the most serious difficulties are practical ones. Assuming it is theoretically possible to distinguish the leader from the demagogue, how is that distinction to be incorporated into the daily operation of political institutions? Wilson offered a threefold response to this query.

First, he claimed his doctrine contained an ethic that could be passed on to future leaders. Wilson hoped that politicians' altered understanding of what constituted success and fame could provide some security. He constantly pointed to British parliamentary practice, urging that long training in debate had produced generations of leaders and few demagogues. Indeed, Wilson had taught at Johns Hopkins, Bryn Mawr, Wesleyan, and Princeton, and at each of those institutions he established debating societies modeled on the Oxford Union.[56]

Second, Wilson placed some reliance on the public's ability to judge character:

Men can scarcely be orators without that force of character, that readiness of resource, that cleverness of vision, that grasp of intellect, that courage of conviction, that correctness of purpose, and that instinct and capacity for leadership which are the eight horses that draw the triumphal chariot of every leader and ruler of freemen. We could not object to being ruled by such men.[57]

According to Wilson, the public need not appeal to a complex standard or theory to distinguish demagoguery from leadership, but could easily recognize "courage," "intelligence," and "correctness of purpose"—signs that the leader was not a demagogue. Wilson did not say why prior publics had fallen prey to enterprising demagogues, but the major difficulty with this second source of restraint is that public understanding of leaders' character would come from their oratory rather than from a history of their political activity or from direct contact with them. The public's understanding of character might be based solely on words.

Third, Wilson suggested that the natural conservatism of public opinion, its resistance to innovation that is not consonant with the speed and direction of its own movement, would afford still more safety:

Practical leadership may not beckon to the slow masses of men from beyond some dim, unexplored space or some intervening chasm: it must daily feel the road to the goal proposed, knowing that it is a slow, very slow, evolution to the wings, and that for the present, and for a very long future also, Society must walk, dependent upon practicable paths, incapable of scaling sudden heights.[58]

Wilson's assurances of security against demagogues may seem unsatisfactory because they did not adequately distinguish the polity in which he worked from others in which demagogues had prevailed, including some southern states in this country. However, his arguments should be considered as much for the theoretical direction and emphases that they implied as for the particular weaknesses they revealed. Wilson's doctrine stood on the premise that the need for more energy in the political system was greater than the risk incurred through the possibility of demagoguery.[59] His view represented a major shift, indeed a reversal, of the founding perspective. If Wilson's argument regarding demagoguery was strained or inadequate, it was a price he was willing to pay to remedy what he regarded as the Founders' inadequate provision for an energetic executive.

Conclusion

Federalist, Constitution proscribe popular leadership
Wilson — prescribes it

Both constitutions were designed to encourage and support an energetic president, but they differ over the legitimate sources and alleged virtues of popular leadership. For the Founders, presidents draw their energy from their authority, which rests on their independent constitutional position. For Woodrow Wilson and for presidents ever since, power and authority are conferred directly by the people. *The Federalist* and the Constitution proscribe popular leadership. Wilson prescribed it. Indeed, he urged the president to minister continually to the moods of the people as a preparation for action. The Founders' president was to look to the people, but less frequently, and to be judged by them, but usually after acting.

The second constitution gained legitimacy because presidents were thought to lack the resources necessary for the energy promised but not delivered by the first. The second constitution did not replace the first, however. Because many of the founding structures persist, while our understanding of the president's legitimate role has changed, the new view should be thought of as superimposed on the old, altering without obliterating the original structure.

Many commentators have noted the tendency of recent presidents to raise public expectations about what they can achieve. Indeed, public disenchantment with government altogether may stem largely from disappointment in presidential performance, inasmuch as the presidency is the most visible and important American political institution. Yet, rather than being the result of the personality traits of particular presidents, raised expectations are grounded in an institutional dilemma common to all modern presidents. Under the auspices of the second constitution, presidents must continually craft rhetoric that pleases their popular audience. Even though presidents are always in a position to promise more, the only additional resource they have to make good on their promises is public opinion itself. Because Congress retains the independent status conferred on it by the first Constitution, it can resist the president.

Naturally, presidents who are exceptionally popular or gifted as orators can overcome the resistance of the legislature. For the political system as a whole, this possibility is both good and bad. To the extent that the system requires periodic renewal through synoptic policies that reconstitute the political agenda, it is good. But the very qualities that are necessary to achieve such large-scale change tend to subvert the deliberative process, which makes unwise legislation or incoherent policy more likely.

Ronald Reagan's major political victories as president illustrate both sides of this systemic dilemma.[60] On the one hand, without the second constitution it would be difficult to imagine Reagan's success at winning tax reform legislation. His skillful coordination of a rhetorical and a legislative strategy overcame the resistance of thousands of lobbies that sought to preserve advantageous provisions of the existing tax code. Similarly, Social Security and other large policies that were initiated by Franklin D. Roosevelt during the New Deal might not have been possible without the second constitution.

On the other hand, Reagan's first budget victory in 1981 and the Strategic Defense Initiative (SDI, also known as Star Wars) illustrate how popular leadership can subvert the deliberative process or produce incoherent policy. The budget cuts of 1981 were secured with virtually no congressional debate. Among their effects was the gutting of virtually all of the Great Society programs initiated by President Lyndon B. Johnson, which themselves were the product of a popular campaign that circumvented the deliberative process.

When Congress does deliberate, as it has on SDI, the debate is often structured by contradictory forms of rhetoric, the product of the two constitutions. The arguments presidents make to the people are different from those they make to Congress. To the people, Reagan promised to strive for a new defense technology that would make nuclear deterrence obsolete. But to Congress, his administration argued that SDI was needed to supplement, not supplant, deterrence.[61] Each kind of argument can be used to impeach the other. President Jimmy Carter found himself in the same bind on energy policy. When he urged the American people to support his energy plan, Carter contended that it was necessary to remedy an existing crisis. But to Congress he argued that the same policy was necessary to forestall a crisis.[62]

The second constitution promises energy, which is said to be inadequately provided by the first. This suggests that the two constitutions fit together to form a more complete whole. Unfortunately, over the long run, the tendency of the second constitution to make extraordinary power routine undermines, rather than completes, the logic of the original Constitution. Garry Wills has described how presidents since John F. Kennedy have attempted to pit public opinion against their own executive establishment. Successors to a charismatic leader then inherit "a delegitimated set of procedures" and are themselves compelled "to go outside of procedures—further delegitimating the very office they [hold]."[63] In Reagan's case, this cycle was reinforced by an ideology opposed to big government. "In the present crisis," Reagan said at his first inaugural, "government is not the solution to our problem; government is the problem." Although fiascoes like the Iran-contra affair are not inevitable, they are made more likely by the logic and legitimacy of the second constitution.

It was hard to imagine that any leader would embrace the second constitution more than Reagan did, but President Bill Clinton surpassed him. According to George Edwards,

The Clinton presidency is the ultimate example of the rhetorical presidency—a presidency based on a perpetual campaign to obtain the public's support and fed by public opinion polls, focus groups, and public relations memos. No president ever invested more in measuring, and attempting to mold, public opinion. [This administration] even polled voters on where it was best for the First Family to vacation. This is an administration that spent $18 million on ads in 1995, a nonelection year! And this is an administration that repeatedly interpreted its setbacks, whether in elections or health care reform, in terms of its failure to communicate rather than in terms of the quality of its initiatives or the strategy for governing. Reflecting his orientation in the White House, Bill Clinton declared that "the role of the President of the United States is message."[64]

The Clinton presidency was a roller coaster of political successes and failures. No doubt it will take scholars decades to make sense of Clinton's political choices and the public's reactions to them. No simple explanation can address how this president, who was the head of his political party when the Democrats were badly defeated in 1994, rebounded so decisively in 1996, or how he came to be impeached by the House in 1998 yet be acquitted by the Senate in 1999. A full analysis of these political undulations and their consequences for the polity would include, at a minimum, accounts of the president's character, his political acumen, the state of the economy and the world, and the actions of the Republican opposition. Without venturing to offer even the beginning of such an analysis, it may be helpful to suggest how the two constitutional presidencies may be a useful backdrop for a fuller narrative. The political dilemmas Clinton faced and the choices he made to contend with them are, at least in part, products of the uneasy conjunction of the two constitutions.

For example, the president's fidelity to the second constitution contributed to the most serious mistake that prompted the impeachment proceeding. Faced with an inquiry into his relationship with Monica Lewinsky, Clinton sought a rhetorical solution to his political difficulty. Oriented to the immediate demands of persuasion in a national plebiscite, Clinton relied on his bully pulpit. On the advice of his former pollster Dick Morris and friend and media adviser Harry Thomason, the president went on national television and forcefully denied that he had "sexual relations" with Lewinsky. That denial, more than the conduct it concealed, fueled congressional opposition and delegitimized his presidency in the eyes of many of his critics and even some of his allies.

Yet presidents are schooled by both constitutions even when they only consciously understand the second. President Carter discovered the Rose Garden strategy of retreating from public view when the demands of foreign policy placed him in a position to see the benefits of a political posture inherent to the first Constitution.[65] Similarly, President Clinton rediscovered the first Constitution as the nation taught itself the constitutional meaning of impeachment.

As the impeachment drama unfolded, Clinton was uncharacteristically mute. He let his lawyers and other surrogates do the talking about impeachment-related matters while he attended to the nation's other business. The nation's resurrection of a nineteenth-century constitutional anachronism, impeachment, placed the president in a position from which he could see the political benefit of acting like a nineteenth-century president. Because the animating charge of the political opposition was that Clinton had disgraced his office—whether through his sexual behavior or his subsequent deceptions and alleged perjury—the president's conduct during the formal proceedings became a rhetorical or dramaturgical refutation of the main charge against him. The one exception to this presidential style, so characteristic of the first Constitution, seemed to prove its significance. When the president emerged from the White House to lead congressional allies in a show of support immediately following the House vote, he was severely criticized for politicizing a constitutional process. Clinton's conscious and seemingly instinctive understanding of leadership conflicted with the model of statesmanship inherent to the constitutional order. After that misstep, the president attempted to recapture the advantages that the dignity of the office provided him.

Although political circumstance encouraged Clinton to rediscover the first Constitution, political crisis led George W. Bush to a more rhetorical presidency than would be his natural inclination. Bush is not a gifted orator. Like his father, he has difficulty expressing himself, is prone to misstatement, and seems unable to master the proper cadences of formal speech. Nevertheless, the terrorist attacks on New York and Washington, Bush's response to them in Afghanistan, and his subsequent war against Iraq required him to lead. In this array of circumstances and responsibilities, one can see both the promise and the pitfall of presidential leadership under the auspices of two constitutions.

Bush's response to the 9/11 terrorist attacks shows how the president's traditional roles under the Constitution can be enhanced by modern rhetorical practices. His leadership of the nation into the war in Iraq reveals how the second constitution sometimes undermines the first.

In the wake of the terrorist attacks on the United States, Bush found it necessary to deliver a number of speeches to a grieving nation. Because it was proper for the president to do this, even under the first Constitution, his words gained in politically constructed authority what they lacked in natural grace. The Constitution, its norms, institutions, and traditions, elevated an ordinary speaker to a station from which he was able to deliver extraordinarily effective leadership.

By contrast, Bush's case for the war in Iraq did not respond to a widely felt crisis. Rather, the president tried to convince the nation that an unseen crisis existed. To do this he developed a public case for war that differed, at least in emphasis, from the real reasons that animated decision makers within the administration. The case for war that prevailed within the administration stood on three basic grounds: the threat from weapons of mass destruction, Iraq's support of terrorism, and the brutality of Iraq's totalitarian practices on its own people. Taken together, these three reasons were all grounded in the nature of the Iraqi regime and therefore were thought to necessitate regime change. Although all three were part of the public case for war,[66] the threat of weapons of mass destruction was the one the administration stressed. When it became apparent that there were no such weapons, the president's policy was, in effect, hoisted by its own rhetorical petard. Bush's credibility was undermined by the rhetorical choices he made to speedily gain popular support for the war and to pressure Congress to authorize the use of force. His "deception" was not, as many commentators alleged, an intentional effort to lie to Congress, to the United Nations, or to the American people. Instead, it was an effort to simplify a complex argument to make it more effective rhetorically. The problem of credibility that hounded the Bush administration toward the end was not the president's personality or moral character. Rather, it was a by-product of a second constitution that lives in tension with the first.

President Barack Obama inherited both the worst economic crisis since the Great Depression and wars in Iraq and Afghanistan. Because he is such a gifted orator, and because the nation needs a president to get it through a genuine crisis, it is reasonable to expect that Obama may perfect the kind of rhetorical leadership that marked the administration of Franklin D. Roosevelt. Obama's policy and political agenda extends the New Deal. In the campaign and early days of the administration, his agenda was marked not by a distinctively original "public philosophy" but rather by one that resembles and invokes Roosevelt's. FDR introduced "fireside chats" and Obama introduced "Organizing for America," a web-based instrument for political education and mobilization. These actions suggest that Obama's leadership follows the path made familiar by the second constitution, in general, and by FDR, in particular. However, Obama's effort to craft a "post-partisan" politics that will change the way politics is conducted in Washington suggests a different possibility, one that more closely resembles the leadership style of Theodore Roosevelt than of FDR. Like the first Roosevelt, Obama disavowed pride of authorship for his economic agenda by offering principles and proposals to Congress and then suspending a public campaign while each house of the legislature crafted its own proposed bill. More generally, Obama campaigned and has governed on behalf of "moderation." He hired a phalanx of lawyers to help restore the Constitution in the Justice Department, and he is a constitutional lawyer himself. Like Theodore Roosevelt, Obama might seek to use the second constitution to restore the first.[67]

It remains to be seen whether the need for emergency action will trump the need for governmental reform. Will the effort to craft a bipartisan economic stimulus bill set in motion a new way of doing business that restores lost elements of the first Constitution, such as a responsible legislature? Or will it devolve into legislative irresponsibility born of familiar partisan conflict between Republicans and Democrats? Will Obama's extraordinary grassroots organization, bolstered by technological savvy, usher in a new era of civic education? Or will it devolve into just another high-tech means to attempt to pressure Congress? These are all plausible futures.

Notes

1. Notable structural changes in the Constitution are the Twelfth, Seventeenth, Twentieth, and Twenty-second Amendments, which deal, respectively, with change in the Electoral College system, the election of senators, presidential succession, and presidential reeligibility. Although all are interesting, only the last seems manifestly inconsistent with the Founders' plan. For a defense of the relevance of the constitutional theory of the presidency to contemporary practice, see Joseph M. Bessette and Jeffrey Tulis, eds., *The Presidency in the Constitutional Order* (Baton Rouge: Louisiana State University Press, 1981); and Joseph M. Bessette and Jeffrey K. Tulis, *The Constitutional Presidency* (Baltimore: Johns Hopkins University Press, 2009). See also David K. Nichols, *The Myth of the Modern Presidency* (University Park: Pennsylvania State University Press, 1994).

2. James W. Ceaser, *Presidential Selection: Theory and Development* (Princeton: Princeton University Press, 1979); Nelson Polsby, *Consequences of Party Reform* (New York: Oxford University Press, 1983); Doris A. Graber, *Mass Media and American Politics,* 6th ed. (Washington, D.C.: CQ Press, 2001); David L. Paletz and Robert M. Entman,

Media, Power, Politics (New York: Free Press, 1981); and Harvey C. Mansfield Jr., *America's Constitutional Soul* (Baltimore: Johns Hopkins University Press, 1991), chap. 12.

3. This essay does not reveal the Founders' personal and political motives except as they were self-consciously incorporated into the reasons offered for their Constitution. The Founders' views are treated on their own terms, as a constitutional theory; Hamilton's statement in the first number of *The Federalist* is taken seriously: "My motives must remain in the depository of my own breast. My arguments will be open to all and may be judged by all." James Madison, Alexander Hamilton, and John Jay, *The Federalist Papers,* ed. Clinton Rossiter (New York: New American Library, 1961), no. 1, 36. For a good discussion of the literature on the political motives of the founding fathers, see Erwin C. Hargrove and Michael Nelson, *Presidents, Politics, and Policy* (New York: Knopf, 1984), chap. 2.

4. The most influential study of the presidency is by Richard Neustadt. See *Presidential Power: The Politics of Leadership from FDR to Carter* (New York: Wiley, 1979), vi: "One must try to view the Presidency from over the President's shoulder, looking out and down with the perspective of his place."

5. Herbert J. Storing, *What the Anti-Federalists Were For* (Chicago: University of Chicago Press, 1981), 83n.

6. *The Federalist,* no. 70, 423.

7. In the first number, "Publius" warns "that of those men who have overturned the liberties of republics, the greatest number have begun their career by paying obsequious court to the people, commencing demagogues and ending tyrants." And in the last essay, "These judicious reflections contain a lesson of moderation to all the sincere lovers of the Union, and ought to put them upon their guard against hazarding anarchy, civil war, and perhaps the military despotism of a victorious demagogue, in the pursuit of what they are not likely to obtain, but from TIME and EXPERIENCE."

8. Ceaser, *Presidential Selection,* 12, 54–60, 166–167, 318–327. See also V. O. Key, *The Responsible Electorate* (New York: Random House, 1966), chap. 2; Stanley Kelley Jr., *Political Campaigning: Problems in Creating an Informed Electorate* (Washington, D.C.: Brookings Institution Press, 1960), 93; Pendleton E. Herring, *Presidential Leadership* (New York: Holt, Rinehart and Winston, 1940), 70; and *The Federalist,* no. 71, 432.

9. *The Federalist,* no. 10, 82; and Ceaser, *Presidential Selection,* 324.

10. Clinton Rossiter, *Constitutional Dictatorship: Crisis Government in the Modern Democracies* (Princeton: Princeton University Press, 1948), chap. 3.

11. *The Federalist,* no. 85, 527.

12. Harvey Flaumenhaft, "Hamilton's Administrative Republic and the American Presidency," in *The Presidency in the Constitutional Order,* ed. Bessette and Tulis, 65–114. The Civil War and turn-of-the-century progressive politics show that Hamilton's "administrative republic" has been punctuated with the sorts of crises and politics Hamilton sought to avoid.

13. *The Federalist,* no. 10, 77; no. 43, 276; no. 51, 323–325; no. 63, 384; and no. 73, 443. Moreover, the factual quest to find a "majority" may be no less contestable than is dispute over the merits of proposals. Contemporary political scientists provide ample support for the latter worry when they suggest that it is often both theoretically and practically impossible to discover a majority will—that is, to count it up—owing to the manifold differences of intensity of preferences and the plethora of possible hierarchies of preferences. Kenneth Arrow, *Social Choice and Individual Values* (New York: Wiley, 1963); and Benjamin I. Page, *Choices and Echoes in Presidential Elections* (Chicago: University of Chicago Press, 1978), chap. 2.

14. *The Federalist*, no. 39, 241; see also Martin Diamond, "Democracy and the Federalist: A Reconsideration of the Framers' Intent," *American Political Science Review* 53 (March 1959): 52–68.

15. *The Federalist*, no. 39, 241; no. 68, 412–423. See also James Ceaser, "Presidential Selection," in *The Presidency in the Constitutional Order*, ed. Bessette and Tulis, 234–282. Ironically, the Founders were proudest of this institutional creation; the Electoral College was their most original contrivance. Moreover, it escaped the censure of, and even won a good deal of praise from, antifederal opponents of the Constitution. Because electors were chosen by state legislatures for the sole purpose of selecting a president, the process was thought more democratic than potential alternatives, such as selection by Congress. Compare Nichols, *Myth of the Modern Presidency*, 39–45.

16. *The Federalist*, no. 72, 435. The empirical judgment that four years would serve the purpose of insulating the president is not as important for this discussion as the principle reflected in that choice, a principle that has fueled recent calls for a six-year term.

17. *The Federalist*, nos. 9 and 10.

18. Gordon Wood, *The Creation of the American Republic: 1776–1787* (New York: Norton, 1969); Michael Parenti, "The Constitution as an Elitist Document," in *How Democratic Is the Constitution?* ed. Robert Goldwin (Washington, D.C.: American Enterprise Institute, 1980), 39–58; and Charles Lindblom, *Politics and Markets* (New York: Basic Books, 1979), conclusion.

19. *The Federalist*, no. 49, 313–317.

20. Ibid., 317.

21. See *The Federalist*, no. 57; Joseph M. Bessette, "Deliberative Democracy," in *How Democratic Is the Constitution?* ed. Goldwin, 102–116; and Michael Malbin, "What Did the Founders Want Congress to Be—and Who Cares?" (paper presented at the annual meeting of the American Political Science Association, Denver, September 2, 1982). On the status of legislative deliberation today, see Joseph M. Bessette, *The Mild Voice of Reason: Deliberative Democracy and American National Government* (Chicago: University of Chicago Press, 1994); William Muir, *Legislature* (Chicago: University of Chicago Press, 1982); and Arthur Maas, *Congress and the Common Good* (New York: Basic Books, 1983).

22. Wood, *Creation of the American Republic*, chap. 5; and Ceaser, *Presidential Selection*, 48.

23. *The Federalist*, no. 62; no. 63, 376–390; and Storing, *What the Anti-Federalists Were For*, chap. 7.

24. *The Federalist*, no. 55, 342.

25. *The Federalist*, no. 71, 432; Madison expresses almost the identical position in no. 63, where he stated,

As the cool and deliberate sense of the community, ought in all governments, and actually will in all free governments, ultimately prevail over the views of its rulers; so there are particular moments in public affairs when the people, stimulated by some irregular passion, or some illicit advantage, or misled by the artful misrepresentations of interested men, may call for measures which they themselves will afterwards be most ready to lament and condemn. In these critical moments how salutary will be [a Senate].

26. John Marshall, *Life of George Washington*, quoted in Charles Thatch, *The Creation of the Presidency* (1923; reprint, Baltimore: Johns Hopkins University Press, 1969), 51; and Max Farrand, ed., *The Records of the Federal Convention of 1787*, 4 vols. (New Haven: Yale University Press, 1966), vol. 2, 35, 22, 32.

27. *The Federalist*, no. 68, 413; no. 71, 433; and no. 73, 442; see also Storing, "Introduction," in Thatch, *Creation of the Presidency*, vi–viii. Thomas Jefferson, "Inaugural Address,"

March 4, 1801, in *The Life and Writings of Thomas Jefferson,* ed. Adrienne Koch and William Peden (New York: Modern Library, 1944), 325.

28. Neustadt, *Presidential Power,* 26, 28–30, 170, 176, 204. See also James Sterling Young, *The Washington Community* (New York: Columbia University Press, 1964), 53. This insight has been the basis of numerous critiques of the American "pluralist" system, which, it is alleged, frustrates leadership as it forces politicians through a complicated political obstacle course. See also Jeffrey K. Tulis, "The President in the Political System: In Neustadt's Shadow," in *Presidential Power: Forging the Presidency for the Twenty-First Century,* ed. Robert Y. Shapiro, Martha Joynt Kumar, and Lawrence R. Jacobs (New York: Columbia University Press, 2000), 265–273.

29. Farrand, *Records,* vol. 1, 66–67; *The Federalist,* no. 47, 360–380; see also U.S. Congress, *Annals of Congress* (Washington, D.C.: Gales and Seaton, 1834), vol. 1, 384–412, 476–608. See generally Louis Fisher, *Constitutional Conflict between Congress and the President* (Princeton: Princeton University Press, 1985).

30. In many discussions of separation of powers today, the meaning of effectiveness is restricted to only one of these objectives—the implementation of policy that reflects popular will. See, for example, Donald Robinson, ed., *Reforming American Government* (Boulder: Westview Press, 1985).

31. See, for example, Lloyd N. Cutler, "To Form a Government," *Foreign Affairs* 59 (Fall 1980): 126–143.

32. Gary J. Schmitt, "Executive Privilege: Presidential Power to Withhold Information from Congress," in *Presidency in the Constitutional Order,* ed. Bessette and Tulis, 154–194; and David Crockett, "Executive Privilege," in *The Constitutional Presidency,* ed. Bessette and Tulis, 203–228.

33. Richard Pious, *The American Presidency* (New York: Basic Books, 1979), 372–415; Gary J. Schmitt, "Separation of Powers: Introduction to the Study of Executive Agreements," *American Journal of Jurisprudence* 27 (1982): 114–138; and Louis Fisher, *Presidential Spending Power* (Princeton: Princeton University Press, 1975), 147–201.

34. Woodrow Wilson, *Congressional Government: A Study in American Politics* (1884; reprint, Gloucester, Mass.: Peter Smith, 1973), preface to 15th printing, introduction; Wilson, *Constitutional Government in the United States* (New York: Columbia University Press, 1908); and Christopher Wolfe, "Woodrow Wilson: Interpreting the Constitution," *Review of Politics* 41 (January 1979): 131. See also Woodrow Wilson, "Cabinet Government in the United States," in *College and State,* ed. Ray Stannard Baker and William E. Dodd, 2 vols. (New York: Harper and Brothers, 1925), vol. 1, 19–42; Paul Eidelberg, *A Discourse on Statesmanship* (Urbana: University of Illinois Press, 1974), chaps. 8 and 9; Harry Clor, "Woodrow Wilson," in *American Political Thought,* ed. Morton J. Frisch and Richard G. Stevens (New York: Scribner, 1971); and Robert Eden, *Political Leadership and Nihilism* (Gainesville: University of Florida Press, 1984), chap. 1.

35. Wilson, *Constitutional Government,* 22, 56; and Wilson, "Leaderless Government," in *College and State,* ed. Baker and Dodd, 337.

36. Wilson, *Congressional Government,* 141, 149, 164, 195.

37. Wilson, *Constitutional Government,* 56.

38. Ibid., 60; see also Wilson, *Congressional Government,* 28, 30, 31, 187.

39. *The Federalist,* nos. 47 and 48, 300–313. Consider Madison's statement in *Federalist* no. 48, 308–309:

Will it be sufficient to mark with precision, the boundaries of these departments in the Constitution of the government, and to trust to these parchment barriers against the encroaching spirit of power? This is the security which appears to have been principally relied upon by the compilers of most of the American Constitutions. But experience assures us that the efficacy of the provision has been greatly overrated; and that some more adequate defense is indispensably necessary for the more feeble against the more powerful members of the government. The legislative department is everywhere extending the sphere of its activity and drawing all power into its impetuous vortex.

40. Schmitt, "Executive Privilege."

41. Wilson, "Leaderless Government," 340, 357; Wilson, *Congressional Government*, 158, 201; and Wilson, "Cabinet Government," 24–25.

42. Wilson, "Leaderless Government," 346; at the time he wrote this, Wilson was thinking of leadership internal to the House, but he later came to see the president performing this same role. Wilson, *Constitutional Government*, 69–77; see also Wilson, *Congressional Government*, 76, 97–98.

43. Eidelberg, *Discourse on Statesmanship*, chaps. 8 and 9; and Ceaser, *Presidential Selection*, chap. 4, conclusion.

44. Woodrow Wilson, *Leaders of Men*, ed. T. H. Vail Motter (Princeton: Princeton University Press, 1952), 39. This is the manuscript of an oft-repeated lecture that Wilson delivered in the 1890s. See also Wilson, *Congressional Government*, 195, 214.

45. Wilson, *Leaders of Men*, 39; and Wilson, *Constitutional Government*, 49. See also Wilson, *Congressional Government*, 78, 136–137.

46. Wilson, "Cabinet Government," 34–35. See also Wilson, "Leaderless Government," 354; and Wilson, *Congressional Government*, 72, 136–137.

47. Wilson, *Congressional Government*, 69, 72.

48. Ibid., 72, 82, 197–198; Wilson, "Cabinet Government," 20, 28–32; and Wilson, *Leaders of Men*, 46.

49. Wilson, *Congressional Government*, 76, and preface to 15th printing, 22–23.

50. Ibid., 187.

51. Wilson, *Constitutional Government*, 49. Today the idea of a mandate as objective assessment of the will of the people has been fused with the idea of leader as interpreter. Presidents regularly appeal to the results of elections as legitimizing the policies they believe ought to reflect majority opinion. On the "false" claims to represent popular will, see Stanley Kelley Jr., *Interpreting Elections* (Princeton: Princeton University Press, 1984).

52. Wilson, *Leaders of Men*, 20, 26.

53. Ibid., 29.

54. I am indebted to Robert Eden for the point about *The Federalist*. See also Ceaser, *Presidential Selection*, 192–197.

55. Wilson, "Cabinet Government," 37; and Wilson, *Leaders of Men*, 45–46.

56. See, for example, Wilson, *Congressional Government*, 143–147.

57. Ibid., 144.

58. Wilson, *Leaders of Men*, 45.

59. Wilson, *Congressional Government*, 144.

60. I discuss this and other dilemmas more fully in *The Rhetorical Presidency* (Princeton: Princeton University Press, 1987). See also Jeffrey K. Tulis, "Revising the Rhetorical Presidency," in *Beyond the Rhetorical Presidency*, ed. Martin Medhurst (College Station: Texas A&M Press, 1996); and Jeffrey K. Tulis, "The Constitutional Presidency in American Political Development," in *The Constitution and the American Presidency*, ed. Martin Fausold and Alan Shank (Albany: State University of New York Press, 1991). For recent criticisms of these ideas along with my rejoinder, see Richard Ellis, ed., *Speaking to the People: The Rhetorical Presidency in Historical Perspective*

(Amherst: University of Massachusetts Press, 1998); and the special issue of *Critical Review* 19, nos. 2–3 (2007).

61. Steven E. Miller and Stephen Van Evera, eds., *The Star Wars Controversy* (Princeton: Princeton University Press, 1986), preface.

62. Sanford Weiner and Aaron Wildavsky, "The Prophylactic Presidency," *Public Interest* 52 (Summer 1978): 1–18.

63. Garry Wills, "The Kennedy Imprisonment: The Prisoner of Charisma," *Atlantic Monthly,* January 1982, 34; and H. H. Gerth and C. Wright Mills, eds., *From Max Weber* (New York: Oxford University Press, 1958), 247–248.

64. George C. Edwards, "Campaigning Is Not Governing: Bill Clinton's Rhetorical Presidency," in *The Clinton Legacy,* ed. Colin Campbell and Bert A. Rockman (New York: Chatham House, 1999), 37. Clinton quoted in Elizabeth Drew, *Showdown: The Struggle between the Gingrich Congress and the Clinton White House* (New York: Simon and Schuster, 1996), 19.

65. Tulis, *Rhetorical Presidency,* 174–175.

66. Deputy Secretary of Defense Paul Wolfowitz interview with Sam Tannenhaus, May 9, 2003, www.defenselink.mil/transcripts/2003/may2003.html.

67. Tulis, *Rhetorical Presidency,* chap.4.

2 Studying the Presidency: Why Presidents Need Political Scientists

Lyn Ragsdale

Political scientists study the presidency, but presidents have not been interested in learning what they have to teach. That's too bad, argues Lyn Ragsdale, because most presidents could learn a great deal. Employing a variety of perspectives and methods, political scientists have uncovered several general patterns in the presidency. Some of these have to do with presidential imagery—for example, "People respond to presidents more through emotions than through rational calculations about the government's performance or presidents' positions on issues." Other generalizations ("Cabinet government does not work") concern the presidential institution. Ragsdale finds that presidents who are ignorant of what political scientists know often make avoidable, sometimes serious mistakes.

American presidents are surrounded by experts. Economists show presidents how to study budgets, inflation figures, and unemployment rates. Domestic policy analysts tell presidents about the details of proposals on civil rights, health care reform, Social Security, and education. Military, foreign relations, and intelligence experts inform presidents about the capabilities of military hardware, defense strategies, international diplomacy, and covert operations. On occasion, historians remind presidents about what past chief executives have accomplished. But political scientists are rarely asked to the White House to instruct presidents about the presidency. Since President Bill Clinton's first term, a team of political scientists has run the White House Transition Project, which offers systematic advice to new presidents' transition teams about specific offices in the White House and the executive departments and what to do and not do when making cabinet and other appointments.[1] But once the transition is complete, political scientists are much less known to American presidents. Few presidents seem ever to have taken a course on the presidency; some seem to have failed one. Presidents typically presume that by virtue of being in office they must know the job's ins and outs. Yet political scientists understand the presidency in a way that other experts cannot. Presidents could benefit from studying the presidency.

This chapter considers what political scientists know about the presidency and what presidents themselves should know. First, two central features of the modern office—imagery and institution—are outlined.[2] Second, several generalizations about the presidency that are related to its imagery and institution are addressed. These generalizations describe what usually happens in the office and outline regular patterns that are difficult for presidents to avoid and equally difficult for them to modify. Third, several episodes of presidential mistakes are examined that might have been avoided had presidents studied the office more carefully. Finally, the issue of what presidents can learn from how political scientists study the presidency is reexamined.

Imagery and Institution

The first thing presidents need to know about the presidency is that it has two major dimensions: imagery and institution. The main image of the presidency is of the president, speaking with a clear lone voice, governing the country. The institution is the complex organization of people that surrounds the president; helps to make presidential decisions; and structures relations with other institutions, such as Congress, the media, the bureaucracy, and the courts.

These two features of the presidency appeared around the beginning of the twentieth century.[3] Image and institution emerged through a philosophical shift from presidential restraint to presidential activism. As proponents of activism, Theodore Roosevelt (1901–1909) and Woodrow Wilson (1913–1921) argued that presidents have the ability to do anything on behalf of the people that does not directly violate the Constitution. Activism thus relies on two concepts, both of which forge the presidential image. First, presidents can do "anything"—they are to be active policymakers and problem solvers. Second, presidents do so on behalf of the people—they are, in Theodore Roosevelt's words, "stewards of the people." The institution is needed to carry out the responsibilities assumed by presidents in the new imagery. The one demands the other.

Neither of these features of the presidency existed in the nineteenth century, when presidents operated under notions of restraint—they exercised only those powers specified in the Constitution and existing laws. As a rule, presidents were neither seen nor heard. George Washington, Thomas Jefferson, Andrew Jackson, James Polk, and Abraham Lincoln aside, presidents before the twentieth century either did not take active roles in policymaking and public leadership or were unsuccessful when they did so; both arenas were thus left to

Congress. For modern presidents the key is to understand more specifically what the image and the institution are like.

On Imagery

The image of the presidency is the single executive image: The president is the most powerful, most important person in the government and in the nation. As the only official elected by the entire country, presidents represent the people. They profess compassion for the average American and passion for the American dream. They are the nation's principal problem solvers, the ones who identify its most daunting challenges and offer solutions. They press their leadership to ensure that the proposed solutions become law. In times of crisis, they single-handedly protect the nation. The image of the president is thus of a person who is omnicompetent (able to do all things) and omnipresent (working everywhere).

An image is a simplification. It is one's mental picture of an object, a product, a situation, or, in this case, a political office. The image usually magnifies certain features while glossing over other relevant details. Reality is typically checked against the image more than the other way around. For example, if you have an image of the perfect cat—big, white, and fluffy—then you are unlikely to enjoy cats who do not match this image. If a scrawny, black, matted feline wanders by, you are much less likely to adopt a new image of the perfect cat to accommodate it. The single executive image is a simplification of both the presidency and American politics. It personalizes the office by embodying all its units, staff, and decisions in one person—the president. In the mind's eye of the nation, the president is the person who matters most. American politics is presidential politics. Many people's recollections of American politics are dominated by the day Truman dropped the bomb, the day John Kennedy was shot, the day Richard Nixon resigned, the day George W. Bush declared war against Iraq, the day after day that Jimmy Carter could not free the hostages in Iran. People often simplify their views of both the presidency and American politics by focusing on the exploits of one person.

To be sure, people are aware that the government is immensely more complex than this—Congress is a powerful and, at times, dominant branch; the bureaucracy seems to do whatever it wants; the Supreme Court announces decisions that tell the rest of the government what to do. Yet citizens look at this assemblage as if it were the scrawny cat. It does not fit their presidential image of the government. Similarly, when they find that presidents appear to be in over their heads with national economic difficulties, dissension within their own party in Congress, or civil wars abroad, they do not modify the single executive image to fit the harsh (and very typical) presidential circumstance. Instead, they revise their opinions of the incumbent chief executive, who comes out the loser in public opinion polls.

Sources of the Single Executive Image. The single executive image arises from three sources: the public, the press, and presidents themselves. Citizens are keenly interested in political figures as individuals, and presidents are the political figures they know best. The political scientist Fred Greenstein observed that people draw on the president as an important cognitive aid to simplify and ultimately understand politics.[4] Many Americans pay little attention to politics, but the one person they do know something about is the president. Many can recall the most trivial details about presidents, from their taste in food—whether it is President Obama's taste for arugula or President Clinton's affinity for McDonald's—to the names of the family pets: Fala (Franklin Roosevelt), King Timahoe (Nixon), Millie (George H. W. Bush), Socks (Clinton), and Barney (George W. Bush). Indeed, when Barack Obama announced to the world on the night he was elected that his daughters would have a puppy in the White House, it set off a frenzy of speculation about what kind of dog the Obamas would get. Thus people simplify the complex operations of government by concentrating on the actions of a single player—the president.

The media help produce the ubiquity of president-watching among the public. The most important national story that the press reports, day in and day out, is about the president. The press covers the presidency as if the persons were the office—what they say, where they go, whom they meet. They too are fascinated with the president as a person. It is not clear which fascination came first—that of the public or that of the press. Much press coverage has become known as the "body watch."[5] Reporters watch the president's every move just in case, as Ronald Reagan put it, the "awful awful" happens. As one television news executive producer observed, "We cover the president expecting he will die."[6] The body watch carries with it a vivid irony. Especially since the Kennedy assassination, the press assumes, probably correctly, that people want to know if a president becomes ill, is injured, or is killed. Yet on most days, nothing catastrophic happens. So the body watch captures the ordinary aspects of the president's life. Otherwise mundane activities, such as taking a morning walk, jogging, playing golf, eating at a restaurant, and boating, become news as part of the body watch. Cameras often captured George W. Bush chopping wood and clearing brush on his ranch in Crawford, Texas, as part of the news. In addition, only when problems arise among members of the White House staff do viewers and readers learn about some of the more than one thousand people who work within the presidency. Most often the president stands alone in daily press coverage.

This press focus on the president was underscored the evening of President Clinton's fourth State of the Union address on February 4, 1997, the same evening a civil jury returned a verdict against former football star O. J. Simpson in the deaths of Simpson's wife and her friend. The television networks had a major decision to make—whether to follow the president or follow the arguably more sensational and dramatic story about Simpson. Consistent with the emphasis on presidential media, the broadcasters decided to cover the president. As Frank Sesno, the Washington Bureau chief for CNN, stated, "If it comes down to it, we go with the president. We don't interrupt the president of the United States."[7]

The press focus on the presidency reinforces the image of the president as omnipresent and omnicompetent. Presidents work to portray particular images of themselves. Many of these images first emerge during the election campaign as the candidates attempt to distinguish themselves from each other and often from the current occupant of the White House. Candidates portray themselves as smart when the predecessor or opponent is depicted as dumb. They portray themselves as energetic, hardworking, and eager for change when the predecessor is shown as lethargic. The personal image of a president also develops while he or she is in office. Some aspects of this image are built quite intentionally by the White House, such as the notion of the smart, calm, family-oriented Barack Obama. Other aspects are shaped more unwittingly through selective media coverage of the president's daily activities, such as Gerald Ford's being typecast as a bumbler after he slipped on ice and hit several errant golf balls. Whether crafted intentionally or occurring accidentally, a president's personal image is measured continually against the single executive image.

How to Study Presidential Imagery. How, then, should presidents study the single executive image so that they can use it most effectively? Presidents may think they know something about imagery from the campaign. It is tempting for them to believe that as long as they stick with what worked then, they will have no problems once in office. But converting campaign imagery into presidential imagery is trickier than many candidates-turned-presidents imagine.

Campaign imagery carries with it a large amount of puffery. Candidates compete to appear as the most convincing omnicompetent player. They make outlandish promises, such as to wipe out a $1 trillion deficit, to impose no new taxes, to implement secret plans to end the war in Vietnam, and to reduce dramatically the role of the federal government in American society. Campaigns operate according to their own laws of physics: almost no promise or accusation is ever too incredible; almost no number of promises or accusations is ever too many. Campaign physics also provides some room for ambiguity and fine tuning during the exceedingly long election season. Candidates can make sweeping commitments but say that the details have not been fully worked out. Or they can say that a proposal has been misunderstood by the media or misrepresented by the opposition.

Campaign imagery is certainly related to the single executive image and derives many of its features from presidential imagery. But the laws of campaign physics do not apply in office. The media now focus not just on the promises made but also on the promises kept. Sweeping commitments must be converted into detailed plans. If presidents back away from promises, compromise them, postpone them, or break them, they violate presidential imagery, because the single executive image suggests that presidents keep their promises and act in the best interest of the nation in doing so. When George H. W. Bush broke his "Read my lips: no new taxes" campaign promise, he later lamented that it was the worst mistake of his presidency. In contrast, when Dwight Eisenhower made good on his campaign pledge to "go to Korea" and bring the warring parties to the peace table, he was heralded as a hero, even though the war ended with the borders unchanged from where they were when the war began three years earlier. Presidents must be constantly aware of the comparison between what was promised during the campaign and what is undertaken in office.

This campaign-office comparison is only one part of the much larger comparison between presidents' personal images and the single executive image. Throughout their terms, all presidents endure a gap between the two images that can never be fully closed. The size of the gap depends on how well presidents present themselves as living up to the single executive image. Part of the gap involves the extent to which campaign promises are kept. But other dimensions include demonstrations of power, success, and American pride.

The wider the image gap, the more the media will depict the president as omnipresent but not omnicompetent. As one example, the failed Bay of Pigs invasion in April 1961—a CIA-directed attempt by Cuban exiles to oust the Communist government of Fidel Castro, which was approved by the Kennedy administration—opened President Kennedy to charges of reckless youth, arrogance, and incompetent decision making. Yet the closer a president's personal image comes to the omnicompetence and omnipresence expected in the single executive image, the less likely the president will end up looking like the scrawny cat. During the Cuban missile crisis in October 1962, when the Soviet Union tried to install missiles in Cuba that were pointed at the United States, Kennedy was praised for his acumen in invoking a naval blockade of the island as well as for the tough yet calm manner in which he did so. Similarly, after George W. Bush, wearing a full pilot suit and helmet, landed in a Navy fighter plane on the aircraft carrier USS Lincoln on May 2, 2003, he tried to embody the single executive image of a leader by boldly proclaiming that the military effort in Iraq had ended while a banner in the background proclaimed "Mission Accomplished." As the war and U.S. involvement continued for another five years, people frequently recalled the aircraft carrier moment. Consequently the gap between Bush's image and the single executive image loomed large. In contrast, immediately after the September 11, 2001, terrorist attacks, Bush made a trip to Ground Zero in New York City to visit the search and rescue teams working at the World Trade Center site. Standing alongside firemen and the American flag, Bush told those assembled that "America today is on bended knee, in prayer for the people whose lives were lost here, for the workers who work here, for the families who mourn."[8] Bush was touted as being caring, sensitive, and bold—all the things required by the single executive image. Thus presidents can study the dimensions of the single executive image to recognize how their personal images will be evaluated by journalists, politicians, and the public.

On the Institution

Although the public, the press, and presidents are at least somewhat familiar with presidential imagery, none of them, not even presidents, are well acquainted with the presidential institution. During the campaign, candidates do not think much about the presidency as an institution; instead, it is a prize to win. They are most likely to invoke imagery that defies the institution: they will do numerous things single-handedly, they will succeed with Congress and the bureaucracy where their predecessors have failed, and they will bring peace to the world and prosperity to the nation. When he took office, President Obama may have been surprised to learn the full extent of what he had inherited: a complex organization consisting of forty-two separate offices, more than sixteen hundred employees, and an annual budget of more than $100 million, officially named the Executive Office of the President (EOP). Outgoing president George W. Bush was undoubtedly more familiar with the organization and also more aware of his limited abilities to change its size and shape. Despite Bush's declared intention to streamline the EOP, he had no more luck in doing so than had most of his predecessors. Indeed, Reagan and Clinton had also announced efforts to trim the office, but with no real success. The number of employees and the budget of the EOP during Clinton's first term looked remarkably similar to those observed during both Bush administrations. The total executive staff averaged 1,727 people under George H. W. Bush, 1,620 under Clinton, and 1,704 during George W. Bush's term.

An institution is an organization of people established to carry out a set of functions. Institutions include schools, corporations, police departments, legislatures, and courts. A peculiar characteristic of an institution is that it acts independently of the people within it. An institution establishes regular patterns of behavior for its members to follow, including divisions of labor (specialization) and standard operating procedures (rules about how things are done). These patterns are followed regardless of who holds positions in the institution, even at the very top.

The contemporary presidency is an institution. It is an organization of people who carry out an array of policy, public, and political functions for which the president is responsible. The presidential institution is no small family business. It operates with a division of labor—offices within the White House specialize in foreign, domestic, and economic policy, the budget, press relations, public appearances, congressional liaison, and group affairs. Through the years the institution has developed standard operating procedures to devise budgets, write and reject legislation, and invoke vetoes. These procedures change only modestly from one president to another. The presidential institution makes many decisions on behalf of the president that the president knows little about.

Not only is the presidential institution elaborate, it is also decentralized. The decentralization means that there is a proliferation of offices, many of which have roughly equal status and the ability to direct, if not determine, presidential decisions. There is less top-down authority in the presidency than one might expect. It is difficult for the president or his senior staff to effectively monitor or even establish the direction for all the work that is done on his behalf. The political scientist Alfred de Grazia remarked, "On a normal issue that comes before the 'President' some dozens of persons are involved. It might be presumptuous to say that more of a collectivity is engaged than when the same type of issue would come before the Congress; but it would be equally presumptuous to say that fewer persons were taken up with the matter."[9]

Institutional Responsibilities. The presidential institution exists to handle three sets of responsibilities, regardless of who is president: policy issues, political targets, and the daily workload. First, units in the EOP handle three broad policy domains: national security, the economy, and domestic affairs. Because each category is so encompassing, several units, each with slightly different jurisdictions, share responsibility for each domain and often compete to exercise their expertise and their control of presidents' ultimate decisions. To make matters even more complicated for presidents, many of the units that have the greatest authority over a particular policy area are not within the EOP but instead are in the departments and agencies of the federal bureaucracy. For example, the National Security Council, the national security adviser, the National Security Council staff, the secretaries of state and defense, the Joint Chiefs of Staff, the director of the Central Intelligence Agency, and in some cases the director of homeland security all participate in making national security decisions. Only the first three are in the EOP.

Second, units in the EOP target political players and other political institutions for presidential persuasion. The job of these units is to convince their targets that what the president wants is what they should want. For example, the Office of Legislative Affairs targets Congress and is the focal point for White House lobbying activities on Capitol Hill. In addition, the White House Press Office targets the press through, among other things, the daily briefing by the press secretary. The Office of Public Liaison and Intergovernmental Affairs targets interest groups, at times pressuring them to support the president's proposals and at other times organizing their support as part of a larger White House lobbying campaign.

Third, key units in the White House—the Office of Administration and the Office of Management and Budget (OMB)—are assigned certain high-volume tasks to ease the presidential workload. The Office of Administration follows routine, computerized procedures for hiring White House and other personnel. OMB is the largest, and arguably the most active, presidential office; it is involved in the preparation of presidents' budgets, sending legislation to Congress, determining whether presidents should sign or veto bills passed by Congress, and reviewing thousands of administrative regulations. OMB's procedures purposely remove presidents from, rather than involve them in, as much daily presidential business as possible.

How to Study the Institution. On entering office, many presidents delight in announcing bold plans to rearrange many of the units within the presidential institution—subtract some, add others. Other presidents proclaim that they will dramatically cut the size and budget of the institution. They do so believing that the presidential institution is a personal organization—one that each president can shape and reshape. To some extent, they are right. Presidents do cut units from the EOP, usually under the guise of getting rid of a holdover from the previous administration. These cuts are more than offset by additions that place the president's own stamp on the EOP. Most of the changes presidents make are at the edges of the presidential institution. For example, George W. Bush ended three EOP offices that Bill Clinton had started: the President's Council on Sustainable Development, the Office of Women's Initiatives and Outreach, and the President's Critical Infrastructure Protection Board. But he replaced them with specialty offices of his own: the White House Office of Faith-Based and Community Initiatives, the Office of Strategic Initiatives, the Office of Homeland Security, USA Freedom Corps, the Office of Global Communications, and the Privacy and Civil Liberties Oversight Board. Similarly, Barack Obama expanded the EOP to include a new Council on Women and Girls, the National Economic Council, and the Privacy and Civil Liberties Oversight Board.

In addition, at the beginning of each president's term there is a grand arrival of new people who scramble for office space following the mass exodus of the previous administration. This rapid turnover leads some observers to suggest that there is no institution at all—instead, just a large staff personally serving a president. But the institution does not grind to a halt every four to eight years. Perhaps nothing better underscores the continuity of the institution than a story about President Nixon's last day in office. On the afternoon that Nixon was to announce his resignation, a congressional staffer phoned the White House and inquired whether several minor pieces of legislation were "in accordance with the president's program."[10] There was no functioning president, nor was there a presidential program that afternoon, but the presidential institution continued to operate—the staffer got an answer. The institution has a fair number of employees who are career civil servants, especially in OMB, and who thus stay on from one president to the next. In addition, the vast array of White House procedures concerning budgeting, legislation, and personnel remain intact. At best, then, the presidential institution is only a quasi-personal organization.

It is also a quasi-formal one. Incoming presidents have less ability to change the size and shape of the institution than they might think. The size, structures, and procedures of the White House breed continuity that is difficult to end. Presidents cannot do without the functions that the EOP provides. Only one president in this century has been able to reduce significantly the number of White House employees. In the aftermath of Watergate, Gerald Ford decreased the EOP by 67 percent—from 5,751 employees in 1974 to 1,910 employees in 1975—by eliminating some offices and councils that had been established during the Nixon years. But he reduced the size of neither the White House Office (the unit closest to the president) nor OMB. (Indeed, both increased slightly.) In addition, Ford's personnel cutbacks in 1975 were countered by large increases in expenditures during 1975 and 1976, especially for the White House Office and OMB. Although Ronald Reagan touted his desire to shrink the size of the federal government, the EOP diminished by little more than one hundred people in his first term and by only seventy-six people in his second term. The overall size crept back up during the George H. W. Bush years. Thus presidents who study the size and shape of the institution learn that the presidency has a life of its own that is quite independent of the people within it, even the president. At a luncheon with former presidents Carter, George H. W. Bush, and Clinton designed to welcome Barack Obama to the Oval Office, George W. Bush reflected that "[a]ll of us who have served in this office understand that the office itself transcends the individual."[11]

Generalizations about Presidential Imagery

What can political scientists tell presidents about image and institution?

Principles of Image Making

Political scientists offer four empirical generalizations about presidential image making.

1. Through their speeches, presidents present themselves as representatives of the people and as moral and religious leaders. Their own words typically portray them as nonpartisan leaders who work alone in the government without the aid of staff, members of Congress, or other executive officials.[12]

2. Public opinion polls show that the public most consistently expects presidents to place the country's interest ahead of politics, be intelligent, exercise sound judgment in a crisis, take firm stands on issues, get the job done, and be concerned about the average citizen.[13]

3. In addition, public opinion polls indicate that people respond to presidents more through emotions than through rational calculations about the government's performance or presidents' positions on issues.[14]

4. Early press coverage, which deals with family stories and future policy plans, is more favorable than subsequent press coverage.[15]

Taken together, these generalizations suggest that the single executive image endures in presidents' own words, public impressions, and press coverage. In their speeches, presidents offer the country the single executive image. They sponsor the dual notions of presidential omnicompetence and omnipresence. They suggest that they alone are linked to the American people, above politics, beyond party, and touched by God. Gerald Ford revealed his connection to the American people on assuming office:

I will be the President of black, brown, red, and white Americans, of old and young, of women's liberationists and male chauvinists and all the rest of us in-between, of the poor and the rich, of native sons and new refugees, of those who work at lathes or at desks or in mines or in the fields, of Christians, Jews, Moslems, Buddhists, and atheists, if there really are any atheists after what we have all been through.[16]

Similarly, the public judges presidents according to the single executive image. As a Nixon aide wrote, "Presidents are measured against an ideal that's a combination of leading man, God, father, hero, pope, king. . . . They want him to be . . . someone to be held up to their children as a model; someone to be cherished by themselves as a revered member of the family."[17]

Early press coverage also reinforces the single executive image by depicting the president as a person of the people (complete with family, furniture, and daily routines) with bold new plans to lead the nation forward. Political scientists Michael Grossman and Martha Kumar found in a study of newspaper, television, and magazine coverage of presidents from 1953 to 1978 that, during the early part of the term, reporters are most attentive to human interest stories about the president. Indeed, a Ford White House official predicted that the first stories about the incoming Carter administration would be personality stories about the president: "First, who is Jimmy Carter? What is his personality? Does he get mad? Does he golf? Does he fish in a pond? How do you find out who somebody is? You look at his friends, his habits, his manner, his character, his personality."[18]

Taking the generalizations together, political scientists reveal two features of the presidential imagery. First, the single executive image rests on symbolism—the president symbolizes the nation, its people, and its government. There is a symbolic equivalence between the president and the public, with the two blurring together as one in presidents' speeches and in media coverage of the office. Presidents frequently use the pronoun *we* to refer to themselves and the American people.[19] As noted previously, human interest news reports depict the president as one of the people. The symbolism is emotionally, not rationally, based. Ordinary citizens, who are often inattentive to government and politically unorganized, find it difficult to obtain tangible benefits from a president, unlike a major industry requesting relief from a regulation or an interest group seeking legislation. Instead, people seek "quiescence" in politics—reassurance that everything is all right or at least that someone is in charge.

People, then, may well be less concerned about what presidents do than how they make them feel. These emotions help to explain the otherwise ironic situations in which presidential failure garners public support. As one example, Kennedy's popularity rose ten points after the ill-fated Bay of Pigs invasion of Cuba in 1961. Had people judged the decision rationally, based on costs and benefits, their response would have been to disapprove of the president's performance. Instead the president benefited in the short term, because people sought quiescence that the "bad guys" were being challenged, no matter what the outcome of the challenge was.

Without studying the presidency, presidents may neglect this emotionally based symbolic connection and expect the American public to evaluate their proposals and achievements on their policy merits. In so doing they confuse objective accomplishment with perceived triumph. Bill Clinton was frustrated, for example, that his numerous legislative successes in 1993 were not accompanied by high public approval ratings. By 1995 Clinton recognized that presidential success is in the eyes of the beholders. In the aftermath of the 1994 midterm congressional elections, in which Republicans gained majorities in both houses of Congress for the first time in forty years, Clinton and the Republican leadership played a tumultuous game of brinkmanship by failing to reach a budget agreement and ultimately shutting down the government for several weeks. Although such deadlock could hardly be deemed an objective success, Clinton gained the upper hand by casting the Republicans as the culprits. His perceived victory boosted his popularity ratings. Following the single executive image, presidents must shape a visceral political experience through telling folksy stories, witnessing human tragedies and triumphs, and offering examples of old-fashioned American values. Presidents who try to behave differently will find the public otherwise engaged.

Second, the single executive image is false. Although the image is a very real part of the American body politic, it is an exaggeration and distortion of grand proportions. The president does not single-handedly lead the people and govern the country. The president may be the single most powerful individual in the country, but Congress as a body is at least as powerful as the president. Presidents surely hold a unique position in the government, but they are not alone, either in the presidential institution or in the larger government.

In two ways the falsehood of the single executive image may perplex presidents who have not adequately studied the presidency. Some presidents fail to see the falsehood. Instead, they act as though they are singularly powerful, flouting regular consultation with Congress and defying laws that prevent unilateral presidential action. In an interview with David Frost after resigning the presidency, Richard Nixon was asked about a president's breaking the law in the best interests of the nation. Nixon responded, "Well, when the President does it, that means that it is not illegal."[20] This was a contorted extension of the single executive image into a claim that the president can do no wrong.

Other presidents who know the image to be false risk pointing out the falsehood at their own peril. Jimmy Carter tried on several occasions to downplay people's expectations by suggesting that he was only one man and could not do it all. Although he was right, the public did not recognize that their expectations were unrealistic. Instead, they judged Carter a failure for not living up to them. Presidents must both recognize the falsehood and live with it just as they must recognize the symbolic connection between the president and the public and do what they can to capitalize on both.

Closing the Image Gap

What can presidents do to capitalize on the single executive image? Political scientists offer four generalizations. (The numbering of these statements continues in sequence from the earlier discussion.)

5. Short successful wars, sudden international crises, and significant diplomatic efforts temporarily improve the president's public approval rating.[21]

6. Major nationally televised addresses also temporarily improve public approval.[22]

7. Protracted wars, domestic riots, public protests and demonstrations, and declining economic conditions diminish public approval.[23]

8. During the course of their terms, presidents face a decline in public approval.[24]

The size of the image gap that presidents endure between their personal images and the single executive image bears directly on presidents' public support—the wider the gap, the lower the public approval rating. Political scientists have recognized two aspects of the image gap: (1) the short-term events, activities, and circumstances that narrow or widen it; and (2) the long-term pattern of public approval during a president's term as it relates to the gap.

In the Short Term. Presidents have a fair degree of control over some ventures that work to their advantage in closing the image gap, such as emergency military interventions, dramatic diplomatic efforts, and well-timed major television addresses. Presidents also face some circumstances beyond their control, such as international crises like the fall of the Berlin Wall and the collapse of the Soviet Union, which may work to their advantage. Whether presidents have control or not, a rally of national support typically takes place. After the terrorist attacks on September 11, 2001, George W. Bush's approval rating soared from 51 percent to 85 percent and peaked at 89 percent. Consistent with the emotional basis of public approval, presidents receive all but unconditional support for actions that place the United States in a clear-cut good-versus-evil, us-against-them position or that envelop the actions or positions of the administration in patriotic trappings.

But other sudden and unforeseen events or conditions at home—such as urban riots, skyrocketing consumer prices, or plummeting job prospects—may leave the public wondering what the president will do. Many of these exigencies will tarnish the president's reputation in relation to the single executive image. The single executive image suggests that presidents are responsible even for things that they cannot predict and over which they have no immediate control. Yet for the very reason that presidents can neither predict nor control what will happen, they are unable to capitalize on these events and conditions. The us-against-them focus changes; it is no longer the United States as a whole against foreign foes. Instead, it is more likely that presidents portray their side as "us" and the opposition as "them," thereby ensuring domestic controversy rather than a popular mandate about how the issues should be handled. George W. Bush's approval rating dropped nearly 10 percentage points overnight, from 48 percent to 39 percent, following Hurricane Katrina because many Americans felt the government's response to the calamity was inadequate.

Generalizations 5, 6, and 7 taken together—the mix of the controlled and the uncontrollable, the presidential rallying of public support, and the public questioning of presidential action—imply that presidents must engage in domestic, foreign, and economic policy making. The single executive image demands attention to all three policy spheres. Although presidents are likely to get less credit in domestic than in foreign affairs because the public rally feature is absent, they may come up short politically if they emphasize foreign over domestic initiatives. For example, because President George W. Bush limited his domestic agenda in order to focus on Iraq, he left himself open to charges of not caring sufficiently about the consequences of Hurricane Katrina on New Orleans. The opposite is also true: it is unwise for presidents to develop high-profile domestic agendas and make short shrift of foreign policy. By doing so, they defy the symbolic importance of acting as the leader of the nation to the world and do not show skills of crisis management, both of which are expected parts of the single executive image. President Clinton initially appeared hesitant in foreign and military affairs, but when criticism about the perceived hesitation mounted, he began to act more decisively. Finally, although economic bad news widens the image gap, economic good news closes it. Even though presidents have limited control over what happens in the economy, they are credited with being economic wizards if the economy is robust. As President Carter observed, "When things go bad you get entirely too much blame. And I have to admit that when things go good, you get entirely too much credit."[25]

In the Long Run. Political scientists have also observed an overall pattern to the shifts in public approval across presidents' terms: approval starts high in the first year, slides during the second and third years, and then rebounds slightly in the fourth year. This pattern denotes three distinct phases to public approval across the term: a honeymoon in some portion of the first year; a period of disillusionment in the middle of the term, when the image gap is at its widest; and a phase of forgiveness at the term's end, when people recognize to some degree that the image is just that and that the president was not so bad after all.

This long-term pattern is one that seems to be an inviolate canon of the office: what starts high must decline. The three phases vary considerably in intensity and duration by president, but the overall pattern is obvious. From Franklin Roosevelt, who was president when public opinion polling first began, to Ronald Reagan, only one president—Dwight Eisenhower—escaped the pattern. Eisenhower's first-term popularity started high and stayed high, although the pattern of decline did occur in his second term. Even presidents who were typically viewed as popular presidents, like Roosevelt and Reagan, nonetheless witnessed the downward pattern during their times in office. George W. Bush also experienced a classic, if precipitous, decline in approval. Despite surging in the aftermath of 9/11, Bush's approval rating dropped throughout his first term and continued to do so during his second term, reaching a historic low of about 25 percent during much of 2008. As unpopular as Bush was, even he experienced the forgiveness phase: his approval rating rose from 25 percent at the time of the November elections to 34 percent as he left office. The cycle began anew with Barack Obama, who entered office with a 68 percent approval rating, a high level of support not seen since Gerald Ford.

Presidents George H. W. Bush and Bill Clinton appear as exceptions to the overall pattern of decline. Neither followed the three phases of support, and it is unclear that future presidents will return to them. Instead, the elder Bush and Clinton faced sharp peaks and valleys in their popularity timed to specific events and presidential actions with little, if any, trend across their terms. Bush's approval started relatively high, soared, and then plummeted. He began office with 69 percent of the American public approving of his job in office. His popularity peaked at 89 percent in February 1991 during the Persian Gulf War, the highest ever recorded for any president. During the war, he had effectively moved his personal image toward the single executive image, getting high marks for exercising good judgment in a crisis and engaging in a large, short, successful military encounter. After the war, there was an expectation on Capitol Hill, in the media, and among many Americans that the president would convert this wave of public support into public deeds, notably on the sluggish economy. Instead, longtime Bush strategist and secretary of state James Baker snapped to reporters, "When you're at 90 percent, you can do what you damn well please." Bush left the impression that he was not willing to do anything about the weak economy or to try to understand the average American's plight. As the economy continued to sour, Bush's image gap widened. His approval sunk to 29 percent by the summer of 1992, a free fall of 60 percent in sixteen months. George H. W. Bush not only achieved the highest approval rating of any president but also incurred the sharpest drop in approval of any president in the shortest period of time.

Clinton's first-term approval started modestly, dropped immediately on taking office, and then rose steadily after the midterm, something no other president has achieved. Clinton began office with 58 percent of Americans approving of his performance in office, but this rating fell sharply to 37 percent by June 1993. Just six months into Clinton's term, his approval ratings had dropped by just over 20 percentage points after bruising battles with Congress over gays in the military, health care reform, and the budget. His ratings remained in the low 40-percent range throughout 1994 and did not break 50 percent again until April 1995. Thereafter, Clinton's approval ratings rose consistently, hitting 60 percent by the end of his first term. During this time, the president appeared to successfully act as the nation's problem solver, consistent with the single executive image, as the White House struck deals with the new Republican-controlled Congress over the budget and welfare reform.

Clinton's second term was marked by still higher ratings in the midst of an impeachment proceeding in the House and a trial in the Senate on charges related to his affair with former White House intern Monica Lewinsky. Clinton's approval rating peaked at 73 percent in December 1998 just after the House voted to impeach him. His ratings remained high during the Senate trial and then, in the months after the Senate failed to convict him, declined somewhat to an average of 60 percent. The public, apparently dismayed by the highly partisan nature of the impeachment process, expressed support for Clinton with strong approval ratings, which then returned to more normal levels as the president returned to more normal business.

In general, three factors appear to be pushing presidents into a new era of volatile relations with the public in which quick swings in approval may occur within the honeymoon-disillusionment-forgiveness sequence. First, the frequency of public opinion polls has increased dramatically. Although American politics has run on public opinion polls for decades, the sheer number of polls and the number of organizations conducting them has never been higher. Polling organizations that used to poll once a month now poll once a week. During periods of presidential crisis, whether related to wars, sex scandals, or critical mistakes, pollsters conduct surveys two to three times a week. On any given news day, several polls may be released by different polling companies and news organizations. In a critical period of the Clinton-Lewinsky scandal in August 1998, when Lewinsky testified before independent counsel Kenneth Starr's grand jury about the nature of her relationship with Clinton, the Gallup Organization conducted separate surveys on August 7, 10, 18, 20, and 21 to monitor any moment-to-moment Clinton approval shifts, which began at 64 percent in the August 7 poll, peaked at 66 percent in the August 18 poll, and dropped slightly to 62 percent by the August 21 poll. The frequency of polling places inordinate attention on *any* approval shift. Even though many of these changes are likely to be within the margin of error of the survey, they are not reported this way.[26] Instead, it appears that the wind has shifted, even if only slightly.

Second, presidents and their advisers have expressly developed political and policy strategies with these omnipresent polls in mind. Although presidents have kept an eye on the polls since the early days of opinion polling, the extent to which presidents have become pollsters is notably more vivid and intense. Dick Morris, one-time polling adviser to President Clinton, commented, "The icons of the past relied on political instinct. Now presidents can use scientific polls and focus groups." Of equal importance, Morris contended that the polls enable a president to take positions that maintain his popularity because "an elected executive—whether president, governor, or mayor—needs a popular majority every day in his term. When [his ratings dip] below 50 percent, he is functionally out of office."[27] Presidents who monitor the polls and make corresponding adjustments to their policies further heighten the significance of polls and quicken the public's response time to these decisions.

Third, presidential news is more instantaneous and comprehensive than in the past. Presidents have long been the single most-covered news figure in American politics, but the growth of the twenty-four-hour news day through CNN and the Internet has greatly accelerated this visibility. This moment-to-moment monitoring of presidential actions and reactions means that presidential failures and successes receive far more microscopic treatment than they once did. Not only the failures and successes but also the depth and length of the treatment become a part of what shifts public approval with swifter reactions and sharper peaks and valleys.

These three factors—more polls taken faster, presidents as pollsters, and all-day news—set up a cycle of presidential action–news–polls–presidential action with a pace that is much faster than when Harry Truman said, "I don't read the polls because they don't mean much." The new metric used to judge a president's job in office may well be how effectively the administration responds to these crises. If presidents encounter a major problem that goes unaddressed, then popularity ratings may be in free fall. If they move effectively to deal with the crisis, they should expect significant increases in approval. Presidents must play the crises with the single executive image in full view or risk appearing ineffectual.

Generalizations about the Presidential Institution

In addition to image, political scientists have examined the presidential institution. They have done so by looking inward to the makeup of the organization and outward to the relations that the presidency has with other institutions, especially Congress, the media, and departments and agencies in the federal bureaucracy.

Inside the Institution

Political scientists offer three generalizations about the internal workings of the presidential institution.

1. Hierarchical staff systems with a single chief of staff are generally more successful than more collegial systems in which every top adviser reports directly to the president.[28]

2. Presidents' own rhetoric to the contrary, cabinet government does not work.[29]

3. Presidents are not solely in charge of the 1,700 people who are employed in the EOP.[30]

In the early weeks after the election, many presidents-elect attempt to wrap their fledgling administrations in democratic expectations. They promise that, unlike past administrations, theirs will be run with great openness. As a symbol of such openness, presidents often promise to take great personal care in the daily running of the White House by granting access to divergent staff voices. As another symbol, presidents announce that the cabinet will meet frequently as a source of information, inspiration, and advice. Neither promise is kept for long.

Why are the promises so quickly abandoned? Political scientists observe that the presidential institution is too large for any of them to be kept. Several recent presidents have learned the hard way that collegial staff configurations lead to presidential overload. To give numerous staff members direct access to the president places a considerable burden on the president to keep abreast of the many major and minor issues being monitored by staff members, not to mention the task of resolving numerous major and minor personality and turf clashes within the staff.

For example, President Ford began his administration with a collegial staff system of nine people reporting directly to him, a spokes-of-the-wheel arrangement, with advisers at the rim of the wheel and the president at its hub. Ford soon bogged down in the collegiality and turned to a hierarchical arrangement, naming Donald Rumsfeld as his chief of staff. Other staff members then filtered information and advice through Rumsfeld rather than going directly to Ford. Dick Cheney, then Ford's second chief of staff and later George W. Bush's vice president, was reminded of the collegial approach at a White House staff party. He received a bicycle wheel mounted on a board with each of its spokes mangled and twisted. A plaque below read, "The spokes of the wheel: a rare form of management artistry as conceived by Don Rumsfeld and modified by Dick Cheney." Cheney left the wheel and a note on his desk as a gift to the incoming adviser to Jimmy Carter, Hamilton Jordan. The note read, "Dear Ham. Beware the spokes of the wheel."[31] But the Carter administration replayed the Ford administration's mistake. It, too, adopted a collegial staff system, which it later abandoned in favor of a more hierarchical one. In Cheney's words, "Someone has to be in charge."[32] The hierarchical approach places a chief of staff between the president and other staff members so that the president will be less overwhelmed by policy and personnel details. Adopting the hierarchical approach does not give presidents any more control over the entire White House apparatus, which remains large and unwieldy, but it does give them more control over the top echelon of the organization, to which they have immediate access. Presidents since Carter have all invested in the hierarchical model. Upon taking office, Barack Obama named Illinois congressman Rahm Emanuel to be his chief of staff. But Obama also designed a novel version of the collegial model for his economic team. In the midst of the gravest economic downturn since the Great Depression, Obama assembled an economic team of well-qualified, talented people but placed no one in charge of the overall economic recovery except himself. As a result, the likelihood of internal division and competition seemed higher than with a more hierarchical approach.

Presidents also find cabinet government to be unworkable. It is cumbersome and unproductive to meet with the cabinet as a whole, let alone to rely on its collective judgment. The cabinet is a body of unequals—some cabinet members enjoy considerably greater access to presidents than do others. In addition, many members of the cabinet are chosen for political reasons—to be a cross-section of the American populace—rather than for their policy expertise. Finally, cabinet members frequently adopt departmental outlooks rather than the more global outlook that might make cabinet government possible. Presidents soon realize that the cabinet is one of the few organizations of government for which the whole is less than the sum of the parts.

The need for coordination at the top and the limited role of the cabinet are symptoms of the internal complexity that marks the presidential institution. Political scientists have uncovered considerable evidence of that complexity as the presidential institution acts independently of the president or the president acts as only one of many players in the institution. For example, although President Kennedy was involved in the decision that gave American approval to the plot by the South Vietnamese military to overthrow President Diem in 1963, the American ambassador to South Vietnam, Henry Cabot Lodge, had considerable control over the matter.[33]

Institutional complexity also permits presidents to hide in the labyrinth of the presidential institution and deny their involvement in schemes that may have backfired, gone awry, or skirted the law. The evidence now suggests that President Reagan knew of the arms-for-hostages agreement with Iran and the channeling of money to the Nicaraguan contra rebels that constituted the Iran-contra affair, but he safely hid his involvement through the "plausible deniability" afforded him by the presidential institution. His national security advisers, first Robert McFarlane and then Adm. John Poindexter, and National Security Council staff members, including Oliver North, acted as screens for the president. They suggested that they had made the decisions without the president's full knowledge, thereby allowing the president to deny any involvement.[34]

Interinstitutional Relations

Political scientists offer presidents generalizations about White House relations with other institutions. The first generalization pertains to what is known about relations between the White House and the departments and agencies of the executive branch; the others describe relations between the White House and Congress.

1. Efforts to politicize the bureaucracy and bureaucratize the White House have only a limited effect on presidents' success in policy implementation.[35]

2. Presidents who establish their legislative agendas early—in the first three to six months of their terms—are more successful at getting specific agenda items passed than are those who wait.[36]

3. The higher presidents' level of legislative activity (that is, the more pieces of legislation on which they take positions), the lower the legislative success. Conversely, the lower the activity, the more successful is the president.[37]

4. Presidential addresses and public approval increase presidents' success in Congress. In turn, presidential success in Congress improves public approval.[38]

Bureaucratic Relations. Many presidents and many citizens are under the misguided impression that the president is the chief executive—the head of the departments and agencies of the executive branch. Nothing could be further from the truth. As Harry Truman complained, "I thought I was the president, but when it comes to these bureaucrats, I can't do a damn thing." In many ways, presidents are satellites of the executive branch. They and their administrations do not share in the values of the various departments and agencies, they operate under different timetables, and they do not know or serve as advocates for clients of the bureaucracy, whether farmers, welfare mothers, or some other group.

In that realization, presidents have attempted three strategies to win the hearts and minds of three million bureaucrats. Presidents Lyndon Johnson and Nixon adopted one strategy—namely, to bring as many decisions about policy implementation as possible into the White House. The Johnson administration created the Office of Economic Opportunity (OEO) in the White House to fight the War on Poverty. The result was a disaster. OEO failed to coordinate community-based poverty programs adequately, leaving many without supervision and leaving the War on Poverty as a whole to flounder. The Nixon administration brought a variety of implementation functions into the White House. Yet the resulting increase in the White House staff was not sufficient to alter bureaucratic patterns of thinking and procedures, especially in the areas of health, welfare, and poverty, over which Nixon sought the greatest control.

President Reagan promoted a second strategy: to groom people for positions in the bureaucracy who espoused the president's philosophy. This strategy met with early success, but as Reagan's term waned so did the strategy. After a year or two, many Reagan recruits returned to the private sector to make more money. In addition, when President George H. W. Bush arrived at the White House with a less firmly defined ideological outlook than Reagan's, hiring people who fit the presidential outlook became difficult. The approach returned with George W. Bush, especially at the Justice Department, where seven U.S. attorneys who were considered to be insufficiently interested in pursuing cases against Democrats were dismissed. In a January 2005 memo to Attorney General John Ashcroft, Kyle Sampson, the Department of Justice's counsel, described the U.S. attorneys who would not be fired: "the vast majority of U.S. Attorneys, 80–85 percent, are doing a great job, are loyal Bushies."[39]

A third strategy, known as administrative clearance, began during the Nixon administration, greatly expanded under Carter, and was heavily relied on by the Reagan White House. It involved OMB's approval of the rules and regulations proposed by departments and agencies. During the Reagan years, the clearance process had a significant effect on the proposed regulations of several agencies, notably the Environmental Protection Agency and the Departments of Housing and Urban Development, Education, and Energy, all of which Reagan disliked. Some agencies refused even to submit certain regulations to OMB for fear they would be shot down. Similarly, many regulations that OMB rejected were never resubmitted.[40]

Administrative clearance shows the greatest promise for putting the presidency into the executive branch loop. It is the first institutionalized effort presidents have made to rein in the bureaucracy. By comparison, the other two strategies were decidedly ad hoc. OMB has established procedures to investigate administrative rules and regulations and acts as a watchdog for the rest of the government. It determines whether rules proposed by a department or an agency in the executive branch are consistent with White House criteria. If they are, the rules are designated as "consistent without change." If they are not, the rules are returned to the agency in one of two ways. First, OMB may issue a "prompt letter" designating the rules as "consistent with change." This requires the agency, which has proposed the rule, to act on the specific modifications requested by OMB in the prompt letter. Second, OMB may issue a "return letter," which asserts that the rule has failed to meet OMB standards. More than 70 percent of agency rules submitted during the George W. Bush administration were deemed "consistent with change" and required modifications based on OMB instructions.[41] As might be expected, because of the institutional nature of the clearance process, presidents have little personal involvement and essentially trust OMB to do what the presidents want.

Congressional Relations. Political scientists have uncovered important lessons for presidents working with Congress. First, presidents must not clutter the legislative agenda with lots of big issues or even lots of small ones. Nor must presidents meet Congress on its own terms, because its agenda is always burdened with large and small issues. Instead, presidents benefit by presenting Congress with a small list of big-ticket items that spell out what the president wants.

Second, presidents must adjust to two kinds of presidential time that dictate many of their most important legislative strategies: electoral time and organizational time. Electoral time is a highly compressed four-year cycle that is geared toward the upcoming election. The electoral clock ticks fast and loudly. As one White House aide put it, "You should subtract one year for the reelection campaign, another six months for the midterms, six months for the start-up, six months for the closing, and another month or two for an occasional vacation. That leaves you with a two-year presidential term."[42] In contrast, many Washington politicians—those elected, those appointed, and those hired—have long time frames for action. Their clocks tick slowly. They have careers—at least a decade but most likely two—in which to finish what they start. Many members of Congress, although they must look toward the next election, enjoy safe seats that ensure their political longevity. Most people in Washington are there to stay. Presidents come and go.

Organizational time is the slower pace at which the White House apparatus gathers information, follows existing procedures, and makes decisions. It reflects the start-up-and-slow-down rhythm of the presidency. Organizational time is at its slowest early in the term, when staff members are just beginning to understand their jobs. It may speed up later in the term as people, including the president, learn the ropes.

Although electoral and organizational time run at opposite speeds, they are linked closely in two ways. In one way, electoral time helps to create the slower organizational time. Because electoral time forces presidents to act in a hurry and to keep acting, it creates a need for a large presidential institution to carry on the action. In such a compressed time frame, it is impossible for presidents and just a few close advisers to develop agendas, see them through Congress, and have the executive branch implement them. They must draw on a presidential institution that operates on its own slow time schedule, made even slower by the coming and going of presidents every four or eight years.

In another way, the joining of electoral and organizational time poses a dilemma for presidents. What is the best time for presidents to put forward their legislative agenda during their terms? Electoral time says the best time to act is early in the term. Organizational time urges presidents to act later, when people are more settled into their jobs. Most presidents and their staffs acknowledge that electoral time takes precedence over organizational time. The organization must try to catch up with demands in the political arena. Electoral time allows presidents to use the single executive image most dramatically if they "hit the ground running" by presenting major policy initiatives to Congress with great public fanfare in the first months of the first year of their terms. "It's definitely a race," stated a Carter aide. "The first months are the starting line. If you don't get off the blocks fast, you'll lose the race."[43]

Yet hitting the ground running is neither easy nor fun. Presidents often stumble in their first months in office and delay their legislative goals. The presidential institution may not be ready to go. Like any large organization, it needs time to work properly. It may even need more organizational time than many institutions because its flow of operation is interrupted every four to eight years by the arrival of a new president and new staff members. The Nixon administration fell into such a trap postponing the announcement of a welfare reform plan. A Nixon aide lamented, "We gave our opponents a great deal of time to fight the Family Assistance Plan. They had at least six months to prepare before the initial announcement. Then, because we were late, the program bogged down in congressional committee. We gave them too many chances to hit us."[44] In addition, if a president has already encountered an era of increasingly volatile public reactions (as discussed previously), then hitting the ground running may not be possible for political as well as organizational reasons. In the absence of a honeymoon period early in the president's term, there is little reason to expect that a major controversial policy initiative is going to sail through Congress.

Finally, the presidential image and the presidential institution intertwine in the legislative process. Presidential addresses and public approval increase presidents' success in Congress on passing various pieces of proposed legislation. In turn, presidential success in Congress increases public approval. These relationships take place within a larger political-economic context. Presidential success in Congress is shaped by the size of the president's party, the year in the term (the later in the term, the less likely the president's position is to prevail), economic circumstances, and international conflicts.[45]

Presidential Mistakes

The fifteen generalizations about imagery and institution embody much of what political scientists know about the presidency. Presidents, like everyone else, make mistakes. But many of them could be avoided if presidents carefully observed these generalizations and the broader discussions of imagery and institution from which they derive.

Presidents' mistakes can be defined as situations in which presidents adopt courses of action that bring about the opposite of what they want or significantly less than what they want. To be sure, mistakes are not always clear-cut. For example, when President Truman fired Gen. Douglas MacArthur for insubordination at the height of an offensive against the Chinese during the Korean War, Truman incurred tremendous political opposition, especially when MacArthur returned to the United States to a hero's welcome. But the decision was not necessarily a military mistake, because MacArthur was pushing for a much wider war with China. Truman replaced MacArthur with Gen. Matthew Ridgway, who was able to correct some of MacArthur's tactical excesses. There are, however, numerous instances in which mistakes are not subject to multiple interpretations. Presidents make mistakes on imagery, on institutional relations, and on the combination of the two.

Mistaken Images

Image mistakes involve the president's failure to live up to some central aspect of the single executive image. Many of these mistakes relate to the president as a person. They often involve small things, such as haircuts, walks on the beach, pets, and trips to the grocery store, because the single executive image depends on the symbolic connection between the president and the American public. People understand the connection best when it is based on activities in daily life that they share with the president. Everyone gets a haircut; everyone goes to the grocery store. As planes reportedly waited on nearby runways at Los Angeles International Airport, President Clinton paid $200 for a haircut by a Beverly Hills stylist aboard *Air Force One.* In a grocery store, President George H. W. Bush was revealed as being unaware of how price scanners worked, indicating that he had not done his own shopping in many years. President Nixon walked on the beach near his home in San Clemente, California, in a tie and dress shoes, looking stiff and uncomfortable. President Johnson played with his pet beagles, Him and Her, by pulling them up by their long floppy ears, outraging dog lovers. Because such image mistakes typically leave the president looking out of touch with average citizens, the gap between the personal image and the single executive image grows.

Image mistakes may also involve the president as a policymaker—breaking a promise, not doing what the single executive image demands under certain policy circumstances, or attempting to revise the image itself. President George W. Bush made image mistakes when he repeatedly suggested not only that Saddam Hussein was aiding al-Qaida and thus was linked to the terrorist attacks on September 11, 2001, but also that Hussein possessed weapons of mass destruction. No evidence supported either claim. This not only weakened Bush's credibility, and thus created significant image problems for him, but also had major policy consequences in defining the impetus for the Iraq war.

As may be imagined, the second type of image mistake is more likely than the first to harm presidents. Although the personal mistakes cause momentary embarrassment and for a time draw considerable press attention, the press and the public soon tire of the topic and move on to something else. The policy mistakes tend to have longer-range consequences and thus are more apt to characterize the failures of an administration.

Institutional Mistakes

Presidents are also prone to mistakes when they fail to address various institutional constraints adequately. Such mistakes involve relations in the White House and relations between the White House and other institutions, such as Congress, the Supreme Court, or a department or an agency in the executive bureaucracy. Within the institution, presidents frequently fail to acknowledge tensions between units that share similar jurisdictions. Several presidents have let animosity fester between the national security adviser and the secretary of state on matters of diplomacy.[46] Information leaks are common occurrences as units within the White House compete with each other to make decisions to their own advantage. In-house scandals or embarrassments also erupt because too many people are going in too many directions to be monitored adequately by the chief of staff or other staff members, let alone the president. Indeed, many of these instances have involved the chiefs of staff themselves, ranging from charges against Eisenhower's chief of staff, Sherman Adams, that he improperly accepted gifts, to those leveled against George H. W. Bush's chief of staff, John Sununu, for using government planes and cars for personal use. Many internal institutional mistakes prompt the question, "Who is minding the store?" And the answer often is, "No one." The mistakes are reflections of the complexity of the presidential institution and the limits to presidents' control over it.

Presidents also make mistakes in relations between the presidency and other institutions. At the base of many of these mistakes is the recent presidential tendency to run against Congress. Presidents charge that Congress is unwieldy, irresponsible, and unable to do what the country needs. Although this tactic may play well with the folks back home, it does not play well with the people on Capitol Hill, who will support or oppose presidential legislative priorities. President Reagan's ill-fated nomination of Robert Bork to the Supreme Court in 1987 revealed several dimensions of interinstitutional mistakes. Although the Reagan administration had been in office for six years, it violated several basic principles of the presidential institution during the nomination battle that lasted for three and one-half months and ended with the Senate's defeat of Bork by the largest margin in history—forty-two to fifty-eight. The Reagan people disregarded fundamental institutional constraints surrounding the nomination of Bork, an activist conservative: The Senate was solidly Democratic;

it was late in Reagan's term; his popularity had slipped; Congress had been angered by the disclosures of the Iran-contra scandal; and several senators, notably Senate Judiciary Committee chair Joseph Biden, were running for president. Institutional miscalculations continued when the Reagan strategists pinned their hopes for victory on southern Democratic senators but did not conduct an aggressive lobbying campaign—either publicly or privately—for Bork until well after the swing senators had been pressured by their constituents not to back Bork. They also gave up a critical timing advantage when Reagan announced the nomination in July. The Senate adjourned for its summer recess in July, and Biden did not call for hearings on the nomination until September. Had the Reagan people anticipated Biden's move, they could have delayed the president's own announcement of the nomination until after the Senate reconvened. This would have prevented Bork's opponents from mobilizing during July and August. Interinstitutional mistakes occur with Congress when presidents fail to take into account its composition, the link between presidential success and public approval, and the idea of timing issues in such a way as to gain the upper hand.

Image-Institutional Mistakes

Presidents also make mistakes that join lapses in imagery with those in institutional relations. Presidents may choose a course of action that widens their image gap. The gap then leaves space for other institutions to gain strategic advantages. President Clinton's attempt to end the forty-eight-year-old ban on gay men and lesbians in the military in 1993 is an example of this kind of image-institution mistake.

Clinton made a campaign promise to end the ban and reiterated the pledge as president-elect. At first glance, one might argue that Clinton did exactly what the single executive image demands. At the earliest possible opportunity—even before being sworn in—he announced that he would issue an executive order lifting the ban. Surely this is the kind of swift, bold action the single executive image requires.

But the single executive image also dictates boundaries within which such swift actions must be taken. They must be done with average Americans in mind and in such a way that citizens either will not be aroused or will be unified. Instead, Clinton chose a highly controversial issue that tapped, among other things, homophobic prejudice both in and out of the military. In doing so, he pushed away his own main agenda item, summarized in his campaign headquarters as "It's the economy, stupid." Nor did the Clinton team lay any rhetorical or public opinion groundwork for the decision. The apt comparison between lifting the gay ban and Truman's executive order desegregating the military was left to several members of Congress and gay rights leaders to make. Furthermore, Clinton announced the decision at a time when few other administration decisions were being made. Indeed, this was the Clinton strategy. The president would look strong lifting the ban early with one stroke of the pen while more intricate plans were being developed for the economic programs at the core of Clinton's agenda. Yet the absence of other presidential news allowed the press to focus intense coverage on the matter of gays in the military rather than on the more typical stories of the new first family moving into the White House and the president's plans for the future. As a result, a public uproar ensued and Clinton lost much of his honeymoon support.

In an attempt to ameliorate the issue, Secretary of Defense Les Aspin announced that he would review the ban and make recommendations to the president in six months. The Clinton people hoped this would be a cooling-off period during which the controversy would diminish. Yet their timing decision set off a series of institutional machinations. Members of the armed forces and members of Congress, especially the Joint Chiefs of Staff and Senate Armed Services Committee chair Sam Nunn, now had a full opportunity to organize against Clinton's proposal. The Joint Chiefs had threatened in November to resign en masse if an executive order not to their liking was forthcoming. Nunn held hearings and visited a submarine to dramatize the close quarters in which sailors, in particular, lived. The Joint Chiefs and Nunn were able to define the issue around their own alternatives. A compromise policy—"Don't ask; don't tell"—was ultimately worked out that permitted gay men and lesbians to serve in the military but not openly to acknowledge their sexual preference. The ban had been modified but not lifted. Thus Clinton began his term with a wide image gap but also allowed two competing institutions—the military and Congress—to define an issue in such a way that the president had to acquiesce to them rather than the other way around.

It is not always the case that presidential mistakes permit other institutions to achieve their goals at the expense of the president. President Clinton's mistakes during the Lewinsky scandal created an immense image gap—he was deceptive when addressing the American people about the affair, he offered a tortured defense of his actions based on a narrow definition of sexual relations, and he did not offer an unequivocal apology for his actions until quite late. These actions were well out of sync with the single executive image, which would expect presidents to be family oriented, honest, and contrite. But two factors saved Clinton from his own mistakes. First, the American public viewed the mistakes as personal in nature. And the public believed they already knew a good deal about this personal side of Clinton, given that rumors about his sexual exploits flew as early as the 1992 campaign. The public knew this in 1992 when they elected Clinton, and they knew it in 1996 when they reelected him, indicating that these matters were not as important as policy matters in defining the importance and visibility of the single executive image. On policy matters, Clinton scored high marks and little gap appeared to exist between his presidential image and the single executive image. The economy was booming, the deficit was gone, Social Security was saved, and welfare reform was in place.

Second, the prosecution of Clinton by independent counsel Kenneth Starr and the impeachment proceedings in the House appeared to be highly partisan. The House, in particular, seemed heedlessly out of step with public opinion. The closer the House moved toward impeachment, the higher went Clinton's approval ratings. In a rather loud statement of dissent to the House, the public indicated in an array of polls that Clinton's transgressions were of a personal nature and did not warrant removal from office. House Republicans created an image gap of their own, appearing to go after the president for their own political gains. Whether Clinton's legacy as president survives his mistakes during the Lewinsky scandal remains a matter for time and history, but it is plain that not all mistakes are equal. Even sensational ones may not spell presidential failure, if the presidential missteps are not policy related and other institutions make their own even more heedless miscalculations.

President George W. Bush made significant image and institutional mistakes in the aftermath of Hurricane Katrina. On August 29, 2005, the day the hurricane made its second, more devastating landfall, Bush interrupted his vacation at his Texas ranch to fly to Arizona for a small birthday party for Republican senator John McCain. The next day he flew on to San Diego to commemorate the sixtieth anniversary of V-J Day, marking the end of the war against Japan in World War II. For those two days, he appeared to be preoccupied not with the storm and its impact, but with other ceremonial and political duties. On August 31, with 80 percent of New Orleans flooded from levees broken by the storm surge, Bush finally cut his vacation short. En route to Washington, he flew over the flooded area of the Gulf coast but did not land. This decision compounded the initial image problem. After first appearing not to care about the situation, he then appeared to avoid direct involvement in its solution.

Not until September 2, five days after the hurricane hit, did Bush visit the region. When he did so, he praised Federal Emergency Management Agency head Michael Brown, "Brownie, you are doing one heck of a job." But it was clear to many Americans watching around-the-clock coverage of the devastation in New Orleans that Brown's management of the recovery effort was seriously flawed. Brown himself did not know for two days that people were stranded at the New Orleans Convention Center, even though it had been reported on all the major news networks. Numerous mix-ups occurred among federal, state, and local agencies, and 47 percent of Americans blamed President Bush directly for the failures of aid and assistance. Institutional breakdowns, then, seemed just as apparent as the image problems. Not only was there a wide image gap as Bush tended to other business while thousands died in the hurricane's wake, but also there were significant institutional failures with little coordination from the White House.

Conclusion: Presidents and Political Scientists

Is it possible that, if President Clinton had a political scientist position in the White House Office or even the Cabinet advising him on the nature of the presidency, the issue of gays in the military would have been resolved in a manner more in keeping with what the White House wanted? Could the Reagan administration have saved the Bork nomination? Could President George H. W. Bush have translated public support into domestic policies after the Persian Gulf War? Political scientists are no more omniscient than presidents or their primary advisers. They would not get it right all of the time. But they have knowledge quite different from that offered by presidents' other advisers, knowledge that is pertinent to every decision that presidents make—namely, how the presidency operates.

Presidents have three main types of advisers. Policy advisers lay out various domestic and international policy problems that presidents may wish to address or may have to address. They also develop positions and programs for presidents to offer as solutions. Economic advisers spell out various options on how to keep the economy robust, how to make the good times return, and how to cut or add to the federal budget. Political advisers consider the politics of a decision—how it will play with the public, how the press will cast the issue, and how other politicians will respond. Political advisers then devise strategies to sell presidents' decisions with these political considerations in mind.

Missing are advisers skilled in telling presidents about the office they hold. Although each type of adviser teaches presidents a good deal about what they need to know to work in the White House, none of them is an expert on the presidency. The generalizations from political science research are not lessons that the other advisers would fully know. Even political advisers, who may be aware of some of the generalizations, such as those on public opinion, are typically not schooled in the presidency per se. Because many political advisers began their stint with the president during the campaign, they often have an electoral framework in mind that is much narrower than that offered by political scientists.

What presidents need is a fourth set of advisers—presidency advisers. Nor will it do to hire only those political scientists who view the presidency from a single perspective or advocate but one method. The generalizations about imagery and institution are a mix of qualitative and quantitative findings. Conclusions about different types of White House staff systems, cabinet government, and the limits to presidents' control of the EOP and the bureaucracy are drawn largely from qualitative accounts. Conclusions about presidential success in Congress, presidential approval, and presidential speeches are drawn primarily from quantitative studies.

The generalizations also reveal the perspectives that political scientists adopt. Studies of presidential dealings with Congress and the public typically adopt the perspective of presidential power. Presidents must persuade members of Congress and the public to give them what they want. Accounts of the relations between presidents and their advisers, cabinet members, and the bureaucracy incorporate historical descriptions, interpretations of the power of presidents, and institutional analyses.

Thus political scientists' understanding of the presidency rests on an accumulation of knowledge that cuts across methods and perspectives. Effective presidency advisers must have studied the office from several perspectives and must be knowledgeable about work using qualitative and quantitative methods. This permits them to understand the full scope of the office and its two central dimensions of imagery and institution. How presidents can succeed at using imagery and the institution is one of the main lessons political scientists offer in studying the presidency.

Notes

1. White House Transition Project, http://whitehousetransitionproject.org.

2. For more details on these two concepts, see Lyn Ragsdale, *Presidential Politics* (Boston: Houghton Mifflin, 1993).

3. Jeffrey Tulis, *The Rhetorical Presidency* (New Haven: Yale University Press, 1987).

4. Fred Greenstein, "What the President Means to Americans," in *Choosing the President,* ed. D. Barber (Englewood Cliffs, N.J.: Prentice Hall, 1974), 144.

5. Michael Grossman and Martha Kumar, *Portraying the President* (Baltimore: Johns Hopkins University Press, 1981).

6. Herbert Gans, *Deciding What's News* (New York: Pantheon, 1979), 145.

7. "Clinton vs. O. J.: Fate Lets Networks, Viewers Off Hook," *Arizona Daily Star,* February 5, 1997, A-12.

8. Rick Hampson, "New York Might Not Be as Inviting as It once Was," *USA Today*, www.usatoday.com/educate/election04/article16.htm.

9. Alfred de Grazia, "The Myth of the President," in *The Presidency*, ed. A. Wildavsky (Boston: Little, Brown, 1969), 50.

10. Hugh Heclo, "Introduction: The Presidential Illusion," in *The Illusion of Presidential Government*, ed. H. Heclo and L. Salamon (Boulder: Westview Press, 1981), 3.

11. "Obama Hails 'Extraordinary Gathering,'" Associated Press, retrieved from www .msnbc.msn.com/id/28535240/?GT1—43001.

12. Barbara Hinckley, *The Symbolic Presidency* (New York: Routledge, 1990); Roderick Hart, *The Sound of Leadership* (Chicago: University of Chicago Press, 1987); and Tulis, *Rhetorical Presidency*.

13. George C. Edwards III, *The Public Presidency* (New York: St. Martin's Press, 1983), 196; Stephen Wayne, "Expectations of the President," in *The President and the Public*, ed. D. Graber (Philadelphia: Institute for the Study of Human Issues, 1982), 17–39.

14. Lyn Ragsdale, "Strong Feelings: Emotional Responses to Presidents," *Political Behavior* 13 (1991): 33–65; and Greenstein, "What the President Means to Americans," 144–145.

15. Grossman and Kumar, *Portraying the President*.

16. "Remarks upon Taking the Oath of Office," *Public Papers of the Presidents, Gerald R. Ford, 1974* (Washington, D.C.: U.S. Government Printing Office, 1975), 1.

17. Quoted in Michael Novak, *Choosing Our King* (New York: Macmillan, 1974), 44.

18. Grossman and Kumar, *Portraying the President*, 275–276.

19. Hinckley, *Symbolic Presidency*.

20. *New York Times*, May 21, 1977, A1.

21. Paul Brace and Barbara Hinckley, *Follow the Leader: Opinion Polls and Modern Presidents* (New York: Basic Books, 1992).

22. Lyn Ragsdale, "The Politics of Presidential Speechmaking," *American Political Science Review* 78 (December 1984): 971–984.

23. Ibid.; Samuel Kernell, "Explaining Presidential Popularity," *American Political Science Review* 72 (June 1978): 506–522; and Charles Ostrom and Dennis Simon, "Promise and Performance: A Dynamic Model of Presidential Popularity," *American Political Science Review* 79 (June 1985): 334–358.

24. John Mueller, "Presidential Popularity from Truman to Johnson," *American Political Science Review* 64 (March 1970): 18–34; James Stimson, "Public Support for American Presidents: A Cyclical Model," *Public Opinion Quarterly* 40 (Spring 1976): 1–21; and Brace and Hinckley, *Follow the Leader*.

25. Quoted in Godfrey Hodgson, *All Things to All Men: The False Promise of the Modern American Presidency* (New York: Simon and Schuster, 1980), 25.

26. Sampling error is created in selecting a group of people from the general population. This error depends on the size of the sample taken and usually is 3 to 4 percentage points on most national public opinion surveys. This means that for a given poll result, say 62 percent approval, and a margin of error of 3 percentage points, the true value of approval falls within the range of 59 percent to 65 percent.

27. Dick Morris, *The New Prince* (Los Angeles: Renaissance Books, 1999).

28. Samuel Kernell and Samuel Popkin, eds., *Chief of Staff* (Berkeley: University of California Press, 1986).

29. Richard Fenno, *The President's Cabinet* (New York: Vintage Books, 1959).

30. John Burke, *The Institutional Presidency* (Baltimore: Johns Hopkins University Press, 1992); Bradley Patterson Jr., *The Ring of Power* (New York: Basic Books, 1988); and

Karen Hult, "Advising the President," in *Researching the Presidency,* ed. George C. Edwards, John Kessel, and Bert Rockman (Pittsburgh: University of Pittsburgh Press, 1993), 111–160.

31. Quoted in James Pfiffner, *The Strategic Presidency* (Chicago: Dorsey Press, 1988), 29.

32. Ibid.

33. See Ragsdale, *Presidential Politics,* 191–196.

34. George Shultz, *Turmoil and Triumph: My Years as Secretary of State* (New York: Scribner, 1993).

35. Richard Nathan, *The Administrative Presidency* (New York: Wiley, 1983).

36. Paul Light, *The President's Agenda* (Baltimore: Johns Hopkins University Press, 1982).

37. Ostrom and Simon, "Promise and Performance."

38. Brace and Hinckley, *Follow the Leader;* Lyn Ragsdale, "Disconnected Politics: The President and the Public," in *Understanding Public Opinion,* ed. Barbara Norrander and Clyde Wilcox (Washington, D.C.: CQ Press, 1996).

39. Allegra Hartley, "Timeline: How the U.S. Attorneys Were Fired," *U.S. News & World Report,* March 21, 2007, www.usnews.com/usnews/news/articles/070321/21Attorneys-timeline.htm.

40. Ragsdale, *Presidential Politics,* 239.

41. Lyn Ragsdale, *Vital Statistics on the Presidency,* 3rd ed. (Washington, D.C.: CQ Press, 2009), 317.

42. Quoted in Light, *President's Agenda,* 17.

43. Ibid., 43.

44. Ibid.

45. Ostrom and Simon, "Promise and Performance."

46. For example, a feud that developed in the Carter administration between Secretary of State Cyrus Vance and National Security Adviser Zbigniew Brzezinski affected the ill-fated helicopter rescue attempt of the American hostages held in Iran.

3 The Presidency in the Eye of the Storm

Marc Landy and Sidney M. Milkis[1]

Although they were written more than two centuries ago, America's founding documents, the Declaration of Independence (1776) and the Constitution (1787), have consistently remained the touchstones of American political development. What keeps these documents relevant, argue Marc Landy and Sidney M. Milkis, are the occasional "refoundings" that certain presidents have wrought in how Americans interpret and apply the documents in changing times. Four presidents in particular—Thomas Jefferson, Andrew Jackson, Abraham Lincoln, and Franklin Roosevelt—each initiated a constitutional refounding by waging a "conservative revolution," which Landy and Milkis define as "a new constitutional teaching, albeit one steeped in the American political tradition."

To properly place the presidency in the context of American political development, three questions are paramount. First, and most fundamentally, how have presidents understood the meaning of executive power and what have been the critical controversies with other branches over conflicting interpretations of that meaning? Second, what role has the president played in the critical episodes that have transformed the American political and constitutional order? Finally, in what ways does the contemporary presidency differ from, and in what ways does it remain the same as, the office envisaged by the Framers?

Presidential Power and Constitutional Refoundings

The president is both the embodiment of the national government and the country's leading political figure. In a sense, this has always been so. In their effort to establish self-government on a grand scale, the architects of the Constitution created the need for such a figure. Alexander Hamilton praised Article II for the way it summoned individuals of great ambition to the office. "The love of fame, the ruling passion of the noblest minds," he wrote in *The*

Federalist No. 72, will "prompt a man to plan and undertake extensive and arduous enterprises for the public benefit."[2]

Hamilton's constitutional justification for granting the president sweeping discretionary power rested in the distinction between how the Constitution vests authority in the legislature and how it vests power in the executive. Article I, Hamilton pointed out, states that "all legislative Powers *herein granted* shall be vested in a Congress of the United States," while Article II does not restrict executive power in that way: "The executive Power shall be vested in a President of the United States of America." The absence of the words "herein granted," he argued, meant that the executive power is both wide ranging and vested exclusively in the president, "subject only to the exceptions and qualifications expressed in the Constitution." This constitutional language, Hamilton insisted, merely confirmed the nature of executive power, which was indispensable to the success of a large and diverse republic.[3]

George Washington put this broad understanding of executive power into practice, establishing a precedent that presidents have followed ever since. In 1793, Washington issued the Neutrality Proclamation, which announced that the United States would not join in the hostilities then taking place between France and Great Britain. Thomas Jefferson and James Madison considered Washington's unilateral executive action to be unconstitutional. A declaration of neutrality was, in effect, a declaration that there should be no war, a decision that rightfully belonged to Congress. To claim that such action was constitutional, Madison argued, was to imply that the executive had a legislative power. Such an argument was "in theory an absurdity—in practice a tyranny."[4]

Hamilton dismissed Madison's view and insisted that in the absence of a declaration of war by Congress the executive had full authority to proclaim and enforce American neutrality. Executive power, he insisted, included the president's duty to take all actions needed to preserve the nation's security unless specifically precluded from doing so by the Constitution. Although political scientists and constitutional scholars are still debating this broad question, Washington *did* declare neutrality, Congress did not contradict him, the country remained at peace, and the power of the president to act unilaterally in emergency circumstances was affirmed.

Much of the conflict between Congress and the president, which has erupted repeatedly in the course of American history, stems from the broad reading of executive power that many presidents have claimed as their own. Jefferson's purchase of Louisiana, which seemed to defy his opposition to executive aggrandizement; Lincoln's suspension of habeas corpus; FDR's prewar provision of military aid to Great Britain and the Soviet Union; Reagan's sale of arms to Iran and provision of arms to the Nicaraguan contras; and George W. Bush's authorization of unwarranted electronic surveillance are prominent examples of actions by presidents who exercised their prerogative in the face of considerable opposition from Congress.

Indeed, support for a sweeping executive power can be found among both defenders and opponents of the Constitution. Hamilton spoke for the Federalists' interpretation of the Constitution, which emphasized that the president is the principal "guardian of the people's interests." As he wrote in the *The Federalist Papers*, "when occasions present themselves in which the interests of the people are at variance with their inclinations," the president has the "duty . . . to withstand the temporary delusion in order to give them time and opportunity for cool and sedate reflection."[5] But even the Anti-Federalists, most of whom considered Hamilton's formula for executive guardianship a recipe for despotism, acknowledged the important role the president would play in holding together a large and diverse society. Their hope was that the president would nurture a sense of patriotism, a vital principle of self-government that would be hard to establish in a large republic. In the words of Cato, "In every large collection of people there must be a 'first man,'" a "visible point serving as a common center of government, towards which to draw their eyes and attachment."[6] George Washington, recognized widely by Federalists and Anti-Federalists alike as the "first man in America," made perhaps his most important contribution to the presidency by serving as this "visible point" of attachment.[7]

Thomas Jefferson developed this idea of "first citizen" into a more capacious view of popular leadership. During his presidency, he argued that the executive was justified in operating outside the law as long as it provided the people with standards for judging its actions. Indeed, when linked securely to popular opinion, the executive would embody American democracy. As Jefferson stated in his first inaugural address, only the president could "command a view of the whole ground" and thus deserved the people's "support against the errors of others, who may condemn what they would not if seen in all its parts."[8]

In short, the essence of the so-called modern presidency, which most scholars associate with the deployment of national administrative power in the name of the people, was there from the beginning. Both Hamilton and Jefferson—the great rivals for the constitutional soul of the American people—prescribed an executive who, when circumstances dictated, could act beyond the law. And even Hamilton, who, as Jeffrey Tulis claims, appeared to "proscribe popular leadership," recognized that the Constitution's celebration of "We, the People" would subject the president to the court of public opinion.[9] As he wrote in defending the unitary, or one-person, executive, "the plurality of the executive tends to deprive the people of the two greatest securities they can have for the faithful exercise of any delegated power, *first,* the restraints of public opinion, which lose their efficacy [to] censure . . . on account of the uncertainty on whom it ought to fall; and *second,* the opportunity of discovering with facility and clearness the misconduct of the person they trust, in order either to their removal from office or to their actual punishment in cases which admit of it."[10] Significantly, it was Hamilton's mentor, Washington, who ensured that the president had the right to speak directly to the people by issuing a Thanksgiving Proclamation, not to Congress but to the people directly.

That the seeds of the modern presidency were there from the start casts doubt on the notion that the presidency, as James Sterling Young has claimed, originally was meant to restrict itself to the constitutional obligation, stated explicitly in the oath of office, "to preserve, protect, and defend the Constitution."[11] Stephen Skowronek's view of the office is more complex and paradoxical but also more credible. Those elected president swear both "to preserve, protect and defend the Constitution," which requires them to affirm the existing order of things, and "to execute the office of the President of the United States," which presupposes their independent intervention in political affairs. This dual obligation creates a strong executive, but one in the grips of a dilemma: it is "a governing institution that is inherently hostile to inherited governing arrangements." As an institution that bridles against order, Skowronek argues, the executive summons not the guardians of ordered liberty whom Hamilton prized but, rather, the ambitious characters Lincoln describes in his Lyceum Address: they are members of the "family of the lion, or tribe of the eagle," who disdain the well-worn path of constitutional government (or any existing path), and seek to use executive power to remake politics and government in their own image. This is true of not just "reconstructive presidents" (who create enduring governing regimes) and "preemptive presidents" (who seek to operate independently of the reigning political order), but also those "loyal sons" who express allegiance to a regime's founder. All presidents, even regime loyalists, are intent on "shattering order."[12]

Yet throughout history, presidents have been restrained by constitutional norms, the separation and division of powers, and political parties. Some presidents, in fact, have strongly resisted allegiance to the prevailing regime, not to "shatter" the existing order but to moderate its excesses in the name of constitutional sobriety. Despite the temptation to expand executive power unduly, presidents who have defined themselves as institutional conservatives—most notably, Grover Cleveland, William Howard Taft, Calvin Coolidge, and Dwight Eisenhower—deserve careful attention, if for no other reason than their critical warnings about the perils of executive aggrandizement. It is especially important to consider these alarms today, a time when recent presidents have broken free of constitutional and partisan constraints.

Even presidents who have left the most indelible marks on the American political order have not simply engaged in "creative destruction." They exerted leadership during major episodes of American political development that were truly conservative revolutions. These "refoundings" required presidents to think constitutionally: to interpret the meaning of the Declaration of Independence, the Constitution, and the relationship between the two for their own time. Lincoln's call for a joining of the principles of the Declaration and the Constitution in a form that condemned slavery to extinction is the most famous. But all of America's most consequential presidents—Jefferson, Jackson, Lincoln, and Franklin D. Roosevelt—have justified regime change in terms of fundamental principles and constitutional norms.

Beyond rhetoric, America's refoundings have been collective engagements. Presidents have been at the center of the storm, but they have not created new regimes on their own. Perhaps most important, regime building has required extraordinary party leadership. To be sure, political parties have not always constrained presidential ambition. Indeed, all of the presidents who instigated regime change were either founders or refounders of political parties. In important respects, as Skowronek suggests, these reconstructive presidents used their parties to remake American politics in their own image. But extraordinary party leadership serves mostly to highlight the collective nature of great political transformations. Political parties have kept presidents faithful to broader interests, even as, episodically, they have given presidents the political strength to embark on ambitious projects of national reform. Moreover, prior to the New Deal, none of the programs that formed the core of a new political regime called for a substantial expansion of executive power.

To dismiss the conventional view of the modern presidency is not to deny that distinctively modern attributes mark the contemporary executive. One such feature involves the decline of the idea of limited constitutional government during the course of the twentieth century. The first to question the idea of limits on the ends and means of government were the Progressives. Theodore Roosevelt, in particular, was dismissive of "parchment barriers" that stood in the way of implementing the people's will. The New Deal prescribed a new understanding of rights that erased many of the traditional impediments to deploying the federal government in the public's service. The use of the federal government by the Great Society to dismantle the ramparts of Jim Crow–style racial segregation further embellished centralized administration. The "steward of the public welfare," as Theodore Roosevelt famously described the modern executive, became the principal object of the public's heightened expectations about what the national government could and should accomplish.

Another characteristic that defines the contemporary presidency is the executive aggrandizement that has followed from the nation's being on a war footing since the start of World War II. Previously, wars were of limited duration and military mobilization was followed by demobilization. As commander in chief, the president has power and responsibilities that expand drastically in time of war. The cold war lasted from the end of World War II to the late 1980s. The war on terror began in earnest in 2001 and shows no signs of abating. The final part of this chapter examines how the president's essential, uneasy place in the American constitutional order has been transformed by the expanded reach of federal public policy and by the permanent war footing on which the country has been placed.

Democratizing the Constitutional Presidency

Washington and John Adams were republicans. They acknowledged that the people were the ultimate source of authority, but they believed that the preservation of liberty required checks on popular rule. Jefferson was a democrat. He believed that the primary defense of liberty was not constitutional checks and balances but majority rule. In response to questions posed by the French *encyclopediste* Jean Baptiste Meusnier, he proudly replied, "This . . . [is] a country where the will of the majority is the law, and ought to be the law."[13]

Thomas Jefferson began and Andrew Jackson completed a major reinterpretation of the meaning of executive power. Their view of the president as the tribune of the people was an essential component of the conservative revolutions they wrought.

Jefferson's View of the Presidency

As Washington understood, the manners adopted by the president are extremely important because they tell the public how it should envisage "the first man." To emphasize the democratic aspect of the presidency, Jefferson jettisoned the presidential coach and rode his own horse. He ignored distinctions of rank at official functions. He dressed in ordinary attire.

But Jefferson's revision of the presidency was more about substance than style. As Jeremy Bailey has demonstrated, Jefferson accepted the expansive view of presidential power put forth by Hamilton but added three critical elements, each of which promoted its democratic aspect. First, the president unifies and thereby embodies the will of the nation. In Jefferson's mind the president was not just the "first man" but, as the only government official elected by the nation as a whole, he was also the instrument of the national will. Second, although Jefferson agreed with Hamilton and Washington that the president must sometimes act outside the law, or even against it, to serve the public good, he insisted that the president must be held accountable for doing so. Once the emergency had passed, it was the president's duty to submit to the people's judgment. Indeed, Jefferson believed that such accountability extended to all presidential actions. Third, the president had to provide a basis for this accountability by explaining to the people what he was proposing to do and why it was in their best interest. Such declarations provided the people with the information and standards of evaluation they needed to judge him adequately.[14]

As the author of the Declaration of Independence, Jefferson relied, not surprisingly, on declarations to explain his views to the people. His first declaration as president was his first inaugural address, which remains his most important presidential utterance. Although the address is most famous for its conciliatory statement that "We are all republicans, we are all federalists," its greatest importance lies in the clear declaration of how Jefferson conceived of his office and what he pledged to accomplish through it. Unlike his predecessors, whose inaugural addresses were perfunctory, Jefferson used his to lay out what he took to be the essential principles of government—"those which ought to shape its administration." He listed fourteen such principles, including three that lie at the heart of democratic government—equal justice for all, free and fair elections, and majority rule. Jefferson admitted that he would make errors of judgment in his fervent efforts to promote democracy, but he also warned that others would misjudge his rightful efforts because their "position will not command a view of the whole ground." Thus, Jefferson implied that only the president, by virtue of his election by the whole nation, commands such a view and can speak authentically for the people as a whole.[15] Jefferson's statement of principles also provided the people with a checklist against which to judge his performance. Because they understood what he intended to do, they could decide whether he succeeded or failed.

Unlike Hamilton, Jefferson never claimed that the vesting clause of Article II gave him sweeping powers; he simply acted as if it did. Lincoln would later assert that the oath of office required him to act against the letter of the Constitution in order to preserve it. Jefferson offered no explicit constitutional rationale for his actions. The most momentous act of his presidency was the Louisiana Purchase, which he admitted, privately at least, was unconstitutional.[16] The Constitution makes no provision for the acquisition and incorporation of new territory. But Jefferson purchased the vast Louisiana territory anyway. John Quincy Adams and others argued that the enormity of the land acquired amounted to a full-fledged "dissolution and recomposition" of the republic and therefore required a constitutional amendment.[17] Jefferson seemed to agree, but he stopped calling for an amendment after receiving reports that Napoleon was having second thoughts about the deal. Jefferson feared that the prolonged amendment process would give the French ruler time to renege.[18]

Instead Jefferson relied on a declaration in his second inaugural address to defend the merits of the Purchase. The Purchase's great expansion of territory would not endanger the republic because the federative principle embodied in the Constitution—the idea of a large republic divided into sovereign states— would prevent any such threat. Jefferson borrowed from Madison's *The Federalist* No. 10 to argue that "the larger our association the less will it be shaken by local passions." He also argued that national security dictated the Purchase: "Is it not better that the opposite bank of the Mississippi should be settled by our own brethren and children than by strangers of another family? With which should we be most likely to live in harmony and friendly intercourse?"[19] Unlike Washington and, later, Lincoln, Jefferson chose not to defend his right to take this fateful action but instead defended the action itself. It would then be up to the people to determine whether his extraconstitutional action merited their censure.

Jackson's View of the Presidency

Andrew Jackson viewed himself as a disciple of Jefferson, but he expanded Jefferson's understanding of executive power in vital ways. Most important, he reconciled Jefferson's democratic understanding of the executive with Washington's conception of the president as defender of the Union. Although Jefferson had invoked national security as a rationale for the Louisiana Purchase, he never renounced the states' rights convictions that, prior to his presidency, had impelled him to draft the Kentucky Resolutions. In his mind the Constitution was a compact among the states that left each state considerable power to resist dictates from the national government. Thus the Kentucky Resolutions urged the states to find some means to challenge the odious Alien and Sedition Acts that Congress passed during the Adams administration.[20]

Jackson shared Jefferson's preference for decentralized government, but he also showed greater respect for his oath of office. When South Carolina claimed the right to nullify a tariff bill that Congress had passed and he had signed, Jackson issued a proclamation stating that no state could defy a legitimate act of Congress and that he would suppress this act of rebellion.[21] Lincoln's successful resistance to secession would have been far more difficult but for the precedent Jackson established.

Jackson's defense of limited government also relied on energetic executive action. He turned the veto power into a potent democratic weapon. With few exceptions, previous presidents, including Jefferson, had used the veto only when they determined that Congress had acted unconstitutionally. Jackson extended its use to include any legislation that he opposed. He vetoed more bills than all six previous presidents combined. His rationale was that since, like Jefferson, he saw himself as the embodiment of the will of the people, he was entitled, even obligated, to use his powers of office to serve that will to the fullest extent possible. The Constitution placed no conditions on the president's use of the veto. Therefore, Jackson's democratic duty was to use it whenever doing so was to the people's benefit.[22]

Conservative Revolutions

Both Jefferson and Jackson placed their democratic understanding of executive power at the service of the conservative revolutions they led. Their radical commitment to majority rule was tempered by a conservative understanding of the proper role of government in a regime dedicated to inalienable individual rights. Jefferson was acutely aware that the greatest threat to those rights was posed by government. It was therefore of critical importance that the president spearhead the campaign to defeat initiatives to enhance the power of the central government, regardless of how benign the purposes of those initiatives might be. Indeed, the most dangerous government encroachments were those that promised to enhance the lives of the people, because they had the greatest seductive power.

A great deal of Jefferson's presidency aimed at repealing Federalist policies that he believed had undermined liberty. By the end of Jefferson's first year in office, Congress had abolished all internal taxes, including the tax on spirits that had sparked the Whiskey Rebellion. Tariffs and the sale of public lands thus became the sole sources of federal revenue, and Congress dedicated a good portion of those funds to paying off the federal debt, further reducing the monies available to fund government activities. Despite this vast reduction in available revenue, Congress reduced spending so much that the government ran a surplus during seven of Jefferson's eight years in office.[23]

Because of Jefferson's commitment to the "federative principle," the Louisiana Purchase did not lead to an aggrandizement of national power. As the habitable portions of the vast territory became populated, the settlers were encouraged to organize territorial governments as a first step to acquiring statehood. An "empire of liberty," the president believed, would be created consisting of state governments that would resist any effort by the federal government to expand its power.[24]

Jackson reinforced Jefferson's assault on centralized power. In the intervening years between their administrations, many limits on federal activity had been relaxed. A second Bank of the United States had been established, and financial support for public improvements had increased. Jackson vetoed the Bank, arguing that it served to entrench economic privilege and was detrimental to the well-being of ordinary people.[25] He adopted a literal interpretation of the Constitution's commerce clause and was therefore willing to fund only those public improvements that were unambiguously interstate in character. Jackson vetoed Congress's appropriation for the Maysville Road because, even though it was part of the interstate Wilderness Road, the Maysville portion fell entirely within the Commonwealth of Kentucky.[26]

The Jacksonian era was more than Jefferson redux. Jackson launched a conservative revolution of his own, the key to which was his political party. Jefferson was the first president to serve simultaneously as party leader. Indeed, the Republican Party that he and Madison created was indispensable to his election and to his program of limited government. But Jefferson, like most of the Founding generation, detested political parties. He hoped that, after it succeeded in restoring constitutional balance, the Republican Party would wither away. For the most part it did. With the demise of the Federalists, one-party rule evolved into no-party rule. In 1820, James Monroe ran for reelection unopposed. The definition of "Republican" became so capacious as to include the son of a Federalist president, John Quincy Adams, whose commitment to an activist federal government was much more akin to Hamilton's than to his adopted party's own founder, Jefferson.

Strongly influenced by Martin Van Buren, Jackson came to see that a Jeffersonian restoration would require a new form of politics. A political party was not a one-time remedy to a one-time problem. The temptation to use government to support economic privilege was ineradicable. The less vigilant and informed the public, the greater the advantages that would accrue to the privilege seekers. Only an active political party could maintain the ongoing level of public concern and mobilization necessary to keep government neutral in the competition for scarce economic goods. To accentuate their commitment to popular political involvement as the key to thwarting the despotism of the rich, Jeffersonian Republicans who were rallied by Jackson and Van Buren gave themselves a new name, the Democrats.

The key to the development of the Democratic Party was the so-called spoils system. The Jacksonian Democrats argued that the government belonged to the people, and therefore no one should consider public office to be an entitlement.[27]

The people gave the offices, and the people could take them away. As instruments of the people, the Democrats would award government posts to those who subjected themselves to party discipline and remove them from office if they failed to obey such discipline. Thus the system both promoted popular participation by encouraging the hope of gaining office and promoted democratic accountability by enabling party leaders to remove those who failed to do the people's bidding.

The spoils system also sustained the decentralized nature of party politics. When state and local party leaders demanded offices as their reward for rallying voters to the national ticket in congressional and presidential elections, even powerful presidents were not inclined to refuse them. Moreover, to keep their jobs, many federal officeholders, particularly those who served in the widely scattered customhouses and post offices, were required to return part of their salaries to the local party organization that sponsored their office, to do party work, and to "vote right" on Election Day. In this way, decentralized Jacksonian parties imitated the "federative principle" of the government with lines of authority reaching up and down from the local to the state to the national party. This highly decentralized and mobilized party system provided a connection between the ordinary citizen and the various levels of government that had been absent in the years of no-party rule.

Thus the presidency emerged from the era of Jefferson and Jackson newly empowered. Jefferson and Jackson's efforts regarding the Louisiana Purchase and nullification, respectively, showed that they would not retreat from Washington's assertion that the president wielded emergency powers. Furthermore, their understanding of themselves as instruments of the popular will caused them to expand the scope of presidential leadership. They would serve as legislative leaders, fighting for new laws that served the public interest and, in Jackson's case, vetoing those that did not. And they would be party leaders, mobilizing, and disciplining the collective efforts on which the success of their democratically inspired efforts depended. But this expansion of presidential power was constrained by the end it was meant to serve: limited constitutional government. Both Jefferson and Jackson saw limited government as the essential safeguard of liberty. Their commitment to small government, reinforced by decentralized parties, was the most important check on presidential power because it constrained any excesses of personal ambition that might arise among Jackson's successors.

Lincoln and the Civil War Refounding

The Civil War refounding is perhaps the most important of America's political transformations. For the leadership he displayed in fostering what he famously termed a "new birth of freedom," Abraham Lincoln won the lasting esteem of the American people as their greatest president. Scholars have shared this celebration of Lincoln's statesmanship. Yet, during his rise to power and throughout his presidency, Lincoln was subjected to ridicule, and even as he gained respect for navigating the uncharted waters of emancipation and a full-scale domestic rebellion, he was frequently charged with being a despot. Even Lincoln's greatest champions have granted that he went beyond the normal bounds of presidential power during the Civil War. Lincoln's bold actions, however, like Jefferson's and Jackson's, did not expand executive power enduringly. Although he espoused a more positive understanding of liberty than these two predecessors, the reform program that Lincoln championed was still bounded tightly by the nation's long-standing commitment to natural rights, limited government, and administrative decentralization.

Indeed, Lincoln was highly critical of the expansion of presidential power wrought by Jackson and his Democratic successors. His invocation of "the family of the lion" and the "tribe of the eagle" in the 1838 Lyceum Address can only be understood as an attack on the Democratic Party's aggrandizement of executive power in peacetime. This was not merely a rhetorical flourish. In the mid-1840s, Lincoln's devotion to settled, standing law informed his opposition to Jackson's protégé, James K. Polk, for initiating and prosecuting the war with Mexico. As a Whig member of the House of Representatives, Lincoln argued that the Constitution gave the "war making power to Congress" and that "the will of the people should produce its own result without examining executive influence."[28]

Nor did Lincoln give any indication that he had abandoned his Whig principles during his rise to political prominence in the Republican Party during the 1850s. To the contrary, as he stated in the Lyceum Address, Lincoln feared that the slavery controversy had made greater the danger of demagogy. "It thirsts and burns for distinction," he said of executive ambition, "and if possible, it will have it, whether at the expense of emancipating the slaves, or enslaving free people."[29] The Republican Party that Lincoln represented in the 1860 presidential election consisted mostly of former Whigs who, like Lincoln, were dedicated to undoing the Jacksonians' expansion of executive power.

Lincoln's rise to power—unlike that of Jefferson, the celebrated author of the Declaration, and Jackson, whose initial fame was born of military glory—was tied inextricably to partisan loyalty and maneuver. Close attachment to his party constrained, even frustrated, Lincoln at times. Just the same, his partisanship provided an indispensable connection to political allies around the country. In no small measure, Lincoln's success stemmed from his extraordinary party leadership. His involvement in party politics both reinforced the conservative nature of the Civil War refounding and ensured that his stewardship, as remarkable as it was, did not expand presidential power in a way that would survive in peacetime.

Lincoln, the Slavery Controversy, and the Constitution

The challenge for Lincoln and the Republican Party in trying to resolve the slavery controversy was to find a constitutional path between the Abolitionists, who celebrated the Declaration's claim that "all men were created equal," and southern leaders like Chief Justice Roger Taney—the author of the notorious *Dred Scott* decision—who believed that the Constitution sanctified slavery as a right of property. Just as the fiery abolitionist William Lloyd Garrison condemned the Constitution as "a covenant with death and an agreement with hell," so did slave hounds such as Taney and even the more moderate Democratic senator from Illinois, Stephen Douglas, wish to confine the freedoms of the Declaration to whites. Lincoln and the GOP sought to escape this conundrum by forging a dynamic relationship between the Declaration and the Constitution that provided opportunities to fulfill America's creed constitutionally as soon as practical circumstances allowed.

A national debate over slavery exploded with the enactment of the 1854 Kansas-Nebraska Act. Sponsored by Douglas, Lincoln's main political rival, and supported by Democratic president Franklin Pierce, the act repealed the Missouri Compromise of 1820 and gave the Kansas and Nebraska territories a choice about whether to allow slavery. Although it passed Congress because of Pierce's heavy-handed use of patronage, it was justified publicly as a logical extension of the Democrats' commitment to local self-government because the voters of each territory would decide whether they should enter the Union as a free or slave state. In his debates with Lincoln during the 1858 Illinois Senate race, Douglas justified northern Democrats' defense of "popular sovereignty" on the grounds that the United States had been "formed on the principle of diversity in the local institutions and laws, and not on that of uniformity . . . [e]ach locality having different interests, a different climate, and different surroundings, required different laws, local policy, and local institutions, adopted to the wants of the locality."[30]

Born of local protest meetings aroused by the Kansas-Nebraska Act, the new Republican Party insisted that Douglas's position defiled the Declaration. Lincoln mocked the idea that "if one man would enslave another, no third man should object," insisting that it was the height of hypocrisy to call that position "popular sovereignty." Proclaiming his "reverence for the constitution and laws," Lincoln conceded that the national government had no power to inter-fere with slavery where it already existed. But he was unwilling to tolerate extending it to the territories, which would undermine the moral foundation of American constitutional government. Drawing on a verse from the Bible's Book of Proverbs—"A word fitly spoken is like apples of gold in pictures of silver"—Lincoln praised the Declaration's principle of "liberty to all" as the essence of American political life. "The assertion of this principle, at the time," he added, "was the word 'fitly spoken' which has proven an 'apple of gold' to us. The Union, and the Constitution, are the pictures of silver, subsequently framed around it. The picture was made, not to conceal, or destroy the apple, but to adorn and preserve it."[31]

Lincoln and the Republicans claimed that they, not the Democrats, were the rightful heirs of Thomas Jefferson because, in tolerating the expansion of slavery by linking popular sovereignty with the infamous Kansas-Nebraska Act, the Democrats had forsaken their Jeffersonian heritage. Indeed, Lincoln insisted that Jefferson had given form to the Framers' opposition to the expansion of slavery into the territories by drafting the Northwest Ordinance of 1787, which banned slavery in the five states—Ohio, Michigan, Indiana, Wisconsin, and Illinois—that composed the Northwest Territory. Prohibiting slavery's expan-sion into the territories, therefore, was true to the principles of the Declaration, as well as to the proper understanding of the Constitution. Equally important, with the enactment of the Missouri Compromise, which prohibited slavery from expanding into the northern part of the Louisiana Territory, this policy became a public doctrine shared by a majority of Americans. Lincoln wanted to restore the Missouri Compromise, not only for the sake of the Union but also for the "sacred right of self-government" and the "restoration of national faith."

The honor Lincoln bestowed on Jefferson was limited, however. He emulated his old foe, Jackson, in believing that the Constitution drew a sharp line between states' rights, which were constitutional, and nullification, which was not. By the time of Lincoln's inauguration, South Carolina and six other southern states—Georgia, Alabama, Mississippi, Florida, Louisiana, and Texas—had seceded. Following Jackson's example, Lincoln used his inaugural address to pronounce the secessionist movement as treasonous: "I hold that in contemplation of uni-versal law and of the Constitution of the Union of these states is perpetual . . . , that no state upon its own mere notion can lawfully get out of the Union." Lincoln declared that he would defend and preserve the Union by enforcing federal laws in all the states, just as the Constitution enjoined him to do.[32]

Moreover, Lincoln reinterpreted the Declaration to invest the Union with a moral—even religious—purpose that gave rise to a new, more positive understanding of liberty. As Daniel Walker Howe has observed, Lincoln's Gettysburg Address transmuted "the proposition that all men are created equal [into] a positive goal for political action, not simply a pre-political state that government should preserve by inaction."[33] The Declaration, Lincoln maintained, "did not mean to assert the obvious untruth, that all were actually enjoying that equality, nor yet, that they were about to confer it immediately upon them. They meant simply to declare the *right,* so that *enforcement* of it might follow as fast as circumstances should permit." The principles of the Declaration, therefore, were to be "constantly looked to, constantly labored for, and even though never perfectly attained, constantly approximated."[34]

Lincoln gave more concrete expression to this new view of liberty in his address to the special session of Congress that convened on July 4, 1861. The Union's struggle, he told Congress, was to maintain that "form and substance of government, whose leading object is, to elevate the conditions of men—to lift artificial weights from all shoulders—to clear the paths of laudable pursuit for all—to afford all, an unfettered start, and a fair chance in the race of life."[35]

The Great American Crisis and Lincoln's Wartime Measures

Lincoln's greatest challenge and opportunity was to stay faithful to this purpose in the face of the most dangerous emergency the country has ever faced. His artful joining of the Declaration and Constitution seemed to promise a moderate position toward slavery and a limited role for the president in resolving the issue. As the *Chicago Tribune* editorialized in boosting Lincoln for president early in 1860, "He has the radicalism which a keen insight into the meaning of the anti-slavery conflict is sure to give; but, coupled with it, that constitutional conservatism which could never fail in proper respect for existing institutions and laws, and which would never precipitate or sanction innovations more destructive than the abuses that they seek to correct."[36] Yet the outbreak of Civil War led Lincoln to suspend his constitutional conservatism. As soon as secession became violent and irrevocable, he believed, his oath to uphold the Constitution allowed, even compelled him to take extraordinary measures, including emancipating the slaves, in order to restore the Union.

From the day after the rebels bombarded Fort Sumter on April 12, 1861, until Congress convened on July 4, everything that Lincoln did to protect the Union and prosecute the war was done on his own authority. Some of his actions, such as mobilizing 75,000 state militia, were clearly within the proper bounds of the president's constitutional authority. Yet Lincoln went well beyond these bounds. Hoping to bring the insurrection to a speedy end, he ordered a naval blockade of the southern coast, enlarged the army and navy (adding 18,000 men to the navy and 22,000 to the army), and suspended the writ of habeas corpus in northern and border states, where rebellious activity was high. This suspension empowered government officials who were acting under the president's authority to make arrests without warrant for offenses undefined in the laws without having to answer for their actions before the regular courts.

Many of Lincoln's measures raised grave doubts about the constitutionality of his prosecution of the war. His unauthorized enlargement of the military seemed to disregard blatantly Congress's clear constitutional power "to raise and support Armies." The president's critics also argued that because the power to suspend the writ of habeas corpus during a national emergency appears in Article I of the Constitution, which defines the authority of the legislature, the right to exercise the power belongs to Congress. Moreover, Lincoln claimed sweeping powers not only to arrest and detain those who were suspected of rebellious activity but also to try them before military tribunals. Lincoln was the first president to authorize the use of these tribunals, which operated outside the rules of evidence and other codes of judicial conduct governing civilian courts.

Lincoln's conception of the president's responsibility to suppress treasonous activity justified both the suspension of habeas corpus and the establishment of martial law in many areas of the country. Indeed, as the Civil War progressed, Lincoln proclaimed even more comprehensive powers for the military authorities, without any apparent thought of seeking congressional authorization. For example, on September 24, 1862, he issued an executive order declaring that all rebels and insurgents and all persons who discouraged enlistment in the Union army, resisted the draft, or engaged in any disloyal practice were subject to martial law and to trial by either a court-martial, which observes rules of evidence similar to those observed by civilian courts, or a military tribunal. This order provoked sharp controversy in the North. It added to the unrest aroused by the draft, which was imposed for the first time during the Civil War. In July 1863, draft riots broke out in New York City, sparking the greatest civil disorder in the nation's history, save for the Civil War itself. Yet resistance to the draft only served to convince Lincoln that military justice and the suspension of habeas corpus were necessary, not only where the war was being fought but also in some peaceful regions of the country.

Lincoln did not assume these extraordinary powers lightly, but only when he believed that his oath of office gave him no choice. As he wrote in an 1864 letter to the Kentucky newspaper editor Albert G. Hodges, domestic rebellion imposed on him an obligation to use "every dispensable means" to "preserve the nation, of which the Constitution was the organic law." It was senseless,

Lincoln argued, to obey legal niceties while the very foundation of the law was threatened: "Was it possible to lose the nation and yet preserve the Constitution? By general law, life and limb must be protected, yet often a limb must be amputated to save a life; but a life is never wisely given to save a limb. It felt that measures otherwise unconstitutional might become lawful by becoming indispensable to the preservation of the nation."[37]

Not surprisingly, the severity of Lincoln's war measures prompted charges of "military dictatorship," even from some Republicans, and has remained the source of considerable debate and controversy. The distinguished presidential scholar Clinton Rossiter described Lincoln's conduct as a "constitutional dictatorship," an apparent contradiction in terms that was meant to capture Lincoln's impressive, if not fully persuasive argument that constitutional government has an unqualified power of self-preservation and that this power was centered in the office of the president. Although Lincoln's use of power during this supreme crisis was eminently defensible, Rossiter warned, it might set a damaging precedent. "If Lincoln could calmly assert: 'I conceive that I may, in an emergency, do things on a military ground which cannot constitutionally be done by Congress,'" Rossiter concluded, then "some future President less democratic and less patriotic might assert the same thing."[38]

Lincoln as Party Leader

Lincoln's crisis presidency was not undertaken *uno solo,* as Rossiter claims. Instead, it was linked to an understanding of the country's constitutional heritage and to a political party dedicated to upholding that heritage. As president-elect, Lincoln strongly resisted any compromise of his party's campaign pledge to prevent the expansion of slavery in the territories. When word leaked that Congress was considering Kentucky senator John J. Crittenden's plan to extend slavery into the Southwest, Lincoln intervened to defeat it. To surrender, under threat, what Lincoln defined as the Republican bedrock would betray those voters who supported the party in the 1860 election. Republicans in Congress agreed. William H. Seward, the former governor of New York, who was Lincoln's chief rival for the Republican presidential nomination, instigated talk of a negotiated settlement, but not a single Republican legislator voted for the Crittenden plan.[39]

Once in office, Lincoln attended to party-building measures that would "bring to life the political philosophy the Republican Party espoused." In the nineteenth century, patronage was central to the task of transforming a political party into an effective instrument of national unity. Lincoln removed Democrats from practically every appointed office they held, and he took full advantage of the enormous growth of government demanded by the war to amplify the effect of patronage appointments. The president prudently distributed these positions to supporters of the leading Republicans in the cabinet and Congress. By letting his fellow partisans, who represented the competing Republican factions, influence patronage, Lincoln ensured that a range of party opinions would be heard. Equally important, joining patronage to the objective of Republican unity inserted party loyalists into every level of government. These political friends included scores of Republican newspaper editors, who were awarded government publishing contracts and positions in government offices. "Editors seem to be in great favor with the party in power," the *Baltimore Evening Patriot* noted, "a larger number of the fraternity having received appointments at its hands than probably under any administration."[40]

In selecting and managing his cabinet, Lincoln also displayed a studied attention to party unity. He appointed Seward as secretary of state not merely to assuage a disappointed rival but also because Seward was a gradualist who prescribed patient acceptance of slavery until the ineluctable advance of nationalism and commercialism gradually extinguished it. Just as Seward represented former Whigs' respect for constitutional formalism, so Salmon Chase of Ohio, whom Lincoln named as secretary of the Treasury, stood for the more vigorous antislavery position in the party. Like Lincoln, Chase viewed the Declaration of Independence as the guiding light of the Constitution. But Chase was more committed than Lincoln to accelerating emancipation, even at the price of weakening constitutional forms. His appointment to the cabinet gave radical Republicans greater confidence that the president's resolve to prevent the expansion of slavery would not waver.

The presence of Seward and Chase created a contest in the cabinet. As each side struggled for Lincoln's favor, the administration risked being paralyzed by continuous bickering between competing party factions. But this was a risk that Lincoln was willing to take to ensure that diverse elements of the newly formed Republican Party would feel included in the administration's counsels. When the tension between Seward and Chase became the center of a great cabinet crisis in late 1862, Lincoln managed the dispute masterfully, maintaining the loyalty of both statesmen and the constituencies they represented. "Lincoln's cabinet represented an ever uneasy alliance, which is why it required so much of his attention," Eric McKitrick wrote. "But in the very process of managing it he was, in effect, at the same time managing the party and fashioning it into a powerful instrument for waging war."[41]

That Lincoln skillfully made the Union's war effort a collective endeavor helps explain the strong support that Congress gave to his controversial emergency actions after the attack on Fort Sumter. In upholding the legality of these actions, the Supreme Court, in the *Prize Cases,* drew attention to legislation Congress passed on July 13, 1861, to ratify Lincoln's orders.[42] The Court's decision supported Lincoln's claim that his conduct was justified not only by the threat the southern rebellion posed to the public safety but also by his expectation that Congress eventually would approve what he did. As Lincoln said in his special message to Congress on July 4, 1861, "These measures, whether strictly legal or not, were ventured upon under what appeared to be a popular demand and a public necessity, trusting then as now, that Congress would ratify them. It is believed that nothing has been done beyond the constitutional competency of Congress."[43] The one exception in Congress's expression of support concerned Lincoln's suspension of habeas corpus. But when Congress finally did act in 1863, it created arrangements to supplement (not replace) those that Lincoln had put in place.[44]

In the final analysis, Lincoln's party leadership succeeded because, in spite of the important differences that divided Republicans, they shared a commitment to free-soil principles. Even the Committee on the Conduct of War, the oversight body formed by Congress in January 1862 that is often portrayed as a thorn in Lincoln's side, served the president's ultimate objective of crushing the southern rebellion and abolishing slavery. Lincoln did not cooperate directly with the radical Republicans who controlled this committee, and he sometimes resisted their most zealous abolitionist tendencies. Nonetheless, he allowed his secretary of war, Edwin Stanton, to collaborate with its members in pressuring recalcitrant Union generals, especially George B. McClellan, whose cautiousness in battle and indifference to emancipation frustrated the president.[45]

Lincoln the Emancipator

The importance of Lincoln's party leadership, and its effect on the Constitution, is revealed most clearly in the struggle for emancipation. His issuance of the Emancipation Proclamation on January 1, 1863, appeared to place the abolition of slavery alongside the restoration of the Union as the primary objectives of the war. But the proclamation was a more limited, cautious measure than some Radical Republicans had hoped it would be. It did not emancipate the slaves everywhere; in fact, Lincoln earlier had voided the declarations of two of his generals freeing slaves in captured territory. Instead, Lincoln, who based the proclamation solely on the "war power" and regarded it as a "fit and necessary war measure for suppressing rebellion," abolished slavery only in the unconquered parts of the Confederacy. Significantly, the proclamation also declared that the door was open for African Americans "to be received into the armed forces of the United States."[46] Nearly 200,000 former slaves became Union soldiers, disrupting the South's labor force and converting part of that force into a northern military asset.

Although the Emancipation Proclamation became a critical part of Union war strategy, it neither condemned slavery as immoral nor guaranteed that it would be abolished after the war. Lincoln vetoed the Wade-Davis bill of 1864, which included sweeping emancipation and Reconstruction measures that he believed the federal government had no constitutional authority to impose on the states. Yet the president realized that to return the emancipated African Americans to slavery would betray the core principle of the Republican Party. When urged to do so by some northern Democrats, who argued that coupling emancipation with restoration of the Union was a stumbling block to peace negotiations with the Confederacy, Lincoln countered that "as a matter of policy, to announce such a purpose, would ruin the Union cause itself."[47] Thus Lincoln's Reconstruction policy, which he announced in December 1863, offered a pardon and amnesty to any white southerner who took an oath of allegiance not only to the Union but also to all of the administration's wartime policies concerning slavery and emancipation.

Emancipation thereby became, as Lincoln had urged in the Gettysburg Address, an end as well as a means of Union victory. But for this cause to become the foundation of a conservative revolution—a true refounding—it had to be endorsed by a popular election and accomplished through regular constitutional procedures. Jefferson and Jackson were content to oversee a fundamental reinterpretation of constitutional principles. Lincoln, seeking to reconcile popular government with devotion to law, worked to achieve abolition by constitutional amendment. In 1864, he took the lead in persuading the Republican National Convention to adopt a platform pledging that, because slavery was "hostile to the principles of republican government, justice and national safety," the GOP would accomplish its "utter and complete extirpation from the soil of the Republic."[48] In stark contrast, the Democratic candidate, the reluctant General McClellan, opposed the Emancipation Proclamation and wanted the Union to continue fighting only until the presecession status quo could be restored.

Reelected in 1864 by large majorities, Lincoln and other Republican leaders moved to enact the Thirteenth Amendment—the Emancipation Amendment— which the president considered the keystone of the party platform. Once the amendment passed, Congress sent it to Lincoln for his signature. The Constitution does not require presidents to sign constitutional amendments, but legislative leaders somehow forgot that Lincoln's endorsement was not needed.[49] This oversight testifies to the importance of Lincoln as a party leader. That the amendment, which was ratified in 1865, was drafted as a pastiche of the Northwest Ordinance must have given Lincoln special satisfaction, because he had been pointing to the earlier document since 1854 as an expression of the Framers' hostility to slavery. Just as surely, the Thirteenth Amendment vindicated Lincoln and his fellow partisans' position that the Republicans, not the Democrats, were the true heirs of Jeffersonian democracy.

Lincoln's disregard for legal constraints on the war power, therefore, went hand in hand with a deep and abiding commitment to the principles and institutions of the Constitution. In his case, popular leadership did not leave a legacy of military dictatorship. Instead, it was dedicated to a conservative revolution—a new constitutional teaching, albeit one steeped in the American political tradition. The Thirteenth Amendment transformed America's scripture, the Declaration of Independence, into a formal constitutional obligation. That obligation was extended by the Fourteenth Amendment, ratified in 1868, which granted all Americans the "privileges and immunities of citizens of the United States," "due process," and "equal protection of the laws." The Fifteenth Amendment, added in 1870, proclaimed that the "right of citizens of the United States to vote shall not be abridged by the United States or any State on account of race, color, or previous condition of servitude."

The three Civil War amendments changed the course of constitutional development and expanded government's obligation to protect the rights of the common citizen. But the political order formed by Lincoln and the Republican Party did not seek to remove all limits on presidential power. Even during the war, Lincoln did not forsake the Whig view of executive power that he had defended in the 1830s and 1840s. Consistent with this view, which most Republicans embraced, Lincoln denied that the president could veto bills merely because he disagreed with them. Only legislation, like the Wade-Davis bill, that he regarded as unconstitutional would be returned to Congress.[50] He deferred almost entirely to Congress on matters unrelated to the war, "contributing little more than his signature" when Republican lawmakers "created a Department of Agriculture, established land grant colleges, passed the Homestead Act (to encourage western settlement), instituted the national income tax, and erected the legislative framework that would lead to the construction of a transcontinental railroad."[51] As the postwar Republican reformer Carl Schurz wrote of Lincoln, "With scrupulous care he endeavored, even under the most trying circumstances, to remain strictly within the constitutional limits of his authority; and whenever the boundary become indistinct, or when the dangers of the situation forced him to cross it, he was equally careful to mark his acts of exceptional measures, justifiable only by the imperative necessities of the civil war, so that they might not pass into history as precedents for similar acts in time of peace."[52]

The powers that Lincoln was willing to accumulate as commander in chief during the Civil War freed him to use the executive office energetically. But Lincoln's assassination and his replacement as president by the bigoted Andrew Johnson severely limited the Civil War refounding. The failure of Reconstruction was also attributable to the Republicans' principled opposition to centralized power. That fear formed a critical backdrop to the notorious "Compromise of 1877," which enabled white majorities in southern states to enact segregation laws that prevented the enforcement of the Fourteenth and Fifteenth Amendments and denied African Americans a full share of citizenship. This debased form of local self-determination severely constrained presidential power for the rest of the nineteenth century, so much so that the self-styled modern reformers who emerged at the end of the nineteenth century overwhelmingly viewed party politics as an obstacle to their ambition to construct an executive-centered "modern" state on American soil.

The New Deal and the Consolidation of Modern Executive Power

Like the other presidents who animated America's refoundings, Franklin D. Roosevelt left more than a record of achievement; he also left a constitutional legacy. The New Deal constitutional order consolidated political developments that led to the rise of mass democracy and the expansion of national administrative power. The relationship between state and society would henceforth be negotiated in critical ways by the "modern presidency," a Progressive era innovation that FDR and his New Deal political allies grafted onto the traditions of natural rights and limited constitutional government that had dominated the polity since the beginning of the nineteenth century. Roosevelt's leadership, like Jefferson's, Jackson's, and Lincoln's, was an indispensable ingredient in a conservative revolution. But the New Deal was the first refounding dedicated to expanding national administrative power and to placing the presidency at the heart of its approach to politics and government. After Roosevelt, this new understanding of executive responsibilities led even conservative Republican presidents to embrace the powers and responsibilities of modern executive leadership.

Redefining the Social Contract

Roosevelt first spoke of the need to modernize elements of the old faith in his Commonwealth Club address, delivered during the 1932 campaign. His theme was that the time had come—indeed, it had come three decades earlier—to recognize the "new terms of the old social contract." It was necessary to rewrite the social contract, FDR argued, to take account of a national economy remade by industrial capitalism and concentrated economic power. This new contract would establish countervailing power in the form of a stronger national state, lest the United States steer "a steady course toward economic oligarchy." Protection of the national welfare must shift from the private citizen to the government. As FDR put it, "The day of enlightened administration has come."[53]

Yet FDR acknowledged that the creation of a national state with expansive supervisory powers would be a "long, slow task." He was sensitive to the uneasy fit between energetic central government and the Constitution. It was imperative, therefore, that the New Deal be informed by a public philosophy in which the new concept of state power would be carefully interwoven with earlier conceptions of American government. The task of modern government, FDR announced, was to assist the development of an "economic declaration of rights, an economic constitutional order."[54] The traditional emphasis in American politics on individual self-reliance—"rugged individualism," as Herbert Hoover put it—must give way to a new understanding of the social contract, in which government guaranteed individual men and women protection from the uncertainties of the marketplace. Government-provided security was to be the new self-evident truth of American political life.

Defending progressive reform in terms of an economic constitutional order was a critical development in the advent of an executive-centered administrative state. Theodore Roosevelt and Woodrow Wilson had anticipated many elements of this argument, but FDR was the first to advocate an ongoing supervisory role for the government that linked this new social contract to constitutional principles. Although Roosevelt's triumph was aided greatly by the economic exigencies of the Great Depression, his deft reinterpretation of the American constitutional tradition was no less important. This reinterpretation went beyond Wilson's New Freedom, which honored decentralized party practices and emphasized initiatives such as antitrust policy and reform activity in the states. FDR's eye was fixed more on his cousin Theodore, who expressed an alternative progressive understanding that envisioned a dominant president serving as the "steward of the public welfare." Theodore Roosevelt's Progressive Party crusade of 1912, which celebrated social justice and the president as the agent of an unvarnished majoritarianism, made an especially strong impression on FDR and his Brains Trust.

FDR called his philosophy "liberalism" rather than "progressivism." He meant to signify that the New Deal would expand rather than subvert the natural rights tradition embedded in the Declaration of Independence. As Roosevelt made clear in the Commonwealth Club address, this new understanding of rights required both a return to and a redefinition of the Declaration, a document in which "rulers were accorded power, and the people consented to that power on consideration that they be accorded certain rights. The task of statesmanship has always been the redefinition of these rights in terms of a changing and growing social order. New conditions impose new requirements upon government and those who conduct government."[55]

Roosevelt reaffirmed the principles of the Commonwealth Club address throughout his presidency. Like Lincoln, FDR believed that this new understanding of the Constitution had to be sanctified by a popular election. He made the "economic constitutional order" the principal message of his first reelection bid in 1936, the decisive triumph that established for a generation the Democratic Party, recast in the New Deal image, as the majority party in American politics. Just as the 1860 and 1864 Republican platforms had celebrated the Declaration as the nation's scripture, so was the 1936 platform, drafted by FDR, written as a pastiche of the Declaration, emphasizing the need for a fundamental reconsideration of rights. As the platform claimed with respect to the 1935 Social Security Act: "We hold this truth to be self evident—that government in a modern civilization has certain inescapable obligations to its citizens," among which is the responsibility "to erect a structure of economic security for [its] people, making sure that this benefit shall keep step with the ever increasing capacity of America to provide a high standard of living for all its citizens."[56]

The new idea of rights—for all intents and purposes, a second Declaration—was not forgotten during World War II. Instead, it became a central rhetorical theme in mobilizing public support for America's participation in the struggle. Roosevelt's Four Freedoms speech, which summoned support for the 1941 Lend-Lease Act, also engaged Congress and the people in a debate about America's role in the world. To the traditional freedoms of speech and religion, Roosevelt added the "freedom from fear," dedicated to "a world-wide reduction of armaments to such a point and in such a fashion that no nation will be in a position to commit an act of physical aggression against any neighbor," and the "freedom from want," the commitment "to economic understandings which will secure to every nation a healthy peace-time life for its inhabitants."[57] The four freedoms soon became, as David Kennedy has written, "a shorthand for America's war aim." More to the point, "they could be taken . . . as a charter for the New Deal itself."[58]

The New Deal Constitutional Program

Roosevelt's redefinition of the social contract had an important influence on laws and institutional change. Historians have generally divided FDR's first term into two periods, each identified by a flurry of legislative activity lasting approximately one hundred days. The first period (1933–1934) was a response to

FDR's call for "bold, persistent experimentation" to meet the great emergency at hand. Among these measures were the Emergency Banking Relief Bill and other legislation establishing the Public Works Administration, the Agricultural Adjustment Administration, and the National Recovery Administration.[59] The second period (1935–1936) brought laws that converted emergency programs, such as the Social Security Act and the National Labor Relations Act, into ongoing obligations of the national government, beyond the vagaries of public opinion and the reach of elections and party politics. As one New Dealer observed hopefully, "we may assume the nature of the problems of American life are such as not to permit any political party for any length of time to abandon most of the collective functions which are now being exercised."[60]

During his second term, FDR pursued a program to thoroughly reconstruct the institutions and practices of constitutional government in the United States. This program—the Third New Deal—was pursued with the understanding that programmatic rights, such as Social Security and collective bargaining, would not amount to much unless new institutional arrangements were established that would reorganize the institutions and redistribute the powers of government.[61] The program included three extremely controversial initiatives: the Executive Reorganization Act, the centerpiece of the program, announced in January 1937; the "court packing" plan, proposed a few weeks later; and the so-called purge campaign, attempted during the 1938 Democratic primary elections. These measures' common objective was to strengthen national administrative power. They marked an effort to transform a decentralized polity, dominated by local parties and court rulings that supported property and states' rights, into a more centralized, even bureaucratic, form of democracy that could deliver the goods championed by New Dealers.[62]

Although the New Deal constitutional program was hostile to localized parties, national partisanship was central to the task of "state building." Indeed, Roosevelt and his New Deal allies recognized that the Democratic Party was a critical means to the creation of the administrative constitution they envisioned. New Deal programmatic rights attracted new groups and interests, such as union members, African Americans, and Jews, who became the key constituencies of the new, more programmatic party. Moreover, Roosevelt viewed partisan maneuvers such as the purge campaign as part of a broader endeavor to transform the Democrats into a national, executive-centered party. In fact, the Third New Deal, especially the administrative reform program, which proposed to significantly expand presidential staff support and greatly extend presidential authority over the executive branch, became at FDR's urging a major focus of party responsibility. The purge campaign focused on conservative Democrats, mostly from border and southern states, who had opposed the executive reorganization and court-packing plans.[63]

Roosevelt suffered damaging political defeats in his pursuit of the Third New Deal, galvanizing opposition that contributed to the heavy losses the Democrats sustained in the 1938 congressional election. The court-packing plan, in particular, served as a lightning rod for FDR's political enemies, spurring a resurgence of congressional independence and the formation of a bipartisan "conservative coalition." The new alliance of Republicans and southern Democrats blocked nearly every major presidential reform initiative from 1937 until the mid-1960s.

Nevertheless, the New Deal did not come to an end in 1938, as many historians and political scientists have claimed. Starting in 1939, FDR rebounded from the defeats he suffered during the first two years of his tempestuous second term and managed to consolidate and institutionalize a political order that reshaped significantly the dynamics of American constitutional government. First, having failed to get his 1937 administrative reform program through Congress, Roosevelt orchestrated the passage of a compromise bill, the Executive Reorganization Act of 1939. Its enactment led to the creation of the Executive Office of the President, including important staff agencies such as the White House Office and the Bureau of the Budget, and enhancing the president's capacity to manage the expanding activities of the executive branch. Consequently, the presidency was no longer merely an office; it was an institution that presidents and their appointees could use to short-circuit the separation of powers. In sum, administrative reforms carried out during the latter part of FDR's second term tended to ratify a process in which public expectations and institutional arrangements established the president, rather than Congress or the political parties, as the principal agent of American democracy.

Second, Roosevelt ran an extraordinary third-term campaign, starting in earnest in the summer of 1938. By then it was clear that FDR's effort to purge conservative Democrats from Congress in a dozen primary contests and replace them with "100% New Dealers" would fail. In contrast to the purge campaign, the bid for a third term was hidden from public view, but it was no less energetic and was perhaps better organized. FDR's shattering of the two-term tradition ratified the subordination of party politics to executive administration. As one aide put it, FDR had "pistol whipped" Democratic Party chieftains into nominating him for a third term and accepting as his running mate Henry Wallace, a militant liberal with virtually no organized support in the Democratic organization. Roosevelt's victory in 1940 ameliorated the bitter defeats the administration suffered during the 1938 elections.

Roosevelt's election to a third term gave him the opportunity to ensure that the New Deal constitutional order would endure. He was able to push through and administer the 1940 Ramspeck Act, which gave him the authority to extend civil service protection to some 200,000 New Deal loyalists who had come to Washington as emergency personnel during his first term to staff the fledgling welfare state. Moreover, Roosevelt remained in the White House to command the nation during World War II. Woodrow Wilson had put business leaders such as Bernard Baruch in charge of industrial mobilization during World War I; in contrast, FDR staffed key wartime positions with New Dealers. With loyalists such as Chester Bowles, who headed the Office of Price Administration, organizing industrial mobilization, "Dr. Win the War" never truly eclipsed "Dr. New Deal." Rather, the New Deal and war effort were melded in such a way as to establish irrevocably the government's responsibility for the welfare of the American people. This synergy was evident in the enactment of the 1944 GI Bill, which entitled veterans to home and business loans, unemployment compensation, and subsidies for education and training.[64]

The Administrative Constitution and Presidential Power

Roosevelt's role in the New Deal refounding surpassed the role played by previous presidents in conservative revolutions. After Roosevelt was elected to a fourth term, death brought his extraordinary stewardship of the nation to an end in April 1945. As Barry Karl has written, FDR's death "set off tremors of disbelief. Caesar was dead." And "whether one feared him as a tyrant or worshipped him as a God," an America without Roosevelt seemed inconceivable.[65] To assure that there would be no more Roosevelts, Republicans and southern Democrats enacted a constitutional amendment that limited future presidents to two terms, the only formal constitutional change that followed in the wake of FDR's path-breaking leadership.

But the New Deal refounding transformed American politics. FDR's constitutional teaching led to a redefinition of the social contract—a new understanding of rights—that caused most Americans to expect that the federal government, with the president in the lead, would remain active in domestic and world affairs. Although Roosevelt bequeathed a stronger executive to his successors than did Jefferson, Jackson, or Lincoln, he did not craft the modern presidency as an imperial office. As a conservative revolution that grafted an activist public philosophy and national administrative apparatus onto a rights-based constitutional system, the New Deal created new obstacles to presidential ambitions. Soon viewed as entitlements, New Deal programs became autonomous islands of power that would constrain presidents no less than natural rights philosophy and localized parties once had. As Martha Derthick has written, the architects of the Social Security program "sought to foreclose the opposition of future generations by committing them irrevocably to a program that promises benefits by rights. . . . In that sense they designed social security to be uncontrollable."[66]

Dwight Eisenhower, the first Republican elected after the New Deal revolution, acknowledged that the new understanding of rights had become an established part of modern American government. When his conservative brother Edgar criticized him privately for carrying on FDR's liberal policies, the president replied bluntly, "Should any political party attempt to abolish social security and eliminate labor law and farm programs, you should not hear of that party again in our political history."[67] In the wake of the New Deal, Oscar Handlin wrote soon after Ike left office, "Eisenhower made palatable to most Republicans the social welfare legislation of the preceding two decades. In the 1950s, the New Deal ceased to be an active political issue and became an accepted part of the American past."[68] Eisenhower also bestowed bipartisan legitimacy on the liberal internationalism practiced by Roosevelt and Harry Truman. He was contemptuous of Republicans—notably, Robert Taft, his main rival for the party's presidential nomination in 1952—who wanted the United States to withdraw into isolation from world affairs.

"Freedom from fear" and "freedom from want"—elaborated as the "Second Bill of Rights"—were not incorporated in a formal constitutional program. Indeed, Roosevelt and most New Dealers were skeptical about the benefits of formal constitutional change. To transform the new understanding of rights into a formal document would deny New Dealers the discretion to administer programs prudently and instead would bind the "economic constitutional order" in a legal straightjacket. Committed to an administrative constitution, the New Deal revolution sought to emancipate the national government from the demands of formal constitutionalism. "The Constitution," FDR insisted in his address celebrating its 150th anniversary, "was not a Lawyers' Contract."[69] It had to be remade so that constitutional policy displaced constitutional obligation.

In the end, however, the administrative constitution did not create the sort of national state that Roosevelt and the architects of the modern presidency had hoped for. Roosevelt's reforms left most New Deal programs exposed to interference not only by Congress and the courts but also by the interest groups that formed to protect these programs. By the 1970s, New Deal liberalism would be condemned as "interest group liberalism," an indictment that inadvertently helped resuscitate conservatism.[70] In the 1980s a serious challenge to the administrative state was mounted by a popular president who was determined to prove that the New Deal had not, after all, "sucked out the meaning of the old slogans of opposition to government activity."[71]

The Post–New Deal President: The Dispersion of Stewardship

The national administrative state, forged on the anvil of the New Deal, has remained the dominant reality of American government and politics ever since its creation. "Freedom from want" is still at the core of American domestic policy, and "freedom from fear" remains the dominant principle of American foreign policy. But after FDR, the president's ability to control the administrative state was constrained by Congress, the courts, and a complex maze of private groups representing an ever more diverse set of interests and ideologies. Post–New Deal Democratic presidents from Truman to Barack Obama have enthusiastically embraced the stewardship model of the American presidency, whose roots go back to Jefferson and Jackson and were embellished by the Roosevelts. But FDR's success in expanding the notion of rights and institutionalizing ambitious interventionist policies within the administrative state deprived his successors of their exclusive claim to be the steward of the people. The expanded rights understanding and the enlarged demands of various segments of society for government aid that were born in the New Deal also strengthened the stewardship claims of Congress and the courts. For example, one of the greatest of all postwar policy changes, school desegregation, was initiated by the Supreme Court. Another extremely important innovation, the development of national environmental policy, was initiated by Congress.

The post–New Deal Republican presidents who preceded Ronald Reagan—Eisenhower, Richard Nixon, and Gerald Ford—performed the stewardship role with less enthusiasm than their Democratic counterparts, but pressure from the Supreme Court and Congress pushed them to adopt it. Thus, it was Eisenhower who sent troops to Little Rock to enforce the Supreme Court's desegregation edict. It was Nixon who established the Environmental Protection Agency to enforce the landmark antipollution laws that Congress passed in the early 1970s. Fearful that the Democrats would defeat him for reelection by outbidding his domestic reform agenda, Nixon went so far as to advocate a guaranteed national income and an expanded affirmative action program.

Theodore Lowi coined the term "interest group liberalism" to describe how private associations and their allies in Congress and the bureaucracy exploited New Deal policies to seize control of specific policy realms. Organized labor gained control of labor policy, farmers of farm policy, and advocates for the poor of the war on poverty. The president had very little say about how these sectors were governed. He lost control of them to the tight-knit coalitions of members of Congress, permanent civil servants, and lobbyists that formed around each domain of public policy.

In the 1970s, new political associations, claiming to be "public interest groups," were able to exploit the rights-endowing aspects of judicial and congressional actions to exert considerable leverage in the new policy realms of the environment, disability, and consumer protection. This variant of interest group liberalism also featured the tripartite alliance of members of Congress (and their staffs), bureaucrats, and lobbyists, but its powerful rights orientation also privileged judges and their clerks. Thus the project of programmatic rights that FDR pioneered flourished in the second half of the twentieth century but morphed into a structure and a set of legal and political dynamics that deprived the president of power to control and direct it.[72]

The Reagan "Revolution"

Not until 1980 was a serious challenge mounted to the rights-endowing interest group liberal expansion of the New Deal political order. In that year, Ronald Reagan was elected president. The central message of his campaign was that "government is the problem." He promised to reduce big government and the tax burdens needed to sustain it. His rhetoric was replete with examples of how the private sector was both more efficient and humane than the public sector and that the discipline and liberty associated with markets was to be highly prized, especially as compared with the straightjacket imposed by government bureaucracy. "The important thing," Hugh Heclo has written, "is not that Reagan said anything fundamentally new," but rather that in the political context created by the New Deal and Great Society, "Reagan continued to uphold something old."[73]

In Reagan's first year in office, his challenge to big government and the interest groups that sustained it scored two major successes. The Professional Air Traffic Controllers Organization (PATCO), one of the very few unions to endorse Reagan, naturally expected to benefit from his victory. When he refused to accept PATCO's contract terms, its members went on strike, fully expecting him to use the disruption they were causing to commercial aviation as an excuse to settle. Instead, Reagan fired them and hired a whole new team of air traffic controllers. No accidents occurred. The strikers were utterly defeated and many never recovered their jobs. This stunning victory for the president was taken by the unions and the public at large as a mark of Reagan's seriousness about resisting both the coercive power of unions and demands for increased spending.

The Republicans gained control of the Senate as well as the presidency in 1980, but the Democrats retained control of the House of Representatives, the more powerful of the two chambers with respect to revenue matters. It thus appeared that Reagan would have little success cutting spending. To do so, he reversed the typical conservative program of cutting taxes only after cutting spending. Instead, he proposed major tax cuts, knowing that most of the spending cuts he proposed had no chance of being enacted. He dared the House to resist the popular idea of tax reduction and was willing to accept the enormous deficits that would result from cutting revenue but not spending. The House did as he hoped, and Reagan happily accepted the resulting deficit. His bet was that the surge in economic activity spurred by the cuts would eventually reduce the deficit. More important, the sheer size of the deficit would act as a deterrent to any new expensive Democratic policy initiatives. He was proved right on both counts.

Reagan's attack on big government did not constitute a refounding in the same sense as those accomplished by Jefferson, Jackson, Lincoln, and FDR. Unlike Roosevelt, Reagan failed to capitalize on his personal popularity to further his broader political ends. He squandered his one great opportunity to create the enduring electoral and congressional Republican majority that would have been required to sustain his revolution. FDR had used his 1936 reelection bid to mobilize support for the entire Democratic ticket. By contrast, Reagan's 1984 campaign was ostentatiously nonpartisan and devoid of serious political content. The theme was "Morning in America," as if, by some obscure diurnal logic, the Democrats could be made to endorse the darkness. The Republicans failed to take control of the House, picking up just fourteen additional seats, and lost two seats in the Senate, presaging the Democratic takeover in 1986. When the Republicans finally gained control of the House and the Senate in 1994, they did so in the middle of the term of Democratic president Bill Clinton, who was reelected in 1996. In the three decades from 1980 to 2010, the Republicans enjoyed undivided control of the presidency and Congress only during the middle four years of George W. Bush's presidency. The Democrats then regained control of Congress in 2006 and took undivided control of the presidency and Congress in 2008.

Despite Reagan's partisan shortcomings, something profound happened as a result of his presidency. A decided shift in public philosophy took place. Reagan's mantra that "government is the problem" clearly resonated in enduring ways. Not since the 1920s had there been such enthusiasm among policymakers and the public at large for free markets and such widespread denigration of government. The greatest complement to Reagan was the extent to which Clinton abetted the turn toward freer markets both practically and rhetorically. In his 1992 campaign, Clinton stated famously that he would "end Welfare as we know it." He did not fulfill this pledge immediately, but after suffering a humiliating defeat to expand the right to health care and seeing his party suffer terrible losses in 1994, Clinton acknowledged that the "era of big government is over." He then kept his 1992 campaign pledge by signing the 1996 Welfare Reform Act, which not only imposed stringent work requirements on welfare recipients but also ended all welfare payments to recipients after five years. This law is the only real retrenchment of the welfare state that has ever taken place. Just as Eisenhower bestowed a form of bipartisan legitimacy on the New Deal, so did Clinton advance a renascent conservatism.

Clinton also joined Presidents Reagan and George H. W. Bush in perpetuating and expanding the deregulation of various sectors of the economy that had begun under President Ford. The Ford administration persuaded Congress to deregulate airlines and trucking, and initiated action by the Supreme Court that led to the divestiture of the AT&T telephone monopoly. Under Reagan, Congress deregulated the savings and loan industry. Under George H. W. Bush, Congress exempted wholesale electricity generators from constraints imposed by one of the key New Deal regulatory statutes, the Public Utility Holding Company Act. In 1999, under Clinton, Congress repealed anticompetitive provisions of another New Deal regulatory stalwart, the Glass-Steagall Act of 1933. The Gramm-Leach-Bliley Financial Services Modernization Act repealed Glass-Steagall's prohibition against commercial banks offering investment and insurance services.[74] As a result, what had been three separate markets—investment banking, commercial banking, and insurance—now became a single, largely unfettered financial services market. The leaders of both parties fought aggressively to open up markets and to constrain federal spending.[75]

Optimism about market competition, as important as it was, did not undermine the essential contours of the New Deal. The welfare program that was eliminated in 1996—Aid to Families with Dependent Children—was never established firmly as an entitlement. All the New Deal programs that were—Social Security, Medicare, and veterans' benefits—remained firmly in place. In 2003, President George W. Bush—who styled himself as a Reagan disciple—joined with a Republican Congress to pass the largest expansion of entitlement spending since the inception of Medicare, when it extended that program to include the provision of prescription drugs. Moreover, in alliance with a liberal icon, Massachusetts senator Edward Kennedy, Bush invoked the right to education in supporting the most important school reform since the Great Society, the No Child Left Behind Act, which dramatically transformed and expanded the role of the federal government in elementary and secondary education. After a brief flirtation with abolishing subsidies, the farm program returned to its former high levels of price supports.

In the end, the Reagan-Clinton-Bush embrace of free markets was selective. It applied to economic regulatory policy and to only one segment of aid to the dispossessed. Otherwise, the rights-based programs of interest group liberalism survived unscathed—indeed, they were expanded in important ways. Thus Reagan's efforts stopped well short of the refoundings undertaken by Jefferson, Lincoln, and FDR. The New Deal was reinterpreted only marginally. There was no broad-scale redefinition of the meaning of constitutional rights allied to the formation of an enduring partisan majority. The limits of the Reagan "revolution" appeared to confirm how New Deal programmatic rights and regulations had won the allegiance, not just of bureaucrats and interest groups, but also of individuals. As Hugh Heclo concludes, Reagan's attack on government as a bureaucratic nightmare was "a partial truth masquerading as the whole. Government also grew to do things that people, in all their variegated ways, really wanted done."[76]

Continual War–Continual War Powers

The greatest and most enduring change in the nature and functioning of the modern presidency has taken place in the realm of foreign policy. Prior to World War II, the United States returned to a peace footing after a war ended. It did not do so after World War II. Throughout the postwar era, military budgets burgeoned, large numbers of men remained in uniform, and fear of a major, probably nuclear conflagration remained omnipresent. Cold war is an apt metaphor for the manner in which the United States and the Soviet Union remained poised for war, provoked each other, and fought small wars through surrogates. Never have two such powerful rivals engaged in such elaborate war preparations and goaded each other so frequently and aggressively without ever going to war.

The cold war changed the concept of commander in chief. The president did not lead a nation into war but presided over military, quasimilitary, and diplomatic activities that were geared toward both maintaining an armed peace and gaining competitive advantage over a dreaded rival. In recognition of the inherent manpower inferiority of the United States compared with the Soviets, a crucial aspect of cold war strategy was to maintain technological superiority. This required massive expenditures, creating the largest peacetime budgets in history. It also necessitated the creation of an extensive and intricate web of relations between the federal government and the many and varied actors involved in the arms race. Eisenhower coined the term "military industrial complex" to describe this new set of relationships, but given the centrality of scientific, engineering, and operations research to the enterprise, he might well have called it the "military–industrial–university–consulting firm complex."

Harry Truman presided over an important government reorganization effort geared toward providing the president with institutional arrangements capable of coping with such massive yet delicate responsibilities. The United States had fought World War II with only the crudest tools for coordinating the activities of the various branches of the armed forces and the civilian departments that also were involved. The 1947 National Security Act reorganized government to provide the president with a better purchase on the management of war making, be it hot or cold. The War Department and Navy Department were grouped in a single Department of Defense under the secretary of defense, along with the newly created Air Force Department.[77] The 1947 act also created the Central Intelligence Agency to serve as the main provider and processor of civilian intelligence. And it established the National Security Council (NSC). The council was composed of the president, vice president, secretary of state, secretary of defense, and other members (such as the director of the Central Intelligence Agency), who met at the White House to discuss long-term problems and handle more immediate national security crises. An initially small NSC staff was hired to coordinate foreign policy materials from other agencies for the president.

Although both the Department of Defense and the NSC were established to improve interagency coordination and cooperation, they also became important sources of rivalry and discord. Over time, the NSC staff grew in size and many presidents came to rely heavily on its director, the national security advisor, to distill the disparate and often conflicting information and advice emanating from the defense department, the state department, the CIA and other agencies with intelligence, military, and diplomatic responsibilities. In many administrations, the national security adviser attained a level of status and influence on a par with the secretary of defense and the secretary of state and used that stature to introduce his or her own initiatives and opinions. Coping with the three-way competition between these senior advisors has proven to be among the president's most serious challenges. The national administrative state's efforts to uphold "freedom from fear" have woven as complex a web of bureaucratic entanglements and rivalries as did its efforts to champion "freedom from want."

Conclusion: Presidential Power and American Democracy

Presidents have been at the center of American political development. They have conveyed a coherent understanding of constitutional change and infused energy into party organizations that have gained them political strength to embark on ambitious projects of national reform. Various refoundings have placed the presidency at the eye of the political storm, but the resolution of these constitutional episodes also has set boundaries on executive authority. By enmeshing the president in a constitutional order dedicated to states' rights and localized parties, those who adhered to Jeffersonian principles hoped to avoid the unified and energetic executive envisioned by Hamilton. Jacksonian Democrats sought to strengthen the executive as the "tribune of the people," but this was accomplished by hitching presidential leadership to a party that enforced collective responsibility for principles that were hostile to centralized power. Jackson's celebrated veto of the bill to recharter the national bank signified that the president's veto power, originally envisioned by the Federalists as a check on democracy, was now an important weapon in the battle to promote equality through limited government. As the failure of Reconstruction showed, even the Civil War refounding did not alter the essential characteristics of a decentralized constitutional order. Rather, Lincoln and the Republican Party gave new life to Whig principles that celebrated natural rights, private property, and legislative supremacy.

The New Deal was the first refounding to place executive power at the center of its reform program. But in forging an alliance between rights and national administration, Roosevelt and his New Deal allies did not abolish the obstacles to a centralized state. The defeats Roosevelt suffered during the Third New Deal did not prevent him from strengthening executive administration. Abetted by the exigencies of World War II, FDR's plans for consolidating the modern presidency were successful. But clothed in the garb of constitutional sobriety, opponents of the New Deal were able to preserve the independence of the courts and Congress to influence the details of administration. The American people came to support executive action in the name of the greater security that New Dealers championed: FDR's "freedom from want" and "freedom from fear." But this support for domestic entitlements and relief from foreign threats did not translate into firm acceptance of executive dominion. Roosevelt himself was somewhat diffident in his support of centralized administration. The New Deal redefinition of rights, he insisted throughout the court-packing ordeal, did not require reducing the constitutional powers of the courts, as Theodore Roosevelt and his Progressive followers had prescribed. The problem was not the Constitution, FDR argued, but "the manner in which it had been interpreted."[78]

America and its leaders are still struggling to come to terms with the legacy of the New Deal. Although the development of the modern presidency and bureaucratic state does not preclude future refoundings, recent developments in the United States appear to encourage pragmatic responses and bureaucratic solutions to global problems, such as the economy, climate change, and home-land security, that diminish somewhat the constitutional struggles that have given rise to previous conservative revolutions. This is not to suggest that America has reached the "end of history." The nation's efforts to cope with the threat of terrorism and the global financial meltdown reveal that presidents will probably continue to face imposing new challenges that will require inno-vative solutions. But the establishment of the president as the principal agent of American democracy, allied to a broad consensus that the national government has the responsibility to protect security at home and abroad, suggests that we still live today, as Morton Keller has written, "in a polity best defined as a lengthened shadow of the New Deal."[79]

Recent presidential politics, in fact, have entailed contests for the soul of the New Deal. Democrats and Republicans, liberals and conservatives, accept the administrative state; they just have different ideas about how to use it. Stated simply, the Democrats celebrate the freedom from want, believing that the welfare and regulatory state must be augmented to sustain freedom. The Republicans' main concern is for freedom from fear, expressed in the strong priority they give to homeland security.[80]

This battle for the meaning of the New Deal suggests that the country is still debating the meaning of rights and how best to protect them. Nevertheless, the rise of the modern executive encourages each president to exploit the full splendor of the office at the expense of responsible public debate and resolu-tion. Caught between the Scylla of bureaucratic indifference and the Charybdis of the public's demand for new rights, the presidency has evolved, or degener-ated, into a plebiscitary form of politics that mocks the New Deal concept of "enlightened administration" and exposes citizens to public figures who exploit their impatience with the difficult tasks of sustaining a healthy constitutional democracy. As the stormy Clinton and Bush presidencies illustrated, the New Deal freed the executive from formal constitutional forms and political parties but at the cost of subjecting it to fractious politics within Washington and vola-tile public opinion outside it.

Recent developments suggest that executive aggrandizement will continue to complicate efforts to recombine presidential power and constitutional democracy. Barack Obama's campaign and the early days of his presidency indicate he has the potential to display uncommon leadership in the hard task of reconciling executive prerogative and democratic accountability. And yet, in a political environment of a seemingly permanent war on terror, a state of perpetual emergency made all the more acute by the worst economic crisis since the Great Depression, presidential prerogative pursued by such a gifted politician may well reduce executive governance to a novel strain of plebiscitary politics that will pose severe threats to liberty. Although Obama may be too decent and moderate a leader to prosecute such a dark chapter in American political development, he must guard against blazing a dangerous path that less responsible leaders might exploit in the future.

Notes

1. The authors thank Emily Charnock of the University of Virginia for her exceptional research support.

2. Alexander Hamilton, James Madison, and John Jay, *The Federalist Papers* (New York: New American Library, 1961), no. 72, 437.

3. *The Papers of Alexander Hamilton,* ed. Harold C. Syrett (New York: Columbia University Press, 1969), vol. 8, 38–39.

4. *Letters of Pacificus and Helvidius on the Proclamation of Neutrality of 1793* (Washington, D.C.: Gideon, 1845), 53–64.

5. Hamilton, Madison, and Jay, *Federalist Papers,* no. 71, 432.

6. *Letters from the Federal Farmer, I,* in *The Antifederalists,* ed. Cecilia M. Kenyon (Indianapolis: Bobbs-Merrill, 1966), 204.

7. Even as he lamented the "aristocratical" tendencies of the delegates who attended the Constitutional Convention in Philadelphia, the Anti-Federalist Federal Farmer acknowledged that Virginia made a "very respectable appointment, and placed at the head of it, the first man in America." Ibid., 204.

8. Thomas Jefferson, "First Inaugural Address," March 4, 1801, in *The Portable Thomas Jefferson,* ed. Merrill D. Peterson (New York: Viking Press, 1975), 294. On Jefferson's view of the relationship between executive power and popular rule, see Jeremy Bailey, *Thomas Jefferson and Executive Power* (New York: Cambridge University Press, 2007).

9. Jeffrey Tulis, *Rhetorical Presidency* (Princeton: Princeton University Press, 1987).

10. Hamilton, Madison, and Jay, *Federalist Papers,* no. 70, 428–429 (emphasis in original).

11. James Sterling Young, "Power and Purpose," *Polity,* 28, 509–516.

12. Stephen Skowronek, *The Politics Presidents Make: Leadership from John Adams to Bill Clinton* (Cambridge: Harvard University Press, 1997), chaps. 1–3.

13. Thomas Jefferson, "Answers to de Meusnier Questions, 1786," in *The Writings of Thomas Jefferson,* memorial ed., ed. Andrew A. Lipscomb and Albert Ellery Bergh, 20 vols. (Washington, D.C., Thomas Jefferson Memorial Association, 1903–1904), vol. 17, 85.

14. Bailey, *Thomas Jefferson and Executive Power,* 9–10.

15. Jefferson, "First Inaugural Address," 290–295.

16. Thomas Jefferson, letters to James Madison, July 1803 and August 24 1803, *The Republic of Letters,* ed. James Morton Smith (New York: Norton, 1995), 1269–1271.

17. John Quincy Adams, *Memoirs of John Quincy Adams,* ed. Charles Francis Adams (New York: AMS Press, 1970), vol. 5, 401. Cited by Bailey, *Thomas Jefferson and Executive Power,* 192.

18. Thomas Jefferson, letter to James Madison, August 18, 1803, in Smith, *Republic of Letters,* 1278. Cited in Bailey, *Thomas Jefferson and Executive Power,* 180.

19. Thomas Jefferson, "Second Inaugural Address," retrieved from www.bartleby.com/124/pres17.html.

20. Thomas Jefferson, "The Kentucky Resolutions of 1798," adopted by the Kentucky legislature on November 10, 1798, retrieved from www.constitution.org/cons/kent1798.htm.

21. Andrew Jackson, "Proclamation Regarding Nullification," December 10, 1832, retrieved from http://avalon.law.yale.edu/19th_century/jack01.asp.

22. Robert Remini, *Andrew Jackson and the Bank War* (New York: Norton, 1967), 81.

23. Leonard White, *The Jeffersonians: A Study in Administrative History, 1801–1829* (New York: MacMillan, 1956), 213–214, 267.

24. Thomas Jefferson, letter to James Madison, April 27, 1809, in Lipscomb and Bergh, *Writings of Thomas Jefferson,* vol. 12, 277.

25. "President Jackson's Veto Message Regarding the Bank of the United States, July 10, 1832," retrieved from http://avalon.law.yale.edu/19th_century/ajveto01.asp.

26. Robert Remini, *Andrew Jackson* (New York: Harper Collins, 1966), 145–146.

27. Andrew Jackson, "First Annual Message to Congress," December 8, 1829, retrieved from www.presidency.ucsb.edu/ws/index.php?pid=29471.

28. Edward S. Corwin, *The President: Office and Powers, 1787–1957,* 4th ed. (New York: New York University Press, 1957), 451.

29. J. B. McClure, ed., *Abraham Lincoln's Speeches* (Chicago: Rhodes and McClure, 1891), 21–22.

30. Robert W. Johannsen, ed., *The Lincoln-Douglas Debates of 1858* (New York: Oxford University Press, 1965), 126–127.

31. Ibid., 131–132. Undated fragment written in early 1861, in *New Letters and Papers of Lincoln,* ed. Paul N. Angle (Boston: Houghton Mifflin, 1930), 241–242. Lincoln's reference is to *Proverbs* 25: 11.

32. Abraham Lincoln, "First Inaugural Address," March 4, 1861, in *The Political Thought of Abraham Lincoln,* ed. Richard N. Current (Indianapolis: Bobbs-Merrill, 1967), 171–172.

33. David Walker Howe, *The Political Culture of American Whigs* (Chicago: University of Chicago Press, 1979), 292.

34. Current, *Political Thought of Abraham Lincoln,* 88–89 (emphasis in original).

35. Ibid., 187–188.

36. *Chicago Tribune,* February 18, 1860, in *Abraham Lincoln: A Press Portrait,* ed. Herbert Mitgang (Athens: University of Georgia Press, 1989), 153.

37. "Abraham Lincoln's Letter to Albert G. Hodges," in *The Evolving Presidency: Addresses, Cases, Essays, Letters, Reports, Resolutions, Transcripts, and Other Landmark Documents, 1787–1998,* ed. Michael Nelson (Washington, D.C.: CQ Press, 1999), 70–74.

38. Clinton L. Rossiter, *Constitutional Dictatorship* (Princeton: Princeton University Press, 1948); see also L. Gerald Bursey, "Abraham Lincoln," in *Popular Images of American Presidents,* ed. William C. Spragens (New York: Greenwood Press, 1988), 77–85.

39. Philip Shaw Paludan, *The Presidency of Abraham Lincoln* (Lawrence: University Press of Kansas, 1994), 33.

40. Ibid.

41. Eric McKitrick, "Party Building and the Union and Confederate War Efforts," in *The American Party System: Stages of Development,* ed. William Nisbet Chambers and Walter Dean Burnham (London: Oxford University Press, 1975), 131.

42. *Prize Cases,* 67 Black 635 (1863).

43. James D. Richardson, ed., *Messages and Papers of the Presidents,* 20 vols. (New York: Bureau of National Literature, 1897), vol. 7, 3225.

44. Bursey, "Abraham Lincoln," 82.

45. Paludan, *Presidency of Abraham Lincoln,* 104–105.

46. Richardson, *Messages and Papers of the Presidents*, vol. 7, 3359.

47. Abraham Lincoln, letter to Charles D. Robinson, August 7, 1864, in *The Collected Works of Abraham Lincoln*, 9 vols., ed. Roy P. Basler (New Brunswick: Rutgers University Press, 1953), vol. 7, 499–500.

48. James M. McPherson, *Abraham Lincoln and the Second American Revolution* (New York: Oxford University Press, 1991), 86.

49. Paludan, *Presidency of Abraham Lincoln*, 297–302.

50. Lincoln took this position in refusing to veto a bill that reduced fees paid to the marshal for the District of Columbia; see Basler, *Collective Works of Abraham Lincoln*, vol. 7, 414–415.

51. Matthew Crenson and Benjamin Ginsberg, *Presidential Power: Unchecked and Unbalanced* (New York: Norton, 2007), 101.

52. Carl Schurz, "Abraham Lincoln," in *Abraham Lincoln*, ed. Carl Schurz (New York: Chautauqua, 1891), 72.

53. *The Papers and Addresses of Franklin D. Roosevelt*, ed. Samuel I. Rosenman, 13 vols. (New York: Random House, 1938–1950), I: 751–752.

54. Ibid., 752.

55. Ibid., 756.

56. "Democratic Platform of 1936," in *National Party Platforms*, ed., Donald Bruce Johnson (Urbana: University of Illinois Press, 1978), 360.

57. Roosevelt, *Public Papers and Addresses*, vol. 9, 671–672.

58. David M. Kennedy, *Freedom from Fear: The American People in Depression and War, 1929–1945* (New York: Oxford University Press, 1999), 469–470.

59. The Works Progress Administration (WPA) was not created during the first hundred days; it was established in January 1935 as the successor to the New Deal's Federal Emergency Relief Agency. Thus the WPA was set during the interregnum between the First and Second New Deals, but its organization and policies were characteristic of the emergence of legislation of the former period. See William Leuchtenburg, *Franklin D. Roosevelt and the New Deal, 1932–1940* (New York: Harper and Row, 1963), chaps. 6 and 7.

60. Joseph Harris, "Outline for a New York Conference," April 8, 1936, in *Papers of the President's Committee on Administrative Management* (Hyde Park, New York: Franklin D. Roosevelt Library).

61. For an overview and critique of the work on the Third New Deal, see John W. Jeffries, "A Third New Deal? Liberal Policy and the American State, 1937–1945," *Journal of Policy History* 8, no. 4 (1996): 387–409; and Sidney M. Milkis, *The President and the Parties: The Transformation of the American Party System since the New Deal* (New York: Oxford University Press, 1993), chaps. 5 and 6.

62. Stephen Skowronek, *Building a New American State: The Expansion of National Administrative Capacities, 1887–1920* (Cambridge: Cambridge University Press, 1982).

63. For a more complete account of New Deal party politics, see Milkis, *President and the Parties*, chaps. 1–4.

64. Ronald Story, "The New Deal and Higher Education," in *The New Deal and the Triumph of Liberalism*, ed. Sidney M. Milkis and Jerome M. Mileur (Amherst: University of Massachusetts Press, 2002); and Suzanne Mettler, *Soldiers to Citizens: The GI Bill and the Making of the Greatest Generation* (New York: Oxford University Press, 2005).

65. Barry Karl, *The Uneasy State: The United States from 1915 to 1945* (Chicago: University of Chicago Press, 1983), 223.

66. Martha Derthick, *Policymaking for Social Security* (Washington, D.C.: Brookings Institution, 1983), 417.

67. Quoted in William E. Leuchtenburg, *In the Shadow of FDR: From Harry Truman to Ronald Reagan,* rev. ed. (Ithaca: Cornell University Press, 1985), 49.

68. Oscar Handlin, "The Eisenhower Administration: A Self-Portrait," *Atlantic Monthly,* November 1963, 68.

69. Roosevelt, *Public Papers and Addresses,* vol. 6, 357–367.

70. Theodore Lowi, *The End of Liberalism: The Second Republic of the United States,* 2nd ed. (New York: Norton, 1979).

71. Harris, "Outline for a New York Conference."

72. R. Shep Melnick, "The Courts, Congress, and Programmatic Rights," in *Remaking American Politics,* ed. Richard A. Harris and Sidney M. Milkis (Boulder: Westview Press, 1989).

73. Hugh Heclo, "Ronald Reagan and the American Public Philosophy," in *The Reagan Presidency: Pragmatic Conservatism and Its Legacies,* ed. Elliot Brownlee and Hugh Davis Graham (Lawrence: University Press of Kansas, 2003), 23.

74. Public Law 106–102, 113 Stat. 1338, enacted November 12, 1999, is an act of the 106th U.S. Congress.

75. For a comprehensive discussion and analysis of various Reagan and Clinton deregulation efforts, see Marc Landy, Martin Levin, and Martin Shapiro, eds., *Creating Competitive Markets: The Politics and Economics of Regulatory Reform* (Washington, D.C.: Brookings, 2007).

76. Heclo, "Ronald Reagan and American Public Philosophy," 34.

77. Each of the three branches maintained their own service secretaries. In 1949 the act was amended to give the secretary of defense more power over the individual services and their secretaries.

78. The conversations concerning the court-packing plan between FDR and his attorney general, Homer Cummings, recorded in the latter's diary, offer important clues to FDR's views on the New Deal constitutional program. See the *Diaries of Homer Stille Cummings,* December 26, 1936, no. 6, 185–194, Homer Cummings Papers, Manuscript Department, Alderman Library, University of Virginia.

79. Morton Keller, "The New Deal and Progressivism: A Fresh Look," in Milkis and Mileur, *New Deal and the Triumph of Liberalism,* 319.

80. In calling for the creation of a new department of government President George W. Bush directly linked the cause of homeland security to the objectives of the New Deal state. Likening his plan to the 1947 National Security Act, which authorized President Harry S. Truman to create the National Security Council and the Department of Defense, he asked Congress to form "a single permanent department with an overriding and urgent mission: securing the homeland of America, and protecting the American people." George W. Bush, Address to the Nation, June 6, 2002, http://whitehouse.gov. The Department of Homeland Security was established in November 2002.

4 Presidential Competence

Paul J. Quirk

The skills of political leadership that a president requires constitute a recurring theme of modern presidential scholarship. Most students of political skill have dwelt on techniques, such as bargaining, persuasion, rhetoric, and management. Paul J. Quirk approaches the subject differently, asking, What must presidents know? Quirk rejects as impossibly demanding the widely advocated "self-reliant" model that is patterned after Franklin Roosevelt. He is even less approving of the "minimalist" model that Ronald Reagan adopted and that George W. Bush pursued. Quirk proposes a "strategic competence" model of the kind practiced, at least part of the time, by Presidents John Kennedy, Gerald Ford, George H. W. Bush, and Bill Clinton. In this model, which early signs indicate that Barack Obama is pursuing, presidents do not need to know everything, but they must make good choices about what to know.

President Barack Obama often displays a great deal of specific knowledge about government and public policy. His immediate predecessor, George W. Bush, was notoriously prone to vagueness and misinformation about such matters. The question is, so what? Did Bush's limited knowledge have something to do with what has been widely considered a failed presidency? Is Obama's erudition reason to expect competent performance?

In this chapter I address a fundamental, yet rarely examined question about American government: What must the president know? To serve the country effectively and achieve political success, must presidents have deep knowledge of the issues and processes of government? Or can they rely on other officials—especially the cabinet and White House staff—to provide the substantive expertise? Considering the enormous complexity of modern government, is the president's direct, personal knowledge even relevant?

Drawing primarily from the experiences of presidents from Franklin Roosevelt to Ronald Reagan, I present three distinct and competing conceptions of the president's personal tasks and expertise—that is, of presidential competence.

I criticize two of these conceptions—one an orthodox approach of long standing, the other associated originally with Reagan. I then offer a third conception, based on a notion of "strategic competence," and discuss its requirements in three major areas of presidential activity. I test the usefulness of the analysis by assessing the performance of the three presidents who followed Reagan—George H. W. Bush, Bill Clinton, and George W. Bush. Finally, I offer some early observations about the methods and apparent competence of President Obama.

The Self-Reliant Presidency

Most commentary on the presidency assumes a concept of the president's personal tasks that borders on the heroic. Stated simply, the president must strive to be self-reliant and personally bear a large share of the burden of governing. And he or, in the future, she must therefore meet intellectual requirements that are correspondingly rigorous.

The classic argument for the self-reliant presidency is presented in Richard Neustadt's *Presidential Power*.[1] In arguing for an enlarged concept of the presidential role, Neustadt stressed that the president's political interests, and therefore his perspective on decisions, are unique. Only the president has political stakes that arguably correspond with the national interest. Thus a president's chances for success depend on what he can do for himself: his direct involvement in decisions, his personal reputation and skill, his control over subordinates.[2]

In this spirit, students of the presidency have often held up Franklin Roosevelt as the exemplary modern president. A perfect "active-positive," in James David Barber's typology of presidential personalities, Roosevelt made strenuous efforts to ensure his thorough understanding of issues and thus increase his control.[3] For example, he often set up competing channels of information and advice. He also looked outside the government for people who could offer additional perspectives.[4] The ideal president, in this view, has a consuming passion for control and thus for information.

This image of the president—as one who makes the major decisions himself, depends on others only in lesser matters, and firmly controls his subordinates—is attractive to most citizens, and presidents seek to project that appearance. But the notion of the self-reliant presidency overlooks the realities of modern government. Even for Roosevelt, self-reliance had costs. In a generally admiring description of his administrative practices, Arthur Schlesinger Jr. concedes that his methods hampered performance in some respects. Roosevelt's creation of unstructured, competitive relations among subordinates caused "confusion and exasperation on the operating level"; it was "nerve-wracking and often positively demoralizing." Because Roosevelt reserved so many decisions for himself, he could not make all of them promptly, and aides often had to contend with troublesome delays.[5]

In later administrations the weaknesses of the self-reliant presidency have emerged clearly. Presidents who have aspired to self-reliance have ended up leaving serious responsibilities badly neglected. Lyndon Johnson, another president with prodigious energy and a need for control, gravitated naturally to the self-reliant approach.[6] Eventually, however, he directed his efforts narrowly and obsessively to the Vietnam War. Meeting daily with the officers in charge, Johnson directed military operations from the Oval Office, at times selecting specific bombing targets. He essentially set aside every other area of presidential concern. In all likelihood, the military officers themselves, guided by the president's civilian subordinates, would have made the military decisions at least as well as Johnson, probably better. Moreover, his direct operational control of military strategy may have impaired Johnson's ability to take a broader, "presidential" perspective on the war. Johnson illustrates a tendency for self-reliance to become an end in itself.

Jimmy Carter, although less psychologically driven than Johnson, preferred self-reliance as a matter of conviction. It led him toward a narrowness of a different kind. From the first month in office, Carter signaled his intention to be thoroughly involved, completely informed, and prompt. "Unless there's a holocaust," he told the staff, "I'll take care of everything the same day it comes in." Thus he spent long hours daily poring over stacks of memoranda and took thick briefing books with him for weekends at Camp David. Initially, he even checked arithmetic in budget documents. Later he complained mildly about the number of long memoranda he had to read, but he still made no genuine effort to curb the flow.[7] Carter's extreme attention to detail cannot have contributed more than very marginally to the quality of his administration's decisions. Yet it took his attention from other, more essential tasks. Carter was criticized as having failed to articulate the broad themes or ideals that would give his presidency a sense of purpose—a natural oversight for a president who was wallowing in detail. He certainly neglected the crucial task of nurturing constructive relationships with other leaders in Washington.[8]

The main defect of the self-reliant presidency, however, is none of these particular risks; rather, it is the blunt, physical impossibility of carrying it out. Perhaps Roosevelt, an extraordinary individual who served when government was still relatively manageable, could achieve an approximation of the ideal. But the larger and more complex government has become, the more presidents have been forced to depend on the judgments of others. Today, any important policy question produces enough proposals, studies, and advocacy papers to keep a policymaker who sought to master it all fully occupied. In any remotely literal sense, therefore, presidential self-reliance is inconceivable.

Even as an inspirational ideal, the self-reliant presidency is more misleading than helpful. It can lead to an obsessive narrowness, and it is too far removed from reality to offer any concrete guidance. Rather than such an ideal, presidents need a conception of what a competent, successful performance would really consist of—one that accepts the nature of government and the limits of normal human ability as they exist.

The Minimalist Presidency

A second approach to presidential competence rejects the heroic demands of self-reliance altogether. In this approach, the president requires little or no understanding of specific issues and problems and instead can rely almost entirely on subordinates to resolve them. This "minimalist" approach has rarely if ever been advocated as an appropriate strategy for presidents in general. Nevertheless, it commands attention both because the Reagan administration relied explicitly on such an approach and because, in certain respects, George W. Bush followed in Reagan's footsteps.

Minimalism does not imply a passive conception of the presidency as an institution, like that of some nineteenth-century American presidents, who subscribed to the Whig theory of government.[9] With the help of an activist White House staff and the various agencies of the Executive Office of the President, a minimalist president can exercise power as expansively as any. Nor does minimalism describe the "hidden-hand" leadership ascribed to Dwight Eisenhower by Fred Greenstein.[10] Long viewed as a passive president, Eisenhower sometimes exercised considerable influence behind the scenes.

The first modern minimalist president was Ronald Reagan, whose administration flatly rejected the self-reliant approach. President Reagan's role in decision making, his spokesmen said during the first year, would be that of a chairman of the board. He would personally establish the general policies and goals of his administration, select cabinet and other personnel who shared his commitments, and then delegate broad authority to them so that they could work out the particulars.[11]

In part, the limited role for the president was designed to accommodate Reagan's limitations—especially his disinclination to do much reading or sit through lengthy briefings—and to answer critics who questioned his ability to serve as president. By expounding a minimalist theory, the Reagan administration was able to defend the president's frequent lapses and inaccuracies in news conferences as harmless and irrelevant. It is a "fantasy of the press," said the communications director, David Gergen, that an occasional "blooper" in a news conference has any real importance.[12]

But the administration presented this minimalist conception not merely as an ad hoc accommodation but as a sensible way for any president to operate. It has at least one claim to be taken seriously: unlike self-reliance, minimalism has the virtue of being attainable. For several reasons, however, the minimalist presidency has serious deficiencies as a general model. Nor was it necessarily satisfactory even in Reagan's case.

Chairman-of-the-board notions notwithstanding, a minimalist president and his administration are likely to have difficulties reaching decisions that serve the president's fundamental goals. Most obvious is that the president's subordinates may have their own agendas. Unless the president is fairly attentive, he will have trouble knowing when an ostensibly loyal subordinate is mainly serving some other constituency. The strategy makes selecting genuinely responsive senior officials exceptionally critical.[13]

But just as important, a minimalist president—or rather, the sort of president who would adopt a minimalist approach—is likely to overestimate his capabilities and judgment. Having neglected the complexities of policy issues over the course of a political career, he would fail to appreciate careful analysis. At least in politics, few people place a high value on discussion or analysis more sophisticated than their own habitual mode of thought.

That President Reagan showed no particular humility about his ability to make policy judgments was most apparent in his decisions about budgets, taxes, and the federal deficit.[14] In late 1981 Reagan's main economic policymakers—Office of Management and Budget (OMB) director David Stockman, Secretary of the Treasury Donald Regan, and White House chief of staff James Baker—recommended unanimously that the president propose a modest tax increase to keep the budget deficit to an acceptable level. But Reagan rejected their recommendation. As a result, the presidential budget was so far in deficit that it was dismissed out of hand even by the Republican Senate, and the president ended up accepting a package of "revenue enhancements" that Congress virtually forced on him.

Moreover, even if a minimalist president is willing to delegate authority and accept advice, his aides and cabinet members may have difficulty making up for his limitations. As they compete for the president's favor, they take cues from his rhetoric and descend to his level of argument. Advocates emerge for almost any policy the president is inclined to support. Such imitation apparently produced the scandals in the Environmental Protection Agency that embarrassed Reagan during his first term and led to the removal of numerous high-level officials. These officials, including the administrator of the agency, Anne Gorsuch Burford, interpreted Reagan's sweeping antiregulatory rhetoric to mean that, requirements of the law notwithstanding, they should hardly regulate at all.

The effect of Reagan's relaxed approach to policy decisions on the quality of debate in his administration is illustrated by a White House meeting on the defense budget in September 1981, recounted in Stockman's revealing memoir.[15] OMB was proposing a moderate reduction in the planned growth of defense spending—still giving the Pentagon an inflation-adjusted increase of 52 percent over five years and 92 percent of its original request. In a presentation that Stockman calls "a masterpiece of obfuscation," Secretary of Defense Caspar Weinberger compared American and Soviet capabilities as if OMB were refusing to endorse any increase. Almost all of his comparisons, displayed in elaborate charts, concerned weapons categories that Stockman was not trying to cut. The secretary concluded his presentation by showing a cartoon depicting OMB's version of the defense budget as "a four-eyed wimp who looked like Woody Allen, carrying a tiny rifle." In the end, Weinberger got his way.

Finally, if a president openly delegates significant decisions and accepts subordinates' advice, the press is likely to shame him into taking charge. Because the public likes presidents who seem in command, it makes good copy for a reporter to charge that aides are assuming the president's job—even when that may be a sensible adaptation to the president's personal limitations. The press sometimes challenged Reagan to demonstrate his involvement in decisions. During summit meetings with Soviet president Mikhail Gorbachev, Reagan took his chances negotiating one-to-one on arms control, a subject of daunting complexity for any president.[16]

It is certainly possible for a minimalist president to resist the temptations and pressures to overstep his capability and impose his own ill-informed decisions, and instead to rely on subordinates to tell him what to do. But such deference to subordinates would require a self-effacing personality—rare among successful politicians—and a willingness to face questioning about who is "the real president." Such a strategy would also make the president exceptionally dependent on his senior aides and cabinet members, who would have extraordinary opportunity to shape the president's goals and agenda according to their own preferences.

Neither self-reliance nor minimalism therefore offers a plausible general route to presidential competence. The question is whether another possible model exists that corrects the defects of both—making feasible demands on the president yet allowing for competent performance.

Strategic Competence

The third conception of presidential competence, set forth in the rest of this chapter, lies between the two extremes of minimalism and self-reliance. But it is not a mere compromise between those extremes. It is based on a notion of *strategic competence.*

The argument is that to perform competently, presidents must have a workable strategy for achieving competence. This strategy must take into account three basic elements of the president's situation:

1. The president's time, energy, and talent, and thus his capacity for direct, personal competence, are scarce resources. Choices must be made concerning what things a president will attempt to know. Delegation is necessary.

2. Depending on the task (for example, deciding issues, promoting policies), the president's ability to substitute the judgment and expertise of others for his own and still get satisfactory results varies considerably. Delegation works better for some tasks than for others.

3. The success of such substitutions will depend on a relatively small number of presidential actions and decisions concerning the selection of subordinates, the general instructions they are given, and the president's interactions with them. How well delegation works depends on how it is done.

Achieving competent performance, then, can be viewed as a problem of allocating resources. The president's personal abilities and time to use them are the scarce resources. For each task, the possibilities and requirements for effective delegation determine how much of these resources should be used and how they should be employed.

In the rest of this chapter, I spell out the implications of strategic competence in three major areas of presidential activity: policy decisions, policy processes, and policy promotion. My claim is that the approach demands only realistic levels of attention and expertise and yet provides a basis for competent performance in each area of presidential activity.

Policy Decisions

When it comes to substantive issues, vast presidential ignorance is simply inevitable. No one understands more than a few significant issues very well. Fortunately, presidents can get by—that is, control subordinates reasonably well and minimize the risk of serious policy mistakes—on far less than a thorough mastery. Some prior preparation, however, is required. And presidents lacking that preparation are likely to have difficulty.

As a matter of course, each president has a general outlook or philosophy of government. His principal aides must share that outlook or represent a variety of views roughly centered on it. The main requirement beyond this is for the president to be familiar enough with the substantive policy debates in each major area to recognize the signs of responsible argument. This familiarity includes having enough exposure to the work of policy analysts and experts in each area to know, if only in general terms, how they reach conclusions and the contribution they make. The point is not that the president will then be able to work through all the facts and arguments about an issue, evaluate them properly, and reach a sound, independent conclusion—that is ruled out if only by lack of time. As he evaluates policy advice, however, such a substantively aware president will at least be able to tell which of his subordinates are making sense. Whatever the subject at hand, the president will be able to judge whether an advocate is bringing to bear the relevant kinds of evidence, considerations, and arguments and citing appropriate authorities.

One can observe the importance of this ability by comparing two—in some respects similar—episodes. Both John Kennedy in 1963 and Ronald Reagan in 1981 proposed large, controversial reductions of the individual income tax, each in some sense unorthodox. But in the role played by respectable economic opinion, the two cases could not be more different.

Kennedy brought to bear the prescriptions of Keynesian economics, which by then had been the dominant school of professional economic thought for nearly three decades. The Kennedy administration took office when the economy was in a deep recession. From the beginning, Walter Heller, a leading academic economist and the chairman of Kennedy's Council of Economic Advisers (CEA), had sought tax reductions to promote economic growth—the appropriate Keynesian response, even though it might increase the federal deficit. Already aware of the rationale for stimulation, Kennedy did not require persuasion on the economic merits, but he did have political reservations. "I understand the case for a tax cut," he told Heller, "but it doesn't fit my call for sacrifice." Nor did it fit the economic views of Congress or the general public— both of which remained faithful on the whole to the traditional belief in an annually balanced budget. But the CEA continued lobbying, and Kennedy— first partially, later completely—went along. Finally, in 1963, Kennedy proposed to reduce income taxes substantially.

The novelty of this proposal, with the economy already recovering and the budget in deficit, alarmed traditionalists. "What can those people in Washington be thinking about?" asked former president Eisenhower in a magazine article. "Why would they deliberately do this to our country?" Congress, which also had doubts, moved slowly but eventually passed the tax cut in 1964. The Keynesian deficits proved right for the time: the tax cut stimulated enough economic activity that revenues, instead of declining, actually increased.[17]

Aside from being a tax cut and being radical, Reagan's proposal bore little resemblance to Kennedy's. Pushed through Congress in the summer of 1981, it represented an explicit break with mainstream economic thinking, both liberal and conservative. The bill embodied the ideas of a small fringe group of economists whose views the conservative Republican economist Herbert Stein dismissed in the *Wall Street Journal* as "punk supply-side economics." In selling the bill to Congress, which was submissive in the aftermath of Reagan's landslide election, the administration made bold, unsupported claims. Despite tax-rate reductions of 25 percent in a three-year period, it promised that the bill would so stimulate investment that revenues would increase and deficits decline. This resembled the claims for the Kennedy bill except that, under the prevailing conditions, nothing in conventional economic models or empirical estimates remotely justified the optimistic predictions. Senate Republican leader Howard Baker, a reluctant supporter, termed the bill "a riverboat gamble." Within a year, policymakers faced deficits in the $200 billion range—twice what they had considered intolerable a short time earlier and enough, nearly all agreed, to damage the economy severely.[18]

A president with some measure of sophistication about economic policy would have dismissed as economic demagoguery the extraordinary claims made for the Reagan tax proposal. He would have been aware of several things: that mainstream economists have worked out methods for estimating the effects of tax policies; that these estimates are imprecise and subject to a range of disagreement; but that they are still the best estimates anybody has. President Reagan presumably knew that most economists did not endorse his proposal. But he had never paid enough attention to serious economic debate to appreciate the difference between ideological faith and empirical measurement.

None of this is to suggest that presidents should set aside their ideologies and simply defer to ideologically neutral experts. Gerald Ford, another conservative president, had a strong belief in free markets and assembled a cabinet and staff largely of individuals who shared that perspective. Yet Ford also insisted that sound professional analysis underlie his decisions and took pains to consider a variety of views. Ford's conservatism shaped the policies of his administration, which held down government spending, stressed controlling inflation more than reducing unemployment, and started the process of economic deregulation.[19] In much the same way, Reagan achieved both conservative goals (cutting tax rates and reducing the tax system's distortion of private economic decisions) and some liberal ones (tax relief for low-income people) in the historic Tax Reform Act of 1986. The president's proposal embodied the consensual judgment among experts both inside and outside of government that the proliferation of credits, exemptions, and deductions in the federal tax code was harmful to the economy.[20]

Adequate policy expertise cannot be acquired in a hurry. A president needs to have been, over the years, the kind of politician who participates responsibly in decision making and debate and who does his homework. This means occasionally taking the time to read some of the advocacy documents (such as congressional hearing testimony and committee reports) that are prepared especially for politicians and their staff. Such documents respect the limits of a politician's expertise and tolerance for detail yet provide a fairly rigorous education.

Policy Processes

In addition to policy issues, presidents must be competent in the processes of policymaking.[21] Most presidential policy decisions are based on advice from several agencies or advisory groups in the executive branch, each with different responsibilities and a different point of view. To be useful to the president, the advice must be brought together in a timely, intelligible way, with proper attention to all the significant viewpoints and considerations. Unfortunately, complex organizational and group decision processes like these have a notorious capacity to produce self-defeating or morally unacceptable results. The specific ways in which they go awry are numerous, but in general terms there are three major threats: intelligence failures, in which critical information is filtered out at lower organizational levels (sometimes because subordinates think the president would be upset by or disagree with it);[22] groupthink, in which a decision-making group commits itself to a course of action prematurely and adheres to it because of social pressures to conform;[23] and noncoordination, which may occur in formulating advice, in handling interdependent issues, or in carrying out decisions.[24]

Many of the frustrations of the Carter administration resulted from its failure to organize decision processes with sufficient care and skill. Carter's original energy proposals, which affected numerous federal programs, were formulated by a single drafting group under the direction of Secretary of Energy James Schlesinger. The group worked in secrecy and isolation, as well as under severe time pressure, which the president had imposed. The resulting proposals had serious flaws that, combined with resentment of the secrecy, led to a fiasco in Congress. Such problems were typical of the Carter administration. Its system of interagency task forces for domestic policymaking generally was chaotic and not well controlled by the White House.[25] Moreover, the White House itself lacked effective coordination.[26]

In foreign policy, the major criticisms of the Carter administration concerned its propensity for vacillation and incoherence. These tendencies resulted largely from its failure to manage the conflict between the national security adviser, Zbigniew Brzezinski, and Secretary of State Cyrus Vance. Despite their different approaches to foreign policy, neither their respective roles nor the administration's foreign policy doctrines were ever adequately clear.[27] The problem was caused in part by Carter's failure to insist that Brzezinski stay within the limits of his assigned role.

In short, serious presidential failures will often result not from individual ignorance—the president's or his advisers'—but from an administration's collective failure to maintain reliable processes for decision. But what must a president know to avoid this danger, and how can he or she learn it?

The effort to design the best possible organization for presidential coordination of the executive branch is exceedingly complex and uncertain—fundamentally, it's a matter of hard trade-offs and guesses, not elegant solutions. Rather than adopt any one organizational plan, a president needs to have a high degree of process sensibility. He should be generally conversant with the risks and impediments to effective decision making and strongly committed to avoiding them. He should recognize the potentially decisive effects of structure, procedures, and leadership methods. And he should be prepared to assign these matters a high priority. In short, the president should treat organization and procedure as difficult matters of vital importance.

The main operational requirements are straightforward. One or more of the president's top-level staff should be a process specialist—someone with experience managing large organizations, ideally the White House, and whose role is defined primarily as a manager and guardian of the decision process, not as an adviser on politics and policy.[28] Certainly, one such person should be the president's chief of staff; others, lower in rank, are needed to manage each major area of policy. A suitable person for each of these roles is one who is sophisticated about the problems of organizational design and the subtleties of human relationships. The president should invest such a person with the support and authority needed to impose a decision-making structure and help him or her insist that everyone adhere to it. Because any organizational arrangement will have weaknesses, some of them unexpected, the president and other senior officials must give the decision-making process continual attention, monitoring its performance and making adjustments.

Finally, if any of this is to work, the president also must be willing to discipline his own participation in decision making. A well-managed, reliable decision-making process sometimes requires the president to perform, so to speak, unnatural acts. In the heat of debate about a major decision, taking the trouble to enforce general plans about structures and roles does not come naturally. Senior officials inevitably will try to bypass established procedures—asking for more control of a certain issue or ignoring channels to give the president direct advice. To enforce the procedures appears to distract from urgent decisions. In any case, the president's temptation is to react according to the substantive outcome he thinks he prefers: if an official who is supposed to be a neutral coordinator has a viewpoint the president likes, let her be heard; if an agency will make trouble over a decision that seems inevitable, stay out of it. Presidents are also tempted to attend primarily to those issues that most interest them, that they understand best, or that they see as promising satisfying results—all of which may fail to reflect their relative importance.

On important decisions that require intensive discussion—decisions in major foreign policy crises, for example—the requirements for presidential self-restraint are even more unnatural. To avoid serious mistakes, it is crucial not to suppress disagreement or close off debate prematurely. Thus, it is important for the president to assume a neutral stance until the time comes to decide. According to psychologist Irving Janis's study of the Kennedy administration's disastrous decision to invade Cuba via the Bay of Pigs, the president unwittingly inhibited debate by his tone and manner of asking questions, which made it obvious that he believed, or wanted to believe, the invasion would work.[29] The president must restrain tendencies that are perfectly normal: to form opinions, especially optimistic ones, before all the evidence is in, and then to want others to relieve his anxiety by agreeing. He must have a strong process sensibility, if only because without it, he will lack the motivation to do his own part.

The performance of Reagan and his aides in organization and policy management was mixed. In establishing effective advisory systems, especially at the outset of the administration, they did well. The administration's principal device for making policy decisions, a system of "cabinet councils," was planned and run largely by Chief of Staff James Baker, who had a knack for organization and previous experience in the Ford administration.[30] Each cabinet council was a subcommittee of the full cabinet, staffed by the White House and chaired by a cabinet member or sometimes the president. The system generally worked well in blending departmental and White House perspectives and reaching decisions in a timely manner, and it kept cabinet members attuned to the president's goals. Inevitably, adjustments were made with the passage of time. The White House Legislative Strategy Group ended up making many of the decisions. Among the cabinet councils, the one assigned to coordinate economic policy, chaired by Treasury Secretary Regan, assumed a broad jurisdiction. To a degree, Reagan played his part in making these arrangements work. He enforced roles—removing a secretary of state, Alexander Haig, who was prone to exceed the limits of his charter—and invested the chief of staff with the authority to run an orderly process.

Nevertheless, the Reagan administration often failed to make decisions through a reasonably sound, deliberate process. One difficulty was that some of the officials Reagan selected to manage decision making lacked the appropriate skills or disposition for the task. In 1985 he allowed an exhausted Baker and an ambitious Regan to switch jobs. Although Regan by then had plenty of experience, he was less suited than Baker to the coordinating role of a chief of staff, and he soon came under attack for surrounding himself with weak subordinates and seeking to dominate the decision process. Until the appointment of Frank Carlucci in December 1986, the administration went through four undistinguished national security advisers—one of them, William Clark, a longtime associate of Reagan's with minimal experience in foreign policy.

On many occasions an even more important source of difficulty was the conduct of the president himself. Instead of exercising self-restraint and fostering discussion, Reagan gave his impulses free rein. He ignored bad news and reacted angrily to unwelcome advice.[31] His role in decisions was unpredictable. Reagan's announcement in March 1983 of the effort to develop a "Star Wars" missile defense system was made, as John Steinbruner says, "without prior staff work or technical definition . . . [and] rather astonished professional security bureaucracies throughout the world."[32] During the 1986 summit meeting with Gorbachev in Reykjavik, Iceland, Reagan again acted without prior staff work when he tentatively accepted a surprise Soviet proposal to do away with long-range nuclear weapons—a utopian notion that ignored the vast superiority of Soviet conventional forces and was soon disavowed by the administration.

Finally, a lack of concern for the integrity of the decision process figured prominently in the Iran-contra scandal that emerged in late 1986, a disaster for U.S. foreign policy and the worst political crisis of the Reagan presidency. The secret arms sales to Iran were vehemently opposed by Secretary of State George Shultz and Secretary of Defense Weinberger, who wrote on his copy of the White House memorandum proposing the plan that it was "almost too absurd for comment." To get around their resistance, the White House largely excluded Shultz and Weinberger from further discussions and carried out the sales, in some degree, without their knowledge. Moreover, to escape the normal congressional oversight of covert activities, the transfers were handled directly by the staff of the National Security Council, designed as an advisory unit, instead of the Department of Defense (DOD) or the Central Intelligence Agency (CIA).

In short, the White House deprived itself of the advice of the two principal cabinet members in foreign policy, the congressional leadership on intelligence matters, and the operational staff of DOD and the CIA—any of whom would have been likely to point out, aside from other serious objections, that the weapons transfers almost inevitably would become public.

Policy Promotion

Good policy decisions, carefully made, are not enough. Presidents also need competence in policy promotion—the ability to get things done in Washington and especially in Congress.[33] For no other major presidential task is the necessary knowledge more complicated or esoteric. Nevertheless, it is also a task in which delegation can largely substitute for the president's own judgment and thus one in which strategic competence places a modest burden on the president.

To promote his policies effectively, a president must make good decisions on complex, highly uncertain problems of strategy and tactics. Which presidential policy goals are politically feasible and which must be deferred? With which groups or congressional leaders should coalitions be formed? When resistance is met, should the president stand firm, perhaps taking the issue to the public, or should he compromise? In all these matters what is the proper timing? Such decisions call for a form of political expertise that has several related elements (all of them different from those involved in winning elections): a solid knowledge of the main coalitions, influence relationships, and rivalries among groups and individuals in Washington; personal acquaintance with a considerable number of important or well-informed individuals; and a fine-grained, practical understanding of how the political institutions work. Clearly, this expertise can be acquired only through substantial and recent experience in Washington. Its lack, however, need not pose much difficulty for a president. Like any technical skill, which in a sense it is, the necessary expertise can easily be hired; the president must only see his need for it.

Because a government as complex as that of the United States has a multitude of jobs that require political skill, people with the requisite experience in policy promotion abound. Many of them (to state the matter politely) would be willing to serve in the White House, and by just asking around a president can get readings on their reputations for effectiveness. Most important, having hired experienced Washington operatives, a president can delegate to them the critical judgments about feasibility, strategy, and political technique. It is not that such judgments are clear-cut, but unlike questions of policy, in these matters the boundary between the realm of expertise and that of values and ideology is easy to discern. Political strategy, in the narrow sense of how to realize policy objectives to the greatest possible extent, is ideologically neutral. It is even nonpartisan: Republican and Democratic presidents attempt to influence Congress in much the same ways.[34] In any case, a political expert's performance in the White House can be measured primarily by short-term results, that is, by how well the administration's policy goals are being achieved.

Both the value and the necessity of delegating policy promotion emerge from a comparison of Carter and Reagan—two presidents who had no prior Washington experience. If there was a single, root cause of the Carter administration's failure (underlying even its mismanagement of decision making), it was the president's refusal to recruit people with successful experience in Washington politics for top advisory and political jobs in the White House.

One of Carter's more unfortunate choices was that of Frank Moore to direct legislative liaison. Although he had held the same job in Georgia when Carter was governor, Moore had no experience in Washington and came to be regarded in Congress as out of his depth. Among Moore's initial staff, which consisted mostly of Georgians, two of the five professionals had worked neither in Congress nor as lobbyists. In organizing them, Moore chose a plan that had been opposed by the former Democratic liaison officials who had been asked for advice. Instead of using the conventional division by chambers and major congressional groups, Moore assigned each of his lobbyists an area of policy. This kept them from developing the stable relationships with individual members of Congress that would enhance trust, and it ignored the straightforward consideration that not all the issues in which the lobbyists specialized would be actively considered at the same time.[35] The Carter administration's reputed incompetence in dealing with Congress could have been predicted: the best of the many Georgians on Carter's staff were able and effective, but others were not, and collectively they lacked the local knowledge to operate skillfully in Washington.[36]

Given this widely condemned failure of his immediate predecessor, it is not surprising that President Reagan avoided the same mistake. But it is still impressive how thoroughly he applied the lesson, even setting aside sectarian considerations for some of the top White House positions. James Baker, who was responsible mainly for political operations during the first term, had been a Ford administration appointee and campaign manager for Reagan's main opponent for the 1980 Republican nomination, George H. W. Bush. Baker was also considered too moderate for a high-level position by many of Reagan's conservative supporters. The congressional liaison director, Max Friedersdorf, was another mainstream Republican, who had worked on congressional relations for Nixon and Ford.[37] In short, the political strategy for policy promotion by which the "Reagan revolution" was pushed through Congress in 1981 was devised and executed by hired hands who were latecomers, at most, to Reaganism. Some change in personnel occurred in subsequent years, including the job switch by Baker and Regan, but the organization and management of this function were essentially stable.[38]

Although the task of formulating strategy for policy promotion can be delegated, much of the hard work cannot. Nothing can draw attention to a proposal and stimulate active public support like a well-presented speech by the president. Furthermore, certain votes are available in Congress if the president makes the necessary phone calls or meets with the right members. The latter task is often tedious, however, if not somewhat demeaning—pleading for support, repeating the same pitch over and over, and promising favors to some while evading requests from others. Presidents therefore often neglect this duty, a source of frustration for their staffs. Carter "went all over the country for two years asking everybody he saw to vote for him," his press secretary complained, "but he doesn't like to call up a Congressman and ask for his support on a bill."[39] Reagan, in contrast, spared no personal effort to pass his program. During the debate on funding for the MX missile in 1985, he had face-to-face meetings with more than two hundred members of Congress and followed up with dozens of phone calls. In 1986, when House Republicans felt they were being ignored in negotiations on tax reform, he went to Capitol Hill to make amends. In the end, a president's effectiveness in lobbying and making speeches depends very much on his basic skills in persuasive communication. A lack of such skills cannot be made up by presidential aides, nor can it be overcome to any great extent by on-the-job learning.

The Possibility of Competence

The presidency is not an impossible job. The requirements for personal knowledge, attention, and expertise on the president's part are manageable— but only if the president has a strategy for competence that carefully puts his own, limited capabilities to use where they are most needed.

With regard to the substance of *policy decisions,* it is enough if over the years the president has given reasonably serious attention to the major national issues and thus has learned to recognize the elements of responsible debate. Inauguration day is too late to begin acquiring this sophistication. In any case, waking before sunrise to read stacks of policy memoranda is neither necessary nor even especially productive.

To maintain an effective *policy process,* the president need not draw the boxes and arrows of organization charts himself. He needs to have a strong process sensibility, that is, a clear sense of the need for careful and self-conscious management of decision making and a willingness to discipline himself as he participates in it. Although the combination of substantive and procedural competence will not ensure that the president always makes the right decision—the one he would make with complete understanding of the issues—it will minimize the likelihood of decisions that are far off the mark.

Finally, the president must know enough to avail himself of the assistance of persons experienced in *policy promotion* in Washington, and especially in dealing with Congress—whether they have been longtime supporters or not. Then he must largely follow their advice and do the often tedious work they ask of him.

Presidential Competence from George H. W. Bush to Barack Obama

The requirements for strategic competence help to account for the successes and failures of the three presidents following Reagan—George H. W. Bush, Bill Clinton, and George W. Bush—and provide insights into the early performance of President Barack Obama. The experience with these presidents provides ample support for the central notions of strategic competence—in particular, the impossibility of self-reliance, the inadequacy of minimalism, and the importance of the president's prior preparation, process sensibility, self-discipline, and strategic use of his own talents.

George H. W. Bush: Self-Indulgence

The presidency of the elder George Bush is typically counted a failure, mostly because he was defeated for reelection.[40] The main source of his loss of popularity, however, did not reflect on his competence. In spring 1991, even as Bush was basking in the glory of American victories in the cold war and the Persian Gulf War, the economy slipped into a recession. Bush refused to support a tax cut or a spending increase to prime the economy, a stance later portrayed by Clinton and the Democrats as showing a lack of concern about the nation's economic distress. In fact, Bush was following the advice of most economists, who warned that increasing an already oversized budget deficit would do harm in the long run.[41] The weak economy hung on through most of 1992; it eroded Bush's standing with the public and, more than anything else, caused his defeat in the election.[42]

Yet Bush's political difficulties also stemmed from his own actions. To be sure, he was highly competent in many respects. He was generally well versed in public policy. He appointed an experienced cabinet and staff and used orderly decision processes.[43] He was an eager self-starter in using his extensive personal contacts to promote his policies in Congress.

Bush fell short of strategic competence, however, in one important respect. Instead of disciplining his participation in decision making, he allowed personal predilections to shape advisory processes and determine decisions. Bush vacillated between extremes of cautiousness and risk taking, and of conciliation and self-assertion. In 1989 Bush surprised observers by caving in, almost meekly, to congressional pressure to end aid to the Nicaraguan contras; but then he invaded Panama under dubious authority of international law. He attacked Iraq with massive force in 1991 but then pulled back without securing a complete victory. One of Bush's riskiest moves was an unconditional "read my lips" promise during the 1988 campaign that he would not raise taxes. His eventual abandonment of the promise and acceptance of tax increases, as part of a 1990 bipartisan deficit-reduction agreement, was a political disaster that placed a major burden on his reelection effort.

Further, Bush had little patience for thinking broadly about plans and purposes. Critics dismissed him as shallow and complained that he had no vision of the country's future. Bush rejected the criticism as irrelevant, belittling what he called "the vision thing." But in fact his relentlessly concrete and narrowly focused thinking constrained deliberation in the White House. Even in the early stages of Bush's term, the staff focused on reacting to events, neglecting broad goals and long-range plans.[44]

Finally, Bush also had little patience for thinking, whether broadly or narrowly, about domestic policy. He had reasons for preferring to spend his time on foreign affairs: his extensive experience in that area (as former U.S. envoy to China and CIA director), the lack of popular support for further conservative reforms in domestic policy, fiscal barriers to new or expanded social programs, and the likelihood of conflict over domestic issues with a Democratic Congress. But instead of exercising self-discipline, Bush allowed his lack of interest in domestic issues to be generally known.[45] Remarkably, he offered no legislative agenda in his first year.[46] Later, some senior officials tried to advance innovative, conservative domestic policies, but they were consistently defeated within the administration.[47]

Bush's lack of a domestic agenda was an effective issue for the Democrats in the 1992 campaign. Bush was reduced to promising that in a second term he would replace his White House staff and work mainly on domestic problems. He did not get the chance.

Bill Clinton: Learning on the Job

Bill Clinton's presidency is difficult to rate as a success or failure. Although Clinton achieved some major policy successes, such as deficit reduction and the

North American Free Trade Agreement, he also experienced major defeats on gay rights and health care reform. He suffered a crushing partisan defeat in the 1994 congressional elections but bounced back to win reelection in 1996 and regain a few seats for his party in the 1998 midterm elections. He eliminated the federal budget deficit but only after Republican prodding. In the most distinguishing episode of his presidency, Clinton was impeached by the House of Representatives on charges of perjury and obstruction of justice in the Monica Lewinsky scandal, but then was acquitted in the Senate trial.

Whatever the ultimate judgment of this mixed record, Clinton's experience differed from his predecessor's on two counts. First, Clinton had better luck with the economy. He enjoyed sustained popularity largely on the strength of an extraordinarily prolonged stretch of economic growth. Although his economic policies generally received reasonably high marks from economists, he also had the good fortune to enter office at the beginning of a major, technology-induced economic boom.[48] Second, although Clinton exhibited marked deficiencies of strategic competence early in his presidency, he learned from his mistakes and made corrections in time to restore his standing with the voters.

In many respects, Clinton was a conspicuously gifted political leader.[49] From the outset of his presidency, he showed an extraordinary grasp of policy issues. In a televised economic summit conference shortly before his first inauguration, Clinton traded ideas, seemingly on equal terms, with leading economists, business leaders, and other experts. He performed with energy and skill in promoting his policies and was an exceptionally effective public speaker.

With respect to one major task, however—management of decision processes—Clinton began abysmally and got his bearings only later. In the first year of his presidency, Clinton failed to exercise strategic competence in managing decision making. His first chief of staff, Thomas "Mack" McLarty, was a lifelong Arkansas friend and successful businessman who had no Washington or government experience. McLarty was out of his element in White House politics. The president's chief counsel, Bernard Nussbaum, was a Wall Street lawyer with minimal experience in Washington.[50] Many Clinton staff members were even less qualified—people in their twenties or early thirties who had limited professional experience of any kind.[51] Strangely, the early Clinton White House also failed to reflect the president's supposed ideological commitments. Dominated by liberal Democrats, it included few of the relatively conservative Democrats for whom Clinton had been a spokesman before the 1992 campaign.[52]

The decision-making process in the early Clinton White House was haphazard, without much explicit management or structure. Decisions were arrived at informally, even mysteriously.[53] In some areas, Clinton practiced an apparently inadvertent self-reliance, making up for the lack of structured advisory processes by investing enormous amounts of time in long-winded discussions with the staff.[54] Not surprisingly, therefore, he was hardly involved at all in other areas, especially foreign policy. In separate episodes, the administration announced major policy changes on Bosnia and Cuba without the president having been apprised of them.[55] In an episode that undermined the central element of his domestic program, Clinton put his wife, Hillary Clinton, and academic policy analyst Ira Magaziner—neither of whom had any experience in executive branch policymaking processes—in charge of developing his 1993 health care reform plan. They set up a bizarre process for designing the proposal, involving dozens of separate task forces and some five-hundred individual participants, and came up with a plan that sunk under the weight of its massive costs and bureaucratic complexity.[56] The disorganized, inexperienced, and ideologically unbalanced White House staff contributed to a legion of political difficulties that beset Clinton in his first two years as president and led to the disastrous Democratic defeat in the 1994 elections.

By the beginning of his second year, however, Clinton had come to understand the costs of careless management and began to bring order and a more moderate direction to the decision process.[57] Clinton found an experienced Washington hand and skilled manager to run the White House: Leon Panetta, OMB director and former chair of the House Budget Committee. In addition, he brought in David Gergen, a former Republican White House aide, to consult on strategy.

After he reformed his decision-making methods, Clinton was generally skillful and effective. Paying more attention to foreign policy, he undertook successful military interventions in Bosnia, Haiti, and Serbia. In political terms, he rarely sounded a wrong note. In 1995 Clinton had a "showdown," as Elizabeth Drew called it, with congressional Republicans over their Contract with America, and especially the budget.[58] Politically, at least, Clinton won, successfully portraying Speaker of the House Newt Gingrich and the Republicans as attacking Medicare and forcing shutdowns of the federal government. In his second term, Clinton worked with congressional Republicans to balance the budget while continuing to exploit their less-popular positions on Medicare and Social Security. In the end, the gravest questions about Clinton's leadership, raised by the Monica Lewinsky scandal, concerned his character, not his competence.

Minimalism Revisited: George W. Bush

Although George W. Bush was the son of one president, his approach to the office resembled more closely that of a different president, Ronald Reagan. Like

Reagan, Bush was a minimalist, who got by as president with modest investments of personal effort in decision making. But his version of minimalism differed from Reagan's in two important respects. On one hand, Bush was more willing than Reagan to defer to subordinates. On the other hand, his subordinates reflected a narrower range of the political spectrum.

Bush's resort to a chairman-of-the-board, minimalist strategy was encouraged, if not required, by his limited interest in substantive issues of government and public policy.[59] In his six years as governor of Texas, Bush rarely dealt with issues in much depth. He insisted on brief meetings and short memoranda and left most issues to his staff.[60] During the 2000 campaign, Bush often revealed a lack of familiarity with major national, and especially international, issues.[61] If Bush had tried to play an active role in assessing the merits of policy debates, he would have lacked the prior experience needed to make discriminating judgments.

Early in his first term, Bush appeared to escape most of the pitfalls of the minimalist approach. Perhaps to compensate for his own limitations, Bush had selected a vice-presidential running mate, Dick Cheney, and had assembled a White House staff and cabinet, who were widely praised as capable and experienced. Many had worked in the campaigns or administrations of previous Republican presidents, especially the elder Bush.[62] Senior political counselor Karl Rove and communications director Karen Hughes were experienced, Bush-family political hands. The chief of staff, Andrew Card, had been deputy chief of staff in the earlier Bush administration.

Card and Rove initially ran the White House as a tight ship, centralizing control of its various offices, focusing attention on priority issues through the new Office of Strategic Initiatives, and making sure that meetings began and ended on time. As appropriate for a chief of staff, Card avoided a high-profile public role and served as an "honest broker" in policy deliberations. In foreign affairs, Bush appointed an academic with only modest governmental experience, Condoleezza Rice, as national security adviser.[63] But Secretary of State Colin Powell and Secretary of Defense Donald Rumsfeld both had had distinguished Washington careers.

Bush largely allowed the vice president, senior aides, and cabinet members to define the direction of his administration. Cheney ran the transition process while Bush waited in the wings at his Texas ranch. After the inauguration, Bush delegated important decisions, often with little specific direction about what he wanted done. When the transition team recommended Paul O'Neill for secretary of the Treasury, Bush met with him and approved the appointment while showing no interest in what O'Neill had to say about economic policy.[64] Bush met with his budget team for a total of about five hours to make all the decisions for his first budget proposal.[65] In general, domestic policy leadership was divided between Cheney, who focused on economic issues, and Rove, the main pipeline to the Christian right, who focused on social issues.

Predictably, Bush's heavy reliance on subordinates led to media criticism and pressure for the president to take on more personal responsibility. Regarding Cheney's extraordinary power, the joke circulated that Bush was "a heartbeat away from the presidency." To counter this image, Bush and his aides tried to create the appearance of hands-on leadership. Describing a two-day gathering of top officials at Camp David the weekend after the 9/11 terrorist attack, Condoleezza Rice told a reporter that, on the first day, Bush sat through seven hours of discussion without speaking, but that on the second day, he met with her in private and dictated an elaborate, multiphase plan, as she took copious notes.[66] A skeptical commentator listed several similar accounts of Bush's supposed hands-on leadership, all based on White House officials' unverifiable reports of private meetings with him.[67]

Nevertheless, unlike with Reagan, there were no reports of Bush overruling his unanimous advisers, barring options they wanted to consider, or catching them off guard with an unexpected decision. On the whole, Bush appeared comfortable in the limited role of a minimalist president. As an adviser described him during the 2000 election campaign, he was "confident enough to show what he doesn't know."[68]

Well into his first year as president, Bush's version of a minimalist presidency appeared to be working. "By and large," I conceded in an earlier version of this chapter, written in late 2001,

the first year of the Bush presidency was counted a political and policy success. Record high public approval ratings reflected the apparent competence and significant successes of the Afghanistan phase of the war on terrorism. And unlike Clinton's first year, there were no scandals or policy fiascoes. In short, the early indications were that, in Bush's case, minimalism worked.[69]

The concession was premature. Bush's minimalist approach eventually contributed to serious difficulties in what was widely regarded a failed, if not calamitous, presidency.[70] His methods had three problematic consequences for his performance. First, whether or not intentionally, Bush allowed very conservative senior officials, especially Cheney, to capture his administration. In addition to letting Vice President Cheney run the transition, and thus play the central role in most of his appointments, he allowed Cheney to establish organizational arrangements for the White House that gave the vice president and his staff essentially unlimited opportunity to participate in presidential decisions. Cheney promoted a hard-right agenda on a wide range of domestic, foreign policy, and constitutional issues.[71] In a mirror image of Clinton's early performance, Bush lurched away from the centrist, "compassionate conservative" posture of his presidential campaign; with few exceptions, especially a major initiative on education, his policy decisions played to the conservative base of the Republican party.[72] He pushed a large tax cut with benefits skewed toward high-income taxpayers, an antimissile defense system, oil and gas drilling in the Alaskan wilderness, withdrawal from the Kyoto accord on global warming, and a ban on federal support for family planning, among other conservative positions. Although he revived the "compassionate conservative" theme for the 2004 campaign, Bush, unlike Clinton, never moved back to the center in his policy decisions.[73]

Second, apart from the ideological direction of his policies, Bush's approach allowed administration officials to neglect serious consideration of facts and evidence. Crucially, he permitted the carefully structured formal advisory processes that he had established nominally to be largely abandoned in practice.[74] Instead of compensating for the president's lack of interest in substantive policy deliberation, Bush's advisers often took cues from the president's approach.[75] Independent reports by two former senior administration officials portray a striking lack of concern for the substantive merits of policy decisions. John DiIulio, a political scientist and former director of the White House Office of Faith-Based Initiatives, reported White House meetings that were supposed to discuss policy decisions but instead addressed only political and public relations considerations. "On social policy and related issues," he added, "the lack of even basic policy knowledge, and the only casual interest in knowing more, was somewhat breathtaking."[76]

After Treasury Secretary O'Neill was forced out of the administration in 2003, he described Bush's indifference to economic analysis of decisions about taxes and the budget.[77] In fact, the Bush administration pushed a series of tax cuts that drove projected long-term budget deficits to alarming levels.[78] It also persistently rejected a growing scientific consensus on the importance of human activity as a cause of global warming. The Bush domestic team confirmed the tendency for White House decision making to mimic a minimalist president's style of thinking.[79]

Third, Bush's methods permitted his administration's foreign-policy-making process to be dominated by advocates of an even narrower ideological perspective, resulting in a lack of exposure to effective criticism. Most of the central figures in Bush's foreign policy apparatus—Cheney, Rice, Defense

Secretary Donald Rumsfeld, and Deputy Secretary Paul Wolfowitz—held a distinct, neoconservative view of the world, a particular stream of conservative thinking, shared by only a fraction of the foreign policy community. From the start, administration neoconservatives favored an aggressive, unilateralist foreign policy; unwavering support for Israel; and, at the first opportunity, war with Iraq to remove Saddam Hussein from power.[80] Even conventional conservatives, such as Secretary of State Colin Powell, were marginalized in White House decision processes. A strategically competent president would have recognized the risks associated with neoconservative doctrines and taken pains to ensure a more balanced foreign policy advisory process.

Bush, Cheney, and Rumsfeld led the nation into a costly and unnecessary war in Iraq, which they also mismanaged in multiple ways.[81] They acted on dubious assumptions about the need for the war and the prospects for success and overlooked discrepant evidence. Perhaps unintentionally, they put pressure on military and intelligence agencies to confirm their beliefs. In the most notorious mistake, they asserted repeatedly and with utmost certitude that Iraq possessed major stockpiles of chemical and biological weapons, had an active program to develop nuclear weapons, and constituted an imminent threat to the region and to the United States.[82]

At a crucial meeting leading up to the invasion, Bush asked CIA director George Tenet for his final assessment of the case for Iraq's possessing weapons of mass destruction. Tenet called it "a slam dunk."[83] On a point of such monumental importance, subject to widespread, public disagreement, a competent president would have asked hard questions about the evidence. But Bush settled for Tenet's assurance. As subsequent investigations found, the evidence was ludicrously weak, consisting mainly of the fact that Iraq had possessed chemical and biological weapons in the mid-1990s and had not documented their removal.[84]

The Bush administration made additional costly misjudgments, mostly reflecting wishful thinking, on a long list of important matters about the war—from the troop levels needed to establish order, to the severity of post-invasion sectarian conflict, to the prospects for a rapid transition to stable self-government in Iraq, among others. On all these issues, the administration's manifest commitment to the case for war probably distorted the intelligence it received.[85] At a minimum, intelligence officials knew which conclusions would best serve their career and organizational interests.

In the final two years of Bush's presidency—following the collapse of his public support and the politically disastrous Democratic sweep in the 2006 midterm congressional elections—he made important changes. He replaced

Rumsfeld with the moderate and experienced Robert Gates as secretary of defense, reduced Cheney's influence, and restored procedural regularity to White House decision making.[86] Bush's policymaking showed signs of being less driven by ideology and wishful thinking. Bush changed course in Iraq, using a 2007 "surge" in troop levels to help improve the security situation there and prepare for an eventual withdrawal of American troops. In the financial crisis that developed in fall 2008, Bush swallowed his ideological objections to government intervention and helped pass a $750 billion financial rescue package. From the standpoint of rescuing Bush's presidency, however, the learning came too late.

Barack Obama: Marks of Competence

Barack Obama entered the White House in 2009 amid the most threatening national conditions that had faced any president since Franklin Roosevelt became president during the Great Depression. American troops were fighting in Iraq and Afghanistan, with no clear path to a successful resolution of either conflict. The nation's economy was sinking rapidly into recession, propelled downward by a collapse of the credit markets, with no reliable means to effect a recovery. With large Democratic majorities in both houses of Congress, Obama had generally good prospects of persuading Congress to adopt his major policies. The central challenge of Obama's presidency, therefore, was to identify policies that would actually work.[87]

Before taking office, Obama had shown evidence of exceptional ability. Despite limited experience in national politics, he had acquired more than enough understanding of policy issues to permit strategic competence in policymaking. Having catapulted into the ranks of presidential contenders with a celebrated speech at the 2004 Democratic National Convention two years before he was elected to the U.S. Senate, Obama had spent much of his four years in national politics campaigning to become president. His limited participation in the Senate's business would not have provided much of an education in national issues for most politicians. But Obama had been the kind of politician who does his homework on public policy from the beginning of his political career. His speeches as an Illinois state senator were criticized by political types as excessively detailed and analytical for the general public—evidence of a serious interest in policy. By the time of the 2008 Democratic primary debates, Obama was giving specific, informed answers to questions about national issues. After the election, he discussed a variety of policy issues in impressive detail when introducing his appointees and in his first press conference only two weeks after the inauguration.[88]

Obama also demonstrated a well developed process sensibility and an appreciation for the value of Washington experience. In an unusual investment of time and effort for a presidential candidate, he quietly worked on plans for his presidency with an unannounced transition team during the last two months of the campaign. After the election, he quickly named a chief of staff, Rahm Emanuel, who had successful experience as deputy chief of staff in the Clinton White House, as a member of the Democratic leadership in the House of Representatives, and as chairman of the House Democratic campaign committee. The selection of Emanuel promised competent staff leadership not only for managing the White House but also for political strategy and policy promotion. Obama's appointees to top economic and foreign policy positions— Lawrence Summers as director of the National Economic Council, Timothy Geithner as secretary of the Treasury, Hillary Clinton as secretary of state, Robert Gates as secretary of defense, and James Jones as national security adviser, among others—were notable for their diverse views, stellar academic and career credentials, and high-level experience in national government.[89] Obama promised that he would make decisions on the basis of vigorous debate between advisers with strong views:

One of the dangers in a White House, based on my reading of history, is that you get wrapped up in groupthink and everybody agrees with everything and there's no discussion and there are no dissenting views. So I'm going to be welcoming a vigorous debate inside the White House. But understand, I will be setting policy as president. I will be responsible for the vision that this team carries out, and I expect them to implement that vision once decisions are made.[90]

Obama's organizational arrangements also had some weaknesses. His appointments operation made some embarrassing early mistakes. It signed off on four individuals for high-level positions who turned out to have tax or other legal problems (three of whom withdrew their names from consideration) and a Republican senator who abandoned his nomination for a cabinet post after concluding that he did not support the president's economic policies. It also failed to fill some key positions in a timely manner, with adverse effects on decision making. When Treasury Secretary Geithner announced his initial plan for stabilizing the banking system a few weeks after the inauguration, he offered so few specifics that his presentation only instilled fears that the administration had no strategy, which produced a sharp drop in the stock market. Observers noted that Geithner was working shorthanded, with no one yet named to most of the other top positions at the Treasury Department.[91] In the long run, Obama's decision to appoint to senior positions numerous high-powered individuals with national reputations, their own constituencies, and diverse policy views posed a danger that his administration would fail to pull together as a team. Hillary Clinton, in particular, had sought to be president herself. Obama may face a major challenge merely to prevent destructive infighting at the top level of his administration.

With respect to organization, Obama adopted a controversial strategy of designating White House "czars" to coordinate policy in several areas—energy and climate change, health care reform, and urban affairs—while also creating new staff positions to coordinate technology and management-performance policies. He appointed Vice President Joe Biden as czar for oversight of the massive economic stimulus program. Congressional critics, especially Sen. Robert Byrd, complained that the czars would avoid the congressional scrutiny that departmental appointees, who are expected to testify in committee hearings, undergo.[92] The czar system undoubtedly reduced the influence of cabinet officials, consistent with the trend of recent presidencies. If carefully managed, it had the potential to enhance the president's ability to shape administration policy, but the added complexity could lead to an unusual amount of conflict and confusion.[93]

Unlike some other energetic presidents, Obama effectively disciplined his own participation in policymaking. He was highly engaged in major decisions, yet largely deferred to his appointed experts. Nor did he become obsessed with details. When military leaders presented an operational plan for sending more troops to Afghanistan, he discussed the issue with them and his advisers in a single, lengthy briefing and then took a few days to ruminate before approving the recommendation.[94]

On the other hand, issues arose in the first months of Obama's presidency about the workability of his methods and strategies for promoting his policies. To be sure, he was fully engaged in the personal tasks of lobbying Congress and making his case to the public. Whereas Jimmy Carter had resisted asking legislators for support, Obama eagerly approached even those legislators and other leaders who were not likely to respond favorably. To promote his $800 billion economic stimulus package, his first major agenda item, Obama met with numerous Republican as well as Democratic members of Congress. He attended a small dinner party for conservative commentators at the home of one of them, George Will. To exploit his popularity, with public approval ratings above 60 percent, he traveled outside of Washington, D.C., every week, visiting places hard hit by the economic crisis, to draw attention to his proposals.

Crucial elements of Obama's political strategy were potentially problematic, however, and may have reflected dubious commitments he made during the campaign to bipartisanship and to an extraordinarily ambitious policy agenda.[95] In Obama's first months in office, he bent over backward trying to build bipartisan coalitions in Congress. Thoughtful observers of American politics often lamented Congress's increasingly bitter partisan conflict of the past two decades. But the intense partisanship was not due to some misunderstanding that could be overcome by skillful peacemaking. It was mainly the effect of long-term trends in electoral politics—especially a realignment of the regional bases of the two political parties that has brought southern conservatives into the Republican Party and northern liberals into the Democratic Party, thereby magnifying the ideological differences between them.[96] Democrats and Republicans increasingly have had irreconcilable goals.

Despite Obama's strenuous efforts to cultivate Republican support, Congress passed his stimulus package without a single Republican vote in the House and with the votes of only the three most moderate Senate Republicans, barely enough to avoid a filibuster. Democrats complained that they had made costly policy concessions to the Republicans on the bill and received nothing but criticism in return. Republicans, however, saw no advantage in supporting a huge spending measure whose beneficial effects would redound to the president's political advantage even if Republicans helped pass it. The episode led Obama to admit that his aspirations for bipartisanship might come to very little. "I am the eternal optimist," he remarked, indicating his intention to continue seeking Republican support, at least for a time. "But I am not a sap."[97]

There were also doubts about the scope of Obama's agenda. In addition to dealing with two wars and the economic crisis (which meant creating and protecting jobs, restoring liquidity to the credit markets, rebuilding a dysfunctional financial system, deciding the fate of the automobile industry, controlling the wave of housing foreclosures, and reforming corporate management, among others), Obama planned major initiatives on health care reform, education, immigration, energy, and climate change, among other controversial matters. Critics argued that he was biting off far more than he or Congress could chew. In defense of the approach, Emanuel quipped that the administration did not want to "waste a good crisis." The need for economic stimulus would strengthen the case for worthy programs of all kinds. Obama also recognized that the first year or two of his presidency offered him the best chance to secure major policy change. The risk, however, was that excessive ambition would result in two years of congressional debate about several major unfinished bills, with very little accomplished.[98]

Facing extraordinarily challenging and uncertain circumstances, Obama encountered criticism, from both the left and the right, and from both the cautious and the bold, on almost every major decision. His presidency held possibilities for either historic achievement or abject failure. That Obama had exceptional skills for leadership, and that he pursued a generally sound strategic approach, improved the prospects, but did not guarantee a successful presidency.

Notes

1. Richard E. Neustadt, *Presidential Power: The Politics of Leadership* (New York: Wiley, 1960).

2. Ibid., chap. 7.

3. James David Barber, *The Presidential Character: Predicting Performance in the White House*, 2nd ed. (Englewood Cliffs, N.J.: Prentice Hall, 1977).

4. Arthur M. Schlesinger Jr., "Roosevelt as Administrator," in *Bureaucratic Power in National Politics*, 2nd ed., ed. Francis E. Rourke (Boston: Little, Brown, 1972), 126–138.

5. Ibid., 132–133, 137.

6. On Johnson's personality and his presidency, see Doris Kearns, *Lyndon Johnson and the American Dream* (New York: Harper and Row, 1976).

7. James Fallows, "The Passionless Presidency," *Atlantic Monthly*, May 1979, 33–48.

8. See Nelson W. Polsby, *The Consequences of Party Reform* (New York: Oxford University Press, 1983), 108–109.

9. See James L. Sundquist, *The Decline and Resurgence of Congress* (Washington, D.C.: Brookings Institution Press, 1981), chap. 2.

10. Fred I. Greenstein, *The Hidden-Hand Presidency: Eisenhower as Leader* (New York: Basic Books, 1982).

11. Dick Kirschten, "White House Strategy," *National Journal*, February 21, 1981, 300–303.

12. Quoted in "The Presidency and the Press Corps," by John Herbers, *New York Times Magazine*, May 9, 1982, 45ff.

13. G. Calvin Mackenzie, *The In-and-Outers: Presidential Appointees and Transient Government in Washington* (Baltimore: Johns Hopkins University Press, 1987).

14. Erwin C. Hargrove, *The President as Leader: Appealing to the Better Angels of Our Nature* (Lawrence: University Press of Kansas, 1999), chap. 6.

15. David A. Stockman, *The Triumph of Politics: How the Reagan Revolution Failed* (New York: Harper and Row, 1986), 276–295.

16. Fred I. Greenstein, *The Presidential Difference: Leadership Style from FDR to Clinton* (Princeton: Princeton University Press, 2001), chap. 10.

17. Arthur M. Schlesinger Jr., *A Thousand Days: John F. Kennedy in the White House* (Boston: Houghton Mifflin, 1965), 628–630, 1002–1008.

18. William Greider, "The Education of David Stockman," *Atlantic Monthly*, December 1981, 27Ff.

19. See A. James Reichley, *Conservatives in an Age of Change: The Nixon and Ford Administrations* (Washington, D.C.: Brookings Institution Press, 1981), chap. 18; Roger Porter, *Presidential Decision Making: The Economic Policy Board* (New York: Cambridge University Press, 1980), chap. 3; and Martha Derthick and Paul J. Quirk, *The Politics of Deregulation* (Washington, D.C.: Brookings Institution Press, 1985), chap. 2.

20. Timothy B. Clark, "Strange Bedfellows," *National Journal*, February 2, 1985. For a penetrating study of the politics of taxation, see John F. Witte, *The Politics and Development of the Federal Income Tax* (Madison: University of Wisconsin Press, 1985).

21. The president's task in managing decision making is more difficult than that of chief executives in some of the parliamentary democracies because they have more elaborate and better institutionalized coordinating machinery. See Colin Campbell and George J. Szablowski, *The Super-Bureaucrats: Structure and Behavior in Central Agencies* (New York: New York University Press, 1979). For insightful analyses of the influences on presidential ability to use information effectively, see John P. Burke and Fred I. Greenstein, *How Presidents Test Reality: Decisions on Vietnam, 1954 and 1965* (New York: Russell Sage Foundation, 1989); and Bert A. Rockman, "Organizing the White House: On a West Wing and a Prayer," *Journal of Managerial Issues* 5 (Winter 1993): 453–464.

22. Harold Wilensky, *Organizational Intelligence: Knowledge and Policy in Government and Industry* (New York: Basic Books, 1967).

23. Irving Janis, *Victims of Groupthink: A Psychological Study of Foreign-Policy Decisions and Fiascoes* (Boston: Houghton Mifflin, 1972).

24. Fundamentally, all organization theory concerns the problem of coordination. See Anthony Downs, *Inside Bureaucracy* (Boston: Little, Brown, 1967), chap. 11; and Jay R. Galbraith, *Organization Design* (Reading, Mass.: Addison-Wesley, 1977). Problems of coordination in the executive branch are emphasized in I. M. Destler, *Making Foreign Economic Policy* (Washington, D.C.: Brookings Institution Press, 1980). For a general treatment of presidential staffing and organization, see James P. Pfiffner, *The Strategic Presidency: Hitting the Ground Running*, 2nd ed. (Lawrence: University Press of Kansas, 1996).

25. Lester M. Salamon, "The Presidency and Domestic Policy Formulation," in *The Illusion of Presidential Government*, ed. Hugh Heclo and Lester Salamon (Boulder: Westview Press, 1982), 177–212.

26. For this and other Reagan-Carter comparisons, see John H. Kessel, "The Structures of the Reagan White House" (paper presented at the annual meeting of the American Political Science Association, Chicago, September 1–4, 1983). More generally on Carter, however, see Kessel, "The Structures of the Carter White House," *American Journal of Political Science* 22 (August 1983).

27. See Cyrus Vance, *Hard Choices: Critical Years in America's Foreign Policy* (New York: Simon and Schuster, 1983); and Zbigniew Brzezinski, *Power and Principle: Memoirs of the National Security Advisor, 1977–1981* (New York: Farrar, Straus, and Giroux, 1983).

28. Alexander George, "The Case for Multiple Advocacy in Making Foreign Policy," *American Political Science Review* 66 (September 1972): 751–785; see also George, *Presidential Decision Making: The Effective Use of Information and Advice* (Boulder: Westview Press, 1980).

29. Janis, *Victims of Groupthink*, chap. 2.

30. James P. Pfiffner, "White House Staff versus the Cabinet: Centripetal and Centrifugal Roles," *Presidential Studies Quarterly* 16 (Fall 1986): 666–690.

31. See Stockman, *Triumph of Politics;* and Laurence I. Barrett, *Gambling with History: Reagan in the White House* (New York: Penguin Books, 1984), esp. 174.

32. John D. Steinbrunner, "Security Policy," in *The New Direction in American Politics*, ed. John E. Chubb and Paul E. Peterson (Washington, D.C.: Brookings Institution Press, 1985), 351.

33. See Barbara Kellerman, *The Political Presidency* (New York: Oxford University Press, 1984); and Mark A. Peterson, *Legislating Together: The White House and Capitol Hill from Eisenhower to Reagan* (Cambridge: Harvard University Press, 1990).

34. For a historical treatment and analysis of organization for White House liaison, see Stephen J. Wayne, *The Legislative Presidency* (New York: Harper and Row, 1978).

35. Eric L. Davis, "Legislative Liaison in the Carter Administration," *Political Science Quarterly* 95 (Summer 1979): 287–302. Eventually, organization of the staff by issues was dropped.

36. Polsby, *Consequences of Party Reform,* 105–114.

37. Dick Kirschten, "Second Term Legislative Strategy Shifts to Foreign Policy and Defense Issues," *National Journal,* March 30, 1985, 696–699.

38. Samuel Kernell, *Going Public: New Strategies of Presidential Leadership,* 3rd ed. (Washington, D.C.: CQ Press, 1997); and Theodore J. Lowi, *The Personal President: Power Invested, Promise Unfulfilled* (Ithaca, N.Y.: Cornell University Press, 1985).

39. Quoted by Polsby, *Consequences of Party Reform,* 109.

40. On the Bush presidency, see Colin Campbell and Bert A. Rockman, eds., *The Bush Presidency: First Appraisals* (Chatham, N.J.: Chatham House, 1991); and Ryan J. Barilleaux and Mary E. Stuckey, eds., *Leadership and the Bush Presidency: Prudence or Drift in an Era of Change?* (Westport, Conn.: Greenwood Press, 1992).

41. See Paul J. Quirk and Bruce Nesmith, "Explaining Deadlock: Domestic Policymaking in the Bush Presidency," in *New Perspectives on American Politics,* ed. Lawrence C. Dodd and Calvin Jillson (Washington, D.C.: CQ Press, 1994), 200–201.

42. See Paul J. Quirk and Jon K. Dalager, "The Election: A 'New Democrat' and a New Kind of Presidential Campaign," in *The Elections of 1992,* ed. Michael Nelson (Washington, D.C.: CQ Press, 1993), 57–88.

43. Richard Cohen, "The Gloves Are Off," *National Journal,* October 14, 1989, 2508–2512; and "Mr. Consensus," *Time,* August 21, 1989, 17–22.

44. Paul J. Quirk, "Domestic Policy: Divided Government and Cooperative Presidential Leadership," in *Bush Presidency: First Appraisals,* 69–92.

45. Robert Shogun, *The Riddle of Power: Presidential Leadership from Truman to Bush* (New York: Penguin Books, 1982), chap. 10.

46. Quirk, "Domestic Policy," 69–92.

47. Burt Solomon, "White House Notebook: Bush Plays Down Domestic Policy in Coasting towards Reelection," *National Journal,* March 30, 1991, 752–753.

48. William D. Nordhaus, "The Story of a Bubble," *New York Review of Books,* January 15, 2004, www.nybooks.com/articles/16878.

49. Fred I. Greenstein, *The Presidential Difference: Leadership Style from FDR to Clinton* (Princeton: Princeton University Press, 2001), chap. 12.

50. W. John Moore, "West Wing Novice," *National Journal,* June 5, 1993, 1339–1343. Two decades earlier, Nussbaum had worked on the Watergate prosecution team.

51. Colin Campbell, "Management in a Sandbox: Why the Clinton Administration Failed to Cope with Gridlock," in *The Clinton Presidency: First Appraisals,* ed. Colin Campbell and Bert A. Rockman (Chatham, N.J.: Chatham House, 1995), 51–87.

52. Fred Barnes, "Neoconned," *New Republic,* January 25, 1993, 14–16.

53. Burt Solomon, "Crisscrossed with Connections . . . West Wing Is a Networker's Dream," *National Journal,* January 15, 1994, 256–257.

54. Elizabeth Drew, *On the Edge: The Clinton Presidency* (New York: Simon and Schuster, 1994).

55. On Clinton's lack of attention to foreign policy, see Larry Berman and Emily O. Goldman, "Clinton's Foreign Policy at Midterm," in *Clinton Presidency: First Appraisals,* 290–324.

56. Paul J. Quirk and Joseph Hinchliffe, "Domestic Policy: The Trials of a Centrist Democrat," in *Clinton Presidency: First Appraisals,* 262–289; Theda Skocpol, *Boomerang* (New York: Norton, 1996), 10; and Lawrence R. Jacobs and Robert Y. Shapiro, *Politicians*

Don't Pander: Political Leadership, Public Opinion, and American Politics (Chicago: University of Chicago Press, 2000), chap. 2.

57. Julie Kosterlitz, "Changing of the Guard," *National Journal*, March 6, 1993, 575; and Burt Solomon, "Boomers in Charge," *National Journal*, June 19, 1993, 1472.

58. Elizabeth Drew, *Showdown: The Struggle between the Gingrich Congress and the Clinton White House* (New York: Simon and Schuster, 1996).

59. For a fuller discussion of Bush's prior experience, see Paul J. Quirk and Sean C. Matheson, "The Presidency: The Election and the Prospects for Leadership," in *The Elections of 2000*, ed. Michael Nelson (Washington, D.C.: CQ Press, 2001), chap. 7.

60. Dan Balz and Terry M. Neal, "Bush as President: Questions, Clues, and Contradiction," *Washington Post*, October 22, 2000, A1.

61. At a campaign appearance, for example, Bush attacked the Democratic ticket for wanting the federal government to control Social Security, "like it's some kind of federal program." It is the largest federal domestic program and is fully administered by the federal government. *Slate*, "Complete Bushisms," at Slate.com.

62. Richard L. Berke, "Bush Shapes His Presidency with Sharp Eye on Father's," *New York Times*, March 28, 2001, A1.

63. Rice had been a member of the staff of the National Security Council in the George H. W. Bush administration. Karen DeYoung and Steven Mufson, "Leaner and Less Visible NSC: Reorganization Will Emphasize Defense, Global Economics," *Washington Post*, February 10, 2001, A1.

64. Ron Suskind, *The Price of Loyalty: George W. Bush, the White House, and the Education of Paul O'Neill* (New York: Simon and Schuster, 2004), chap. 1.

65. Richard L. Berke, "Bush Is Providing Corporate Model for White House," *New York Times*, March 11, 2001, A1.

66. Jane Perlez, David E. Sanger, and Thom Shanker, "A Nation Challenged: The Advisers; From Many Voices, One Battle Strategy," *New York Times*, September 23, 2001, A1.

67. Howard Kurtz, "What Bush Said and When He Said It," *Washington Post*, October 1, 2001, C1.

68. Balz and Neal, "Bush as President."

69. Paul J. Quirk, "Presidential Competence," in Michael Nelson, ed., *The Presidency and the Political System*, 8th ed. (Washington, D.C.: CQ Press, 2002), 161.

70. For a balanced assessment of the Bush presidency, see Robert Maranto, Tom Lansford, and Jeremy Johnson, eds., *Judging Bush* (Palo Alto: Stanford University Press, 2009), especially chap. 1. For the widespread negative assessment, see Robert S. McElvaine, "HNN Poll: 61% of Historians Rate the Bush Presidency Worst," April 1, 2008, http://hnn.us/articles/48916.html.

71. Shirley Anne Warshaw, "The Cheneyization of the Bush Administration," in Maranto et al., *Judging Bush*, chap. 3; James P. Pfiffner, "President Bush and the Use of Executive Power," in Maranto et al., *Judging Bush*, chap. 4; Pfiffner, *Power Play: The Bush Presidency and the Constitution* (Washington, D.C.: Brookings Institution Press, 2008); Michael Nelson, "Richard Cheney and the Power of the Modern Vice Presidency," in *Ambition and Division: Legacies of the George W. Bush Presidency*, ed. Steven E. Schier (Pittsburgh: University of Pittsburgh Press, 2009).

72. Dana Milbank and Ellen Nakashima, "Bush Team Has 'Right' Credentials: Conservative Picks Seen Eclipsing Even Reagan's," *Washington Post*, March 25, 2001, A1; Richard Stevenson, "Political Memo: Bush's Moves to Assure Right Ignite Storm on Left," *New York Times*, April 8, 2001, A22; and Juliet Eilperin, "For GOP House Moderates

a Season of Discontent," *Washington Post,* July 22, 2001, A6; Paul Pierson and Jacob S. Hacker, *Off Center: The Republican Revolution and the Erosion of American Democracy* (New Haven: Yale University Press, 2005). For the major exception to Bush's rightward drift, see Frederick Hess and Patrick McGuinn, "Bush's Great Society: No Child Left Behind," in Maranto et al., *Judging Bush,* chap. 9.

73. Dan Balz, "The GOP's Challenge: Softening the Edges," *Washington Post,* September 1, 2004, A1.

74. Karen Hult, David B. Cohen, and Charles Walcott, "The Bush White House and Bureaucracy," in Maranto et al., *Judging Bush,* chap. 7.

75. Gary Mucciaroni and Paul J. Quirk, "Deliberations of a 'Compassionate Conservative': George W. Bush's Domestic Presidency," in *The George W. Bush Presidency: Appraisals and Prospects,* ed. Colin Campbell and Bert A. Rockman (Washington, D.C.: CQ Press, 2003), chap. 7.

76. Ron Suskind, "Why Are These Men Laughing?" *Esquire,* January 2003, 96–105 (quote on 99).

77. Suskind, *Price of Loyalty,* 116–118.

78. Jeffrey E. Cohen and Costas Panagopoulos, "George W. Bush and Economic Policy: A Study in Irony," in Maranto et al., *Judging Bush,* chap. 10.

79. Associated Press, "Experts Decry Bush Science Policies," *USA Today,* February 2, 2005, www.usatoday.com/news/washington/2005–02–20-bush-science_x.htm.

80. Lawrence Korb and Laura Conley, "Forging an American Empire," in Maranto et al., *Judging Bush,* chap. 13; Suskind, *Price of Loyalty;* and Richard A. Clarke, *Against All Enemies: Inside America's War on Terror* (New York: Free Press, 2004).

81. Thomas E. Ricks, *Fiasco: The American Military Adventure in Iraq* (New York: Penguin Press, 2006).

82. U.S. Senate, *Report of the Select Committee on Intelligence on the U.S. Intelligence Community's Prewar Assessments on Iraq,* 108th Congress, 2nd Session, Senate Report 108–301, July 9, 2004.

83. Bob Woodward, *Plan of Attack* (New York: Simon and Schuster Paperbacks, 2004), 247–250.

84. U.S. Senate, *Report of the Select Committee on Intelligence.*

85. Ibid., 272–285; Thomas Powers, "How Bush Got It Wrong," *New York Review of Books,* September 23, 2004, www.nybooks.com/articles/article-preview?article_id=17413. There has been a partisan debate about whether Bush (intentionally) "misled" the country in his claims about Iraq's possessing weapons of mass destruction. In fact, no credible evidence has indicated that Bush himself ever doubted that Iraq had such weapons. However, he clearly exaggerated the shaky grounds for that belief, and either knowingly or recklessly misrepresented important evidence to support his claims.

86. Hult, Cohen, and Walcott, "The Bush White House and Bureaucracy."

87. Paul J. Quirk and Bruce Nesmith, "The Presidency: The Unexpected Competence of the Barack Obama Administration," in Michael Nelson, ed., *The Elections of 2008* (Washington: CQ Press, 2009), chap. 4.

88. Fred I. Greenstein, "The Leadership Style of Barack Obama: An Early Assessment," *The Forum* 7, no. 1 (2009), Article 6.

89. Quirk and Nesmith, "The Presidency: Unexpected Competence."

90. Quoted in Greenstein, "The Leadership Style of Barack Obama: Early Assessment," 8, from Obama's response to a reporter during the press conference announcing his national security team, December 1, 2008.

91. David Prosser, "Geithner Is Fast Running Out of Time and Excuses," *The Independent,* March 23, 2009, www.independent.co.uk/news/business/analysis-and-features/david-prosser-geithner-is-fast-running-out-of-time-and-excuses-1651731.html.

92. Noelle Straub, "Byrd Questions Obama's Use of Policy 'Czars,'" *Greenwire,* February 25, 2009, www.greenwire.com.

93. Personal communication, James P. Pfiffner, March 3, 2009.

94. Helene Cooper and Eric Schmitt, "White House Debate Led to Plan to Widen Afghan Effort," *New York Times,* March 27, 2009, www.nytimes.com/2009/03/28/us/politics/28Prexy.html?_r=1&scp=1&sq=obama%20afghanistan&st=cse.

95. Quirk and Nesmith, "The Presidency: Unexpected Competence."

96. Richard Fleisher and Jon R. Bond, "The Shrinking Middle in the U.S. Congress," *British Journal of Political Science* 34, no. 3 (July 2004): 429–451.

97. William Schneider, "For Divided Congress, Making Up Is Hard to Do," *National Journal,* February 28, 2009, www.nationaljournal.com.

98. Jonathan Rauch, "Is Obama Repeating Bush's Mistakes?" *National Journal,* March 28, 2009, www.nationaljournal.com.

5 The Psychological Presidency

Michael Nelson

Several delegates to the Constitutional Convention of 1787 noted during the first week of debate that to invest power in a unitary office was to invest power in one person. Not until James David Barber wrote The Presidential Character, *however, was a systematic effort made to explore the psychological consequences of that important truism. Michael Nelson examines this influential book, along with another that Barber wrote about the voters' supposed contributions to the "psychological presidency,"* The Pulse of Politics. *Although Nelson finds Barber's theories wanting (the healthiest of Barber's character types, for example, are not always successful presidents), he praises Barber for drawing scholars' attention to the psychological aspects of the presidency and for encouraging political journalists to do the same in their coverage of presidential campaigns.*

The United States elects its president every four years, which makes it almost unique among democratic nations. During several presidential election campaigns in the 1970s and 1980s, *Time* magazine ran a story about James David Barber, which makes him equally singular among political scientists. The two quadrennial oddities are not unrelated.

The first *Time* article, which appeared in 1972, was about Barber's just-published book, *The Presidential Character: Predicting Performance in the White House,* in which he argued that presidents could be divided into four psychological types: "active-positive," "active-negative," "passive-positive," and "passive-negative." What's more, according to Barber via *Time,* by taking "a hard look at men before they reach the White House," voters could tell in advance what candidates would be like if elected: healthily "ambitious out of exuberance," like the active-positives; pathologically "ambitious out of anxiety," like the active-negatives; "compliant and other-directed," like the passive-positives; or "dutiful and self-denying," like the "passive-negatives." In the 1972 election, Barber told *Time,* the choice was between an active-positive, George McGovern, and a psychologically defective active-negative, Richard M. Nixon.[1]

Nixon won the election, but Barber's early insights into Nixon's personality won notoriety for both him and his theory, especially in the wake of Watergate. So prominent had Barber become by 1976 that White House correspondent Hugh Sidey used his entire "Presidency" column in the October 4 issue of *Time* to tell readers that Barber was refusing to type candidates Gerald R. Ford and Jimmy Carter this time around. "Barber is deep into an academic study of this election and its participants, and he is pledged to restraint until it is over," Sidey reported solemnly.[2] Actually, more than a year before, Barber had told *U.S. News & World Report* that he considered Ford an active-positive.[3] Carter, who read Barber's book twice when it came out, was left to tell the *Washington Post* that active-positive is "what I would like to be. That's what I hope I prove to be."[4] And so Carter would be, wrote Barber in a special postelection column for *Time.*[5]

The 1980 election campaign witnessed the appearance of another Barber book, *The Pulse of Politics: Electing Presidents in the Media Age,* and, in honor of the occasion, two *Time* articles. This was all to the good because the first, a Sidey column in March, offered more gush than information: "The first words encountered in the new book by Duke's Professor James David Barber are stunning: 'A revolution in presidential politics is under way.' . . . Barber has made political history before."[6] A more substantive piece in the magazine's May 19 "Nation" section described the new book's cycle theory of presidential elections. According to Barber ever since 1900, steady four-year beats in the public's psychological mood, or "pulse," have caused a recurring alternation among elections of "conflict," "conscience," and "conciliation." *Time* went on to stress, although not explain, Barber's view of the importance of the mass media, both as a reinforcer of this cycle and as a potential mechanism for helping the nation to break out of it.[7]

In subsequent years Barber, who died in 2004, wrote for and was written about in numerous other national publications. But it was *Time*'s infatuation with Barber that brought him a level of fame that comes rarely to political scientists. For Barber, fame came at some cost. Although widely known, his ideas were little understood. The media's cursory treatment of them made them appear superficial or even foolish—instantly appealing to the naive, instantly odious to the thoughtful. Partly as a result, Barber's reputation in the intellectual community as an *homme sérieux* suffered. In the backrooms and corridors of scholarly gatherings, one heard "journalistic" and "popularizer," the ultimate academic epithets, muttered along with his name. Indeed, in a 1991 assessment of contemporary scholarly research on the presidency, Paul Quirk observed of the whole field of presidential psychology that "researchers seem to have kept their distance from the subject as if to avoid guilt by association" with Barber.[8]

This situation is in need of remedy. Barber's theories may be seriously flawed, but they are serious theories. For all their limitations—some of them self-confessed—they offer one of the most significant contributions a scholar can make: an unfamiliar but useful way of looking at a familiar subject that we no longer see very clearly. In Barber's case, the familiar thing is the American presidency, and the unfamiliar way of looking at it is through the lenses of psychology.

Psychological Perspectives on the Presidency

Constitutional Perspectives

To look at politics in general, or the American presidency in particular, from a psychological perspective is nothing new. Although deprived of the insights of modern psychology, the Framers of the Constitution constructed their plan of government on a foundation of Hobbesian assumptions about what motivates *homo politicus*. (They called what they were doing moral philosophy, not psychology.) James Madison and most of his colleagues at the Constitutional Convention assumed that "men are instruments of their desires"; that "one such desire is the desire for power"; and that "if unrestrained by external checks, any individual or group of individuals will tyrannize over others."[9] Because the Framers believed these things, a basic tenet of their political philosophy was that the government they were designing should be a "government of laws and not of men." Not just psychology but history had taught them to associate liberty with law and tyranny with rulers who depart from law, as had George III and his colonial governors.

In the end the convention yielded to those who urged, on grounds of "energy" in the executive, that the Constitution lodge the powers of the executive branch in a single person, the president.[10] There are several reasons why the delegates were willing to put aside their doubts and inject such a powerful dose of individual character into the new plan of government. One is the Framers' certain knowledge that George Washington would be the first president. They knew that Washington aroused powerful and, from the standpoint of winning the nation's support for the new government, vital psychological responses from the people. As Seymour Martin Lipset has shown, Washington was a classic example of what sociologist Max Weber called a charismatic leader, a man "treated [by the people] as endowed with supernatural, superhuman, or at least specifically exceptional powers or qualities."[11] Marcus Cunliffe noted,

[B]abies were being christened after him as early as 1775, and while he was still President, his countrymen paid to see him in waxwork effigy. To his admirers he was "godlike Washington," and his detractors complained to one another that he was looked upon as a "demigod" whom it was treasonous to criticize. "Oh Washington!" declared Ezra Stiles of Yale (in a sermon of 1783). "How I do love thy name! How have I often adored and blessed thy God, for creating and forming thee the great ornament of human kind!"[12]

Just as Washington's "gift of grace" would legitimize the new government, the Framers believed, so would his personal character ensure its republican nature. The powers of the president in the Constitution "are full great," wrote Pierce Butler, a convention delegate from South Carolina, to a British kinsman,

and greater than I was disposed to make them. Nor, entre nous, do I believe they would have been so great had not many of the delegates cast their eyes towards General Washington as President; and shaped their Ideas of the Powers to be given to a President, by their opinions of his Virtue.[13]

The Framers were not so naive or shortsighted as to invest everything in Washington. To protect the nation from power-mad tyrants after he left office, they provided that the election of the president, whether by electors or members of the House of Representatives, would involve selection by peers—personal acquaintances of the candidates who could screen out those of defective character. And even if someone of low character slipped through the net and became president, the Framers believed that they had structured the office to protect the nation from harm. "The founders' deliberation over the provision for indefinite reeligibility," Jeffrey Tulis has shown, "illustrates how they believed self-interest could sometimes be elevated."[14] As Alexander Hamilton argued in *The Federalist*, whether presidents are motivated by "avarice," "ambition," or "the love of fame," they will behave responsibly to secure reelection to the office that allows that desire to be fulfilled.[15] Underlying this confidence was the assurance that in a relatively slow-paced world, mad or wicked presidents could do only so much damage before corrective action could remove them. As John Jay explained, "So far as the fear of punishment and disgrace can operate, that motive to good behavior is amply afforded by the article on the subject of impeachment."[16]

Scholarly Perspectives

The Framers' decision to inject personality into the presidency was a conscious one. But it was made for reasons that eventually ceased to pertain. The destructive powers at a modern president's disposal are ultimate and swift; the impeachment process now seems uncertain and slow. Peer review never took hold in the Electoral College. The rise of the national media makes the president's personality all the more pervasive. In sum, most of the Framers' carefully conceived defenses against a president of defective character are gone.

Clearly, then, a sophisticated psychological perspective on the presidency was overdue in the late 1960s, when Barber began offering one in a series of articles and papers that culminated in *The Presidential Character*.[17] Presidential scholars had long taken it as axiomatic that the American presidency is an institution shaped in some measure by the personalities of individual presidents. But rarely had the literature of personality theory been brought to bear, in large part because scholars of the post–Franklin D. Roosevelt period no longer seemed to share the Framers' reservations about human nature, at least as far as the presidency was concerned. Instead, historians and political scientists exalted not only presidential power but also presidents who are ambitious for power. Richard Neustadt's influential book *Presidential Power*, published in 1960, was typical in this regard:

The contributions that a president can make to government are indispensable. Assuming that he knows what power is and wants it, those contributions cannot help but be forthcoming in some measure as by-products of his search for personal influence.[18]

As Erwin Hargrove reflected in post-Vietnam, post-Watergate 1974, this line of reasoning was the source of startling deficiencies in scholarly understandings of the office: "We had assumed that ideological purpose was sufficient to purify the drive for power, but we forgot the importance of character."[19]

Scholars also had recognized for some time that Americans' attitudes about the presidency, like presidents' actions, are psychologically as well as politically rooted. Studies of schoolchildren indicated that they first come into political awareness by learning of, and feeling fondly toward, the president. As adults, they rally to the president's support, both when they inaugurate a new one and in times of crisis.[20] Popular nationalistic emotions, which in constitutional monarchies are directed toward the king or queen, are deflected in American society onto the president. Again, however, scholars' awareness of these psychological forces manifested itself more in casual observations (Dwight D. Eisenhower was a "father figure"; the "public mood" is fickle) than in systematic investigation.

The presidencies of John F. Kennedy, Lyndon B. Johnson, and Richard Nixon altered this scholarly quiescence. Surveys taken shortly after the Kennedy assassination recorded the startling depth of the feelings that Americans have about the presidency. A large share of the population experienced symptoms classically associated with grief over the death of a loved one. Historical evidence suggests that the public has responded similarly to the deaths of all sitting presidents, young or old, popular or not, whether by murder or natural causes.[21]

If Kennedy's death illustrated the deep psychological ties of the public to the presidency, the experiences of his immediate successors showed even more clearly the importance of psychology in understanding the connection between president and presidency. Johnson, the peace candidate who rigidly pursued a self-defeating policy of war, and Nixon, who promised "lowered voices" only to angrily turn political disagreements into personal crises, seemed to project their personalities onto policy in ways that were both obvious and destructive. The events of the 1960s and 1970s brought students of the presidency up short. As they paused to consider the "psychological presidency," they found Barber standing at the ready with the foundation and first floor of a full-blown theory.

James David Barber and the Psychological Presidency

Barber's theory offers a model of the presidency as an institution shaped largely by the psychological mix between the personalities of individual presidents and the public's deep feelings about the office. It also proposes methods of predicting what those personalities and feelings are likely to be in particular circumstances. These considerations govern *The Presidential Character* and *The Pulse of Politics,* books that will be examined in turn. The question of how we can become masters of our own and of the presidency's psychological fate is also treated in these books, but it receives fuller exposition in other works by Barber.

Presidential Psychology
The primary danger of the Nixon administration will be that the President will grasp some line of policy or method of operation and pursue it in spite of its failure. . . . How will Nixon respond to challenges to the morality of his regime, to charges of scandal and/or corruption? First such charges strike a raw nerve, not only from the Checkers business, but also from deep within the personality in which the demands of the superego are so harsh and hard. . . . The first impulse will be to hush it up, to conceal it, bring down the blinds. If it breaks open and Nixon cannot avoid commenting on it, there is a real setup here for another crisis.

James David Barber was more than a little proud of that prediction, mainly because he made it in a talk he gave at Stanford University on January 19, 1969, the eve of Nixon's first inauguration. It was among the earliest in a series of speeches, papers, and articles whose purpose was to explain his theory of presidential personality and how to predict it, always with his forecast for Nixon's future prominently, and thus riskily, displayed. The theory received its fullest statement in *The Presidential Character*.

Character, in Barber's usage, is not quite a synonym for "personality," but it comes close.[22] To be sure, a politician's psychological constitution also includes two other components: an adolescence-born *worldview,* which Barber defines as "primary, politically relevant beliefs, particularly his conceptions of social causality, human nature, and the central moral conflicts of the time"; and a *style,* or "habitual way of performing three political roles: rhetoric, personal relations, and homework," which develops in early adulthood. But clearly Barber considered character, which forms in childhood and shapes the later development of style and worldview, to be "the most important thing to know about a president or candidate." As he defined the term, "character is the way the President orients himself toward life—not for the moment, but enduringly." It "grows out of the child's experiments in relating to parents, brothers and sisters, and peers at play and in school, as well as to his own body and the objects around it." Through these experiences, the child—and thus the adult to be—arrives subconsciously at a deep and private understanding of his or her fundamental worth.

For some, this process results in high self-esteem, the vital ingredient for psychological health and political productiveness. Others must search outside themselves for evidence of worth that at best will be a partial substitute. Depending on the source and nature of their limited self-esteem, Barber suggested, they will concentrate their search in one of three areas: the affection from others that compliant and agreeable behavior brings, the sense of usefulness that comes from performing a widely respected duty, or the deference attendant with dominance and control over other people. Because politics is a vocation rich in opportunities to find all three of these things—affection from cheering crowds and devoted aides, usefulness from public service in a civic cause, dominance through official power—it is not surprising that some insecure people are attracted to a political career.

This makes for a problem, Barber argued. If public officials, especially presidents, use their office to compensate for private doubts and demons, it follows that they will not always use it to serve public purposes. Affection seekers will be so concerned with preserving the goodwill of those around them that they seldom will challenge the status quo or otherwise rock the boat. The duty-doers will be similarly hidebound, although in their case inactivity will result from the feeling that to be useful they must be diligent guardians of time-honored practices and procedures. Passive presidents of both kinds may provide the nation with "breathing spells, times of recovery in our frantic political life," or even "a refreshing hopefulness and at least some sense of sharing and caring." Still, in Barber's view, their main effect is to "divert popular attention from the hard realities of politics," thus leaving the country to "drift." And "what passive presidents ignore, active presidents inherit."[23]

Power-driven presidents pose the greatest danger. They will seek their psychological compensation not in inaction but in intense efforts to maintain or extend their personal sense of domination and control through public channels. When things are going well for power-driven presidents and they feel they have the upper hand with their political opponents, problems may not arise. But when matters cease to go their way, as eventually will happen in a democratic system, the power-driven president's response almost certainly will take destructive forms, including rigid defensiveness and aggression against opponents. Only those with high self-esteem will be secure enough to lead as democratic political leaders should lead, with persuasion and flexibility as well as action and initiative.

Perhaps more important than the theoretical underpinnings of Barber's character analysis is the practical purpose that animates *The Presidential Character*: to help citizens choose their presidents wisely. The book's first words heralded this purpose:

When a citizen votes for a presidential candidate he makes, in effect, a prediction. He chooses from among the contenders the one he thinks (or feels, or guesses) would be the best president. . . . This book is meant to help citizens and those who advise them cut through the confusion and get at some clear criteria for choosing presidents.

How, though, in the heat and haste of a presidential election, with candidates notably unwilling to bare their souls for psychological inspection, are we to find out what they are really like? Easy enough, argues Barber. To answer the complex question of what motivates a political leader, just answer two simpler questions in its stead: active or passive? ("How much energy does the man invest in his presidency?") and positive or negative? ("Relatively speaking, does he seem to experience his political life as happy or sad, enjoyable or discouraging, positive or negative in its main effect?").

According to Barber, the four possible combinations of answers to these two questions turn out to be almost synonymous with the four psychological strategies that people use to enhance self-esteem. The *active-positives* are the healthy ones in the group. Their high sense of self-worth enables them to work hard at politics, enjoy what they do, and thus be fairly good at it. Of the four eighteenth- and nineteenth-century presidents and the sixteen twentieth-century presidents whom Barber typed, he placed Thomas Jefferson, Franklin D. Roosevelt, Harry S. Truman, Kennedy, Ford, Carter, George H. W. Bush, and Bill Clinton in this category. The *passive-positives* (James Madison, William H. Taft, Warren G. Harding, Ronald Reagan) are the affection seekers. Although not especially hardworking, they enjoy their time in office. The *passive-negatives* (Washington, Calvin Coolidge, Eisenhower) neither work nor play; it is duty, not pleasure or zest, that gets them into politics. Finally, there are the power-seeking *active-negatives,* who compulsively and with little satisfaction throw themselves into their presidential chores.

In Barber's view, active-negative presidents John Adams, Woodrow Wilson, Herbert Hoover, Lyndon Johnson, and Richard Nixon all shared one important personality-rooted quality: They persisted in disastrous courses of action (Adams's repressive Alien and Sedition acts, Wilson's League of Nations battle, Hoover's depression policy, Johnson's Vietnam, Nixon's Watergate) because to have conceded error would have been to lose their sense of control, something their psychological constitutions would not allow them to do. Table 5.1 summarizes Barber's four types and his categorizations of individual presidents.

Not surprisingly, *The Presidential Character* was extremely controversial when it came out in 1972. Many argued that Barber's theory was too simple, that his four types did not begin to cover the range of human complexity. At one level, this criticism is as trivial as it is true. In spelling out his theory, Barber stated clearly that "we are talking about tendencies, broad directions; no individual man exactly fits a category." He offered his character typology as a method for sizing up potential presidents, not for diagnosing and treating them. In the midst of image-laden election campaigns, a reasonably accurate shorthand device is about all we can hope for. The real question, then, is whether Barber's shorthand device is reasonably accurate.

Barber's intellectual defense of his typology's soundness, quoted in full, is not altogether comforting:

Why might we expect these two simple dimensions [active-passive, positive-negative] to outline the main character types? Because they stand for two central features of anyone's orientation toward life. In nearly every study of personality, some form of the active-passive contrast is critical; the general tendency to act or be acted upon is evident in such concepts as dominance-submission, extraversion-introversion, aggression-timidity, attack-defense, fight-flight, engagement-withdrawal, approach-avoidance. In every life we sense quickly the general energy output of the

Table 5.1 Barber's Character Typology, with Presidents Categorized According to Type

Energy directed toward the presidency	Affect toward the presidency	
	Positive	Negative
Active	Thomas Jefferson Franklin Roosevelt Harry Truman John Kennedy Gerald Ford Jimmy Carter George H. W. Bush Bill Clinton	John Adams Woodrow Wilson Herbert Hoover Lyndon Johnson Richard Nixon
	"consistency between much activity and the enjoyment of it, indicating relatively high self-esteem and relative success in relating to the environ-ment.... shows an orientation to productiveness as a value and an ability to use his styles flexibly, adaptively."	"activity has a compulsive quality, as if the man were trying to make up for something or escape from anxiety into hard work.... seems ambitious, striv-ing upward, power-seeking.... stance toward the environment is aggressive and has a problem in managing his aggressive feelings."
Passive	James Madison William Taft Warren Harding Ronald Reagan	George Washington Calvin Coolidge Dwight Eisenhower
	"receptive, compliant, other-directed character whose life is a search for affection as a reward for being agree-able and cooperative.... low self-esteem (on grounds of being unlovable)."	"low self-esteem based on a sense of uselessness ... in politics because they think they ought to be.... tendency is to withdraw, to escape from the conflict and uncertainty of politics by empha-sizing vague principles (especially pro-hibitions) and procedural arrangements."

Sources: Barber's discussions of all presidents but Clinton are in *The Presidential Character: Predicting Performance in the White House,* 4th ed. (Englewood Cliffs: Prentice Hall, 1992). Clinton is characterized by Barber in Doyle McManus, "Key Challenges Await Clinton," *Los Angeles Times,* January 20, 1993, A6. See also James David Barber, "Predicting Hope with Clinton at Helm," *Raleigh News and Observer,* January 17, 1993.

people we deal with. Similarly we catch on fairly quickly to the affect dimension—whether the person seems to be optimistic or pessimistic, hopeful or skeptical, happy or sad. The two baselines are clear and they are also independent of one another: all of us know people who are very active but seem discouraged, others who are quite passive but seem happy, and so forth. The activity baseline refers to what one does, the affect baseline to how one feels about what one does.

Both are crude clues to character. They are leads into four basic character patterns long familiar in psychological research.[24]

In the library copy of *The Presidential Character* from which I copied this long passage, there is a handwritten note in the margin: "Footnote, man!" But there is no footnote to the psychological literature, here or anywhere else in the book. Casual readers might take this to mean that none was necessary, and they would be right if Barber's types really were "long familiar in psychological research" and "appeared in nearly every study of personality."[25] But they are not and they do not. As Alexander George has pointed out, personality theory itself is a "quagmire" in which "the term 'character' in practice is applied loosely and means many different things."[26] Barber's real defense of his typology—it works; look at Nixon—is not to be dismissed, but one wishes he had explained better why he thinks it works.[27]

Barber's typology also has been criticized for not being simple enough, at least not for purposes of accurate preelection application. Where, exactly, is one to look to discover whether deep down candidate Jones is the energetic, buoyant person her image makers say she is? Barber was quite right to warn analysts away from their usual hunting ground—the candidate's recent performance in other high offices. These offices "are all much more restrictive than the Presidency is, much more set by institutional requirements,"[28] and thus much less fertile cultures for psychopathologies to grow in. This was Barber's only real mention of what might be considered a third, equally important component of the psychological presidency: the rarefied, courtlike atmosphere—well described in George Reedy's *The Twilight of the Presidency*[29]—that surrounds presidents and allows those whose psychological constitutions so move them to seal themselves off from harsh political realities.

Barber's alternative to performance-based analysis—namely, a study of the candidate's "first independent political success," or FIPS, during which he or she developed a personal formula for success in politics—is not very helpful either. How, for example, is one to tell which IPS was first? According to Barber's appropriately broad definition of *political,* Johnson's first success was not his election to Congress but his work as a student assistant to his college's president. Hoover's was his incumbency as student body treasurer at Stanford. Sorting through a candidate's life with the thoroughness necessary to determine his or her FIPS may or may not be an essential task. But it is clearly not a straightforward one.

Further difficulties arise from the unevenness of the evidence about presidents that is available when they are still candidates or even while they are in office. Clinton's behavior as president, for example, persuaded Fred Greenstein that he (and Barber) had been wrong in their initial assessment of his character. "The ever-smiling, hyperactive Clinton has all of the outward signs of an active-positive character," Greenstein wrote near the end of Clinton's second term. "Yet his actions, particularly in the Monica Lewinsky affair, reveal him to be as emotionally deficient as any active-negative president."[30] Similarly, Greenstein's immersion in the Eisenhower papers, which did not become available until long after the president left office, allowed him to demonstrate that Ike was an active rather than a passive president. Eisenhower's public passivity represented a leadership strategy of reassurance; in truth, Greenstein found, he pursued a vigorous behind-the-scenes, "hidden-hand presidency."[31]

Some scholars question not only the scientific basis or practical applicability of Barber's psychological theory of presidential behavior but also the importance of psychological explanation itself. Psychology appears to be almost everything to Barber, as this statement from his research design for *The Presidential Character* reveals:

What is de-emphasized in this scheme? Everything which does not lend itself to the production of potentially testable generalizations about presidential behavior. Thus we shall be less concerned with the substance or content of particular issues . . . less concern[ed] for distant phenomena, such as relationships among other political actors affecting events without much reference to the president, public opinion, broad economic or historical trends, etc.—except insofar as these enter into the president's own approach to decision-making.[32]

But is personality all that matters? Provocative though Barber's theory may be, it seems to unravel in the application. A "healthy" political personality turns out to be no guarantee of presidential success. Barber classed Ford, Carter, and Bush early in their presidencies as active-positives, for example. Carter, in fact, seemed to take flexibility—a virtue characteristic of active-positives—to such an extreme that it approached vacillation and inconsistency, almost as if in reading *The Presidential Character* he had learned its lessons too well.

Nor, as Table 5.2 shows, does Barber's notion of psychological unsuitability seem to correspond to failure in office. The ranks of the most successful presidents in four recent surveys by scholars include some whom Barber classified as active-positives (Jefferson, Truman, Kennedy, and Franklin Roosevelt), but also several active-negatives (Wilson, Lyndon Johnson, and John Adams) and others whom Barber labeled passive-negative (Washington and Eisenhower) or passive-positive (Reagan).[33] The most perverse result of classifying presidents by this standard involves Abraham Lincoln, whom Jeffrey Tulis, correctly applying Barber's theory, found to be an active-negative.[34]

Table 5.2 "Great" Presidents and Barber's Character Typology

	Positive	Negative
Active	Thomas Jefferson	John Adams
	Franklin Roosevelt	Woodrow Wilson
	Harry Truman	Lyndon Johnson
	John F. Kennedy	[Abraham Lincoln]
Passive	Ronald Reagan	George Washington
		Dwight Eisenhower

Note: For purposes of this table, a "great" president is defined as one who ranked among the first ten in at least one of these five polls of scholars: Steve Neal, "Our Best and Worst Presidents," *Chicago Tribune Magazine,* January 10, 1982, 9–18; Robert K. Murray and Tim H. Blessing, *Greatness in the White House: Rating the Presidents, Washington through Carter* (University Park: Pennsylvania State University Press, 1988); David L. Porter, letter to author, January 15, 1982; Arthur M. Schlesinger Jr., "The Ultimate Approval Rating," *New York Times Magazine,* December 15, 1996, 47–51; and "C-Span 2009 Historians' Presidential Leadership Survey," www.c-span.org/Presidential>Survey/Overall-Ranking .aspx. Four others who achieved this ranking (Jackson, Polk, T. Roosevelt, and McKinley) are not included because Barber did not classify them according to his typology. Lincoln's name is bracketed because Jeffrey Tulis classified him using Barber's typology.

Hargrove found the active-positive category equally unhelpful because it is too broad:

Active-positive presidents vary so as individuals that the category lacks the capacity to analyze and explain actions of presidential leadership. A schema that puts Franklin Roosevelt and Jimmy Carter in the same cell tells us that they shared high self-esteem and the capacity to learn and adapt to circumstances, but it says nothing about the great differences in political skill between them or the psychological bases for such differences.[35]

One could raise similar doubts about categories that lump together Harding and Reagan (passive-positive) or Coolidge and Eisenhower (passive-negative).

Clearly, personality is not all that matters in the presidency. As Tulis noted, Lincoln's behavior as president can be explained much better by his political philosophy and leadership skills than by his personality. Similarly, one need not resort to psychology to explain the failures of active-negatives Hoover and, in the latter years of his presidency, Lyndon Johnson. Hoover's unbending opposition to instituting massive federal relief in the face of the Great Depression may have stemmed more from ideological convictions than psychological rigidity. Johnson's refusal to change his administration's policy in Vietnam could be interpreted as the action of a self-styled consensus leader trying to steer a moderate course between hawks who wanted full-scale military involvement and doves who wanted unilateral withdrawal.[36] These presidents' actions were ineffective but not necessarily irrational.

Theoretical and practical criticisms such as these are important, and they do not exhaust the list. Observer bias is another. Because Barber's published writings provide no clear checklist of criteria by which to type candidates, subjectivity is absolutely inherent. But the criticisms should not blind us to his major contributions in *The Presidential Character:* a concentration (albeit excessive) on the importance of presidential personality in explaining presidential behavior, a sensitivity to the role of personality as a variable (power does not always corrupt, nor does the office always "make the man"), and a boldness in approaching the problems voters face in predicting what kind of president a candidate will be if elected.

Public Psychology

The second side of the psychological presidency—the public's side—was Barber's concern in *The Pulse of Politics: Electing Presidents in the Media Age.* The book is about elections, those occasions when, because citizens are deciding who will fill the presidency, they presumably feel (presidential deaths aside) their emotional attachment to the office most deeply. Again Barber presented a typology. The public's election moods come in three varieties, he argued: *conflict* ("we itch for adventure, . . . [a] blood-and-guts political contest"), *conscience* ("the call goes out for a revival of social conscience, the restoration of the constitutional covenant"), and *conciliation* ("the public yearns for solace, for domestic tranquility").[37] In this book the types appear in recurring order as well, over a twelve-year cycle: conflict, conscience, then conciliation.

Barber's question in *The Pulse of Politics*—what is "the swirl of emotions" with which Americans surround the presidency?—is as important and original as the questions he posed in *The Presidential Character.* But again, his answer is as puzzling as it is provocative. Although Barber's theory applies only to American presidential elections since 1900, he seemed convinced that the psychological "pulse" has been beating deeply, if softly, in all humankind for all time. Barber discovered conflict, conscience, and conciliation in the "old sagas" of ancient peoples and in "the psychological paradigm that dominates the modern age: the *ego,* instrument for coping with the struggles of the external world [conflict]; the *superego,* warning against harmful violations [conscience]; the *id,* longing after the thrill and ease of sexual satisfaction [conciliation]." He found this primordial pulse firmly reinforced in American history. Conflict is reflected in our emphasis on the war story ("In isolated America, the warmakers repeatedly confronted the special problem of arousing the martial spirit against distant enemies. . . . Thus our history vibrates with *talk* about war"). Conscience is displayed in America's sense of itself as an instrument of divine providence ("our conscience has never been satisfied by government as a mere practical arrangement"). Conciliation shows up in our efforts to live with each other in a heterogeneous "nation of nationalities." In the early twentieth century, Barber argued, these three themes became the controlling force in the political psychology of the American electorate, so controlling that every presidential election since the conflict of 1900 has fit its place within the cycle: conscience in 1904, conciliation in 1908, conflict again in 1912, and so on. What caused the pulse to start beating so strongly, he feels, was the rise of national mass media.

The modern newspaper came first, just before the turn of the century. "In a remarkable historical conjunction, the sudden surge into mass popularity of the American daily newspaper coincided with the Spanish-American War." Because war stories sold papers, daily journalists also wrote about "politics as war"—that is, as conflict. In the early 1900s national mass circulation magazines arrived on the scene, taking their cues from the Progressive reformers who dominated the politics of that period. "The 'muckrakers'—actually positive thinkers out to build America, not destroy reputations"—wrote about "politics as a moral enterprise," an enterprise of conscience. Then came the broadcast media, radio in the 1920s and television in the 1950s. What set them apart was their commercial need to reach not just a wide audience but the widest possible audience. "Broadcasting aimed to please, wrapping politics in fun and games ... conveying with unmatched reach and power its core message of conciliation."

As for the cyclic pulse, the recurring appearance of the three public moods in the same order, Barber suggested that the dynamic is internal: Each type of public mood generates the next. After a conflict election ("a battle for power ... a rousing call to arms"), a reaction sets in. Conscience calls for "the cleansing of the temple of democracy." But "the troubles do not go away," and four years later "the public yearns for solace," or conciliation. After another four years, Barber claimed, "the time for a fight will come around again," and so on.

In *The Pulse of Politics*, difficulties arise not in applying the theory (a calendar will do: if it's 2012, this must be a conciliation election) but in the theory itself. Barber needed an even more secure intellectual foundation for the cyclic pulse than for the character typology, because this time he not only classified all presidential elections into three types but also asserted that they recur in a fixed order. Once again, however, one finds no footnotes. If Barber grounded his theory in scholarly sources, then it is impossible to tell—and hard to imagine—what they are. Nor does the theory stand up sturdily under its own weight. If, for example, radio and television are agents of conciliation, why did we not have more conciliating elections after they became our dominant political media? Perhaps that is why some of the "postdictions" to which Barber's theory leads are as questionable as they are easy to make. Did conscience really typify the mean-spirited campaign between Vice President Al Gore and Texas governor George W. Bush in 2000, conciliation the mutually disdainful 2004 contest between Bush and Sen. John F. Kerry of Massachusetts, or conflict the civil, substantive 2008 election involving Arizona senator John McCain and Sen. Barack Obama of Illinois?

The most interesting criticism pertinent to Barber's pulse theory, however, was made in 1972 by a political scientist concerned with the public's presidential psychology, which he described as a "climate of expectations" that "shifts and changes." This scholar wrote,

Wars, depressions, and other national events contribute to that change, but there is also a rough cycle, from an emphasis on action (which begins to look too "political") to an emphasis on legitimacy (the moral uplift of which creates its own strains) to an emphasis on reassurance and rest (which comes to seem like drift) and back to action again. One need not be astrological about it.

A year earlier the same scholar had written that although "the mystic could see the series . . . marching in fateful repetition beginning in 1900 . . . [but] the pattern is too astrological to be convincing." Careful readers will recognize the identity between the cycles of action-legitimacy-reassurance and conflict-conscience-conciliation. Clever ones will realize that both passages were written by James David Barber.[38]

Person, Public Mood, and the Psychological Presidency

A good deal about the public's political psychology, in fact, is sprinkled through *The Presidential Character,* and the more of it one discovers, the more curious things get. Most significant is the brief concluding chapter, "Presidential Character and the Moods of the Eighth Decade" (reprinted in the three subsequent editions of the book, most recently in 1992), which contains Barber's bold suggestion of a close fit between the two sides of his model. For each type of public psychological climate, Barber posited a "resonant" type of presidential personality. This seems to be a central point in his theory of the presidency. "Much of what [a president] is remembered for," he wrote, "will depend on the fit between the dominant forces in his character and the dominant feelings in his constituency." Furthermore, "the dangers of discord in that resonance are severe."[39]

What is the precise nature of this fit? When the public cry is for action (conflict), Barber argued, "it comes through loudest to the active-negative type, whose inner struggle between aggression and control resonates with the popular plea for toughness. . . . [The active-negative's] temptation to stand and fight receives wide support from the culture." In the public's reassurance (conciliation) mood, he wrote, "they want a friend," a passive-positive. As for the "appeal for a moral cleansing of the Presidency," or legitimacy (conscience), Barber suggested that it "resonates with the passive-negative character in its emphasis on *not* doing certain things." This leaves the active-positive, Barber's president for all seasons.[40] Blessed with a "character firmly rooted in self-recognition and self-love," Barber's "active-positive can not only *perform* lovingly or aggressively or with detachment, he can *feel* those ways."[41]

What Barber first offered in *The Presidential Character,* then, was the foundation for a model of the psychological presidency that was not only two-sided but integrated as well, one in which the "tuning, the resonance—or lack of it" between the public's "climate of expectations" and the president's personality "sets in motion the dynamic of his Presidency." Barber concentrated on the personality half of his model in *The Presidential Character,* then firmed it up and filled in the other half—the public's—in *The Pulse of Politics.* And this is where things become especially puzzling. Most authors, when they complete a multi-volume opus, trumpet their accomplishment. Barber did not. In fact, one finds in *The Pulse of Politics* no mention at all of presidential character, of public climates of expectations, or of "the resonance—or lack of it"—between them.[42]

At first blush, this seems doubly strange, because there is a strong surface fit between the halves of Barber's model. As Table 5.3 indicates, in the twenty-three twentieth-century elections after Roosevelt's in 1904 (Barber did not type twentieth-century presidents before Taft or after Clinton), presidential character and public mood resonated sixteen times. The exceptions—active-negative Wilson's election in the conscience year of 1916, passive-negative Coolidge's in conflictual 1924, active-negative Hoover's in the conscience election of 1928, passive-negative Eisenhower's in the conciliating election of 1956, active-negative Johnson's in conscience-oriented 1964, active-negative Nixon's in conciliating 1968, and passive-positive Reagan's in conflict-dominated 1984—perhaps could be explained by successful campaign image management, an argument that would also support Barber's view of the media's power in presidential politics. In that case, a test of Barber's model would be: Did these "inappropriate" presidents lose the public's support when people found out what they were really like after the election? In every presidency but those of Coolidge, Eisenhower, and Reagan, the answer would have been yes.

On closer inspection, however, it also turns out that in every case but these, the presidents whose administrations were unsuccessful were active-negatives. But, Barber tells us, active-negative presidents fail for reasons that have nothing to do with the public mood. As for the model's overall success rate of sixteen

Table 5.3 Resonance of Character Type and Public Mood in Presidential Elections, 1908–1996

	Election		Winning presidential candidate	
Year	Public mood	"Resonant" character types	Name	Character type
1908	Conciliation	Passive–positive (Active–positive)	Taft	Passive–positive
1912	Conflict	Active–negative (Active–positive)	Wilson	Active–negative
1916	Conscience	Passive–negative (Active–positive)	Wilson	Active–negative
1920	Conciliation	Passive–positive (Active–positive)	Harding	Passive–positive
1924	Conflict	Active–negative (Active–positive)	Coolidge	Passive–negative
1928	Conscience	Passive–negative (Active–positive)	Hoover	Active–negative
1932	Conciliation	Passive–positive (Active–positive)	Roosevelt	Active–positive
1936	Conflict	Active–negative (Active–positive)	Roosevelt	Active–positive
1940	Conscience	Passive–negative (Active–positive)	Roosevelt	Active–positive
1944	Conciliation	Passive–positive (Active–positive)	Roosevelt	Active–positive
1948	Conflict	Active–negative (Active–positive)	Truman	Active–positive
1952	Conscience	Passive–negative (Active–positive)	Eisenhower	Passive–negative
1956	Conciliation	Passive–positive (Active–positive)	Eisenhower	Passive–negative
1960	Conflict	Active–negative (Active–positive)	Kennedy	Active–positive
1964	Conscience	Passive–negative (Active–positive)	Johnson	Active–negative
1968	Conciliation	Passive–positive (Active–positive)	Nixon	Active–negative
1972	Conflict	Active–negative (Active–positive)	Nixon	Active–negative
1976	Conscience	Passive–negative (Active–positive)	Carter	Active–positive
1980	Conciliation	Passive–positive (Active–positive)	Reagan	Passive–positive
1984	Conflict	Active–negative (Active–positive)	Reagan	Passive–positive
1988	Conscience	Passive–negative (Active–positive)	Bush	Active–positive
1992	Conciliation	Passive–positive (Active–positive)	Clinton	Active–positive
1996	Conflict	Active–negative (Active–positive)	Clinton	Active–positive

Sources: Compiled by the author; data from James David Barber, *The Presidential Character: Predicting Performance in the White House* (Englewood Cliffs: Prentice Hall, 1972, 1977, 1985, 1992) and *The Pulse of Politics: Electing Presidents in the Media Age* (New York: Norton, 1980).

out of twenty-three, it includes ten elections that were won by active-positives who, he says, resonate with every public mood. A good hand in wild-card stud poker is seldom a good hand in Texas Hold 'Em; Barber's success rate in the elections not won by active-positives was only six of thirteen. In conscience elections, only once did a representative of the resonant type (passive-negative) win, while purportedly less-suitable active-negatives won three times.

Barber's Prescriptions

In *The Presidential Character* and *The Pulse of Politics* Barber developed a suggestive and relatively complete model of the psychological presidency. Why he failed even to acknowledge the connection between the theories in each book, much less present them as a unified whole, remains unclear. Perhaps he feared that the lack of fit between his mood and personality types—the public and presidential components—would have distracted critics from his larger points.

In any event, the theoretical and predictive elements of Barber's approach to the presidency are sufficiently provocative to warrant him a hearing for his prescriptions for change. Barber's primary goal for the psychological presidency was that it be "de-psychopathologized." He wanted to keep active-negatives out of the White House and put healthy active-positives in. He wanted the public to become the master of its own political fate, breaking out of its electoral mood cycle, which is essentially a cycle of psychological dependency. Freed of their inner chains, the president and the public, Barber claimed, will be able to forge a "creative politics" or "politics of persuasion," as he variously dubbed it. Just what this kind of politics would be like is not clear, but apparently it would involve greater sensitivity on the part of both presidents and citizens to the ideas of the other.[43]

It will not surprise readers to learn that Barber, by and large, dismissed constitutional reform as a method for achieving his goals. After all, if the presidency is as shaped by psychological forces as he said it is, then institutional tinkering will be, almost by definition, beside the point.[44] Change, to be effective, will have to come in the hearts and minds of the people: in the information they get about politics, the way they think about that information, and the way they feel about what they think. Because of this, Barber argued, the central agent of change will have to be the most pervasive—namely, media journalism, especially its coverage of presidential elections.[45]

It is in his prescriptive writings that Barber was on the most solid ground and that his answers were as good as his questions. Unlike many media critics, he did not assume imperiously that the sole purpose of newspapers, magazines, and television is to elevate the masses. Barber recognized that the media are made up of commercial enterprises that must sell papers and attract viewers and visitors. He recognized, too, that the basic format of news coverage is the story, not the scholarly treatise. Barber's singular contribution was his argument that the media can improve the way they do all of these things at the same time, and that better election stories will attract bigger audiences in more enlightening ways.

The first key to better stories, Barber argued, is greater attention to the candidates. Election coverage that ignores the motivations, developmental histories, and basic beliefs of its protagonists is as lifeless as dramas or novels would be if they neglected these crucial human attributes. Such coverage is also uninformative. Elections, after all, present the voters with choices among people, and as Barber showed, the kinds of people that the candidates are influences the kinds of presidents they would be. Good journalism, according to Barber, would "focus on the person as embodying his historical development, playing out a character born and bred in another place, connecting an old identity with a new persona—the stuff of intriguing drama from Joseph in Egypt on down. That can be done explicitly in biographical stories."[46]

Barber was commendably diffident; he did not expect reporters to master and apply his own character typology. But he did want them to search the candidates' lives for patterns of behavior, particularly the rigidity that characterizes active-negatives. (Of all behavior patterns, rigidity, he believed, "is probably the easiest one to spot and the most dangerous one to elect.")[47] With public interest ever high in "people" stories and in psychology, Barber probably was right to think that this kind of reporting would not only inform readers but would engage their interest as well.

As *Washington Post* editors Leonard Downie and Robert Kaiser point out, press coverage of recent elections has sometimes tried to fulfill Barber's expectations.[48] During the nomination stage of the 1988 campaign, the "character" issue drove two Democratic candidates from the field, much to the relief of most political leaders and (eventually) most voters. Former senator Gary Hart's extramarital escapades, which were revealed by the *Miami Herald,* were politically harmful less because of his moral weakness than because of the recklessness the incidents illuminated in his character. Serious doubts also were raised about Sen. Joseph Biden's intellectual and personal depth when the press discovered that he had lied to voters about his success in school and then tried to pass off stories from an autobiographical speech by a British politician as events drawn from his own life. As for the Republican nominee in 1988, George H. W. Bush, he triumphed in part because he was able to lay to rest the so-called wimp factor—that is, the suspicion that he was too weak to be a successful president.

Coverage of the character issue took a different and, from Barber's perspective, lamentable turn in the 1990s. Moral, not psychological, character became the media's obsession. In 1992 Clinton's truthfulness and fidelity were called into question when an Arkansas acquaintance, Gennifer Flowers, publicly charged that she and Clinton had engaged in a long-standing extramarital affair while he was governor. Clinton denied the charge but conceded that he and his wife had endured some marital problems in the past. Soon after, letters in Clinton's own hand were published suggesting that he had dodged the draft during the Vietnam War. In contrast to their strong response to the candidates whose psychological character was questioned in 1988, however, voters overcame their doubts about Clinton's moral character and elected him—an active-positive, in Barber's reckoning[49]—as president. Coverage of the 1996 election, which matched two well-established figures, the incumbent Clinton and the long-familiar Senate Republican leader Robert Dole, was less character centered than its recent predecessors. But in 1998, Clinton's affair with former White House intern Monica Lewinsky dominated the national agenda.

In campaigning for their parties' presidential nominations in 2000, Al Gore and George W. Bush each worked hard to persuade the voters that he was a leader of strong moral character. Gore emphasized that he was a family man who regarded Clinton's affair with Lewinsky as "inexcusable." Bush did his best to inoculate himself against character charges by admitting long before the first vote was cast that he had been morally lax as a younger man. He regularly ended campaign speeches by raising his hand skyward and declaring, "Should I be fortunate enough to win, when I put my hand upon the Bible, I will swear to uphold the dignity and honor of the office." The *Post* "printed book-length series of articles about the lives and careers of both men."[50]

Character concerns of the psychological sort went a long way toward determining the outcome of the 2000 general election. Gore carried into the campaign a reputation as an aggressive, experienced, and skillful debater, a reputation Bush lacked. Yet Bush ended up benefiting considerably more from their three nationally televised debates than Gore did. In the first debate, Gore treated his opponent with disdain, often speaking condescendingly when it was his turn and sighing and grimacing while Bush spoke. Chastened by the adverse public response, Gore was deferential, almost obsequious during the second debate. He hit his stride in the third debate, but the inconsistency of his behavior from one debate to the next fed voters' doubts about who Gore really was. Bush was not strongly impressive in any of the debates, but voters saw the same man in all three of them. Gore, who entered the debate season leading Bush by around five percentage points in the polls, left it trailing by five points.[51]

Although neither Bush nor Kerry made character a major issue in any form in 2004, their supporters did. Documentary filmmaker Michael Moore's *Fahrenheit 9/11*, an election year box-office hit, portrayed Bush sometimes as stupid, sometimes as evil, but always as a man of dangerously defective character. Kerry's character came under assault from a new political group called Swift Boat Veterans for Truth. In television commercials, the Swift Boat Veterans attacked Kerry's record as a swift boat commander in the Vietnam War, sowing doubts about his truthfulness and courage. The character of John McCain and Barack Obama was also emphasized by their supporters in 2008, but in a more positive way. McCain's heroic "grace under pressure" as a prisoner of war in North Vietnam and Obama's reflective search for identity and meaning as the son of a white American mother and a black Kenyan father became much-celebrated features of their candidacies for president.

Engaging readers' interest was Barber's final key to better journalism. What voters need in order to make decisions is the same as what they want—namely, information about who the candidates are and what they believe. According to a study of network evening news coverage of the 1972 election campaign, which Barber cited, almost as much time was devoted to the polls, strategies, rallies, and other "horse-race" elements of the election as to the candidates' personal qualifications and issue stands combined. As Barber noted, "The viewer tuning in for facts to guide his choice would, therefore, have to pick his political nuggets from a great gravel pile of political irrelevancy."[52] Critics who doubt the public's interest in long, fleshed-out stories about what candidates think, what they are like, and what great problems they would face as president would do well to check the thirty-five years of ratings for CBS's *60 Minutes*.

An electorate whose latent but powerful interest in politics is engaged by the media will become an informed electorate because it wants to, not because it is supposed to. This was Barber's strong belief. So sensible a statement of the problem was this, and so attractive a vision of its solution, that one can forgive him for cluttering it with types and terminologies.

Notes

1. "Candidate on the Couch," *Time*, June 19, 1972, 15–17; James David Barber, *The Presidential Character: Predicting Performance in the White House* (Englewood Cliffs: Prentice Hall, 1972); a second edition was published in 1977, a third edition in 1985, and a fourth edition in 1992. Unless otherwise indicated, the quotations cited in this essay appear in all four editions, with page numbers drawn from the first edition.

2. Hugh Sidey, "The Active-Positive Searching," *Time*, October 4, 1976, 23.

3. "After Eight Months in Office—How Ford Rates Now," *U.S. News & World Report*, April 28, 1975, 28.

4. David S. Broder, "Carter Would Like to Be an 'Active Positive,'" *Washington Post*, July 16, 1976, A12.

5. James David Barber, "An Active-Positive Character," *Time*, January 3, 1977, 17.

6. Hugh Sidey, "'A Revolution Is Under Way,'" *Time*, March 31, 1980, 20.

7. "Cycle Races," *Time*, May 19, 1980, 29.

8. Paul J. Quirk, "What Do We Know and How Do We Know It? Research on the Presidency," in *Political Science: Looking to the Future*, ed. William J. Crotty and Alan D. Monroe, vol. 4 (Evanston: Northwestern University Press, 1991), 52. Psychologists, on the other hand, have been paying more attention to the presidency. See, for example, Dean Keith Simonton, *Why Presidents Succeed: A Political Psychology of Leadership* (New Haven: Yale University Press, 1987); and Harold M. Zullow, Gabriele Oettingen, Christopher Peterson, and Martin E. P. Seligman, "Pessimistic Explanatory Style in the Historical Record," *American Psychologist* 43 (September 1988): 673–681.

9. Robert A. Dahl, *A Preface to Democratic Theory* (Chicago: University of Chicago Press, 1956), 6–8.

10. The phrase is Alexander Hamilton's. See Alexander Hamilton, James Madison, and John Jay, *The Federalist Papers*, with an introduction by Clinton Rossiter (New York: New American Library, 1961), no. 70, 423.

11. Seymour Martin Lipset, *The First New Nation* (New York: Basic Books, 1963), chap. 1; and Max Weber, *The Theory of Social and Economic Organization* (New York: Oxford University Press, 1947), 358.

12. Marcus Cunliffe, *George Washington: Man and Monument* (New York: New American Library, 1958), 15. See also Richard Brookhiser, *Founding Father: Rediscovering George Washington* (New York: Free Press, 1996).

13. Max Farrand, *The Records of the Federal Conventions of 1787*, 4 vols. (New Haven: Yale University Press, 1966), vol. 1, 65.

14. Jeffrey Tulis, "On Presidential Character," in *The Presidency in the Constitutional Order*, ed. Jeffrey Tulis and Joseph M. Bessette (Baton Rouge: Louisiana State University Press, 1981), 287.

15. *Federalist*, nos. 71 and 72, 431–440.

16. Ibid., no. 64, 396.

17. See, for example, James David Barber, "Adult Identity and Presidential Style: The Rhetorical Emphasis," *Daedalus* 97 (Summer 1968): 938–968; Barber, "Classifying and Predicting Presidential Styles: Two 'Weak' Presidents," *Journal of Social Issues* 24 (July 1968): 51–80; Barber, "The President and His Friends" (paper presented at the annual meeting of the American Political Science Association, New York, September 1969); and Barber, "The Interplay of Presidential Character and Style: A Paradigm and Five Illustrations," in *A Source Book for the Study of Personality and Politics*, ed. Fred I. Greenstein and Michael Lerner (Chicago: Markham, 1971), 383–408.

18. Richard E. Neustadt, *Presidential Power: The Politics of Leadership* (New York: Wiley, 1960), 185.

19. Erwin C. Hargrove, *The Power of the Modern Presidency* (New York: Knopf, 1974), 33.

20. See, for example, Fred I. Greenstein, *Children and Politics* (New Haven: Yale University Press, 1965); and John E. Mueller, *War, Presidents, and Public Opinion* (New York: Wiley, 1973).

21. Paul B. Sheatsley and Jacob J. Feldman, "The Assassination of President Kennedy: Public Reactions," *Public Opinion Quarterly* 28 (Summer 1964): 189–215. See also Michael Nelson, "Evaluating the Presidency," in *The Presidency and the Political System*, 8th ed., ed. Michael Nelson (Washington, D.C.: CQ Press, 2006), 1–27.

22. Unless otherwise indicated, all quotes from Barber in this section are from *The Presidential Character*, chap. 1.

23. Ibid., 145, 206. In more recent writings, Barber's assessment of presidential passivity has grown more harsh. A passive-positive, for example, "may . . . preside over the cruelest of regimes." *Presidential Character*, 3rd ed., 529–530.

24. Barber, *Presidential Character*, 12.

25. Thirteen years after *The Presidential Character* was first published, in an appendix to the third edition, Barber described a variety of works to show that his character types "are not a product of one author's fevered imagination," but rather keep "popping up in study after study." In truth, most of the cited works are not scholarly studies of psychological character at all, nor are they claimed to be by their authors.

26. Alexander George, "Assessing Presidential Character," *World Politics* 26 (January 1974): 234–282.

27. Ibid. George argued that Nixon's behavior was not of a kind that Barber's theory would lead one to predict.

28. Barber, *Presidential Character*, 99.

29. George Reedy, *The Twilight of the Presidency* (New York: New American Library, 1970). See also Bruce Buchanan, *The Presidential Experience: What the Office Does to the Man* (Englewood Cliffs: Prentice Hall, 1978).

30. Fred I. Greenstein, *The Presidential Difference: Leadership Style from FDR to Clinton* (New York: Free Press, 2000), 3.

31. Fred I. Greenstein, *The Hidden-Hand Presidency* (New York: Basic Books, 1982).

32. James David Barber, "Coding Scheme for Presidential Biographies," January 1968, mimeographed, 3.

33. The surveys are reported in Steve Neal, "Our Best and Worst Presidents," *Chicago Tribune Magazine*, January 10, 1982, 9–18; Robert K. Murray and Tim H. Blessing, *Greatness in the White House: Rating the Presidents, Washington through Carter* (University Park: Pennsylvania State University Press, 1988); David L. Porter, letter to author, January 15, 1982; Arthur M. Schlesinger Jr., "The Ultimate Approval Rating," *New York Times Magazine*, December 15, 1996, 47–51; and "C-Span 2009 Historians' Presidential Leadership Survey," www.c-span.org/PresidentialSurvey/Overall-Ranking.aspx.

34. Tulis, "On Presidential Character."

35. Erwin C. Hargrove, "Presidential Personality and Leadership Style," in *Researching the Presidency: Vital Questions, New Approaches*, ed. George C. Edwards III, John H. Kessel, and Bert Rockman (Pittsburgh: University of Pittsburgh Press, 1993), 96.

36. Erwin C. Hargrove, "Presidential Personality and Revisionist Views of the Presidency," *Midwest Journal of Political Science* 17 (November 1973): 819–836.

37. James David Barber, *The Pulse of Politics: Electing Presidents in the Media Age* (New York: Norton, 1980). Unless otherwise indicated, all quotes from Barber in this section are from chapters 1 and 2.

38. The first quote appears in *Presidential Character*, 9; the second in "Interplay of Presidential Character and Style," n2.

39. Barber, *Presidential Character*, 446.

40. Ibid., 446, 448, 451.

41. Ibid., 243.

42. Barber did draw a connection between the public's desire for conciliation and its choice of a passive-positive in the 1980 election: "Sometimes people want a fighter in the White House and sometimes a saint. But the time comes when all we want is a friend, a pal, a guy to reassure us that the story is going to come out all right. In 1980, that need found just the right promise in Ronald Reagan, the smiling American." James David Barber, "Reagan's Sheer Personal Likability Faces Its Sternest Test," *Washington Post,* January 20, 1981, 8.

43. James David Barber, "Tone-Deaf in the Oval Office," *Saturday Review/World,* January 12, 1974, 10–14.

44. James David Barber, "The Presidency after Watergate," *World,* July 31, 1973, 16–19.

45. Barber, *Pulse of Politics,* chap. 15. For other statements of his views on how the press should cover politics and the presidency, see James David Barber, ed., *Race for the Presidency: The Media and the Nominating Process* (Englewood Cliffs: Prentice Hall, 1978), chaps. 5–7; Barber, "Not Quite the *New York Times:* What Network News Should Be," *Washington Monthly,* September 1979, 14–21; and Barber, *Politics by Humans: Research on American Political Leadership* (Durham: Duke University Press, 1988), chaps. 17–18.

46. Barber, *Race for the Presidency,* 145.

47. Ibid., 171, 162–164.

48. Leonard Downie Jr. and Robert G. Kaiser, *The News about the News: American Journalism in Peril* (New York: Knopf, 2002), 36.

49. James David Barber, "Predicting Hope with Clinton at Helm," *Raleigh News and Observer,* January 17, 1993. For a different view of Clinton, one that offers examples of "the driven investments of energy" characteristic of active-negatives, see Stanley A. Renshon, "A Preliminary Assessment of the Clinton Presidency: Character, Leadership and Performance," *Political Psychology* 15 (1994): 331–394.

50. Downie and Kaiser, *News about the News,* 36.

51. Barber, *Race for the Presidency,* 174, 182–183.

52. Michael Nelson, "The Election: Ordinary Politics, Extraordinary Outcome," in *The Elections of 2000,* ed. Michael Nelson (Washington, D.C.: CQ Press, 2001), 78–79.

6 The Presidency and the Nominating Process: Politics and Power

Richard M. Pious

The Constitution defines the pool of possible presidents in any election as consisting of every "natural born Citizen" who has "attained to the Age of thirty-five Years, and been fourteen Years a Resident within the United States"—more than one hundred million people. Historically, it has been the job of the major political parties to narrow the field of possible presidents to the two candidates from whom the voters make their final choice. During the early nineteenth century, congressional caucuses did this job on behalf of their parties. Caucuses were then replaced by national party conventions dominated by state party bosses. The conventions continue to meet every four years, but since the 1970s they have been dominated by delegates chosen by the voters in primaries. In this chapter, Richard M. Pious analyzes the kinds of candidates that different nominating methods have favored. He argues that in the primaries-dominated process, "those who emerge with the nomination lack national executive experience, a situation that rarely occurs in other nations." Pious suggests that restoring "some peer review and a greater role for party professionals and members of Congress"—the same groups that dominated earlier nominating processes—might yield more qualified presidential nominees.

Americans have never been satisfied with the way parties nominate presidential candidates. By a margin of nearly five to one, voters in 2000 thought that party politicians and big contributors had more say than ordinary citizens about the candidates the Democrats and Republicans would select, and they felt powerless to affect a process they thought was too long, too boring, and too uninformative.[1] How can the nominating contests attract the best politicians? How can parties select their nominees in a way that engages the voters, as well as fosters the legitimacy and increases the democratic mandate of those who win? Throughout American history, parties have experimented with different answers to these questions, but what remains constant in American politics is that no approach to candidate selection has been able simultaneously to maximize both voter participation and the responsibility of the contenders' peers to judge their qualifications.

Transformation of the Nominating Processes

The Framers of the Constitution knew that George Washington would be chosen unanimously as the first president. They assumed that from then on the Electoral College would "nominate" five candidates for the presidency, each probably representing one of the larger states, and that the House of Representatives would choose from among this group. During Washington's and John Adams's presidencies, however, politicians coalesced into "factions" and then into the beginnings of national parties. If elections were to be decided by the Electoral College, the parties would need to nominate candidates.

King Caucus: Nomination by Congressional Party

Between 1800 and 1824 the nomination of presidential candidates was entrusted to party members in Congress. They would meet after the congressional session was over, with Federalists in one party caucus and Republicans (the name taken by the Anti-Federalists) in another. Each caucus would endorse a contender by plurality vote of those present and send word of its endorsement to the state parties.

The congressional caucuses gave an advantage to Washington insiders, such as cabinet secretaries and congressional leaders, who were known personally to members of Congress and who could lobby directly at the Capitol for the nomination. Governors and other officials in the states were at a disadvantage, and none ran for president during this period. The Founders themselves were at the forefront of presidential politics: two-thirds of those receiving electoral votes in the first eight presidential elections had been members of the Congresses convened under the Articles of Confederation during the 1780s.

Each of the presidents in the caucus era—Thomas Jefferson, James Madison, James Monroe, and John Quincy Adams—had served previously as secretary of state, with all but Jefferson serving in his immediate predecessor's administration. Each secretary of state was able to win the Republicans' congressional caucus endorsement by defeating cabinet or congressional rivals. Each promised cabinet positions to prominent congressional party leaders or their friends. Within each cabinet, ambitious men jockeyed for the next nomination and tried to consolidate their influence in Congress by tailoring their policies and appointments to please legislators from their party.

The result was a kind of cabinet government. The president was surrounded by cabinet secretaries with their own followings in Congress. To get anything done, the president had to win the cabinet's support. Important presidential decisions were made in council, with presidents reading formal state papers outlining their arguments to the cabinet, followed by spirited discussion and then a vote on the president's proposal. If a president received little or no support in the cabinet, he would often postpone the decision or abandon the policy.

Although the presidents who served in this period were all experienced and intelligent, cabinet government was a prescription for a weak and indecisive presidency. James Madison, who at the constitutional convention had wanted a "council of state" to diffuse executive power, governed between 1809 and 1817 through the system of cabinet consensus, and the resulting power vacuum was filled by congressional "hawks" eager for war with Great Britain. With the president reluctant and indecisive, the country suffered military defeats in Canada and a British raid that destroyed the Capitol and the White House during the War of 1812. The situation improved only when the desperate Madison nominated his secretary of state, James Monroe, to serve simultaneously as secretary of war, putting an end to cabinet decision making and bringing some coherence to government policy.

Nominating Conventions: Nomination by State Party Organizations

The rise of Jacksonian democracy in the 1820s led to the abandonment of the congressional caucus and with it an end to cabinet government. In the presidential election of 1824, Andrew Jackson did not win the congressional caucus endorsement, but he nonetheless won pluralities of the popular and Electoral College votes. In the contingency election that followed, the House chose John Quincy Adams, who also had not won the congressional caucus endorsement. Adams in turn picked House Speaker Henry Clay to be his secretary of state and thus his presumed successor. An enraged Jackson charged that a corrupt bargain between Adams and Clay had denied him the White House.

Jackson ran again in 1828, promising to sweep away the remnants of the corrupt Republican Party. He did not even try to win the endorsement of "King Caucus" but instead accepted endorsements from some state conventions and state legislatures. Jackson was elected, and the consequences for presidential governance were enormous. Because he had not been nominated by members of Congress, he felt no accountability to a congressional party. As president he exercised constitutional prerogatives to block the legislature's majority, using the veto to make policy of his own. Because he had not needed to put congressional leaders in his cabinet to win nomination, he downgraded the cabinet, not even meeting with it for much of his first term. Jackson established the principle that a president could issue orders to cabinet secretaries and fire them if they did not follow his policies, greatly expanding presidential powers over the departments.

King Caucus was gone, but what would replace it? The answer was provided by advances in water and rail transportation that by the 1830s made interstate travel along the eastern seaboard safe, comfortable, quick, and inexpensive. Anti-Masons convened the first national convention in 1830 to organize themselves as a political party, and held a presidential nominating convention in 1831. The new national Republican Party held a convention in December 1831, and the Democratic Party met in the Baltimore Athenaeum in May 1832. The Democrats nominated Martin Van Buren as Jackson's second-term vice president and passed a resolution concurring in the "nominations" for reelection that Jackson had received "in various parts of the Union" by Democratic state parties. By 1836 all the candidates of major parties were nominated by the convention system.

Conventions were not democratic expressions of the will of the rank-and-file delegates. "Less than one hundred men in any convention . . . really dictate what occurs," Bronx County's Democratic Party boss Ed Flynn admitted years later.[2] State and local party bosses held the delegates' proxies. In many states a "unit rule" required each delegation to caucus (hold a meeting off the convention floor), and a majority of delegates, under the guidance of these leaders, then determined how the entire state's votes were to be cast. Some delegations would remain uncommitted, voting for a "favorite son" governor or senator, until the bosses completed their bargaining with a leading candidate's manager and threw their support his way. "I authorize no bargains and will be bound by none," Abraham Lincoln telegraphed his managers at the 1860 Republican convention in Chicago's Wigwam Hall. "Damn Lincoln," one of his zealous managers responded, and won Indiana by offering to make Caleb Smith secretary of the interior; Pennsylvania by giving Simon Cameron the War Department; and New York by offering Salmon Chase the Treasury Department. In 1932 Franklin Roosevelt's campaign manager, Jim Farley, made a deal with Virginia to put Sen. Claude Swanson in the cabinet; won Missouri by offering patronage to the Pendergast machine in Kansas City; won Louisiana by seating a delegation headed by its governor, Huey Long, who was involved in a credentials fight with a rival Louisiana faction; and won Texas by offering Roosevelt's main rival, John Nance Garner, the vice presidency.

During the era of boss-dominated conventions, the front-runner would try to build a winning coalition over several ballots by convincing uncommitted delegations to join his bandwagon. Other candidates might gang up to encourage defections from the front-runner's coalition. (From 1832 to 1936, Democrats required a two-thirds vote for nomination in order to block any nominee who could not appeal to both the North and South.) A rival coalition might challenge the credentials of some of the front-runner's delegates, start a platform fight to try to split his coalition, or raise a divisive procedural issue. In the end, a deadlocked convention might reject all the leading contenders and choose a "dark horse": of those, all but Republican Wendell Willkie in 1940 won the subsequent election—which may say something for the political acumen of the bosses behind them.

"What the party wants," observed James Bryce, a noted British commentator on American politics, late in the nineteenth century, "is not a good president but a good candidate."[3] Delegates favored nominees of mediocre ability who often lacked national government experience but whom state party bosses knew to be reliable team players. Between 1836 and 1900, serious contenders— that is, candidates whose base of support extended beyond their own states—at the major-party conventions included thirteen governors and ten Union generals, most of whom initially had received their military commissions because they were state politicians. Only two cabinet secretaries received delegate votes, although twenty senators—themselves elected by the state legislatures—contended. The convention system offered an open invitation to bosses to engage in influence peddling and corruption in the administration of a president they had handpicked.

In the early and mid-twentieth century, as the United States assumed the global responsibilities of a great power, party bosses rose to the occasion and nominated distinguished public servants, including Theodore Roosevelt, William Howard Taft, Woodrow Wilson, Herbert Hoover, Franklin Roosevelt, and Dwight Eisenhower. Even then they sometimes slipped back to old habits—witness their nomination of Warren Harding, a mediocre man who tolerated massive corruption in his administration. The pattern of governors and senators dominating the field continued: between 1900 and 1968, nineteen senators and twenty-one governors, but only three cabinet secretaries, two members of the House, and two generals, received a significant number of votes at either party's convention.

The Primary and Caucus System: Nomination by the Party in the Electorate

A second set of changes in nominating politics arose from the erosion of the legitimacy and authority of the post–New Deal Democratic Party in the 1960s, caused by the unpopularity of the Vietnam War with party activists, the mobilization of newly enfranchised African American voters in the South, and the student movement on university campuses. Between 1968 and 1972 the Democrats transferred the power to decide on the composition of a state's convention delegation from the state party organization to its supporters in the electorate—that is, from the bosses to the voters.

The mechanism that made this transfer possible was the primary contest— that is, a vote within a state party to determine the presidential preferences of its members. The first presidential primary had been held in Florida in 1904. It was a "preference primary" that allowed voters to indicate their choice for the presidential nomination, although the convention delegates were still chosen by party leaders. By 1916, twenty states had established primaries, but many were still Florida-style "beauty contests." In the 1920s, because of high cost and low voter participation, eight states dropped primaries and returned to the closed caucus system.

Because so few states permitted the voters to select convention delegates, only two-fifths of the top vote-getters in the primary season were nominated by the conventions between 1912 and 1968. Matters reached a crisis point in 1968, when Vice President Hubert Humphrey won the Democratic nomination without entering a single Democratic primary; his support came from party bosses who controlled more than 60 percent of the delegates. To many rank-and-file Democrats, especially the antiwar activists supporting Sen. Eugene McCarthy, the system seemed outrageously undemocratic. Journalists focusing on "smoke-filled rooms" and boss-dominated conventions joined them in attacking the system's legitimacy.

The Democrats subsequently established the Commission on Party Structure and Delegate Selection (the McGovern-Fraser Commission) and adopted dramatically different rules for 1972. The state parties were required either to hold primaries to select delegates to the national convention or to hold open caucuses (meetings at which any registered Democrat could participate) to select delegates to state conventions that would choose delegates to the national convention. Using either system, rank-and-file voters, not party bosses, would select the convention delegates. Delegations could no longer be bound by the unit rule, which the Democrats repealed in 1968. Unified state delegations controlled by party bosses gave way to divided delegations in which several candidates could gain convention votes if they did well in the open state contests. The Republicans soon followed suit with similar rules changes, and most state legislatures opted for primaries rather than open caucuses. The number of primaries zoomed from fifteen in 1968, to twenty-seven by 1976, and to forty by 1992. In 2008, thirty-nine states held Democratic primaries that together chose approximately three-quarters of the elected convention delegates, with caucuses choosing the remainder; on the Republican side, thirty-eight states held primaries.

Under the current system a politician can run for president without the backing of state party leaders by appealing to voters directly in primaries and caucuses. Individuals who run for convention delegate in primaries and caucuses have been selected by, and remain loyal to, a particular contender's organization, not to a local or state party. These delegates take their direction from the contender's organization at the convention.

The primary system has transformed the field of contenders. Physical and mental endurance, personal wealth or access to well-heeled contributors, name recognition, organizational abilities, and ease in dealing with the media are essential. No group of bosses meeting in a convention back room can now determine the ideal qualities of the party nominee for the next election, much less choose the candidate. It makes no sense to speak of "Republicans choosing an outsider" or "Democrats deciding on a centrist" in an era when the decisions about who will run are made by politicians who see the ideal president in the bathroom mirror.

The way candidates are nominated today does nothing to enhance the authority of the presidency, and in some ways it detracts from the power of incumbent presidents. Nominees are beholden to special interests and large campaign contributors, as well as to organizers of so-called 527 committees that raise money for issue advertisements that can help their campaign (although nominally acting independently). Candidates cannot even think of mounting a run for the nomination without access to huge amounts of campaign cash. The length of the primary season means they must engage in an exhausting endurance contest. They are encouraged by their media advisers to deal with issues tactically rather than substantively. If they change their mind about issues, they are characterized by the media and voters as mere "politicians" who have no principles and who "flip-flop." Each nominee's character and private life are subject to media scrutiny often based on rumor and innuendo.

Who Gets Nominated?

Does the nominating process attract the most qualified candidates? Contenders usually come from a small group of career politicians, most of whom have experience in public office, access to large amounts of money, and experience in running a media campaign. What they often do not have is experience in national government, particularly within the executive branch they aspire to lead, or much expertise in conducting foreign or economic policy.

Contenders with Prior Political Experience

Incumbent presidents, the only contenders with experience in the office, won twenty-four convention renominations between 1836 and 2008. (Even before the convention era, Adams, Jefferson, Madison, Monroe, John Quincy Adams, and Jackson were their party's choice for a second term.) But not all incumbents want a second term, nor are all renominated by their parties. Several pre–Civil War presidents, such as James Polk, Millard Fillmore, Franklin Pierce, and James Buchanan, pledged to serve a single term or were discouraged by their parties from seeking reelection. John Tyler and Andrew Johnson were sympathetic to the opposition party and therefore were ditched at the first opportunity. Later, in the post–Civil War period, incumbents' chances for renomination improved. Republican presidents dominated the largely African American party organizations in the southern states through their control of federal patronage, and this enabled them to amass a great lead in convention delegates and virtually assure themselves renomination. Partly because of the increase in federal patronage and contracts channeled through state parties, vice presidents who succeeded to the presidency after Theodore Roosevelt found it fairly easy to win the support of state party leaders and capture their party's nomination. But in the current era of primary contests, presidents who are unpopular with the party rank and file are vulnerable to challenges within their own party: Gerald Ford in 1976 and Jimmy Carter in 1980 had to stave off intraparty challengers who nearly defeated them. As a result of the splits in their parties, both candidates lost in the general election.

A party that does not renominate its incumbent president usually has no chance to win. When Polk was not renominated in 1848, opposition Whigs won with Zachary Taylor; when Fillmore was dropped in 1852, opposition Democrats won with Pierce; when Buchanan retired in 1860, opposition Republicans won with Abraham Lincoln. Similarly, when Harry Truman and Lyndon Johnson faced stiff opposition for renomination and withdrew from the contests in 1952 and 1964, their weakness presaged victory by the Republicans.

A president may try to pass the nomination to an heir apparent or to block another contender, but most such attempts do not work. Calvin Coolidge was unable to derail the presidential ambitions of his secretary of commerce, Herbert Hoover, in 1928. Dwight Eisenhower wanted Treasury Secretary Robert Anderson in 1960, but Anderson declined to run, allowing Vice President Richard Nixon to assume the mantle of heir apparent. Some presidents have helped heirs win the nomination and election, as Ronald Reagan did George H. W. Bush in 1988. But often the heir apparent loses the election, as did Hubert Humphrey in 1968 and Al Gore in 2000. The president can make it clear that he is sympathetic to their efforts during the primary season, help them raise funds, and give them credit for accomplishments in the administration. But it may be difficult for both president and heir to make the transition after the nomination because each may view himself as the head of the party, entitled to speak for it and set its policy. In 1960 Nixon pleaded with Eisenhower to take measures against a crippling recession, and in 1968 Humphrey wanted Johnson to stop the bombing in Vietnam, but neither president complied until it was too late. In 2000 Gore and President Bill Clinton were unable to mesh their campaign efforts successfully, and considerable friction developed between them and their staffs. In 2008, due to an unpopular war in Iraq and a weak economy, the last thing John McCain wanted was to be seen as Bush's heir, and he went out of his way to distance himself from the Bush administration.

Vice presidents have become viable contenders for the presidential nomination because they have been transformed from marginal figures with little to do in Washington into important presidential advisers, policy implementers, and party campaigners. Until the twentieth century most vice presidents were not presidential contenders. Between 1789 and 1900, only seven vice presidents became president, three by winning party nominations and being elected (John Adams, Thomas Jefferson, and Martin Van Buren) and four by succession when the president died (John Tyler, Millard Fillmore, Andrew Johnson, and Chester Arthur). Of those who became president by succession, none subsequently won the party's presidential nomination.

Between 1901 and 2008, seven vice presidents became president. Theodore Roosevelt, Coolidge, Truman, and Lyndon Johnson succeeded to the office and subsequently were nominated and elected. Richard Nixon was nominated for president and lost the election in 1960; eight years later he was nominated and elected. Gerald Ford became vice president through the appointment procedures of the Twenty-fifth Amendment, succeeded to the presidency when Nixon resigned in 1974, and won the presidential nomination of his party in 1976. George H. W. Bush was not only nominated but also elected in 1988—the first time this had happened since Van Buren did it in 1836. Three other vice presidents won their party's presidential nomination but lost the general election: Hubert Humphrey in 1968, Walter Mondale in 1984 (four years after leaving office), and Al Gore in 2000.

One might expect that secretaries of state, defense, and Treasury, as heads of the most important cabinet departments, would be likely candidates to win presidential nominations. But department secretaries were favored only in the congressional caucus system. Since the 1830s only five cabinet secretaries have been viable contenders at a national convention. In the modern era of media politics, some cabinet members (such as Colin Powell) have been mentioned as potential contenders, but few have made the race, and since 1824 only Taft in 1908 and Hoover in 1928 have won major-party nominations while serving in the cabinet. Most presidents have never served in the cabinet and come into office without any national executive experience—as Obama did after the 2008 election.

Some presidents have been members of Congress, but the majority take office having few connections to the legislators with whom they will have to work.[4] One or more senators are almost always in the field of contenders (seventy through 2008), but hardly any become president. Only one senator in the nineteenth century (Benjamin Harrison) and two in the twentieth (Warren Harding and John Kennedy) were elected directly from the Senate. Just after Kennedy became president, some political scientists—generalizing from a sample of one—argued that senators were likely to win presidential nominations because they served in Washington, received national media attention, had high name recognition, and dealt with important national issues. For a time this generalization held up: between 1960 and 1972, every major-party nominee was a current or former senator. Yet in 1964 and 1972, the nominee who was a sitting senator (Barry Goldwater in 1964 and George McGovern in 1972) lost the presidential election by a huge margin. The anti-Washington mood of the voters made such candidates, who were steeped in windy, arcane legislative language and practices, less attractive to voters than the incumbent president seeking reelection—a pattern repeated in 2004 by John Kerry but broken in 2008, when both John McCain and Barack Obama won their parties' nominations while serving in the Senate.

Only ten serious contenders have run for a presidential nomination while serving in the House. Of these, just one, James Garfield, has been elected president, and that was in 1880. Several presidential nominees have served in the House at some point in their careers, but they moved on to other public office or returned to private life before running for the White House.

Governors have executive experience but not in the national government. Nevertheless, they have done well in winning presidential nominations. With the end of King Caucus, governors became part of the field, and forty-four were serious contenders for their party's nomination between 1844 and 2008. In the nineteenth century, four won the presidency, including James Polk, Rutherford Hayes, Grover Cleveland, and William McKinley. Six were elected in the twentieth century: Wilson, Franklin Roosevelt, Carter, Reagan, Clinton, and George W. Bush. Four of the six most recent presidents have been governors.

Governors usually win nomination when they can exploit an anti-Washington mood in the electorate: they portray themselves as Washington outsiders ready to shake up the capital and as vigorous executives who know how to solve problems and not just talk about them. Governors also seem to be better able to organize efficient campaigns and fund them adequately, often relying on a core of in-state private and corporate contributors who must deal with their state governments.

Military Officers

Military officers rarely win presidential nominations. Sixteen have contended for a nomination through 2008, but only six career generals, who were successful commanders in major wars, became president: Washington, Jackson, William Henry Harrison, Taylor, Ulysses Grant, and Eisenhower. (Six others had the rank of general but were not career military men.) In the nineteenth and twentieth centuries, a number of less-distinguished officers sought or won nomination, but those who were nominated were defeated in the general election: the potential or actual nominees included Winfield Scott, John Fremont, George McClellan, Winfield Hancock, Leonard Wood, and Douglas MacArthur. These men tended to be arrogant and unable to compromise, had difficulties with their civilian superiors, and lacked political skills. Each had been relieved of his command or sidelined in his career.[5] As the unsuccessful candidacy of retired general Wesley Clark demonstrated in 2004, the media skills a contender needs are usually not acquired in a military career: When asked if he would have voted for the resolution in Congress authorizing war against Iraq, Clark first said yes, then said no, and finally called to his press secretary for help.

Geographical Politics

From 1800 to 1820, all the nominees of the congressional caucus were Virginians. In the era of boss-dominated conventions, between 1836 and 1968, eleven of the Whig and Republican nominees came from Ohio and six from New York. Fourteen of the Democratic nominees were from New York alone. Of the sixty-eight major-party nominations in the convention era, Republicans gave only four to candidates from small states, all of whom subsequently lost the election. Democrats nominated only three small-state candidates: Two of them were elected (Franklin Pierce of New Hampshire, in 1852, and Harry Truman of Missouri, in 1948), but William Jennings Bryan of Nebraska squandered three nominations (1896, 1900, and 1908). Before the Civil War, several nominees chosen or endorsed by conventions came from the South, including Jackson, William Henry Harrison, Polk, and Taylor. After the Civil War, southerners were excluded from consideration. Until Carter's nomination in 1976, the only southerners chosen were Wilson (born in Virginia, but his political career was spent in New Jersey) and Lyndon Johnson, a Texan who emphasized his western rather than southern roots.

Since the reforms of 1972, the geographic spread has expanded: candidates can come from anywhere, and being from the South or a small state does not exclude one from the talent pool, as Bill Clinton (from Arkansas, a small southern state) and John McCain (from Arizona, which has a relatively small population) demonstrated. For the Republicans, the old New York–Ohio combination has given way to a succession of candidates from large Sun Belt states, especially California (Nixon and Reagan) and Texas (both Bushes). For Democrats, the picture is less clear, but between 1964 and 2004 the party won the White House only when it nominated southern centrists (Johnson, Carter, and Clinton). One reason for the geographic switch from the North to the South and West is that since the early 1980s the Sun Belt states have gained population and electoral votes at the expense of the Snow Belt states.

Do parties need to nominate experienced Washington insiders who have lengthy track records in national politics? Until 2004 there was no evidence that voters cared about this trait. Since the mid-twentieth century, the outsider who ran against the insider politics of Washington has been more likely to win the election. The victors include Eisenhower, Carter, Reagan, Clinton, and the younger Bush. In the thirteen contests between 1952 and 2000, the candidate with less Washington experience won four times and lost twice; one race involved two Washington outsiders; and six involved two insiders. But in 2004 John Kerry attracted Democratic voters in primaries precisely because he had more national experience than his rivals Howard Dean and John Edwards—although Dean won many hearts with his passionate attacks on the Bush administration and Edwards's cheerful personality attracted voters, Kerry won support from those concerned with "electability": as one bumper sticker put it, "I dated Dean but married Kerry." Then in 2008, Barack Obama, with less than four years of experience as a U.S. senator, defeated the front-runner, Hillary Clinton. Questions about Obama's experience—or the lack thereof—dominated the nominating contest. Clinton claimed that her experience in the Senate (and as first lady) should give her the edge; Obama countered that it was judgment—he, unlike Clinton, had opposed the 2003 invasion of Iraq from the start—and not experience that should count.

The Nominating Season

The presidential nominating process is a two-year marathon. Within each party, a large group of potential participants is winnowed to a small field of contenders from which a winner eventually emerges. Is this lengthy process, with its emphasis on media relations, polls, organizations, and the ability to raise huge amounts of money, the best way to ensure that good candidates are nominated?

David Broder, a columnist for the *Washington Post,* once argued that an "inner club" of political journalists could identify presidential possibilities that party professionals might otherwise overlook. Although early attention from the "club" of pundits may help a campaign establish its credibility, especially with large campaign contributors, changes in public attitudes have made such endorsement as much a liability as an asset. Many voters consider columnists part of the Washington establishment. Contenders may therefore prefer to bypass tough scrutiny on national issues by informed journalists, in favor of "soft" interviews on late-night television and all-day radio talk shows, in which empathy rather than knowledge bonds them to viewers and listeners. In 1992 Bill Clinton went on Arsenio Hall's late-night television program and played jazz riffs on the saxophone in front of a national audience of millions. That image alone was worth far more than thousands of words from newspaper columnists.

On those occasions when journalists and pundits could have been useful in providing peer review (that is, a judgment by people who have observed the candidate closely and are qualified to evaluate his or her competence and character), they have tended to falter. An examination of mainstream media coverage of contenders just before the primary season starts indicates that only a tiny percentage of stories explore the candidates' records, and only one-quarter deal with their positions on issues. A majority of stories are concerned with fund raising and political strategy and tactics—the horse race.[6] The proliferation of campaign blogs, with their endless reports on the activities of campaign staffers, has only increased the attention paid to trivial, "inside the beltway" campaigning games at the expense of significant examination of the issues.

Until the most recent elections, prenomination polls had a mixed record of predicting the nominees. Only five or six politicians achieve contender status in the preconvention polls in any election.[7] In some nominating seasons, a contender comes out of nowhere to win a nomination; high standing in the early polls does not guarantee victory to anyone. Jimmy Carter, an obscure former governor of Georgia, won the Democratic nomination and the presidency in 1976, even though he had not been included in the polls the previous year. In 1986 Michael Dukakis's name did not appear on a list of eighteen likely Democratic candidates in the Gallup polls, yet in 1988 he won the Democratic nomination. Preprimary polls sometimes overstate a front-runner's strength: in 1984 the *New York Times* published poll results before the first primaries, indicating that Walter Mondale held a commanding lead. Shortly thereafter, Mondale was in the fight of his life against Gary Hart. In 1996 and 2000, a combination of preprimary polls, early fund raising, cash reserves, and regional strength was the best predictor of who would win the nomination.[8] This pattern did not hold in 2004, however, when the candidacy of Howard Dean, the leader in polls just prior to the first delegate contests, collapsed in Iowa and then in New Hampshire as a result of voters' doubts about his personality. Not only did pollsters not catch on to Dean's collapse, they later failed to pick up a surge for John Edwards against John Kerry in Wisconsin.

Until 2008 the conventional wisdom of political scientists was that, given the increasingly "front-loaded" primary season, contenders must become political heavyweights before entering the nominating contests. They cannot rely on pulling themselves up by their bootstraps once the voting begins, although those chasing a front-runner can benefit from that candidate's collapse.[9] In 2008 this conventional wisdom was upended: Hillary Clinton was a heavy favorite to win the Democratic nomination, with advantages in name recognition, funding, and staffing. Yet, by tapping into the desire of young people and antiwar activists for change, Barack Obama was able to raise more money and outspend Clinton, out-organize her in caucus states, and out-strategize her in developing campaign themes. Similarly, John McCain, after running a poorly organized and badly funded campaign in 2007, managed to right his sinking campaign organization and defeat a better-funded and well-organized Mitt Romney to win the nomination. The 2008 contests in both parties cast considerable doubt on the claim that the nominating process has become overly compressed. Both contests resulted in the front-runner's defeat, and the Democratic contest lasted through the final rounds of primaries and caucuses.

The best way to become a political heavyweight is to attract campaign contributions. That was how Obama attracted notice late in 2007, even before the voting in primaries was under way. "You need three things to run for public office," former House Speaker Tip O'Neill used to say, "money, money and money." Nowhere is this truer than in presidential nominating politics. The Federal Election Campaign Amendments of 1974 placed a spending limit on each contender's prenomination campaign. The law also limited campaign contributions. No individual could contribute more than $1,000, and no political action committee or political party committee could contribute more than $5,000, to a contender in the preconvention period. The figure for individual donations increased to $2,000 in 2004 and $2,300 in 2008.

Each contender is eligible for matching funds from the federal Treasury, if he or she raises $5,000 in each of twenty states in amounts of $250 or less. The

Treasury then matches, dollar for dollar, all contributions of $250 or less. Candidates who receive less than 10 percent of the vote in two consecutive state primary contests lose their eligibility for federal funding. In effect, the law helps winnow out the weaker candidates by drying up their funding almost immediately, thus narrowing the field to two or three within a few weeks after the first contests are held. In 2004 candidates were spending $10 million per month once the primaries began, and Wesley Clark, Sen. Joe Lieberman, and Rep. Dick Gephardt all found it impossible to continue after early defeats. Because the Supreme Court ruled that a contender who chooses not to accept matching funds is not subject to the expenditure ceiling, the system favors contenders (such as Bush in 2000, Kerry in 2004, and Obama in 2008) who, by raising large amounts of money before the primary season begins, can then reject public funding and its overall spending limits and raise and spend unlimited amounts. In 2004 that amounted to $150 million for Kerry.[10] In 2008 Obama, relying heavily on small contributions and those solicited over the Internet, raised $338 million in the primary season, almost half in contributions of less than $200. The money advantage is real and decisive: Since 1980 every contender (with the exception of Kerry in 2004) who eventually won a major-party nomination led the field in funds raised on December 31 of the year prior to the convention.

Caucus-Convention and Primary Contests: Are They Democratic?

The reforms of the 1970s were designed to put more power into the hands of the voters in each party. Have they done so?

Caucuses have become open-participation events, rather than closed gatherings of party leaders and their supporters. Some states, such as Iowa, attracted as much as 17 percent of registered party voters in 2008, but overall participation averages around 3 percent. With such low turnout, caucuses are less an exercise in mass voter mobilization than a forum for organized interests who can get their members to the meetings.[11] The Iowa caucuses are the first contest held by any state for convention delegates. The winner and second-place finisher in Iowa receive much more media coverage than other contenders and usually enjoy a surge in campaign contributions. In 1984, for example, Gary Hart took second place in Iowa, and George McGovern finished third, with fewer than fifteen hundred votes separating them. Hart received a boost in his campaign from the press, while McGovern was ignored and soon dropped out. Doing poorly in Iowa usually means quitting the race within a month: only one party nominee ever finished lower than third, and that was Bill Clinton, who didn't campaign in the state in deference to Iowa's favorite son contender, Sen. Tom Harkin.

Proponents of state primaries argue that since 1972 these contests have become mass participation exercises in intraparty democracy, with tens of millions of voters taking part.[12] One-quarter to one-third of the eligible voters turn out in most competitive state contests. But turnout declined after the 1970s, and in 2004 it was only 10 percent of eligible voters. And fewer Americans said they were paying attention to media coverage of the primary season; the percentage dropped from 28 percent in February 1988 to 18 percent in February 2000, though it rose again in 2004.[13] In 2008 voter participation and voter interest in primaries rose dramatically, especially within the Democratic Party. Turnout in New Hampshire was up by 50 percent over 2004, in Missouri by 47 percent, in New Jersey by 69 percent, and in Massachusetts by 48 percent. Whether this was a one-time phenomenon due to Obama's ability to mobilize new voters, or a fundamental change in turnout rates, remains to be seen.

By tradition (and now by national party rules), the first primary is held in New Hampshire. It is a small state, and candidates campaign in person, in living rooms, and in high school auditoriums. "You get to ask one on one about issues you care about," one voter observed. "You see body language, inflection, and get a sense of what they're like as a person. And through your vote you transmit that to the American people."[14] Because of the enormous media exposure the New Hampshire results generate for the winner, it is one of the most important contests.[15] Turnout is always high: about 80 percent of registered Democrats in 2004 and close to 85 percent in 2008. Victory in New Hampshire is no guarantee of success, however; it must be followed by many other primary victories. Conversely, losing in New Hampshire need not be fatal, as Walter Mondale demonstrated in 1984 and George W. Bush did in 2000. In 1992 Bill Clinton did not win the state, but by coming in second to the favored New England candidate (Sen. Paul Tsongas of Massachusetts), he won the contest in the eyes of the media.

One political scientist has referred to Iowa and New Hampshire as a "Venus flytrap," because candidates "pour more and more of their time, money, people and strategic options into the gaping mouth of the plant, until, at the very moment of victory, it snaps shut on their ability to win subsequent contests."[16] But the primary electorate in these states is unrepresentatively skewed toward voters from higher socioeconomic groups. Nor does the primary electorate represent the racial diversity of the population. Iowa and New Hampshire are disproportionately white (92.6 percent and 95.1 percent, respectively). These states winnow the field of candidates down to a small number, and they disadvantage voters from states with more minority and urban voters that hold contests later. Nationally, the biggest distortions are ideological: Democratic primary voters are more likely to be liberal than all Democratic registered voters, and Republican primary voters are heavily skewed toward the conservative end of the party's spectrum.

Defenders of the primaries counter that in all cases since 1972 the winner of the primary season (and the eventual nominee) has become the first choice of the party's voters as expressed in public opinion polls. The primary winner is transformed into the leader of the party by virtue of subjecting himself (and someday herself) to the endurance contest and emerging victorious.[17] This was true of Kerry, for example, who started with about 10 percent support from Democrats in polls before the primary season but had about 60 percent support in early March, once he had won a majority of convention delegates in the primaries and caucuses. But the same was not necessarily true for Barack Obama. Hillary Clinton won about as many votes as Obama in the primaries, including a large number of primary victories toward the end of the contest. Obama won the nomination because he had won more caucus states and because "superdelegates" (discussed in the next section) tilted in his direction.

National Conventions

Convention delegates chosen through primary and caucus contests no longer exercise independent judgment; instead they simply confirm the results of the primary and caucus contests. Nevertheless, conventions still have significant functions: delegates must agree on a platform and approve the candidate's choice of a running mate. For a second-term incumbent's party, the convention symbolizes a ritual transfer of party leadership from the president to the candidate.

The most important thing the delegates must do at the convention is win over a national television audience that has tuned in for a coronation and not a confrontation. Intense intraparty friction or a convention bloodbath makes it difficult for a candidate to win the White House. In contrast, a unified, well-managed convention that symbolizes party unity and delivers the party's message—the kind put on by Bush in 2004 and McCain in 2008 can be advantageous to the candidate: in 2008, McCain's selection of Sarah Palin for the vice presidential candidate electrified the convention and for a time reshaped the race.

Delegate Demographics

The nominee at the convention must appeal to a television audience that is quite different demographically and ideologically from the convention delegates. Compared with most voters, the delegates are better educated (four-fifths are college graduates, and more than half the Democrats and one-third of the Republicans hold advanced degrees) and more affluent (more than two-thirds have a family income of $75,000 or more). One-quarter of the Democratic delegates are union members, compared with 11 percent of the workforce. Democrats have more Catholic, Jewish, and African American delegates at their conventions than do Republicans, and far fewer evangelical Christians (13 percent to 33 percent in 2004), reflecting differences in the parties' electoral coalitions. Because the Democratic convention may appear to viewers to be too weighted toward minorities (23 percent of Democratic delegates were African American in 2008) and the Republican convention may appear to have too many whites (93 percent of delegates in 2008), each party has to find a way to make its convention "look like America," and they do so with minority speakers emphasizing diversity.

In most Republican conventions a majority of the delegates call themselves conservatives (63 percent in 2004, with the remainder self-described as moderates). In the Democratic conventions, delegates are now fairly evenly divided between liberals and moderates (the split was 41 percent liberal and 52 percent moderate in 2004).[18] Democrats have to deal with "cultural politics" and the agendas of women, young delegates, and gays and lesbians, as well as those of many ethnic minorities. The danger is that some voters may assume that the Democrats do not represent white "middle Americans" or their values. Republicans must manage their convention to avoid the charge that they are a lily-white party insensitive to minorities. They have done so in part by increasing the percentages of minority delegates (6 percent African American, 7 percent Hispanic, and 2 percent Asian American in 2004, but far fewer in 2008).

Until the 1970s many governors and members of Congress attended conventions as leaders of their state delegations and could play an important role in forging the nominee's winning coalition and moderating party platforms. But after the 1972 reforms, members of the party-in-government stopped attending because they felt uncomfortable and unwelcome in the midst of so many ideological activists.[19] In 1968, 39 percent of Democratic House members and 68 percent of Democratic senators were delegates, but in 1980 only 15 percent of House Democrats and 14 percent of Senate Democrats attended. In their place, a growing number of delegates (99 for the Democrats and 121 for the Republicans in 2004) are leading campaign and party fund-raisers, who ratify the nomination they have already funded.

To provide more representation of the party-in-government, Democrats since 1984 have provided seats in state delegations for "superdelegates": most Democratic members of the House and Senate are added automatically to their state delegations, along with each state's members of the Democratic National Committee. Since 1992 the proportion of superdelegates has been fixed at 18 percent of all delegates.[20] Their presence is supposed to restore some element of peer review to the nominating process—that is, to expose candidates to the judgment of the politicians who know them and have worked with them. In theory the superdelegates could hold the balance of power if no contender came into the convention with a majority of the elected delegates. But because the superdelegates had always voted heavily for the front-runner, congressional peer review played no role in the selection of a candidate—until 2008.

The contest between Obama and Clinton in 2008 eventually came down to the preferences of superdelegates. Initially a majority favored Clinton, even among African American legislators serving as superdelegates. But as Obama won more and more caucus and primary states, and as his claim to represent the will of the party's voters began to resonate, many superdelegates began to reassess the situation. They faced a dilemma of representation: should they consult the primary or caucus results that reflected their own congressional districts? Or their state? Or results nationwide reflecting the will of the party as a whole? Or should they act, not as delegates implementing the will of voters, but as "politicos" who trade their vote for tangible benefits for their constituents? Or should they act as "trustees" in the best interest of the party, by thinking independently and autonomously about which of the contenders would be the strongest candidate? In the end, although a combination of these factors was likely in play, most superdelegates seemed to take the position that Obama—by virtue of winning more delegates in the primaries and caucuses, was the choice of the party rank and file and, therefore, should be their choice, as well.

The "Scripted" Convention

How the delegates conduct themselves at the convention may divide or unify the party, bring it new supporters from the television audience, or alienate voters and show a party in disarray. Voters use conventions as cues either to decide, or to reinforce a standing disposition, to vote for a candidate; they hope the convention will allow them to get to know the candidate better. Guided by the campaign managers of the presumptive nominee, the national party committee organizes the convention's business into staged segments, or "podium events," including addresses by party notables (the text reviewed in advance by the nominee), showcasing of candidates running for other offices, presentation of documentary films about the nominee and past presidents, and floor demonstrations. At the 2004 convention, Democrats used their speakers to show that they were firm on national security (considered their weakness); Republican speakers emphasized patriotism; firmness in the war on terror; and "compassionate conservatism," to counter the impression that they do not care about the disadvantaged. In 2008 Obama moved his acceptance speech out of the convention hall and into a large stadium, emphasizing his connection with the people. Republicans suspended their convention for a day to focus on fund raising for hurricane relief efforts in Louisiana, to emphasize their compassion for those in need.

In the past the party platform was subject to traditional politicking by delegates with different ideas, though this could be politically dangerous. The unscripted 1972 Democratic convention, in which the delegates were able to write the platform, seemed too extreme for most voters, and McGovern's support in the polls declined from 41 percent to 39 percent. Republicans had similar difficulties writing their platforms in 1976, 1992 and 1996, with similar results. By 2008, platforms were written in advance by the candidate's team, to control the message, or as they now put it, to "introduce the brand" to the voting "consumers."

If the nominee gives a good acceptance speech, the scripted convention helps obtain a short-term "bounce" in the form of higher poll ratings. Since 1964 the upward surge in the postconvention polls has averaged 6.8 percentage points for Democrats and 7.3 percentage points for Republicans, with the record held by Bill Clinton, who gained sixteen points in 1992.[21] In 2004 Kerry had a small bounce (between zero and four points, depending on the poll), and Bush countered with what was likely a larger bounce (between two and seven percentage points, depending on the poll). In 2008 Obama gained six to eight points from the convention, but this lead was reversed when McCain chose Sarah Palin as his running mate, and Republicans won back the points and then took a few more in the next weeks. But a candidate can also be damaged if the viewing audience dislikes the script: Barry Goldwater destroyed his chances in 1964 when he told his cheering supporters that "extremism in the defense of liberty is no vice," thus allowing Lyndon Johnson to paint him as an extremist who would start World War III. After the convention, when Goldwater commercials appealed to voters with the slogan, "In your heart, you know he's right," Democrats retorted with the line, "In your guts, you know he's nuts."

With suspense drained out of conventions, they have lost much of their audience. Prime-time convention coverage in 1976 by the three major broadcast networks ran 142 hours; by 1996 it was down to less than 20 hours, with each network averaging an hour or so of programming per night, as they have ever since. ABC's Ted Koppel left the 1996 Republican convention in disgust, saying there was no news to be covered there. That year a third-time *Seinfeld* rerun outdrew the three networks' convention coverage by three to one. In 2004 only

24.7 million voters watched the last night of the Democratic convention, down from 27 million in 1992.[22] Only 28 million viewers watched Bush accept his nomination in 2004.[23] "If we were on for three hours a night, in a lot of places a test pattern would get better ratings," former CBS anchor Dan Rather admitted.[24] The scripted convention is now so obsolete that Kerry floated a trial balloon suggesting that he accept the nomination after the convention, so that he could continue to raise and spend funds for another month before the federal campaign expenditure ceiling of $75 million began to apply.[25] In 2008 some television networks, to save money, decided not to build expensive anchor booths. Yet the networks miscalculated: because of Obama's fresh themes (and the fact that he was the first African American nominee of a major party), the audience for his convention speech topped 38.4 million people. On the Republican side, McCain's speech drew 38.93 million from the networks (these figures do not include viewers of PBS or C-Span, which might add another 3 million). Even before that, Sarah Palin's vice presidential acceptance speech was watched by 37.24 million people). These huge audiences—more than any in American history—are bound to challenge the conventional wisdom that conventions have become obsolete and expensive white elephants for the parties.

Nominating Politics and Governance in the Twenty-first Century

Every few years a small cottage industry of political scientists, media commentators, and professional campaign experts arises to talk about reforming the presidential nominating system.[26] One study has found that a majority (57 percent) of the public would prefer a national primary over the present system, to reinforce the power of the voters.[27] In this view, holding a primary on a single day would increase turnout and make the process more representative. About one-fifth of the voters hold that it is useful to have primaries in stages, so that no well-funded candidate can deliver an immediate knockout punch on a single day. They believe that a long primary period enables other candidates to catch up and nullify the advantage of the front-runner, so that the candidate who demonstrates the best organizational and media ability over a lengthy period will emerge victorious. Polls do not show that any of the proposed rearrangements of the contests (such as regional groupings, or small states followed by large states) has majority support from the voters, however.[28]

Some critics of the primary system would prefer less democracy and more peer review by politicians who know the contenders personally and can assess their character and abilities.[29] These critics argue that the self-selected field of candidates emphasizes the wrong kind of experience and downgrades expertise based on a long apprenticeship in national government. They believe that peer review by professional politicians is needed to filter out intellectually or ethically weak contenders, as well as those who are too inexperienced, too ignorant about governance, or flawed by unsuitable personality traits.

Critics also note the irony that efforts to democratize the nominating process through the primary system have created a need for huge amounts of money to fund television commercials, thereby providing wealthy individuals and groups with opportunities to trade campaign cash for favored treatment. The need to develop a large campaign organization means that the staffers who surround candidates are too inclined to equate media savvy with effective governance, and the newly elected president is encouraged to appoint a *West Wing* sort of White House staff that is too young and inexperienced in anything other than campaign tactics. The grueling fund-raising and primary marathon itself discourages some individuals with extensive experience and excellent character from running. Put another way, Broder's Law (named for columnist David Broder) states that any candidate willing to do what it now takes to win the nomination should not be trusted with the office. If a candidate is not self-centered to begin with, the current emphasis on biographical politics (according to which, voters make decisions based on the candidates' life stories rather than on their stances on issues) will surely promote narcissistic personality traits that may do more harm than good in office.

Primaries promote an individualistic, media-centered approach to presidential politics, rather than encouraging the president to work closely with the congressional and state parties. When candidates win the nomination by going over the heads of party leaders and communicating directly to voters, they may decide they owe nothing to those leaders—and the feeling will be reciprocated. They may repudiate their presidential or congressional parties and claim the mantle of change or the identity of "maverick," but in doing so they will alienate members of the party with whom they will have to work once in office. To the extent that incompetent, inexperienced, egocentric, and unscrupulous campaign staffers attempt to use the news media to fool voters, the authority of the presidency is diminished—especially when the "hooks" that journalists use in their reporting on the nominating campaign emphasize candidates' manipulation of the voters and the funding role of special interests.

One reform often called for by critics of the nominating process is a return to party politics at the conventions. Some argue that as many as half of each state's convention delegation should consist of uncommitted delegates chosen by the state's party professionals. The primary and caucus contests could winnow the roster of contenders, but the politicians would make the final choice, and that in turn would force contenders to forge close links with their party organizations.

Defenders of the current system claim that the news media expose phonies. They point out that peer review and the politicking that goes with it often led to mediocre nominees, that the constraints party bosses once placed on presidents hardly served the public interest, and that we are better off without the horse trading and corruption that attended old-style convention politics. They argue that making candidates run a lengthy gauntlet of primaries gives voters the chance to find out about their personality, character, and perseverance and that the system provides for "voter peer review"—particularly in small states such as Iowa and New Hampshire, where candidates meet voters personally.

Perhaps the most serious problem with the nominating system is that those who emerge with nominations lack national executive experience, a situation that rarely occurs in other nations. (It is a sobering thought that, in 2008, Sarah Palin's eighteen months as governor of Alaska gave her more executive experience than the other three members, all senators, of both major-party tickets.) In European parliamentary systems, most party and government leaders serve long apprenticeships in a national government before heading it. European prime ministers start on the "backbenches" as rank-and-file legislators and demonstrate their talents in minor assignments. They then become junior ministers, assisting senior colleagues in running a department and defending its policies in debates, or they hone their skills as "shadow ministers" assigned to debate with the government on particular issues. In Germany they often have experience in state government and then in a national ministry, a pattern similar to that found in France. Similarly, in Russia and China, those who ascend to power have served long apprenticeships and have extensive executive experience. But in the United States, there is no orderly line of succession, no opposition leader unifying the party and preparing for the time the electorate returns it to power. The prior careers of most presidents have not prepared them for the challenges of working within the Washington community, particularly running the departments and exercising executive power. And those who come from Congress are usually not the most experienced or the ones who have held its leadership positions—a description that applied in 2008 to both nominees for president, McCain (a "maverick" in his party) and Obama (a novice).

It may be that lengthy preparation does not produce better decisions and policies in the European countries to which the United States is usually compared. And, on balance, it may be better to have a nominating system that is open to new talent, however inexperienced, because it may produce leaders who are responsive to new trends rather than enmeshed in the ways of the

Washington establishment. The contributions to the 2004 debate made by Gov. Howard Dean, who rocked the Democratic establishment and energized the party's base by appealing to antiwar sentiment, suggest the need to keep the process open, even when such a contender doesn't win the nomination. But it also seems reasonable to assume that the complexities of managing the U.S. economy and providing for national security in an age of terrorist threats are strong arguments for a nominating system that chooses candidates who are both experienced and responsive.

The argument between proponents and opponents of the modern nominating system has raged for close to four decades.[30] In that time, divisive intraparty battles, media campaigns, and critical media coverage have had their effects. The appeal of the nominees to the voters has declined sharply, as have the turnouts in primaries and caucuses. The need to raise enormous amounts of money has increased. Have the trade-offs between intraparty democracy and accountability, on the one hand, and effective presidential leadership of party and Congress, on the other, become unacceptable? Returning some peer review and a greater role for party professionals and members of Congress to the nominating system might be a means to restore its vitality.

Notes

1. Shorenstein Center Poll, "Vanishing Voter Project," news releases, June 1 and June 16, 2000; and CBS News/*New York Times* Poll, May 10–13, 2000, in which only 21 percent of respondents thought they, rather than party leaders (26 percent) or contributors (46 percent), had the most influence on nominations.

2. Ed Flynn, *You're the Boss* (New York: Collier Books, 1962), 111.

3. James Bryce, "Why Great Men Are Not Elected President," in *The American Commonwealth*, ed. Louis M. Hacker (New York: Putnam's, 1959), 27–34.

4. The following data are based on the author's calculations; "contenders" are defined as those receiving delegate votes at national nominating conventions.

5. Jean Edward Smith, "Beware Generals Bearing a Grudge," *New York Times*, February 13, 2004, A31.

6. Project for Excellence in Journalism, Pew Center for the People and the Press, January 2000.

7. William Keech and David Matthews, *The Party's Choice* (Washington, D.C.: Brookings Institution Press, 1976), 14–19; and Arthur Hadley, *The Invisible Primary* (Englewood Cliffs, N.J.: Prentice Hall, 1976).

8. Randall E. Adkins and Andrew J. Dowdle, "Break Out the Mint Juleps?" *American Political Quarterly* 28 (April 2000): 251–269; and Randall E. Adkins and Andrew J. Dowdle, "How Important Are Iowa and New Hampshire to Winning Post-Reform Presidential Nominations?" *Political Research Quarterly* 54 (June 2001): 431–444.

9. Randall E. Adkins and Andrew J. Dowdle, "Is the Exhibition Season Becoming More Important to Forecasting Presidential Nominations?" *American Politics Research* 29 (May 2001): 283–288.

10. *Buckley v. Valeo*, 424 U.S. 1 (1976).

11. See Austin Ranney, "Participation in Precinct Caucuses," in *Presidential Politics*, 2nd ed., ed. James I. Lengle and Byron E. Shafer (New York: St. Martin's, 1983), 175.

12. For data on 2004 primaries, see www.fairvote.org/turnout/primaryturnout2004. htm.

13. Pew Research Center for the People and the Press, "Public Attentiveness to News Stories in Primary Season," 2000.

14. Elisabeth Rosenthal, "Who's That at the Next Table? Ho-Hum, It's a Candidate," *New York Times*, January 19, 2004, A13.

15. Gary Orren and Nelson Polsby, *Media and Momentum* (Chatham, N.J.: Chatham House, 1987).

16. Craig Allan Smith, "The Iowa Caucuses and Super Tuesday Primaries Reconsidered," *Presidential Studies Quarterly* 22 (Summer 1992): 524.

17. William H. Lucy, "Polls, Primaries and Presidential Nominations," *Journal of Politics* 35 (November 1973): 837; later calculations by author.

18. Data from CBS News and *New York Times* poll of delegates.

19. Jeane Kirkpatrick, "Dismantling the Parties" (Washington, D.C.: American Enterprise Institute, 1978), 10.

20. Michael Goldstein, *Guide to the 1992 Presidential Election* (Washington, D.C.: CQ Press, 1991), 26.

21. For data on bounces, see Rick Lyman, "First the Convention, Then the Inevitable Expectations Game," *New York Times*, July 29, 2004, A12.

22. For Nielson Media Research ratings since 1960, see "Eyes of the Nation," *New York Times*, July 26, 2004, P7.

23. Data from Nielson Media Research, September 4, 2004.

24. Steve Gorman, "Bare Bones DNC Coverage Draws Lower Ratings," Reuters, August 28, 2004.

25. Until Franklin Roosevelt in 1936, those nominated did not attend the convention and accepted days or weeks after, but modern practice has been for candidates to attend and to accept in a speech to the delegates on the day after the roll call vote.

26. For a history of the proposal and the issues involved, see www.nationalprimary. info.

27. "Vanishing Voter Project," Shorenstein Center Poll, January 12–16, 2000.

28. CBS/*New York Times* Poll, May 10–13, 2000.

29. See the incisive critique of James Ceasar, *Presidential Selection* (Princeton: Princeton University Press, 1979).

30. For a comprehensive discussion of reform proposals, see www.nationalprimary. info.

7 The Faulty Premises of the Electoral College

George C. Edwards III

Political parties control the nomination of presidential candidates, but the Constitution spells out how the president will be chosen from among these nominees. Few issues vexed the delegates to the Constitutional Convention more than presidential selection. The method they eventually came up with—after rejecting proposals to have the president chosen by Congress, the people, or even the state governors—was the Electoral College. Modern supporters of the Electoral College defend it with arguments that, according to George C. Edwards III, are unpersuasive and inaccurate on their own terms, and that neglect the foundational democratic principle of political equality. Edwards argues instead for a system of direct election of the president.

Political equality lies at the core of democratic theory. Robert Dahl, the leading democratic theorist, includes equality in voting as a central standard for a democratic process: "Every member must have an equal and effective opportunity to vote, and all votes must be counted as equal."[1] Indeed, it is difficult to imagine a definition of democracy that does not include equality in voting as a central standard.

Because political equality is a central standard for democratic government, we must evaluate any current or proposed mechanism for selecting the president against it. A popular misconception is that electoral votes simply aggregate popular votes. In reality, the electoral vote regularly deviates from the popular will as expressed in the popular vote—sometimes merely in curious ways, usually by strengthening the victory margin of the popular vote leader, but at other times in such a way as to deny the presidency to the people's preferred candidate.

The percentage of electoral votes received by a candidate nationwide rarely coincides with the candidate's percentage of the national popular vote for several reasons, the most important of which is the winner-take-all (or unit-vote) system.[2] All states except Maine and Nebraska have a winner-take-all system in which they award *every* electoral vote to the candidate who receives the most popular votes in that state. In effect, the system assigns to the winner the votes of the people who voted *against* the winner.

The operation of the winner-take-all system effectively disenfranchises voters who support losing candidates in each state. In the 2000 presidential election, nearly three million people voted for Al Gore in Florida. Because George W. Bush won 537 more votes than Gore, however, he received all of Florida's electoral votes. A candidate can win some states by very narrow margins, lose other states by large margins (as Bush did by more than one million votes in California and New York in 2000), and so win the electoral vote while losing the popular vote. Because there is no way to aggregate votes across states, the votes for candidates who do not finish first in a state play no role in the outcome of the election.

African Americans, who are the nation's most distinctive minority group, are concentrated in the Deep South. They rarely vote for the Republican candidates who win their states. Thus, their votes are wasted because they are never added up across the country. It is not surprising that presidential candidates have generally ignored these voters in their campaigns.[3]

In a multi-candidate contest such as the ones in 1992, 1996, and 2000, the winner-take-all system may suppress the votes of the majority as well as the minority. In 1996, less than a majority of voters decided how the electoral votes of twenty-six states would be cast. In 2000, pluralities rather than majorities determined the allocation of electoral votes in eight states, including Florida and Ohio. In each case, less than half the voters determined how all of their state's electoral votes were cast. One result of these distorting factors is that there is typically a substantial disparity in almost all elections between the share of the national popular vote a candidate receives and that candidate's percentage of the electoral vote. In 1876, 1888, 2000 and, arguably, 1960,[4] the candidate who finished second in the popular vote won the election.

The unit-vote system also allows even small third parties to siphon more votes from one major-party candidate than the other and thus determine the outcome in a state, as Ralph Nader did in both Florida and New Hampshire in 2000. Indeed, by taking more votes from Gore than from Bush, Nader determined the outcome of the entire election. The results distorted the preferences of the voters, because the preferred candidate in both Florida and New Hampshire in a two-person race was Al Gore, not George W. Bush, who ultimately won the states.

If no candidate wins a majority of the electoral votes, as happened in 1800 and 1824, the House of Representatives chooses the president. Here, each state delegation receives one vote, allowing the seven smallest states, with a population of about 5 million, to outvote the six largest states, with a population of about 123 million. It is virtually impossible to find any defenders of this constitutional provision, which is the most egregious violation of democratic principles in American government.

The Electoral College violates political equality. It is not a neutral counting device. Instead, it favors some citizens over others, depending solely upon the state in which they live. The Electoral College is not just an archaic mechanism for counting the votes; it is also an institution that aggregates popular votes in an inherently unequal manner.

What good reason is there to continue such a system in an advanced democratic nation in which the ideal of popular choice is the most deeply ingrained principle of government?

Constitutional Consistency

Some defenders of the Electoral College argue that its violations of majority rule are just an example of constitutional provisions that require supermajorities to take action.[5] For example, it takes the votes of two-thirds of the senators present to ratify a treaty. The Framers designed all such provisions, however, to allow minorities to prevent an action. The Electoral College is different. It allows a minority to take an action—that is, to select the president. As such, it is the only device of its kind in the Constitution.

Defending Interests

One common justification for the Electoral College and its violations of political equality is that it protects important interests that a system of direct election by the people would overlook or even harm. Advocates argue that allocating electoral votes by state, and states casting their votes as units, ensures that presidential candidates will be attentive to and protective of states' interests, especially the interests of states with small populations. Most supporters of the Electoral College also maintain that it is an essential bulwark of federalism and that electing the president directly would undermine the federal system.[6]

On their face, such claims seem far-fetched. In practice, candidates allocate proportionately more campaign stops and advertisements to competitive and large states than to small ones.[7] Because these justifications for the Electoral College are so common, however, we must investigate them more systematically. (It is illuminating—and frustrating—that advocates of the Electoral College virtually never offer systematic evidence to support their claims.)

Proponents of the view that one of the major advantages of the Electoral College is that it forces candidates to be more attentive to and protective of state interests, especially the interests of states with small populations, base their argument on the premises that (1) states have interests as states, (2) these interests require protection, and (3) interests in states with smaller populations both require and deserve special protection from federal laws.

State Interests

States do not have coherent, unified interests. Even the smallest state has substantial diversity within it. No state includes just one point of view. That is why Alaska may have a Republican governor and one or more Democratic senators, and why "conservative" states like Montana and North and South Dakota vote Republican for president but sometimes send liberal Democrats to the U.S. Senate. As historian Jack Rakove argues, "States have no interest, as states, in the election of the president; only citizens do." He adds:

The winner-take-all rule might make sense if states really embodied coherent, unified interests and communities, but of course they do not. What does Chicago share with Galena, except that they both are in Illinois; Palo Alto with Lodi in California; Northern Virginia with Madison's home in Orange County; or Hamilton, N.Y., with Alexander Hamilton's old haunts in lower Manhattan?[8]

James Madison, recognizing how diverse states are, opposed counting the presidential vote by state (as in the unit rule) and hoped that, at the least, votes would be counted by district within states. Disaggregating the statewide vote and allowing districts within states to support the same candidate would encourage cohesiveness in the country and counter the centrifugal tendencies of regionalism.[9] Moreover, Madison did not want candidates to make appeals to special interests. As he proclaimed at the Constitutional Convention, "Local considerations must give way to the general interest"—even on slavery.[10]

Judith Best, who is perhaps the most diligent defender of the Electoral College, recognizes that heterogeneity exists within states but nevertheless argues that the citizens of each state share a common interest in managing their state's resources, including roads, parks, schools, local taxes, and the like. True enough. She also argues that these interests are as or more important than the characteristics people in a state share with people in other states, such as race, gender, religion, and ethnicity.[11] Many women, blacks, Hispanics, farmers, and members of other groups would be surprised to hear that local roads and parks are more important to their lives than the place they occupy in the economic and social structure of the country.

Equally important, Best makes a series of either logically or empirically incorrect statements about the relation between community interests and the election of the president. First, she confuses local communities with states. Her examples are largely of local, not state, issues, even though the policies of local governments vary widely within each state. Second, she argues that the president must be responsive to state interests to be elected and that candidates must "build [the] broadest possible coalitions of local interests" to win.[12] No evidence exists to support these assertions, and Best provides none. "State interest" is a dubious concept. Best cannot offer a single example of such an interest.

Do presidents focus on local interests when building their electoral coalitions? They do not. As we will see, candidates ignore most of the country in their campaigns, and they do not focus on local interests where they do campaign. Similarly, nowhere in the vast literature on voting in presidential elections has any scholar found that voters choose candidates on the basis of their stands on state and local issues. Indeed, candidates avoid such issues because they do not want to be seen by the rest of the country as pandering to special interests. In addition, once elected, the president has little to do with the issues that Best raises as examples of the shared interests of members of communities. There is no reason, and certainly no imperative, to campaign on these issues.

The Need for Protection

The Constitution places many constraints on the actions a simple majority can take. Minorities have fundamental rights to organize, communicate, and participate in the political process. The Senate greatly overrepresents small states and, within that chamber, the filibuster is a powerful extraconstitutional tool for thwarting majorities. Moreover, more than a simple majority is required to overcome minority opposition by changing the Constitution.

With these powerful checks on simple majorities already in place, do some minority rights or interests require additional protection from national majorities? If so, are these minorities concentrated in certain geographic areas? (Because it allocates electoral votes on the basis of geography, the Electoral College protects only geographically concentrated interests.) Does anything justify awarding interests in certain geographic locations—namely, small states—additional protections in the form of extra representation in the electoral system that citizens in other states do not enjoy?[13]

Two of the most important authors of the Constitution, James Wilson and James Madison, understood well both the diversity of state interests and the need to protect minorities that are embodied in the Constitution. They saw little need to confer additional power to small states through the Electoral College.

"Can we forget for whom we are forming a government?" Wilson asked. "Is it for *men*, or for the imaginary beings called *States?*"[14] Madison declared that experience had shown no danger of state interests being harmed by a national majority[15] and that "the President is to act for the *people* not for *States.*"[16]

Congress, whose members are elected by districts and states, is designed to be responsive to constituency interests. The president, as Madison pointed out, is supposed to take a broader view. When advocates of the Electoral College express concern that direct election of the president would suppress local interests in favor of the national interest, they are in effect endorsing a presidency that is responsive to parochial interests in a system that already offers minority interests extraordinary access to policymakers and opportunities to thwart policies they oppose.

Interestingly, supporters of the Electoral College almost never specify what geographically concentrated rights or interests need special protection through the Electoral College. They certainly have not developed a general principle to justify additional protections for some interests rather than others. Nevertheless, we can do our own analysis of the distribution of interests in the United States.

The Interests of Small States

Do the states with small populations that receive special consideration in the Electoral College have common interests to protect? In the Constitutional Convention, Madison pointed out that it was not necessary to protect small states from large ones because the large ones—Virginia, Massachusetts, and Pennsylvania—had such different economic, religious, and other interests. Their size did not constitute a common interest. Indeed, rivalry was more likely to occur among large states than coalition.[17] Madison was prescient. The great political battles of American history—in Congress and in presidential elections—have been fought by opposing ideological and economic interests, not by small states and large states.

A brief look at the seventeen states with the fewest electoral votes (that is, three, four, or five) shows that they are quite diverse.[18] Maine, Vermont, New Hampshire, and Rhode Island are in New England; Delaware and West Virginia are in the Middle Atlantic region; North and South Dakota, Montana, and Nebraska are in the Great Plains; New Mexico is in the Southwest; and Nevada, Wyoming, Utah, and Idaho are in the Rocky Mountain region. Alaska and Hawaii are regions unto themselves.

Some of these states have high average levels of income and education, and others have considerably lower levels. Some are quite liberal and others are very conservative, and their policies and levels of taxation reflect these differences. Several of the states are primarily urban, but many others are rural. They represent a great diversity of core economic interests, including agriculture, mining, gambling, chemicals, tourism, and energy. Even their agricultural interests are quite diverse, ranging from grain and dairy products to hogs and sheep. In sum, small states do not share common interests. It is not surprising that their representatives do not vote as a bloc in Congress and that their citizens do not vote as a bloc for president.

Even if small states share little in common, are there some interests that occur only in states with small populations? Not many. The first interest that may come to mind is agriculture, with visions of small farmers tilling the soil of small states. But most farmers live in states with large populations. The market value of the agricultural production of California, Texas, Florida, and Illinois alone substantially exceeds that of all seventeen of the smallest states combined.[19]

For that matter, agriculture does not lack for powerful champions, especially in Congress, which has taken the lead in providing benefits, principally in the form of subsidies, for agriculture. Rather than competing to give farmers more benefits, presidents of both parties have attempted to restrain congressional spending on agriculture. The Electoral College has not turned presidents into champions of rural America.

It is difficult to identify interests that are centered in a few small states. Even if we could, however, the question remains whether these few interests out of the literally thousands of interests in the United States deserve special protection. What principle would support such a view? Why should those who produce wheat and hogs have more say in electing the president than those who produce vegetables, citrus, and beef? Is not the disproportionate Senate representation of states in which wheat and hogs are produced enough to protect these interests? There is simply no evidence that interests like these deserve or require additional protection from the electoral system.

Attention to State Interests

As we have seen, a core justification for the Electoral College and its violations of political equality is that allocating electoral votes by state forces candidates to pay attention to state-based interests in general and the interests of small states in particular. In their enthusiasm for the status quo, some advocates go further and claim that, under the Electoral College, "all states are 'battlegrounds'" in the presidential election.[20]

Although defenders of the Electoral College almost never specify what interests the Electoral College is protecting, they nevertheless argue that candidates would ignore these interests if the president were chosen in a direct popular election. They base this argument on the premise that candidates appeal directly to state interests and give disproportionate attention to those of small states.

Do presidential candidates focus on state-level interests in their campaigns? Do they devote a larger percentage of their campaign efforts to small states than they would if the president were elected directly? To answer these questions, we need to see what candidates actually do and whether there is evidence that the Electoral College encourages candidates to be more attentive to small states. If candidates are not more oriented to small states and the interests within them than we would expect in a system of direct election, then we have reason to reject one of the principal justifications for the Electoral College's violation of political equality.

Candidates' Speeches

One prominent way that a candidate could attend to the interests of a state is by addressing them in speeches to that state's voters. What do candidates actually say when they campaign in the various states?

The presidential election of 2000 provides an excellent test of the hypothesis that the Electoral College motivates candidates to focus on state-based interests. Because the outcome in every single state that year was crucial to the outcome of this extraordinarily close election, each candidate had the maximum incentive to appeal to state interests. Nevertheless, neither George W. Bush nor Al Gore focused on state interests in their speeches, and they certainly did not focus on small state interests.[21]

Was the presidential election of 2000 unique in this way? Apparently not. A study of the campaign speeches of Bill Clinton and Robert Dole during the 1996 campaign found that they also did not focus their speeches on local interests.[22]

Candidates' Visits[23]

The most direct means for candidates to appeal to voters is to visit their states and address them directly. Modern transportation has made it relatively easy for candidates to crisscross the nation in search of votes. Proponents of the Electoral College argue that one of its principal advantages is that it forces candidates to pay attention to small states that would otherwise be neglected in a national election and to build a broad national coalition by appealing to voters in every region.

During the presidential election of 2000, only one of the seven states with three electoral votes had a visit from a presidential candidate—a single visit by Al Gore to Delaware. The six states with four electoral votes received a total of seven visits from the presidential candidates, including George W. Bush's vacation trips to Maine. Four more states had five electoral votes, and two of them had no visits from the candidates. New Mexico and West Virginia, small but highly competitive, were the two exceptions. In sum, presidential candidates did not visit eleven of the seventeen smallest states at all, and only one candidate visited two of the other six states.

Among the eleven states with six, seven, or eight electoral votes, Arkansas, Iowa, Oregon, and Kentucky were highly competitive, and presidential candidates paid them multiple visits. The candidates visited only one of the other seven states in this group, however—a single visit by George W. Bush to Arizona. Thus, presidential candidates did not visit seventeen of the twenty-eight smallest states. Three others received a single visit from the candidate of only one party.

Vice presidential candidates' visits tell a similar story. In 2000, they visited the ten smallest states a total of only four times. Eight of the seventeen smallest states did not receive a visit from a single presidential or vice presidential candidate of either party.

Bush's and Gore's emphasis on competitive states in 2000 is not unusual.[24] In the 2004 general election, no presidential candidate visited any of the seven states with only three electoral votes, and the only visit from a vice presidential candidate came when Dick Cheney went to his home state of Wyoming. Presidential candidates did not visit twelve of the seventeen smallest states, nor did vice presidential candidates visit ten of them.

Candidates also ignored the three states with six electoral votes in 2004, except for a single vice presidential candidate visit to Arkansas. Indeed, presidential candidates appeared at campaign events in only nine of the twenty-nine smallest states during the entire general election campaign. In two of these nine states, only one candidate visited, making a single visit in each case. The presidential candidates also avoided eight of the thirteen states with ten to fifteen electoral votes.

On the other hand, the candidates lavished attention on the thirteen competitive states: New Hampshire, West Virginia, New Mexico, Nevada, Iowa, Colorado, Minnesota, Wisconsin, Missouri, Michigan, Ohio, Pennsylvania, and Florida.

In addition to its failure to encourage candidate visits to small states, the Electoral College provides incentives to ignore many larger states. In 2004, the total number of campaign visits to the highly populated states of California, Texas, New York, and Illinois for both parties' presidential and vice presidential candidates was two. One of these visits was a home state rally for George W. Bush in Texas on the last night of the campaign. New Mexico and Iowa, with a total of only twelve electoral votes, received as many visits as the other thirty of the smallest thirty-two states combined. They also received more visits than California, Texas, New York, Illinois, Michigan, and New Jersey combined.

The 2008 election followed a similar pattern. Barack Obama campaigned in only fourteen states and John McCain in just nineteen states. Joseph Biden and Sarah Palin each campaigned in eighteen states. Each of the four candidates campaigned in the competitive small states of New Mexico, Nevada, and New Hampshire. Presidential candidates Obama and McCain went to none of the fourteen other small states. Palin added a single visit to Maine and her home state of Alaska, while Biden visited Montana, West Virginia, and his home state of Delaware. In addition, with the exception of a single McCain event in New York (where he had to be for other reasons), none of the candidates campaigned in the four large states of California, Texas, New York, and Illinois.

In the course of overlooking most states, candidates also avoid entire regions of the country. Democrats have little incentive to campaign in the heavily Republican Great Plains and Deep South, and Republicans have little incentive to visit most of Democratic New England.

In sum, the Electoral College provides no incentive for candidates to pay attention to small states and take their cases directly to their citizens. Indeed, it is difficult to imagine how presidential candidates could be *less* attentive to small states than they already are. Candidates are not fools. They go where the Electoral College makes them go, and it makes them go to competitive states, especially large competitive states. They ignore most small states; in fact, they ignore most of the country.

Candidates' Advertising

Candidates reach most voters through television advertising. Technology makes it easy to place ads in any media market in the nation at short notice. Do candidates operating under the Electoral College compensate for their lack of visits to small or noncompetitive states by advertising there?

No. In 2000, for example, advertising expenditures in each state closely tracked the number of candidate appearances in that state. Some voters were bombarded with television advertising; others saw none at all. The candidates essentially ignored twenty-six states and the District of Columbia. In doing so, they bypassed major American cities such as Phoenix, Denver, Indianapolis, Washington, Baltimore, New York, Charlotte, Houston, and Dallas/Ft. Worth. The Gore campaign also bypassed Los Angeles, San Francisco, and San Diego.[25]

Focusing advertising on competitive states is nothing new.[26] Thus, as in the case of candidate visits, the idea that the Electoral College forces candidates to take their cases to small states and build coalitions from all regions of the country is erroneous.

In sum, the fundamental justification of the Electoral College—that it forces candidates to be attentive to particular state interests, especially those concentrated in small states—is based on a faulty premise. In reality, the Electoral College discourages candidates from paying attention to small states and to much of the rest of the country, as well. In 2004, neither George W. Bush nor John Kerry ran a single national television advertisement.

Preserving Federalism

One of the most serious assertions by those opposed to abolishing the Electoral College and instituting direct popular election of the president is that doing so would undermine the federal nature of the constitutional system. Defenders of the Electoral College base this assertion on the premise that the Electoral College is a key underpinning of federalism. In truth, it is unclear what federalism has to do with the presidency, the one elective part of the government that is designed to represent the nation as a whole rather than as an amalgam of states and districts. Federalism is certainly an important component of the constitutional system, but does federalism need the Electoral College to maintain it?

A Federal Principle?

The Founders did not design the Electoral College on the federal principle. The Electoral College does not enhance the power or sovereignty of the states. Moreover, the Founders expected electors to exercise their individual discretion when casting their votes. They did not expect electors to vote as part of any state bloc. No delegate at the Constitutional Convention referred to the Electoral College as an element of the federal system or even as important to the overall structure of the Constitution.

Similarly, the Founders did not regard the Electoral College as a means of implementing the Connecticut Compromise, which created a House of Representatives apportioned according to population and a Senate in which each state has two seats. The allocation of two electoral votes to each states corresponding to its Senate representation were not to further federalism Instead, the extra votes were to serve as a corrective for large state power. The federative principle would have required that these extra electors be organized like the Senate as a separate body with an independent voice in the choice of the president.

The Electoral College was not designed to protect state interests. If it were, the Founders would have insisted that state legislatures choose electors, who would be agents of the state governments. But, they did not do so. Indeed, the Electoral College was "an anti-states-rights device," designed to keep the election of the president away from state politicians.[27]

Essential for Federalism?

Even if the Electoral College was not designed as an aspect of federalism, is it essential for preserving federalism? We have already seen that the Electoral College does not cause presidential candidates to devote attention to the states as states in general or to small states in particular. Neither the existence nor the powers and responsibilities of state governments depend in any way on the existence of the Electoral College. If it were abolished, states would have the same rights and duties they have now. Federalism is deeply embodied in congressional elections, in which two senators represent each state just because it is a state and in which members of the House are elected from districts within states. Direct election of the president would not alter these federalism-sustaining aspects of the constitutional structure. A leading expert on federalism, Neal Peirce, has said it best: "The vitality of federalism rests chiefly on the constitutionally mandated system of congressional representation and the will and capacity of state and local governments to address compelling problems, not on the hocus-pocus of an eighteenth-century vote count system."[28]

Greater National Control of the Electoral Process?

Occasionally, a defender of the Electoral College laments the prospect that direct election of the president would foster greater national control of the electoral process. But this has already occurred. The Fifteenth, Eighteenth, Nineteenth, Twenty-third, Twenty-fourth, and Twenty-sixth Amendments to the Constitution all expanded the electorate. Federal, not state, law effectively determines who is eligible to vote now, and in the wake of the vote-counting debacle in Florida in the 2000 election, federal law dictates the rules for voter registration, voter access to the polls, counting votes, correcting voters' errors on their ballots, resolving challenges to a citizen's right to vote, and ensuring that voting systems have minimal rates of error. The federal government also provides aid to states to improve their voting machinery and registration lists.

Federal standards are here to stay—within the framework of the Electoral College. Moreover, Americans and their elected representatives overwhelmingly support these laws and constitutional amendments. If anything, the enormous disparity in ballot designs across the states, many of which are needlessly complex, makes a strong case for greater uniformity.[29] The Caltech/MIT Voting Technology Project concluded that four to six million votes were lost in the 2000 election as a result of problems with ballots, voting equipment, and registration databases.[30] As President George W. Bush said when he signed the Help America Vote Act of 2002, "The administration of elections is primarily a state and local responsibility. The fairness of all elections, however, is a national priority."[31]

Protecting Non-State-Based Minority Interests

Some observers claim that the Electoral College ensures a "proper distribution" of the vote, in which the winning candidate receives majority support across social strata, thus protecting minority interests.[32] This claim is nonsense. In 2000, George W. Bush did not win a larger percentage than Al Gore of the votes of women, African Americans, Hispanics, and Asian Americans; voters aged 18–29 or those aged 60 or older; the poor; members of labor unions; those with less than $50,000 of household income; those with a high school education or less and those with postgraduate education; Catholics, Jews, and Muslims; liberals and moderates; urbanites; or those living in the East and West.[33]

It strains credulity to claim that Bush's vote represents concurrent majorities across the major strata of American society. What actually happened in 2000 was that the Electoral College imposed a candidate supported by white male Protestants—the dominant social group in the country—over the objections not only of a plurality of all voters but also of most "minority" interests in the country. This anti-democratic outcome is precisely the opposite of what defenders of the Electoral College claim for the system.

Why Not Elect Everyone by the Same Rules?

A common refrain by advocates of the Electoral College goes something like this: "If you insist on majority—or at least plurality—rule, why don't you insist on abolishing the Senate, in which seats are allocated to states rather than people?" The answer is straightforward. The Founders designed the Senate explicitly to represent states and the interests within them. The presidency is designed to do something quite different. The president is supposed to rise above parochial interests and represent the entire nation. Perhaps the most compelling argument that the president should be elected by direct popular vote is that the president and vice president are the only national officials in the country who represent the people as a whole and that the candidate who wins the most votes best approximates the choice of the people.

Similarly, some defenders of the Electoral College ask, "If you are so concerned that the people choose the president, what about all the nonelected judges and other officials in government? Shouldn't we elect them as well?" Of course not. It is not feasible to elect department heads and other executive officials, no matter how the president is selected. The issue is not electing additional officials. The issue is letting a plurality of voters elect the president who nominates judges and executive officials.

Advantage of Direct Election

It is difficult to see whose interests the Electoral College protects. Rather than protecting the interests of states and minorities, it reduces the incentives for people to vote in states that are safe for the locally dominant party's candidate. It also weakens the incentive for either the majority or minority party to attempt to persuade citizens to go to the polls and support its national ticket. Under the Electoral College, it makes no sense for candidates to allocate scarce resources to states they either cannot win or are certain to win, in which case, the size of their victory is irrelevant.

Candidates would be much more attentive to small states and minorities with direct election than they are with the Electoral College. Because every vote counts in a direct election, candidates would have an incentive to appeal to all voters and not just those strategically located in swing states.[34] An extra vote in Massachusetts or Texas would count as much as one in Michigan or Florida.

Presidential and vice presidential candidate Robert Dole explained that, under direct election, candidates also would have to pay attention to areas within states that are now ignored because they are safe for one party or the other. Thus, "the voters in the majority of States would receive greater attention and the objective of federalism would be served better."[35]

With these incentives, candidates would find it easy to spread their attention more evenly across the country. Because the cost of advertising is mainly a function of market size, it does not cost more to reach 10,000 voters in Wyoming than it does to reach 10,000 voters in a neighborhood in Queens or Los Angeles. Actually, it may cost less to reach voters in smaller communities because larger markets tend to run out of commercial time, increasing the price of advertising.[36] Politicians know this, even if advocates of the Electoral College do not. That is why, in the election of 2000, the candidates "devoted nearly as much advertising to Yakima as in Seattle, as much to Traverse City as to Flint, as much to Wausau as to Milwaukee" when they campaigned within states.[37]

Direct election of the president also would provide the incentive for candidates to encourage all of their supporters, no matter where they live, to go to the polls, because under direct election, every vote counts. Conversely, under the

Electoral College, it does not matter how many votes a candidate receives in a state as long as the number of votes surpasses that any opponent receives. The goal is to win states, not voters. As Douglas Bailey, the media manager of the 1976 Ford-Dole campaign, put it, "There is a vast population [outside urban areas], with every vote counting, that you cannot ignore in a direct election."[38]

It is possible, but by no means certain, that some candidates would find it more cost-effective under direct election to mobilize votes in urban areas or to visit urban areas where they would receive free television coverage before large audiences. Such actions would do nothing to undermine the argument against the Electoral College, however. Small states cannot be worse off than they are now, because under the Electoral College, candidates rarely visit or campaign there. Direct election of the president cannot diminish campaign efforts that do not exist. Instead, direct election would provide increased incentives for candidates to campaign in most small states, as well as increased incentives to campaign in many large and medium-sized states. Direct election would disperse campaign efforts rather than deprive small states of them.

Direct election, unlike the Electoral College, thus encourages citizens to participate in elections and candidates to take their campaigns to these citizens, enhancing our civic life. Direct election would increase voter turnout and stimulate party-building efforts in the weaker party, especially in less competitive states.

Some critics of direct election mistakenly claim that it would splinter the two-party system. Their criticism is based on the premise that direct election would require a runoff between the two leading candidates. But it would not. Under the Electoral College, victorious presidential candidates—including, most recently, Kennedy (1960), Nixon (1968), Clinton (1992 and 1996), and George W. Bush (2000)—have received less than a majority of the national popular vote about 40 percent of the time since 1824, and there is no relation between the vote they received and their later success in, say, dealing with Congress. Some of our strongest presidents, including Polk, Lincoln, Cleveland, Wilson, Truman, and Kennedy, received a plurality, but not a majority, of the popular vote.

Nor is the Electoral College the basis of the two-party system. Single-member districts and plurality election are, and the nation would be one electoral district under direct election. Thus, direct election would not splinter the party system.

By contrast, direct election would protect the country from the mischief of third parties. The Electoral College's unit rule encourages third parties, especially those with a regional base, because by winning a few states they may deny either major-party candidate a majority of the electoral vote. Such a result was certainly the goal of Strom Thurmond in 1948 and George Wallace in 1968. Imagine giving these racist candidates leverage to negotiate with the leading candidates before the electoral votes were officially cast. Moreover, even without winning any states, Ralph Nader inadvertently distorted the vote and determined the outcome of the 2000 election.

Conclusion

A core justification offered by defenders of the Electoral College, and its violations of political equality, is that it is necessary to protect important interests that would be overlooked or harmed by a system of direct election of the president. Yet such claims are based on faulty premises. States—including states with small populations—do not embody coherent, unified interests and communities, and they have little need for protection. Even if they did, the Electoral College does not provide it. Contrary to the claims of the institution's supporters, candidates do not pay attention to small states. The Electoral College distorts the presidential campaign so that candidates ignore many large and most small states and devote most of their attention to a few competitive states.

The Electoral College is also not a bastion of federalism. It is not based on federative principles and is not essential for the continuance of a healthy federal system. As former Senate majority leader and Republican presidential nominee Robert Dole put it, direct election is "commonsense federalism."[39]

Notes

1. Robert A. Dahl, *On Democracy* (New Haven: Yale University Press, 2000), 37. See also Robert A. Dahl, *Democracy and Its Critics* (New Haven: Yale University Press, 1989), 110.

2. See George C. Edwards III, *Why the Electoral College Is Bad for America* (New Haven: Yale University Press, 2004), chap. 2.

3. Darshan J. Goux and David A. Hopkins, "The Empirical Implications of Electoral College Reform," *American Politics Research* 36 (November 2008): 860–864.

4. For a discussion of the 1960 election, see Edwards, *Why the Electoral College Is Bad for America*, 48–51.

5. See, for example, Tara Ross, *Enlightened Democracy: The Case for the Electoral College* (Los Angeles: World Ahead, 2004).

6. Ross, *Enlightened Democracy*, 53; Judith A. Best, *The Choice of the People?: Debating the Electoral College* (Lanham, Md.: Rowman & Littlefield, 1996), 55; William C. Kimberling, "The Electoral College," retrieved from www.fec.gov/pdf/eleccoll.pdf; James R. Stoner Jr., "Federalism, the States, and the Electoral College," in Gary L. Gregg, ed., *Securing Democracy: Why We Have an Electoral College* (Wilmington, Del.: ISI Books, 2001), 51–52.

7. Raymond Tatalovich, "Electoral Votes and Presidential Campaign Trails, 1932–1976," *American Politics Quarterly* 7 (October 1979): 489–497; Scott C. James and Brian L. Lawson, "The Political Economy of Voting Rights Enforcement in America's Gilded Age: Electoral College Competition, Partisan Commitment, and the Federal Election Law," *American Political Science Review* 93 (March 1999): 115–131; Daron R. Shaw, "The Methods behind the Madness: Presidential Electoral College Strategies, 1988–1996," *Journal of Politics* 61 (November 1999): 893–913, Daron R. Shaw, *The Race to 270* (Chicago: University of Chicago Press, 2007).

8. Jack Rakove, "The Accidental Electors," *New York Times,* December 19, 2000, A35.

9. James Madison to George Hay, August 23, 1823. In Gaillard Hunt, ed., *The Writings of James Madison,* vol. 9 (New York: G. P. Putnam's Sons, 1900–1910), 47–55.

10. Max Farrand, ed., *The Records of the Federal Convention of 1787,* rev. ed., vol. 2 (New Haven: Yale University Press, 1966), 111.

11. Best, *Choice of the People?,* 37.

12. Ibid., 35.

13. See Robert A. Dahl, *How Democratic Is the American Constitution?* (New Haven: Yale University Press, 2001), 50–53, 84.

14. Max Farrand, ed., *The Records of the Federal Convention of 1787,* rev. ed., vol. 1 (New Haven: Yale University Press, 1966), 483.

15. Farrand, ed., *Records of the Federal Convention of 1787,* vol. 1, 447–449.

16. Farrand, ed., *Records of the Federal Convention of 1787,* vol. 2, 403.

17. Farrand, ed., *Records of the Federal Convention of 1787,* vol. 1, 447–449.

18. I have omitted Washington, D.C., from this analysis because it is limited to the number of electoral votes of the least populous state and is not overrepresented in the Electoral College.

19. U.S. Department of Agriculture, *2007 Census of Agriculture,* vol. 1, chap. 2, table 2. (This census occurs every five years.)

20. Ross, *Enlightened Democracy,* 41, 87; Michael M. Uhlman, "Creating Constitutional Majorities: The Electoral College after 2000," in Gregg, ed., *Securing Democracy,* 106; Paul A. Rahe, "Moderating the Political Impulse," in Gregg, ed., *Securing Democracy,* 63.

21. Edwards, *Why the Electoral College Is Bad for America,* 101–102.

22. The speeches are provided by the *Annenberg/Pew Archive of Presidential Campaign Discourse* (CD-ROM), 2000. The results are reported in Edwards, *Why the Electoral College Is Bad for America,* 102–103.

23. The author collected the data for 2000, 2004, and 2008. The data for 2000 are reported in Edwards, *Why the Electoral College Is Bad for America,* 103–109.

24. Stanley Kelley Jr., "The Presidential Campaign," in Paul T. David, ed., *The Presidential Election and Transition 1960–1961* (Washington, D.C.: Brookings Institution, 1961), 70–72; Daron R. Shaw, "The Effect of TV Ads and Candidate Appearances on Statewide Presidential Votes, 1988–96," *American Political Science Review* 93 (June 1999): 359–360; Edwards, *Why the Electoral College Is Bad for America,* 103–109. See also Larry M. Bartels, "Resource Allocation in a Presidential Campaign," *Journal of Politics* 47 (August 1985): 928–936; Steven J. Brams and Morton D. Davis, "The 3/2's Rule in Presidential Campaigning," *American Political Science Review* 68 (March 1974): 113–134; Claude S. Colantoni, Terrence J. Levasque, and Peter C. Ordeshook, "Campaign Resource Allocation under the Electoral College," *American Political Science Review* 69 (March 1975): 141–154; Steven J. Brams and Morton D. Davis, "Comment on 'Campaign Resource Allocations under the Electoral College,'" *American Political Science Review* 69 (March 1975): 155–156.

25. Edwards, *Why the Electoral College Is Bad for America,* 109–114.

26. "Testimony of Hon. Hubert H. Humphrey, U.S. Senator from the State of Minnesota," *The Electoral College and Direct Election: Hearings before the Committee on the Judiciary, United States Senate,* January 27, February 1, 2, 7, and 10, 1977, 95th Congress, 1st sess., 25, 35; "Testimony of Douglas Bailey," *The Electoral College and Direct Election: Hearings before the Subcommittee on the Constitution of the Committee on the Judiciary, Supplement, United States Senate,* July 20, 22, 28, and August 2, 1977, 95th Congress, 1st sess., 267, 258–273; as well as the testimony at the same hearings by Sen. Robert Dole ("Testimony of Hon. Robert Dole, U.S. Senator from the State of Kansas," *The Electoral College and Direct Election: Hearings before the Subcommittee on the Constitution of the Committee on the Judiciary, Supplement,* 30), who also stressed the campaign distortions created by the Electoral College. See also Bartels, "Resource Allocation in a Presidential Campaign"; Shaw, "The Effect of TV Ads and Candidate Appearances on Statewide Presidential Votes, 1988–96"; Shaw, *Race to 270,* chap. 4.

27. Martin Diamond, *The Electoral College and the American Idea of Democracy* (Washington, D.C.: American Enterprise Institute, 1977), 4.

28. Twentieth Century Fund, *Winner Take All* (New York: Holmes & Meier, 1978), chap. 6.

29. See Richard G. Niemi and Paul S. Herrnson, "Beyond the Butterfly: The Complexity of U.S. Ballots," *Perspectives on Politics* 1 (June 2003): 317–326.

30. Caltech/MIT Voting Technology Project, *Voting: What Is, What Could Be* (2001).

31. Remarks of President George W. Bush at signing ceremony for the Help America Vote Act of 2002, The White House, October 29, 2002.

32. Ross, *Enlightened Democracy,* 41, 87, 109, 142, 182, 187, 170, 188; Uhlman, "Creating Constitutional Majorities"; Rahe, "Moderating the Political Impulse"; Best, *Choice of the People?,* 14, 21, 23–24, 27, 36–37.

33. Voter News Service Exit Polls; Gallup News Service, "Candidate Support by Subgroup," News Release, November 6, 2000 (Based on 6-Day Average, October 31–November 5, 2000).

34. See Eric R. A. N. Smithy and Peverill Squire, "Direct Election of the President and the Power of the States," *Western Political Quarterly* 40 (March 1987): 29–44.

35. *Electoral College and Direct Election,* 40.

36. Goux and Hopkins, "The Empirical Implications of Electoral College Reform."

37. Michael Hagen, Richard Johnston, and Kathleen Hall Jamieson, "Effects of the 2000 Presidential Campaign" (paper delivered at the annual meeting of the American Political Science Association, August 29–September 1, 2002), 3.

38. Quoted in U.S. Congress, Senate, Committee on the Judiciary, *Report on Direct Popular Election of the President and Vice President of the United States,* 95th Congress, 1st sess., 1967, 124.

39. *Electoral College and Direct Election,* 39.

8 The Presidential Spectacle

Bruce Miroff

To govern successfully, presidents have always needed support from the public.
What is new in the modern presidency is how hard they work to achieve it.
As Bruce Miroff argues, the modern president "not only responds to popular
demands and passions but also actively reaches out to shape them." The president
does so in speeches and in symbol-laden events, which Miroff, borrowing from
the language of cultural anthropology, calls "spectacles." Understood properly, for
example, the highly popular war against Iraq that George H. W. Bush launched
in February 1991 resembled nothing so much as a professional wrestling match, in
which the audience (the American people) was gratified by the sight of the good
guy (President Bush) overpowering the bad guy (Iraqi leader Saddam Hussein).
In prosecuting the post-9/11 war against terrorism and the recent war against
Iraq, George W. Bush even adopted the costume of a good guy, dressing sometimes
in military garb, which previous commanders in chief almost never have done.

One of the most distinctive features of the modern presidency is its constant cultivation of popular support. The Framers of the Constitution
envisioned a president substantially insulated from the demands and passions
of the people by the long term and dignity of the office. The modern president,
in contrast, not only responds to popular demands and passions but also
actively reaches out to shape them. The possibilities opened up by modern
technology and the problems presented by the increased fragility of institutional coalitions lead presidents to turn to the public for support and strength.
If popular backing is to be maintained, however, the public must believe in the
president's leadership qualities.

Observers of presidential politics have come to recognize the centrality of
the president's relationship with the American public. George Edwards has
written of "the public presidency" and argued that the "greatest source of influence for the president is public approval."[1] Samuel Kernell has suggested that
presidential appeals for popular support now overshadow more traditional

methods of seeking influence, especially bargaining. Presidents today, Kernell argues, are "going public," and he demonstrates their propensity to cultivate popular support by recording the mounting frequency of their public addresses, public appearances, and political travel. These constitute, he claims, "the repertoire of modern leadership."[2]

This new understanding of presidential leadership can be carried further. A president's approach to, and impact on, public perceptions are not limited to overt appeals in speeches and appearances. Much of what the modern presidency does, in fact, involves the projection of images whose purpose is to shape public understanding and gain popular support. A significant—and growing—part of the presidency revolves around the enactment of leadership as a spectacle.

To examine the presidency as a spectacle is to ask not only how a president seeks to appear but also what the public sees. We are accustomed to gauging the public's responses to a president with polls that measure approval and disapproval of overall performance in office and effectiveness in managing the economy and foreign policy. Yet these evaluative categories may say more about the kind of information that politicians or academic researchers want than about the terms in which most members of a president's audience actually view the president. A public that responds mainly to presidential spectacles will not ignore the president's performance, but its understanding of that performance, as well as its sense of the overarching and intangible strengths and weaknesses of the administration, will be colored by the terms of the spectacle.

The Presidency as Spectacle

A spectacle is a kind of symbolic event, one in which particular details stand for broader and deeper meanings. What differentiates a spectacle from other kinds of symbolic events is the centrality of character and action. A spectacle presents intriguing and often dominating characters not in static poses but through actions that establish their public identities.

Spectacle implies a clear division between actors and spectators. As Daniel Dayan and Elihu Katz have noted, a spectacle possesses "a narrowness of focus, a limited set of appropriate responses, and . . . a minimal level of interaction. What there is to see is very clearly exhibited; spectacle implies a distinction between the roles of performers and audience."[3] A spectacle does not permit the audience to interrupt the action and redirect its meaning. Spectators can become absorbed in a spectacle or can find it unconvincing, but they cannot become performers. A spectacle is not designed for mass participation; it is not a democratic event.

Perhaps the most distinctive characteristic of a spectacle is that the actions that constitute it are meaningful not for what they achieve but for what they signify. Actions in a spectacle are gestures rather than means to an end. What is important is that they be understandable and impressive to the spectators. Roland Barthes illustrates this distinction between gestures and means in his classic discussion of professional wrestling as a spectacle. Barthes shows that professional wrestling is completely unlike professional boxing. Boxing is a form of competition, a contest of skill in a situation of uncertainty. What matters is the outcome, and because that is in doubt, we can wager on it. But in professional wrestling, the outcome is preordained; it would be senseless to bet on who is going to win. What matters in professional wrestling are the gestures made during the match, gestures by performers portraying distinctive characters, gestures that carry moral significance. In a typical match, an evil character threatens a good character, knocks him down on the canvas, abuses him with dirty tricks, but ultimately loses when the good character rises up to exact a just revenge.[4]

It may seem odd to approach the presidency through an analogy with boxing and wrestling—but let us pursue it for a moment. Much of what presidents do is analogous to what boxers do: they engage in contests of power and policy with other political actors, contests in which the outcomes are uncertain. But a growing amount of presidential activity is akin to pro wrestling. The contemporary presidency is presented by the White House (with the collaboration of the media) as a series of spectacles in which a larger-than-life main character and a supporting team engage in emblematic bouts with immoral or dangerous adversaries.

A number of contemporary developments converged to foster the rise of spectacle in the modern presidency. The mass media have become its principal vehicle. Focusing more of their coverage on presidents than on any other person or institution in American life, the media keep them constantly before the public and give them unmatched opportunities to display their leadership qualities. Television provides the view most amenable to spectacle; by favoring the visual and the dramatic, it promotes stories with simple plotlines over complex analyses of causes and consequences. But other media are not fundamentally different. As David Paletz and Robert Entman have shown, nearly all American journalists "define events from a short-term, anti-historical perspective; see individual or group action, not structural or other impersonal long run forces, at the root of most occurrences; and simplify and reduce stories to conventional symbols for easy assimilation by audiences."[5]

The mass media are not, to be sure, always reliable vehicles for presidential spectacles. Reporters may frame their stories in terms that undermine the meanings the White House intends to convey. Their desire for controversy can feed off presidential spectacles, but it also can destroy them. The media can contribute to spectacular failures in the presidency as well as to successful spectacles.

Spectacle has also been fostered by the president's rise to primacy in the American political system. A political order originally centered on institutions has given way, especially in the public mind, to a political order that centers on the person of the president. Theodore Lowi wrote, "Since the president has become the embodiment of government, it seems perfectly normal for millions upon millions of Americans to concentrate their hopes and fears directly and personally upon him."[6] The "personal president" that Lowi described is the object of popular expectations; those expectations, Stephen Wayne and Thomas Cronin have shown, are both excessive and contradictory.[7] The president must attempt to satisfy the public by delivering tangible benefits, such as economic growth, but these will almost never be enough. Not surprisingly, then, presidents turn to the gestures of the spectacle to satisfy their audience.

To understand the modern presidency as a form of spectacle, we must consider the presentation of presidents as spectacular characters, the role of their teams as supporting performers, and the arrangement of gestures that convey the meaning of their actions to the audience.

A contemporary president is, to borrow a phrase from Guy Debord, "the spectacular representation of a living human being."[8] An enormous amount of attention is paid to the president as a public character; every deed, quality, and even foible is regarded as fascinating and important. The American public may not learn the details of policy formulation, but they know that Gerald Ford bumps his head on helicopter door frames, that Ronald Reagan likes jellybeans, and that Bill Clinton enjoys hanging out with Hollywood celebrities. In a spectacle, a president's character possesses intrinsic as well as symbolic value; it is to be appreciated for its own sake. The spectators do not press presidents to specify what economic or social benefits they are providing; nor do they closely inquire into the truthfulness of the claims presidents make. (To the extent that they do evaluate the president in such terms, they step outside the terms of the spectacle.) The president's featured qualities are presented as benefits in themselves. Thus John Kennedy's glamour casts his whole era in a romanticized glow, and Reagan's amiability relieves the grim national mood that had developed under his predecessors.

The president's character must be not only appealing in itself but also magnified by the spectacle. The spectacle makes the president appear exceptionally decisive, tough, courageous, prescient, or prudent. Whether the president is in fact all or any of these things is obscured. What matters is that he or she is presented as having these qualities, in magnitudes far beyond what ordinary citizens can imagine themselves to possess. The president must appear confident and masterful before spectators whose very position, as onlookers, denies them the possibility of mastery.[9]

The presidential qualities most likely to be magnified will be those that contrast dramatically with the attributes that drew criticism to the previous president. Reagan, following a president perceived as weak, was featured in spectacles that highlighted his potency. The elder Bush, succeeding a president notorious for his disengagement from the workings of his own administration, was featured in spectacles of hands-on management. Clinton, supplanting a president who seemed disengaged from the economic problems of ordinary Americans, began his administration with spectacles of populist intimacy. The younger Bush, replacing a president notorious for personal indiscipline and staff disorder, presented a corporate-style White House where meetings ran on time and proper business attire was required in the Oval Office. Obama, coming after a president disparaged widely as intellectually incurious and ideologically stubborn, emphasizes his openness to dialogue and pragmatism.

Presidents are the principal figures in presidential spectacles, but they have the help of aides and advisers. The star performer is surrounded by a team. Members of the president's team can, through the supporting parts they play, enhance or detract from the spectacle's effect on the audience. For a president's team to enhance the spectacles, its members should project attractive qualities that either resemble the featured attributes of the president or make up for the president's perceived deficiencies. A team will diminish presidential spectacles if its members project qualities that underscore the president's weaknesses.

A performance team, Erving Goffman has shown, contains "a set of individuals whose intimate cooperation is required if a given projected definition of the situation is to be maintained."[10] The team can disrupt presidential spectacles in a number of ways. A member of the team can call too much attention to himself or herself, upstaging the president. This was one of the disruptive practices that made the Reagan White House eager to be rid of Secretary of State Alexander Haig. A team member can give away important secrets to the audience; Budget Director David Stockman's famous confessions about supply-side economics to a reporter for the *Atlantic* jeopardized the mystique of economic innovation that the Reagan administration had created in 1981. Worst of all, a member of the team can, perhaps inadvertently, discredit the central meanings that a presidential spectacle has been designed to establish. The revelations of Budget Director Bert Lance's questionable banking practices deflated the lofty moral tone established at the beginning of the Carter presidency.

The audience watching a presidential spectacle, the White House hopes, is as impressed by gestures as by results. Indeed, the gestures are sometimes preferable to the results. Thus, a "show" of force by the president is preferable to the death and destruction that are the results of force. The ways in which the invasion of Grenada in 1983, the bombing of Libya in 1986, and the seizing of the Panamanian dictator Manuel Noriega in 1990 were portrayed to the American public suggest an eagerness in the White House to present the image of military toughness but not the casualties from military conflict—even when they are the enemy's casualties.

Gestures overshadow results in a presidential spectacle. They also overshadow facts. But facts are not obliterated. They remain present; they are needed, in a sense, to nurture the gestures. Without real events, presidential spectacles would not be impressive; they would seem contrived, mere pseudoevents. Some of the facts that emerge in the course of an event, however, might discredit its presentation as spectacle. Therefore, a successful spectacle, such as Reagan's "liberation" of Grenada, must be more powerful than any of the facts on which it draws. Rising above contradictory or disconfirming details, the spectacle must transfigure the more pliant facts and make them carriers of its most spectacular gestures.

Presidential spectacles are seldom pure spectacles in the sense that a wrestling match can be a pure spectacle. Although they may involve a good deal of advance planning and careful calculation of gestures, they cannot be completely scripted in advance. Unexpected and unpredictable events will occur during a presidential spectacle. If the White House is fortunate and skillful, it can capitalize on some of those events by using them to enhance the spectacle. If the White House is not so lucky or talented, such events can detract from, or even undermine, the spectacle.

Also unlike wrestling or other pure spectacles, the presidential variety often has more than one audience. Its primary purpose is to construct meanings for the American public. But it also can direct messages to those whom the White House has identified as its foes or the sources of its problems. In 1981, when Reagan fired the air traffic controllers of the Professional Air Traffic Controllers Organization (PATCO) because they engaged in an illegal strike, he presented to the public the spectacle of a tough, determined president who would uphold the law and, unlike his predecessor, would not be pushed around by grasping interest groups. The spectacle also conveyed to organized labor that the White House knew how to feed popular skepticism about unions and could make things difficult for a labor movement that became too assertive.

As the PATCO firing shows, some presidential spectacles retain important policy dimensions. One could imagine a continuum on which one end represents pure policy and the other pure spectacle. Toward the policy end one would find behind-the-scenes presidential actions, including quiet bargaining over domestic policies (such as Lyndon Johnson's lining up of Republican support for civil rights legislation) and covert actions in foreign affairs (such as the Nixon administration's use of the CIA to "destabilize" a socialist regime in Chile). Toward the spectacle end would be presidential posturing at home (law and order and drugs have been handy topics) and dramatic foreign travel (from 1972 until the 1989 massacre in Tiananmen Square, China was a particular presidential favorite). Most of the president's actions are a mix of policy and spectacle.

The Triumph of Spectacle: Ronald Reagan

The Reagan presidency was a triumph of spectacle. In the realm of substantive policy, it was marked by striking failures as well as significant successes. But even the most egregious of the failures—public exposure of the disastrous covert policy of selling arms to Iran and diverting some of the profits to the Nicaraguan contras—proved to be only a temporary blow to the political fortunes of the most spectacular president in decades. With the help of two heartwarming summits with Soviet leader Mikhail Gorbachev, Reagan recovered from the Iran-contra debacle and left office near the peak of his popularity. His presidency, for the most part, floated above its flawed processes and failed policies, secure in the brilliant glow of its successful spectacles.

The basis of this success was the character of Ronald Reagan. His previous career in movies and television made him comfortable with and adept at spectacles; he moved easily from one kind to another.[11] Reagan presented to his audience a multifaceted character, funny yet powerful, ordinary yet heroic, individual yet representative. His was a character richer even than Kennedy's in mythic resonance.

Coming into office after Jimmy Carter, a president who was widely perceived as weak, Reagan as a spectacle character projected potency. His administration featured a number of spectacles in which Reagan displayed his decisiveness, forcefulness, and will to prevail. The image of masculine toughness was played up repeatedly. The American people saw a president who, even though in his seventies, rode horses and exercised vigorously, a president who liked to quote (and thereby identify himself with) movie tough guys such as Clint Eastwood and Sylvester Stallone. Yet Reagan's strength was balanced nicely by his amiability; his aggressiveness was rendered benign by his characteristic one-line quips. The warm grin took the edge off the toughness, removed any intimations of callousness or violence.

Quickly dubbed "the Great Communicator," Reagan presented his character not through eloquent rhetoric but through storytelling. As Paul Erickson has demonstrated, Reagan liked to tell tales of "stock symbolic characters," figures whose values and behavior were "heavily colored with Reagan's ideological and emotional principles."[12] Although the villains in these tales ranged from Washington bureaucrats to Marxist dictators, the heroes, whether ordinary people or inspirational figures like Knute Rockne, shared a belief in America. Examined more closely, these heroes turned out to resemble Reagan himself. Praising the heroism of Americans, Reagan, as the representative American, praised himself.

The power of Reagan's character rested not only on its intrinsic attractiveness but also on its symbolic appeal. The spectacle specialists who worked for Reagan seized on the idea of making him an emblem for the American identity. In a June 1984 memo, White House aide Richard Darman sketched a reelection strategy that revolved around the president's mythic role: "Paint RR as the personification of all that is right with or heroized by America. Leave Mondale in a position where an attack on Reagan is tantamount to an attack on America's idealized image of itself."[13] Having come into office at a time of considerable anxiety, with many Americans uncertain about the economy, their future, and the country itself, Reagan was an immensely reassuring character. He had not been marked by the shocks of recent U.S. history—and he denied that those shocks had meaning. He told Americans that the Vietnam War was noble rather than appalling, that Watergate was forgotten, that racial conflict was a thing of the distant past, and that the U.S. economy still offered the American dream to any aspiring individual. Reagan (the character) and America (the country) were presented in the spectacles of the Reagan presidency as timeless, above the decay of aging and the difficulties of history.

The Reagan team assumed special importance because Reagan ran what Lou Cannon has called "the delegated presidency."[14] As the public knew, Reagan's team members carried on most of the business of the executive branch; his own work habits were decidedly relaxed. Reagan's team did not contain many performers who reinforced the president's character, as Kennedy's youthful, energetic New Frontiersmen had. But it featured several figures whose spectacle role was to compensate for Reagan's deficiencies or to carry on his mission with a greater air of vigor than the amiable president usually conveyed.

David Stockman was the most publicized supporting player in the first months of 1981. His image in the media was formidable. *Newsweek,* for example, marveled at how "his buzz-saw intellect has helped him stage a series of bravura performances before Congress" and acclaimed him "the Reagan

Administration's boy wonder."[15] There was spectacle appeal in the sight of the nation's youngest budget director serving as the right arm of the nation's oldest chief executive. More important, Stockman's appearance as the master of budget numbers compensated for a president who was notoriously uninterested in data. Stockman faded in spectacle value after his disastrous confession in fall 1981 that budget numbers had been doctored to show the results the administration wanted.

As Reagan's longtime aide, Edwin Meese III was one of the most prominent members of the president's team. Meese's principal spectacle role was not as a White House manager but as a cop. Even before he moved from the White House to the Justice Department, Meese became the voice and the symbol of the administration's tough stance on law-and-order issues. Although the president sometimes spoke about law and order, Meese took on the issue with a vigor that his more benign boss could not convey.

The Reagan administration developed an effective balance of images in foreign affairs in the persons of Secretary of Defense Caspar Weinberger and Secretary of State George Shultz. Weinberger quickly became the administration's most visible cold war hard-liner. As the tireless spokesperson and unbudging champion of a soaring defense budget, he was a handy symbol for the Reagan military buildup. Nicholas Lemann noted that although "Weinberger's predecessor, Harold Brown, devoted himself almost completely to management, Weinberger . . . operated more and more on the theatrical side."[16] His grim, hawk-like visage was as much a reminder of the Soviet threat as the alarming, book-length reports on the Russian behemoth that his Defense Department issued every year. Yet Weinberger sometimes could seem too alarming, feeding the fears of those who worried about Reagan's war-making proclivities.

In contrast to Weinberger, Shultz was a reassuring figure. He was portrayed in the media in soothing terms: low-key, quiet, conciliatory. In form and demeanor he came across, in the words of *Time*, "as a good gray diplomat."[17] Shultz was taken to be the voice of foreign policy moderation in an administration otherwise dominated by hard-liners. Actually, Shultz had better cold war credentials than Weinberger, having been a founding member of the hard-line Committee on the Present Danger in 1976. And he was more inclined to support the use of military force than was the secretary of defense, who reflected the caution of a Pentagon gun-shy after the Vietnam experience. But Shultz's real views were less evident than his spectacle role as the gentle diplomat.

The Reagan presidency benefited not only from a spectacular main character and a useful team but also from talent and good fortune in enacting spectacle gestures. The Reagan years were sprinkled with events—the PATCO strike, the Geneva summit, the Libyan bombing, and others—whose significance lay primarily in their spectacle value. The most striking Reagan spectacle of all was the invasion of Grenada. As the archetypal presidential spectacle, Grenada deserves a close look.

Reagan ordered American forces to invade the island of Grenada in October 1983. Relations had become tense between the Reagan administration and the Marxist regime of Grenada's Maurice Bishop. When Bishop was overthrown and murdered by a clique of more militant Marxists, the Reagan administration began to consider military action. It was urged to invade by the Organization of Eastern Caribbean States, composed of Grenada's island neighbors. And it had a pretext for action in ensuring the safety of the Americans—most of them medical students—on the island. Once the decision to invade was made, U.S. troops landed in force, evacuated most of the students, and seized the island after encountering brief but unexpectedly stiff resistance. Reagan administration officials announced that, in the course of securing the island, U.S. forces had discovered large caches of military supplies and documents indicating that Cuba planned to turn Grenada into a base for the export of communist revolution and terror.

The details that eventually came to light cast doubt on the Reagan administration's claims of a threat to the American students and a buildup of "sophisticated" Cuban weaponry in Grenada. Beyond such details, there was the sheer incongruity between the importance bestowed on Grenada by the Reagan administration and the insignificance of the danger it posed. Grenada is a tiny island, with a population of 100,000, a land area of 133 square miles, and an economy whose exports totaled $19 million in 1981.[18] That U.S. troops could secure it was never in question; as Richard Gabriel has noted, "In terms of actual combat forces, the U.S. outnumbered the island's defenders approximately ten to one."[19] Grenada's importance did not derive from the military, political, and economic implications of America's actions, but from its value as a spectacle.

What was this spectacle about? Its meaning was articulated by a triumphant President Reagan: "Our days of weakness are over. Our military forces are back on their feet and standing tall."[20] Reagan, even more than the American military, came across in the media as "standing tall" in Grenada.

The spectacle actually began with the president on a weekend golfing vacation in Augusta, Georgia. His vacation was interrupted first by planning for an invasion of Grenada and then by news that the U.S. Marine barracks in Beirut had been bombed. Once the news of the Grenada landings replaced the tragedy in Beirut on the front page and television screen, the golfing angle proved to be an apt beginning for a spectacle. It was used to dramatize the ability of a relaxed and genial president to rise to a grave challenge. And it supplied the White House with an unusual backdrop to present the president in charge, with members of his team by his side. As Francis X. Clines reported in the *New York Times,*

The White House offered the public some graphic tableaux, snapped by the White House photographer over the weekend, depicting the President at the center of various conferences. He is seen in bathrobe and slippers being briefed by Mr. Shultz and Mr. McFarlane, then out on the Augusta fairway, pausing at the wheel of his golf cart as he receives another dispatch. Mr. Shultz is getting the latest word in another, holding the special security phone with a golf glove on.[21]

Pictures of the president as decision maker were particularly effective because pictures from Grenada itself were lacking; the Reagan administration had barred the American press from covering the invasion. This move outraged the press but was extremely useful to the spectacle, which would have been subverted by pictures of dead bodies or civilian casualties or by independent sources of information with which congressional critics could raise unpleasant questions.

The initial meaning of the Grenada spectacle was established by Reagan in his announcement of the invasion. The enemy was suitably evil: "a brutal group of leftist thugs." America's objectives were purely moral—to protect the lives of innocent people on the island, namely American medical students, and to restore democracy to the people of Grenada. And the actions taken were unmistakably forceful: "The United States had no choice but to act strongly and decisively."[22]

But the spectacle of Grenada soon expanded beyond this initial definition. The evacuation of the medical students provided one of those unanticipated occurrences that heighten the power of spectacle. When several of the students kissed the airport tarmac to express their relief and joy at returning to American soil, the resulting pictures on television and in the newspapers were better than anything the administration could have orchestrated. They provided the spectacle with historical as well as emotional resonance. Here was a second hostage crisis—but where Carter had been helpless to release captive Americans from Iran, Reagan had swiftly come to the rescue.

Rescue of the students quickly took second place, however, to a new theme: the claim that U.S. forces had uncovered and uprooted a hidden Soviet-Cuban base for adventurism and terrorism. In his nationally televised address, Reagan did not ignore the Iran analogy: "The nightmare of our hostages in Iran must never be repeated." But he stressed the greater drama of defeating a sinister communist plot. "Grenada, we were told, was a friendly island paradise for tourism.

Well, it wasn't. It was a Soviet-Cuban colony being readied as a major military bastion to export terror and undermine democracy. We got there just in time."[23] Grenada was turning out to be an even better spectacle for Reagan: He had rescued not only the students but the people of all the Americas as well.

As the spectacle expanded and grew more heroic, public approval increased. The president's standing in the polls went up. *Time* reported that "a post-invasion poll taken by the *Washington Post* and ABC News showed that 63% of Americans approve the way Reagan is handling the presidency, the highest level in two years, and attributed his gain largely to the Grenada intervention."[24] Congressional critics, although skeptical of many of the claims the administration made, began to stifle their doubts and chime in with endorsements in accordance with the polls. An unnamed White House aide, quoted in *Newsweek,* drew the obvious lesson: "You can scream and shout and gnash your teeth all you want, but the folks out there like it. It was done right and done with dispatch."[25]

In its final gestures, the Grenada spectacle actually commemorated itself. Reagan invited the medical students to the White House and, predictably, basked in their praise and cheers. The Pentagon contributed its symbolic share, awarding some eight thousand medals for the Grenada operation—more than the number of American troops that had set foot on the island. In actuality, Gabriel has shown, "the operation was marred by a number of military failures."[26] Yet these were obscured by the triumphant appearances of the spectacle.

That the spectacle of Grenada was more potent and would prove more lasting in its effects than any disconfirming facts was observed at the time by Anthony Lewis. Reagan "knew the facts would come out eventually," wrote Lewis. "But if that day could be postponed, it might make a great political difference. People would be left with their first impression that this was a decisive President fighting communism."[27] Grenada became for most Americans a highlight of Reagan's first term. Insignificant in military or diplomatic terms, as spectacle it was one of the most successful acts of the Reagan presidency.

A Schizoid Spectacle: George H. W. Bush

Time magazine accorded George Herbert Walker Bush a unique honor: it named him its "Men of the Year" for 1990. There were really two President Bushes, the magazine explained, a strong and visionary leader in international affairs and a directionless fumbler at home.[28] The split in Bush's presidency that *Time* highlighted was as evident in the realm of spectacle as in the realm of policy. The foreign affairs spectacle of the first Bush presidency featured a masterful leader, a powerhouse team, and thrilling gestures. The domestic spectacle featured a confused leader, a colorless team, and gestures of remarkable ineptitude. Together, they created a schizoid spectacle.

Critics could find much to fault in the substance of Bush's foreign policy, but as spectacle, his foreign policy leadership was an unalloyed triumph.[29] The main character in the Bush administration's foreign policy spectacle was experienced, confident, decisive, in charge. Bush seemed bred to foreign policy stewardship in a patrician tradition dating back to Theodore Roosevelt and Henry Stimson. He came across to the public as the master diplomat, successfully cajoling and persuading other world leaders through well-publicized telephone calls; in truth, he moved easily among international elites, obviously in his element. He was an even more triumphant spectacle character when featured in winning tableaux as commander in chief of Operation Desert Storm, which drove occupying Iraqi troops out of Kuwait in 1991.

The foreign policy team made a superb contribution to the global side of the Bush spectacle. Not since the administration of Richard Nixon had a president's skill at diplomacy been magnified so effectively by his top civilian advisers; not since World War II had a commander in chief been blessed with such popular military subordinates. James Baker, Bush's onetime Houston neighbor and longtime political manager, was both courtly and canny as secretary of state. Dick Cheney was a cool, cerebral secretary of defense, with an air of mastery reminiscent of Robert McNamara. Colin Powell, chair of the Joint Chiefs of Staff, radiated dignity and authority as the highest ranking African American in the history of the military and was almost universally admired. General Norman Schwarzkopf was the feisty commander of Desert Storm—an appealing emblem for a military finally restored to glorious health after two decades of licking its Vietnam wounds.

More than anything else, military gestures produced exciting drama in the Bush foreign affairs spectacle. Panama was the prelude to the Persian Gulf War. It featured, in Panamanian leader Manuel Noriega, a doubly immoral adversary—a drug smuggler as well as a dictator. The U.S. military operation to depose Noriega was swift and efficient, and victory was assured once the Panamanian strongman was seized and transported to the United States to face drug-trafficking charges.

The Gulf War victory dwarfed Panama, not only as a significant policy accomplishment but also as spectacle. Bush depicted Iraqi dictator Saddam Hussein as a second Hitler, a figure whose immense record of evil made Noriega look like a small-time thug. To be sure, Operation Desert Storm lacked the satisfying climax of destroying the evil adversary, but as a military display it provided Americans with numerous scenes to cheer. The indisputable favorites were Defense Department videos of laser-guided bombs homing in on Iraqi targets with pinpoint accuracy. In the cinematic terms that President Reagan had made popular, Desert Storm was not the cavalry rescue of Grenada or the capture of the pirate captain in Panama; it was high-tech epic, the return of the American Jedi.

Bush's foreign policy spectacle was successful—perhaps too successful. Once the Soviet Union crumbled and Iraq was militarily humiliated, foreign policy seemed much less relevant to most Americans. According to Walter Dean Burnham, "In 1992 foreign policy issues and public concerns about them played the smallest role in any American presidential election since 1936."[30] As Americans began to focus almost exclusively on the home front, they witnessed a domestic Bush spectacle utterly unlike the foreign affairs version.

The domestic Bush was an uncertain, awkward character, especially in the electorally decisive field of economic policy. Inheriting what he had once derided as Reagan's "voodoo economics," Bush presided over an economic crisis when the policy's magic failed. In the face of this crisis, which was evident by the second year of his administration, Bush drifted, seemingly clueless about how to restore the economy to health. The only economic prescription he ever put forward with any conviction was a cut in the capital gains tax rate that would have most directly benefited wealthy investors. Comfortable dealing with the problems that beset his fellow world leaders, Bush seemed ill at ease with the economic problems plaguing ordinary Americans.

Bush's economic team only magnified his weaknesses. His secretary of the Treasury, Nicholas Brady, and chair of the Council of Economic Advisers, Michael Boskin, were pale, dim figures who barely registered in the public's consciousness. To the extent that anyone did notice them, they seemed to epitomize inaction. A more visible economic team member was the budget director, Richard Darman. But he was portrayed in the media as arrogant and abrasive, epitomizing the antagonism between the Bush White House and Capitol Hill that resulted in domestic policy gridlock.

It was through a series of small gestures, some intended and others inadvertent, that Bush's disengagement from the economic difficulties of ordinary people was demonstrated most dramatically. Touring a grocery store, the president expressed amazement at the electronic scanners that read prices. To those who stood by every week as these scanners recorded their food purchases, here was a president unfamiliar with how families struggled to pay their grocery bills. Visiting a suburban mall in 1991, on the day after Thanksgiving (the busiest shopping day of the year), Bush brought along reporters, who publicized his purchases: athletic socks for himself, Christmas presents for his family. Bush's shopping expedition seemed designed to convey the message that Americans could lift themselves out of recession just by taking a few more trips to the mall. The most telling gesture of disengagement came early in 1992 at a campaign stop in New Hampshire, when Bush blurted out a stage cue from one of his speechwriters: "Message: I care." The message that came through instead was that the president had to be prompted to commiserate with the economic woes of the American people.

Real economic fears and pains denied Bush reelection in 1992. But the fears and pains were made worse by the ineptitude of his domestic spectacle. The president who lacked not only a credible economic plan but also credible gestures that would communicate concern and effort to restore economic health went down to a landslide defeat, with 63 percent of the electorate voting against him. The schizoid spectacle of George H. W. Bush, triumphant in its foreign policy performance, disastrous in its domestic policy performance, was over.

A Postmodern Spectacle: Bill Clinton

George H. W. Bush had two disparate spectacles; Bill Clinton had many. Clinton's was a postmodern spectacle. A postmodern spectacle, previously more familiar in popular culture than in presidential politics, features fleeting images and fractured continuity, surfaces without depths, personae rather than personalities. Characters in a postmodern spectacle succeed not by capturing the lasting admiration or trust of their audience but by artfully personifying the changing fashions that fascinate it.

Depictions of Clinton by close observers in the media tended to agree on his shape-shifting presidential performance but to differ about whether it should evoke moral indignation or neutral evaluation. One caustic Clinton watcher, *New York Times* columnist Maureen Dowd, called the president "the man of a thousand faces."[31] Other commentators preferred cool, postmodern terms such as *makeover* and *reinvention,* the same words used to describe the diva of contemporary pop culture, Madonna.[32]

Clinton's presidency had important elements of constancy, including the successful economic course he first charted in 1993 and his underlying attachment to government as a potentially positive force in society. The frequent changes of course during Clinton's two terms owed as much to the formidable political constraints he faced as to the opportunities for spectacle he seized.[33] Moreover, historical precedents for Clinton's "mongrel politics" may be found in the administrations of presidents such as Woodrow Wilson and Richard Nixon, who also were accused of opportunistic borrowing from ideological adversaries in eras when the opposition party set the reigning terms of political discourse.[34] Nonetheless, Clinton's repeated redefinitions of himself and his presidency made these predecessors seem almost static by comparison. Sometimes awkwardly, sometimes nimbly, Clinton pirouetted across the presidential stage as no one before him.

Clinton's first two years in office were largely a failure of spectacle. The promising populist intimacy he displayed in the 1992 campaign quickly gave way to a spectacle of Washington elitism: social life among the rich and famous (including an infamous $200 haircut by a Beverly Hills stylist) and politics among the entrenched and arrogant (the cozy alliance with the Democratic congressional leadership). The new president seemed simultaneously immature (the undisciplined decision delayer aided by a youthful and inexperienced White House staff) and old-fashioned (the big-government liberal with his bureaucratic scheme to reform the health care system). The crushing rebukes that Clinton suffered in 1994—the failure of his health care plan even to reach the floor of either house of Congress and the Republican takeover of both houses in the midterm elections—showed how little he had impressed his audience. Yet a postmodern irony was at work for Clinton—his defeats freed him. Not having to implement a large-scale health care plan, Clinton was able to dance away from the liberal label. Not having to tie himself to his party's congressional leadership in a bid for legislative achievement, he was able to shift his policy stances opportunely to capitalize on the excesses of the new Republican agenda.

In his first two years, Clinton lacked an important ingredient of many presidential spectacles: a dramatic foil. Bush had Manuel Noriega and Saddam Hussein, but the post–cold war world was too uninteresting to most Americans to supply foreign leaders ripe for demonization. (That would change after September 11, 2001.) The hidden blessing of the 1994 elections for Clinton was that they provided him with a domestic foil of suitably dramatic proportions: Speaker of the House Newt Gingrich. Gingrich was often compared to Clinton—and the comparison worked mostly in Clinton's favor. Shedding the taint of liberalism, Clinton pronounced himself a nonideological centrist saving the country from Gingrich's conservative extremism. Before, Clinton had talked and shown off too much in public; now, in comparison to the grandiose garrulousness of Gingrich, he seemed almost reticent—and certainly more mature. Attacked as too soft in his first two years, Clinton could turn the image of compassion into a strength by attacking a foil who proposed to reduce spending for seniors on Medicare and to place the children of welfare mothers in orphanages. Lampooned as spineless in his first two years, Clinton could display his backbone by winning the budget showdown with Gingrich and the Republicans in the winter of 1995–1996.[35]

In a postmodern spectacle, a president can try on a variety of styles without being committed to any one of them. As the 1996 election season commenced (and as Gingrich fled the spotlight after his budget defeat), Clinton executed another nimble pirouette by emulating the patron saint of modern Republicans, Ronald Reagan. Clinton's advisers had him watch Reagan videotapes to study "the Gipper's bearing, his aura of command."[36] His campaign team found a model for 1996 in the 1984 Reagan theme of "Morning in America," in which a sunny president capitalized on peace and prosperity while floating serenely above divisive issues. Like Reagan in 1984, Clinton presented himself in 1996 as the benevolent manager of economic growth, the patriotic commander in chief, and the good father devoted to family values. Unlike Reagan, he added the images of the good son protecting seniors and the good steward protecting the environment. Clinton's postmodern appropriation of Reagan imagery helped to block the Republicans from achieving their goal of a unified party government fulfilling Reagan's ideological dreams.

Clinton's postmodern spectacle shaped the public's impressions of his team. With a man of uncertain character in the White House, strong women in the cabinet drew special attention: Attorney General Janet Reno at the outset of his first term, Secretary of State Madeleine Albright at the outset of his second. But no members of Clinton's cabinet or staff played as important a supporting role in his spectacle as his wife, Hillary, and his vice president, Al Gore. Hillary Rodham Clinton appeared as an updated, postfeminist version of Eleanor Roosevelt, a principled liberal goad pressing against her husband's pragmatic instincts. Like Eleanor, she was a hero to the liberal Democratic faithful and a despised symbol of radicalism to conservative Republican foes. Al Gore's spectacle role was to be the stable and stolid sidekick to the quicksilver president. Even his much-satirized reputation as boring was reassuring when counterpoised to a president who sometimes appeared all too eager to charm and seduce his audience.

A postmodern spectacle is best crafted by postmodern spectacle specialists. When Clinton's presidential image began taking a beating, he turned for help to image makers who previously had worked for Republicans but who were as ideologically unanchored as he was. In 1993 Clinton responded to plunging poll ratings by hiring David Gergen, the White House communications chief during Reagan's first term. But the amiable Gergen was unable to reposition Clinton as a centrist nearly so effectively as Dick Morris, Clinton's image consultant after the 1994 electoral debacle. Morris had worked before for Clinton but also for conservative Republicans such as Senate majority leader Trent Lott. As a *Newsweek* story described him, Morris "was a classic mercenary—demonic, brilliant, principle-free."[37] It was Morris's insight, as much as Clinton's, that rhetoric and gesture, supported by the power of the veto, could turn a presidency seemingly moribund after 1994 into a triumphant one in 1996.

The remarkable prosperity the nation enjoyed during Clinton's second term purchased an unusual stretch of calm (some called it lethargy) for his administration—until the Monica Lewinsky storm threatened to wreck it in early 1998. Numerous Americans of all political persuasions were appalled by Clinton's sexual escapades and dishonest explanations in the Lewinsky affair. But for Clinton-haters on the right, long infuriated by the successful spectacles of a character who symbolized (for them) the 1960s culture they despised, the Lewinsky scandal produced a thrill of self-confirmation. See, they proclaimed, his soul *is* the moral wasteland we always said it was. The unwillingness of most Americans to concur with conservative Republicans that Clinton's moral failures necessitated his ouster from the presidency only made his impeachment and conviction more urgent for the right. If strong support for Clinton in the polls indicated that the public was following him down the path toward moral hollowness, then removing him became a crusade for the nation's soul, an exorcism of the moral rot jeopardizing the meaning of the Republic.

But the moralistic fulminations of the right were no match for the power of spectacle. It was not spectacle alone that saved the Clinton presidency. Clinton was protected by prosperity and by Americans' preference for his centrist policies over the conservative alternatives. He was aided, too, by the inclination of most Americans to draw a line between public rectitude and private freedom. Nonetheless, Clinton's eventual acquittal by the Senate owed much to spectacle. To be sure, his own spectacle performance in the Year of Lewinsky was hardly his best. Perhaps no role suited Clinton so little as that of repentant sinner. But he was blessed by even worse performances from his adversaries. Just as Newt Gingrich had been necessary to resuscitate Clinton from the political disaster of 1994, so was Kenneth Starr, the independent counsel in hot pursuit of the president, essential to his rescue from the personal disaster of 1998. Starr's self-righteous moralism disturbed most Americans more than Clinton's self-serving narcissism.

In the end, the shallowness of the postmodern spectacle that had characterized the Clinton presidency from the start supplied an ironic benefit in the Lewinsky scandal. Had Clinton possessed a stable, respected character, revelations of secret behavior that violated that character might have startled the public and shrunk its approval of his performance in office. His standing in the polls might have plummeted, as President Reagan's did after the disclosure that his administration was selling arms to terrorists. But because a majority of Americans had long believed, according to the polls, that Clinton was not very honest or trustworthy, his misbehavior in the Lewinsky affair came as less of a shock and was diluted quickly by frequent reminders of his administration's popular achievements and agenda. Postmodern spectacle is not about character, at least not in a traditional sense; it is about delivering what the audience desires at the moment. Personality, political talent, and a keen instinct for survival made Bill Clinton the master of postmodern spectacle.

The Souring of Spectacle: George W. Bush

George W. Bush scored the highest Gallup approval rating in history after the terrorist attacks on September 11, 2001—and the highest Gallup disapproval rating ever during his final year in office. Bush's was a spectacle that soared briefly, then soured worse than that of even his most beleaguered predecessors.[38]

Although Bush promised the novelty of "compassionate conservatism" during the campaign, his administration's original agenda mainly followed the familiar priorities of the Republican right. But Bush's conservatism ran deeper than his policy prescriptions. In its characters, its styles, and its gestures, the Bush administration was determined to reach back past the postmodern spectacle of Bill Clinton and restore the faded glories of contemporary conservatism.

One fund of recycled images and themes upon which Bush drew was the Reagan spectacle. As a presidential character, Bush enjoyed many affinities with Reagan. He presented himself as a Reagan-style nonpolitician whose optimism and bonhomie would brighten a harsh and demoralizing political environment. His principal policy prescriptions for the nation also recycled Reaganesque themes and gestures. Like Reagan, Bush rapidly pushed through Congress a massive tax cut that favored the wealthy in the guise of an economic stimulus, using "fuzzy math" to promise Americans the pleasure of prosperity without the pain of federal deficits. Like Reagan, too, Bush promoted a national missile defense system that would use cutting-edge (and still nonexistent) technology to restore the ancient dream of an innocent America invulnerable to the violent quarrels that beset the rest of the world. Even the Bush administration's most politically costly stance in its early months, presidential decisions favoring private interests over environmental protection, was couched in the Reagan-style claim of protecting the pocketbooks of ordinary citizens. Revising a Clinton rule that would have mandated higher efficiency for central air conditioners, Bush's secretary of energy, Spencer Abraham, indicated that his goal was to save low-income consumers from having to pay more to cool their homes or trailers.[39]

Recycled images and themes from his father's administration were equally evident in the early months of Bush's presidency. They were especially useful as emblems of the new president's "compassionate" side. Like his father, "W" trumpeted his conciliatory stance toward congressional opponents and set out to be an "education president." Bush's recycling of paternal gestures also was apparent in his meetings with representatives of the groups that had opposed his election most strongly. Just as the father had met with Jesse Jackson after winning the White House, the son invited the Congressional Black Caucus. Neither Bush expected to win over African American voters through these gestures. Instead, each hoped to signal to moderate whites that he was a "kinder, gentler" (George H. W. Bush) or "compassionate" (George W. Bush) conservative who exuded tolerance and goodwill.

On September 11, 2001, when al-Qaida terrorists killed thousands of Americans in a twisted spectacle of their own by piloting hijacked airliners into the World Trade Center and the Pentagon, Bush was given the chance to stage a more politically potent spectacle. The recycled conservative became the warrior president. Clumsy in his first public responses to the horror of September 11, 2001, Bush quickly hit his stride in what would be remembered as iconic moments of his presidency: his visit with rescue workers at Ground Zero in New York and his impressive speech to Congress on September 20, which struck a delicate balance between a forceful response to terrorism, a compassionate response to tragedy, and a teaching of tolerance toward followers of the Islamic faith. These moments would be further etched in the public mind during Bush's campaign for reelection. For example, in narrating the president's 9/11 heroics near the site of the tragedy, the 2004 Republican convention in New York City was skillfully designed to link Bush inextricably with Americans' determination to defeat the nation's terrorist enemies.

After the initial success of the military campaign against al-Qaida and the Taliban regime that harbored it in Afghanistan, the delicate balance in Bush's approach to September 11 gave way to a consistently martial tone. Paced by Secretary of Defense Donald Rumsfeld, the Bush administration began to feature a spectacle of muscular globalism. In his State of the Union address in January 2002, the commander in chief previewed an expansion of the war on terror to combat an "axis of evil," composed of North Korea, Iran, and especially Iraq.[40] Bush's dramatic phrase, which made headlines around the world, rhetorically invoked both the nation's Axis enemies in World War II and the Soviet "evil empire" of the cold war to amplify the peril posed by new adversaries in the Middle East and Asia. In its emphasis on eliminating the regime of Saddam Hussein in Iraq, the phrase gestured toward the spectacular completion by the son of the mission in which the father, it now seemed, had sadly fallen short. The speech began the buildup to the war against Iraq that was launched a year later, as the Bush administration mustered its political and rhetorical resources to portray Saddam's regime, with its alleged weapons of mass destruction and ties to al-Qaida, as a sinister threat to American security.

The war in Iraq was far more serious and deadly than Reagan's invasion of Grenada, and Bush's spectacle specialists were on the lookout for even more gripping gestures that would display a president "standing tall." As Elisabeth Bumiller noted in the *New York Times,* "[T]he Bush administration, going far beyond the foundations in stagecraft set by the Reagan White House, is using the powers of television and technology like never before."[41]

Copiloting an S-3B Viking onto the deck of the aircraft carrier *Abraham Lincoln* on May 1, 2003, President Bush starred in what was instantly recognized as a new classic of presidential spectacles; the press quickly dubbed it Bush's *Top Gun* affair, recalling the Tom Cruise movie. The White House used the carrier as its stage to announce that major combat operations in Iraq were over; a banner over the president's head was emblazoned, "Mission Accomplished." Every detail of the event was meticulously planned for how it would look on television and in newspaper photos. The landing of the Viking at sea highlighted the degree of risk, with the fighter jet brought to a halt by the last of the four cables that catch planes on the carrier deck. Members of the *Lincoln* crew were garbed in varied but coordinated shirt colors as they surrounded the president—reminiscent of a football halftime ceremony. At the center of this massive stage was President Bush, who played his part with evident relish. *New York Times* columnist Maureen Dowd described the moment: "He flashed that famous all-American grin as he swaggered around the deck of the aircraft carrier in his olive flight suit, ejection harness between his legs, helmet tucked under his arm, awe-struck crew crowding around."[42]

Through these gestures, Bush's spectacle specialists implanted his image as a warrior president while eliding the realities on the ground in Iraq. Adhering to the tradition of civilian control of the military, Bush's predecessors had generally eschewed military garb. But his choice of martial clothing on the *Abraham Lincoln* and at subsequent appearances with soldiers deployed to Iraq played up his oneness with the American armed forces. The tailhook landing on the carrier suggested that Bush, as copilot, was willing to share some of the risks to which his decisions as commander in chief exposed American troops. No matter how controversial the war in Iraq might be, the one aspect of it that aroused consensus among Americans was the steadfast courage of the armed forces. Amalgamating himself with the troops through warrior spectacles, Bush signified that this virtue was his, too.

Subsequent media inquiries unearthed details that called into question this signification. Viewers of Bush's dramatic flight to the *Abraham Lincoln* had witnessed what appeared to be a risky jet landing at sea. Later it was revealed by the press that the aircraft carrier was close to San Diego and could have been reached by helicopter; in fact, the ship had sailed a bit further out into the Pacific so that the California coastline would not be visible on television.[43] The president also was derided later on for the "Mission Accomplished" banner, whose sentiment turned out to be wildly premature.

Although the premises with which Bush had taken the nation to war in Iraq were soon shown to be false, his 9/11 image as America's protector against terrorists and his identification through spectacle with American troops were formidable assets when he faced the voters in 2004. At the hands of the president's campaign managers (some of whom had designed his Iraq spectacles), John Kerry, a decorated war hero in Vietnam, was re-created as a foreign-policy weakling compared with George W. Bush, who had avoided Vietnam but had become a spectacle warrior.

Yet if Bush's spectacle specialists had hoped to portray the invasion and occupation of Iraq as an adventure tale, by the time of Bush's reelection, it was beginning to turn into a horror story instead. The "bad guys" in Iraq, with their suicide bombings and beheadings, perpetrated such sickening violence that Americans began to wonder what had happened to the Bush administration's prediction that Iraqis would greet U.S. forces as liberators. Even worse for the Bush spectacle was horror on the American side. American guards at the Abu Ghraib prison abused and sexually humiliated Iraqi prisoners. Meanwhile, American troops, many left poorly protected due to insufficient armor, were subjected to grievous wounds from insurgent explosive devices in Iraq, and when they were shipped home, they were housed in shabby medical facilities. Most Americans continued to perceive the troops as virtuous, but it was increasingly difficult to find virtue in the civilian leaders who had sent them into such a hell.

September 11, 2001, was an unexpected event that allowed Bush's spectacle to soar. Hurricane Katrina in 2005 was an equally unexpected event that compounded Bush's failures in Iraq and soured his presidency for the remainder of his term. The hurricane that devastated New Orleans and the Gulf Coast was among the worst natural disasters in American history. But it was also a political disaster for the Bush presidency. Television, the tool of presidential spectacle, now savagely undermined it. Heart-wrenching pictures of hurricane victims, most of them poor and black, were powerful as well for what was absent: the federal rescue effort that could have saved many. Irate media commentators suggested that the president had abandoned his people.

President Bush's personal role in the Hurricane Katrina story contributed to that message. On vacation when the hurricane struck the Gulf Coast, Bush was urged by his top political adviser, Karl Rove, to fly over New Orleans and survey the damage. But unlike his "Mission Accomplished" landing, this was no *Top Gun* immersion in the thick of action. Photos of Bush soaring high above New Orleans in the comfort and safety of *Air Force One,* his press secretary Scott McClellan later observed, fostered "an image of a callous, unconcerned president."[44] Accompanying stories of incompetence on the part of Bush's subordinates in response to the hurricane, the pictures suggested a president who poorly comprehended what was happening either at home or abroad.

Bush's team made its own contributions to the souring of his spectacle. The hapless supporting player in the Hurricane Katrina story was Michael Brown, the lightweight head of the Federal Emergency Management Agency. Leading roles in the Iraq fiasco were played by administration heavyweights, especially Vice President Dick Cheney and Secretary of Defense Donald Rumsfeld. Both Cheney and Rumsfeld became notorious in the media for the arrogance with which they wielded power and dismissed criticism. Cheney was prone to cheery pronouncements about Iraq that had no connection to events on the ground, as when he proclaimed that the insurgency was in its "last throes" just before it reached new depths of violence. Rumsfeld was inclined to disparage discontent in the military's ranks, replying to one soldier who bemoaned the lack of armor for trucks: "You go to war with the army you have, not the army you might want. . . ."[45] Bush eventually dumped Rumsfeld, but he could not fire the vice president, whom critics compared to the grimmest authoritarian in modern film: Darth Vader.

Changes in the media also played a part in the souring of the Bush spectacle. Jeffrey Cohen has demonstrated that today's 24/7 news media, especially cable television, are not as favorable to presidential prospects as the media were in the "golden age" of network television. Presidents now receive less coverage than before, the coverage they do receive is more likely to be negative in tone, and the audience for broadcast presidential speeches has shrunk.[46] President Bush did have help from a cable network, FOX News, which tends to cheer on Republicans. On the other side of the ledger were numerous cable (and Internet) commentators who picked apart all of the Bush administration's flaws. Perhaps the deadliest blows to Bush were struck by Comedy Central's satirists of spectacle, Jon Stewart and Stephen Colbert.

By his final months in office, Bush's spectacle had become so sour that the president was nearly ignored by the media. As the extraordinary election contest between Barack Obama and John McCain took center stage in 2008, Bush seemed more spectator than performer. A small and unexpected occurrence during the president's last visit to Iraq in December 2008 encapsulated the fate of his spectacle. Infuriated by what had happened to his country after Bush invaded it, an Iraqi journalist threw both of his shoes (a gesture of extreme contempt in his culture) at the American president during a news conference. At the heyday of his spectacle, aboard the *Abraham Lincoln*, Bush had emulated Reagan in "standing tall" as a warrior. Now, he was reduced to ducking footwear hurled by someone who represented many in their scorn for him.[47]

Conclusion

It is tempting to blame the growth of spectacle on individual presidents, their calculating advisers, and compliant journalists. It is more accurate, however, to attribute the growth of spectacle to larger, structural forces: the extreme personalization of the modern presidency, the excessive expectations of the president that most Americans have, and the media coverage that fixes on presidents and treats American politics largely as a report of their adventures. Indeed, presidential spectacles can be linked to a culture of consumption in which spectacle is the predominant form that relates the few to the many. Spectacle, then, is more a structural feature of the contemporary presidency than a strategy of deception adopted by particular presidents.

Is there any escape from spectacle, with its promotion of gesture over accomplishment, its obfuscation of presidential accountability, and its encouragement of passivity on the part of ordinary citizens? As the presidency of Barack Obama begins, the prospects are ambiguous. The failures of George W. Bush have set the stage for Obama to offer appealing contrasts in the realm of spectacle. More important, Obama appears to have the potential for the most impressive spectacle since Reagan. As the first black president, he represents a fundamental break with an exclusionary racial tradition and an extraordinary affirmation of the American dream. His charisma and eloquence, so often on display during the 2008 election, have already made him a larger-than-life figure not only at home but around the world. In the enormous crowds that flock to see and hear Obama, presidential spectacle may even reach new heights.

On the other hand, Obama is the first president with a background as a community organizer. No previous president has expressed such a strong belief in grassroots politics and its axiom that change comes from the bottom up. His campaign for the White House featured innovative, web- and email-based methods to engage and activate millions of supporters, and he vows to seek input from ordinary citizens throughout his administration. The structural demands of presidential spectacle may prompt Obama to provide only lip service to these participatory values while cultivating the power that spectacle can bring when it is most successful. But if he upholds the political faith that he has professed in the past, a presidential spectacle may, for the first time, support and not supplant the democratic arts of self-government.

Notes

1. George C. Edwards III, *The Public Presidency: The Pursuit of Popular Support* (New York: St. Martin's, 1983), 1. In his more recent work Edwards documents the difficulties that presidents face when they attempt to gain public support for their policy proposals. See George C. Edwards III, *On Deaf Ears: The Limits of the Bully Pulpit* (New Haven: Yale University Press, 2003).

2. Samuel Kernell, *Going Public: New Strategies of Presidential Leadership*, 3rd ed. (Washington, D.C.: CQ Press, 1997), 106. For historical perspective on the president's relationship with the public, see Jeffrey K. Tulis, *The Rhetorical Presidency* (Princeton: Princeton University Press, 1987); Richard J. Ellis, ed., *Speaking to the People: The Rhetorical Presidency in Historical Perspective* (Amherst: University of Massachusetts Press, 1998); and Michael J. Korzi, *A Seat of Popular Leadership: The Presidency, Political Parties, and Democratic Government* (Amherst: University of Massachusetts Press, 2004).

3. Daniel Dayan and Elihu Katz, "Electronic Ceremonies: Television Performs a Royal Wedding," in *On Signs*, ed. Marshall Blonsky (Baltimore: Johns Hopkins University Press, 1985), 16.

4. Roland Barthes, *Mythologies* (New York: Hill and Wang, 1972), 15–25.

5. David L. Paletz and Robert M. Entman, *Media Power Politics* (New York: Free Press, 1981), 21.

6. Theodore J. Lowi, *The Personal President* (Ithaca, N.Y.: Cornell University Press, 1985), 96.

7. See Stephen J. Wayne, "Great Expectations: What People Want from Presidents," in *Rethinking the Presidency*, ed. Thomas E. Cronin (Boston: Little, Brown, 1982), 185–199; and Thomas E. Cronin, *The State of the Presidency*, 2nd ed. (Boston: Little, Brown, 1980), 2–25.

8. Guy Debord, *Society of the Spectacle* (Detroit: Black and Red, 1983), para. 60.

9. On the confidence of the public personality and the anxiety of his audience, see Richard Sennett, *The Fall of Public Man* (New York: Knopf, 1977).

10. Erving Goffman, *The Presentation of Self in Everyday Life* (Garden City, N.Y.: Anchor Books, 1959), 104.

11. See Michael Rogin, *Ronald Reagan, the Movie, and Other Episodes in Political Demonology* (Berkeley: University of California Press, 1987), 1–43.

12. Paul D. Erickson, *Reagan Speaks: The Making of an American Myth* (New York: New York University Press, 1985), 49, 51, 52.

13. Quoted in ibid., 100.

14. Lou Cannon, *Reagan* (New York: Putnam, 1982), 371–401.

15. "Meet David Stockman," *Newsweek*, February 16, 1981.

16. Nicholas Lemann, "The Peacetime War," *Atlantic*, October 1984, 88.

17. "Coolly Taking Charge," *Time*, September 6, 1982.

18. "From Bad to Worse for U.S. in Grenada," *U.S. News and World Report*, October 31, 1983.

19. Richard A. Gabriel, *Military Incompetence: Why the American Military Doesn't Win* (New York: Hill and Wang, 1985), 154.

20. Quoted in "Fare Well, Grenada," *Time,* December 26, 1983.
21. *New York Times,* October 26, 1983.
22. Ibid.
23. *New York Times,* October 28, 1983.
24. "Getting Back to Normal," *Time,* November 21, 1983.
25. "'We Will Not Be Intimidated,'" *Newsweek,* November 14, 1983.
26. Gabriel, *Military Incompetence,* 186.
27. Anthony Lewis, "What Was He Hiding?" *New York Times,* October 31, 1983.
28. "A Tale of Two Bushes: One Finds a Vision on the Global Stage; the Other Still Displays None at Home," *Time,* January 7, 1991.
29. See, for example, Larry Berman and Bruce W. Jentleson, "Bush and the Post–Cold War World: New Challenges for American Leadership," in *The Bush Presidency: First Appraisals,* ed. Colin Campbell and Bert A. Rockman (Chatham, N.J.: Chatham House, 1991), 93–128.
30. Walter Dean Burnham, "The Legacy of George Bush: Travails of an Understudy," in *The Election of 1992: Reports and Interpretations,* ed. Gerald M. Pomper et al. (Chatham, N.J.: Chatham House, 1993), 21.
31. Maureen Dowd, "Bubba Don't Preach," *New York Times,* February 9, 1997.
32. Howard Fineman and Bill Turque, "How He Got His Groove," *Newsweek,* September 2, 1996; and Garry Wills, "The Clinton Principle," *New York Times Magazine,* January 19, 1997.
33. See Bert A. Rockman, "Leadership Style and the Clinton Presidency," in *The Clinton Presidency: First Appraisals,* ed. Colin Campbell and Bert A. Rockman (Chatham, N.J.: Chatham House, 1996), 325–362.
34. Stephen Skowronek, *The Politics Presidents Make: Leadership from John Adams to Bill Clinton* (Cambridge: Harvard University Press, 1997), 447–464.
35. Elizabeth Drew, *Showdown: The Struggle between the Gingrich Congress and the Clinton White House* (New York: Simon and Schuster, 1996).
36. Fineman and Turque, "How He Got His Groove."
37. Evan Thomas et al., "Victory March," *Newsweek,* November 18, 1996.
38. "Bush's 69% Job Disapproval Rating Highest in Gallup History," www.gallup.com/poll, April 22, 2008.
39. Matthew L. Wald, "Bush Relaxes Clinton Rule on Central Air-Conditioners," *New York Times*, April 14, 2001.
40. Quoted in *New York Times*, January 30, 2002.
41. Elisabeth Bumiller, "Keepers of Bush Image Lift Stagecraft to New Heights," *New York Times*, May 16, 2003.
42. Maureen Dowd, *Bushworld: Enter at Your Own Risk* (New York: Putnam's, 2004), 356. For details about the carrier event, see David E. Sanger, "In Full Flight Regalia, the President Enjoys a 'Top Gun' Moment," *New York Times,* May 2, 2003.
43. Paul Krugman, "Man on Horseback," *New York Times*, May 6, 2003.
44. Scott McClellan, *What Happened? Inside the Bush White House and Washington's Culture of Deception* (New York: Public Affairs, 2008), 274.
45. Quoted in Frank Rich, *The Greatest Story Ever Sold: The Decline and Fall of Truth in Bush's America* (New York: Penguin Books, 2007), 177, 156–157.
46. Jeffrey E. Cohen, *The Presidency in the Era of 24-Hours News* (Princeton: Princeton University Press, 2008).
47. Sudarsan Raghavan and Dan Eggen, "Shoe-Throwing Mars Bush's Baghdad Trip," *Washington Post,* December 15, 2008.

9 The Presidency and the Press: The Paradox of the White House Communications War

Lawrence R. Jacobs

Most contemporary presidents face a conundrum: high expectations from the public about what they can and should do to remedy the nation's problems and a limited ability to meet those expectations in the face of often-recalcitrant members of Congress preoccupied with compiling their own records and entrenched opposition by vocal and well-organized interest groups. The standard approach presidents take to overcome this conundrum is to "go public"—that is, to appeal directly to the American people in an effort to mobilize them to pressure members of Congress to support the president. Chief executives and their advisers devote much of their time trying to shape news coverage and, increasingly, web-based discussion of their policy initiatives in the hope of crowding out congressional critics and opposing pressure groups. But, as Lawrence R. Jacobs warns, this communications assault often breeds political backlash and public doubt and suspicion. Bill Clinton's campaign to reform health care and George W. Bush's presidency offer lessons for the Barack Obama administration as it takes advantage of new web technology. In particular, the strategy of "pounding the press" and exploiting the web by launching a "communications war" often produces the paradoxical effect of amplifying the prominence of independent and critical sources in press reports and on the web. Jacobs points to the political payoffs of less adversarial and more collaborative strategies of communications through the web and the press.

Bill Clinton's victory in the 1992 presidential election, along with Democratic victories in races for Congress that put them in the majority in both the House of Representatives and the Senate, seemed to offer a remarkable opportunity to move the party's agenda after a dozen years of Republican control of the White House and, at times, the Senate. These initial hopes for unified party government quickly gave way to a series of controversies over Clinton's campaign promise to legalize gays in the military, a designer haircut that jumped off

236

the gossip pages onto the front pages as an illustration of presidential vanity and extravagance, and the near defeat of his first significant legislative proposals: the budget and a package of economic stimulus measures. The inaugural bunting was just coming down, yet Clinton's honeymoon was vaporized and his political bank account was already overdrawn.

Clinton's aides and friends traced his political problems to hostile media coverage and his team's failure (as Sen. Jay Rockefeller privately counseled Hillary Rodham Clinton) to bring journalists into a "crafted information flow" that incorporated friendly sources and supportive messages.[1] Health care reform—one of Clinton's top legislative priorities during his first two years in office—epitomized the president's political quagmire. Clinton's advisers blamed the rough going on the opposition's success in portraying reform as "more taxes and government control"; the critics outmaneuvered the White House in recruiting reporters who were "ripe for manipulation" to "serve as the vehicle for attacks." White House aides criticized the press not only for uncritically conveying the attack messages of the opposition but also for using a horse-race prism for all coverage about the president. The media either reduced Clinton's policy initiatives to his "concern about getting elected" or ignored his less controversial but significant policy proposals because "it's not confrontational [and] it's not conflict."[2] The debilitating outcome of this cycle of damaging media coverage was to fuel the public's fear that they would "pay more [and] get less."[3]

The solution, the White House decided, was to launch a "communications war," "us[ing] the power of the White House to control the message" through presidential speeches and actions that would dominate press reporting and drown out critical commentary by journalists and political opponents.[4] The key to political success, Clinton explained after his first year in office, was the president's unparalleled "access to the people through the communications network." The ability to dominate press coverage, he believed, gave any chief executive the ability to "create new political capital all the time."[5] Clinton's aides were blunter: the president and his advisers could "get away with anything provided you believe in something, you say it over and over again, and you never change."[6] Political redemption, as they saw it, lay in a "massive public communications campaign" that was aimed at the press and that "deliberately and relentlessly communicate[d]" the president's "program to the public."[7]

Although George W. Bush led the opposite political party and harbored a quite different political philosophy, he adopted a similar approach to managing public communications and the press. One reason for the similarity is that Bush had made the same diagnosis as his Democratic predecessor: the media put a higher premium on grabbing audiences and hyping disagreements than on accurate reporting. Karl Rove, the president's principal political adviser for most of his term in office, complained that the press is preoccupied with "get[ting] a headline or get[ting] a story that will make people pay attention to their magazine, newspaper, or television." "The nature of the news business," another Bush adviser explained, "is that conflict is news."[8]

To control what it saw as the media's natural inclination toward hype and conflict, the Bush White House declared a communications war of its own to rally the public and win passage of its legislative agenda. The president insisted that members of his administration "tal[k] about what we want to talk about, not what the press wants to talk about." The White House imposed a top-to-bottom process to "control your message" and to "get everyone on the same song sheet." The process began with clear instructions from the president and his senior advisers, which were relayed throughout the White House and executive departments. The result was a "funnel of information" that created a "mind meld" and, in the view of President Ronald Reagan's communications chief, Michael Deaver, "the most disciplined White House in history." From the perspective of the press, the White House had erected a "fortress" or "wall" to keep information among the insiders and out of the hands of reporters.

Barack Obama shared his predecessor's self-assurance and, indeed, began his term with even more confidence in his White House's ability to use strategic communications to protect and widen his influence on policymaking. His campaign's pioneering use of the Internet was expected by his advisers and by independent observers to equip the Obama White House with the political influence needed to enact policies that would reverse the sharpest economic downturn in a generation, as well as the direction of costly wars in Iraq and Afghanistan. Creating a "wired presidency" was—according to the Obama transition team—"our first priority" and would, in the view of a Democratic strategist, make Obama the "first president to be connected . . . directly with millions of Americans."[9] In particular, the new administration planned to introduce a transformative type of Internet governing by building on the campaign's innovative use of the web to distribute information, mobilize grassroots efforts to contact and turn out voters, and raise more money online than ever before. (During the campaign, about 3.1 million individuals donated $500 million online.) Media observers and Internet experts harbored supersized hopes that the Obama administration would "transform the way the U.S. president interacts with the citizenry" and become the "first global leader of the digital age."[10]

Although Obama's embrace of the Internet may inaugurate a qualitatively different era of presidential communications, his political calculus was the same as his two predecessors': effective political communications is the linchpin of presidential power and the operational core of modern presidential political strategy. Like Clinton and Bush, Obama focused on designing an effective apparatus to capitalize on the presidency's unique vantage point to dominate news reporting and the Internet in order to tame opposing individuals and institutions. One analysis of presidential public statements shows that the "modern president now spends much of his time trying to out-think the media" by "grabbing at persuasive opportunities [and] constructing persuasive ground rules before their opponents or the media have a chance to do so."[11] Strategic communications gives rise to a plethora of tactics for "pounding" the press and, increasingly, the web with carefully calibrated messages that are repeated endlessly by the president, administration officials, and their offices.

The three most recent presidents converged on a similar strategy because they were propelled by a common conundrum haunting all modern presidents: they are elected to satisfy the nation's expectations for peace and prosperity but operate in a constitutional system and political process that disperse power and invite political rivalry, division, and stalemate. As modern presidents struggle to loosen the institutional stranglehold on their initiatives, they zero in on the press and the Internet as decisive tools to augment their scarce political power by promoting themselves and their policies. The White House develops a "full-time rhetorical manufacturing plant" not simply to provide neutral information but also as an instrument for political advantage.[12]

Despite the persistence of presidential optimism about this strategy, public communications rarely deliver the political capital that presidents and their aides imagine. Clinton's and Bush's approaches to public communications and their subsequent disappointments present sobering lessons to the early Obama White House as it seeks to enhance its influence by capitalizing on the broad and widening use of the web.

Presidential Uses of Public Communications: From Analog to Digital

The dance of presidential aspirations and the evolving technology of communications cut a sharp path through American political development. The scope and intensity of presidential communications increased over time as strategic need converged with new technology, prompting William McKinley to seize on national newspapers at the turn of the century, Franklin Roosevelt to embrace the radio during the 1930s, and John Kennedy to welcome television into his press conferences in the early 1960s.

Presidents used their public communications to attempt to accomplish three distinct political goals. First, presidents plan their activities and speeches to increase the volume of media coverage and Internet interactions devoted to specific policy areas of their choosing. The Clinton White House had two purposes in relentlessly communicating its health care reform proposal. One was to increase coverage of the administration's proposal, and the other was to shift media attention away from more troublesome issues such as the president's abandoned campaign promise of a middle-class tax cut and the controversy over the Whitewater land deal in Arkansas. The Bush White House pinned its second-term hopes of passing historic Social Security reform on dominating the airwaves to create the perception that a crisis demanded immediate action and to minimize the costs of reform, which (they calculated) would drown out attention to incremental solutions, a sizable hike in the budget deficit, and reductions in benefits.

The Obama administration came into office intent not only on continuing to boost press coverage of topics of its choosing but also on taking the innovative step of driving web activity to focus on these topics. The administration's embrace of the Internet was propelled by its success during the 2008 campaign in distributing one billion emails to millions of voters, including the 13 million individuals who shared their email addresses with the campaign. Obama's transition team anticipated that the campaign's web capacity would "increase the size of his megaphone" and make it feasible to "reach . . . a larger audience of people who wouldn't normally pay attention to policy."[13] Some experts projected that more than 50 million Americans would sign up for Obama's White House web site within six months and thereby create the largest network in political history, a powerful political instrument for guiding public as well as personal discussions among family, friends, and workplace colleagues.[14]

The Obama administration's hope of steering public discussions toward its agenda of issues was premised on certain shifts in how the president communicates. The Obama White House sought to transform the White House web page from a static digital depository of documents and materials to an interactive engine that reaches more Americans in more intimate and meaningful ways. The White House's web site features, for instance, legislative proposals that are readily searchable, a blog, and a suggestion form. In addition, the Obama team plans to take the initiative by sending information to individuals who sign up. Indeed, nearly half of Obama's online campaign supporters indicated that they want to hear directly from the new president and other officials, with one-third expecting to receive emails and other communications. Millions of Americans expect the Obama administration to use the Internet to make them "part of the action" and to keep them in "direct contact."[15] The Obama administration also sought to capitalize on the Internet to tailor information to the particular interests and perspectives of individuals rather than sending impersonal mass communications through the media or bulk emails. Administration efforts to focus attention on health care reform might, for instance, involve sending emails to Medicare recipients tailored to their potential concerns and thereby attempt to preempt scare tactics by reform opponents.[16] In short, Obama's application of new technology may create a new "personal democracy" to efficiently deliver individualized information that focuses the attention of Americans on the administration's agenda.

The second political goal of presidential communications is to increase the media's use of administration officials and allies as news sources and to keep the opposition from making news. The president's calculus is that getting the media to select friendly sources will steer stories toward advancing the president's ideas and interests; opponents or disinterested sources, in contrast, presumably would raise hostile, unhelpful, or distracting questions. Think of Senator Rockefeller's advice to Hillary Clinton: to create an "information flow" in which journalists would rely upon President Clinton's supporters for their stories.

Obama intends to complement his predecessors' media strategy by using the Internet to elevate his own and administration officials and allies' personal presence in the public debate. In addition to negotiating for television time and maneuvering print media to convey the White House's message, Obama decided to use YouTube to speak in a direct and unfiltered manner to millions of people about subjects of his choosing. He plans to stream sections of cabinet meetings live on the Internet to create a much more visible platform for his administration's department heads. The administration is also taking advantage of the Internet—as Obama signaled during the campaign—to create "21st-century fireside chats [that] spea[k] directly to the American people on video streams . . . [to] allow me to interact with them directly."[17] It is posting on YouTube analyses of the president's economic stimulus package by administration officials as well as by carefully selected experts outside government. The Obama White House is capitalizing on new technology to leverage the unparalleled visibility of the president in an effort to unilaterally establish him and administration officials and allies as prominent and, in some cases, dominant voices in the public arena.

Third, even as they gear up for "communications wars," presidents expect the press to steer away from coverage of political strategizing in favor of reports on the substance of their initiatives. Presidents calculate (accurately) that press stories about political strategy and conflict breed cynicism among Americans, but news reports that portray presidential actions in terms of substantive policy convey seriousness and constructiveness about the nation's interests.[18] The Bush White House barely took a break after the grueling November 2004 elections before gearing up a massive public communications campaign to promote the president's second-term agenda and to focus news coverage on what it saw as the facts about Social Security's financing. Only a month after the election, the administration orchestrated what it called a "conference" to highlight its wholesome concern for the program's financial solvency. The press, of course, suspected (also accurately) that the White House's rollout of information on Social Security was part of a broader communications strategy, leading to a kind of Kabuki theater in which the administration presented an outward face of solemn devotion to fact that was devoid of strategic calculation.

Obama ran into a similar dynamic. His efforts to win quick passage of his massive economic stimulus package were portrayed by the press through a political lens of strategic machinations to out-maneuver dueling factions. For example, press reports framed the president's public expressions of sympathy with those who "might be skeptical of [his stimulus] plan" as "statements [that] are coded to appeal to budget hawks in both parties."[19] Obama countered by openly encouraging "collaboration" with congressional Democrats and Republicans and by posting on YouTube scholarly presentations by economic advisers.

The Obama White House both extended his predecessors' established communications practices and introduced profound changes in them. It continued to pursue what had become standard objectives of the modern presidency—dominating the agenda with its issues, drawing journalists to friendly sources, and steering coverage away from political maneuvering. But it also came to office with more radical intentions to use the Internet to qualitatively change strategic communications. The purpose, according to one Democratic strategist, was to make an "extraordinary reinvention of *how* the president connects with the people . . . [and] define[s] his relationship with the American people" (emphasis added).[20] Another Democratic operative speculated that "Obama could become the most powerful presidency that we have ever seen" by "communicat[ing] directly to people using the social networking and Web-based tools such as YouTube that his campaign mastered" and in the process becoming "more directly connected to millions of Americans than any president."[21] To Republicans, the model was breathtaking, representing a "real vision . . . [for] sophisticated and . . . bottom-up, open-source [communications]." Obama's dramatic departure was to spark a "resurgence of populism" and, for the first time, "put individual voters truly in charge of the information they receive."[22]

In pursuit of these three goals, the Obama administration made three qualitative breakthroughs in strategic communications: soliciting advice from and listening to Americans, mobilizing supporters to engage in specific political activities to advance the administration's agenda, and bypassing the established print and broadcast media. The old model of presidential communications was unidirectional: the president talks and the audience listens. One of the most significant changes introduced by the Obama administration was to structure its web presence to cultivate two-way exchanges and thus to "make sure that every American voice is heard," that "the American people [have] a seat at the table, and that we receive the benefit of their feedback." Google CEO and Obama adviser Eric Schmidt heralds the higher quality decisions that result when the president solicits advice, which Schmidt likens to the "open source collaboration" found in computer software development: "An open system means more voices; more voices mean more discussion, which leads to a better decision."[23]

Although reaching "better decisions" may result from Obama's new model of web-based communication, the White House's primary consideration was to develop tools of political influence. The strategic payoff of advice-seeking is engagement and its political corollary, support. "People want to be listened to . . . [even if you] don't agree with them all the time," explains an admiring Republican operative. Advice is also expected to generate a sense of efficacy or, as Obama transition officials promised, a belief that change is "fueled by your ideas and your passion." People are welcome to share views that will "help shape the future of this movement."[24] This drive for advice has taken a number of forms, ranging from soliciting suggestions about which of the nation's challenges are most pressing and, as the transition web site asked, "what worries you most about the health care system," to creating, as Obama promised during the campaign, an online "comment period" on proposed legislation. One invitation for advice prompted more than 3,600 comments from health care professionals, scholars, and consumers.[25]

Obama's second communications breakthrough was to leverage the Internet's potential to mobilize millions of individuals to organize support for the president and his policies. A survey after the 2008 election found that 62 percent of Obama voters indicated that they would encourage others to support the new administration's policies during the coming year.[26]

When communications relied entirely on the traditional print and broadcast media, the White House's mobilization strategy amounted to a kind of "Paul Revere" approach of literally calling for help, as was the case when presidents used nationally televised addresses to ask viewers to contact their members of Congress. The Obama administration broke from this model's treatment of individuals as passive receptacles to be dragged out of their slumber by barrages of requests. Instead, it embraced the web's capacity for building social networks to create a web of communication and engagement. Tellingly, Obama's networking approach was shaped by the cofounder of Facebook, who worked as a strategist for the campaign.

The core idea of Obama's networking approach is to use web communications to coalesce otherwise isolated and disconnected individuals into organized associations based on exchanging ideas, working together, and, at times, interacting face-to-face. Obama's innovation is not simply seizing the latest techie device or even compiling a massive list of email addresses. Rather, the innovation is using these new capabilities to bring together people who do not know each other and may not share much in common other than their support for Obama. One Internet expert explained that "anyone who imagines that all power is in who controls the lists misunderstands that we are no longer in the age of lists, we are in the age of networks."[27] The Obama campaign anticipated that the Internet would be a critical tool to build the "broad coalition of Americans organizing their own communities to build support for the change we need." Its postelection web network is the administration's tool to "leverage the work [of] our supporters . . . to support the policy agenda they rallied around during the campaign" in order to pressure "elected officials [who] . . . aren't going to bring change to Washington."[28]

The practical payoff of web-inspired mobilization is the ability to efficiently ignite blitzes by hundreds of individuals who show up to cheer the president or to unleash an avalanche of emails and other communications against administration foes. This capacity was used during the campaign to organize massive rallies, register millions to vote, and turn out millions of voters on Election Day through phone calls and door knocking.[29] Obama's strategists translated these campaign tactics into White House governing strategies, one transition team document explained, to "mobilize communities to place pressure on key legislators when major issues are on the table." Members of Congress who oppose an administration proposal will face, a Democratic strategist predicted, "millions of Americans . . . pounding on them, calling them, e-mailing and knocking on their district office doors." Although earlier presidents could unleash hundreds or thousands of calls and letters, as Ronald Reagan famously did during his early budget battles with Congress, Obama's supporters are convinced that "no president . . . has been that directly connected to that many millions of Americans."[30] In addition to lobbying legislators, everyday citizens also were seen as valuable emissaries to their neighbors to explain the administration's proposals.

Web-mobilization not only offers a potentially dramatic expansion of the president's leverage over uncertain neighbors and recalcitrant members of

Congress, it also makes it possible to reward supportive legislators and interest groups. The Obama White House laid plans to use its Internet networks to raise campaign funds and drive turnout for legislative supporters during the 2010 midterm elections.[31]

One of the defining powers of the modern White House—its ability and willingness to appeal over the heads of Washingtonians to rally the American people—may be going viral, exponentially expanding the scope and perhaps the influence of the public presidency. The political punch of web-harnessing millions of citizens is striking: the payoff from a trip by an administration official to a Midwestern city to stir up constituent pressure for the president's stimulus plan may pale in comparison to a million emails inundating the offices of a few stubborn members of Congress. Obama's new web approach may redefine what it means for the president to "go public," as well as the strategy's rate of return in terms of the volume of constituent "voice." Members of Congress and other influential figures in Washington may recalibrate their estimates of the political punishment that will result from defying the new web presidency, as well as the rewards of being supportive.

The third radical innovation of Obama's web communication strategy is to bypass or at least supplement the White House's previous dependence on traditional print and broadcast media. The foundation for this transition from traditional to new media has been paved by new patterns of news consumption. A November 2008 survey found that 59 percent of voters reported that they used the web during the campaign to send political email, read political blogs, or research candidates.[32] The use of the traditional media was smaller: 34 percent read a newspaper, 39 percent watched cable news, and 29 percent viewed network news. With younger Americans even more likely to rely on the Internet for news, the proportion of voters who do so will only rise over time.[33]

The Obama White House's use of the Internet to provide information and deliver news challenges the traditional press's control over political communications. Even if traditional media are reluctant to drop their scheduled programming to allow the president to deliver a national address, the Obama White House can release a 30-minute YouTube speech whenever it chooses. The posting will directly reach millions of Americans, and the traditional press will still cover it, further expanding its reach. Of greater importance, the Obama White House's use of the web to communicate directly diminishes the traditional media's gatekeeping role. President George W. Bush complained that the traditional press was a "filter" that stood between him and the general public. Obama's use of the web equips his White House to sidestep the press to speak directly to Americans about issues of his choosing in ways that he prefers.

Costs of Communications Warfare

Rival politicians and interest groups in a complex information environment make it all but impossible for presidents to dominate the news. The experiences of the Clinton and Bush presidencies offer a consistent and sober warning to the Obama White House: although the introduction of new technology offers new opportunities for the White House, opponents or even allies with perspectives of their own are unlikely to lag far behind in exploiting the Internet. The net effect of the Internet on the White House's communications strategy is unlikely to dramatically favor the Obama administration to the extent it assumed at the outset of its term. Obama will probably learn a lesson that both Clinton and Bush came to understand: White House expectations to dominate political communications, more often than not, will be frustrated.

On contentious issues that divide the political parties, presidential efforts to launch and win communications wars do increase attention to their policy initiatives but in ways that work against the president's goals. Perversely, these efforts often increase press and web attention to opposition sources and to the president's political strategy rather than to friendly sources and policy substance. The paradox is that the more the president publicly promotes controversial policies to create favorable news, the more likely is an increase in the volume of damaging press coverage and web chatter. One of the troubling consequences of the White House's excessive confidence is that it can seduce presidents into embracing policy proposals that overshoot their political support in Congress.

Presidential strategies to promote contentious policy initiatives by dominating political communications generate three paradoxical patterns. First, an escalation in presidential communications increases the volume of press reports and Internet attention to them.[34] This pattern fulfills, in part, the strategic intentions of presidents but it also opens the door to the opposition. Second, the president's decision to say more about a contentious issue in order to dominate public discussion of it paradoxically results in a notable rise in press interviews with independent voices and authoritative government opponents, as well as in critical and questioning web commentary by opponents and ambivalent supporters. Third, the president's declaration of a communications war to promote a contentious policy prompts the press to diminish its reporting on substantive policy issues and to expand its coverage of the motivations, intentions, and strategic behavior of the White House. Bloggers and organized web opponents eagerly seize on White House hypocrisy in claiming the high ground of substantive concern for the country's welfare while practicing the arts of political strategizing, including orchestrated photo ops and backroom deals with balky legislators.

In short, when the White House launches a communications war on a contested policy, it provokes just the kind of press coverage and Internet reaction that it set out to avoid—increased attention to opposition voices and to its own political maneuverings. The next section of the chapter reviews highly contentious campaigns by Clinton and Bush to illustrate the general hurdles facing the Obama administration.

Clinton's Waterloo—Health Care Reform

Bill Clinton came into office in January 1993 committed to comprehensive reform of the American health care system as one of his top legislative priorities. As a candidate, Clinton effectively articulated the public's widespread unhappiness with the existing health care system, but as president he faced a dense thicket of organized opponents and ambivalent allies. In a story familiar in American politics, the stakeholders in the status quo generated greater intensity and more organizational activity than did the supporters of reform or the potential recipients of reform's diffuse benefits.

In Sync: The White House Media Campaign and the Volume of Press Reports. President Clinton became bogged down during much of his first half-year in office in passing his budget and designing his proposal for health care reform. But by September 1993 the budget was approved and the outlines of his health reform proposal were set. The White House then switched gears and prepared an elaborate launch of the proposal that culminated with the quintessence of the media-based, promotional presidency: an electrifying, prime-time-televised speech to Congress and the nation from the House of Representatives and a deluge of public presidential statements about health care reform.[35] Carefully staged visits to congressional committees by the first lady, who had overseen the development of the president's proposal, continued the administration's choreographed trumpeting of its health reform initiative.

The White House campaign ignited counterstrategies by other political actors. The president's closest congressional allies—members of his own party—splintered into different camps and in some cases conspired against him. Democrats who were miffed at the president's version of health care reform capitalized on the media's hunger for leaks by feeding reporters a politically damaging early draft of his plan. Other Democrats battled over which committee would review the legislation and thereby share the national spotlight with the president. Some Republican members of Congress rushed forward with their own bill to prevent the White House from monopolizing press coverage. More than half of the Republican senators and House members endorsed their party's proposal, even though they had no intention of passing a health care reform bill that President Clinton would sign. In addition, interest groups—especially opponents of the president's proposal—launched their own national media campaign, including a series of television advertisements featuring "Harry and Louise," a fictional couple who offered folksy criticism.[36]

Press reporting of health issues paralleled the political and policy developments. Detailed content analysis of a dozen print and broadcast media tracked the number of lines of press coverage devoted to health care during 1993 and 1994.[37] This content analysis reveals a consistent pattern: the total monthly volume of press coverage rose and fell depending on when Clinton devoted his own time and energy to promoting reform publicly. The first of three main periods of extensive reporting occurred in September 1993, when Clinton publicly launched his plan and government officials in both political parties and interest group opponents mobilized in response. By November and December, press reports declined and bottomed out, revealing a rarely acknowledged but intrinsic flaw in presidential media campaigns: they are nearly impossible to sustain. In Clinton's case, the White House's meticulously choreographed "game plan" to relentlessly communicate the president's health plan was tripped up by unplanned delays in transmitting the administration's specific legislative proposal to Congress, by foreign policy emergencies, including an attack on American troops in Somalia, and by unrelated domestic controversies, especially the Whitewater land deal charges that followed the Clintons from Arkansas. While the president was distracted from promoting his health care proposal, his critics remained "on message" and eager to take advantage of his absence from the debate by hammering his plan and outlining their alternative plans.

The second peak in press reporting was propelled by Clinton's televised, prime-time State of the Union address in January 1994, which he used to refocus Congress and the public on moving his legislation through the committee process. His dramatic attempts to rouse Americans included theatrically flourishing the pen with which he promised to veto any legislation that fell short of universal health care coverage.

Heading the Republican opposition, Senate minority leader Robert Dole then stepped into the spotlight that Clinton had shone on health care reform. In his most direct and open challenge to Clinton's crusade, Dole downplayed the urgency of reform, insisting that there was no crisis in health care and underscoring the "Harry and Louise" ads' theme that the president's plan was bureaucratic and overly complicated. After these January fireworks, the White House's carefully scripted plans for sustaining its media onslaught faltered again as health reform was swallowed up in the byzantine world of the legislative process. Not surprisingly, press coverage declined during the spring to one of its lowest levels.

The third and final surge in press coverage of Clinton's campaign to reform health care came in the period May to August 1994, in response to the quickening pace and seriousness of the congressional lawmaking process. All the major committees met and voted. Several of them approved the major components of the Clinton proposal, but the most important committees voted down critical elements. The Senate conducted a heated floor debate but did not approve any legislation. Throughout this period, Senate majority leader George Mitchell and other congressional leaders conducted intense but ultimately futile negotiations to try to stitch together a majority for health care reform. Clinton once again escalated his public statements in an attempt to pressure Congress, but the Republicans remained steadfastly opposed, backing away from the proposal they had embraced earlier and even from minor reforms such as revising insurance rules. Several Democrats also defected from the president's corner. By the fall of 1994, press reporting on health care plummeted, with virtually no coverage of it during the 1994 midterm elections. In the end, a Congress that was controlled by the president's party never even voted on one of his top domestic priorities.

In short, the volume of press coverage of health care reform in 1993 and 1994 paralleled the cycles of debate among government officials in ways that defied the White House's well-hatched plans. Clinton's fervent public campaign to promote his ideas through press coverage succeeded at times in drawing unusual attention to the issue, as the White House had hoped. But that success opened the door for critics of Clinton's plan to grab the spotlight and undermine his message.

Sharing the Mic. The tempo and character of the policy debates on health care reform were reflected not only in the changing volume of press reports but also in the media's varying sources and frames—variations on the White House's intended themes that contradicted the administration's strategy. A principal motivation for the Clinton White House's communications war was to create an "information flow" that connected journalists with friendly sources—namely, the president, administration officials, and Democratic Party allies—who would deliver supportive messages. The White House strategy did attract significant attention to the president, but it also increased press attention to opponents of his plan and to journalists and policy experts who raised questions that undermined his message. Close analysis of press reports in 1993 and 1994 shows that the president and administration officials were the source of 14 percent of news reports on health reform, as measured by the number of lines of coverage.

Members of the Democratic Party such as Senators Rockefeller and Mitchell drew another 8 percent of the media's references. By margins of three to one and even four to one, the press cited congressional Democrats as offering supportive rather than critical comments. But the friendly sources that the White House hoped would dominate news reports were not entirely dependable: the president's partisans and subordinates were also sources of a substantial number of critical press reports, leaking damaging information to the press.

The success of the White House juggernaut in attracting press attention created an opportunity for the president's critics. The press turned to interest groups, most of which criticized the Clinton plan, in 22 percent of its coverage. Most of these interest groups represented hospitals and doctors or were advocacy groups such as AARP, the seniors' lobby. An additional 6 percent of press reports used Republican officials as sources. In the battle over whom journalists turned to for interviews and information, the White House declaration of war created a slight edge for its opponents or, at best, a draw.

In addition to the sources most prone to criticize Clinton's plan, the press also regularly used sources who were inclined to offer "nonpartisan" reactions, and these tended to raise questions and issues that distracted from or contradicted the administration's carefully crafted message. The media's search for independent arbiters of an acrimonious debate meant that 7 percent of journalists' sources were policy experts. On top of that, journalists, press commentators, and political pundits were the source in 22 percent of media coverage. The willingness of journalists to narrate or insert their own observations about the health reform debate into news coverage is part of a larger pattern of reporters' substituting their own commentary and interpretations for standard sources and the actual words of politicians.[38] In 1993 and 1994, journalists were not shy about offering their rendition of what they saw as the White House's contrivances, usually doing so in a critical tone.

The reality concerning which sources journalists turned to was far from the White House's initial strategy of cajoling reporters to use friendly sources who would convey the White House's finely tuned rhetoric through the press and ignite public support. The media's actual behavior reversed the White House's expectations: the president's communications offensive led the press to expand the range of viewpoints by giving greater attention to Republicans and interest groups. Once again, the White House's choreographed message was shot down by hostile return fire or obscured in a haze of expert or journalist commentary.

Putting Politics First. Part of the art of politics is to present policies that benefit particular groups as the actions of a beneficent and public-spirited leader who has put aside crass political calculations in the interests of the country's good. One of the core objectives of the Clinton White House was to focus reporters on the substance of its health care reform proposal rather than on its self-serving political strategizing. Once again, however, White House expectations were reversed, and plans to dominate media coverage were frustrated.

Press reporting of health care reform was analyzed closely to determine whether journalists presented, or framed, their reports in substantive terms (for example, the content of Clinton's plan) or in terms of political conflict and strategy (the horse-race prism that so bothered Clinton's aides—and many critics of the press).[39] From 1993 to 1994, press attention was divided equally between coverage framing the debate in terms of substantive issues and coverage focusing on political strategy and conflict.[40] This overall pattern, however, masks critical variations over time. During the first nine months of Clinton's term, when his health care reform plan was being designed, the media devoted greater attention to substance than to politics. In August 1993, for instance, substance was the focus of 70 percent of press reports. The White House offensive fell apart after September, however, when press reports began to be dominated by accounts of political strategy and bickering. Consider the *Washington Post*'s coverage on September 23, 1993, after Clinton made his first prime-time speech. Ruth Marcus and Ann Devroy kicked off their report by highlighting the "fundamental differences" and "grueling fight" that had already developed. In another *Washington Post* story, Spencer Rich catalogued the positions of competing interest groups.[41]

The November 1993 and January 1994 surges in the media's tendency to frame the health care reform debate in terms of dueling strategies reflected the debate's increasingly political character. Dole shifted his response to Clinton's plan from receptiveness to direct opposition, and Clinton countered the Republican and interest group attacks with a carefully crafted State of the Union address. Far from deferring to the White House preference for rich, substantive content, the press conveyed the genuine acceleration of political disagreement and maneuvering.

The third and largest spike in strategic framing began in May 1994, paralleling the culmination of the policy debates among members of Congress. The press conveyed the genuine struggle between Democratic leaders' frantic but vain efforts to build a supportive coalition and reform opponents' maneuverings to defeat those efforts.

Little in the health care reform campaign resembled the elaborate, step-by-step White House plan for presidential dominance of press coverage. The White House consistently underestimated the media's tendency to cover controversial presidential initiatives by increasing their use of critics and independent voices as sources and by focusing on political conflict and strategy.

Bush's Failed Campaign to Privatize Social Security

The George W. Bush White House declared the kind of communications war for Social Security reform that Clinton had unleashed unsuccessfully for health care reform. For Bush, reforming Social Security so that individuals could establish private investment accounts would be a landmark accomplishment, ranking—according to Karl Rove's assistant—as "one of the most significant conservative governing achievements ever." White House officials also believed that it could be a winning issue for Republican candidates, one that could attract younger and independent voters to the GOP if presented carefully.[42]

The White House's Media Strategy Opens the Door for Critics. From Bush's first presidential campaign in 2000 to the start of his second term in 2005, he and his aides pinned their hopes of enacting partial privatization of Social Security on an effective communications strategy that would saturate the airwaves with carefully crafted messages by the president and administration officials and thereby rally Americans to their side and glue together a coalition in Congress. Only days after Bush was reelected in 2004, the White House launched an election-style campaign for Social Security. "It's going to be a battle royal," one administration ally put it, "very much like an election campaign but over an issue rather than a candidate."[43]

Winning Americans over to Social Security reform by dominating press coverage required, in the White House's view, a simple and compelling presentation that would dominate news reports and communicate a consistent, focused message. This communications strategy had three steps. The first was to convey through the press a sense of urgency and induce reporters to treat the administration's proposal as a necessary reform rather than compare it unfavorably to the status quo. The primary challenge, Bush explained consistently, was to "convince people that there is a problem that needs to be addressed" and that "we can postpone action no longer." To instill this sense of urgency, the president and his spokesmen warned repeatedly of a looming "crisis," of a system that was "going bankrupt," of a "dangerous" situation in which "people pay a lifetime of high taxes for a Social Security benefit that . . . they'll never receive."[44]

The second step in the White House's communications strategy was to saturate Americans with carefully selected words while downplaying others. Bush touted Social Security reform as heralding an "ownership society" that would introduce "choice" and "control." Retirement taxes would "belong" to and be "owned" by individuals, not government. As the president stressed in his 2001 State of the Union address, "Ownership, access to wealth, and independence should not be the privilege of a few. They are the hope of every American, and we must make them the foundation of Social Security."[45]

The White House and its supporters believed that accentuating words that extolled the benefits of reform would dominate press coverage, overshadowing and challenging the costs that its opponents would flag. Republican messages on Social Security reform were tailored—at the recommendation of party pollsters—to include "constant acknowledgment of the importance of Social Security to seniors and near-seniors," while "repeatedly saying that the candidate will never support any plan that would cut Social Security benefits." Central to this disavowal of cuts was banning the phrase "Social Security privatization" because it "carries connotations of dismantling the publicly run Social Security system, or sending participants out to fend for themselves," according to a Republican communications specialist. Although the president's chief political adviser, Karl Rove, used the phrases "Social Security privatization" and "private personal retirement accounts" synonymously before polls reported their damaging effect on public support, the White House came to insist that "personal accounts are not privatization . . . [but] simply directing the government to invest some of your savings."[46]

The third step in the White House's strategy to promote Social Security reform by dominating press coverage was to organize a powerful coalition of allies to reinforce its public communications. "The idea," a Bush supporter explained, "is to coalesce the reform groups around a much larger reform plan, to build so much momentum behind it that that's what they have to adopt." The backers of the president's initiative who ponied up millions of dollars for an election-style advertising blitz included established conservative advocates such as the Club for Growth and newly formed lobbying and advocacy groups such as the Alliance for Worker Retirement Security. Conservative research groups such as the Heritage Foundation and the Cato Institute also joined in the White House's efforts. To give the campaign a populist look, the president's presentations often included testimonials from "regular folks," carefully recruited by allies.[47]

Heading into 2005, the White House was confident that its public communications strategy combined with the president's reelection would produce a reform of Social Security that established personal retirement accounts. Although the enormous public support for Social Security had previously earned it a reputation as the "third rail" of American politics, a White House ally declared that "the third rail is dead" and even Democrats conceded that "George Bush touched what was supposed to be the 'third rail' and wasn't electrocuted."[48]

But the vigorous communications war launched by the White House and its allies also ignited critical reactions from Republicans, Democrats, and interest groups, which increased press coverage of the challenges to the president and his messages. Bush's closest Capitol Hill allies—Republican members of Congress—splintered into different and at times warring camps, prompting one House Republican strategist to declare in fall 2004 that passage of reform would be a "very difficult goal to achieve." One "deep split" within the Republican Party concerned the size of the private accounts, with some advocating a maximalist approach that would allow workers to redirect about two-thirds of the payroll taxes that they pay. Others wanted to take a more cautious approach, redirecting one-third or less. Other Republicans did not share the White House's political confidence. Former House Speaker Newt Gingrich warned that Bush's effort to reform Social Security was "political suicide."[49]

Republican doubts were amplified by the ferocious criticism from Democrats and their allies in organized labor and among powerful organizations of seniors, notably AARP. These organizations' antireform effort gelled in a coalition of one hundred organizations dubbed the New Century Alliance for Social Security.[50]

As with Clinton's efforts on health reform, Bush's promotion of his Social Security reform initiative had a paradoxical effect: its success in increasing the volume of press coverage also generated a crescendo of criticism that the press dutifully reported. The nature of the press coverage is illustrated by a *New York Times* article. The headline pleased the White House by conveying one of the president's principal messages: "Bush Says Social Security Plan Would Reassure Markets." Eleven of the article's paragraphs explained the arguments in favor of partial privatization, often quoting the president directly. But the article balanced its coverage of the White House's case by devoting twelve paragraphs to criticisms of the president's approach.[51]

One of the main antireform messages the media reported was that the need for change in Social Security was modest rather than urgent. After the 2004 elections, one critic charged that the "whole idea that Social Security needs to be fixed is false." Democratic presidential candidate John Kerry's spokesman warned that the "administration's blitz on Social Security is eerily reminiscent of the way they made their case for war."[52]

Critics also stepped into the media spotlight to highlight the costs of reform, which Bush had downplayed consistently. Congressional Democratic leaders "welcome[d] a debate" to "expose" the financial costs and benefit cuts that reform would bring. AARP's chief took to the airwaves to emphasize that the president's "new system could require as much as $2 trillion or more in benefit cuts, new taxes, or more debt." Under growing press scrutiny, Republicans acknowledged to reporters that "[a]nyone that tells you there is a painless way to fix Social Security simply isn't telling the whole truth." By 2005, when Bush launched his campaign, the candor of congressional Republicans and the criticism of opponents forced the administration to concede the costs of reform. The opening sentence in a *Washington Post* story announced that the administration would "cu[t] promised benefits by nearly a third in the coming decades," and the *New York Times* ran a leaked email from Karl Rove's top aide acknowledging that benefit cuts were necessary.[53]

Dueling Messengers. While the White House constructed its communications strategy for channeling the press toward sympathetic sources, press coverage ended up expanding attention to opponents of Social Security reform and to journalists and policy experts who raised questions about it, with the result that the surge in press coverage of the president's message was offset significantly by reporting that challenged or undermined it. Journalists repeatedly turned for comment to Democrats, who persistently warned that taxpayers and Social Security beneficiaries would be "left high and dry" by partial privatization.[54] Reporters also ferreted out information from nonpartisan experts in the Government Accountability Office, the Congressional Budget Office, and even the International Monetary Fund, all of whom challenged the administration's case for reform.[55]

Journalists and editors were also eager to share the klieg lights that the White House's communications war had turned on. Editorialists and commentators ran essays with headlines such as "The Social Security Fear Factor," "Reckonings: Fabricating a Crisis," "A Biased Social Security Report," and "The Social Security Shell Game."[56]

Raw Politics. President Bush and his leading advisers understood the media's tendency to focus on political strategy and conflict and designed the launch of their Social Security plan to highlight its substance and thus build public confidence that they were promoting the national interest. But the White House's plans not only failed to conceal the genuine divisions among Republicans, Democrats, and their allies, but also fed media suspicions about the administration's motives. The strategies and counterstrategies of the proponents of partial privatization and their rivals led one advocate to worry that "both sides are priming the public to be against anything that is real reform" because "they have done a good job making the debate . . . more partisan, more contentious and less beneficial to the public."[57]

Press accounts highlighted the partisan divide, informing their audiences that "[m]ost Republicans in Congress support the idea of private accounts . . . [and]

[m]ost Democrats oppose private accounts." One of a series of *New York Times* stories on the dueling political strategies was headlined, "Two Sides Rally to Shape Social Security Discussion." It catalogued the "maneuvering" and high "political stakes" surrounding Bush's initiative. Seeking to capture the political battlefield, press reports described critics of the administration's plan as eager to "portray Mr. Bush as a lackey of moneyed special interests" while administration supporters armed for combat were convinced that "you can't just hold back and let the other guys shoot."[58] Commentators seized on the political dueling to spin their own scenarios, with liberal *New York Times* columnist Paul Krugman warning of "the administration's political strategy . . . to sell private accounts with false advertising"[59] and the *Washington Post* editorial page calling for "political bravery" in the face of the ferocious battle to "talk calmly about Social Security."[60]

In short, as in Clinton's health care reform effort, a persistent pattern emerged: well-laid White House plans produced the very outcomes the administration sought to avoid. Presidential promotions increased coverage not just of the administration's approach but also of the criticisms of opponents and of each side's dueling strategies, inevitably feeding public cynicism about politics and reform.

Obama's Trojan Horse

Clinton's and Bush's approaches to public communications and their subsequent disappointments present sobering lessons concerning Obama's early hopes to enhance his influence by capitalizing on the public's broad and widening use of the web. For all their hopes, the Obama White House's use of the web and the traditional media may create a kind of Trojan horse effect: its efforts to capitalize on the Internet may unleash three politically damaging and unpredictable dynamics that will reverse or frustrate its efforts to set the public agenda, frame policy issues, and mobilize its supporters.

First, action breeds reaction. Obama's success is motivating a furious drive by Republicans and their allies to emulate the Democrat's use of the Internet for political benefit. Conservative blogs and political networking efforts increasingly accept that "online organizing is by far the most efficient way to transform our party structures to be able to compete."[61]

Second, short-term success can sow the seeds of future failure. Success by the Obama White House in mobilizing pressure on members of Congress may generate resentment that diminishes the White House's long-term influence by alienating moderate Republicans and irritating fence-sitting Democrats, who often provide the key swing votes in building legislative majorities. Drawing on his own experience, Rove warned the Obama administration that "strong-arming irritates allies, infuriates fence sitters and enrages opponents in Congress." Although Democrats may reflexively dismiss Rove's advice, it does strike at the reality that the White House's relations with legislators are ongoing and not simply a one-shot affair. Using the Internet to pressure legislators on one bill may make them "livid" (as Rove put it) and complicate future efforts to build supportive coalitions on other issues that Congress handles.[62]

The third and perhaps most daunting challenge facing the Obama administration is the tumult and confusion its use of the Internet will stir up publicly among Obama's allies. The Internet's power—open and free-flowing dialogue and networking—introduces a host of political headaches. One problem is that Obama's supporters (not to mention Republicans and other rivals) can use the web to organize opposition to his actions. For example, the backlash against the transition team's selection of conservative evangelist Rick Warren to give the inauguration's opening prayer blossomed on Obama's own web site. One Democratic web strategist warned the Obama team that "people who have helped you . . . can also organize in opposition to your policies."[63] The Internet both empowers presidential communication and facilitates presidential criticism. It not only widens Obama's communication potential but also enhances and indeed even creates "rallying point[s] for critics."[64]

The Internet's enormous capabilities and its fostering of a sense of connection to the Obama White House may also generate unrealistic or unattainable expectations of what the president chooses to accomplish. Obama's strategy of welcoming advice from the grassroots may lead to a sense of unresponsiveness if administration policy does not follow the proposed direction. "Listening to grass-roots supporters is easy," explained a political strategist, "[but] [m]aking them feel heard is the challenge."[65]

In short, the enormous new capabilities for presidential communications introduced by the Internet create a double-edged sword that both enhances the scope and control of the White House message and invites broad dissent. There may well be a contradiction in Obama's web presidency—the power of the bully pulpit lies in the one-way flow of information from the president to his audience whereas the Internet is fundamentally interactive and based on two-way exchanges.

Collaborative Presidential Leadership

Presidents and their advisers enter the White House as political victors. To get elected, they have overcome stiff competition and long odds. Once ensconced in the West Wing, they quickly come to appreciate that institutional and political constraints on governing make it difficult to fulfill all of their campaign promises. The blend of supreme confidence and inadequate political resources both motivates the White House to try to expand the president's support and convinces it that administration officials possess the skills and temperament needed to win any communications war they decide to wage.

In reality, however, concerted efforts by presidents to dominate press coverage and portray themselves and their policies in a good light are unlikely to produce the results they anticipate. Such efforts are more likely to generate press coverage and Internet exchanges that dwell on the inevitable disagreements that emerge among the president, his allies, and his opponents. Both Bush's drive for partial privatization of Social Security and Clinton's crusade for health care reform generated press reports that were preoccupied with political conflict and strategy. The Obama administration may find itself pinned down by an unexpected backlash against its bold new communications strategy.

The exaggerated confidence that presidents and their advisers have in their ability to define political communications routinely produces two surprises for them. First, their fixation on the potential benefits of media warfare distorts and overtakes their evaluation of the cost of this style of leadership—namely, significant public attention to the views of critics and to the unattractive business of strategizing.[66] Presidents who choose to become communications warriors invariably inflict political damage on themselves.

Second, presidential schemes to dominate press coverage of divisive domestic policies often result in wasted opportunities and political deadlock. White House hubris in its ability to control information encourages the executive to embrace policy initiatives that reach well beyond what the public and legislators are willing to accept. Unquestioned faith in spin control was one of the reasons the Clinton and Bush White Houses produced legislative initiatives on health care and Social Security that far outstretched their support among the public and Congress, resulting in humiliating defeats and squandered opportunities to make progress on critical policy challenges.

Although the political power of presidential communications is more modest and conditional than the White House and political observers appreciate, the president and the country can benefit from presidential public appeals that are less confrontational. For the president, public leadership through the press is a tool for setting the policy agenda by directing attention to his priorities. For the country, public presidential leadership expands the volume of information distributed to the people and broadens the range of voices and viewpoints that they hear. This in turn increases the probability that Americans will be able to identify policy advocates and their interests, understand the costs and benefits of proposed policy changes (and how these are distributed), and, because of the increased scrutiny of public claims, evaluate the reliability of information. Presidential leadership draws into the light of day the policy debates that are normally cloistered in government offices and congressional committees.

The implication of the paradox of presidential communications wars— namely, that they generate public attention to critics and to political conflict and strategy—is not that presidents should abandon the bully pulpit. Instead, they should reconsider one particular leadership style—communications warfare—in favor of another—institutionally based cooperative leadership. Cooperative leadership rests on a philosophy of shared governance, common institutional interests, and a focus on issues already of interest to other government officials. Cooperative presidential leadership means sharing the national spotlight, rather than scheming to smother critics and their viewpoints, and using this common platform to accommodate competing perspectives in a spirit of compromise. Cooperative leadership by presidents increases the volume of press coverage and web dialogues, broadens the range of its sources, and encourages public attention to substantive issues. Presidents who fully appreciate the constraints and costs of communications warfare will place a greater premium on the modest (but realistic) benefits of cooperative leadership.

Notes

1. Memo to first lady from Sen. Jay Rockefeller, May 26, 1993, regarding "Health Care Reform Communications," confidential.

2. Interviews with Clinton administration officials by Lawrence R. Jacobs (LRJ), June 28, 1994, August 2, 1994, August 31, 1994, December 6, 1994, December 8, 1994, and June 19, 1995.

3. "A Winning Strategy for Health Care Reform" for first lady by Ira Magaziner, Jeff Eller, and Bob Boorstin, July 1993; memo to first lady from Michael Lux, regarding "positioning ourselves on health care," May 3, 1993.

4. Memo from Lux to the president, December 15, 1993.

5. Sidney Blumenthal, "The Education of a President," New Yorker, January 24, 1994, 31–43; interview with Clinton administration officials by LRJ, August 1, 1994, and July 17, 1995.

6. Interview with Clinton administration officials by LRJ, June 28, 1994, August 2, 1994, and December 6, 1994.

7. Interview with Clinton administration officials by LRJ, December 6, 1994, and December 8, 1994; report by Magaziner, "Preliminary Work Plan for the Interagency Health Care Taskforce," January 26, 1993; memo to first lady from Magaziner, May 3, 1993, regarding "what is ahead and how to organize for it"; memo to distribution from Jennings and Ricchetti, April 14, 1993, regarding "congressional update and strategy for health care reform"; memo to first lady from Boorstin and Lois Quam, February 6, 1993, regarding health care communications 100-day strategy.

8. Unless otherwise noted, the quotations and material relating to the Bush White House's relations with the media are drawn from Ken Auletta, "Fortress Bush: How the White House Keeps the Press Under Control," *New Yorker,* January 19, 2004, 53–65.

9. Joe Trippi, quoted in Sheryl Gay Stolberg, "A Rewired Bully Pulpit," *New York Times,* November 23, 2008; Martha T. Moore, "Volunteers for Obama Plan to Keep in Touch," *USA Today,* November 21, 2008.

10. Richard S. Dunham, Dwight Silverman, and Kyle Pendergast, "Obama's Preferred Address Begins with http, Not 1600," *Houston Chronicle,* November 9, 2008.

11. Roderick Hart, "Some Footnotes on the Role of Public Communication in Incumbent Politics," in *Communications Yearbook,* ed. Margaret McClaughlin (Beverly Hills: Sage, 1987), 143, 120.

12. William Bennett and Robert Entman, "Mediated Politics: An Introduction," in *Mediated Politics: Communication in the Future of Democracy,* ed. William Bennett and Robert Entman (New York: Cambridge University Press, 2001); Timothy Cook, "The Future of the Institutional Media," in *Mediated Politics,* ed. Bennett and Entman; Timothy Cook, *Governing with the News: The News Media as a Political Institution* (Chicago: University of Chicago Press, 1998); and Samuel Kernell, *Going Public: New Strategies of Presidential Leadership,* 3rd ed. (Washington, D.C.: CQ Press, 1997).

13. Jen Psaki, quoted in Stolberg, "A Rewired Bully Pulpit."

14. Dunham, Silverman, and Pendergast, "Obama's Preferred Address"; Omar Wasow, quoted in Frank Davies, "Obama Ready to Embrace Internet as Tool for Persuasion and Participation," *San Jose Mercury News,* November 14, 2008.

15. The Pew Research Center for People and the Press survey interviewed 2,254 adults about their Internet use and was conducted from November 20 to December 4, www.pewinternet.org/PPF/r/271/report_display.asp.

16. Philip Elliott, "Obama Online Supporters Key to Pushing His Agenda," Associated Press, December 30, 2008; Frank Davies, "Obama Team Shifts from Online Campaigning to More Accessible Government," *San Jose Mercury News,* December 12, 2008.

17. Davies, "Obama Ready to Embrace Internet."

18. Cappella and Jamieson present evidence that press reporting on political strategy and conflict corresponds with increased cynicism among Americans. Joseph N. Cappella and Kathleen H. Jamieson, *Spiral of Cynicism: The Press and the Public Good* (New York: Oxford University Press, 1997).

19. Jennifer Loven, "Obama Warns of Dire Consequences without Stimulus," Associated Press, January 8, 2009.

20. Simon Rosenberg, quoted in Dunham, Silverman, and Pendergast, "Obama's Preferred Address."

21. Joe Trippi, quoted in Chris Cillizza, "Obama Makes a Point of Speaking of the People, to the People," *Washington Post,* December 14, 2008.

22. David Ho, "Obama White House to Embrace New Web Tools and Reach," *Cox News Service,* November 26, 2008; Davies, "Obama Ready to Embrace Internet."

23. Daniel Lyons and Daniel Stone, "President 2.0," *Newsweek,* December 1, 2008.

24. Stolberg, "A Rewired Bully Pulpit"; Davies, "Obama Team Shifts"; Davies, "Obama Ready to Embrace Internet"; Christina Bellantoni, "Obama Site a Haven for Fans, Critics," *Washington Times,* December 27, 2008.

25. Peter Overby, "The Fate of Obama's Net Roots Network," NPR "All Things Considered," December 2, 2008.

26. Pew Research Center for People and the Press survey.

27. Micah Sifry, quoted in Peter Overby, "The Fate of Obama's Net Roots Network."

28. Ben LaBolt, quoted in Paul West, "Obama Keeps the Machine Humming," *Baltimore Sun,* November 23, 2008.

29. Shailagh Murray and Matthew Mosk, "Under Obama, Web Would Be the Way," *Washington Post,* November 10, 2008.

30. Joe Trippi, quoted in David Ho, "Obama White House to Embrace New Web Tools and Reach."

31. Murray and Mosk, "Under Obama, Web Would Be the Way."

32. Pew Research Center for People and the Press survey.

33. Ibid.

34. Herbert Gans, *Deciding What's News* (New York: Random House, 1979); Lance Bennett, "Toward a Theory of Press-State Relations in the United States," *Journal of Communication* 40 (Spring): 103–125; Timothy Cook, *Making Laws and Making News: Media Strategies in the U.S. House of Representatives* (Washington, D.C.: Brookings Institution, 1989); Leon Sigal, *Reporters and Officials* (Lexington, Mass.: D. C. Heath, 1973); and Gaye Tuchman, *Making News* (New York: Free Press, 1978).

35. Jacobs and Shapiro, *Politicians Don't Pander,* 112–114, 173.

36. Lawrence R. Jacobs, "Manipulators and Manipulation: Public Opinion in a Representative Democracy," *Journal of Health Politics, Policy and Law* 26 (December 2001): 1361–1374.

37. The analysis of press coverage of health care draws on data collected for my book with Bob Shapiro, *Politicians Don't Pander,* chaps. 5 and 6. See this book for more details on coding and research design.

38. Joseph Cappella and Kathleen Hall Jamieson, *Spiral of Cynicism* (New York: Oxford University Press, 1997); Kathleen Hall Jamieson, *Dirty Politics* (New York: Oxford University Press, 1992); Thomas E. Patterson, *Out of Order* (New York: Knopf, 1994); and Catherine Steele and Kevin Barnhurst, "The Journalism of Opinion: Network News Coverage of U.S. Presidential Campaigns, 1968–1988," *Critical Studies in Mass Communications* 13 (September 1996): 187–209.

39. For instance, a news account of Clinton's health care reform campaign that focused on the president's calculation that passing his plan would boost the Democratic Party's prospects in the 1994 election represents a strategic frame, while a news report on the content of the president's plan or on national health care expenditures on hospital and physician services and their rate of increase over the past decade represents a substantive frame.

40. The use of a particular frame is presented as a proportion of the total number of lines the press devoted to reporting on health care issues each month. This proportional measure controls for the overall upsurges in coverage that periodically catapulted health care into the spotlight; it makes it possible to detect changes in coverage over time that were independent of the rising volume of reports on either issue.

41. Ruth Marcus and Ann Devroy, "Clinton Stamps 'Urgent Priority' on Health Plan," *Washington Post,* September 23, 1993; Spencer Rich, "Who Stands Where on Health Care," *Washington Post,* September 23, 1993.

42. Quoted in Richard Stevenson, "GOP Divide as Bush Views Social Security," *New York Times,* January 6, 2005; Edwin Chen, "Now Directing Attention to Revamping Social Security," *Los Angeles Times,* November 30, 2003.

43. David Morgan, "Bush Plans a Media Blitz on Social Security," Reuters, December 22, 2004; Richard Stevenson, "Bush Says Social Security Plan Would Reassure Markets," *New York Times,* December 17, 2004.

44. John Havemann, "Some Find Strong Pulse in Social Security," *Los Angeles Times,* December 12, 2004; Stevenson, "Bush Says Social Security Plan Would Reassure Markets";

Richard Stevenson, "Social Security Panel Faces Challenges," *New York Times,* May 3, 2001.

45. Edmund Andrews, "Most G.O.P. Plans to Remake Social Security Involve Deep Cuts to Tomorrow's Retirees," *New York Times,* December 14, 2004; President Bush's speech to a joint session of Congress, *Washington Post,* February 28, 2001; Mike Allen and Amy Goldstein, "Bush to Tout 'Retirement Security' Proposals," *Washington Post,* February 28, 2002; Jonathan Weisman, "'In Politics, Words Matter,' Social Security Memo Says," *Washington Post,* September 13, 2002; Mike Allen and Juliet Eilperin, "Wary Words on Social Security, GOP Shunning Use of 'Privatization,'" *Washington Post,* May 11, 2002.

46. Morgan, "Bush Plans"; Allen and Eilperin, "Wary Words on Social Security"; Weisman, "In Politics, Words Matter."

47. Leigh Strope, "Bush Soc. Sec. Plan to Allow Tax Diversion," Associated Press, January 4, 2005; Morgan, "Bush Plans"; Edmund Andrews, "Clamor Grows in the Privatization Debate," *New York Times,* December 17, 2004; Edmund Andrews, "Bush Puts Social Security at Top of Economic Conference," *New York Times,* December 16, 2004; Jonathan Weisman, "Bush Faces Pressure on Social Security," *Washington Post,* December 28, 2003.

48. Janet Hook, "GOP Divided over Pushing Reform of Social Security," *Los Angeles Times,* December 7, 2003; Susan Page, "Social Security Debate May Be Ready to Reignite," *USA Today,* December 3, 2002; Leigh Strope, "Election Shifts Social Security Impetus," *Boston Globe,* November 9, 2002; Dan Balz, "Bush Lays Out Ambitious Plan for Long Term," *Washington Post,* May 6, 2001.

49. Ramesh Ponnuru, "The Case against Benefit Cuts," *National Review Online,* January 7, 2005; Morgan, "Bush Plans"; Andrews, "Bush Puts Social Security"; Robin Toner and David Rosenbaum, "Social Security Poses Hurdles for President," *New York Times,* September 18, 2004; Stevenson, "GOP Divide"; Jim VandeHei and Juliet Eilperin, "Bush's Plan for Social Security Loses Favor," *Washington Post,* August 13, 2002; Hook, "GOP Divided."

50. Andrews, "Bush Puts Social Security" and "Clamor Grows."

51. Stevenson, "Bush Says Social Security Plan Would Reassure Markets."

52. Ibid.; Morgan, "Bush Plans."

53. Jonathan Weisman and Mike Allen, "Social Security Formula Weighed, Bush Plan Likely to Cut Initial Benefits," *Washington Post,* January 4, 2005; and Richard Stevenson, "GOP Divide as Bush Views Social Security," *New York Times,* January 6, 2005.

54. Stevenson, "Bush Says Social Security Plan Would Reassure Markets"; Janet Yellen, "The Binge Mentality in the Federal Budget," *New York Times,* July 22, 2002.

55. Andrews, "GOP Plans to Remake Social Security."

56. *New York Times* editorials, January 3, 2005, July 27, 2001; Paul Krugman, *New York Times,* August 21, 2001; *Washington Post,* editorial, December 2, 2002; Bob Kerrey and Warren Rudman, "Social Security Shell Game," *Washington Post,* August 12, 2002.

57. Weisman, "GOP Disavows Social Security 'Privatization.'" *Washington Post,* September, 13, 2002.

58. Richard Stevenson, "Two Sides Rally to Shape Social Security Discussion," *New York Times,* June 18, 2001, and "House Social Security Bill Shows Trade-Offs for Bush," *New York Times,* July 29, 2001.

59. Paul Krugman, "Fear of All Sums," *New York Times,* June 21, 2002; Krugman, "Nothing for Something," *New York Times,* August 8, 2001.

60. Editorial, "A Chance for Discussion," *Washington Post,* December 2, 2002.

61. Murray and Mosk, "Under Obama, Web Would Be the Way."

62. Karl Rove, "Now Obama Has to Govern," *Wall Street Journal,* November, 20, 2008.

63. Peter Daou, quoted in Murray and Mosk, "Under Obama, Web Would Be the Way."

64. Peter Daou, quoted in Bellantoni, "Obama Site a Haven for Fans, Critics"; Philip Elliott, "Obama Seeks Peace Between New, Traditional Backers," Associated Press, December 9, 2008.

65. Liz Morningstar (aide to Governor Deval Patrick of Massachusetts), quoted in Scott Helman, "Obama Backers Look for Ways to Carry Out the Call for Change," *Boston Globe,* December 9, 2008.

66. Research on presidential influence on press reporting repeatedly points to constraints imposed by outside events, as well as to alternative interpretations by other elites and the media's framing of those outside developments and alternative interpretations. George Edwards and B. Dan Wood, "Who Influences Whom? The President, Congress, and the Media," *American Political Science Review* 93 (1999): 327–344; Richard Nadeau, Richard Niemi, David Fan, and Timothy Amato, "Elite Economic Forecasts, Economic News, Mass Economic Judgments, and Presidential Approval," *Journal of Politics* 61 (1999): 597–611.

10 The Presidency and Interest Groups: Allies, Adversaries, and Policy Leadership

Daniel J. Tichenor

Images of presidents are prominent in American iconography—think of memorials, such as the Washington Monument and Mount Rushmore, or of the faces of presidents on coins and currency. Interest groups inhabit a less-favored place in American popular culture. Political candidates brand each other, not themselves, as "tools" of the "special interests." Yet because interest groups have political resources that presidents need if they are to govern successfully in the domain of domestic policy, no president can avoid developing relationships with many of these groups. As Daniel J. Tichenor uses historical evidence to show, one key variable affecting president–interest group relations is whether organized interests are affiliated or unaffiliated with the president's political party. The other is whether historical circumstances have granted the president a broad or a narrow capacity to exercise policy leadership. The four possible combinations of answers to these two questions range from the highly productive "collaborative breakthrough politics" to the stagnant "adversarial politics-as-usual."

From the earliest days of his run for the presidency, Barack Obama condemned special interests and highly paid lobbyists for turning the national government "into a game only they can afford to play," one that was rigged to favor their narrow agendas over the collective good. "In a democracy, the price of access and influence should be nothing more than your voice and your vote," Obama told supporters while endorsing ethics reform and vowing that special interests "will not run my White House."[1] These appeals were hardly novel: Presidential candidates routinely get good political mileage from telling appreciative crowds that the interests of ordinary citizens must be defended against the welter of Washington lobbying groups that bedevil good government.[2]

Yet if electoral assaults on special interests are nothing new, Obama seized upon this theme with unusual frequency in his presidential bid as a potent retort in the change-versus-experience debate. After routinely lamenting that

"George Bush and Dick Cheney have turned divisive, special interest politics into an art form," he struck hard against more seasoned opponents like Hillary Rodham Clinton and John McCain, "who tout their experience working the system in Washington."[3] Promising to change how business gets done in Washington, Obama pledged to refuse money from federal lobbyists and railed against the lobbyists in the upper echelons of McCain's campaign. But this war against special interests did not mean that interest groups sat on the sidelines during the election. Liberal and conservative interest groups made their presence known in mobilization efforts during the contentious primary contests; in the drafting of the party platforms; on the convention floors in Denver and Minneapolis; in campaign ads broadcast on radio and television; in massive fund raising; and in grassroots efforts to motivate members and persuade voters through direct mail advertisements, phone banks, door-to-door canvassing, and other get-out-the-vote methods.

Usually, once the dust settles on an election, the victor tones down his populist rhetoric against the Washington lobbying community. Obama, however, did not let up on his attacks against special interests and their well-heeled lobbyists. Indeed, even before taking office, he demonstrated his devotion to transparency and good government by establishing ethics guidelines that banned federal lobbyists from donating to the transition process and prohibited the transition staff from lobbying the administration for one year.[4] After his inauguration, one of Obama's first executive orders imposed new ethics rules for former lobbyists working in his administration, new barriers for White House staffers who leave the government for lobbying jobs, and bans on gifts from lobbyists. Touting his imposition of "stricter limits" on special interest groups and registered lobbyists than those of "any other administration in history," the new president promised to protect "good ideas and good plans" from the sinister influence of "secret meetings and campaign checks."[5]

Despite Obama's vigorous efforts to distance his administration from powerful organized interests, neither interest groups nor lobbyists are as marginalized or constrained as his rhetoric may suggest. During the campaign, Obama repeatedly said that lobbyists "won't find a job in my White House." Yet after the election, he allowed prominent lobbyists to serve on his transition team and appointed people who once had worked as Washington influence-seekers with powerful lobbying firms even though they had not formally registered as federal lobbyists.[6] The reality is that many former officials of both major parties have lobbied when out of power, and to exclude all such seasoned figures would decimate the pool of potential appointees who have valuable political and policy experience.

Obama also issued executive orders early in his presidency that were favored by some of his party's strongest interest group allies, ranging from organized labor to reproductive rights groups.[7] He worked to reach beyond his party's core more aggressively than his predecessors, instructing his advisers to meet dozens of times during both his transition and his first months in office with business groups like the U.S. Chamber of Commerce, Business Roundtable, and the National Association of Manufacturers.[8] In short, the new Obama administration has been as careful to cultivate the support of important national interest groups as to publicly promote new ethics rules designed to trim the sails of special interests and federal registered lobbyists. The attention that Obama has devoted to Washington lobbying groups underscores a basic fact of contemporary American political life: the national interest group system is as much a fixture in Washington as the modern presidency. Both were born in the protean decades of the early twentieth century, and their relationship to one another has often been uneasy, contentious, and inevitable.

At first blush, modern chief executives appear to have ample incentive to keep their distance from organized interests. Although millions of ordinary citizens either belong to or contribute to various interest groups, most Americans view organized interests in national politics with a level of contempt and suspicion not unlike that of the Constitution's wary architects.[9] As the only officials elected by the entire nation, modern presidents often have cast themselves as guardians of the common good against a host of selfish vested interests. "Fifteen million people in the United States are represented by lobbyists," Harry Truman was fond of saying. "The other 150 million have only one man who is elected at large to represent them—that is, the President of the United States."[10] Likewise, administrations that seem too closely aligned with particular groups risk being charged with serving special interests, as President George W. Bush learned early in his first term when his stands on issues such as Arctic drilling, arsenic levels in drinking water, and global warming provoked criticism that he was cozying up to well-heeled corporate powers.[11] Presidential wariness of organized interests is accentuated by the fact that entrenched Washington lobbies routinely frustrate the president's programmatic goals.

For their part, interest groups would appear to have good reason to concentrate their energies on government institutions other than the presidency. Members of Congress and federal bureaucrats typically enjoy long tenures in office, but a president's hold on power is comparatively brief. The average tenure of postwar presidents has been just over six years. Furthermore, gaining access to the White House can be a tall order for a lobbyist because of the severe constraints on the time and attention of presidents and their advisers. In contrast, the size and specialized work of Congress and the federal agencies make them more accessible to interest groups. As one political insider put it, "There are 535 opportunities in Congress and only one in the White House. Where would you put your effort?"[12] In short, interest group relationships with members of Congress and federal bureaucrats are likely to be longer lasting and more reliable than those with presidents and their top aides.

Despite these significant disincentives to close relations between presidents and interest groups, rarely can either disregard the other. Indeed, they do so at their political peril. Organized interests are crucial elements of presidents' electoral coalitions. In an era of candidate-centered campaigns, interest groups provide money, organizational support, and votes for presidential hopefuls during their primary and general election bids.[13] Once in office, modern presidents largely stake their claims as successful leaders on whether they can build supportive coalitions for their policies with any regularity. Along with political parties, organized interests can offer the White House a potent and efficient means of expanding support for the president's agenda in Congress and other venues. Presidents must also consider, however, that interest groups can just as surely serve as sources of mobilized opposition.

In turn, interest groups cannot ignore the enormous power that modern executives wield in agenda setting, policy formation, budget making, and policy implementation. Presidents can even alter the prevailing interest group system. They can encourage the creation of new organized interests, actively work to demobilize others, and influence how interest groups frame their preferences in the first place.[14] In short, the modern presidency presents interest groups with significant opportunities and constraints. Whether as allies or as rivals, policy-minded presidents and interest groups cannot discount each other in a political system constitutionally designed with the imperative that "ambition must be made to counteract ambition."[15]

One of the most revealing views of the relationship between national interest groups and the White House is provided by their interactions in domestic policymaking. In the next section, I present a theoretical model of president–interest group relations based on the disposition of organized interests toward the president's party (affiliated versus unaffiliated) and on the relative capacities of different presidents to exercise policy leadership in varying historical circumstances (broad versus narrow). From this model, I derive four distinctive forms of president–interest group interaction: collaborative breakthrough politics, adversarial breakthrough politics, collaborative politics-as-usual, and adversarial politics-as-usual. In the rest of the chapter I offer case studies that illuminate each type of interactive politics.

As we shall see, collaboration with the president is frequently less rewarding (and opposition more beneficial) for interest groups than is commonly presumed. Indeed, opposing groups sometimes translate White House antagonism into new sources of organizational vitality. At the same time, modern executives have good reason to frustrate the policy ambitions of even their strongest interest group allies. Presidents often find that the national interest group system can pose major extraconstitutional impediments to their programmatic goals, compounding the challenges of policy leadership in a political system replete with barriers to change. It is little wonder that tensions and resentments abound in president–interest group interactions concerning domestic policymaking, with each side prone to blame the other for lost opportunities.

Friends, Foes, and Policy Leadership: A Framework of President–Interest Group Relations

The first decades of the twentieth century witnessed an evolution in the presidency that tied executive authority and power to previously scorned forms of rhetorical leadership.[16] During the same period, an unprecedented number and variety of organized interests became actively engaged in Washington lobbying.[17] As Figure 10.1 illustrates, never before had so many organized interests attempted to influence federal policymaking. Conflict and ambivalence characterized modern president–interest group relations from the start. Early activists such as Theodore Roosevelt and Woodrow Wilson frequently warned the public of the sinister influence of organized interests in national politics and spoke eloquently of the president's duty to champion the public good. "The business of government is to organize the common interest against the special interest," Wilson told appreciative voters.[18]

Both Roosevelt and Wilson, however, found it difficult to ignore organized interests that could help them govern. During his second term Roosevelt confided to a close friend that his principled refusal to nurture relationships with corporate interests made leadership challenging. "I am genuinely independent of the big monied men in all matters where I think the interests of the public are concerned . . . ," he noted. "But . . . it is out of the question for me to expect them to grant favors to me in return. The sum of this is that I can make no private or special appeals to them, and I am at my wits' end how to proceed."[19] Wilson's administration, by contrast, nurtured close working relationships with business and labor groups during World War I to coordinate industrial production. As the political scientist E. Pendleton Herring observed soon after the war, "In mobilizing the full strength of the country these special interest

Figure 10.1 Appearances of Private Corporations and Interest Groups at Congressional Hearings, 1833–1917

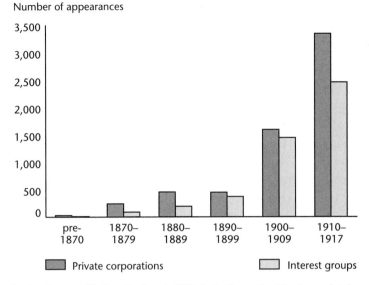

Number of appearances

Private corporations   Interest groups

Source: Based on data created by the author from the CIS Index for Congressional Hearings, 23rd–64th Congresses (Washington, D.C.: Government Printing Office, 1985).

units gave the government cohesive and responsible organizations with which to deal."[20]

Likewise more than a few organized interests in the Progressive Era perceived the rise of the modern presidency as a potentially important opportunity to advance their agendas. Consider, for example, the considerable energy and resources that woman suffrage groups such as the National American Woman Suffrage Association and the Congressional Union focused on winning White House support in the 1910s. Inspired by Roosevelt's transformation of the presidency into a "popular steward" of the people, suffragists saw the executive office as a new source of policy dynamism in an often staid American polity. "We knew that [the presidency], and perhaps it alone, would ensure our success," suffragist leader Alice Paul later explained.[21] Wilson was hounded by suffragist groups from his first inauguration in 1913 until the waning days of his second term. Significantly, the tactics that suffragist organizations employed in their pursuit of presidential support included not just conciliatory lobbying but also highly disruptive anti-administration protests.[22] As modern presidents and interest groups emerged as fixtures in national political life, their ability to recast each other's political calculations and policy fortunes was unmistakable.

To capture president–interest group relations in their full richness and complexity would require separate accounts of how each president has dealt with interest groups. But one way to generalize about the interactions between modern presidents and interest groups—that is, to identify patterns and deduce analytical insights about their reciprocal relations—is to focus on two factors that help structure president–interest group politics: (1) the relationship of interest groups to the president's party, and (2) the varying opportunities for presidential policy leadership.

It is an old saw of political science that vigorous political parties and interest groups are fundamentally at odds with one other.[23] In truth, both major American parties are linked to interest groups, and each nurtures interest group coalitions that will help its candidates win office and its officeholders govern. "Whether observed in the electoral or lobbying arenas," Mark Peterson notes, "a significant portion of the interest group community reflects ideological positions, takes stands on the issues of the day, or represents constituencies whose orientations are at least compatible with one of the two major parties."[24] While reassuring the general public of their eagerness to stand up to "special interests," modern presidents and their political advisers readily understand the importance of party-affiliated interest groups in constructing successful electoral coalitions and governing majorities. Franklin Roosevelt, for example, established mechanisms by which White House staff members could attend to the groups that made up his loose New Deal coalition, including organized labor, nationality groups, and small farmers.[25] Subsequent presidents have followed suit.[26] Naturally not every interest group pursues access to, or an alliance with, the White House. For ideological and strategic reasons, groups unaffiliated with the president's party may advance outsider strategies, such as campaigns to garner media attention and public support. For the purposes of our analytical model, the relationship of interest groups to the president's party (ranging from closely affiliated to staunchly unaffiliated) is crucial because it takes into account both collaborative and adversarial forms of interaction.

What are the implications of collaborative and adversarial relations when the opportunities for modern executives to advance their domestic policy agendas are broad or narrow? By most accounts, a few presidents have enjoyed a broad opportunity to dominate the policymaking process and to advance their agendas (breakthrough politics). Presidential scholars tend to agree that the political context was exceptionally favorable for Woodrow Wilson, Franklin Roosevelt, Lyndon Johnson, and Ronald Reagan to exercise policy leadership.[27] Most modern presidents have had to struggle with more challenging leadership

Table 10.1 Presidents and Interest Groups: A Model of Interactive Politics

President's capacity to exercise policy leadership	Relationship of interest groups to the president's party	
	Affiliated (Collaborative strategies)	Unaffiliated (Adversarial strategies)
Broad (Breakthrough politics)	Collaborative breakthrough politics *Roosevelt's New Deal for labor* *Reagan and the Christian right*	Adversarial breakthrough politics *Roosevelt and the Liberty League* *Reagan's assault on liberal citizens' groups*
Narrow (Politics-as-usual)	Collaborative politics-as-usual *George H. W. Bush and the Competitiveness Council* *George W. Bush and air quality*	Adversarial politics-as-usual *Carter and energy reform* *Clinton and health care reform*

circumstances in which their opportunities to reshape public policy have been relatively narrow (politics-as-usual).

As Table 10.1 illustrates, four types of interactive politics emerge when we consider together the relationship of interest groups to the president's party (affiliated or unaffiliated) and the relative capacity of a president to exercise policy leadership (broad or narrow).[28] One may predict that collaborative breakthrough politics will involve White House sponsorship and co-optation of interest group allies. When the agendas or behavior of interest groups are at odds with politically dominant presidents, these groups are likely to be marginalized.

Adversarial breakthrough politics places interest group opponents in the difficult position of challenging presidents who have enormous political capital. If these groups are politically effective, they likely will face intense White House assaults. Even when confronted by powerful White House antagonism, however, oppositional groups may find alternative sources of support in Congress or the bureaucracy because of the fragmented structure of the political system. Indeed White House antagonism may inspire sympathy for a threatened cause that groups can use to attract new supporters and acquire fresh resources.

The dynamics of collaborative politics-as-usual can produce either weak or strong ties between presidents and the interest groups affiliated with their party. Weak alliances are likely when the president offends affiliated groups by moving toward the political center to secure policy achievements and an independent public image. Presidents who pursue this strategy may presume that, as captives of the president's party, affiliated groups have few alternatives but to maintain at least tacit support for the administration. Nevertheless, strong alliances are possible if the constrained presidents are eager to shore up support from their ideological base by pursuing the policy initiatives endorsed by affiliated interest groups. Collaborative politics-as-usual seems likely to be inhospitable to affiliated groups seeking major policy innovations but more opportune for groups satisfied with incremental policy change.

Finally, adversarial politics-as-usual predictably affords oppositional interest groups numerous chances to frustrate the policy designs of politically constrained presidents by mobilizing grassroots resistance, exploiting alliances with supporters in other branches and levels of government, and pursuing other forms of veto politics. When presidents do not dominate the policymaking process, oppositional groups will play a significant role in helping to set the public agenda and shape new policy initiatives. Under these circumstances the White House may decide to follow the lead of interest groups championing popular causes. To illuminate these distinctive patterns of interactive politics, I next examine several cases of president–interest group relations.

Franklin Roosevelt and Industrial Unionism: Collaborative Breakthrough Politics I

Interest groups are attentive to new political openings for their policy goals. During the 1930s organized labor could not resist linking its fortunes to the activist presidency of Franklin Roosevelt and his ambitious New Deal agenda. Labor leaders, such as John Lewis of the United Mine Workers (UMW), especially welcomed opportunities to translate New Deal legislative and administrative initiatives into growth for their unions. In particular, these labor leaders hoped to organize unskilled industrial workers who had been largely neglected by the American Federation of Labor (AFL). In 1933 the Roosevelt administration invited a large number of organized interests—including business and labor groups—to participate in drafting the National Industrial Recovery Act (NIRA). Labor activists such as W. Jett Lauck, a Lewis lieutenant, persuaded the White House to include a vague provision in NIRA, Section 7(a), that recognized the right of workers to bargain collectively. Although corporate leaders were reassured by their lawyers that the provision included no administrative mechanism for enforcement, Lauck reported to Lewis that Section 7(a) "will suit our purposes." After NIRA sailed through Congress, Lewis and other union organizers aggressively exploited the popularity of Roosevelt and NIRA to attract more miners to the UMW. "The president wants you to join the union," UMW literature and speakers told workers.[29] Tens of thousands of miners signed union cards and formed lodges with names such as "New Deal" and "Blue Eagle." After only one year of invoking the celebrated names of Roosevelt and the New Deal, the UMW's membership rolls had swollen from 150,000 to more than 500,000.[30]

Lewis and other labor organizers orchestrated a dramatic break with the AFL in 1934, forming the Congress of Industrial Organizations (CIO) to represent millions of unskilled industrial workers.[31] Publicly, CIO leaders professed unwavering support for Roosevelt and the New Deal. In private, they noted the aloof posture that the White House assumed when Sen. Robert Wagner, D-N.Y., championed legislation to protect unionizing efforts. Roosevelt tepidly endorsed the Wagner Act of 1935, organized labor's Magna Carta, only at the eleventh hour.[32] Although he understood that organized labor was a crucial element of his electoral and governing coalitions, the president took pains to publicly assert his independence of both labor and business interests. During major strikes, for example, Roosevelt was known to tell reporters that labor activists "did silly things." He often sounded centrist tones in urging employers and disgruntled laborers to embrace "common sense and good order."[33]

Lewis and the CIO recognized Roosevelt's lack of enthusiasm for union radicalism but also appreciated that labor reforms such as the Wagner Act and the National Labor Relations Act were powerful catalysts for union organizing and collective bargaining. In 1936 Lewis, David Dubinsky, George Berry, Sidney Hillman, and other labor activists entered into a political marriage of convenience between the CIO and the Democratic Party to reelect Roosevelt. CIO unions contributed significant financial and logistical support to the president's reelection campaign; in fact, Lewis's UMW was the Democratic Party's largest financial benefactor in 1936. In forming the Labor Nonpartisan League, however, Lewis hoped that union votes could be marshaled in future elections to support whichever party or candidate best served the CIO's interests.[34]

After his landslide victory, it became clear that Roosevelt expected organized labor to follow his lead and not the reverse. Like other presidents who have dominated the policy process, Roosevelt intended to dictate the terms of any alliances between the White House and interest groups. Amid labor confrontations with "little steel" in 1937 and 1938, Roosevelt stunned many labor supporters with his comment on the killing of ten steelworkers who were demonstrating in Chicago against Republic Steel Corporation. Denouncing management and unions alike as sponsors of senseless violence, Roosevelt declared "a curse on both your houses." In a Labor Day radio address to millions of listeners, Lewis rebuked the president: "It ill behooves one who has supped at labor's table and who has been sheltered in labor's house to curse with equal fervor and fine impartiality both labor and its adversaries when they become locked in deadly embrace."[35] By the end of the 1930s, Lewis and a few other CIO leaders were convinced that the National Labor Relations Board (NLRB), the courts, and the White House were limiting the labor movement's larger aims. In 1940, Lewis worked in vain to derail FDR's reelection, fearing that it would bring about American entry into war and the concomitant demise of labor's agenda for progressive change. After vain efforts first to launch a third-party challenge and then to back the Republican candidate, Wendell Willkie, in the election, Lewis stepped down as CIO president.[36]

Eager to marginalize and defuse Lewis-style CIO militancy, the Roosevelt White House embraced moderate "labor statesmen" like Sidney Hillman, president of the Amalgamated Clothing Workers of America and a founder of the CIO. Hillman, in contrast to Lewis, was an unflinching Roosevelt loyalist. He oversaw the creation of the CIO's political action committee, which further cemented the ties between organized labor and the Democratic Party.

After Pearl Harbor, wartime imperatives required extraordinary industrial production and coordination. Labor leaders such as Philip Murray, the new CIO president, and Walter Reuther of the United Auto Workers proposed "industrial councils" that would facilitate efficient wartime production while giving organized labor real influence—along with business and the government—in supervising industries and the workforce. The Roosevelt administration eschewed such ideas. In the end, the AFL, the CIO, and other unions agreed to a no-strike pledge during the war and merely hoped that the war agencies would exercise their robust power over industrial workers benevolently.[37] "Instead of an active participant in the councils of industry," historian Alan Brinkley notes, "the labor movement had become, in effect, a ward of the state."[38] As the war drew to a close, Lewis's vision of an independent labor movement engaged in militant activities was overshadowed by broad CIO and AFL support for a more conciliatory posture. Heartened by the gains and protections that unions had secured during Roosevelt's administration, leaders of organized labor pinned their hopes on a permanent alliance with the Democratic Party.

Presidents with broad opportunities to shape domestic policy are unlikely to leave the interest group system the way they found it. It is hardly surprising that chief executives who have the ability to remake American politics and governance are equally capable of reconstructing the interests that are closest to them. Although Roosevelt did not explicitly favor union expansion or the meteoric rise of the CIO, his influence in those developments was unmistakable. Organized labor benefited a great deal from its ties to a president blessed with the exceptional opportunity to advance major policy changes, but

Roosevelt exercised enormous control over the terms of their alliance and the nature of reform. Co-optation was the price of labor's programmatic collaboration, as union militancy and independence gave way to a moderate, bureaucratic style of labor organization.

Reagan and the Christian Right: Collaborative Breakthrough Politics II

During the late 1970s the Christian right emerged as a new force in conservative politics. For decades after the Scopes trial of 1925 and the repeal of Prohibition in 1933, religious conservatives had retreated from the political sphere into a separate subculture of churches and sectarian educational and social institutions.[39] In the 1960s and 1970s many social and political changes deeply offended Christian fundamentalists, evangelicals, Pentecostals, and charismatics, who strongly believed that they must resist culturally liberal government policies that favored "secular humanism" over faith-based morality. Organizations formed to advocate what leaders of the new Christian right described as a pro-family agenda, including tax credits for private school tuition, promotion of school prayer, and restrictions on abortion and pornography. The most prominent new group was the Moral Majority, led by televangelist Jerry Falwell. Other new organizations included the Religious Roundtable, which brought together reform-minded fundamentalist and evangelical clergy, the National Christian Action Council, Christian Voice, and Pat Robertson's Freedom Council.[40]

During the presidential campaign of 1980, Ronald Reagan openly courted conservative Christian leaders. Sharing their enthusiasm for restoring traditional values, Reagan pledged his support for their social agenda. He won an early endorsement from Christian Voice, which organized an effective political action committee—Christians for Reagan—on his behalf. The Religious Roundtable invited Reagan to address more than fifteen thousand ministers at one of its public affairs briefings in summer 1980, another event that helped to coalesce conservative Christians behind his candidacy. The Moral Majority and other groups mobilized voters at the fundamentalist and evangelical grassroots, urging followers to express their religious convictions at the polls.[41] Reagan openly appealed to conservative religious leaders and constituents by supporting the removal of a pro–Equal Rights Amendment plank from the Republican platform and the insertion of an antiabortion plank.[42] His 1980 presidential bid served as an important catalyst for unifying and mobilizing the Christian right, making it a formidable electoral force in American politics.

As president, Reagan appointed a number of Christian right activists to visible administration positions. Morton Blackwell, who served as a liaison between evangelicals and the Reagan campaign organization, was named a special assistant on the White House staff. Robert Billings, the former executive director of the Moral Majority, received a prominent post in the Department of Education. Gary Bauer, a future director of the Family Research Council, became domestic adviser in Reagan's second term. Reagan also used his "bully pulpit" to advocate Christian right causes, including frequent endorsements of constitutional amendments to prohibit abortion and restore school prayer.[43] Reagan exercised his executive powers to bar the disbursement of public funds to any family planning organization that discussed abortion as an option with patients. The White House also threw its support behind fundamentalist Bob Jones University in its lawsuit against the Internal Revenue Service, which had revoked the institution's tax-exempt status because of alleged racially discriminatory practices.[44]

If Christian right activists expected the Reagan administration to expend significant political capital on behalf of their social reform agenda, however, they soon discovered that the White House had other priorities. Reagan strategists focused instead on economic issues and a defense buildup. James Baker, the politically moderate White House chief of staff, and Robert Michel, the House Republican leader, set the tone early by serving notice that social issues would not be the administration's top priority. Reagan even reneged on a campaign promise to appear at the 1981 March for Life in Washington, offering instead to meet privately with antiabortion leaders in the Oval Office. Several of them boycotted the meeting in protest. Paul Weyrich, a central figure in the Christian right movement, organized a conference call among conservative religious leaders in hopes of rallying them to press their social policy goals with the president. Yet few of these leaders were prepared to battle the Reagan White House. Falwell, for instance, argued that to antagonize the administration would be self-defeating.[45] Significantly, at the same time the White House was placing Christian right issues on the back burner, the Moral Majority and other conservative religious organizations dutifully joined a broad coalition of conservative interest groups in rallying behind the president's 1981 Omnibus Budget Reconciliation Act and his Economic Recovery Tax Act.[46] In 1984, although they had few tangible policy gains to show for their alliance with Reagan, prominent Christian right groups threw their full support behind the president's reelection campaign.

The Reagan presidency gave the Christian right and its conservative social agenda enormous symbolic recognition. It also forged an enduring alliance between conservative religious groups and the Republican Party: in every presidential election since 1980, the Christian right has focused its energies on electing the Republican candidate. Ralph Reed, a prominent movement figure, credits Reagan with leading religious conservatives "out of the wilderness" and "giving their concerns a viability in the political system that they had never had before."[47] To be sure, he and many other Christian right activists also lament that they received little more from the Reagan administration than "consolation prizes like speeches by the Gipper to their annual conventions or schmooze sessions in the Roosevelt Room."[48] Yet the Christian right had few alternatives but to remain loyal. Presidents who dominate the political system for a time, such as FDR and Reagan, largely control the terms of their sponsorship of interest group allies. Co-optation is often the price interest groups pay for their engagement in collaborative breakthrough politics. Sometimes the price is high. Unlike organized labor in the 1930s, which benefited from the reform program that Roosevelt framed, however, the Christian right accepted a form of co-optation from Reagan that ensured that its policy goals would be frustrated.

Roosevelt and the American Liberty League: Adversarial Breakthrough Politics I

When a president dominates the national policymaking process as thoroughly as Roosevelt did during his first term as president, oppositional groups often have little choice but to shift their political efforts from working with the administration to challenging it with aggressive publicity campaigns and electoral battles. The American Liberty League's crusade against Roosevelt and the New Deal provides an apt illustration of adversarial breakthrough politics.

Early in his presidency, Roosevelt hoped that his administration and its economic recovery experiments would earn the approval of a broad coalition of interests. He was particularly eager to win the support of the business community. But business leaders began to mobilize against Roosevelt when New Deal reformers unveiled a 1934 stock exchange measure that made clear the administration's determination to regulate high finance.[49] In summer 1934, defiant business leaders launched the American Liberty League to serve as an anti–New Deal interest group. The new organization was dominated by prominent executives and corporate lawyers from banking, oil, steel, transportation, automaking, and other industries.[50] The league boasted especially close ties to General Motors and the Du Pont family's financial empire. Claiming to be nonpartisan, the league took pains to include among its officers a handful of conservative Democrats who loathed the New Deal, most notably Al Smith, the 1928 Democratic presidential nominee.[51] All of these officers, including Smith, soon bolted from the Democratic Party, however, which led Arthur Krock of the *New*

York Times to conclude that the league's nonpartisanship was a fiction. Instead, he informed readers that the Liberty League was the aegis of Republican patricians determined to guard their business civilization.[52]

League officers initially crowed that their organization would enlist two to four million in its crusade to defend nineteenth-century economic liberalism against the New Deal. Their efforts fell woefully short: at its peak, the league could claim roughly 75,000 members. Its principal activities focused on reshaping what one leader called "the collective expression of public opinion."[53] The league established offices in the National Press Club building in Washington; issued a profusion of pamphlets, bulletins, and newspaper editorials; and made extensive use of radio to challenge New Deal principles. League spokespersons warned radio listeners that the New Deal threatened "the individual freedom of the worker . . . to sell his own labor on his own terms" and unfairly seized "the accumulation of the thrifty" to distribute it to "the thriftless and unlucky."[54]

Roosevelt handled the league adeptly. He told reporters that he was delighted to learn that its officers were evaluating the New Deal in light of the Ten Commandments. Unfortunately, he noted, they had forgotten the commandment from Jesus to "love thy neighbor as thyself."[55] In his January 1936 message to Congress, Roosevelt declared his pride in having "earned the hatred of entrenched greed," "the unscrupulous money-changers," and the "discredited special interests." In a much-publicized speech to well-heeled members of the Liberty League at Washington's Mayflower Hotel a few weeks later, Al Smith excoriated New Dealers for betraying traditional American ideals in favor of socialist notions of government control and radical collectivism.[56] The choice was clear, Smith declared. Was it to be "Washington or Moscow, the Stars and Stripes or the red flag and the hammer and sickle, the 'Star Spangled Banner' or the 'Internationale'?"

During the 1936 election campaign, as the Republican National Committee and its presidential candidate, Alfred Landon, did their best to strike moderate-to-liberal postures, the Liberty League provided Roosevelt a perfect foil. Landon hoped to distance his party from the Liberty League by running on progressive issues, and he pointedly asked the organization not to publicly endorse his candidacy. Nevertheless, league members contributed lavish sums to defeat Roosevelt and stepped up their anti–New Deal publicity efforts during the campaign. To the chagrin of the Landon team, these high-profile activities only helped New Dealers to brand the Republican Party the tool of wealthy, antigovernment elites. Throughout the 1936 campaign, Roosevelt railed against "economic royalists" who cared little about the plight of most Americans. For his last campaign address outside his home state of New York in 1936, FDR went to

Wilmington, the Delaware home of the Du Pont empire, to speak about liberty. He used the occasion to recount a parable of Lincoln's about a wolf who, after being pulled off the neck of a lamb by the shepherd, denounced the shepherd for destroying liberty. "Plainly, the sheep and the wolf are not agreed upon a definition of the word liberty," Lincoln quipped.[57]

Not long after Roosevelt won his landslide reelection, the Liberty League chose to shut down rather than retreat into political obscurity. Its failed effort to derail the New Deal illustrates the difficulties oppositional groups can face when squaring off against breakthrough presidents, especially if they lack a large membership base. As we shall see in President Reagan's struggle with liberal citizens' organizations, however, oppositional groups sometimes can prove resilient and even mount effective challenges to breakthrough presidents.

Reagan's Assault on Liberal Citizens' Groups: Adversarial Breakthrough Politics II

Ronald Reagan, the first modern conservative president with abundant political resources, declared war on liberal advocacy groups concerned with the environment, consumer protection, civil rights, poverty, and other policy issues. Reaganites made no effort to conceal their disdain for these groups, viewing them as "a bunch of ideological ambulance chasers" who profited from bloated government and stood in the way of "regulatory relief."[58] Government retrenchment, the Reagan White House resolved, would require a concerted effort to decrease the groups' resources, size, and influence. The administration set out to demobilize its interest group opponents in 1981 by shrinking government programs they favored, limiting their access to important federal agencies, and eliminating federal grants and contracts that supported their activities.[59]

The Reagan offensive was devastating for some advocacy groups, especially antipoverty organizations. The administration's 1981 social welfare budget cuts spared programs for the elderly, thereby neutralizing senior citizens' lobbies that might have served as powerful allies of advocacy organizations for the poor.[60] Instead, Reagan's effort to "defund the left" by eliminating government grant programs that supported liberal groups took its heaviest toll on a small cluster of poor people's lobbies.[61] When these groups shifted their energies from political advocacy to providing services, however, a number of new groups concerned with the homeless arose and made the Reagan administration's assault on the welfare state the focal point of contentious politics. Organizations associated with the emerging homeless movement of the 1980s engaged in confrontational anti-Reagan protests, building shantytown "Reaganvilles," reminiscent of the

Hoovervilles of the Great Depression, and staging attention-getting demonstrations that cast the White House as insensitive to the poor.[62] Ironically, the Reagan administration's constriction of established antipoverty organizations dating back to the Great Society opened the door for new groups to challenge the president's agenda. Presidential antagonism inadvertently encouraged the formation of liberal interest groups.

Beyond its partially effective assault on a handful of antipoverty organizations, the White House plan to enervate liberal groups failed. Reagan's strategists had largely ignored the possibility that resourceful opposition groups might transform open hostility from a powerful, conservative president into a catalyst for liberal organizational growth. National environmental groups, for example, prospered during the 1980s. Denied access to once-friendly federal agencies,[63] environmental organizations launched an effective drive that included aggressive fund raising, publicity, and coordinated action with congressional allies. As private donations to these groups increased, environmental leaders quipped that James Watt, Reagan's unpopular, anticonservation secretary of the interior, was the "Fort Knox of the environmental movement."[64] The membership rolls of organizations such as the Wilderness Society and the Sierra Club doubled between 1980 and 1985.[65] Finally, environmental groups drove from office two prominent Reagan appointees (Watt and Environmental Protection Agency director Anne Gorsuch) and mounted a successful challenge to the administration's plans for environmental deregulation. Clearly, adversarial breakthrough politics can give oppositional groups the chance to expand and exert influence if they enjoy strong, broad-based constituencies and alternative bases of support within the government.

George H. W. Bush, Centrist Reform, and the Competitiveness Council: Collaborative Politics-as-Usual

Presidents with narrow opportunities to exercise domestic policy leadership often have strong political incentives to embrace centrist reforms. By moving toward the political center, these presidents can gain credit among voters for advancing popular, often bipartisan initiatives. In the process, however, they may alienate their party's core interest group allies. George H. W. Bush's endorsements of popular bipartisan measures on the environment and civil rights illustrate this trade-off.

Bush's opportunities for policy leadership were severely limited when he became president in 1989. His party held only 175 seats in the House of Representatives, the fewest of any modern president at the start of a term.

Operating within this constrained political environment, the Bush administration hoped to prove its capacity to govern by introducing major environmental reform legislation that would draw considerable congressional, media, and popular support. During his 1988 election campaign, Bush pledged a "kinder, gentler" America and promised to be an "environmental president." As he proclaimed on the campaign trail, "Those who think we are powerless to do anything about the 'greenhouse effect' are forgetting about the 'White House effect.'"[66]

Once in office, Bush stayed on the environmental bandwagon; like Richard Nixon before him, Bush hoped to outmaneuver—or at least keep pace with—congressional Democrats on an issue of enormous popular concern. In July 1989 he sent to Congress an ambitious clean air bill, which was enacted in early 1990 after successful negotiations with Senate majority leader George Mitchell, D-Maine. The Clean Air Act amendments proved to be Bush's most significant domestic policy achievement.[67] Along the way, however, his administration was required to marginalize traditional Republican interest group allies in business and industry.

At about the same time, the Bush White House endorsed another major centrist reform, the Americans with Disabilities Act (ADA), which had the solid support of the public and liberal political actors but was viewed with dread by many in the business community. The ADA sought to add the disabled to the list of groups protected against discrimination by the 1964 Civil Rights Act. At the urging of a broad coalition of advocates for disability rights, civil rights, and labor, the ADA also required that new or remodeled facilities be made accessible to disabled persons seeking jobs or hoping to make use of public accommodations; existing facilities were to be made accessible whenever "readily achievable." The potential financial costs of complying with ADA requirements were enormous, and Bush administration officials attempted to soften the blow on business by pressuring legislators to eliminate language from the bill permitting aggrieved parties to sue for damages. Congressional Democrats refused, then passed the ADA unaltered. With polls indicating overwhelming public support for civil rights reform on behalf of the disabled, Bush signed the ADA into law.[68]

Conservative critics assailed the Bush administration for approving the Clean Air Act amendments and the ADA.[69] Business groups and other conservative organizations warned administration officials that, in time of recession, new regulatory burdens placed "significant drags on the country's economic recovery."[70] Troubled by those attacks, Bush hoped to appease business groups outside the gaze of the media by limiting the regulatory reach of the Clean Air Act, the ADA, and other initiatives in the implementation process. To this end, Bush created the Council on Competitiveness within the Executive Office of the President. The council, chaired by Vice President Dan Quayle, was to review regulations issued by federal agencies and try to make them less burdensome for the relevant industry. "The president would say that if we keep our hand on the tiller in the implementation phase," recounted a member of the council, "we won't add to the burdens of the economy."[71]

In closed-door meetings, the Competitiveness Council focused on agency regulations that industry representatives complained were excessive. When the Department of Housing and Urban Development proposed ADA-related regulations on how to make apartments more accessible to the disabled, for instance, the council pressured the department to ease the regulations at the behest of construction and real estate interests. As Jeffrey Berry and Kent Portney found, "The new rules were more sympathetic to the industry, and lobbyists for the home builders claimed that hundreds of millions of dollars would be saved each year in aggregate building costs."[72]

The success of some business groups in winning regulatory relief from the Bush administration illustrates perhaps the most promising strategy for interest group allies of politically constrained presidents to achieve incremental policy gains. Avoiding the glare of television lights, interest groups are most likely to benefit from collaborative politics-as-usual by winning favorable regulatory decisions through executive orders or by mobilizing White House pressure on federal agencies for friendly implementation of existing laws. The Competitiveness Council, however, was ultimately unable to operate in secrecy. Liberal public interest groups, media scrutiny, and congressional opponents eventually hamstrung its activities.[73] As the Bush years suggest, the relationship between presidents with limited political power and their party's interest group coalition is often unproductive. And it does not matter which party controls the White House. Liberal interest groups closely aligned with the Democratic Party were frustrated during the Clinton administration when popular centrist reforms were on the agenda. Clinton's support for the North American Free Trade Agreement (alienating organized labor), the Personal Responsibility and Work Opportunity Reconciliation Act (alienating antipoverty and civil rights groups), and the Defense of Marriage Act (alienating gay and lesbian groups) underscores the incentives constrained executives have to associate themselves with centrist initiatives even if they estrange interest group allies by doing so.

Clinton and Health Care Reform: Adversarial Politics-as-Usual

Shortly after his unexpected 1948 election, President Truman launched an aggressive campaign to secure national health insurance. Hoping to make the most of his modest political opportunity for programmatic leadership, Truman vigorously nurtured popular support for his ambitious health proposal. The American Medical Association (AMA) and other groups that viewed national health insurance as inimical to their interests launched an intense public relations campaign to depict Truman's plan as socialistic and corrosive of quality medical care. Spending an unprecedented $1.5 million for its publicity counteroffensive, the AMA ran ads claiming that national health insurance would place government bureaucrats between patients and their physicians. Already constrained by the slim Democratic majorities in Congress and by strong resistance from the conservative southern wing of his party, Truman was helpless to save his health plan when public support dwindled.[74]

More than four decades later, Bill Clinton, another Democrat constrained by limited political capacity to remake domestic policy, made universal health care the centerpiece of his administration's reform agenda. He ran effectively on the issue during the 1992 election, receiving a warm reception from voters who agreed that the health care system was in crisis. After a lengthy policy-planning process, in late 1993 Clinton unveiled his much-anticipated Health Security Act, whose name was meant to associate his proposal with one of the federal government's most popular programs, Social Security. In substance, the act called for a new public-private partnership involving "managed competition" and employer mandates.[75] Politically, it made important concessions to large companies and health insurance providers to win their support, while promising universal coverage and limits on soaring medical costs to attract the elderly, consumer groups, unions, religious organizations, and groups representing women, children, and minorities. When the AMA, the U.S. Chamber of Commerce, and several large employers voiced support for principal features of the Health Security Act, it seemed that the Clinton administration had assembled a powerful left-right coalition.

By mid-1994 Clinton's crusade for sweeping health care reform was dead. Critics point to the plan's eye-glazing complexity, resistance from Democrats on the relevant congressional committees, Clinton's failure to streamline his policy agenda, his unwillingness to work with reform-minded Republicans, and high levels of public distrust in government, among other explanations.[76] For our purposes, however, it is useful to concentrate on the significant role that Clinton's interest group adversaries played in derailing health care reform.

Initially, the strongest group opposition to the administration's health care package came from two national organizations with large grassroots constituencies: the Health Insurance Association of America (HIAA) and the National Federation of Independent Businesses (NFIB). The HIAA represented midsize and small health insurance companies, many of which would go out of business if the Health Security Act became law. Large employers stood to benefit from the Clinton plan, but small businesses represented by the NFIB found intolerable the proposal's mandate that employers pay 80 percent of their employees' health premiums.[77] The Pharmaceutical Research and Manufacturers of America (PhRMA), representing drug companies that stood to lose profits under the Clinton scheme, also joined the opposition. Then, late in 1993 Republican strategists led by William Kristol, of the Project for the Republican Future, campaigned to persuade a broad set of conservative interest groups to mobilize against even a compromise version of the Health Security Act. Anything but an all-out effort to defeat health care reform, Kristol argued, would jeopardize the political future of the Republican Party and its interest group coalition. Passing the Clinton plan, he insisted, would "relegitimize middle-class dependence for 'security' on government spending and regulation" and thereby revive the Democratic Party's appeal "as the generous protector of middle-class interests."[78] The Christian Coalition, antitax groups, and a variety of other conservative interest groups responded by channeling new resources into the effort to kill health care reform, coordinating their activities with HIAA, NFIB, and PhRMA.

Clinton's interest group adversaries devoted considerable funds to advertising. HIAA spent approximately $14 million on its public relations blitz, which included the "Harry and Louise" television ads, in which a middle-class couple expresses its angst about the Clinton proposal. PhRMA devoted roughly $20 million to its own political advertising campaign. The antireform advertising crusade was designed to minimize public concerns about a health crisis while arousing fears that the president's plan would reduce the quality of medical care, eliminate individual choice of health care providers, encourage bloated government, and dramatically increase taxes to cover the cost of universal coverage. For its part, the 600,000-member NFIB focused on grassroots mobilization, including direct mail and phone bank assaults on the Clinton plan.[79] Against this backdrop, the White House received only modest support for its health care initiative from traditionally Democratic interest groups. The AFL-CIO and other labor groups, for example, had already expended considerable resources fighting one of Clinton's treasured centrist achievements, NAFTA.[80]

Adversarial politics took its toll on public support for Clinton's health care reform, which drifted downward from 67 percent in a September 1993 *Washington Post*/ABC News poll to 44 percent in February 1994.[81] Destined for defeat, the Health Security Act was never put to a vote in either the House or the Senate. The failure of Clinton's major domestic policy initiative presaged the Republican takeover of Congress in November. Many analysts trace the demise of health care reform in 1993 and 1994 to the Clinton administration's strategic missteps, of which there were many. Placed within the context of our theoretical model, however, Clinton's failure to achieve major health care reform reflects the formidable challenges faced by politically constrained presidents who pursue large-scale policy change. It also illustrates the enormous opportunities for interest group adversaries to block the programmatic ambitions of modern presidents in periods of politics-as-usual.

George W. Bush's First Term: Mastering Collaborative Politics-as-Usual

Like his predecessor, George W. Bush came into office with his party in control of Congress. Yet he received fewer popular votes than his Democratic opponent in the 2000 election, and his Electoral College victory hinged on the controversial intervention of a conservative Supreme Court majority. Moreover, Bush's party lost seats in the congressional elections, leaving Republicans a narrow 221–211 majority in the House and an evenly split Senate that remained Republican thanks only to the vice president's tiebreaking vote. Although Bush was hardly in a position to claim a mandate for bold shifts in public policy, he secured his top priority of a huge tax cut by pursuing a highly partisan strategy.[82] But the Bush administration's opportunities to dramatically reshape domestic policy remained relatively narrow in the first term, even with an ideologically cohesive Republican congressional party and, after September 11, 2001, an unprecedented national security crisis that lent the president new clout. As with his father and Clinton before him, Bush's other successful domestic initiatives—most notably education reform in 2001 and Medicare reform in 2003—were centrist measures that relied on compromise and bipartisan coalitions. The administration's more controversial legislative proposals, such as its initiative to involve faith-based organizations in the delivery of government-funded social services and its efforts to authorize oil drilling in Alaska's Arctic National Wildlife Refuge, were largely frustrated.

Stymied on the legislative front, the Bush White House shifted its attention to regulatory change. As the bastion of politically constrained presidents who hope to alter domestic policies, regulatory action allows an administration to advance its agenda and assist allied organized interests unilaterally, incrementally, and with little public or media attention. In contrast to high-profile lawmaking efforts such as Clinton's ill-fated campaign for sweeping health care reform, an administration can write or revise regulations largely on the president's own authority. Although the Bush White House was certainly not the first to pursue its policy goals through regulation, it proved exceptionally aggressive and successful in its use of this strategy during the first term.

The administration's air quality policies are illustrative. During the 2000 presidential race, Bush pledged to impose controls on power plant emissions of carbon dioxide. In her first days as Bush's director of the Environmental Protection Agency (EPA), Christie Todd Whitman, a former Republican governor of New Jersey, announced plans to carry out this promise. Interest groups representing electric power companies expressed alarm. One of their main lobbyists, Haley Barbour, a former Republican Party chairman, threw down the gauntlet in a memorandum to Vice President Dick Cheney: "The question is whether environmental policy still prevails over energy policy with Bush-Cheney, as it did with Clinton-Gore." Barbour urged Cheney, who was heading a task force established by President Bush to conduct a broad review of energy policy, to show that environmental issues did not "trump good energy policy."[83] In March 2001 Bush announced that he would not impose carbon dioxide controls, explaining that "the reality is that our nation has a real problem when it comes to energy."[84]

Industry lobby groups such as the Edison Electric Institute and Electric Reliability Coordinating Council soon pressed the White House for new regulatory changes. One of their targets was a set of rules known as the New Source Review program, which required companies to add new pollution controls when they upgraded or expanded their plants. In a memorandum to Cheney, Whitman warned that any administration effort to undercut New Source Review rules would make it "hard to refute the charge that we are deciding not to enforce the Clean Air Act." In November 2002, however, the administration quietly released a statement from EPA's assistant administrator outlining revisions of the New Source Review program. The rules stipulated that companies would not have to add new pollution control devices if their plant upgrades and construction projects did not cost more than 20 percent of the plant's total value. The rules changes also raised the amount of pollution permitted an entire facility, rather than targeting emissions from individual pieces of equipment, and exempted plants that had installed modern pollution controls from having to make further improvements for ten years, regardless of their emission levels. Twelve states, twenty cities, and numerous environmental groups sued the EPA in response. "Our powerful, bipartisan court challenge says to this administration: 'No, you cannot repeal the federal Clean Air Act by dictatorial edict,'" declared Connecticut attorney general Richard Blumenthal.

Even as opponents of Bush's air quality policies fought these rules changes in the courts, environmental groups noted that lax regulatory enforcement had already paid huge dividends for affected power companies.[85] In addition to loosening air quality controls, Bush's EPA has proved far less vigorous than previous administrations in cracking down on companies that violate federal environmental laws. The number of lawsuits initiated against companies for environmental violations during Bush's first term declined 75 percent from the number initiated during the last four Clinton years. The $56.8 million in civil penalties that the EPA collected in fiscal 2004 is the lowest amount since 1990.[86]

The Bush White House's approach to environmental policy does not represent an isolated example. New regulations adopted during Bush's first term revised health rules, work safety standards, product safety disclosure requirements, energy regulations, and other measures in a manner that usually favored business and industry allies and drew fire from interest groups representing consumers, labor, the elderly, medical patients, racial minorities, and other constituencies. At the behest of automakers, the National Highway Traffic Safety Administration published a regulation forbidding the public release of some data related to unsafe motor vehicles because the information might cause "substantial competitive harm" to manufacturers. The Mine Safety and Health Administration proposed a new regulation that would dilute rules intended to protect coal miners from black lung disease. Responding to industry complaints, the Department of Labor dropped a rule requiring employers to keep a record of employees' ergonomic injuries. A rule that required hospitals to install facilities to protect workers against tuberculosis was also jettisoned by the administration. In response to lobbying by groups representing lumber and paper companies, Forest Service managers were authorized to approve logging in federal forests without the usual environmental reviews.

These regulatory initiatives inspired little or no public attention. Indeed, it is the unilateral, low-profile character of regulatory change that makes it so attractive to presidents whose efforts to get what they want from Congress are frustrated. During his tenure, George W. Bush honed the skills of collaborative politics-as-usual by regularly winning favorable policy outcomes for his administration and its interest group allies through incremental, regulatory means.

Conclusion

Political interactions between presidents and national interest groups are an intrinsic feature of contemporary American politics. By studying president–interest group relations as a function of executive leadership opportunities and the partisan and ideological affiliations of interest groups, we can recognize patterns across time, much as Stephen Skowronek's emphasis on regime cycles enables us to forge analytical links between presidents from different historical periods who faced similar political circumstances.[87] The existing scholarly literature underscores the recent development of the institutional resources and political strategies the White House can use to deal with the interest group system.[88] These findings sometimes have led presidential scholars to regard all modern presidents as equally well situated to orchestrate successful relations with organized interests. For example, according to Peterson, "Modern presidents have the institutional means, and have demonstrated the willingness, to influence the interest group system to their own advantage."[89] Our model of interactive politics offers a decidedly different portrait of president–interest group relations, one in which modern executives are frequently confounded in their efforts both to coax allies into supportive coalitions and to thwart opposition groups. Except for rare moments of presidential dominance, interest groups orchestrate effective strategic politics of their own.

Presidents with transformational policy aspirations but ordinary leadership opportunities have routinely found interest group relations trying. Oppositional groups are usually in a good position to frustrate the president's most ambitious programmatic goals, as Clinton's ill-fated crusade for health care reform illustrates. Nurturing and aiding interest group allies can also prove difficult for politically constrained presidents. These executives have strong incentives to endorse centrist measures that are popular but less bold because enactment allows them to point to tangible policy achievements. In the process, however, they routinely alienate affiliated interest groups, as George H. W. Bush learned when he supported the Clean Air Act amendments and the ADA. Indeed, the political allure of such popular centrist initiatives frequently saps the ability of politically constrained presidents to build strong coalitions to support their more partisan measures. During periods of politics-as-usual, they instead may quietly provide succor to their interest group allies through administrative means. But the intense scrutiny that the media and opposition groups devote to White House activities guarantees that such efforts rarely remain secret. When publicized, they may subject the president to charges of catering to special interests and may be contested by interest group adversaries in the federal courts and Congress.

Although most interest groups allied to presidents with constrained leadership opportunities receive fewer tangible benefits than many assume, oppositional groups often find the adversarial politics that prevails during such presidencies hospitable to vibrant and effective activism. As interest groups opposed to Clinton's Health Security program discovered in the 1994 midterm election, countermobilization can have surprising transformational possibilities.

Obviously, interest groups are most rewarded for collaborative relations with the White House during those rare historic moments when breakthrough presidents dominate American governance. But as the Christian right found during the Reagan revolution, such alliances are no guarantee of programmatic achievement. Breakthrough presidents set the terms of collaboration with their allied interest groups, and groups whose goals may jeopardize more important White House objectives may find themselves marginalized in the policy process. Even when the transformational goals of breakthrough presidents and allied interest groups are nearly the same, as was the case with Roosevelt and labor activists in the 1930s, co-optation is typically the price these groups pay to secure dramatic gains for their constituencies.

The sorry history of the American Liberty League illustrates the precarious situation of organized interests that oppose the programmatic ambitions of politically dominant presidents. It is telling, however, that Ronald Reagan, the most recent breakthrough president, dominated domestic policymaking for only a year and that his interest group adversaries prospered during most of his tenure. The scale and variety of the interest group system since the 1970s have been greater than ever before. This important development, as Graham Wilson argues, is part of what forces presidents today to contend with "a thicker structure of constraining institutions (in this case, interest groups)."[90] Thus the likelihood of strained relations between modern presidents and interest groups is greater than ever.

The Obama administration's reform agenda is exceptionally ambitious, reflecting its intention to translate unusually broad political warrants and opportunities into major economic domestic policy breakthroughs in areas ranging from the economy and health care to education, energy, and the environment. It also likely will have to tackle nettlesome questions such as illegal immigration, the failed drug war, and the future of Social Security. For all of these issues, the White House will gain support, absorb pressure, and endure opposition from the dense network of interest groups that are gathered in the nation's capital, including diverse citizens' groups, trade associations, corporations, labor unions, professional associations, and intergovernmental lobbies.

Thus far, Obama has used a repertoire of strategies in dealing with the Washington lobbying community. In a manner akin to other recent presidents, he has unflinchingly used executive orders to advance policies that are favorable to some of his party's strongest organized allies, such as new regulations on federal contractors endorsed by labor unions and federations; the reversal of Bush administration restrictions on funding for international family planning organizations that provide information, counseling, or referrals for abortion services that won praise from reproductive rights lobbies; and restoration of Endangered Species Act protections supported by environmental groups.[91] He has reached out to traditionally conservative business groups for support on domestic agenda items, such as health care reform, that will require bipartisan support.

Yet Obama also has been willing to introduce surprising game-changers to national interest group politics, like an unprecedented White House directive barring registered lobbyists from talking or meeting with administration officials about specific projects or applicants in the nearly $800 billion stimulus package. Lobbyists are permitted to submit written statements about stimulus projects to federal agencies, which must make these communications available online for the public to see within three days. These lobbying rules drew fire from the American Civil Liberties Union as a violation of First Amendment rights and from the trade group the American League of Lobbyists as "discrimination, segregation, and unconstitutional action against a class of Americans," but the public sided with the president.[92] Even as lobby groups vowed to fight these restrictions in court, the Treasury Department drew up plans for similar rules limiting lobbying on behalf of recipients of bank bailout money. For its part, the Obama administration clarified that its goal was not to curtail interest group lobbying but to make it more open and public. "The goal is full transparency," the White House explained, by "ending closed-door lobbyist deal-making in favor of sunlight."[93]

Despite the animosities unleashed by these new limits, interest groups in Washington have adapted to the power shift in predictable fashion. Organized interests aligned with the Democratic Party hope for rich programmatic rewards during the Obama presidency, but they have limited ability to challenge the White House when it pursues a more centrist or bipartisan policy course. Conservative interest groups have wasted little time in pursuing adversarial strategies in response to Obama's most significant domestic reform blueprints, and they already have profited from fund-raising efforts within their base. One of the most intriguing questions is whether Obama's dominance over the policymaking process will be as long as FDR's or as short-lived as Reagan's. Whichever the case, Obama's battles and collaborations with national lobbying groups will profoundly shape both policy outcomes and the character of American politics.

Notes

1. Lynn Sweet, "Not in My White House," *Chicago Sun-Times*, December 16, 2007; "Obama Vows Ethics Reforms," Associated Press, June 22, 2007; Alexander Bolton, "Senator Obama Finesses His Lobbyist Ties," *The Hill*, April 19, 2007. It bears noting that before entering the presidential contest, Obama emerged in 2006 as the Democrats' point-person on attacking a Republican "culture of corruption" in the wake of the Jack

Abramoff scandal. See "Obama Says It's Time to Clean Up Politics," ABCNews.com, January 18, 2006.

2. See, for example, Lee Walczak, "John Kerry: Already on the GOP Firing Line," *Business Week*, February 16, 2004; and Keith Koffler, *Congress Daily*, September 17, 2004, 5.

3. "Barack Obama Sharpens Special Interest Message," Associated Press, September 3, 2007; Leslie Wayne, "Outside Groups Aid Obama, Their Vocal Critic," *New York Times*, January 30, 2008.

4. David Kirkpatrick, "In Transition, Ties to Lobbying," *New York Times*, November 15, 2008; and Michael Kranish, "Obama Softens Ban on Hiring Lobbyists," *Boston Globe*, November 12, 2008.

5. Stewart Powell, "Obama's Vow to Rein in Lobbying Will Face Challenges," *Houston Chronicle*, January 20, 2009.

6. David Kirkpatrick, "Obama's Pick of Daschle May Test Conflict-of-Interest Pledge," *International Herald Tribune*, November 20, 2008; David Kirkpatrick, "In Transition, Ties to Lobbying," *New York Times*, November 15, 2008; Matthew Mosk, "Ex-Lobbyists Have Key Obama Roles," *Washington Post*, November 15, 2008.

7. David Stout, "Obama Moves to Reverse Bush Labor Policies," *New York Times*, January 30, 2009; "Obama Issues Executive Order Reversing GOP Abortion Policy," *CNN Political Ticker*, January 23, 2009.

8. Tom Hamburger and Peter Wallsten, "Obama Faces Choices among Special Interests," *Los Angeles Times*, January 19, 2009.

9. See Jeffrey Berry, *The Interest Group Society* (Glenview, Ill.: Scott, Foresman, 1989), 2–3; and Mark Petracca, "The Rediscovery of Interest Group Politics," in *The Politics of Interests: Interest Groups Transformed*, ed. Mark Petracca (Boulder: Westview Press, 1992), 7–11.

10. Quoted in James Deakin, *The Lobbyists* (Washington, D.C.: Public Affairs Press, 1966), 7.

11. "Is Bush Poisoning His Well?" *National Journal*, April 14, 2001, 1120–1121.

12. Lyndon Johnson adviser, quoted in Paul Light, *The President's Agenda* (Baltimore: Johns Hopkins University Press, 1999).

13. Stephen Wayne, "Interest Groups on the Road to the White House: Traveling Hard and Soft Routes," in *The Interest Group Connection*, ed. Paul Herrnson, Ronald Shaiko, and Clyde Wilcox (Chatham, N.J.: Chatham House Publishers, 1998), 65–79.

14. See Benjamin Ginsburg and Martin Shefter, "The Presidency and the Organization of Interests," in *The Presidency and the Political System*, 5th ed., ed. Michael Nelson (Washington, D.C.: CQ Press, 1988).

15. See Alexander Hamilton, James Madison, and John Jay, *The Federalist Papers*, ed. Clinton Rossiter (New York: New American Library, 1961).

16. Jeffrey Tulis, *The Rhetorical Presidency* (Princeton: Princeton University Press, 1987).

17. See Elisabeth Clemens, *The People's Lobby: Organizational Innovation and the Rise of Interest Group Politics in the United States, 1890–1925* (Chicago: University of Chicago Press, 1997); and Richard Harris and Daniel Tichenor, "Organized Interests and American Political Development," *Political Science Quarterly* (Spring 2003).

18. Quoted in Lewis Eigen and Jonathan Siegel, *The Macmillan Dictionary of Political Quotations* (New York: Macmillan, 1993), 382.

19. Ibid., 381.

20. E. Pendleton Herring, *Group Representation before Congress* (Baltimore: Johns Hopkins University Press, 1929), 51.

21. Quoted in Christine Lunardini and Thomas Knock, "Woodrow Wilson and Woman Suffrage: A New Look," *Political Science Quarterly* 95 (Winter 1981): 671.

22. Daniel Tichenor, "The Presidency, Social Movement, and Contentious Change: Lessons from the Woman's Suffrage and Labor Movements," *Presidential Studies Quarterly* 29 (March 1999): 14–25.

23. Robert Dahl, *Dilemmas of Pluralist Democracy* (New Haven: Yale University Press, 1982), 190.

24. Mark Peterson, "Interest Mobilization and the Presidency," in *The Politics of Interests: Interest Groups Transformed*, ed. Mark Petracca (Boulder: Westview Press, 1992), 239–240.

25. Joseph Pika, "Interest Groups and the White House under Roosevelt and Truman," *Political Science Quarterly* 102 (Fall 1987): 4, 647–668.

26. Bradley Patterson Jr., *The Ring of Power* (New York: Basic Books, 1988), 200–212.

27. William Lammers and Michael Genovese, *The Presidency and Domestic Policy* (Washington, D.C.: CQ Press, 2000); David Mayhew, *Divided We Govern* (New Haven: Yale University Press, 1991); and Erwin Hargrove and Michael Nelson, *Presidents, Politics and Policy* (New York: Knopf, 1984).

28. For an excellent typology of interest group liaison (governing party, consensus building, outreach, and legitimation), see Mark Peterson, "The Presidency and Organized Interests: White House Patterns of Interest Group Liaison," *American Political Science Review* 86 (September 1992): 3.

29. Robert Zeiger, *John L. Lewis: Labor Leader* (Boston: Twayne, 1988), 64.

30. William Leuchtenburg, *Franklin Roosevelt and the New Deal* (New York: Harper and Row, 1963), 106–107.

31. Ibid., 86.

32. Bruce Miroff, *Icons of Democracy* (New York: Basic Books, 1993), 262.

33. Ibid., 260–262.

34. Leuchtenburg, *Franklin Roosevelt*, 189.

35. Zeiger, *John L. Lewis*, 105–106.

36. Marc Landy, "FDR and John L. Lewis: The Lessons of Rivalry," in *Modern Presidents and the Presidency*, ed. Marc Landy (Lexington, Mass.: D. C. Heath, 1985), 106–112; and Zeiger, *John L. Lewis*, 109.

37. Alan Brinkley, *The End of Reform: New Deal Liberalism in Recession and War* (New York: Knopf, 1995), 201–226.

38. Ibid., 212.

39. Eric Larson, *Summer for the Gods* (Cambridge: Harvard University Press, 1997), 232–235.

40. John C. Green, "The Spirit Willing: Collective Identity and the Development of the Christian Right," in *Waves of Protest*, ed. Jo Freeman and Victoria Johnson (New York: Rowman and Littlefield, 1999), 156–159.

41. Kenneth Wald, *Religion and Politics in the United States* (Washington, D.C.: CQ Press, 1992), 234–235.

42. See Ralph Reed, *Active Faith: How Christians Are Changing the Soul of American Politics* (New York: Free Press, 1996), 113–114.

43. A. James Reichley, *Religion in American Public Life* (Washington, D.C.: Brookings Institution, 1985), 324–325.

44. Duane Oldfield, *The Right and the Righteous: The Christian Right Confronts the Republican Party* (New York: Rowman and Littlefield, 1996), 118–121.

45. See Reed, *Active Faith*, 114–115.

46. Reichley, *Religion in American Public Life*, 325.

47. Reed, *Active Faith*, 116.

48. Ibid., 115.

49. Leuchtenburg, *Franklin Roosevelt*, 90.

50. See Frederick Rudolph, "The American Liberty League, 1933–1940," *American Historical Review* 56 (October 1950): 19–33.

51. Albert Fried, *FDR and His Enemies* (New York: St. Martin's Press, 1999), 90–91, 120–125.

52. Krock is quoted in Rudolph, "The American Liberty League," 22–23.

53. Ibid., 25.

54. Ibid., 24, 28.

55. Fried, *FDR and His Enemies*, 90.

56. Leuchtenburg, *Franklin Roosevelt*, 178–179.

57. Rudolph, "The American Liberty League," 25.

58. The quote is Reagan's; see Michael S. Greve, "Why 'Defunding the Left' Failed," *Public Interest* 89 (Fall 1987): 91.

59. Peterson, "Interest Mobilization and the Presidency," 226–230.

60. Douglas R. Imig, "American Social Movements and Presidential Administrations," in *Social Movements and American Political Institutions*, ed. Ann Costain and Andrew McFarland (New York: Rowman and Littlefield, 1998), 151–162.

61. Douglas R. Imig, *Poverty and Power* (Lincoln: University of Nebraska Press, 1996), 49–54.

62. Imig, "American Social Movements," 167–169.

63. Mark Peterson and Jack Walker have shown that Reagan ushered in "a virtual revolution" in the access of interest groups to bureaucratic agencies of the federal government. See Peterson and Walker, "Interest Group Responses to Partisan Change," in *Interest Group Politics*, 2nd ed., ed. Allan J. Cigler and Burdett A. Loomis (Washington, D.C.: CQ Press, 1986), 172.

64. Greve, "Why 'Defunding the Left' Failed," 99.

65. See Christopher Bosso, "The Color of Money: Environmental Groups and the Pathologies of Fund Raising," in *Interest Group Politics*, 4th ed., ed. Allan J. Cigler and Burdett A. Loomis (Washington, D.C.: CQ Press, 1995), 104; and Richard Waterman, *Presidential Influence and the Administrative State* (Knoxville: University of Tennessee Press, 1989), 134.

66. John Holusha, "Bush Pledges Aid for Environment," *New York Times*, September 1, 1988.

67. Richard Cohen, *Washington at Work: Back Rooms and Clean Air* (New York: Macmillan, 1992); and Norman Vig, "Presidential Leadership and the Environment from Reagan to Clinton," in *Environmental Policy: New Directions for the Twenty-First Century*, 4th ed., ed. Norman Vig and Michael Kraft (Washington, D.C.: CQ Press, 2000), 104–107.

68. See David Mervin, *George Bush and the Guardianship Presidency* (New York: St. Martin's, 1996), 98–101.

69. See Richard Harris and Sidney Milkis, *The Politics of Regulatory Change: A Tale of Two Agencies* (New York: Oxford University Press, 1996), 292–293.

70. Mervin, *George Bush*, 100.

71. Quoted in Harris and Milkis, *Politics of Regulatory Change*, 289.

72. Jeffrey Berry and Kent Portney, "Centralizing Regulatory Control and Interest Group Access: The Quayle Council on Competitiveness," in *Interest Group Politics*, 4th ed., ed. Cigler and Loomis, 320.

73. Ibid., 336–340.

74. One of the best accounts of this struggle is provided by Paul Starr, *The Social Transformation of American Medicine* (New York: Basic Books, 1982), 350.

75. Jacob Hacker, *Road to Nowhere: The Genesis of President Clinton's Plan for Health Security* (Princeton: Princeton University Press, 1997).

76. Theda Skocpol, *Boomerang: Health Care Reform and the Turn against Government* (New York: Norton, 1997), 133–188; Allen Schick, "How a Bill Didn't Become a Law," in *Intensive Care: How Congress Shapes Health Policy*, ed. Thomas Mann and Norman Ornstein (Washington, D.C.: Brookings Institution Press, 1995), 240–251; and Darrell West and Burdett Loomis, *The Sound of Money* (New York: Norton, 1999), 75–108.

77. West and Loomis, *Sound of Money*, 78–82.

78. Skocpol, *Boomerang*, 143–146.

79. West and Loomis, *Sound of Money*, 83–85.

80. Ibid., 79–80.

81. Ibid., 92–93.

82. Douglas Jehl, "Rejoicing Is Muted for the President in Budget Victory," *New York Times*, August 8, 1993, 1, 23; and *Congressional Quarterly Weekly Report*, May 26, 2001, 1251–1254.

83. Christopher Drew and Richard Oppel Jr., "Air War: Remaking Energy Policy," *New York Times*, March 6, 2004, A1.

84. Ibid.

85. Matthew Wald, "E.P.A. Says It Will Change Rules Governing Industrial Pollution," *New York Times*, November 23, 2002, A1; Drew and Oppel, "Air War," 1; and Don Hopey, "Groups Score Bush on Environment," *Pittsburgh Post-Gazette*, November 10, 2004, 1.

86. Hopey, "Groups Score Bush on Environment," 1.

87. Stephen Skowronek, *The Politics Presidents Make* (Cambridge: Harvard University Press, 1993).

88. For an excellent review of this literature, see Joseph Pika, "Interest Groups: A Doubly Dynamic Relationship," in *Presidential Policymaking: An End-of-Century Assessment*, ed. Steven Shull (New York: M. E. Sharp, 1999), 59–78.

89. It is telling that Peterson focuses on the political activities of Lyndon Johnson and Ronald Reagan, presidents with exceptional political opportunities to advance policy breakthroughs. See Peterson, "Interest Mobilization and the Presidency," 237.

90. Graham K. Wilson, "The Clinton Administration and Interest Groups," in *The Clinton Presidency: First Appraisals*, ed. Colin Campbell and Bert Rockman (Chatham, N.J.: Chatham House, 1996), 231.

91. Stout, "Obama Moves to Reverse Bush Labor Policies."

92. Kenneth Vogel, "Obama Order Worries Speech Groups," Politico.com, March 28, 2009; Kevin Bogardus, "New Rules on Stimulus Make Lobbyists Bristle," *The Hill*, March 23, 2009.

93. Ibid.

11 The Presidency and Political Parties

Sidney M. Milkis

The modern presidency has been anything but supportive of today's Republican and Democratic Parties. According to Sidney M. Milkis, most presidents, starting with Franklin Roosevelt, have found the traditional party system too grounded in state and local organizations to be of much help in the effort to forge presidential policies and programs. Indeed, to the extent that the parties have exercised influence through Congress, presidents have sometimes perceived them to be an impediment to national leadership. FDR, Lyndon Johnson, and Richard Nixon each took steps to replace party influence with administration centralized in the bureaucracy and the White House. Ronald Reagan and George H. W. Bush tried to restore some (but not all) of the traditional importance of the political parties, Milkis argues, by "refashioning them into highly untraditional but politically potent national organizations." Their efforts were uneven and met with limited success. Although Bill Clinton did little to sustain the Democratic Party, George W. Bush contributed to, and benefited from, the development of the more national and programmatic Republican Party that emerged with the resurgence and transformation of conservatism during the Reagan presidency. Bush's militant partisanship ultimately became an albatross for his party; nevertheless, national parties are likely to be an important feature of American politics in the foreseeable future. Indeed, the 2008 election made clear that Barack Obama and the Democrats learned a great deal from the political tactics employed by the Republicans.

The relationship between the presidency and the American party system has always been difficult. The architects of the Constitution established a non-partisan president who, with the support of the judiciary, was intended to play the leading institutional role in checking and controlling the "violence of faction" that the Framers feared would rend the fabric of representative democracy. Even after the presidency became a more partisan office in the early nineteenth century, its authority continued to depend on an ability to transcend party politics.

The president is nominated by a party but, unlike the British prime minister, is not elected by it.

The inherent tension between the presidency and the party system reached a critical point during the 1930s. The institutionalization of the modern presidency, arguably the most significant constitutional legacy of Franklin Roosevelt's New Deal, ruptured the limited but significant bond that linked presidents to their parties. In fact, the modern presidency was crafted with the intention of reducing the influence of the party system on American politics. In this sense Roosevelt's extraordinary party leadership contributed to the decline of the American party system. This decline continued—even accelerated—under the administrations of subsequent presidents, notably Lyndon Johnson and Richard Nixon. Under Ronald Reagan, however, the party system showed signs of transformation and renewal. Reagan and his successor, George H. W. Bush, supported efforts by Republicans in the national committee and the congressional campaign organizations to restore some of the importance of political parties by refashioning them into highly untraditional but politically potent national organizations. George W. Bush further advanced and benefited from the more national and programmatic party that arose with the resurgence and transformation of conservatism during the Reagan presidency. Although Bush ultimately became an albatross for the Republican Party in the 2008 election, his experience suggests that vigorous presidential leadership in the present configuration of executive and party has the defects of its virtues. In the hands of an overweening executive, the party may simply become a means to the president's end, sapping the organization of both its autonomy and its ability to adapt to changing political circumstances. It remains to be seen, therefore, whether national programmatic parties can perform the parties' historic function of moderating presidential ambition and mobilizing public support for political values and government policies.

New Deal Party Politics, Presidential Reform, and the Decline of the American Party System

The New Deal seriously questioned the adequacy of the traditional natural-rights liberalism of John Locke and the Framers, which emphasized the need to limit constitutionally the scope of government's responsibilities. The modern liberalism that became the public philosophy of the New Deal entailed a fundamental reappraisal of the concept of rights. As Roosevelt first indicated in a 1932 campaign speech at the Commonwealth Club in San Francisco, effective political reform would require, at a minimum, the development of "an economic declaration of rights, an economic constitutional order," grounded in a commitment to guarantee a decent level of economic well-being for the American people. Although equality of opportunity had traditionally been promoted by limited government interference in society, Roosevelt argued, recent economic and social changes, such as the closing of the frontiers and the growth of industrial combinations, demanded that America now recognize "the new terms of the old social contract."[1]

Establishing a new constitutional order would require a reordering of the political process. The traditional patterns of American politics, characterized by constitutional mechanisms that impede collective action, would have to give way to a more centralized and administrative government. As Roosevelt put it, "The day of enlightened administration has come."[2]

The concerns Roosevelt expressed at the Commonwealth Club are an important guide to understanding the New Deal and its effects on the party system. The pursuit of an economic constitutional order presupposed a fundamental change in the relationship between the presidency and the party system. In Roosevelt's view, the party system, which was essentially based on state and local organizations and interests and therefore was suited to congressional primacy, would have to be transformed into a national, executive-oriented system organized on the basis of public issues.

In this understanding Roosevelt was no doubt influenced by the thought of Woodrow Wilson. The reform of parties, Wilson believed, depended on extending the influence of the presidency. The limits on partisanship inherent in American constitutional government notwithstanding, the president represented the party's "vital link of connection" with the nation: "He can dominate his party by being spokesman for the real sentiment and purpose of the country, by giving the country at once the information and statements of policy which will enable it to form its judgments alike of parties and men."[3]

Wilson's words spoke louder than his actions; like all presidents after 1800, he reconciled himself to the strong fissures within his party.[4] Roosevelt, however, was less willing to work through existing partisan channels, and more important, the New Deal represented a more fundamental departure than did Wilsonian progressivism from traditional Democratic policies of individual autonomy, limited government, and states' rights.

While president-elect, Roosevelt began preparations to modify the partisan practices of previous administrations. For example, convinced that Wilson's adherence to traditional partisan politics in staffing the federal government was unfortunate, Roosevelt expressed to Attorney General Homer Cummings his desire to proceed along somewhat different lines, with a view, according to

Cummings's diary, "to building up a national organization rather than allowing patronage to be used merely to build Senatorial and Congressional machines."[5] Roosevelt followed traditional patronage practices during his first term, allowing the chair of the Democratic National Committee (DNC), James Farley, to coordinate appointments in response to local party organizations and Democratic senators. After Roosevelt's reelection in 1936, however, the recommendations of these organizations were not followed as closely. Beginning in 1938 especially, as Edward Flynn, who became the DNC chair in 1940, indicated in his memoirs, "the President turned more and more frequently to the so-called New Dealers," so that "many of the appointments in Washington went to men who were supporters of the President and believed in what he was trying to do, but who were not Democrats in many instances, and in all instances were not organization Democrats."[6]

Wilson had taken care to consult with congressional party leaders in the development of his policy program, but Roosevelt relegated his party in Congress to a decidedly subordinate status. He offended legislators by his use of press conferences to announce important decisions and, unlike Wilson, eschewed the use of the party caucus in Congress. Roosevelt rejected as impractical, for example, the Wilsonian suggestion of Rep. Alfred Phillips Jr. "that those sharing the burden of responsibility of party government should regularly and often be called into caucus and that such caucuses should evolve party policies and choice of party leaders."[7]

The most dramatic aspect of Roosevelt's attempt to remake the Democratic Party was his twelve-state effort, involving one gubernatorial and several congressional primary campaigns, to unseat conservative Democrats in 1938. Such intervention was not unprecedented; William Taft and Wilson had made limited efforts to remove recalcitrants from their parties. But Roosevelt's campaign took place on a scale that was never before seen and, unlike previous efforts, made no attempt to work through the regular party organization. His action was viewed as such a shocking departure from the norm that the press labeled it "the purge," a term associated with Adolf Hitler's attempt to weed out dissension from Germany's National Socialist Party and Joseph Stalin's elimination of "disloyal" members from the Soviet Communist Party.

In 1936 the Roosevelt administration successfully pushed to abolish the Democratic National Convention rule that required support from two-thirds of the delegates for the nomination of the president and vice president. This rule had been defended in the past because it guarded the most loyal Democratic region—the South—against the imposition of an unwanted ticket by the less habitually Democratic North, East, and West.[8] To eliminate the rule, therefore, would weaken the influence of southern Democrats (whom Thomas Stokes, a liberal journalist, described as "the ball and chain which hobbled the Party's forward march") and facilitate the adoption of a national reform program.[9]

After the 1938 purge campaign, columnist Raymond Clapper noted that "no President ever has gone as far as Mr. Roosevelt in striving to stamp his policies upon his party."[10] Roosevelt's massive partisan effort began the process of transforming the parties from local to national and programmatic organizations. At the same time, the New Deal made partisanship less important. Roosevelt's partisan leadership ultimately was based on forging a personal link with the public that would better enable him to make use of his position as leader of the nation, not just of the party that governed the nation.[11] For example, in all but one of the 1938 primary campaigns in which he participated personally, Roosevelt chose to make a direct appeal to public opinion rather than attempt to work through, or reform, the regular party apparatus. This strategy was encouraged by earlier reforms, especially the direct primary, which had begun to weaken the grip of party organizations on the voters. Radio broadcasting also had made direct presidential appeals an enticing strategy, especially for as popular a president with as fine a radio presence as Roosevelt. After his close associate Felix Frankfurter urged him to go to the country in August 1937 to explain the issues that gave rise to the bitter Court-packing controversy, Roosevelt, perhaps anticipating the purge campaign, responded, "You are absolutely right about the radio. I feel like saying to the country—'You will hear from me soon and often. This is not a threat but a promise.'"[12]

In the final analysis the "benign dictatorship" that Roosevelt sought to impose on the Democratic Party was more conducive to corroding the American party system than to reforming it. His prescription for party reform—extraordinary presidential leadership—posed a serious if not intractable dilemma. On the one hand, the decentralized character of politics in the United States could be modified only by strong presidential leadership; on the other, a president determined to alter fundamentally the connection between the executive and the party eventually would shatter party unity.[13]

Roosevelt, in fact, was always aware that the extent to which his goals could be achieved by party leadership was limited. He felt that a full revamping of partisan politics was impractical, given the obstacles to party government that are so deeply ingrained in the American political experience. The immense failure of the purge campaign reinforced this view: in the dozen states in which the president acted against entrenched incumbents, he was successful in only two—Oregon and New York.[14] Moreover, Roosevelt and his fellow New Dealers did not view the welfare state as a partisan issue. The reform program of the

1930s was conceived as a "second bill of rights" that they meant to establish as much as possible in permanent programs beyond the vagaries of public opinion and elections. The new rights that Roosevelt pledged the federal government to protect included "the right to a useful and remunerative job" and "the right to adequate protection from the fears of old age, sickness, accident and unemployment."[15] These new rights were never formally ratified as part of the Constitution, but they became the foundation of political dialogue, redefining the role of the national government and requiring major changes in American political institutions.

Thus, the most significant institutional reforms of the New Deal did not promote party government but fostered instead a program that would help the president to govern in the absence of party government—to enable him to become, in Theodore Roosevelt's capacious phrase, "the steward of the public welfare."[16] This program, as embodied in the 1937 executive reorganization bill, would have greatly extended presidential authority over the executive branch, including the independent regulatory commissions. The president and the executive agencies would also be delegated extensive authority to govern, making unnecessary the constant cooperation of party members in Congress. As a presidential committee report put it, with administrative reform the "brief exultant commitment" to progressive government that was expressed in the elections of 1932 and, especially, 1936 would now be more firmly established in "persistent, determined, competent, day by day administration of what the Nation has decided to do."[17]

Interestingly, the reorganization bill, which was intended to make politics less necessary, became, at Roosevelt's urging, a party government–style "vote of confidence" for the administration in Congress.[18] Roosevelt initially lost this vote in 1938, when the bill was defeated in the House of Representatives, but he did manage, through the purge campaign and other partisan actions, to keep administrative reform sufficiently prominent in party councils that a compromise version passed in 1939. Although considerably weaker than Roosevelt's original proposal, the 1939 Executive Reorganization Act was a significant measure. It not only provided authority to create the Executive Office of the President, which included the newly formed White House Office and a strengthened and refurbished Bureau of the Budget, but also enhanced the president's control of the expanding activities of the executive branch. The reorganization act represents the genesis of the institutional presidency, which was equipped to govern independently of the constraints imposed by the regular political process.

The civil service reform that the Roosevelt administration carried out was another important part of the effort to replace partisan politics with executive administration. The original reorganization proposals of 1937 contained provisions to make the administration of the civil service more effective and to expand the merit system. Although the reorganization bill passed in 1939 was shorn of this controversial feature, Roosevelt found it possible to accomplish extensive civil service reform through executive action and other legislation. He extended merit protection to personnel appointed by the administration during its first term, four-fifths of whom had been brought into government outside of merit channels.[19] Patronage appointments had traditionally been used to nourish the party system; the New Deal celebrated an administrative politics that fed instead an executive branch oriented to expanding liberal programs. As the administrative historian Paul Van Riper has noted, the new practices created a new kind of patronage, "a sort of intellectual and ideological patronage rather than the more traditional partisan type."[20]

Roosevelt's leadership transformed the Democratic Party into a way station on the road to administrative government. As the presidency developed into an elaborate and ubiquitous institution, it preempted party leaders in many of their limited, but significant, duties: providing a link from government to interest groups, staffing the executive department, contributing to policy development, organizing election campaigns, and communicating with the public.[21] Moreover, New Deal administrative reform was directed not just to creating presidential government but also to embedding progressive principles in a bureaucratic structure that would insulate reform and reformers from electoral change.

Lyndon Johnson's Great Society and the Transcendence of Partisan Politics

Roosevelt's leadership during the New Deal prepared the executive branch to be a government unto itself and established the presidency rather than the party as the locus of political responsibility. World War II and the Cold War greatly augmented this shift. With the Great Depression giving way to war, another expansion of presidential authority took place, as part of the national security state, further weakening the executive's ties with the party system. As the New Deal prepared for war, Roosevelt spoke not only of the government's obligation to guarantee "freedom from want" but also of its responsibility to provide "freedom from fear"—to protect the American people, and the world, against foreign aggression. The obligation to uphold "human rights" became a new guarantee of security, which presupposed a further expansion of national administrative power.[22] The new requirements of internationalism allowed Harry Truman to persuade Congress to enact an additional administrative reform in 1947, increasing the powers of, and centralizing control over, the national security state.

Called the National Security Act, it created the National Security Council, the Central Intelligence Agency, and the Department of Defense.[23]

But the modern presidency was created to chart the course for, and direct the voyage to, a more liberal America. Roosevelt's pronouncement of a "second bill of rights" had begun this task, and it fell to Lyndon Johnson, as one journalist noted, to "codify the New Deal vision of a good society."[24] Johnson's Great Society program entailed expanding the economic constitutional order with policy innovations such as Medicare and, even more significant, extending those benefits to African Americans.

Johnson's attempt to create the Great Society marked a significant extension of programmatic liberalism and accelerated the effort to transcend partisan politics. Johnson, who came to Congress in 1937 in a special House election as an enthusiastic supporter of the New Deal, well remembered Roosevelt's ill-fated efforts to guide the affairs of his party. He took Roosevelt's experience to be the best example of the generally ephemeral nature of party government in the United States, and he fully expected the cohesive Democratic support he received from Congress after the 1964 election to be temporary.[25] Johnson, like Roosevelt, looked beyond the party system toward the politics of "enlightened administration."

Although Johnson avoided any sort of purge campaign and worked closely with Democratic congressional leaders, he took strong action to de-emphasize the role of the traditional party organization. For example, the Johnson administration undertook a ruthless attack on the DNC beginning in late 1965, slashing its budget to the bone and eliminating several of its important programs, such as the highly successful voter registration division. The president also ignored the pleas of several advisers to replace the amiable but ineffective John Bailey as DNC chair. Instead, he humiliated Bailey, keeping him but turning over control of the scaled-back committee's activities to Marvin Watson, the White House political liaison.[26]

Journalists and scholars explain Johnson's lack of support for the regular party organization by invoking his political background and personality. Some observers have suggested that Johnson was afraid the DNC might be built into a power center capable of challenging his authority on behalf of the Kennedy wing of the party.[27] Others have pointed to Johnson's roots in the one-party system of Texas, an experience that inclined him to emphasize a consensus style of politics, based on support from diverse elements of the electorate that spanned traditional party lines.[28]

These explanations are not without merit. Yet to view Johnson's failures as a party leader in purely personal terms is to ignore the imperative of policy reform that influenced his administration. Like Roosevelt, Johnson "had always regarded political parties, strongly rooted in states and localities, capable of holding him accountable, as intruders on the business of government."[29] Moreover, from the beginning of his presidency Johnson had envisioned the enactment of an ambitious program that would leave its (and his) mark on history in the areas of government organization, conservation, education, and urban affairs. Such efforts to advance the New Deal goal of economic security and also to enhance the "quality of American life" necessarily brought Johnson into sharp conflict with established elements of the Democratic Party, such as the national committee and local machines.[30] As one Johnson aide put it, "Because of the ambitious reforms [LBJ] pushed, it was necessary to move well beyond, to suspend attention to, the party."[31]

Considerable evidence exists that the Johnson administration lacked confidence in the Democratic Party's ability to act as an intermediary between the White House and the American people. For example, an aide to Vice President Hubert Humphrey wrote to Marvin Watson that "out in the country most Democrats at the State and local level are not intellectually equipped to help on such critical issues as Vietnam and the riots." After a meeting with district party leaders from Queens, New York, White House domestic adviser Joseph Califano reported that "they were . . . totally unfamiliar with the dramatic increases in the poverty, health, education and manpower training areas."[32] The uneasy relationship between the Johnson presidency and the Democratic Party was particularly aggravated by the administration's aggressive commitment to civil rights, which created considerable friction with local party organizations, especially, but not exclusively, in the South. It is little wonder, then, that when riots began to erupt in the cities in the mid-1960s, the president had his special assistants spend time in ghettos around the country instead of relying on the reports of local party leaders.[33]

Lack of trust in the Democratic Party encouraged the Johnson administration to renew the New Deal pattern of institutional reform. In the area of policy development, one of Johnson's most significant innovations was to create several task forces under the supervision of the White House Office and the Bureau of the Budget. These working groups were made up of leading academics throughout the country, who prepared reports in virtually all areas of public policy. The specific proposals that came out of these groups, such as the Education Task Force's elementary education proposal, formed the heart of the Great Society program. The administration took great care to protect the task forces from political pressures, even keeping their existence secret. Moreover, members were told to pay no attention to political considerations; they were not to worry about whether their recommendations would be acceptable to Congress and party leaders.[34]

The de-emphasis of partisan politics that marked the creation of the Great Society was also apparent in the personnel policy of the Johnson presidency. As his main talent scout, Johnson chose not a political adviser but John Macy, who was also chair of the Civil Service Commission. Macy worked closely with the White House staff, but especially during the early days of the administration, he was responsible for making recommendations directly to the president. As the White House staff rather grudgingly admitted, Macy's "wheel ground exceedingly slow but exceedingly fine."[35] He uncovered candidates with impressive credentials and experience after careful national searches.

The Johnson administration's strong commitment to merit greatly disturbed certain advisers who were responsible for maintaining the president's political support. James Rowe, who was Johnson's campaign director in 1964 and 1968, constantly hounded Macy, without success, to consider political loyalists more carefully. Rowe believed that Johnson's personnel policy was gratuitously inattentive to political exigencies. At one point he ended a memo to Macy by saying, "Perhaps you can train some of those career men to run the political campaign in 1968. (It ain't as easy as you government people appear to think it is.)" Macy never responded, but the president called the next day to defend his personnel director and to chastise Rowe for seeking to interfere in the appointment process.[36]

The rupture between the presidency and the party made it difficult to sustain political enthusiasm and organizational support for the Great Society. The Democrats' poor showing in the 1966 congressional elections precipitated a firestorm of criticism about the president's inattention to party politics, criticism that continued until Johnson withdrew from the presidential campaign in 1968. Yet Johnson and most of his advisers felt that they had to de-emphasize partisanship if the administration was to achieve programmatic reform and coordinate the increasingly unwieldy activities of government. During the early days of the Johnson presidency, one of his more thoughtful aides, Horace Busby, wrote the president a long memo in which he stressed the importance of establishing an institutional basis for the Great Society. About a year later, Busby expressed great satisfaction that Johnson had confounded his critics by achieving notable institutional changes. In fact, these changes seemed to mark the full triumph of the Democrats as the party to end party politics:

Most startling is that while all recognize Johnson as a great politician his appointments have been the most consistently free of politics of any President—in the Cabinet or at lower levels.

On record, history will remember this as the most important era of nonpartisanship since the "Era of Good Feeling" more than a century ago at the start of the nineteenth century. Absence of politics and partisanship is one reason the GOP is having a hard time mounting any respectable offense against either Johnson or his program.[37]

As in the case of the New Deal, however, the institutional innovations of the Great Society did not eliminate "politics" from the activities of the executive branch. Rather, the Great Society extended the merging of politics and administration that had characterized executive reform during the 1930s. For example, to improve his use of the appointment process as a tool of executive administration, Johnson issued an executive order to create a new category of positions in the executive branch, called noncareer executive assignments (NEAs). In recognition of their direct involvement in policymaking, the NEAs were exempted from the usual civil service requirements.

To be sure, the NEAs gave Johnson a stronger foothold in the agencies.[38] But the criteria his administration used to fill these positions emphasized loyalty to Johnson's program rather than a personal commitment to the president. As a consequence, Johnson's active role as manager of the federal service, which John Macy considered unprecedented for a "modern-day Chief Executive," helped to revive the high morale and programmatic commitment that had characterized the bureaucracy during the 1930s.[39] As White House aide Bill Moyers urged in a memo to the president regarding the newly created Department of Housing and Urban Development, the goal of the Great Society was to renew "some of the zeal—coupled with sound, tough executive management of the New Deal days."[40]

The legacy of Johnson's assault on party politics was apparent in the 1968 election. By 1966 Democratic leaders no longer felt that they were part of a national coalition. As 1968 approached, the Johnson administration was preparing a campaign task force that would work independently of the regular party apparatus.[41] These actions greatly accelerated the breakdown of the state and local Democratic machinery, placing party organizations in acute distress in nearly every large state.[42] By the time Johnson withdrew from the election in March 1968, the Democratic Party was already in the midst of a lengthy period of decay that was accentuated, but not really caused, by the conflict over the Vietnam War.

Thus, the tumultuous 1968 Democratic convention and the reforms of the nominating process, spawned by the McGovern-Fraser Commission, that followed in its wake should be viewed as the culmination of long-standing efforts to free the presidency from traditional partisan influences. In many respects, the expansion of presidential primaries and other changes in nomination politics that the commission initiated were a logical extension of the modern presidency. The very quietness of the revolution in party rules that took place during the 1970s is evidence in itself that the party system was forlorn by the end of the Johnson era. Those changes could not have been accomplished over the opposition of alert and vigorous party leaders.[43]

Johnson was well aware that the collapse of the regular party apparatus was under way by 1968. From 1966 on, his aides bombarded him with memos warning of the disarray in the Democratic Party organization. Johnson also was informed that reform forces in the states were creating "a new ball game with new rules." These memos indicated that by exploiting the weakened party apparatus, an insurgent with as little national prominence as antiwar senator Eugene McCarthy could mount a head-on challenge to Johnson.[44] The president expressed his own recognition of the decline of party politics in a meeting with Humphrey on April 5, 1968, a few days after he announced his decision not to run for reelection. Although indicating his intention to remain publicly neutral, Johnson wished the vice president well. But he expressed concern about Humphrey's ability to win the support of the party organization: "This the president cannot assure the vice president because he could not assure it for himself."[45] Like Roosevelt, Johnson had greatly diminished his partisan capital in pursuit of programmatic innovation.

Richard Nixon, Nonpartisanship, and the Demise of the Modern Presidency

Considering that the New Deal and Great Society were established by replacing traditional party politics with administration, it is not surprising that when a conservative challenge to liberal reform emerged, it entailed the creation of a conservative "administrative presidency."[46]

Until the late 1960s, opponents of the welfare state were generally opposed to the modern presidency, which had served as the fulcrum of liberal reform. Nevertheless, by the end of the Johnson administration it was clear that a strong conservative movement would require an activist program of retrenchment to counteract the enduring effects of the New Deal and Great Society.[47] Opponents of liberal public policy, most of them Republicans, decided that, ideologically, the modern presidency could be a two-edged sword.

The administrative actions of the Nixon presidency were a logical extension of the practices of Roosevelt and Johnson. Nixon's centralization of authority in the White House and reduction of the regular Republican organization to perfunctory status were hardly unprecedented.[48] The complete autonomy of the

Committee for the Re-Election of the President (CREEP) from the Republican National Committee (RNC) in Nixon's 1972 campaign was but the final stage of a long process of White House preemption of the national committee's political responsibilities. And the administrative reform program that was pursued after Nixon's reelection, in which he concentrated executive authority in the hands of White House operatives and four cabinet "supersecretaries," was the culmination of a long-standing tendency in the modern presidency to reconstitute the executive branch as a formidable instrument of government.[49]

Thus, just as Roosevelt's presidency anticipated the Great Society, Johnson's presidency anticipated the administrative presidency of Richard Nixon. Indeed, the strategy of pursuing policy goals through administrative entities, which had been created for the most part by Democratic presidents, was considered especially suitable by a minority Republican president who faced a Congress and bureaucracy intent on preserving his predecessors' programs. Nixon actually surpassed previous modern presidents in viewing the party system as an obstacle to effective governance.

Yet, mainly because of the Watergate scandal, Nixon's presidency had the effect of strengthening opposition to the unilateral use of presidential power, even as it further attenuated the bonds that linked presidents to the party system. The evolution of the modern presidency now left the office in complete institutional isolation. This isolation continued during the Ford and Carter years, so much so that by the end of the 1970s scholars were lamenting the demise of the presidency as well as of the party system.

The Reagan Presidency and the Revitalization of Party Politics

Although the emergence of the modern presidency fostered a serious decline in the traditional, local and state patronage-based parties, some developments during the Reagan presidency suggested that a phoenix was emerging from the ashes. The erosion of old-style partisan politics allowed a more national and issue-oriented party system to develop, forging new links between presidents and their parties.

The Republican Party in particular developed a formidable organizational apparatus, which displayed unprecedented strength at the national level.[50] The refurbishing of the Republican organization was due largely to the efforts of William Brock, who, during his tenure as chair of the RNC from 1976 to 1980, set out to rejuvenate and ultimately to revolutionize the national party. After 1976 the RNC and the two other national Republican campaign bodies, the National Republican Senatorial Committee and the National Republican Congressional

(House) Committee, greatly expanded their efforts to raise funds and provide services for the party's state and local candidates. Moreover, these efforts carried the national party into activities, such as publishing public policy journals and distributing comprehensive briefing books for candidates, that demonstrated its interest in generating programmatic proposals that might be politically useful. The Democrats lagged behind in party-building efforts, but the losses they suffered in the 1980 elections encouraged them to modernize the national political machinery, openly imitating some of the devices used by the Republicans. As a result, the traditional apparatus of both parties, based on patronage and state and local organizations, gave way to a more programmatic party politics, based on the national organization. Arguably, a party system had finally evolved that was compatible with the national polity forged on the anvil of the New Deal.[51]

The revival of the Republican Party as a force to counter government-by-administration reinforced the development of a new American party system. The nomination and election of Ronald Reagan, a far more ideological conservative than Richard Nixon, galvanized the GOP's commitment to programs, such as "regulatory relief" and "new federalism," that challenged the institutional legacy of the New Deal. At the same time, Reagan broke with the tradition of the modern presidency and identified closely with his party. The president worked hard to strengthen the Republicans' organizational and popular base, surprising his own political director with his "total readiness" to shoulder partisan responsibilities such as making numerous fund-raising appearances for the party and its candidates.[52] After having spent the first fifty years of his life as a Democrat, Reagan brought the enthusiasm of a convert to Republican activities.

The experience of the Reagan administration suggested how the relationship between the president and the party could be mutually beneficial. A strong Republican Party provided Reagan with the support of a formidable institution, solidifying his personal popularity and facilitating support for his program in Congress. As a result, the Reagan presidency was able to suspend the paralysis that had seemed to afflict the executive office in the 1970s, even though the Republicans still lacked control of the House of Representatives. In turn, Reagan's popularity served the party by strengthening its fund-raising efforts and promoting a shift in voters' party loyalties, placing the Republicans by 1985 in a position of virtual parity with the Democrats for the first time since the 1940s.[53] It may be, then, that the 1980s marked the watershed both for a new political era and for a renewed link between presidents and the party system.

Yet the Reagan presidency frequently pursued its program with acts of administrative discretion that short-circuited the legislative process and weakened efforts to carry out broadly based party policies. From the start, in fact, the Reagan White House often pursued programmatic change by using the administrative tactics that characterized the Nixon years. Not only was policy centered in the White House Office and other support agencies in the Executive Office of the President, but much care was taken to plant White House loyalists in the departments and agencies—people who could be trusted to ride herd on civil servants and carry forth the president's program. Most significant, a wide range of policies to deregulate business were pursued, not through legislative change but by administrative inaction, delay, and repeal. President Reagan's Executive Orders 12291 and 12498 mandated a comprehensive review of proposed agency regulations and centralized the review process in the Office of Management and Budget (OMB).[54] Reagan also appointed the Task Force on Regulatory Relief, headed by Vice President George H. W. Bush, to apply cost-benefit analyses to existing rules. As for the Iran-contra scandal, it was not simply a matter of the president's being asleep on his watch; rather, it also revealed the Reagan administration's determination to assume a more forceful anticommunist posture in Central America in the face of a recalcitrant Congress and bureaucracy.[55]

In sum, Reagan did not transform Washington completely. Rather, he strengthened the Republican beachhead in the nation's capital, solidifying his party's recent dominance of the presidency and providing better opportunities for conservatives in the Washington community. Reagan's landslide reelection in 1984 did not prevent the Democrats from maintaining control of the House of Representatives; nor did his plea to the voters during the 1986 congressional campaign to elect Republican majorities prevent the Democrats from recapturing control of the Senate. The 1988 election, in which Vice President Bush defeated the Democratic Massachusetts governor, Michael Dukakis, appeared to confirm the limits of the Reagan revolution, reflecting in its outcome the underlying pattern that had characterized American politics since 1968: Republican dominance of the White House, Democratic ascendancy almost everywhere else. In fact, the 1988 election represented an extreme manifestation of the pattern. Never before had a president been elected while the other party gained ground in the House, the Senate, the state legislatures, and the state governorships. Never before had voters given a newly elected president fewer fellow partisans in Congress than they gave George H. W. Bush.[56]

Reagan's two terms witnessed a revitalization of the struggle between the president and Congress; indeed, his conservative program became the foundation for more fundamental philosophical and policy differences between the two branches than in the past. The Iran-contra affair and the battles to control regulatory policy were marked not just by differences between Reagan and Congress about policy but also by the efforts of each to weaken the other. The pursuit of conservative policies through the administrative presidency continued with Bush's elevation to the White House. Facing hostile Democratic majorities in the House and Senate, the Bush administration imposed the burden of curbing environmental, consumer, and civil rights regulations on the Competitiveness Council, chaired by Vice President Dan Quayle. Like its predecessor, the Task Force on Regulatory Relief, the Competitiveness Council required administrative agencies to justify the costs of existing and proposed regulations. The efforts of Republican presidents to compensate for their party's inability to control Congress by seeking to circumvent legislative restrictions on presidential conduct were matched by Democratic initiatives to burden the executive with smothering legislative oversight.[57] Conservatives opposed to liberal reform, then, did not challenge national administrative power but fought a raw and disruptive battle to control its services.

A major, if not the main, forum for partisan conflict during the Reagan and Bush years was a sequence of investigations in which Democrats and Republicans sought to discredit one another. To be sure, ongoing legal scrutiny of public officials was in part a logical response to the Watergate scandal. To prevent another Nixon-style "Saturday Night Massacre," Congress passed the Ethics in Government Act of 1978, which provided for the appointment of independent counsels to investigate allegations of criminal activity by executive officials. Not surprisingly, divided government encouraged the exploitation of the act for partisan purposes. In the 1980s congressional Democrats frequently demanded criminal investigations and possible jail sentences for their political opponents. When Bill Clinton became president in 1993, congressional Republicans turned the tide with a vengeance. As a consequence, political disagreements were readily transformed into criminal prosecutions. Moreover, investigations under the independent counsel statute tended to deflect attention from legitimate constitutional policy differences and to focus the attention of Congress, the press, and citizens alike on scandals. Disgrace and imprisonment thus joined electoral defeat as risks of political combat in the United States.[58]

Bill Clinton and the Politics of Divided Democracy

The 1992 election contained both optimistic and pessimistic portents for linking the modern presidency and national parties. The Democrats ran an effective campaign; the party not only captured the presidency but also preserved its majorities in the House and Senate, ending twelve years of divided rule in Washington. Indeed, Bill Clinton's victory over George H. W. Bush seemed to represent more than a rejection of the incumbent president; in part, it expressed the voters' hope that the institutional conflict they had witnessed during the era of divided government would now come to an end.[59] This hope was encouraged by Clinton's promise to govern as a "new Democrat," an "agent of change" who would restore consensus to American politics.

Nevertheless, the strong support for independent candidate Ross Perot reflected the continuing erosion of partisan loyalties in the electorate. Perot's campaign, which garnered 19 percent of the popular vote (the most serious electoral challenge to the two-party system since Theodore Roosevelt's 1912 Progressive Party candidacy), suggested just how much presidential politics had become detached from the constraints of party. Perot, a successful businessman, had never held political office of any kind, and his campaign, dominated by thirty-minute infomercials and hour-long appearances on television talk shows, set a new standard for direct, plebiscitary appeals to the voters that threatened to sound the death knell of the party campaign. "Perot hints broadly at an even bolder new order," historian Alan Brinkley wrote in July 1992, "in which the president, checked only by direct expressions of popular desire, will roll up his sleeves and solve the nation's problems."[60]

In the end, however, the American people invested their hope for constructive change more cautiously, in the possibility that Clinton embodied a new form of Democratic politics that could correct and renew the progressive tradition as shaped by the New Deal. During the mid-1980s, Clinton had headed the Democratic Leadership Council (DLC), a group of party moderates who developed many of the ideas that became the central themes of his run for the presidency. As Clinton declared frequently during the campaign, these ideas represented a new philosophy of government, a "new covenant" that in the name of opportunity, responsibility, and community would seek to constrain the demands for economic rights that had been unleashed by the New Deal. The essence of Clinton's message was that the long-standing liberal commitment to guarantee economic welfare through entitlement programs such as Social Security, Medicare, Medicaid, and Aid to Families with Dependent Children had gone too far. The main objective of the new covenant was to correct the tendency of Americans to celebrate individual rights and government entitlements without acknowledging the mutual obligations they had to one another and to their country.[61]

Clinton pledged to dedicate his party to the new concept of justice he espoused. But his commitment to control government spending and recast the welfare state was obscured during the early days of his presidency by many traditional liberal actions. No sooner had he been inaugurated than Clinton announced his intention to lift the long-standing ban on homosexuals in the military. The president soon learned, however, the difficulty of resolving such a divisive social issue through "the stroke of a pen." To be sure, the development of the administrative presidency gave chief executives more power to make domestic policy autonomously. Yet when presidents tried to extend national administration to issues that shaped the character of American public life, this power proved inadequate.[62]

Most damaging for Clinton was that the issue became a symbol of his inability to revitalize progressive politics as an instrument to redress the economic insecurity and political alienation of the middle class. The bitter partisan fight over the administration's budget, in summer 1993, reinforced doubts about Clinton's ability to lead the nation in a new, more harmonious direction. Even though his budget plan promised to reduce the deficit, it included new taxes and an array of social programs that Republicans and conservative Democrats perceived as standard "tax and spend" liberalism. In August 1993 Congress enacted a modified version of the plan, albeit by a razor-thin margin and without any support from Republicans, who voted unanimously against it in the House and Senate. Clinton won this narrow, bruising victory only after promising moderate Democrats that he would put together another package of spending cuts in the fall. But this uneasy compromise failed to dispel his political opponents' charge that Clinton was a wolf in sheep's clothing—a conventional liberal whose commitment to reform had expired as soon as he was elected.[63]

The deference that Clinton displayed toward traditional liberal causes was, to an extent, understandable; it was a logical response to the modern institutional separation between the presidency and the party. The moderate wing of the party that he represented—including the DLC—was a minority wing. The majority of liberal interest group activists and Democratic members of Congress still preferred "entitlements" to "obligations" and "regulations" to "responsibilities." The media-driven caucuses and primaries, a legacy of the McGovern-Fraser reforms, had given Clinton the opportunity to seize the Democratic nomination as an outsider candidate, but they offered him no means to effect a transformation of his party when he took office. To bring about the new version of progressivism that he advocated during the campaign, Clinton would have had to risk a brutal confrontation with the major powers in the Democratic Party.[64]

No president had risked such a confrontation with his party since Roosevelt's failed purge campaign in 1938. It is not surprising, therefore, that Clinton's allies in the DLC urged him to renew his "credentials as an outsider" by going over the heads of his party's leaders in Congress and taking his message directly to the people. The new president could "break gridlock," they argued, only by appealing to the large number of independents in the electorate who had voted for Perot—that is, by "forging new and sometimes bipartisan coalitions around an agenda that moves beyond the polarized left-right debate."[65]

In fall 1993 Clinton took a page from his former DLC associates by successfully campaigning to secure congressional approval of the North American Free Trade Agreement (NAFTA) with Canada and Mexico. The fight for NAFTA caused Clinton to defend free enterprise ardently and to oppose the protectionism favored by labor unions, one of the most important constituencies in the national Democratic Party. Clinton's victory owed partly to the support of the Republican congressional leadership. No less important was Vice President Al Gore's inspired performance in a debate with Perot, the leading opponent of NAFTA. Gore's optimistic defense of free markets was well received by a large television audience, rousing enough public support for the treaty to persuade a majority of legislators in both houses of Congress to approve it.[66]

But health care, not trade policy, became the defining issue of Clinton's first two years in office. The administration's health care proposal promised to "guarantee all Americans a comprehensive package of benefits over the course of an entire lifetime." The formulation of this program appeared to mark the apotheosis of New Deal administrative politics; it was designed by First Lady Hillary Rodham Clinton and the president's longtime friend Ira Magaziner behind closed doors. Moreover, it would have created a new government entitlement program and an administrative apparatus that signaled the revitalization rather than the reform of the traditional welfare state.[67] Although Clinton made conciliatory overtures to the plan's opponents, hoping to forge bipartisan cooperation on Capitol Hill and a broad consensus among the general public, the possibilities for comprehensive reform hinged on settling differences about the appropriate role of government that had divided the parties and the country for the past two decades. In the end, this proved impossible.[68]

By proposing such an ambitious health care reform bill, Clinton angered conservatives. By failing to deliver on his proposal, he dismayed the ardent liberals of his party. Most significant, the defeat of the health care program created the overwhelming impression that Clinton had not lived up to his campaign promise to transcend the bitter philosophical and partisan battles of the Reagan and Bush years.

Clinton and his party paid dearly for this failure in the 1994 midterm elections. The Republicans gained fifty-two seats in the House and eight in the Senate, taking control of Congress. Moreover, they won dramatic victories at the state and local levels: Republicans increased their governorships to thirty (their first majority since 1970) and approached parity in state legislatures, a status they had not enjoyed since 1968. The Republicans achieved this victory in an off-year campaign that was unusually partisan and ideological, thanks largely to the remarkable leadership of the House minority whip, Rep. Newt Gingrich of Georgia. Gingrich, his party's choice to be the new Speaker of the 104th Congress, persuaded more than three hundred House candidates to sign a Republican Contract with America, a "covenant" with the nation that promised to rein in government by eliminating programs, ameliorating regulatory burdens, and cutting taxes. Clinton's attack on the Republican program during the campaign backfired, serving only to abet Republicans in their effort to highlight the president's failure to reform government.[69]

Yet the dramatic Republican triumph in the 1994 midterm elections brought back divided government and with it the institutional confrontation between the president and Congress that Clinton had promised to resolve. The first session of the 104th Congress, in 1995, quickly degenerated into the same sort of administrative politics that had corroded the legitimacy of political institutions in the United States since Nixon's presidency. This time, however, the struggle between the branches assumed a novel form: a Democratic White House versus a Republican Congress.

The battle between Clinton and Congress became especially fierce over legislation to balance the budget. More than any other idea celebrated in the Contract with America, Republicans believed that legislation balancing the budget would give them their best opportunity to control Congress for years to come. The most controversial part of the GOP's program was a proposal to scale back the growth of Medicare, a federal health insurance program for the elderly, by encouraging beneficiaries to enroll in health maintenance organizations and other private managed health care systems. Rallied by their most militantly partisan members in the House, Republicans sought to pressure Clinton to accept their budget priorities by twice shutting down federal government offices and even threatening to force the U.S. Treasury into default. Clinton effectively countered these confrontational tactics. His veto in December 1995 of a sweeping Republican budget bill that not only would have overhauled Medicare but also remade decades of federal social policy roused popular support for the administration. In attacking Medicare and other popular Democratic social policies, such as environmental programs, the Republicans' assault on programmatic liberalism went beyond what was promised by the Contract with America and gave Clinton the opportunity to take a political stand that most of the country supported.

When Congress returned for the second session of the 104th Congress in January 1996, it was not to Speaker Gingrich's agenda of reducing the role of Washington in the society and economy but to the measured tones of Clinton's third State of the Union message. The president, having outmaneuvered the Republican Congress, now co-opted its most popular theme, declaring that "the era of big government is over."[70] This was not merely a rhetorical flourish. Withstanding furious criticism from liberal Democratic members of Congress and interest group activists, Clinton signed welfare reform legislation in August that replaced the existing entitlement to cash payments for low-income mothers and their dependent children with temporary assistance and a strict work requirement.[71] Clinton conceded that the act was flawed, cutting too deeply into nutritional support for low-income working people and denying support unfairly to legal immigrants. Nevertheless, by requiring welfare recipients to take jobs, it served the fundamental principle Clinton had championed in the 1992 campaign of "re-creating the Nation's social bargain with the poor."[72]

Warning that "we cannot go back to the time when our citizens were left to fend for themselves," however, Clinton called for a halt to Republican assaults on popular liberal programs dedicated to providing economic security, educational opportunity, and environmental protection.[73] Using DNC funds, the White House had orchestrated a national media blitz toward the end of 1995 that excoriated the Republicans' program to reform Medicare and presented the president as a figure of national reconciliation who favored welfare reform and a balanced budget but who also would protect middle-class entitlements, education, and the environment.[74] Clinton's carefully modulated State of the Union message underscored this media campaign, revealing the president as a would-be healer eager to bring all sides together.

Throughout his 1996 reelection campaign, Clinton held firmly to the centrist ground he had staked out after the 1994 elections, campaigning on the same "new" Democratic themes of "opportunity, responsibility, and community" that had served him well during his first run for the White House. He won 49 percent of the popular vote, to Republican nominee Robert Dole's 41 percent and Perot's 8 percent, and 379 electoral votes to Dole's 159.

Clinton was the first Democratic president since FDR to be elected to a second term, but by focusing on his own campaign he did little to help his party. The Democrats lost two seats in the Senate and gained only a modest nine seats in the House, failing to regain control of either chamber. In truth, Clinton's campaign testified to the fragility of the nationalized party system that arose during the 1980s. The president's remarkable political comeback in 1995 was supported by so-called soft money that by law was designated for party-building activities.[75] But these funds were used mostly to mount television advertising campaigns that championed the president's independence from partisan conflicts. Clinton scarcely endorsed the election of a Democratic Congress in 1996; moreover, he raised funds for the party's congressional candidates only late in the campaign. Adding insult to injury, the administration's dubious fund-raising methods led to revelations during the final days of the campaign that reduced Clinton's margin of victory and undermined the Democrats' effort to retake the House.[76]

Clinton's wayward effort to forge a "third way" between the two parties is suggestive of the modern presidency's dominant but uneasy place in contemporary American politics. The disjuncture between the bitter partisanship on Capitol Hill and the weakening of partisan affiliation outside it helped to win Clinton a certain following in the country.[77] Yet as the House's impeachment and the Senate's trial of Clinton dramatically revealed, the "extraordinary isolation" of the modern presidency has its limits.[78] Hoping to become a great president in the tradition of Franklin Roosevelt, Clinton instead became the first elected chief executive to be impeached. (Andrew Johnson, the only other president to suffer such an indignity, inherited the office after Lincoln was assassinated.) Just as Reagan and Bush were plagued by independent counsels who investigated alleged abuses in their administrations under the authority of the Ethics in Government Act, so did Clinton have troubles of his own with independent counsels.[79] In early January 1998 Kenneth Starr was authorized to pursue allegations that the president had lied under oath about having an affair with a White House intern, Monica Lewinsky, and that at Clinton's urging his close associate Vernon Jordan had encouraged Lewinsky to perjure herself about the matter.

With Clinton facing an impeachment trial, nearly every political expert predicted that the Republicans would emerge from the 1998 elections with a tighter grip on Congress and, by implication, on the president's political fate.[80] But having been preoccupied by the Lewinsky scandal for the entire year, the Republicans were left without an appealing campaign message. Indeed, as the Lewinsky scandal unfolded throughout 1998, the public continued to express overwhelming approval of Clinton's performance in office, especially his management of the economy.[81] The Republicans were unable to increase their 55–45 majority in the Senate and lost five seats in the House, leaving them with a slim 223–211 majority. Clinton, the first Democrat since FDR to be reelected, now became the first president since Roosevelt in 1934 to see his party gain seats in a midterm election. Ironically it was Gingrich, the hero of the GOP's 1994 ascent to power, and not Clinton, who was forced from office. After the elections, watching his fellow Republicans fall into soul-searching and mutual recriminations, Gingrich announced that he was giving up not only his leadership position but also his seat in Congress.

Still, whatever authority the president had at the beginning of his administration to establish a new covenant of rights and responsibilities between citizens and their government was shattered by public disrespect for his morality.[82] Moreover, the virulent partisanship that characterized the impeachment process forced Clinton to seek fellowship among the Democrats in Congress and to abandon plans to pursue entitlement reform as the capstone of his presidency.[83] In the wake of the impeachment debacle, Clinton positioned himself as the champion of Social Security and Medicare, urging Congress to invest a significant share of the mounting budget surplus in these unreconstructed liberal programs.[84] Clinton's extraordinary resilience, it seemed, was achieved at the cost of failure to fulfill his promise to correct and renew the progressive tradition.

George W. Bush, the War on Terrorism, and the Advance of Executive-Centered Partisanship

The 2000 election testified to the modern presidency's fragile governing authority. Neither the Democratic nominee, Vice President Gore, nor the Republican, Gov. George W. Bush of Texas, took positions that offered a way out of the fractious state of American politics. Instead, both candidates adapted a centrist, pragmatic stance during the general election campaign that was designed to shore up the principal programs of the welfare state. The activist cores of the Democratic and Republican Parties differed starkly on issues such as abortion and the environment, reflecting their fundamental disagreements about the role of government and the relationship between church and state. But the two candidates sought to distance themselves from their parties, each of them seeking a strategic center between Democratic liberalism and Republican conservatism. The election ended in a virtual tie, a deadlock ultimately resolved by the Supreme Court. The controversial conclusion to the election bitterly divided policy activists, but not the American people, many of whom, consistent with the recent pattern of low-turnout elections and public indifference toward politics, had stayed away from the polls.

Like his predecessor, Bill Clinton, candidate Bush sought to forge a "third way," signifying the modern presidency's dominant but uneasy place in contemporary American politics. At its best, Clinton's third way pursued a broad consensus for a limited but energetic national government. All too often, however, his approach degenerated into a politics of expediency that substituted polls and focus groups for leadership. Bush's "compassionate conservatism" seemed to have the same strengths and weaknesses as Clinton's "new covenant." Indeed, Bush's campaign speeches in 2000 bore a striking resemblance to Clinton's during the 1992 and 1996 elections. The Bush administration programs that embodied these values—especially his reform proposals for education, social services, and welfare—invoked many of the ideas incubated at the DLC, the centrist Democratic group that gave rise to several of Clinton's policy initiatives.[85]

Important differences marked Bush's and Clinton's stances toward partisanship, however. Clinton never made clear how his third-way politics would serve the core principles of the Democratic Party; in fact, he and the DLC were highly ambivalent, if not avowedly hostile, toward partisanship. But in compassionate conservatism Bush embraced a doctrine that he and his close advisers hoped would strengthen the appeal of the Republican Party. Bush's rhetoric and policy proposals, his top political strategist, Karl Rove, claimed, were a deliberate attempt to play to conservative values without being reflexively antigovernment.[86] Bush's call for substantial tax cuts appealed to the right's hostility toward government. But the president also acknowledged, columnist E. J. Dionne observed, "that most people do not draw meaning from the marketplace alone, and that the marketplace is not the sole test or most important source of virtue."[87] "The invisible hand works many miracles," Bush said in July 1999. "But it cannot touch the human heart. . . . We are a nation of rugged individuals. But we are also the country of the second chance—tied together by bonds of friendship and community and solidarity."[88]

In part, the moral commitment Bush envisioned would be served by empowering nonprofit institutions that worked outside of government. For example, he proposed changes in federal and state regulations that would allow private, "faith-based" charitable organizations to play a larger role in providing government social services to the poor. The national government would play an important role in sustaining moral values as well. As Michael Gerson, Bush's principal speech writer, argued, the president's rhetoric did not try to "split the difference between liberalism and conservatism." Rather, Bush's speeches sought to convey how "activist government could be used for conservative ends."[89] The Reagan presidency had also made use of national administrative power, but the Bush administration was prepared to take big government conservatism much further. Although Reagan and his conservative allies once talked of eliminating the Department of Education, Bush proposed to make the nation's public schools more accountable to the department by linking federal aid to national standards of learning. Social conservatives had long sought to advance morality by opposing abortion. Bush professed to be staunchly "pro-life," but he called for a more "incremental" attack on abortion. More important, he proposed to buttress conservative religious values with affirmative government efforts to help the poor, promote marriage, and ensure that "every child will be educated."[90]

Bush's ambition to redefine Republican conservatism entailed a difficult balancing act between partisanship and bipartisan cooperation. This task was made all the more difficult by the tenuous hold the Republicans had on government. The Senate was evenly split between Democrats and Republicans when Bush took office, with Vice President Dick Cheney breaking the tie. But like Clinton at the beginning of his administration, Bush chose to cooperate with his party's strongly ideological leaders in Congress. Like Clinton, too, Bush preferred to solidify his base in the party before reaching out to independent voters. The president's emphasis on traditional conservative issues such as tax cuts, regulatory relief, energy production, and missile defense risked alienating moderate Republicans, a dwindling but pivotal group in the closely divided House and Senate. The president and his party paid dearly for this approach in May 2001, when Sen. James Jeffords of Vermont announced that he was transferring his allegiance from the Republican to the Democratic caucus, giving control of the Senate to the Democrats.[91]

Facing the prospect of partisan obstruction by Senate Democrats, the Bush administration intensified its efforts to consolidate political and policy responsibility within the White House. The first President Bush's top political strategist, Lee Atwater, had worked at the RNC rather than at the White House, helping to sustain for a time the status and independence of the national party organization. In contrast, George W. Bush's principal political consultant, Karl Rove, an Atwater protégé, became a top White House adviser. He staffed a new Office of Strategic Initiatives that oversaw a nearly complete melding of presidential and partisan politics. Rove granted that the national parties that had emerged since the 1980s "were of great importance in the tactical and mechanical aspects of electing a president." But they were "less important in developing a political and policy strategy for the White House." In effect, he said, parties served as a critical "means to the president's end." The emergence of the modern executive office presupposed that "the White House had to determine the administration's objectives" and by implication the party's.[92] Rove assumed political responsibility that undercut the power of RNC chair James Gilmore III, who was replaced with the more compliant Mark Raciot. Politics was joined to policy as Rove sought to position the president as a nontraditional Republican. By the end of his first summer in the White House, Bush was preparing to stress education and values, not taxes and defense.[93]

Bush-style compassionate conservatism promised to soften the Republican Party's harsh antigovernment edge. It also gave the president a platform to act independently of his party. Programs such as faith-based initiatives and educational reform were not pursued within Republican councils. Rather, as has been the custom since the development of the modern presidency, the White House advanced these objectives through executive orders and bipartisan cooperation.[94] The education bill in particular seemed less a use of government to serve conservative principles than an uneasy compromise between liberal demands for more spending and conservative insistence on standards. Bush trumpeted his alliance with the liberal Democratic icon Sen. Edward Kennedy in passing education reform legislation in 2001.

The president's attention shifted dramatically away from matters such as faith-based initiatives and educational reform when the United States was struck by terrorists of the al-Qaida network on September 11, 2001. In the aftermath of the first attack on the American continent since the War of 1812, and the most deadly in the nation's history, the country appeared to unite overnight. Citizens gave generously to relief funds to aid the families of those who lost their lives. The American flag was unfurled everywhere, and patriotic hymns, especially, "God Bless America," were sung repeatedly. Polls showed a remarkable and immediate jump in support for Bush, from 51 percent approval of the job he was doing as president to 90 percent approval within days of the September 11 attack. A strong consensus quickly formed in support of his military response to the terrorist assault.

In the short term, the war on terrorism strengthened the modern presidency and greatly tempered the polarized partisanship that had plagued it during the previous three decades. Hardly a discouraging word was heard when the Bush administration created a White House Office of Homeland Security, imposed tighter restrictions on airports, and embraced deficit spending to help the economy and fight a war in Afghanistan, which harbored the al-Qaida leaders. Highlighting the need for bipartisanship in a time of national crisis, Bush justified the war on terrorism in words that echoed Franklin Roosevelt. "Freedom and fear are at war," he told a joint meeting of Congress on September 20, 2001. "The advance of human freedom—the great achievement of our time, and great hope of every time—now depends on us. Our nation—this generation—will lift a dark threat of violence from our people and our future. We will rally around the world to this cause by our efforts, by our courage."[95]

As the president prepared the nation for new responsibilities at home and abroad, presidential scholars and public officials dusted off concerns from the 1960s and 1970s about an imperial presidency. Already executive centered in its

approach to politics and policy, the Bush White House became even more insulated from Congress and the Republican Party as it planned and fought the war
against terrorism.[96] For a time these complaints failed to penetrate the aura of
invincibility that Bush had enjoyed since September 11. But the roots of congressional resentment ran deep. Beginning in spring 2002 Bush administration
officials, and then the president himself, openly pursued the possibility of
another military venture: an invasion of Iraq that, unlike the Persian Gulf War
of 1991, would involve a "preemptive" attack and had as its mission the removal
of Saddam Hussein from power. Recognizing the country's obsession with
homeland security and reluctant to thwart a popular president as the midterm
elections approached, Congress passed a resolution in October 2002 authorizing the president to use military force against Iraq "as he determines to be
necessary." In doing so, legislators sustained the Bush administration's revival
of the Cold War–era belief that an overriding cause—the containment of communism then, the war against terrorism now—justified the expansive use of
presidential power around the globe.

Risking the bipartisan support that accrued in the aftermath of 9/11, Bush
threw himself into the 2002 midterm election campaign earlier and more energetically than any president in history. Unlike his predecessors, Bush had experienced both united and divided government during his first two years in office.
He was convinced long before the 2002 election campaign began that his best
strategy for leading Congress was to regain control of the Senate for the
Republican Party.

In seeking a Republican Senate, Bush faced a daunting challenge: the average
loss for the president's party in post–World War II midterm elections was four
Senate seats. Even worse from the Republicans' standpoint, their party was
more exposed in 2002 than the Democrats: twenty Republican seats were at
stake in the election, compared with fourteen Democratic seats. No president's
party had taken control of the Senate away from the other party in a midterm
election since 1882.

Bush, on Rove's advice, decided well in advance of the elections to become
actively involved in the campaign for a Republican majority in Congress. He
and Rove recruited strong Republican challengers to incumbent Democratic
senators, even to the point of intervening in state party politics to do so. The
president's strenuous efforts to raise a campaign war chest and his numerous
appearances for GOP candidates strengthened his influence over his party.
Several of his appearances were in states where the Republican candidate was
trailing and where, if the Democrats had won, Bush risked being blamed for
defeat.[97] The results of the election vindicated Bush's decision to take this risk.

The Republicans gained two seats in the Senate, transforming them from minority to majority status, and increased their majority in the House of Representatives. An election eve poll indicated that 50 percent of the voters were basing their decision on their opinion of the president, many more than the 34 percent who had done so in 1990 or the 37 percent who had done so in 1998. Of the 50 percent, 31 percent were pro-Bush and only 19 percent opposed him.[98]

Political analysts were quick to describe the historic nature of the Republican victory and to credit Bush as the most successful party-building president since Franklin Roosevelt.[99] Not only did the 2002 elections mark the first time in more than a century that the president's party had regained control of the Senate at midterm, it also represented the first time since FDR that a president saw his party gain seats in both houses of Congress in a first-term midterm election. The GOP also emerged from the elections with more state legislature seats than the Democrats for the first time in half a century; and even though the number of Republican governors declined from twenty-nine to twenty-seven during Bush's first term, Arnold Schwarzenegger's victory in the 2003 California recall election gave the Republican Party control of the governorships of the four most populous states: California, Texas, New York, and Florida.

Bush could not take all the credit for the Republican gains. Since the late 1970s the party had been developing into a formidable national organization in which the RNC, rather than state and local organizations, was the principal agent of party-building activities. This top-down approach to party building appeared to many critics to be too centralized and too dependent on television advertising to perform the party's traditional role of mobilizing voters and popular support for government programs. But the Bush White House and the RNC, believing that it had been out-organized "on the ground" by Democrats in the 2000 election, began to put together a massive grassroots mobilizing strategy in 2002. Democrats since the New Deal had relied on auxiliary party organizations such as labor unions to get out the vote. But the GOP created its own national organization to mobilize supporters. Depending on volunteers, albeit closely monitored ones, and face-to-face appeals to voters, the Republicans built on their success in 2002 to mount the most ambitious national grassroots campaign in the party's history for the 2004 elections.[100]

Bush not only benefited from the development of what might be considered the first national party machine in history, he also played a critical role in strengthening it. The White House recruited candidates, raised money to fund their campaigns, and helped to attract volunteers to identify Republican voters and get them out to vote. Just as Ronald Reagan had played a critical part in laying a philosophical and political foundation that enabled the Republican

Party to become a solidly conservative and electorally competitive party by 1984, so did Bush make an important contribution in enlarging the core supporters of the party. During his first term, Bush broke Reagan's record for attracting first-time contributors to the Republican Party: under Reagan, 853,595 people donated to the Republican Party for the first time; by the time Bush stood for reelection, he had already attracted more than one million new donors to the GOP.[101] More important, although Reagan never converted his personal popularity into Republican control of Congress or the states, Bush approached reelection in 2004 with his party in charge of the House, the Senate, and most governorships. Indeed, the Republican Party had more political control than at any time since the 1920s.

Nevertheless, the centrality of the Bush White House in policymaking, as well as in mobilizing support and framing issues in both the 2002 and 2004 campaigns, suggests that modern presidential politics continues to subordinate partisan to executive responsibility. Reagan made extensive use of executive administration at a time when Congress was usually in the hands of the Democrats. That Bush also made considerable use of administrative mechanisms to achieve his goals, even when his party controlled both houses of Congress, suggests that the administrative presidency may impede the emergence of a more collaborative, party-centered policy process even under the most favorable circumstances. Indeed, subscribing to the "unitary executive" prescribed by Vice President Cheney, Bush became a more zealous defender of presidential prerogatives than his Republican predecessors, and his position only hardened as he fought the war on terrorism.

In domestic policy, the president's staffing practices and aggressive use of OMB's powers of regulatory review were gauged to maximize presidential control over the civil service. Particularly in areas such as environmental and health and safety regulation, Bush made extensive use of executive orders, signing statements, and regulatory rulemaking to achieve significant departures from past policies. The president also used executive orders to make headway on controversial social issues, such as limiting funding for stem-cell research and denying funds to overseas family-planning organizations that offered abortion counseling. Although these efforts often enjoyed the support of congressional Republicans, they also suggested that the Bush administration preferred to transcend institutions of collective responsibility rather than work through them to achieve compromise or consensus. Even when the administration sought to work with congressional Republicans, it tended to do so in a heavy-handed manner that elicited resentment among GOP legislators. For example, Vice President Cheney, sometimes with Karl Rove in tow, frequently attended the Senate Republicans' weekly strategy sessions, an unusual intrusion that attested to the Bush administration's determination to make the Republican Party on Capitol Hill an arm of the White House.[102]

Bush's administrative strategy not only impeded the emergence of a more collaborative, party-centered policy process, it also contributed directly to the party's declining fortunes after 2004. The administration's ineffectual response to the Hurricane Katrina disaster in 2005 undermined the claim to administrative competence that had previously bolstered the White House and the Republican Party. The negative consequences of Bush's administrative overreaching for the GOP were most evident in the fallout from the White House's imperious management of the war in Iraq and the broader war on terrorism. Determined to wage war on its own terms, the Bush administration, bolstered by solid and largely passive Republican congressional support, made a series of unilateral decisions that departed from historic and legal convention. It chose to deny "enemy combatants" captured in the war on terrorism habeas corpus rights to challenge their detainment in civilian courts, to abrogate the Geneva Conventions and sanction rough treatment (or torture) of detainees during interrogations, and to engage in warrantless surveillance of American citizens suspected of communicating with alleged terrorists abroad. When these controversial decisions were revealed, they provoked widespread condemnation and damaged the GOP's public support. More broadly, the administration's insistence on a free hand to manage the war in Iraq ultimately resulted in the erosion of public confidence in the Republican Party as it became clear that the administration had badly botched postwar reconstruction efforts.

As the 2006 elections revealed, well before the economic crisis that began two years later overwhelmed all other issues, the administration's and the party's prestige was severely (and, in the case of the president, irreparably) wounded by the war. According to a national exit poll taken after the midterm congressional contests, about six in ten voters (59 percent) said they were dissatisfied (30 percent) or angry (29 percent) with President Bush. By a margin of more than two to one, those dissatisfied with Bush supported the Democratic candidate in their district (69 percent to 29 percent); and among those angry with the president, the margin was more than fifteen to one (92 percent to 6 percent).[103] Moreover, several studies appeared to show that general unhappiness with the White House and the war in Iraq contributed not only to the Democrats' taking control of the House and Senate but also to the substantial gains they made in gubernatorial and state legislative races.[104]

Thus, just as previous modern presidents demonstrated insufficient attention to party-building, Bush's experience illustrated the risks posed by overweening presidential partisanship. Ironically, the vigor of the Bush administration's party leadership—and the evident dependence of the GOP on Bush's stewardship—endangered the integrity of the Republican Party. Between 2001 and 2005, the GOP relied heavily for its political sustenance on Bush's personal popularity and prestige as a wartime leader. Both the 2002 and the 2004 elections celebrated executive power, turning on issues of international and domestic security that emphasized the modern presidency's place at the center of government.

The White House also played a dominant role in organizing the massive grassroots efforts that marked Bush's 2004 reelection campaign and in stimulating public participation in these efforts. Campaign officials designed and implemented grassroots programs, concentrated efforts in the battleground states, and deliberately bypassed state and local party leaders to mount a national party offensive.[105] This approach reaped political dividends for GOP candidates in the short run; Bush won 51 percent of the popular vote to Sen. John Kerry's 48 percent, and the Republicans gained three seats in the House and four in the Senate. But it threatened to make the party subservient to presidential authority and to enervate its capacity to hold the president accountable to broader principles. As Stephen Skowronek has warned, the modern GOP appeared to signal a political future in which the party "in effect [becomes] whatever the president needs it to be, and whatever capacity it had to hold its leaders to account would accordingly be lost."[106] The ironic denouement of this development was revealed after the 2008 presidential election, when many Republicans blamed Bush, whom they had previously followed with alacrity, for casting them into the political wilderness.

Barack Obama, the 2008 Presidential Election, and the Ratification of Executive-Centered Parties

Democratic senator Barack Obama of Illinois offered the voters "Change We Can Believe In" during the 2008 presidential campaign. But his extraordinary two-year quest for the White House left unclear what kind of change he proposed. Calling on the people to trust in the "audacity of hope," Senator Obama ran an idealistic campaign that sought to reprise the modern presidency's role as "steward of the public welfare." He pledged to bring Americans together and to overcome the raw partisanship that had polarized the Washington community for nearly two decades and that had begun to divide the country during George W. Bush's eight years in office. "In the face of despair, you believe there can be hope," he told the large, enthusiastic audience that gathered in Springfield, Illinois, in February 2007, to hear him announce his candidacy for the presidency.

"In the face of politics that's shut you out, that's told you to settle, that's divided us for too long, you believe we can be one people, reaching for what's possible, building that more perfect union."[107] As the child of a white mother from Kansas and a black father from Kenya, a man of color raised in Hawaii and Indonesia, and a reformer schooled in Chicago politics as a member of the post–civil rights generation, Obama seemed to embody the aspirations of the entire nation—to transcend, as no previous modern president could, the racial, ethnic, religious, and economic differences that long had divided the country.

To be sure, Obama aroused considerable opposition among conservatives, who dismissed him as a doctrinaire liberal posing as a statesman who could lift the nation out of the muck of partisan rancor. His candidacy was also heavily criticized by his chief rival for the Democratic nomination, Sen. Hillary Clinton of New York, the former first lady who, as the first strong woman candidate for president, also had a legitimate claim to inherit the progressive mantle. To a remarkable degree, however, Obama overshadowed Clinton in inspiring the admiration of the country: he was cast perfectly, it seemed, to play the role chartered by the architects of the modern presidency.

Yet Obama and his leading advisers also saw enormous potential in the national party politics that George W. Bush had practiced. His organizational efforts, in fact, were modeled on the techniques that Republicans had pioneered in 2004. Eschewing the Democrats' traditional reliance on organized labor and other constituency organizations to mobilize the party faithful, Obama promised to strengthen the national party apparatus. He vowed to wage a fifty-state campaign, build grassroots organizations in every state, help elect Democrats down the ballot, and register millions of new voters who would support the party's commitment to depart from the domestic and foreign policies of the previous eight years. Obama's organizational strategy, which combined Internet-based recruiting of volunteers, the use of data files to carefully target potential loyalists, and old-fashioned door-to-door canvassing, elaborated on the tactics that had worked successfully for Bush and the GOP in 2002 and, especially, 2004. The remarkable effectiveness of Obama's fund-raising operation, which drew heavily on Internet-solicited donations, further reflected lessons learned from the Bush campaign. Especially adept at soliciting small donations, Obama became the first major-party candidate to refuse public funds for the general election campaign.[108]

Like the formidable Bush-Cheney machine of 2004, the Obama-Biden organization relied in part on the regular party apparatus. DNC chairman Howard Dean decided in 2006 to strengthen Democratic organizations throughout the country, an approach that state and local party leaders credited with abetting the party's impressive victories then and in 2008.[109] Just as the Bush-Cheney machine of 2004 resulted in a wide-ranging Republican victory, the Obama-Biden campaign of 2008 yielded not just a decisive triumph at the presidential level but also substantial gains in House and Senate races. This success was in large measure the result of voters' unhappiness with Bush, who had mired the country in an unpopular war and a severe financial crisis. But Obama's sophisticated grassroots campaign linked a vast network of volunteers, elicited enormous enthusiasm among potential supporters, and mobilized the highest voter turnout since 1968. Coming on the heels of the substantial increase in voter participation in the 2004 election, the 2008 campaign appeared to confirm the emergence of a national party system that was ameliorating the chronic voter apathy that had afflicted the presidency-centered administrative state.[110]

Nevertheless, the further development of an executive-centered party system has not eliminated the tension between presidential and party leadership. Hoping to reap the benefits of their party-building efforts during the election, Obama campaign officials announced in January 2009 that the new administration intended to maintain the grassroots campaign in order to press the president's agenda and lay the groundwork for his reelection. "Organizing for America" would be housed in the DNC, now headed by Virginia governor Timothy Kaine, who had endorsed Obama's candidacy early in the primary fight and provided critical support for his general election campaign. Dubbed "Barack Obama 2.0" by insiders, the plan called for hiring full-time organizers to mobilize the Internet-based grassroots network forged during the presidential campaign, which had generated a database of 13 million email addresses and tens of thousands of phone bank volunteers and neighborhood coordinators. Organizing for America's purpose would be to pressure wavering Democrats and moderate Republicans to enact administration-sponsored legislation on the economy, health care, energy, and other subjects. Such a plan clearly could provoke tensions with members of Congress, who would not welcome the idea that Obama's political network was targeting them from within their own states and districts. Moreover, although some state-level Democratic officials were enthusiastic about embedding Obama's machine in the DNC because they viewed Organizing for America as an extension of Dean's fifty-state strategy, others expressed concern that it could become a competing political force that revolved around the president's ambitions while diminishing the needs of other Democrats.[111]

Obama's aides, including his highly regarded campaign manager, David Plouffe, denied that Obama 2.0 was merely a permanent campaign to advance the president's fortunes. They insisted that the grassroots network's purpose was to deliver on the reform that Obama and his party had promised during the 2008 election. Moreover, the president's political aides assured their partisan brethren that Obama 2.0 would be a force in mobilizing support for Democratic candidates in the 2010 congressional and state races.[112] Congressional Republicans' near-unanimous resistance to the president's overtures for bipartisan support of his emergency economic stimulus bill in February 2009 appeared to confirm the need to sustain a strong Democratic organization.[113]

It remains to be seen, however, whether the vaunted Obama machine can be transformed into a durable organization that simultaneously strengthens the administration and bolsters the Democratic Party. Like the Bush-Cheney machine, the Obama-Biden campaign organization benefited other Democratic candidates. At the same time, just as the 2004 Republican campaign was directed by Bush-Cheney strategists, so was the 2008 Democratic grassroots effort run out of the Obama-Biden headquarters. The architects of the Obama campaign praised Dean's fifty-state strategy, but they relied almost completely on their own staff, money, and organization, not only to compete in battleground states but also to make incursions into traditional Republican territory. And just as the Bush-Cheney machine relied on volunteers whose principal loyalty was to the president, so did the Obama-Biden grassroots organization rest in the volunteers' deep admiration for the Democratic standard-bearer.[114] As one liberal blogger fretted toward the end of the 2008 election, "Power and money in the Democratic Party is being centralized around a key iconic figure. [Obama] is consolidating power within the party." Embedding the Obama campaign organization in the DNC only served to reinforce this concern, arousing fears that Obama was building an "Obama party."[115]

Beyond the 2008 election, then, the Democrats will be challenged to sustain a collective commitment independent of their devotion to Obama. The Bush administration was split between presidential loyalists and those who wanted to meld the campaign organization with the GOP. The Obama administration, following a campaign that promised to bring about a "post-partisan age," is likely to be even more divided between advisers who want to integrate the campaign into the party structure and those who view the vast network of activists, neighborhood organizers, and volunteers as a force that should remain "an independent entity—organized around the 'Obama brand.'"[116]

The question remains, therefore, whether the profound revival of the modern executive's governing authority in the wake of 9/11 has brought a national party system to fruition or continued the long-term development of a modern presidency that renders collective partisanship impractical. Indeed, there is a real sense that the "new" party system may be a creature of, and dependent on, the modern presidency. When asked how his initial appointments to administrative positions, many of whom were old Washington hands, would carry out the campaign's promise to transform national politics, President-elect Obama replied, "What we are going to do is combine experience with fresh thinking. But understand where vision for change comes from first and foremost. It comes from me."[117] This assertion of presidential prerogative dovetailed with Obama's plan to concentrate more power in the West Wing than any president since Nixon. In organizing the White House Office, he assembled a group of policy "czars" who would have broad programmatic authority to "cut through—or leapfrog—the traditional bureaucracy" in matters of national security, climate change, economic policy, health care, housing, and education.[118] Similarly, President Obama's early days in the White House saw him reverse a number of important domestic and foreign policies with the stroke of the pen, including an executive order that banned the use of controversial CIA interrogation tactics.[119]

Recent developments thus suggest that executive aggrandizement will likely continue to complicate efforts to achieve greater collective responsibility for policymaking. More significantly, the very vigor of strong party leaders such as George W. Bush and Barack Obama threatens the integrity of political parties as collective organizations with a past and a future. During the Progressive era, at the dawn of the modern presidency, Herbert Croly noted that Woodrow Wilson's effort to put his stamp on the Democratic Party suggested that aggressive executive partisanship might erode the integrity of collective responsibility, even as it strengthens party organization in the short term: "At the final test, the responsibility is his [the president's] rather than the party's. The party which submits to such a dictatorship, however benevolent, cannot play its own proper part in the system of government. It will either cease to have any independent life or its independence will eventually assume the form of revolt."[120] Croly's observation about the inherently antagonistic relationship between collective responsibility and executive dominion was made in a context when localized, decentralized parties prevailed. Yet it still may provide guidance for analyzing the dynamics of the relationship between the president and parties in an era of modern administration and nationalized, programmatic parties.

Notes

1. Franklin D. Roosevelt, *Public Papers and Addresses*, 13 vols. (New York: Random House, 1938–1950), vol. 1, 751–756.

2. Ibid., 752.

3. Woodrow Wilson, *Constitutional Government in the United States* (New York: Columbia University Press, 1908), 68–69.

4. Arthur S. Link, "Woodrow Wilson and the Democratic Party," *Review of Politics* 18 (April 1956): 146–156. Wilson effectively established himself as the principal voice of the Democratic Party. But he accepted traditional partisan practices concerning legislative

deliberations and appointments in order to gain support for his program in Congress, thus failing to strengthen either the Democratic Party's national organization or its fundamental commitment to progressive principles. After 1914, Wilson embraced many elements of progressive democracy, such as direct leadership of public opinion, national administration of commercial activity, and civil service reform. Wilson thus overcame some of the Democratic Party's antipathy toward national administrative power and showed that with the growing prominence of presidential candidates, party leaders in Congress were willing to sacrifice programmatic principles to win the White House. See Scott James, *Presidents, Parties, and the State: A Party System Perspective on Democratic Regulatory Choice, 1884–1936* (New York: Cambridge University Press, 2000). In the end, however, this conversion to advanced progressivism only exposed the yawning gap between, on the one hand, Wilson's pretense to serving as a national progressive leader and, on the other, his allegiance to a decentralized and patronage-based party. See Daniel Stid, *The President as Statesman: Woodrow Wilson and the Constitution* (Lawrence: University Press of Kansas, 1998), esp. chaps. 6, 8.

5. *Personal and Political Diary of Homer Cummings*, January 5, 1933, box 234, no. 2, 90, Homer Cummings Papers (no. 9973), Manuscripts Department, University of Virginia Library, Charlottesville.

6. Edward J. Flynn, *You're the Boss* (New York: Viking, 1947), 153.

7. Alfred Phillips Jr. to Franklin D. Roosevelt, June 9, 1937; and Roosevelt to Phillips, June 16, 1937, President's Personal File, 2666, Franklin D. Roosevelt Library, Hyde Park, New York.

8. Franklin Clarkin, "Two-Thirds Rule Facing Abolition," *New York Times*, January 5, 1936, IV, 10.

9. Thomas Stokes, *Chip off My Shoulder* (Princeton: Princeton University Press, 1940), 503. For an assessment of Roosevelt's role in the abolition of the two-thirds rule that also addresses the significance of this party reform, see Harold F. Bass Jr., "Presidential Party Leadership and Party Reform: Franklin D. Roosevelt and the Abrogation of the Two-Thirds Rule" (paper presented at the annual meeting of the Southern Political Science Association, Nashville, Tennessee, November 7–9, 1985).

10. Raymond Clapper, "Roosevelt Tries the Primaries," *Current History*, October 1938, 16.

11. Morton Frisch, *Franklin D. Roosevelt: The Contribution of the New Deal to American Political Thought and Practice* (Boston: S. T. Wayne, 1975), 79.

12. Frankfurter to Roosevelt, August 9, 1937, box 210, Papers of Thomas G. Corcoran; Roosevelt to Frankfurter, August 12, 1937, reel 60, Felix Frankfurter Papers; both in Manuscript Division, Library of Congress, Washington, D.C.

13. Herbert Croly, a fellow Progressive, criticized Wilson's concept of presidential party leadership along these lines. Although he shared Wilson's view that executive power needed to be strengthened, Croly argued that the "necessity of such leadership [was] itself evidence of the decrepitude of the two-party system." Croly believed that Theodore Roosevelt's 1912 Progressive Party campaign, which scorned the two-party system, championed candidate-centered campaigns, and prescribed that presidents seek political support through direct appeals to public opinion, represented the wave of the future. The emergence of a modern executive and the destruction of the two-party system, he wrote, "was an indispensable condition of the success of progressive democracy." *Progressive Democracy* (New York: Macmillan, 1914), 345, 348. On the Progressive Party and its legacy, see Sidney M. Milkis and Daniel J. Tichenor, "'Direct Democracy' and Social Justice: The Progressive Party Campaign of 1912," *Studies in American Political*

Development 8 (Fall 1994): 282–340; and Sidney M. Milkis, *Theodore Roosevelt, the Progressive Party, and the Transformation of American Democracy* (Lawrence: University Press of Kansas, 2009).

14. The purge campaign galvanized opposition to Roosevelt throughout the nation, apparently contributing to the heavy losses the Democrats sustained in the 1938 general elections.

15. The term "second bill of rights" comes from Roosevelt's 1944 State of the Union message, which reaffirmed the New Deal's commitment to an economic constitutional order. Roosevelt, *Public Papers and Addresses*, vol. 13, 40.

16. The term comes from Theodore Roosevelt's New Nationalism speech, a 1910 address, which foretold of many developments that would guide both Wilson's and FDR's presidencies. See Theodore Roosevelt, The *Works of Theodore Roosevelt*, 26 volumes (New York: Scribner's, 1926), vol. 17, 19–20.

17. *Report of the President's Committee on Administrative Management* (Washington, D.C.: U.S. Government Printing Office, 1937), 53. This committee, headed by Louis Brownlow, played a central role in the planning and politics of executive reorganization from 1936 to 1940. For a full analysis of the commission, see Barry Karl, *Executive Reorganization and Reform in the New Deal* (Cambridge: Harvard University Press, 1963).

18. So strongly did Roosevelt favor this legislation that House majority leader Sam Rayburn appealed for party unity before the critical vote on the executive reorganization bill, arguing that its defeat would amount to a "vote of no confidence" in the president. *Congressional Record*, 75th Congress, 3rd sess., April 8, 1938, pt. 5, 5121.

19. Memorandum, "Extending the Competitive Classified Civil Service," Herbert Emmerich to Louis Brownlow, June 29, 1938; and Civil Service Commission statement regarding executive order of June 24, 1938, extending the merit system; both in *Papers of the President's Committee on Administrative Management*, Roosevelt Library; see also Richard Polenberg, *Reorganizing Roosevelt's Government* (Cambridge: Harvard University Press, 1966), 22–23, 184. With the passage of the Ramspeck Act in 1940, the convulsive movement to reshape the civil service was virtually completed. The Ramspeck Act authorized the president to extend the merit system to nearly 200,000 positions previously exempted by law, many of them occupied by supporters of the New Deal. Roosevelt took early advantage of this authorization in 1941. By executive order he extended the coverage of civil service protection to include about 95 percent of the permanent service. Leonard White, "Franklin Roosevelt and the Public Service," *Public Personnel Review* 6 (July 1945): 142.

20. Paul Van Riper, *History of the United States Civil Service* (Evanston, Ill.: Row, Peterson, 1958), 327. The merging of politics and administration took an interesting course as a result of the 1939 Hatch Act. Until passage of this bill, which barred most federal employees from participating in campaigns, the Roosevelt administration made use of the growing army of federal workers in state and local political activity, including some of the purge campaigns. Even though the Hatch Act curtailed Roosevelt's ability to continue these activities, the president signed the legislation. He was more interested in orienting the executive branch as an instrument of programmatic reform than he was in developing a national political machine, and the insulation of federal officials from party politics was not incompatible with such a purpose.

21. The task of communicating with the public encouraged FDR and those who staffed the newly created Executive Office of the President to make use of surveys. With the help of the respected pollster Hadley Cantril, the Roosevelt administration learned

that the American people viewed the idea of a "second bill of rights" favorably. Oscar Cox to Hadley Cantril, May 3, 1943; Hadley Cantril to Oscar Cox, April 30, 1943; Memorandum, Hadley Cantril to David Niles, James Barnes, and Oscar Ewing, April 30, 1943; "Public Opinion: The NRPB Report and Social Security," Office of Public Opinion Research, April 28, 1943. Roosevelt Library, Oscar Cox Papers, box 100, Lend-Lease Files. On the Roosevelt administration's use of polls, see Robert Eisenger and Jeremy Brown, "Polling as a Means toward Presidential Autonomy: Emil Hurja, Hadley Cantril and the Roosevelt Administration," *International Journal of Public Opinion Research* 10 (1998): 239–256; and Theodore Lowi, *The Personal President: Power Invested, Promise Unfulfilled* (Ithaca, N.Y.: Cornell University Press, 1985), 62–66.

22. Roosevelt, *Public Papers and Addresses*, vol. 9, 671–672.

23. Martin Shefter, "War, Trade, and U.S. Party Politics," in *Shaped by War and Trade*, ed. Ira Katznelson and Martin Shefter (Princeton: Princeton University Press, 2002), 123.

24. Richard A. Rovere, "A Man for This Age Too," *New York Times Magazine*, April 11, 1965, 118. For an account of the influence of Roosevelt and the New Deal on Johnson's presidency, see William E. Leuchtenburg, *In the Shadow of FDR: From Harry Truman to Ronald Reagan*, rev. ed. (Ithaca: Cornell University Press, 1985), chap. 4; and Sidney M. Milkis, *President and the Parties* (New York: Oxford University Press, 1993), chaps. 7 and 8.

25. Lyndon Baines Johnson, *The Vantage Point: Perspectives of the Presidency, 1963–1969* (New York: Holt, Rinehart and Winston, 1971), 323.

26. Theodore White, *The Making of the President, 1968* (New York: Atheneum, 1969), 107.

27. Rowland Evans and Robert Novak, "Too Late for LBJ," *Boston Globe*, December 21, 1966, 27.

28. David Broder, "Consensus Politics: End of an Experiment," *Atlantic Monthly*, October 1966, 62.

29. Doris Kearns, *Lyndon Johnson and the American Dream* (New York: New American Library, 1976), 256.

30. In a memorandum about one of the early strategy sessions that led to the Great Society, Larry O'Brien, Johnson's chief legislative aide, expressed concern about the acute political problems he anticipated would result from such an ambitious program. Memorandum, Larry O'Brien to Henry Wilson, November 24, 1964, Henry Wilson Papers, box 4, Lyndon Baines Johnson Library, Austin, Texas.

31. Interview with Horace Busby, June 25, 1987.

32. Memorandum, William Connel to Marvin Watson, August 27, 1967, Marvin Watson Files, box 31; Memorandum, Joseph Califano to the president, March 27, 1968, Office Files of the President (Dorothy Territo), box 10; both in Johnson Library.

33. Memorandum, Harry C. McPherson Jr. and Clifford L. Alexander to the president, February 11, 1967, Office Files of Harry McPherson; Memorandum, Sherwin Markman to the president, February 17, 1968, White House Central Files, Subject File, "WE9 (welfare), Exec. February, 1968," box 38; Sherwin J. Markman, Oral History, by Dorothy Pierce McSweeny, tape 1, May 21, 1969, 24–36; all in Johnson Library. Many local Democrats felt threatened by the community action program with its provision for "maximum feasible participation." See Daniel P. Moynihan, *Maximum Feasible Misunderstanding* (New York: Free Press, 1970), 144–145.

34. William E. Leuchtenburg, "The Genesis of the Great Society," *Reporter*, April 21, 1966, 38.

35. Memorandum, Hayes Redmon to Bill Moyers, May 5, 1966, box 12, Office Files of Bill Moyers, Johnson Library. For an excellent book-length treatment of Johnson's

personnel policy, see Richard L. Schott and Dagmar S. Hamilton, *People, Positions, and Power: The Political Appointments of Lyndon Johnson* (Chicago: University of Chicago Press, 1983).

36. Memorandum, James Rowe to John W. Macy Jr., April 28, 1965, John Macy Papers, box 504; James H. Rowe, Oral History, by Joe B. Frantz, interview 2, September 16, 1969, 46–47; both in Johnson Library. Rowe's battles with Macy are noteworthy and ironic: as a charter member of the White House Office, he had performed Macy's role for the Roosevelt administration, upholding the principle of merit against the patronage requests of DNC chair James Farley and his successor, Ed Flynn.

37. On the importance of institutional reform, see Draft Memorandum, Horace Busby to Mr. Johnson, n.d., box 52, folder of memos to Mr. Johnson, June 1964; Busby quote is from Memorandum, Horace Busby for the president, September 21, 1965, box 51, Office Files of Horace Busby, Johnson Library.

38. Terry Moe, "The Politicized Presidency," in *The New Direction in American Politics*, ed. John E. Chubb and Paul E. Peterson (Washington, D.C.: Brookings Institution Press, 1985), 254.

39. Memorandum, Horace Busby to the president, April 21, 1965, and attached letter from John Macy (April 17, 1965), box 51, Office Files of Horace Busby, Johnson Library; Joseph Young, "Johnson Boost to Career People Called Strongest by a President," *Washington Post*, May 16, 1965; Eugene Patterson, "The Johnson Brand," *Atlanta Constitution*, April 30, 1965; and Raymond P. Brandt, "Johnson Inspires the Civil Service by Appointing His Top Aides from among Career Officials," *St. Louis Dispatch*, May 2, 1965. For a comprehensive treatment of Johnson's management of the bureaucracy, see James A. Anderson, "Presidential Management of the Bureaucracy and the Johnson Presidency: A Preliminary Exploration," *Congress and the President* 1 (Autumn 1984): 137–163.

40. Memorandum, Bill Moyers to the president, December 11, 1965, box 11, Office Files of Bill Moyers, Johnson Library.

41. James Rowe became quite concerned on hearing of the task force proposal. He warned the White House staff that this might further weaken the regular party apparatus, which was "already suffering from shellshock both in Washington and around the country because of its impotent status." James Rowe, "A White Paper for the President on the 1968 Presidential Campaign," n.d., Marvin Watson Files, box 20, folder of Rowe, O'Brien, Cooke, Criswell Operation, Johnson Library.

42. Allan Otten, "The Incumbent's Edge," *Wall Street Journal*, December 28, 1967.

43. Byron E. Shafer, *Quiet Revolution: The Struggle for the Democratic Party and the Shaping of Post-Reform Politics* (New York: Russell Sage Foundation, 1983). In 1969 the DNC, acting under a mandate from the 1968 Chicago Convention, established the Commission on Party Structure and Delegate Selection. Under the chairmanship first of Sen. George McGovern and, after 1971, of Rep. Donald Fraser, the commission developed guidelines for the state parties' selection of delegates to the national conventions. Their purpose was to weaken the prevailing party structure and to establish a more direct link between presidential candidates and the voters. The DNC accepted all the commission's guidelines and declared in the call for the 1972 convention that they constituted the standards that state Democratic parties, in qualifying and certifying delegates to the 1972 Democratic National Convention, must make "all efforts to comply with." The new rules eventually caused a majority of states to change from selecting delegates in closed councils of party regulars to electing them in direct primaries. Although the Democrats initiated these changes, many were codified in state laws that affected the Republican Party almost as much. For a discussion of the long-term forces

underlying the McGovern-Fraser reforms, see David B. Truman, "Party Reform, Party Atrophy, and Constitutional Change," *Political Science Quarterly* 99 (Winter 1984–1985): 637–655.

44. Memorandum, John P. Roche for the president, December 4, 1967, White House Central Files, PL (Political Affairs) folder; Memorandum, Ben Wattenberg to the president, December 13, 1967, Marvin Watson Files, box 10; Memorandum, Ben Wattenberg to the president, March 13, 1968, Marvin Watson Files, box 11; all in Johnson Library.

45. Memorandum of conversation, April 5, 1968, White House Famous Names, box 6, Robert F. Kennedy folder, 1968 Campaign, Johnson Library.

46. Richard Nathan, *The Administrative Presidency* (New York: Wiley, 1983).

47. Stephen Teles, "Conservative Mobilization against Entrenched Liberalism," in Paul Pierson and Theda Skocpol, eds., *The Transformation of American Government: Activist Government and the Rise of Conservatism* (Princeton: Princeton University Press, 2007).

48. On Nixon's party leadership as president, see the Ripon Society and Clifford Brown, *Jaws of Victory* (Boston: Little, Brown, 1973), 226–242.

49. Nathan, *Administrative Presidency*, 43–56. Toward the end of the Johnson presidency, the administration tried to consolidate further the president's control of the activities of the executive branch. Johnson's second task force on government organization—the Heineman task force—made many recommendations in 1967 that formed the basis of the Nixon administrative reform program. For example, it called for the reorganization of executive departments and agencies into a smaller number of "superdepartments" that would be "far more useful and much more responsive to, and representative of, Presidential perspectives and objectives than the scores of parochial department and agency heads who now share the line responsibilities of the executive branch." Johnson favored the Heineman task force's central recommendations and planned to implement some of them after his reelection in 1968, but his retirement came sooner than expected. Task Force on Government Organization, "The Organization and Management of the Great Society Programs," June 15, 1967, and "A Recommendation for the Future Organization of the Executive Branch," September 15, 1967, both reports located in Outside Task Forces, box 4, Task Force on Government Organization folder, Johnson Library. See also Peri Arnold, *Making the Managerial Presidency: Comprehensive Reorganization Planning, 1905–1980* (Princeton: Princeton University Press, 1986), 268.

50. Daniel Galvin argues that Republican presidents since the New Deal have been more committed to party building than their Democratic counterparts. See Daniel J. Galvin, *Presidential Party Building* (Princeton: Princeton University Press, forthcoming).

51. A. James Reichley, "The Rise of National Parties," in *New Direction in American Politics*, ed. Chubb and Peterson, 191–195. By the end of the 1980s, Reichley was less hopeful that the emergent national parties were well suited to perform the parties' historic function of mobilizing public support for political values and government policies. See his richly detailed study, *The Life of the Parties: A History of American Political Parties* (New York: Free Press, 1992), esp. chaps. 18–21.

52. Rhodes Cook, "Reagan Nurtures His Adopted Party to Strength," *Congressional Quarterly Weekly Report*, September 28, 1985, 1927–1930; David S. Broder, "A Party Leader Who Works at It," *Boston Globe*, October 21, 1985, 14; and interview with Mitchell Daniels, assistant to the president for political and governmental affairs, June 5, 1986.

53. Thomas E. Cavanaugh and James L. Sundquist, "The New Two-Party System," in *New Direction in American Politics*, ed. Chubb and Peterson.

54. Nixon transformed the Bureau of the Budget into the Office of Management and Budget by executive order in 1970, adding a cadre of presidentially appointed assistant directors for policy between the OMB director and the bureau's civil servants. As a consequence, the budget office attained additional policy responsibility and became more responsive to the president. In the Reagan administration, the OMB was given a central role in remaking regulatory policy. See Richard A. Harris and Sidney M. Milkis, *The Politics of Regulatory Change: A Tale of Two Agencies*, 2nd ed. (New York: Oxford University Press, 1996).

55. As the minority report of the congressional committees investigating the Iran-contra affair acknowledged, "President Reagan gave his subordinates strong, clear, and consistent guidance about the basic thrust of the policies he wanted them to pursue toward Nicaragua. There is some question and dispute about *precisely* the level at which he chose to follow the operational details. There is no doubt, however, . . . [that] the President set the U.S. policy toward Nicaragua, with few if any ambiguities, and then left subordinates more or less free to implement it." *Report of the Congressional Committees Investigating the Iran-Contra Affair*, 100th Cong., 1st sess., House Report 100–433, Senate Report 100–216 (Washington, D.C.: U.S. Government Printing Office, 1987), 501 (emphasis in original).

56. Michael Nelson, "Constitutional Aspects of the Elections," in *The Elections of 1988*, ed. Michael Nelson (Washington, D.C.: CQ Press, 1989), 195.

57. Benjamin Ginsberg and Martin Shefter, *Politics by Other Means: The Declining Importance of Elections in America* (New York: Basic Books, 1990).

58. Linda Greenhouse, "Ethics in Government: The Price of Good Intentions," *New York Times*, February 1, 1988; and Cass R. Sunstein, "Unchecked and Unbalanced: Why the Independent Counsel Act Must Go," *The American Prospect* (May–June, 1998): 20–27.

59. An exit poll revealed that a plurality of voters now preferred to have the presidency and Congress controlled by the Democratic Party. See William Schneider, "A Loud Vote for Change," *National Journal*, November 7, 1992, 2544.

60. Alan Brinkley, "Roots," *New Republic*, July 27, 1992.

61. William Clinton, "The New Covenant: Responsibility and Rebuilding the American Community" (speech delivered at Georgetown University, Washington, D.C., October 23, 1991).

62. On President Clinton's use of executive orders, his attempt to carry out policy "with the stroke of a pen," see Thomas Friedman, "Ready or Not, Clinton Is Rattling the Country," *Washington Post*, January 31, 1993. The proposal to lift the ban on gays and lesbians in the military plagued Clinton throughout the critical early months of his presidency. Intense opposition from the respected head of the Joint Chiefs of Staff, Colin Powell, and the influential chair of the Senate Armed Services Committee, Sam Nunn, D-Ga., forced Clinton to defer his executive order for six months while he sought a compromise solution. But the delay and the compromise aroused the ire of gay and lesbian activists, who had given strong financial and organizational support to Clinton during the election campaign. The controversy also forced the president to betray his campaign promise to focus "like a laser" on the economy. Ann Devroy and Ruth Marcus, "President Clinton's First Hundred Days: Ambitious Agenda and Interruptions Frustrate Efforts to Maintain Focus," *Washington Post*, April 29, 1993, A1.

63. Douglas Jehl, "Rejoicing Is Muted for the President in Budget Victory," *New York Times*, August 8, 1993, 1, 23; and David Shribman, "Budget Battle a Hollow One for President," *Boston Globe*, August 8, 1993, 1, 24.

64. Indeed, during the early days of his presidency, Clinton sought to identify with his party's leadership in Congress and the national committee—partly, one suspects, to avoid the political isolation from which Carter had suffered. Carter kept party leaders in Congress and the national committee at arm's length, but Clinton sought both to embrace and to empower the national organization. The White House lobbying efforts on Capitol Hill focused almost exclusively on the Democratic caucus; and the administration relied heavily on the DNC to marshal public support for its domestic programs. Interviews with David Wilhelm, DNC chair, October 18, 1993, and Craig Smith, DNC political director, October 19, 1993; and Rhodes Cook, "DNC under Wilhelm Seeking a New Role," *Congressional Quarterly Weekly Report*, March 13, 1993, 634. For a critical analysis of the DNC's lobbying efforts on behalf of Clinton, see Kathryn Dunn Tenpas, "Promoting President Clinton's Policy Agenda: DNC as Presidential Lobbyist," *The American Review of Politics* 17 (Fall 1996): 283–298.

65. Al From and Will Marshall, "The Road to Realignment: Democrats and the Perot Voters," in *The Road to Realignment: Democrats and the Perot Voters* (Washington, D.C.: Democratic Leadership Council, 1993).

66. A majority of Republicans in the House and Senate supported the free trade agreement, and a majority of Democrats, including the House majority leader and majority whip, opposed it. David Shribman, "A New Brand of D.C. Politics," *Boston Globe*, November 18, 1993, 15; and Gwen Ifill, "56 Long Days of Coordinated Persuasion," *New York Times*, November 19, 1993, A27.

67. Address to Congress on health care plan, printed in *Congressional Quarterly Weekly Report*, September 25, 1993, 2582–2586; and Robin Toner, "Alliance to Buy Health Care: Bureaucrat or Public Servant?" *New York Times*, December 5, 1993, 1, 38.

68. Adam Clymer, "National Health Program, President's Greatest Goal, Declared Dead in Congress," *New York Times*, September 27, 1994, A1. For a comprehensive treatment of the Clinton health care program, see Cathie Jo Martin, "Mandating Social Change within Corporate America" (paper presented at the annual meeting of the American Political Science Association, New York, 1994). Martin's study shows that health care reform became the victim of "radically different world views about the state and corporation in modern society," 1.

69. Examining exit polls that suggested that a "massive anti-Clinton coalition came together" to produce the "revolution" of 1994, the political analyst William Schneider wrote of the voters' desire for change, "If the Democrats can't make government work, maybe the Republicans can solve problems with less government." Schneider, "Clinton, the Reason Why," *National Journal*, November 12, 1994, 2630–2632.

70. William Clinton, State of the Union address, January 23, 1996, printed in *Congressional Quarterly Weekly Report*, January 27, 1996, 258–262.

71. Many public officials and journalists claimed that the new law put an end to "a sixty-one-year-old entitlement to welfare." In truth, the Aid to Families with Dependent Children program (AFDC) never existed as an entitlement in the sense that Social Security and Medicare did. The program only guaranteed federal matching funds to states that established AFDC programs. See R. Shep Melnick, "The Unexplained Resilience of Means-Tested Programs" (paper delivered at the annual meeting of the American Political Science Association, Boston, September 3–6, 1998).

72. William Jefferson Clinton, "Remarks on Signing the Personal Responsibility and Work Opportunity Reconciliation Act," August 22, 1996, *Weekly Compilation of Presidential Documents*, no. 1484.

73. Clinton, State of the Union address, January 23, 1996.

74. Bob Woodward, *The Choice* (New York: Simon and Schuster, 1996), 344.

75. Anthony Corrado, "Financing the 1996 Elections," in *The Election of 1996*, ed. Gerald Pomper (Chatham, N.J.: Chatham House, 1997). In 2002, Congress enacted the Bipartisan Campaign Reform Act, which prohibited the national political parties from raising or spending soft money.

76. Michael Nelson, "The Election: Turbulence and Tranquility in Contemporary American Politics," in *The Elections of 1996*, ed. Michael Nelson (Washington, D.C.: CQ Press, 1997), 52; Gary Jacobson, "The 105th Congress: Unprecedented and Unsurprising," in *Elections of 1996*, ed. Nelson, 161; and Kathryn Dunn Tenpas, "The Clinton Reelection Machine: Placing the Party Organization in Peril," *Presidential Studies Quarterly* 28, no. 4 (Fall 1998): 761–768.

77. Clinton's gift for forging compromise was displayed in May 1997, when the White House and the Republican congressional leaders agreed on a plan to balance the budget by 2002. In part, this uneasy deal was made possible by a revenue windfall caused by the robust economy, which enabled the negotiators to avoid the sort of hard choices concerning program cuts and higher taxes that had animated the bitter struggles of the 104th Congress. Richard W. Stevenson, "After Years of Wrangling, Accord Is Reached on Plan to Balance the Budget by 2002," *New York Times*, May 3, 1997, 1. Even so, this rapprochement, which brought about the first balanced budget in three decades, testified to the potential of modern presidents to advance principles and pursue policies that defy the sharp cleavages that pervade the party system. Indeed, Clinton's third way was emulated abroad as well, with leaders in Britain, Germany, Italy, and Holland attempting to fashion programs that combined market efficiency and social justice. See Jim Hoagland, "Third Way Politics," *Washington Post*, May 20, 1999. In the face of these developments, DLC president Al From, who had often been critical of Clinton's inconsistent commitment to the "third way," credited the president with "modernizing progressive politics for the world." Interview with Al From, June 7, 1999. For a more critical and historical analysis of Clinton's third-way politics, see Stephen Skowronek, *The Politics Presidents Make: Leadership from John Adams to Bill Clinton* (Cambridge: Harvard University Press, 1997), 447–464.

78. The term *extraordinary isolation* is Woodrow Wilson's. See *Constitutional Government in the United States*, 69.

79. Republicans had long opposed reauthorization of the independent counsel statute, considering it an unconstitutional infringement on the executive's prosecutorial authority. But their resistance to Democratic efforts to reauthorize the statute came to an end in 1993, when the Whitewater scandal emerged. Katy J. Harriger, "Independent Justice: The Office of the Independent Counsel," in *Government Lawyers: The Federal Bureaucracy and Presidential Politics* (Lawrence: University Press of Kansas, 1995), 86.

80. Janny Scott, "Talking Heads Post-Mortem: All Wrong, All the Time," *New York Times*, November 8, 1998, A22.

81. The controversy of the Clinton impeachment process led to bipartisan opposition to the Ethics in Government Act, which Congress failed to reauthorize when the act lapsed in the summer of 1999.

82. Voters distinguished sharply between Clinton, the chief executive, of whom they approved, and Clinton, the man, whom they regarded as immoral and untrustworthy. Just 20 percent of those interviewed in a January 1999 Gallup poll thought Clinton provided good moral leadership, and only 24 percent characterized him as honest and trustworthy, new lows for his presidency. "Good Times for Clinton the President, but Personal Reputation Hits New Low," Gallup News Service, January 23, 1999, www.gallup.com.

83. Interview with Will Marshall, president, Progressive Policy Institute, June 14, 1999.

84. David E. Rosenbaum, "Surplus a Salve for Clinton and Congress, *New York Times*, June 29, 1999.

85. New Democrats accused Bush of trying to steal their politics. As DLC president Al From wrote in spring 1999, Bush's effort to call himself a "compassionate conservative" appeared to be an effort by Republicans "to do for their party what New Democrats did for ours in 1992—to redefine and capture the political center." Al From, "Political Memo," *The New Democrat*, 11 (May/June 1999): 35. Many Republicans agreed. One skeptical conservative revealed that if he wanted to know the Bush campaign's position on a particular issue, he would consult the DLC magazine, *The New Democratic Blueprint*. Interview with Bush campaign adviser, not for attribution, November 13, 2001.

86. Interview with Karl Rove, November 15, 2001.

87. E. J. Dionne Jr., "Conservatism Recast," *Washington Post*, January 27, 2002.

88. George W. Bush, "Duty of Hope," speech, Indianapolis, Indiana, July 22, 1999, www.georgewbush.com.

89. Interview with Michael Gerson, November 15, 2001.

90. Rove interview; remarks by Governor Bush, June 12, 1999, Cedar Rapids, Iowa, www.georgewbush.com.

91. Tish Durkin, "The Scene: The Jeffords Defection and the Risk of Snap Judgments," *National Journal*, May 26, 2001.

92. Rove interview. Rove believed that Atwater, a friend of his for twenty years, had made a mistake by going to the RNC. Political power fell into the hands of White House Chief of Staff John Sununu. A leading conservative in Washington who worked in the Bush administration indicated that he strongly urged Rove to work at the White House, not the RNC, "where organizational frustrations were rampant." Interview with conservative journalist, not for attribution, November 13, 2001.

93. Fred Barnes, "The Impresario: Karl Rove, Orchestrator of the Bush White House," *Weekly Standard*, August 20, 2001.

94. On January 29, 2001, Bush created a White House office to, among other things, "eliminate unnecessary legislative, regulatory, and other bureaucratic barriers that impede faith-based and other community efforts to solve social problems." Executive Order 13199, "Establishment of Faith-Based and Community Initiatives." He also ordered the Departments of Labor, Education, Health and Human Services, and Housing and Urban Development, as well as the attorney general's office, to establish Centers for Faith-Based and Community Initiatives within their departments. These centers would perform internal audits, identifying barriers to the participation of faith-based organizations in providing social services and forming plans to remove those barriers. Executive Order 13198, "Agency Responsibilities with Respect to Faith-Based and Community Initiatives," January 29, 2001. As for education, from the start Bush and his advisers viewed it as the central issue distinguishing Bush as a different kind of Republican. George W. Bush, State of the Union address, January 29, 2002, www.whitehouse.gov; and Rove interview.

95. George W. Bush, address to the joint session of Congress and the nation, January 20, 2002, www.whitehouse.gov.

96. David Nather and Jill Barshay, "Hill Warning: Respect Level from White House Too Low," *CQ Weekly*, March 9, 2002.

97. Bush was the featured attraction at sixty-seven fund-raising events that raised a record $141 million in campaign contributions for the Republican Party and its

candidates. Moreover, throughout the fall, Bush campaigned ardently for Republican nominees. For example, in the five days leading up to the election, he traveled 10,000 miles to speak at Republican rallies in seventeen cities in fifteen states.

98. Adam Nagourney and Jane Elder, "In Poll, Americans Say Both Parties Lack Vision," *New York Times*, November 3, 2002. An election eve Gallup Poll reported that 53 percent would be using their vote "in order to send a message that you support [or oppose] George W. Bush." Of these, 35 percent said they would vote to support him and 18 percent said they would vote to express their opposition. David W. Moore and Jeffrey M. Jones, "Late Shift toward Republicans in Congressional Vote," November 4, 2002, www.gallup.com.

99. Rhodes Cook, "Bush, the Democrats, and 'Red' and 'Blue' America," *Rhodes Cook Newsletter*, October, 2003, www.rhodescook.com.

100. Interview with Matthew Dowd, political strategist for the Bush-Cheney Campaign, July 8, 2004; see also, Matt Bai, "The Multilevel Marketing of the President," *New York Times Magazine*, April 25, 2004. Dowd insisted that a centralized grassroots campaign was not an oxymoron. The "ground war" was built with community volunteers, but "once they volunteered, we ask them to do certain things. A national organization has to have a consistent message and mechanics. If the message is not consistent, if tasks are not systematically assigned, the campaign will implode. This was the message of the [failed Howard] Dean campaign: letting people loose can get the candidate in trouble. The message and organization must be relatively disciplined." The centralized grassroots campaign was not without spontaneity, however. "The campaign headquarters gave people tasks, but volunteers on the ground had some flexibility in determining how to carry out those tasks. It was local volunteers, for example, who learned that model homes in subdivisions were a good place to register new voters."

101. The average contribution of the new donors was less than $30. RNC press release, October 1, 2003. Personal interview with Christine Iverson, RNC press secretary, July 7, 2004.

102. Jonathan Mahler, "After the Imperial Presidency," *New York Times Magazine*, November 9, 2008.

103. Bush was much more of a drag on his party's candidates than was former president Clinton in 1994. More than a third (36 percent) of the electorate said they voted to oppose Bush; compare that with the 27 percent who voted to oppose Clinton in 1994, and the 21 percent who voted likewise in 1998, the year Congress impeached the president. "Centrists Deliver for Democrats," Pew Research Center, November 8, 2006.

104. Ralph Thomas and Andrew Garber, "Even in State Races, Anti-Bush Mood Played Major Role," *Seattle Times*, November 9, 2006.

105. Sidney M. Milkis and Jesse Rhodes, "George W. Bush, the Republican Party, and the 'New' American Party System," *Perspectives on Politics* 5, no. 3 (September 2007): 461–488.

106. Stephen Skowronek, "Leadership by Definition: First Term Reflections on George W. Bush's Leadership Stance," *Perspectives on Politics* 3, no. 4 (December 2005): 829.

107. Barack Obama, Announcement for President, February 10, 2007, www.barack obama.com.

108. Alec MacGillis, "Obama Camp Relying Heavily on Ground Effort," *Washington Post*, October 12, 2008.

109. Ari Berman, "The Dean Legacy," *The Nation*, February 28, 2008. Former aide to Vice President Gore and Harvard professor Elaine Kamarck offers preliminary evidence

that Dean's contributions did make a difference in the 2006 campaigns. See Kamarck, "Assessing Dean's Fifty-State Strategy in the 2006 Midterm Elections," *Forum* 4, no. 3 (2006), www.bepress.com/forum/vol4/iss3/art5.

110. "Voting Turnout," http://elections.gmu.edu/voter_turnout.htm.

111. Peter Wallsten, "Retooling Obama's Campaign Machine for the Long Haul," *Los Angeles Times*, January 14, 2008.

112. Lisa Taddeo, "The Man Who Made Obama," *Esquire*, February 2, 2009.

113. The House vote was 246 to 183, with just 7 Democrats joining all 176 Republicans in opposition. In the Senate, the vote, 60 to 38, was similarly partisan. Only three centrist Republicans joined fifty-five Democrats and two independents in favor. David M. Herszonhorn, "Recovery Bill Gets Final Approval," *New York Times*, February 13, 2009. The party-line schism, coupled with the withdrawal of Republican senator Judd Gregg, Obama's nominee to be secretary of commerce, appeared to demonstrate the futility of the president's effort to move Washington toward post-partisanship at a time when the parties are so divided on the most important issues facing the country. See Peter Baker, "Bipartisanship Isn't So Easy, Obama Sees," *New York Times*, February 13, 2009.

114. Adam Nagourney, "Dean Argues His 50-State Strategy Helped Obama Win," *International Herald Tribune*, November 12, 2008.

115. Dana Goldstein and Ezra Klein, "It's His Party," *The American Prospect*, August 18, 2008.

116. Peter Wallsten and Tom Hamburger, "Obama's Army May Get Drafted," *Los Angeles Times*, November 14, 2008.

117. David Corn, "This Wasn't Quite the Change We Pictured," *Washington Post*, December 7, 2008.

118. Michael D. Shear and Cici Connolly, "Obama Assembles Powerful West Wing," *Washington Post*, January 8, 2009.

119. Dan Eggen and Michael D. Shear, "The Effort to Roll Back Bush Policies Continues," *Washington Post*, January 27, 2009.

120. Croly, *Progressive Democracy*, 346.

12 The Institutional Presidency

John P. Burke

Not until 1857 did Congress appropriate funds for a White House staff—one clerk. More than a half-century later, President Woodrow Wilson had only seven full-time aides. Growth in the size of the White House staff began in earnest during the presidency of Franklin Roosevelt, and with occasional lapses, the growth has yet to abate. The major challenge for presidents—not just for Roosevelt and his Democratic successors, such as Bill Clinton and Barack Obama, but also for conservative Republicans like Ronald Reagan and George W. Bush—has been to keep pace with an ever-expanding bureaucracy. Ironically, John P. Burke argues, the size and complexity of the modern presidential staff have caused the White House itself to take on "the character of a bureaucratic organization." Burke chronicles a number of the strategies presidents have adopted—with varying success—to make good use of their staffs.

Analysis of the workings of the White House staff, both by people who have served on it and by scholars, has a peculiar if not schizophrenic quality. For some, the staff is simply a reflection of the personality, style, and managerial skills of the incumbent president. Others emphasize characteristics of the presidency that seem to endure from administration to administration. Both of these perspectives have some merit. Presidents do seem to leave their imprint—for better or for worse—on the office. The formal and hierarchical arrangements of the Dwight Eisenhower, Richard Nixon, Ronald Reagan, George H. W. Bush, and George W. Bush presidencies and the more collegial, informal, ad hoc patterns in the John Kennedy, Lyndon Johnson, and Bill Clinton White Houses can be linked to the organizational preferences and "work ways" of each of these chief executives. Yet the White House staff, now made up of some two thousand employees in significant policy-making positions, also serves as an organizational context that can—just as in any bureaucracy—set limits on what a president can do and sometimes thwart even the best of presidential intentions. For the skillful president, the White House staff is like very hard clay that can be molded only with great effort, patience, and understanding; for the less skilled it can become a hard rock, if not a brick wall, that resists presidential management and control.

A full analysis of how presidents have succeeded or failed at this "organizational artistry" would require a detailed account of the presidential staff system that has evolved since the late 1930s and a close examination of the efforts of each of the presidents from Franklin Roosevelt through Barack Obama to organize and manage the institutional presidency. What follows is only part of that larger project: an outline of some of the institutional characteristics of the modern presidency and the managerial challenges they present to incumbent presidents.[1]

One point that deserves mention is how odd the need for organizational leadership would have seemed to presidents in the nineteenth and early twentieth centuries. Thomas Jefferson managed his office with one secretary and a messenger. Sixty years later, in the administration of Ulysses Grant, the size of the staff had grown to three. By 1900 the staff consisted of a private secretary (formally titled "secretary to the president"), two assistant secretaries, two executive clerks, a stenographer, three lower-level clerks, and four other office personnel. Under Warren Harding the size of the staff grew to thirty-one, but most staff members were clerical. Herbert Hoover managed to persuade Congress to approve two more secretaries to the president, one of whom he assigned the job of press aide.

It was common practice for early presidents to hire immediate family and other relatives as their secretaries, an indication that their few staff members functioned as personal aides rather than as substantive policy advisers. John Quincy Adams, Andrew Jackson, John Tyler, Abraham Lincoln, and Ulysses Grant all engaged their sons as private secretaries. George Washington, James Polk, and James Buchanan employed their nephews. James Monroe employed his younger brother and two sons-in-law. Zachary Taylor hired his brother-in-law.

Early presidents also paid the salaries of their small staffs out of their own pockets. Not until 1857 did Congress appropriate money ($2,500) for a presidential clerk—one. As recently as the Coolidge presidency, the entire budget for the White House staff, including office expenses, was less than $80,000.[2] By 1963 it had climbed to $12 million. In 2009 the corresponding figure for the Executive Office of the President was estimated conservatively at $375 million. Other estimates, taking into account items that are paid for by departments and agencies, put the total at over $1 billion.[3]

As demands on the presidency mounted, more help was needed. Grappling with the Great Depression of the 1930s, President Roosevelt's solution was to "muddle through." Early in his administration he experimented with a form of cabinet government but quickly became dissatisfied with its members' parochial perspectives, infighting, and tendencies to leak information to the press—problems encountered by many of Roosevelt's successors who also took office thinking that the cabinet would play a central role in their policymaking. Roosevelt then moved to a series of coordinating bodies that included relevant cabinet officers and the heads of the new agencies that were created as part of the New Deal. Another of FDR's managerial strategies was to borrow staff from existing departments and agencies; these employees remained on their home agencies' personnel budgets while they were "detailed" to the White House. In fact, the legislative whirlwind of Roosevelt's first hundred days was the product of a loosely organized group of assistants, many of whom did not have formal positions on the White House staff.

Roosevelt's patchwork arrangement worked, but just barely. In an interview with a group of reporters shortly after his reelection in 1936, Roosevelt publicly attributed his victory to the failure of his Republican opponent, Gov. Alfred Landon of Kansas, to seize on the president's chief weakness. "What is your weakness?" one of the reporters asked. "Administration," replied the president.[4] Clearly something needed to be done.

Roosevelt had already taken steps to rectify his administrative problems by forming the Committee on Administrative Management, headed by Louis Brownlow. Roosevelt's creation of the Brownlow Committee was not the first presidential effort to seek administrative advice on how to make the presidency work more effectively. But it was the Brownlow Committee that most clearly and directly focused on the need for a larger, reorganized White House staff.[5]

Concluding that "the President needs help," Brownlow and his associates proposed that "to deal with the greatly increased duties of executive management falling upon the president, the White House staff should be expanded."[6] After initially rejecting the then-controversial proposal, Congress passed the revised recommendations of the Brownlow Committee in the Reorganization Act of 1939.[7] Significant increases in the staff resources available to the president also followed passage of the Employment Act of 1946, which created the Council of Economic Advisers, and the National Security Act of 1947, which led to the development of the National Security Council and its staff, and the recommendations of the 1947 Hoover Commission on the Reorganization of the Executive Branch.[8] During Eisenhower's presidency, existing units within the White House Office (itself the core unit of the White House staff) were more clearly defined, and new offices were created. Eisenhower also designated Sherman Adams as the first White House chief of staff and assigned him significant authority to oversee and coordinate the domestic policy component of the staff system.[9]

From the handful of aides that Roosevelt and his predecessors could appoint, the numbers have increased steadily in each succeeding administration. By 1953 the size of the White House Office was about 250. Twenty years later, it had grown to almost five hundred. In 1977, criticizing the size of the staff as a symptom of the "imperial presidency," Jimmy Carter reduced it by a hundred employees, mostly by moving them to other parts of the executive bureaucracy. By 1980, Carter's last year in office, the size of the staff had inched back up to five hundred, and it has remained at about that size ever since. When other administrative units under direct presidential control (the larger Executive Office of the President) are included—such as the Office of Management and Budget (OMB), the National Security Council, and the Council of Economic Advisers—the number of staff swells to about two thousand. Physically, the Executive Office of the President has spilled out from the East and West wings of the White House to occupy first the Old Executive Office Building next door, which was once large enough to house the Departments of State, War, and Navy, and then the New Executive Office Building on the north side of Pennsylvania Avenue, as well as other, smaller buildings in the vicinity.

A marked change in the character of the presidency has thus occurred. By recognizing that the American executive is an institution—a presidency, not merely a president—we can better understand the office, how it operates, the challenges it faces, and how it affects our politics.

The Institutional Presidency

If the presidency is best understood as an institution, then clearly it should embody some of the characteristics of an institution. But what do terms such as *institution, institutional,* and *institutionalization* mean? Our concern is the organizational character of the presidency—its growth in size, the complexity of its work ways, and the general way in which it resembles a large, well-organized bureaucracy. More specifically, an institution is complex in what it does (its functions) and how it operates (its structure); and it is well bounded—that is, differentiated from its environment.[10]

Complex Organization

Institutions are complex: they are relatively large in size; each part performs a specialized function; and some form of central authority coordinates the parts' various contributions to the work of the whole. The first aspect of

Table 12.1 The White House Office, 1939

Secretary to the president	Stephen Early
Secretary to the president	Brig. Gen. Edwin M. Watson
Secretary to the president	Marvin H. McIntyre
Administrative assistant	William H. McReynolds
Administrative assistant	James H. Rowe Jr.
Administrative assistant	Lauchlin Currie
Personal secretary	Marguerite A. LeHand
Executive clerk	Rudolph Forster

Source: United States Government Manual, 1939 (Washington, D.C.: U.S. Government Printing Office, 1939).

complexity—the increase in size of the institutional presidency—can easily be seen by comparing the White House staff available to President Roosevelt in 1939, before the adoption of the Brownlow Committee's recommendations, with the staff at work in the Clinton, Bush, or Obama White House. The eight-person list of members of the White House staff in the 1939 *United States Government Manual* (see Table 12.1) is dwarfed by the long list of staff members currently serving under President Barack Obama. A comparison of the Roosevelt and Obama staffs also illustrates the second aspect of organizational complexity: increasing specialization of function. Roosevelt's aides were, by and large, generalists; they were simply called "secretary to the president" or "administrative assistant." The staff list for the Obama White House includes titles such as deputy assistant to the president for communications, deputy assistant to the president for legislative affairs, deputy assistant to the president and director of media affairs, special assistant to the president for public liaison, associate counsel to the president, and many others.

Other units of the White House staff operate within functionally defined, specialized areas, such as national security or environmental quality. In fact, one of the primary causes of the growth of the White House staff has been the addition of these units: the Bureau of the Budget (created in 1921, transferred from the Treasury Department in 1939, and reorganized as OMB in 1970), the Council of Economic Advisers (1946), the National Security Council (1947), the Office of the United States Trade Representative (1963), the Office of Policy Development (1970), the Council on Environmental Quality (1970), the Office of Science and Technology Policy (1976), the Office of Administration (1977), and the Office of National Drug Control Policy (1989). All told, the once relatively simple tasks of the president's staff—writing speeches, handling correspondence, and orchestrating the daily schedule—have evolved into substantive duties that affect the policies presidents propose and the ways they deal with the steadily increasing demands placed on the office.

The final characteristic of institutional complexity is the presence of a central authority that coordinates the contributions of the institution's functional parts. For the presidency, such authority resides nominally in the president. Since the 1950s, however, coordinating authority has gradually been taken over by the White House chief of staff—Sherman Adams under Eisenhower; H. R. Haldeman under Nixon; Hamilton Jordan and Jack Watson under Carter; James Baker, Donald Regan, Howard Baker, and Kenneth Duberstein under Reagan; John Sununu and Samuel Skinner under George H. W. Bush; Thomas "Mack" McLarty III, Leon Panetta, Erskine Bowles, and John Podesta under Clinton; Andrew Card Jr. and Joshua Bolten under George W. Bush; and Rahm Emanuel under Obama. The chief of staff performs substantive roles in policymaking and, in most cases, wields day-to-day authority over the workings of the White House staff.

Differentiation from Environment

The complexity of the presidency and its reliance on expert advice have given the institution a unique place in the policy process, differentiating it from its political environment. One way this has occurred is through increased White House control of new policy initiatives. Presidents now routinely try to shape the nation's political agenda, and the staff resources they have at their disposal make it possible for them to do so. John Kennedy, Lyndon Johnson, and especially Richard Nixon, with his creation of the Domestic Council, emphasized White House control of policy formulation, de-emphasizing the involvement of the cabinet and the bureaucracy. Carter and Reagan began their terms of office by promising to rely more on the cabinet. They quickly found that goal unworkable in practice and turned inward to the White House staff for policy advice. Clinton, George W. Bush, and Obama followed this pattern, and their domestic and economic initiatives were largely the work of their White House staffs.

Those outside the White House—Congress, the bureaucracy, the news media, and the public—have responded to presidential direction of the national agenda by expecting more of it. Political lobbying and influence seeking, especially by those directly involved in Washington politics, focus on the president. Although American politics remains highly decentralized, incremental, and open to multiple points of access, those seeking to influence national politics try to cultivate the people who have the most to do with policy proposals: the White House staff.

A second aspect of the presidency that differentiates it from the surrounding political environment is the way parts of the staff are organized explicitly to manage external relations with the media, Congress, and various constituencies.

The press secretary and staff coordinate, and in many cases control, the presidential news passed on to the media.[11] Since 1953 specific staff assistants also have been assigned to lobby Congress on the president's behalf. Today White House lobbying efforts are formally organized within the large, well-staffed Office of Legislative Affairs. The establishment of special channels of influence for important constituent groups is another way presidents manage their relations with the political environment. This practice began in the administration of Harry Truman, when David Niles became the first staff aide explicitly assigned to serve as a liaison to Jewish groups. Eisenhower hired the first black presidential assistant, E. Frederic Morrow, and added a special representative from the scientific community as well. In 1970 Nixon created the Office of Public Liaison as the organizational home within the White House staff for the aides serving as conduits to particular groups. By the time Jimmy Carter left office in 1981, special staff members were assigned to consumers, women, the elderly, Jews, Hispanics, white ethnic Catholics, Vietnam veterans, and gay men and lesbians, as well as to such traditional constituencies as African Americans, labor, and business.[12]

In George W. Bush's White House, liaison to constituency groups took on particular importance with the appointment of Karl Rove as "senior adviser" to the president. Rove not only was placed in charge of the public liaison and political affairs offices, but also was made the contact for conservative, business, and religious groups. Those contacts played an important role in Bush's successful reelection effort. The pattern continued in the Obama White House when the president appointed Valerie Jarrett, a longtime member of his inner circle, as "senior adviser" in charge of both the public liaison and intergovernmental affairs offices.

The increasing differentiation of the presidency as a discrete entity thus complements its increasing complexity and reliance on expertise as evidence of its status as an institution.

Effects of an Institutional Presidency

Even if the presidency bears the marks of an institution, do its distinctly institutional characteristics—as opposed to the individual styles, practices, and idiosyncrasies of each president—matter? Despite the tremendous growth in the size of the president's staff, perhaps it remains mainly a cluster of aides and supporting personnel, with their tasks, organization, and tenure varying greatly from administration to administration, even changing within the tenure of each president. After all, observers of the presidency, both scholarly and journalistic, have noted enormous differences between the Kennedy and Eisenhower White Houses, between Johnson and Nixon, Carter and Reagan, Reagan and George H. W. Bush, George W. Bush and Obama, and even Bush father and Bush son. It is the personality, character, and distinctive behavior of each of these presidents that have generally attracted the attention of press and public.

Some of these observations are accurate, but to the extent that the institutionalized daily workings of the presidency transcend the personal ideologies, character, and idiosyncrasies of those who work within it (especially the president), it makes sense to analyze the presidency from an institutional perspective. Not only do many of the presidency's institutional characteristics affect the office, but the effects are negative as well as positive. The institutional presidency can help determine the success or failure of a particular president.

External Centralization: Presidential Control of Policymaking

The creation of a large presidential staff has centralized much policymaking power within the presidency. This development has both positive and negative aspects. On the positive side, an institutional presidency that centralizes control of policy can protect the programs that the president wishes to foster. The Washington political climate is usually not receptive to new political initiatives, which must compete for programmatic authority and budget allocations against older programs that are generally well established in agencies and departments, have strong allies on Capitol Hill, and enjoy a supportive clientele of special interest groups.

In creating the Office of Economic Opportunity (OEO), Lyndon Johnson, a president whose legislative skills were unsurpassed, recognized precisely this problem. The OEO was designed to be a central component of Johnson's War on Poverty. As Congress was considering the legislation to create the OEO, three departments—Commerce; Labor; and Health, Education, and Welfare—lobbied to have it administratively housed within their respective bailiwicks. Johnson, recognizing that this would subordinate the OEO to whatever other goals a department might pursue, lobbied Congress to set up the OEO so that it would report directly to the president. Johnson was especially swayed by the views of Harvard economist John Kenneth Galbraith, who warned, "Do not bury the program in the departments. Put it in the Executive offices, where people will know what you are doing, where it can have a new staff and a fresh man as director."[13]

The centralization of power in presidents' staffs has not always redounded to their advantage. One of the worst effects of increasing White House control of the policy process, especially in foreign policy, has been to diminish or even exclude other sources of advice. Since the creation of the National Security

Council (NSC) in 1947, presidents have tended to rely for advice on the council's staff, especially the president's assistant for national security (also known as the NSC adviser). Ironically, Congress's intent in creating the NSC was to check the foreign policy power of the president by creating a deliberative body whose members would provide an alternative source of timely advice to the president.

Except during Eisenhower's presidency, the NSC has not generally functioned as an effective deliberative body. What has developed instead is a large, White House–centered NSC staff, headed by a highly visible national security assistant, that often dominates the foreign policy-making process.[14] The reasons why the NSC staff and the national security assistant have come to dominate are plain: proximity to the Oval Office, readily available staff resources, and a series of presidents whose views about decision-making processes differed from Eisenhower's. Beginning with McGeorge Bundy under Kennedy and continuing with Walt Rostow under Johnson, Henry Kissinger under Nixon, and Zbigniew Brzezinski under Carter, most national security assistants not only have advocated their own policy views but also have eclipsed other sources of foreign policy advice, especially the secretary of state and the State Department.

Perhaps the best testimony to the problems created by centralizing control of foreign policy in the NSC staff can be found in the memoirs of three recent secretaries of state. Cyrus Vance, who served under Carter, repeatedly battled Brzezinski. Vance's resignation as secretary of state in 1980, in fact, was precipitated by the administration's ill-fated decision—from which Vance and the State Department were effectively excluded—to try to rescue the American hostages in Iran.[15]

Alexander Haig, Reagan's first secretary of state, encountered similar problems with the NSC. In his memoirs, Haig claims he had only secondhand knowledge of many of the president's decisions. In a chapter tellingly titled, "Mr. President, I Want You to Know What's Going on around You," Haig reported,

William Clark, in his capacity as National Security Adviser to the President, seemed to be conducting a second foreign policy, using separate channels of communications . . . bypassing the State Department altogether. Such a system was bound to produce confusion, and it soon did. There were conflicts over votes in the United Nations, differences over communications to heads of state, mixed signals to the combatants in Lebanon. Some of these, in my judgment, represented a danger to the nation.[16]

George Shultz, Haig's successor as secretary of state, also found himself cut out of a number of important decisions by the NSC staff. The most notable was the Reagan administration's secret negotiations with Iran to exchange arms for the release of American hostages in Lebanon and its covert, illegal use of the profits generated by the arms sales to fund the contra rebels in Nicaragua. The arms deal violated standing administration policy against negotiating for hostages, and the disclosure of the secret contra funds undermined congressional support for Reagan's policies in Central America. The affair not only bespoke Shultz's conflicts with the NSC but also was politically damaging to the president.

Some exceptions have been noted to the general pattern of NSC dominance in foreign policy-making: one occurred during the Ford administration, another in the elder Bush's presidency. In both cases a reasonable balance was struck in the advisory roles of the State Department and the NSC. But the two cases are revealing about the conditions under which excessive centralization can be avoided. In both presidencies the same individual, Brent Scowcroft, served as the NSC adviser, and he deliberately crafted his job to be a "neutral" or "honest" broker of the foreign policy-making process.[17] Furthermore, in both administrations the secretaries of state had extensive White House staff experience. Kissinger had served under Nixon as NSC adviser, and for part of his tenure in the Nixon and Ford administrations he was simultaneously NSC adviser and secretary of state. Bush's secretary of state, James Baker, had served as White House chief of staff and as secretary of the Treasury under Reagan.

Foreign and national security policy making in George W. Bush's presidency offers another variant. During the first term, NSC adviser Condoleezza Rice, a longtime Bush confidant, was generally considered both a policy coordinator and a policy adviser, much like her mentor Brent Scowcroft in the George H. W. Bush presidency. George W. Bush, however, had other powerful voices in his inner circle during his first term: Secretary of State Colin Powell, Secretary of Defense Donald Rumsfeld, and Vice President Dick Cheney, all of whom had served in previous administrations. Rumsfeld and Cheney were chiefs of staff under Ford, and Powell was Reagan's NSC adviser. Rumsfeld and Cheney also had served as defense secretary, and Powell had been chairman of the Joint Chiefs of Staff.

The events of September 11, 2001, radically transformed many of the internal dynamics of the Bush presidency. Although a foreign policy-making process with substantial participation by the cabinet developed after September 11, the White House staff remained a powerful force. According to one account, the "outline of the war plan often emerge[d] from the private conversations" of Bush and Rice.[18] The NSC added two new offices to deal with counterterrorism and computer security, and other White House units were created as well. Most notably, Bush signed an executive order creating the Office of Homeland Security, with a mandate to coordinate federal efforts to prevent and respond to domestic terrorism. The White House unit predated the establishment of a cabinet-level Department of Homeland Security in December 2002 (which Chief of Staff Andrew Card and members of his staff played the major role in creating). However, the White House's Office of Homeland Security remained in place after the department came into being.[19]

In domestic and economic policy, Bush generally centralized policymaking in the White House.[20] During Bush's first term, the White House staff was the dominant force in such areas as tax reform, education, the patients' bill of rights, and the faith-based initiatives proposal. In fact, in at least one of these issue areas, education policy, reports surfaced that the secretary of education was not pleased with the dominant role taken by the White House.[21] After Bush was reelected in 2004, one aide observed that the pattern would likely continue: "The Bush brand is a few priorities, run out of the White House, with no interference from the cabinet."[22] Departmental compliance with the White House's agenda, coupled with Bush's own emphasis on loyalty and discipline, was further exemplified (and bolstered) with Bush's nomination of three White House aides to cabinet positions in his second term: Rice as secretary of state, White House legal counsel Alberto Gonzales as attorney general, and Margaret Spellings (the White House domestic adviser who had largely devised the education reform proposals) as secretary of education. According to one account, "Bush and senior adviser Karl Rove are determined to 'implant their DNA throughout the government,' as one official put it."[23]

Despite his sharp policy differences with Bush, President Obama also centralized policymaking in the White House. Three longtime associates, David Axelrod, Peter Rouse, and Valerie Jarrett, were given the title of "senior adviser" to the president. New White House offices were created to coordinate energy, health care, and urban policy initiatives; a White House–based "performance evaluation" office was also added. As one account noted during the transition, although Obama built "a cabinet of prominent and strong willed players . . . he is putting together a governing structure that will concentrate more decision making over his top domestic priorities in the White House" than in the departments. These changes "shift the political center of gravity farther away from the cabinet, a trend that has accelerated under presidents of both parties in recent years."[24] The appointment of Lawrence Summers, a former secretary of the Treasury, to head the National Economic Council, also indicated a significant White House role in shaping economic policy.

Internal Centralization: Hierarchy, Gatekeeping, and Presidential Isolation

The centralization of policy-making power by the White House staff has been accompanied by a centralization of power within the staff by one or two chief aides. This internal centralization is further evidence of the institutional character of the presidency, and it too affects the way the institutional presidency operates, providing both opportunities and risks for the president.

On the positive side, centralization of authority within a well-organized staff system can ensure clear lines of responsibility, well-demarcated duties, and orderly work ways. When presidents lack a centralized, organized staff system, the policy-making process suffers.

The travails of Franklin Roosevelt's staff illustrate the problems that can arise from lack of effective organization. Roosevelt favored a relatively unorganized, competitive staff system, one in which the president acted as his own chief of staff. But rather than establishing regular patterns of duties and assignments and an orderly system of reporting and control, Roosevelt often gave several of his staff assistants the same assignment, pitting them against each other.

Some analysts have argued that redundancy—two or more staff members doing the same thing—can benefit an organization.[25] But in Roosevelt's day, staff resources were minimal. Worse, his staff arrangements generated jealousy and insecurity among his aides, neither of which is conducive to sound policy advice or effective administration. As Patrick Anderson observes, "Roosevelt used men, squeezed them dry, and ruthlessly discarded them. . . . The requirement [for success] was that they accept criticism without complaint, toil without credit, and accept unquestioningly Roosevelt's moods and machinations."[26]

In addition to making the staff more effective, a system in which one staff member serves as chief of staff or is at least *primus inter pares* (first among equals) is advantageous to a president for other reasons. It can protect the president's political standing, for example. A highly visible staff member with a significant amount of authority within the White House can act as a kind of lightning rod, handling politically tough assignments and deflecting political controversy from the president to himself or herself.

Perhaps the best example of this useful division of labor comes from the Eisenhower presidency. Part of Eisenhower's success as president derived from a leadership style in which he projected himself as a chief of state who was above the political fray, while allowing his assistants, especially Sherman Adams, the flinty former governor of New Hampshire who was Eisenhower's chief of staff, to seem like prime ministers concerned with day-to-day politics. A 1956 *Time* magazine feature on Eisenhower's staff reported that Adams's scrawled "O.K., S.A." was tantamount to presidential approval. Although it was really Eisenhower who made the decisions, Adams's reputation as the "abominable 'No!' man" helped to "preserve Eisenhower's image as a benevolent national and international leader" and protect his standing in the polls.[27]

A well-organized, centralized staff can also work against a president. Corruption and the abuse of power are among the dangers of elevating one assistant to prominence and investing that person with a large amount of power. Sherman Adams proved politically embarrassing to Eisenhower when he was accused of accepting gifts from a New England textile manufacturer. Eisenhower found it personally difficult to ask his trusted aide to resign and delegated the job to Vice President Nixon. The political and personal problems Eisenhower experienced through relying on, and then having to fire, Adams seem to be part of a pattern: Truman and Harry Vaughan, Johnson and Walter Jenkins, Nixon and Haldeman, Reagan and Donald Regan, and George H. W. Bush and John Sununu.

Another two-edged consequence of a centralized staff system is that a highly visible assistant with a large amount of authority can act as a gatekeeper, controlling and filtering the flow of information to and from the president. Both Jordan under Carter and Regan under Reagan were criticized for limiting access to the president and selectively screening the information and advice the president received. Joseph Califano Jr., Carter's secretary of health, education, and welfare, had repeated run-ins with Jordan. While lobbying Dan Rostenkowski, the Democratic representative from Illinois and influential chair of the Health Subcommittee of the House Ways and Means Committee, on a hospital cost containment bill, Califano found that Rostenkowski also resented the treatment he was receiving from Jordan. "He never returns a phone call, Joe," Rostenkowski complained. "Don't feel slighted," Califano replied. "He treats you exactly as he treats most of the Cabinet."[28] In July 1979 Carter fired Califano and promoted Jordan.

Donald Regan, who succeeded James Baker as Reagan's chief of staff in 1985, acquired tremendous power in domestic policy-making, played a major role in important presidential appointments, and was even touted in the media as Reagan's prime minister. Immediately on taking office, Regan flexed his political muscles by revamping the cabinet council system, substituting instead two streamlined bodies: the Economic Policy Council and the Domestic Policy Council. Regan retained control of the two councils' agendas. Subsequent council reports to President Reagan also flowed through Regan: "The simplified system strengthened Regan's direct control over policy, establishing him as a choke point for issues going to the President."[29]

Regan certainly was effective at centralizing power in his hands, but his attempts to exercise strong control over the policy-making process did not always serve the president's interests. In the realm of domestic policy, the tactics of Regan and his staff frequently upset House Republicans: Regan "ignored them while shaping a tax bill with [Democratic] House Ways and Means Chairman Dan Rostenkowski." President Reagan salvaged tax reform with a personal appeal to his party in Congress, "but the specter of the president traveling to Capitol Hill like a supplicant to plead for Republican House votes plainly raised doubts about the quality of White House staff work."[30]

In the realm of foreign affairs, Regan was the first chief of staff to play a major role in both making and implementing policy. His attempts to influence foreign policy precipitated the resignation of Robert McFarlane, the national security adviser, and led to the selection of Adm. John Poindexter, a Regan ally, as his replacement. The Regan-dominated, Poindexter-led NSC soon embroiled the Reagan administration in the politically embarrassing Iran-contra affair.[31]

Although George H. W. Bush was more personally involved in the policy process than Reagan, his management style fared little better. In foreign affairs he tended to operate with a close-knit group of advisers, especially his trusted longtime associate, Secretary of State James Baker. Trying simultaneously to be at the center of the decision process but avoid micromanagement of the U.S. efforts to depose Panamanian dictator Manuel Noriega and to win the Persian Gulf War, Bush appears to have been vulnerable to some of the problems Irving Janis has identified in his theory of "groupthink." These include a tendency for the leader to announce his preferences before the group has fully explored alternatives, the exclusion of dissenting opinions (for example, Colin Powell, chairman of the Joint Chiefs of Staff, was absent from several meetings soon after Iraq invaded Kuwait), and a certain degree of like-mindedness in the views of the participants.[32] Bush avoided decision fiascoes, however, because of his own foreign policy expertise and experience and his ability to reach out to other world leaders to forge effective coalitions, especially during the Gulf War.

Bush clearly preferred foreign affairs to domestic policy, largely delegating the latter to Chief of Staff John Sununu. He and OMB director Richard Darman quickly asserted control over Bush's domestic and economic policy operations, locking out cabinet secretaries and other staff members and leading to, according to Walter Williams, a "domestic policy regency."[33]

Centralized authority of the kind that Regan and Sununu practiced is preferable to organizational anarchy. But as hierarchy and centralization develop within the White House staff, presidents can find themselves isolated, relying on a small core group of advisers. If that occurs, the information the president gets will already have been selectively filtered and interpreted. Discussions and deliberations will be confined to an inner circle of like-minded advisers. Neither development is beneficial to the quality of presidential decision making or to the formulation of effective policy proposals.

George W. Bush centralized domestic policy making, but less in Chief of Staff Andrew Card than in Karl Rove, his chief political and policy adviser. Drawing on their shared experience with the elder Bush's management style, the president and Card were well aware of the dangers of investing too much power in the chief of staff position. Moreover, in planning for his new administration, Bush and Card sought to build stronger political and communications operations into the White House policy process than had existed in the first Bush White House. These operations were initially headed by Rove (politics) and Karen Hughes (communications), both of whom were longtime aides and advisers to Bush. The division of labor initially proved reasonably effective, although Rove's political contacts and advice were often subject to media scrutiny. But when Hughes resigned in April 2002, Rove's influence and visibility increased. Media accounts did not indicate any heightening of internal conflict, but questions were raised about the White House's overemphasis on loyalty and discipline, its ideological insularity, and the need for Bush to have other channels of information and advice.[34]

President Bush's response to the events of September 11 and his decisions to wage war in Afghanistan and Iraq were not the products of a deliberative process driven by the White House staff, although NSC adviser Rice's private counsel remained important to Bush. Considering the presence of such powerful and experienced players as Cheney, Powell, and Rumsfeld, a staff-driven process was unlikely to develop. Moreover, most accounts of Bush's decision making after September 11 stressed his deep personal involvement in the details of policy and his frequent meetings with the war cabinet.[35] What was problematic was whether intelligence had been properly shared, analyzed, and vetted before September 11 about a potential terrorist attack. With Iraq, the intelligence issue arose again, first with respect to the falsely reported presence of weapons of mass destruction and then with respect to the difficulties postwar reconstruction would encounter. Perhaps Rice would have served the president better by acting more assertively as an honest broker of the decision process: testing assumptions, challenging evidence for its reliability, questioning deeper ideological commitments, making sure a full range of policy options was on the table, coordinating information, and fostering bureaucratic cooperation. Greater White House involvement of this sort might have contributed to a more thorough decision-making process.

Barack Obama's selection of Rahm Emanuel as chief of staff brought on board someone with impressive credentials who was likely to hew to the strong chief of staff model. Emanuel had been Clinton's chief White House political adviser (akin to Rove), he had strong political credentials as the fourth-ranking

Democrat in the House of Representatives, and he had a reputation as a tough and demanding manager and fierce partisan infighter. If all works out well, he may serve as a policy adviser and a tough but effective manager along the lines of Leon Panetta and James Baker. If not, the difficulties experienced under John Sununu or Don Regan are likely to emerge. The situation is complicated by the appointment of three longtime Obama advisers—Axelrod, Jarrett, and Rouse—as "senior advisers" to the president with authority over various units of the staff. How well Emanuel and these senior advisers work together will have major consequences for the Obama presidency.

Bureaucratization

As the top levels of the White House staff have gained authority and political visibility, the rest of the staff has taken on the character of a bureaucratic organization. Among its bureaucratic characteristics are complex work routines, which often stifle originality and reduce differences on policy to their lowest common denominator. Drawing on his experience in the Carter White House, Greg Schneiders complained that if one feeds "advice through the system . . . what may have begun as a bold initiative comes out the other end as unrecognizable mush. The system frustrates and alienates the staff and cheats the President and the country."[36] Schneiders also noted that the frustrations of staffers do not end with the paper flow:

There are also the meetings. The incredible, interminable, boring, ever-multiplying meetings. There are staff meetings and task force meetings, trip meetings and general schedule meetings, meetings to make decisions and unmake them and to plan future meetings, where even more decisions will be made.[37]

"All of this might be more tolerable," Schneiders suggested, "if the staff could derive satisfaction vicariously from personal association with the President." But few aides have any direct contact with the president: "Even many of those at the highest levels—assistants, deputy assistants, special assistants—don't see the President once a week or speak to him in any substantive way once a month."[38] Similarly, Karen Hult observes that "So much of it is symbolic." In her view, staff members "want to get close to the president because it signals . . . the person really has the president's ear. Now, of course, the more people you have like that, the less likely they really are to have the president's ear."[39]

What develops as a substitute for work satisfaction or personal proximity to the president are typical patterns of organizational behavior: "bureaucratic" and "court" politics. With regard to court politics, for example, White House staff members often compete for assignments and authority that serve as a measure of their standing and prestige on the staff and ultimately with the president. Sometimes these turf battles are physical in character, with staff members competing for larger office space and closer proximity to central figures in the administration, especially to the president and the Oval Office in the West Wing. At the beginning of each presidential term, journalists take an intense interest in the size of staff offices and their location in relation to the president; these are taken as signs of relative power and influence by the Washington political community.

Not only are staff members concerned about their standing within the White House, but they also care about how they are perceived by outsiders. Patterns of behavior—bureaucratic politics—can develop that relate to a staff member's place in the organization: "Where one stands depends on where one sits." Staff members often develop allies on the outside—members of the press, members of Congress, lobbyists, and other political influentials—who can aid the programs and political causes of particular parts of the institutional presidency or the personal careers of staffers. Conversely, they can also create hostility and enmity among those outside the staff who compete with them for the president's attention. One classic example of this is the "us versus them" attitude that develops between White House staff members (inside) and the regular departments (outside) in domestic and economic policy and between the NSC staff (inside) and the State Department (outside) in foreign policy. In part, such attitudes may stem from different views and perspectives of a personal nature. But these attitudes may also inhere in the endemic bureaucratic competition and politics that any complex, bureaucratic institution generates.

Politicization

As a response to the bureaucratization of the White House staff, presidents are increasingly politicizing the institutional presidency. That is, they are attempting to make sure that staff members heed their policy directives and serve the president's political needs, rather than their own.

In most cases, the president's reasons for politicizing the staff are understandable. The Constitution's system of shared powers deals presidents a weak hand in Washington. To advance their goals, presidents need broad agreement among their aides and assistants with their political programs and policy goals. President Nixon, for example, created the Domestic Council as a discrete unit within the White House staff to serve as his principal source of policy advice on domestic affairs because he feared that the agencies and departments were staffed with unsympathetic liberal Democrats.

The difficulty for presidents comes in determining to what extent they should politicize their staffs. Excessive politicization can limit the range of opinions among (and thus the quality of advice from) the staff. Taken to extremes, politicization may result in a phalanx of like-minded sycophants.

Excessive politicization can also weaken the objectivity of the policy analysis at the president's disposal, especially if the newly politicized staff unit has a tradition of neutral competence and professionalism. As Terry Moe summarized the argument, "Politicization is deplored for its destructive effects on institutional memory, expertise, professionalism, objectivity, communications, continuity, and other bases of organizational competence."[40]

The part of the president's staff in which politicization has been most noticeable—and the debate over politicization most charged—is OMB. When Nixon created the Domestic Council he also reorganized the old Bureau of the Budget into the present OMB. Although the Bureau of the Budget was an arm of the presidential staff and certainly not wholly above politics, it was regarded as a place where neutral competence was paramount—that is, "a place where you were both a representative for the President's particular view and the top objective resource for the continuous institution of the Presidency."[41]

Nixon increased the number of political appointees in OMB. Moreover, some functions once assigned to professionals were given to political appointees; for example, presidentially appointed program associate directors were placed in OMB's examining divisions.[42] The effects of these changes have been noticeable: greater staff loyalty to political appointees, less cooperation with other parts of the White House staff and with Congress, and reduced impartiality and competence in favor of ideology and partisanship. The role of OMB in the policy process has also changed: it now gives substantive policy advice—not just objective budget estimates—and takes an active and visible role in lobbying Congress.

The experience of the Reagan administration is particularly revealing of the risks of excessive politicization in budget making, an area where expertise and objective analysis must complement the policy goals expressed in the president's budget proposal. Reagan relied heavily on OMB, especially during the directorship of David Stockman, both in formulating an economic policy and in trying to get its legislative provisions passed by Congress. Stockman himself concluded—and announced that conclusion in the title of his memoirs—that the so-called Reagan revolution failed.[43] Part of Stockman's thesis was that Reagan was done in by normal Washington politics, which is particularly averse to a budget-conscious president. But Stockman's own words reveal a politicized, deprofessionalized OMB, which may not have been able to give the president the kind of objective advice that he needed, at times, to win over his critics and political opponents:

The thing was put together so fast that it probably should have been put together differently. . . . We were doing the whole budget-cutting exercise so frenetically . . . juggling details, pushing people, and going from one session to another. . . . The defense program was just a bunch of numbers written on a piece of paper. And it didn't mesh.[44]

The politicization of OMB cannot explain all of Stockman's difficulties. But as Stockman's account attests, Reagan and his advisers needed hard questioning, objective analysis, and criticism of the sort that the old Bureau of the Budget, but not the new OMB, could provide a president.

Putting the President Back In

Since its inception under Franklin Roosevelt, the institutional presidency has undoubtedly offered presidents some of the important resources they need to meet the complex policy tasks and expectations of the office. But as we have seen, the by-products of an institutional presidency—centralization of policy-making in the president's staff, hierarchy, bureaucratization, and politicization—have detracted from as well as served presidents' policy goals.

Presidents are not, however, simply at the mercy of the institution. Having emphasized the institutional character of the presidency, we should not neglect the presidential character of the institution. Although the presidency is an institution, it is an intensely personal one, which can take on a different character from administration to administration, from one set of staff advisers to another. Presidents and their staffs are by no means hostages to the institution. They have often been able to benefit from the positive resources it provides while deflecting or overcoming the institutional forces that detract from their goals.

The most obvious management task a president faces is to recognize on first being elected that organizing and staffing the White House are matters of highest priority. All of Washington and the media wait in eager anticipation for the president-elect to announce the names of the new cabinet. But it is how presidents-elect organize the White House staff and select the people who work for them that will make or break their presidencies.[45]

Clinton's difficulties during his first years as president can be attributed in great measure to his failure, during the transition period before he took office, to understand what it takes to create an effective staff system. According to one report, "Though it had studied the operations of every other major government agency, [Clinton's transition team] assigned no one to study the workings of the White House."[46] This failure was "an insane decision," according to one senior Clinton aide. "We knew more about FEMA [Federal Emergency Management

Agency] and the Tuna Commission than we did about the White House. We arrived not knowing what was there, had never worked together, had never worked in these positions."[47]

Clinton's early appointments of top aides exhibit another pattern of which presidents need to be wary: the tendency to offer staff positions to longtime political loyalists and campaign workers. As one Clinton aide noted, "Unable to shift from a campaign mode, it [Clinton's transition team] made staffing decisions with an eye to rewarding loyal campaign workers instead of considering the broader task of governing."[48] Presidents surely need assistants who are personally loyal to them and share their deeply held political views. But presidents also need aides who are adept in Washington politics or have expertise in a particular policy area. Too many friends from Little Rock, Sacramento, or rural Georgia can doom a presidency very quickly.

In contrast, George W. Bush had a more successful transition to office, despite the unusual circumstances of determining who won the 2000 election. Much preliminary planning had been undertaken before the election, including the selection of a chief of staff. Furthermore, even as the uncertainty over how Florida voted dragged on (not to be settled until December 12), transition planning was well under way in the Bush camp. Bush made a particularly wise choice in placing Cheney in charge of the transition. Cheney was not only a veteran of past administrations but also a participant in the outgoing Ford and senior Bush transitions. Bush's early selection of Card as chief of staff enabled White House planning and organization to proceed on course. By the end of the first week of January, Bush was only a week behind where Clinton had been in picking his cabinet, and he was well ahead in announcing White House appointments.[49]

Like Bush, Barack Obama used his transition period wisely in preparing to take office. During summer 2008, John Podesta, a former Clinton chief of staff, was assigned to head Obama's preelection transition. Podesta ambitiously began by developing lists of potential nominees, formulating a legislative agenda, reviewing President Bush's executive orders, planning for Obama's first 100 days in office, and organizing the postelection transition. On November 6, two days after the election, Obama tapped Rahm Emanuel as chief of staff, and in the ensuing weeks key White House staff appointments were announced. Cabinet appointments also were swiftly made public, often in teams that stressed Obama's agenda and priorities.

Obama was somewhat less surefooted in his choice of department heads. On the one hand, by December 19 his roster of cabinet nominees was complete. No transition since Nixon's in 1968 had made swifter progress. But this progress came at a price. Two of Obama's appointees—Bill Richardson as secretary of commerce and Tom Daschle as secretary of health and human services—withdrew when serious ethical questions emerged after their nominations were announced. His next choice as commerce secretary, New Hampshire Republican senator Judd Gregg, first accepted and then declined a nomination, citing "irresolvable conflicts" with the president on public policy. Not until spring 2009 were the two seats filled. The Senate confirmed former Washington governor Gary Locke as secretary of commerce on March 24, 2009. One month later, on April 28, Kansas governor Kathleen Sebelius was confirmed to head the Department of Health and Human Services.

Beyond striking a good balance between loyalty, on the one hand, and Washington experience and policy expertise on the other, presidents must also be aware of the strengths, and especially the weaknesses, of the various ways of organizing the staff members they have selected. For example, to reduce some of the negative effects of relying on a large White House staff, Eisenhower complemented his use of the formal machinery of the NSC and Adams's office with informal channels of advice. In foreign affairs, he turned not just to his trusted secretary of state, John Foster Dulles, but also to a network of friends and associates with political knowledge and substantive experience, such as his brother Milton Eisenhower and Gen. Alfred Gruenther, the supreme allied commander in Europe. Eisenhower also held regular meetings with his cabinet and with congressional leaders to inform them of his actions, to garner their support, and to hear their views and opinions.[50]

When dealing with his staff, Eisenhower encouraged his aides to air their disagreements and doubts in a candid and straightforward manner. He especially emphasized the need to avoid expressing views that simply reflected departmental or other bureaucratic interests. Herbert Brownell, his attorney general from 1953 until 1957, recalls that "time after time" Eisenhower would tell his cabinet members, "You are not supposed to represent your department, your home state, or anything else. You are my advisers. I want you to speak freely and, more than that, I would like to have you reflect and comment on what other members of the cabinet say."[51] Minutes of Eisenhower's NSC meetings reveal a president who was exposed to the policy divisions within his staff and who engaged in lively discussions with Dulles, Nixon, Harold Stassen, Henry Cabot Lodge, and others. But Eisenhower was also careful to reserve for himself the ultimate power of decision. Although they had a voice in the process, neither the NSC nor Adams decided for the president.

Kennedy dismantled most of the national security staff that had existed under Eisenhower, preferring instead to use smaller, more informal and collegial decision-making forums. Kennedy's abandonment of more formal procedures may have been unwise, but his experience with the "Ex-Com" (his executive committee of top foreign policy advisers) offers lessons about how presidents can make good use of informal patterns of seeking and giving advice. In April 1961 Kennedy's advisers performed poorly, steering him into an ill-conceived, poorly planned, hastily decided, and badly executed invasion of Cuba—the Bay of Pigs disaster. In the aftermath of that fiasco, Kennedy commissioned a study to find out what had gone wrong. On the basis of its findings, he reorganized his decision-making procedures—including major changes in the Central Intelligence Agency—and explored the faults in his own leadership style. By the time of the Cuban missile crisis, in October 1962, Kennedy and his advisers had become an effective decision-making group. Information was readily at hand, the assumptions and implications of policy options were probed, pressures that could lead to a false group consensus were avoided, and Kennedy deliberately concealed his own policy preferences—sometimes absenting himself from meetings—to facilitate candid discussions and to head off a premature decision.

In addition to developing a suitable leadership style, presidents can also take steps to deal with the bureaucratic tendencies that crop up in their staffs. Kennedy's New Frontier agenda, for example, included a number of programs, such as the Peace Corps, that did not resemble traditional bureaucracies; and his personal style generated loyalty and trust. Eisenhower lacked the youthful vigor of his successor, but his broad organizational experience made him a good judge of character with a sure instinct for what and how much he could delegate to subordinates and how best to organize and use their various talents. As with members of his cabinet, Eisenhower emphasized to his staff aides that they worked for him, not for the NSC, Adams, or anyone else.

Finally, although the tendencies toward centralization of policymaking within the White House and politicization of the advisory process have been powerful, all presidents have the capacity to choose how they will act and react within a complex political context populated by other powerful political institutions, processes, and participants. Too much politicization weakens any special claims of expertise, experience, and institutional primacy that the president might make in a particular policy area. Too much centralization eclipses the role of other political actors in a system that is geared to share, rather than exclude, domains of power; it may also set in motion a powerful reaction against the president.

Presidents would be well-advised not to neglect the observation about presidential success that Richard Neustadt made nearly fifty years ago: "Presidential power is the power to persuade."[52] But what presidents also need to know is that the character and intended audience of that persuasion must be tailored not just to the requirements of legislative bargaining and enhancing popular support but to the institutional character of the presidency itself.

Notes

1. For a fuller account, see John P. Burke, *The Institutional Presidency: Organizing and Managing the White House from FDR to Clinton* (Baltimore: Johns Hopkins University Press, 2000).

2. Stephen J. Wayne, *The Legislative Presidency* (New York: Harper and Row, 1978), 30.

3. Bradley H. Patterson, *To Serve the President: Continuity and Innovation in the White House Staff* (Washington, D.C.: Brookings Institution, 2008), 31–32.

4. Quoted in Louis Brownlow, *A Passion for Anonymity: The Autobiography of Louis Brownlow*, vol. 2 (Chicago: University of Chicago Press, 1958), 392.

5. I use the term *larger* to refer to the Brownlow Committee's recognition that the president needed greater staff resources and its recommendations that the Bureau of the Budget be brought over from the Treasury Department and that the Executive Office of the President be created. In its advice on increasing the size of the president's immediate staff, the committee's recommendations were rather modest: the addition of six administrative aides who would avoid the political spotlight and have a "passion for anonymity." These new positions added a more formal structure to the Roosevelt White House and set out new responsibilities for the once–ad hoc staffing arrangement. It is also interesting to note that Roosevelt rejected Brownlow's recommendations that the position of a chief of staff be created and that a more hierarchical, formally organized White House be established; their implementation would await FDR's successors. For further analysis of FDR and the institutional presidency, see Matthew J. Dickinson, *Bitter Harvest: FDR, Presidential Power, and the Growth of the Presidential Branch* (Cambridge: Cambridge University Press, 1997). For fuller discussion of earlier reorganization efforts, see Peri Arnold, *Making the Managerial Presidency: Comprehensive Reorganization Planning, 1905–1980* (Princeton: Princeton University Press, 1986).

6. President's Committee on Administrative Management, *Administrative Management in the Government of the United States* (Washington, D.C.: U.S. Government Printing Office, 1937), 4.

7. The initial Brownlow Committee recommendation for reorganizing the executive branch also included proposals to redefine the jurisdiction of cabinet departments, regroup autonomous and independent agencies and bureaus, and give the president virtually unchecked authority to determine and carry out the reorganization and any needed in the future. The more controversial proposals were either dropped or made more palatable in the reorganization act passed by Congress in 1939.

8. For further discussion of the Brownlow and Hoover Commissions, as well as other efforts at reorganizing the presidency, see Arnold, *Making the Managerial Presidency*.

9. On the growth of the White House staff during the Eisenhower presidency, see John Hart, "Eisenhower and the Swelling of the Presidency," *Polity* 24 (1992): 673–691.

10. The characteristics of institutionalization are adapted, in part, from Nelson Polsby, "The Institutionalization of the U.S. House of Representatives," *American Political Science Review* 52 (1968): 144–168. On the notion of the presidency as an institution, also see Lester Seligman, "Presidential Leadership: The Inner Circle and Institutionalization," *Journal of Politics* 18 (1956): 410–426; *The Institutionalized*

Presidency, ed. Norman Thomas and Hans Baade (Dobbs Ferry, N.Y.: Oceana Press, 1972); Robert S. Gilmour, "The Institutionalized Presidency: A Conceptual Clarification," in *The Presidency in Contemporary Context*, ed. Norman Thomas (New York: Dodd, Mead, 1975), 147–159; John Kessel, *The Domestic Presidency: Decision-Making in the White House* (North Scituate, Mass.: Duxbury Press, 1975); Lester Seligman, "The Presidency and Political Change," *Annals* 466 (1983): 179–192; John Kessel, "The Structures of the Carter White House," *American Journal of Political Science* 27 (1983): 431–463; John Kessel, "The Structures of the Reagan White House," *American Journal of Political Science* 28 (1984): 231–258; Colin Campbell, *Managing the Presidency* (Pittsburgh: University of Pittsburgh Press, 1986); and Peri Arnold, "The Institutionalized Presidency and the American Regime," in *The Presidency Reconsidered*, ed. Richard Waterman (Itasca, Ill.: F. E. Peacock, 1993), 215–245.

11. On White House relations with the media, see Martha J. Kumar, *Managing the President's Message: The White House Communications Operation*, (Baltimore: Johns Hopkins University Press, 2007).

12. For further discussion, see Joseph Pika, "Interest Groups and the Executive: Federal Intervention," in *Interest Group Politics*, ed. Allan J. Cigler and Burdett A. Loomis (Washington, D.C.: CQ Press, 1983), 298–323.

13. Galbraith quoted in Lyndon Johnson, *Vantage Point: Perspectives of the Presidency, 1963–69* (New York: Holt, Rinehart and Winston, 1971), 76. For a more extensive analysis of White House centralization, see Andrew Rudalevige, *Managing the President's Program: Presidential Leadership and Legislative Policy Formulation*, Princeton: Princeton University Press, 2002).

14. On the development of the role of NSC adviser, see John P. Burke, *Honest Broker? The National Security Advisor and Presidential Decision Making* (College Station: Texas A&M University Press, 2009).

15. Cyrus Vance, *Hard Choices: Critical Years in America's Foreign Policy* (New York: Simon and Schuster, 1983), 409–410.

16. Alexander Haig, *Caveat: Realism, Reagan, and Foreign Policy* (New York: Macmillan, 1984), 306–307.

17. On Scowcroft's role as honest broker, see Burke, *Honest Broker?*, 151–197.

18. Jane Perlez, David Sanger, and Thom Shanker, "From Many Voices, One Battle Strategy," *New York Times*, September 23, 2001.

19. For further discussion on centralization post–September 11, see John P. Burke, *Becoming President: The Bush Transition, 2000–2003* (Boulder: Lynne Rienner, 2004), 175–180, 186–188.

20. There were, however, some exceptions. Early in the new administration Vice President Cheney was asked to develop a comprehensive energy program. Bush also chose a special task force to flesh out his campaign proposals for Social Security reform.

21. See, for example, Noam Scheiber, "Rod Paige Learns the Hard Way," *New Republic*, July 2, 2001; and Diana Schemo, "Education Chief Seeks More Visible Role," *New York Times*, August 5, 2001.

22. Quoted in Jim VandeHei and Glenn Kessler, "President to Consider Changes for New Term," *Washington Post*, November 5, 2004.

23. Mike Allen, "Bush to Change Economic Team," *Washington Post*, November 29, 2004.

24. Peter Baker, "Reshaping White House with a Domestic Focus," *New York Times*, December 20, 2008.

25. Martin Landau, "Redundancy, Rationality, and the Problem of Duplication and Overlap," *Public Administration Review* 29 (1969): 346–358.

26. Patrick Anderson, *The President's Men* (Garden City: Anchor Books, 1969), 10.

27. Fred I. Greenstein, *The Hidden-Hand Presidency* (New York: Basic Books, 1982), 147. Adams's counterpart in foreign affairs was Secretary of State John Foster Dulles.

28. Joseph A. Califano Jr., *Governing America: An Insider's Report from the White House and the Cabinet* (New York: Simon and Schuster, 1981), 148.

29. Ronald Brownstein and Dick Kirschsten, "Cabinet Power," *National Journal*, June 28, 1986, 1589.

30. Bernard Weinraub, "How Donald Regan Runs the White House," *New York Times Magazine*, January 5, 1986, 14.

31. On the involvement of the chief of staff in foreign policy, see David A. Cohen, Chris J. Dolan, and Jerel A. Rosati, "A Place at the Table: The Emerging Foreign Policy Roles of the White House Chief of Staff," *Congress and the Presidency* 29 (2002): 119–149.

32. Irving Janis, *Groupthink: Psychological Studies of Policy Decisions and Fiascoes*, 2nd ed. (Boston: Houghton Mifflin, 1982). On possible problems with Bush's small-group decision making in the Gulf War, see Bob Woodward, *The Commanders* (New York: Simon and Schuster, 1991); Daniel P. Franklin and Robert Shepard, "Analyzing the Bush Foreign Policy" (paper presented at the annual meeting of the American Political Science Association, Washington, D.C., August 29–September 1, 1991); and Cecil V. Crabb Jr. and Kevin V. Mulcahy, "The Elitist Presidency: George Bush and the Management of Operation Desert Storm," in *Presidency Reconsidered*, 275–300. On problems in the Panama invasion of 1989, see John Broder and Melissa Healy, "Panama Operation Hurt by Critical Intelligence Gaps," *Los Angeles Times*, December 24, 1989, 1.

33. Walter Williams, "George Bush and White House Policy Competence" (paper presented at the annual meeting of the American Political Science Association, Chicago, September 3–6, 1992), 12–13.

34. See, for example, Ron Suskind, *The Price of Loyalty: George W. Bush, the White House, and the Education of Paul O'Neill* (New York: Simon and Schuster, 2004).

35. On the response to September 11 and the war in Afghanistan, see, for example, Bob Woodward, *Bush at War* (New York: Simon and Schuster, 2002); on the war in Iraq, see Bob Woodward, *Plan of Attack* (New York: Simon and Schuster, 2004).

36. Greg Schneiders, "My Turn: Goodbye to All That," *Newsweek*, September 24, 1979, 23.

37. Ibid.

38. Ibid.

39. Quoted in Baker, "Reshaping White House with a Domestic Focus."

40. Terry M. Moe, "The Politicized Presidency," in *The New Direction in American Politics*, ed. John Chubb and Paul Peterson (Washington, D.C.: Brookings Institution Press, 1985), 235.

41. Hugh Heclo, "OMB and the Presidency: The Problem of 'Neutral Competence,'" *Public Interest* 38 (1975): 81.

42. Ibid., 85.

43. David A. Stockman, *The Triumph of Politics: Why the Reagan Revolution Failed* (New York: Harper and Row, 1986).

44. Quoted in William Greider, *The Education of David Stockman and Other Americans* (New York: Dutton, 1982), 33, 37.

45. For an analysis of the Carter through Clinton transitions, see John P. Burke, *Presidential Transitions: From Politics to Practice* (Boulder: Lynne Rienner, 2000). For an

early analysis of the Obama transition, see John P. Burke, "The Obama Presidential Transition: An Early Assessment," *Presidential Studies Quarterly* 39, no. 3 (September 2009): 572–602

46. Jack Nelson and Robert Donovan, "The Education of a President," *Los Angeles Times Sunday Magazine*, August 1, 1993, 14.

47. Quoted in ibid.

48. Ibid.

49. For further analysis of the George W. Bush transition, see Burke, *Becoming President.*

50. On Eisenhower's "binocular" use of informal and formal patterns of advice, see Greenstein, *Hidden-Hand Presidency*, 100–151. On his decision-making processes, see John P. Burke and Fred I. Greenstein, with Larry Berman and Richard Immerman, *How Presidents Test Reality: Decisions on Vietnam, 1954 and 1965* (New York: Russell Sage, 1989).

51. Herbert Brownell with John P. Burke, *Advising Ike: The Memoirs of Attorney General Herbert Brownell* (Lawrence: University Press of Kansas, 1993), 294.

52. Richard E. Neustadt, *Presidential Power: The Politics of Leadership* (New York: Wiley, 1960).

13 The Presidency and the Bureaucracy: The Levers of Presidential Control

David E. Lewis and Terry M. Moe

"Chief executive" is not a presidential title that appears in the Constitution. Indeed, the constitutional separation of powers grants considerable authority over the executive branch, or bureaucracy, to Congress as well as to the president. Nonetheless, modern presidents work hard to maximize their control of the bureaucracy and to shift the balance of political power in their own favor. David E. Lewis and Terry M. Moe explain why presidents seek to make themselves "chief executives"; and, after reviewing the constitutional and historical aspects of the relationship between the presidency and the bureaucracy, they offer case studies in the areas of personnel, budgets, and regulatory review to illuminate how presidents do it—and why they usually succeed.

At 8 p.m. on Friday, December 30, 2005, President George W. Bush sent an email. In it was a simple "signing statement," written to guide administrative agencies and the courts in their interpretation of a new bill that he had just signed into law.[1]

This was no ordinary legislation. It included a provision called the Detainee Treatment Act, sponsored by Sen. John McCain in response to harrowing revelations about the Abu Ghraib prison scandal and the interrogation tactics employed in the president's war on terror.[2] Bush had publicly opposed the act with veto threats and aggressive lobbying, arguing that it impinged on his constitutional powers and limited the discretion he required to keep the nation safe from terrorists. Nonetheless, the bill overwhelmingly passed both the Senate (90–9) and the House (308–122).[3] Confronted with veto-proof majorities, the president relented and, in a public meeting with Senator McCain, agreed to sign the bill.[4]

Bush's email, however, unilaterally unraveled the legislation McCain had fought so hard to secure. The signing statement read, "The Executive Branch shall construe ... the Act, relating to detainees, in a manner consistent with the constitutional authority of the President to supervise the unitary Executive Branch and as Commander in Chief and consistent with the constitutional limitations on the judicial power."[5] In other words, detainee treatment practices would not be governed by the legislation Congress had enacted, but rather by the president's interpretation of his authority under the Constitution. Detainee treatment practices in the defense and intelligence bureaucracy—the parts of the government that were charged to carry out the law and give it meaning— would proceed as the president instructed, not as Congress had sought to require.

It is tempting to see this episode through a very narrow lens—the presidency of George W. Bush—and to think that, because Bush was one of the nation's least popular presidents, excoriated by his many critics for excessive uses of presidential power, there must be something off-the-charts about his legislation-gutting email. But in fact, Bush's action was not unusual at all. Presidents have been issuing signing statements since James Monroe, and modern presidents have used them with increasing frequency.[6] Congress doesn't like it. But presidents do.

What was Bush trying to achieve when he attached his signing statement to the Detainee Treatment Act? By telling the bureaucratic agencies charged to implement the new law what he considered its language to mean, and thus how he expected it to be carried out, Bush was attempting to exercise control over the bureaucracy—and in so doing, to shape the content and outcomes of public policy.

Writ large, this is what all modern presidents do. Sometimes they use signing statements, but far more often they rely upon other levers of presidential power, such as appointments, budgets, and regulatory review, that are better known. Whatever the mechanisms, all presidents routinely and systematically take actions throughout their terms of office that are designed to bring the bureaucracy more fully under their control. Indeed, they have little choice but to do so. Almost all important policies are carried out by public agencies of one kind or another—and precisely because this is unavoidably true, the bureaucracy makes up virtually the entire corpus of government. Any president who hopes to be a strong leader and put his stamp on the nation's public policy must control the bureaucracy. Or at least gain as much control as possible.

Throughout our nation's history, presidents have made a good deal of progress on this front. During the nineteenth century, there was very little bureaucracy because the departments and agencies of the executive branch were few in number and small in size and scope. Presidents tended to be weak and Congress strong. But as the federal government began actively addressing the burgeoning problems of industrial society during the early decades of the twentieth century, particularly during the New Deal of the 1930s, American bureaucracy grew enormously. And as the bureaucracy grew, so did the presidency, which evolved into a complex institution whose specialized components—the Office of Management and Budget (OMB), the National Security Council, the White House domestic policy staff, the White House appointments unit, and many others—are devoted largely to providing the president with the capacity to impose centralized control on the bureaucracy.[7] These developments are among the defining features of modern American government: a government that is bureaucratic and presidentially led.

Yet presidential control is far from complete. Precisely because bureaucracy is so central to public policy, Congress cares about the bureaucracy too. Indeed, this is putting it mildly. Congress knows that, unless it can shape the substance of bureaucratic action, the laws its legislators write and the benefits they attempt to bring home to constituents and powerful interest groups are worth little more than the paper on which they are written. Congress has formidable weapons to employ, moreover, in bringing its preferences to bear: it authorizes bureaucratic agencies' programs, supplies the money for agencies to operate, and oversees their behavior.

The stage is set, then, for an ongoing struggle between the president and Congress over which branch controls the bureaucracy—a struggle that is guaranteed, even encouraged, by a Constitution that puts no single branch in charge, and indeed barely deals with the bureaucracy at all. Any effort to understand presidential leadership must understand the nature of this perpetual battle over the bureaucracy, how presidents have responded to it, and how well they have done—and can be expected to do—in gaining the upper hand.

The challenge facing presidents is a daunting one. But despite the obstacles that the American system of checks and balances purposely puts in their way, and despite the awesome powers of a turf-conscious Congress, presidents have inherent advantages in the struggle to control the federal bureaucracy—advantages that have allowed them, slowly but surely, to outmuscle Congress (much of the time) and play the predominant role in harnessing the bureaucracy toward their own ends. We are not saying that presidents reign supreme. We are saying instead that, although the separation of powers is naturally brutal to presidents, they have made it less so through strategic and aggressive action.

In the first part of the chapter, we show that a distinctive logic governs this struggle for control. Along the way, we explain how decisions about the bureaucracy are made in the political process, the relative roles that the president and Congress play, and the forces that give rise to key presidential advantages. In the second part, we detail how presidents have used their inherent advantages through various levers of power. Specifically, they have increased their strategic use of presidential appointees across the government, they have extended their control over the federal budget, and they have centralized the review of agency rulemaking in their own hands. Through these actions they have gained more control over the nation's bureaucracy, and over its policies and governance, than the constitutional fragmentation of power would otherwise provide.

The President, the Congress, and the Dynamics of Control

To understand the dynamics of control, we need to start at the beginning with how the bureaucracy is organized. Although this topic may seem sterile and far removed from politics, it is anything but. Organization matters. Everyone in the political process knows that the specifics of agency organization—mandates, structures, personnel systems, locations in the hierarchy of government, and more—have profound consequences for how policies are interpreted and carried out, as well as for which politicians and groups are in a position to exercise control. Because decisions about organization are matters of strategy and struggle, they are intensely political.[8]

Within Congress, the legislative designers of public agencies tend to view the bureaucracy in parochial terms. As individual actors in a fragmented system, legislators and interest groups are not held responsible for the performance of the bureaucracy as a whole, as presidents are. They have little concern for broad issues of management, efficiency, and coordination, as presidents do. Interest groups have their eyes on their own interests and not much else. Legislators have their eyes on their own electoral fortunes, and thus on the special (often local) interests that can bring them security and popularity in office. For both interest groups and legislators, politics is not about the system. It is about the pieces of the system, and about ensuring the flow of benefits to constituents and special interests. As we see in the following sections, political parties modify these tendencies somewhat. But the tendencies remain fundamental.

What are the implications for how the bureaucracy gets organized? In any particular case, of course, a winning legislative coalition wants an agency that will carry out its favored policies effectively. But this is not simply a matter of designing organizations to be effective. For what an agency actually does will depend on who controls it and what they want it to do. If control of the agency falls into the "wrong" hands, the most effective organization in the world will not help. The key challenge a legislative coalition faces is to ensure its own control, and to insulate against the control of others.

The way to accomplish such control most directly is to specify the agency's organization in great detail by establishing decision procedures, standards, timetables, personnel rules, and other structural features. A strategically designed compendium of such rules serves to tell the agency precisely what to do and how to do it. In this way, the legislative coalition that passes the law is able to exercise control *ex ante*, embedding its interests in formal restrictions that, by giving the "right" direction to agency behavior, also insulate it from future influence by opponents. The benefits of insulation do not come cheap, because restrictive rules can easily undermine the agency's effectiveness by denying it the discretion it needs to do a "good" job. But in a world of political uncertainty, where enemies abound, this is a price worth paying if the agency is to be protected.

Presidents are prime targets of this strategy, even when legislative coalitions regard the current incumbent as friendly. The reason is that all presidents, for institutional reasons, use their power in ways that are threatening to legislators and groups. As national leaders with a broad, heterogeneous constituency, presidents think in grander terms than members of Congress about social problems and the public interest, and they tend to resist specialized appeals. Moreover, because presidents are held uniquely responsible by the public for virtually every aspect of national performance, and because their leadership turns on effective governance, they have strong incentives to seek centralized control of the bureaucracy, both for themselves and for their policy agendas.

Legislative coalitions often have reason, then, to try to insulate agencies from presidential influence. All the formal restrictions mentioned here help to do that: by specifying the features of agencies' organization—and thus the rules that ultimately guide their behavior—in excruciating detail, they help to insulate agencies from external control, including presidential control. Other restrictions are aimed directly at presidents themselves. The independent commission, for example, is a popular structural form that restricts presidents' appointment and removal powers, as well as their budgetary and managerial reach. Similarly, legislation is sometimes crafted to limit the number of presidential appointees in an agency, and to use civil service hiring procedures and professional credential requirements as protections against presidential control.

So although presidents are nominally in charge of the entire executive branch, the American political system makes it very difficult for them to exercise genuine control. This is a built-in problem, ultimately traceable to the constitutional separation of powers and its far-reaching consequences for politics. The bureaucracy is a product of this politics. It is heavily influenced by the fragmented, decentralized forces that animate congressional decision making, and it is slowly pieced together over time—agency by agency, program by program, unit by unit, procedure by procedure—with little overarching concern for the whole, and with conscious, strategic effort to insulate its components from possible opponents. The bureaucracy is not designed to be centrally controlled by presidents, or by anyone else. Yet controlling it is essential to presidential leadership.

What can presidents do?

Presidential Discretion and Unilateral Power

There is actually quite a lot that presidents can do to control the bureaucracy. In the fractious, often chaotic politics that separation of powers tends to generate, presidents enjoy important advantages over Congress in the ongoing struggle for control. Over time, these advantages have allowed presidents to move the structure of the bureaucratic system, however haltingly and episodically, along a presidential trajectory—shifting the balance of power in their favor, and giving them greater (if still very imperfect) control.

Presidents are greatly advantaged by their position as chief executive, which gives them many opportunities to make unilateral decisions about structure and policy. If they want to develop their own institutional capacity (by beefing up the apparatus of the institutional presidency), review or revise agency decisions, coordinate agency actions, make changes in agency leadership, or otherwise impose their views on the bureaucracy, they can simply act—claiming the legal right to do so—and leave it to Congress and the courts to react. For reasons discussed later, Congress often finds this difficult or impossible to do, and the president wins by default. The ability to win by default is a cornerstone of the presidential advantage.

Why do presidents have powers of unilateral action?[9] Part of the answer is constitutional. The Constitution, rather than spelling out their authority as chief executive in detail through specific enumerated powers—a strategy favored by those among the Framers who were most concerned with limiting the executive—is largely silent on the nature and extent of presidential authority, especially in domestic affairs. It broadly endows presidents with the "executive power" and charges them to "faithfully execute the laws," but says little else. This very ambiguity, as Richard Pious notes, "provided the opportunity for the exercise of a residuum of unenumerated power."[10] The proponents of a strong executive at the Constitutional Convention were well aware of that.

The question of what the president's formal powers really are, or ought to be, will always be controversial among legal scholars. But two things seem reasonably clear. One is that if presidents are to perform their duties effectively, they must be (and in practice are) regarded as having certain legal prerogatives that allow them to do what executives do: manage, coordinate, staff, collect information, plan, reconcile conflicting values, and so on. This is what it means, in practice, to have the executive power.[11] The other is that, although the content of these prerogative powers is often unclear, presidents have been aggressive in pushing an expansive interpretation: rushing to claim the gray areas of the law, asserting their rights of control, and exercising them—whether or not other actors, particularly in Congress, happen to agree.[12] Many of the same arguments can be made for the president's role as commander in chief, but the presidential advantages are stronger and more obvious when it comes to war and foreign policy—so we continue to highlight the grounds for unilateral presidential action in the domestic realm, and in governance generally.[13]

The courts, which have the authority to resolve ambiguities about the president's proper constitutional role, generally have not chosen to do so. Certain contours of presidential power have been clarified by major court decisions—on the removal power, for instance, and executive privilege—and justices have sometimes offered their views on the president's implied or inherent powers as chief executive. But the political and historical reality is that presidents have largely defined their own constitutional role by pushing out the boundaries of their prerogatives.[14]

Congress can do nothing to eliminate presidents' executive power. Presidents are not Congress's agents. They have their own constitutional role to play and their own constitutional powers to exercise, powers that are not delegated to them by Congress and thus cannot be taken away. Any notion that Congress makes the laws and that the president's job is simply to execute them—to follow orders, in effect—overlooks what separation of powers is all about: presidents have authority in their own right, coequal to Congress and not subordinate to it.

Precisely because presidents are chief executives, however, what they can and cannot do is also shaped by the goals and requirements of the laws they are charged to execute. And Congress has the right to be as specific as it wants in writing these laws, as well as in designing the agencies that administer them. If Congress likes, it can specify policy and structure in enough detail to narrow agency discretion considerably, and with it the scope of presidential control. It can also impose requirements that explicitly qualify and limit how presidents may use their prerogative powers—as it has done, for example, in protecting members of independent commissions from removal and in mandating civil service protections.[15]

Yet these sorts of restrictions ultimately cannot contain presidential power. To begin with, presidents are powerful players in the legislative process, and because discretion is the foundation of their power and ultimate success in controlling the bureaucracy, they will fight for statutes that give them as much discretion as possible, and they can veto those that don't. All legislation, as a result, is inevitably shaped to some degree by the presidential drive to increase administrative discretion.[16] In addition, legislators have their own incentive to craft bills that delegate considerable discretion to agencies and presidents in order to pursue their own goals. Legislators' main concern, politics aside, is for the effective provision of benefits to their constituents. For problems of even moderate complexity, especially in an ever-changing and increasingly interdependent and complicated world, this requires putting most aspects of policy and organization in the hands of agency professionals and allowing them to use their expert judgment to flesh out the details. It requires, in other words, the delegation of discretion. And once this is done—as it regularly is, year in and year out—presidents and agencies do the actual governing, not Congress.

Thus, although legislators and groups may try to protect their agencies by burying them in rules and regulations, a good deal of agency discretion will remain, and presidents cannot readily be prevented from turning it to their own advantage. They are centrally and supremely positioned in the executive, they have great flexibility to act, they have a vast array of powers and mechanisms at their disposal, they have informal means of persuasion and influence—and they, not Congress, are the ones who are ultimately responsible for day-to-day governance. Even when Congress directly limits a presidential prerogative, such as the removal power, presidents have the flexibility simply to shift to other avenues of discretionary action.

In part, Congress's problem is analogous to the classic problem a board of directors faces in trying to control management in a private firm.[17] The board, representing owners, tries to impose rules and procedures to ensure that management will behave in the owners' best interests. But managers have their own interests at heart, and their expertise and day-to-day control of operations allow them to strike out on their own. Congress faces the same problem with presidents. However much it tries to structure things, presidents can use their own institution's—and through it, the bureaucracy's—informational and operational advantages to promote the presidential agenda.

Yet Congress's situation is even worse than the corporate analogy would suggest. In business settings, the owners may well have control problems, but they also have supreme authority over their managers, whom they have the right to hire and fire—and thus they have major levers for gaining the upper hand. In American politics, Congress has no such authority. Its executive officers—presidents—have all the resources for noncompliance that corporate managers do, and in addition they are not Congress's agents in the scheme of government. Presidents have formal authority in their own right. Congress does not hire them, it cannot fire them short of impeachment, and it cannot structure their powers and incentives in any way it might like. Yet Congress is forced to entrust them with the execution of the laws. From a control standpoint, this is your basic nightmare.

It is also important to recognize that, although Congress can try to limit presidential prerogatives by enacting statutes, presidents are greatly empowered through statutory law whether Congress intends it or not. Some legislative grants of power to the presidency are explicit, such as the negotiation of tariffs and the oversight of mergers in the foreign trade field. But the most far-reaching additions to presidential power are implicit. When new statutes are passed, almost regardless of what they are, they increase presidents' total responsibilities and give them a formal basis for extending their authoritative reach into new realms. At the same time, the new statutes add to the total discretion available for presidential control, as well as to the resources contained within the executive.

It may seem that the proliferation of statutes would tie presidents in knots as they pursue the execution of each one. But the opposite is true: the aggregate effect of all these statutes on presidents is liberating and empowering. Presidents, as chief executives, are responsible for *all* the laws—and, inevitably, those laws turn out to be interdependent and conflicting in ways that the individual statutes themselves do not recognize. As would be true of any executive, the president's proper role is to rise above a myopic focus on each statute in isolation, to coordinate policies by taking account of their interdependence, and to resolve statutory conflicts by balancing their competing requirements. All of this affords presidents substantial discretion, which they can use to impose their own priorities on government.[18]

Congress's Collective Action Problems

Another major source of presidential advantage deserves equal emphasis. Presidents are unitary actors who sit alone atop their own institution, the Executive Office of the President. Within that institution, what they say goes. In contrast, Congress is a collective body that can make decisions only through the laborious aggregation of member preferences. As such, it suffers from serious collective action problems that presidents not only avoid, but can exploit.

This crucial fact of political life is too often overlooked. Scholars and journalists tend to reify Congress, treating it as an institutional actor like the president and analyzing their interbranch conflicts accordingly. The president and Congress are portrayed as fighting it out, head to head, over matters of institutional power and prerogative. Each is seen as defending and promoting its own institutional interests. The president wants power, Congress wants power, and they struggle for advantage.

This portrayal misconstrues things. Congress is made up of hundreds of members, each a political entrepreneur, each dedicated to reelection, each serving a district or state. Although they have a common stake in upholding the institutional power of Congress, this is a collective good, not an individual one, and as such can only weakly motivate their behavior.[19] Members of Congress are trapped in a classic prisoner's dilemma: all of them might benefit if they could cooperate in defending or advancing Congress's power, but each has a strong incentive to free ride if supporting the collective good is politically costly to them as individuals. Just as most citizens, absent taxation, would not voluntarily pay for their share of the national defense, so most legislators will not flout the interests of their constituents or key interest groups if that is the price of protecting congressional power. If a legislator is offered a dam or a veterans' hospital or a new highway in exchange for supporting a bill that, among other things, happens to reduce Congress's power relative to the president's, there is little mystery as to where the stronger incentives would lie.

The internal organization of Congress, especially its party leadership, imposes a modicum of order and gives it a certain capacity to guard its power.[20] Indeed, in recent decades, with the parties ever more ideologically polarized and party-line votes increasingly common, it may appear that party leaders have been strong enough to stifle the fractious inclinations of their members, coordinate and direct behavior, and get Congress to defend itself by acting coherently as an institution. But there is less institutional strength here than meets the eye.

What has happened in recent decades, more fundamentally, is that the constituencies within each party have become more homogeneous, mainly because the conservative South has become more Republican and the liberal Northeast has become more Democratic. Party leaders—who are elected by their members and highly sensitive to their needs—have been better able to mobilize them to vote together because there are many more issues on which they already agree. Not so, however, when they don't agree. Constituency is still in the driver's seat, and much of what looks like the power of leaders is really a reflection of shared constituency concerns and ideology. Leaders have no license to force members to do what they don't want to do, or don't really care about—such as taking costly action to protect Congress's institutional power relative to the president's—in the face of competing inducements to behave otherwise.[21]

The party that doesn't occupy the presidency, of course, does have an electoral reason—although it is not directly related to protecting Congress as an institution—for challenging the president on some occasions. If its members can make him look bad, and if they are able to tarnish his party's label, then they are more likely to win the next election. In addition to the forces of constituency, then—which can easily be centrifugal, and thus can be played upon by presidents—legislators have a "shared electoral fate" that shapes at least part of their political calculus and may induce them to stand up to the president when he tries to enhance his power. There is a flip side to this phenomenon, however, that works in the opposite direction and undercuts its efficacy: legislators in the president's own party have a shared electoral fate in seeing that he wins—and they have an incentive to undermine any effort by Congress to strike back at him or foil his plans. This is just another example of how complex the congressional decision process is, and how many collective action problems stand in the way of strong, coherent legislative action.

Presidents are not hobbled by collective action problems. Supreme within their own institution, they can simply make authoritative decisions about what to do—and then do it. On occasion, their interests as individuals may conflict with those of the presidency as an institution. The short-term pressures on them to enhance the loyalty of an agency like OMB, for example, could cause them to overly politicize it, and this could undercut the institutional presidency's long-term capacity for expertise and competence.[22] But most of the time, presidents' personal drive for leadership almost always motivates them to do things that actively promote and nurture the power of their institution—because it is through their institutional power that they are able to get things done, and to succeed. Thus not only is the presidency a unitary institution, but there is also substantial congruence between the president's individual interests and the interests of the institution.

In sum, presidents have both the will and the capacity to promote the power of their own institution, but individual legislators have neither and cannot be expected to promote the power of Congress in a coherent and forceful way. This basic imbalance means that presidents will behave imperialistically and opportunistically, but that Congress will not do the same by formulating an offensive of its own, and indeed will not even be able to mount a consistently effective defense of its authority against presidential encroachment.

Congress's situation is all the worse because its collective action problems do more than weaken its will and disable its capacity for action. They also allow presidents to manipulate legislative behavior to their own advantage by getting members to support or at least acquiesce in the growth of presidential power. One reason for this has already been established by political scientists: in any majority-rule institution with a diverse membership, so many different majority coalitions are possible that, with the right manipulation of the agenda, outcomes can be engineered to allow virtually any alternative to win against any other.[23] Put more simply, agenda setters can take advantage of the collective action problems inherent in majority-rule institutions to get their own way.

Presidents have at least two important kinds of agenda-setting power. First, because Congress is so fragmented, presidentially initiated legislation is the most coherent force in setting the legislative agenda. The issues Congress deals with each year are fundamentally shaped by the issues presidents decide are salient.[24] Second, presidents set Congress's agenda when they or their appointees in the bureaucracy act unilaterally to alter the status quo—by making the Environmental Protection Agency less aggressive in enforcing the Clean Air Act, for example, or by having the Occupational Safety and Health Administration conduct fewer on-site inspections of worker safety. This sort of thing happens all the time, and Congress is forced to react or acquiesce. In either case, presidents can choose their positions strategically, with an eye to the various majorities in Congress, and engineer outcomes more beneficial to the presidency than they could if dealing with a unified opponent.[25]

Presidential leverage is greatly enhanced by the maze of obstacles that stand in the way of each congressional decision. A bill must pass through subcommittees, committees, and floor votes in both the House of Representatives and the Senate; it eventually must be passed in identical form by both houses; and it is threatened along the way by rules committees, filibusters, holds, and other procedural roadblocks. Every one of these veto points must be overcome if Congress is to act. Presidents, in contrast, need to succeed with only one to ensure that their newly determined status quo will prevail.

More generally, the transaction costs of congressional action are enormous. Not only must coalitions somehow be formed among hundreds of legislators across two houses and a variety of committees—a challenge that requires intricate coordination, persuasion, trades, promises, and all the rest—but owing to scarce time and resources, members must also be convinced that the issue at hand is more deserving than the hundreds of other issues competing for their attention. Party leaders and committee chairs can help, but the obstacle-strewn process of generating legislation remains incredibly difficult and costly. And because it is, the best prediction for most issues most of the time is that Congress will take no positive action at all. Whatever members' positions on an issue, the great likelihood is that *nothing will happen*.

When presidents use unilateral powers and discretion to shift the status quo, what they want most from Congress is no formal response at all—which is exactly what they are likely to get. This would be so in any event, given the multiple veto points and high transaction costs that plague congressional choice. But it is especially likely when presidents and their agents enter the legislative process on their own behalf—dangling rewards, threatening sanctions, offering side payments, and perhaps most important, mobilizing the legislators in their own party to come to their support.[26] Presidents are especially well-situated and endowed with political resources to do this. And again, blocking congressional action is fairly easy—especially given that, should all else fail, presidents can use their veto.

Whether presidents are trying to block or to push for legislation, the motivational asymmetry between them and Congress adds mightily to their cause. Presidents are strongly motivated to develop an institutional capacity for controlling the bureaucracy as a whole, and, when structural issues are in question, they take the larger view. How do these structures contribute to or detract from the creation of a presidential system of control? Legislators are driven by localism and special interests, and they are little motivated by these sorts of systemic concerns. This basic motivational asymmetry has a great deal to do with what presidents are able to accomplish when they attempt to block or steer congressional outcomes.

On issues affecting the institutional balance of power, then, presidents care intensely about securing changes that promote their institutional power, whereas legislators typically do not. Members of Congress are unlikely to oppose incremental increases in the relative power of presidents unless the issue in question directly harms the special interests of their constituents—which, if presidents play their cards right, can often be avoided. On the other hand, legislators are generally unwilling to do what is necessary to develop Congress's own capacity for strong institutional action. Not only would doing so often require that they put constituency concerns aside for the sake of the common good, which they have strong incentives not to do, but it also would tend to call for more centralized control by party leaders and less individual member autonomy, which they find distinctly unattractive.

When institutional issues are at stake in legislative voting, then, presidents have a motivational advantage: they care more about their institution than legislators do about theirs. This asymmetry means that they will invest more of their political clout in getting what they want. It also means that the situation is ripe for trading. Legislators may fill the airwaves with rhetoric about the dangers of presidential power, but their weak individual stakes in overcoming these dangers allow them to be bought off with the kinds of particularistic benefits (and sanctions) that they really do care about. This does not mean that presidents can perform magic. If what they want requires affirmative congressional action, the obstacles are many and the probability of success is low. But their chances are still much better than they otherwise would be, absent the motivational asymmetry between them and legislators. And if all presidents want to do is block congressional action, which often is all they need to preserve their control over the bureaucracy, then the asymmetry can work wonders in cementing presidential *faits accomplis*.

The Levers of Presidential Control: Three Cases

Presidents have used their institutional advantages to enhance their control over the bureaucracy. In this section, we describe three important examples of how they have done this—in the areas of personnel, budgets, and regulatory review. In each case, Congress has been either unwilling or unable to protect its own power, and the net result has been a shift in the balance of power toward presidents.

Personnel

During the middle and late 1800s, members of Congress were actively involved in the spoils system, which, in doling out government jobs to the party faithful, was the foundation of the American party system. Control of spoils gave them control over appointments to the bureaucracy, and thus substantial control over the bureaucracy itself. American society, however, was undergoing disruptive changes—industrialization, immigration, urbanization—and these changes gave rise to massive social problems, as well as to new political groups demanding governmental action to solve them. A government that traditionally had done very little, and could get away with being staffed by appointees who lacked expertise and experience, was now expected to perform at a much higher level.

As a result, Congress was under pressure to adopt a merit system for government personnel. The first step came with the Pendleton Act in 1883, which created the Civil Service Commission and brought 10.5 percent of federal jobs under the umbrella of merit appointment. The proportion of merit-protected civil servants then grew, decade by decade, as did the protections afforded federal employees under the system. Presidents had the authority to add jobs to the merit system and, at the end of their terms, often "blanketed in" their political appointees, ensuring that the latter couldn't be fired en masse by the next president. Meanwhile, business and civic groups continued the drumbeat for civil service expansion, as did the emerging federal employee unions, and Congress responded by adding new classes of employees to the system. By the 1930s, more than 80 percent of federal jobs had become part of civil service.[27]

During the Great Depression, Franklin Roosevelt led the federal government into new areas of economic and regulatory activity. Scores of new agencies were created to counter the depression and, later, to mobilize for World War II. The bureaucracy grew by leaps and bounds. Federal employment soared.[28] Most of the new jobs were originally filled with appointees recommended by Democratic Party officials; but these positions were then blanketed in as the New Deal drew to a close, thus protecting them from future dismissal.[29]

The expansion of bureaucracy presented all subsequent presidents with a fundamental challenge. If they wanted to be strong leaders, they needed to control the tangle of departments, agencies, boards, and commissions that populated the government and carried out policy. This was especially true for Dwight Eisenhower, the first Republican to become president in twenty years—because upon assuming office in 1953, he faced a bureaucracy filled with Democrats.

Supported by a Republican Congress hungry for jobs, President Eisenhower acted through executive order to create 800–1,000 new appointed positions, hoping to rein in the sprawling New Deal bureaucracy.[30] Prior to this order, high-level federal jobs—such as director and assistant director of the U.S. Fish and Wildlife Service, director of the National Park Service, and chief and deputy chief of the Soil Conservation Service—were filled by career employees who had worked their way up through the agency.[31] After Eisenhower issued his order, these jobs could be filled by presidential appointees. And they were.[32]

Subsequent presidents have continued to add appointees to the federal personnel system. And more fundamentally, they have worked to develop the president's institutional capacity to find, recruit, and select loyal appointees. The number of political appointees has nearly doubled from 1,778 at the end of the Eisenhower administration to about 3,250 in 2008. These increases have come under both Democratic and Republican presidents, with the largest increase occurring during the presidency of Jimmy Carter—for reasons we soon discuss.

Why wouldn't Congress simply forbid modern presidents to expand the numbers of appointees? One reason is evident in the Eisenhower experience. He entered office with Republican majorities in Congress. They wanted him to be successful and, with Republicans in high-level executive positions, to move policy in a more conservative direction. They also knew that, as members of the president's party, they could recommend candidates for appointment and, when successful, win the appreciation of the appointees and their group supporters—along with their endorsements and campaign support.

When the president is from the opposing party, needless to say, Congress often resists presidential efforts to increase the number of appointees. It is common for them to communicate their displeasure to the White House informally—but they can also go public. For example, in 1987 several Democratic members of Congress, backed by a General Accounting Office (now the Government Accountability Office) report, complained that President Ronald Reagan was "packing" the bureaucracy with appointees, particularly in the agencies that manage the government, such as the Office of Personnel Management (personnel), the General Services Administration (facilities), and OMB (finances).[33] During Bill Clinton's administration, Republicans publicly complained about an increase in appointees in the Commerce Department, and Commerce Secretary William Daley agreed to cut the number.[34]

Not surprisingly, the data show that during periods of unified government—when the presidency and Congress are controlled by the same party—significantly larger increases in the number of political appointees occur than during periods of divided government.[35] Yet even when Congress is controlled by the opposition party, serious efforts to reduce the number of appointees have gained little traction. This is true despite repeated claims by think tanks, academics, and former government officials that there are too many political appointees in the bureaucracy, threatening its expertise and "neutral competence."[36] Congress's problem is that, because the president can veto any legislation he doesn't want, a fair portion of his own party would have to go along if the number of appointees were to be cut—and they are unlikely to do that. In addition, the majority party's willingness to cut the number of appointees is inhibited by the hope that its own candidate will win the presidency in the next election.

The dynamic at work here, therefore, favors the president. Congress is not a unified institution intent on maximizing its power relative to the president's. It is a factionalized institution rife with collective action problems, and it is vulnerable to presidential imperialism. Historically, Congress has occasionally resisted presidential efforts to increase the number of political appointees, and it has occasionally succeeded in pressuring presidents to reduce the numbers in specific agencies. But overall, presidents have increased the penetration of appointees in the bureaucracy quite dramatically.

Targeting Management Agencies. The career civil service, whose members are neither hired nor fired by presidents, is obviously a major impediment to presidential leadership of the bureaucracy. Presidents took strategic action *within* the existing federal personnel system to affect the numbers and placement of political appointees. But until Jimmy Carter, no modern president had seriously tried to change the system itself. Civil service reform had been contemplated in broad reorganization packages, notably under Roosevelt (via the Brownlow Committee) and Eisenhower (via the second Hoover Commission), but such reform had never been a high priority on its own.[37] This isn't so surprising: genuine reform requires controversial new legislation, which is extraordinarily difficult and politically costly to achieve. With so many other ways to enhance their power over the bureaucracy through unilateral action, presidents have had little incentive to pursue it.

Carter's situation was different from that of his predecessors. With the massive growth of government in the 1960s under Lyndon Johnson's Great Society, followed in the early 1970s by the dramatic expansion of federal regulation—with the creation of the Environmental Protection Agency and the Occupational Safety and Health Administration, for example—Carter oversaw a bureaucracy much bigger, more complex, and more expensive than they had. And by the mid-1970s, in a worsening atmosphere of stagflation and energy shortages, Americans were fed up. Strong antigovernment, antitax sentiments swelled within the electorate, and politicians—including Carter—responded with pledges of reform.[38]

It was easy to portray civil service reform as part of this broad movement for better, more effective government. But for Carter it was much more than that: it was a way to make the civil service system more responsive to the presidency, and thus to enhance the president's capacity to control the bureaucracy. The kind of reform he had in mind amounted to nothing less than a clear shift in the balance of institutional power.

In the early spring of 1978, barely a year after assuming office, Carter placed a comprehensive proposal for civil service reform before Congress.[39] Among other things, he aimed to divide the Civil Service Commission into two parts. One, the Office of Personnel Management (OPM), would be headed by a single presidential appointee and given substantial discretion in crafting personnel policies for federal employees. The other, the Merit Systems Protection Board, would be an adjudicatory agency for handling employee appeals and grievances. In addition, Carter pushed for the creation of the Senior Executive Service (SES), a flexible corps of about 8,000 high-level administrators who could be moved from job to job at the discretion of the president and his subordinates and whose ranks would include some 800 political appointees.[40]

Nothing about this proposal could have fooled legislators into seeing civil service reform as a simple attempt to achieve "good government." It was also—and obviously—a bold attempt to expand presidential power over personnel and thus over the entire bureaucracy. Congress responded just as we would expect. Legislators simply did not care much about the balance-of-power issue and, with a few exceptions, did not oppose this clear shift in authority and discretion to the president. Virtually all the political controversy was stimulated by other aspects of the bill that were tangential to the power issue but affected veterans' organizations and public sector unions—constituency interests that, unlike the collective good of institutional power, motivate members of Congress to take action.[41]

The dynamics of control favored the president. Carter had a Democratic majority in Congress and so was in a strong position to begin with. Plus, most of the political conflicts between the president and Congress, and within Congress itself, centered on special-interest concerns—which excited negative votes even among many Democrats at points along the way—but not on whether Congress was yielding too much authority to the president in an institutional power struggle. In the end, Carter compromised on the veterans' and labor issues and won on what he really cared about. The Civil Service Reform Act transferred governance of the federal personnel system from an independent commission to a presidential agency (OPM) headed by a political appointee and endowed with greater discretion; it increased the number of appointees in OPM from six to twelve; it embedded them more deeply into the structure of the agency; and it created the SES—a hugely important innovation that allowed presidents to move thousands of high-level careerists from job to job, and gave them hundreds of additional appointees to work with as well. All in all, the act resulted in a tremendous boost for presidential power.

Strengthening the White House Personnel Operation. Along with the increase in the number of political appointees, the White House personnel operation has grown more sophisticated in how it fills these positions.[42] Truman was the first president to have a White House aide designated specifically to handle personnel issues. And up through the Eisenhower administration, it was common for the national party to have an office close to the White House to handle appointments. With the advent of John Kennedy's administration, however, a dedicated White House staff emerged both to recruit appointees and to manage the patronage pressures on the new administration.

Since that time, presidents have increasingly professionalized and institutionalized the personnel process.[43] President Kennedy employed three personnel officials. President Nixon employed twenty-five to thirty. Today the number is higher still, and can exceed one hundred when new presidents are transitioning into office. Starting with Nixon, presidents began employing professional recruiters to help identify qualified persons for top executive posts. Recent presidents have also regularized a process for handling patronage requests from campaign staff, the party, interest groups, and influential members of Congress through an ever more formal division between policy and patronage efforts.

The growing sophistication of the personnel operation has allowed presidents to take more and more control of the appointments process—leaving less to their party and their department and agency heads. Throughout much of the twentieth century, presidents were involved directly in filling only the top executive positions. In recent decades, they have increasingly sought to assert their influence over all appointed positions. One Clinton personnel official, for example, recounted that the president's nominees for cabinet posts were told, "These positions are Bill Clinton's, and he appoints them—the Senate-confirmed positions, the non-career SES positions, and the Schedule C positions—he selects them."[44] Similarly, a George W. Bush personnel official said, "This is not a beauty contest. The goal is pick the person who has the greatest chance of accomplishing what the principal [that is, the president] wants done,"[45] emphasizing the importance of both loyalty to the president's program and the ability to do what the president (not Congress) wants.

Congress hasn't done anything to slow the development of the White House personnel operation. In part, legislators recognize that presidents need to make appointments and thus need to get organized for that purpose. But of course, bigger issues are at stake. The president's institutional capacity is related directly to his ability to shift the balance of power with Congress in his favor. Congress could have tried to keep the president's institutional capacity to a minimum—for example, by restricting the amount of money appropriated for presidential operations, or by restricting his discretion (much of it grounded in OPM and the SES) in allocating appointees across the bureaucracy. But it hasn't done these things. In the final analysis, presidents hold most of the cards: they can veto anything Congress enacts, members of their own party support them anyway, and power issues just don't mobilize legislators to rise up and defend their institution.

Budgets

In the late 1800s and early 1900s, as government became bigger, more bureaucratic, and more complex in the course of responding to the nation's growing social problems, Congress began to have serious difficulties dealing with the national budget.[46] Its own fragmented organization was part of the problem. Congress was divided into policy-based committees, and bureaucratic agencies each submitted their budgetary requests to these committees directly, without coordination. This diffusion of control made it difficult for Congress to establish priorities in its spending, or even to reconcile expenditures with revenues—leading to frequent deficits.

These problems came into sharp relief in the aftermath of World War I, precipitating a fiscal crisis that pushed the nation's debt from $1 billion to $25 billion. Congress responded by enacting the Budget and Accounting Act of 1921, which created the Bureau of the Budget (BOB) within the Treasury Department, authorized it to pull together the budget estimates of every agency into a single federal budget, and made presidents responsible for improving the economy and efficiency of administration. The intention was to compensate for Congress's collective action problems by creating a more coherent, coordinated structure for the budget.[47]

The BOB, however, soon became a foundation for the expansion of presidential power. With authority not only to collect agency budget estimates but also to revise them—and thus to bring them into line with his own priorities and policy goals—the president now had a far stronger institutional capacity for directing national policy. Presidents gradually began to use the budget as a policy tool by adjusting budget estimates to promote their own legislative goals. The budget evolved into a document that described presidential aspirations for what government should do and how it should do it. By the end of the New Deal and World War II, after two decades of Democratic presidents and Democratic congressional majorities, a general expectation had emerged that presidents would take the lead on the budget, and that Congress would use the president's budget as a starting point for its own deliberations. This deference to the president was bolstered by the fact that the BOB had far-reaching expertise and detailed inside knowledge about what the bureaucracy was (and was not) doing, and how much its programs actually cost—which gave the president's team an information advantage over Congress.

Presidential control of the budgetary process—and through it, public policy—received another boost in 1939. Franklin Roosevelt, worried that the inability to manage the fast-growing New Deal bureaucracy might threaten his reelection, as well as the New Deal itself, asked Congress to help him create an institutional apparatus for housing agencies that would be truly presidential—and not really part of the larger bureaucracy, where they would be vulnerable to more congressional intervention. Large Democratic majorities agreed to empower their president by authorizing the creation of the Executive Office of the President and placing the BOB under its rubric. The Budget Bureau was now, in every sense, an arm of the presidency.

When Republicans finally regained control of both branches in 1953, they could have acted to roll back the BOB and the power of the presidency. But they didn't, because the power was now theirs. Over time, the BOB grew in size, and its career staff gained greater and greater influence in matters ranging from the details of administration and spending to the broader contours of public policy. The bureau also became an important source of institutional memory for the president, as well as for Congress. It provided vital transition advice to new presidents, monitored the management performance of different bureaucratic agencies, and helped presidents use the budget to accomplish their larger political goals. The BOB viewed its mission as serving the presidency as an institution, rather than any one individual president.

But presidents, characteristically, wanted more. In particular, they wanted the BOB to be responsive to their individual needs and political agendas; they also wanted it to be a more powerful control mechanism overall. The vehicle for change was Richard Nixon's Reorganization Plan no. 2, which, under "reorganization authority" granted to the president by Congress, would become law unless disapproved by either the House or the Senate. Nixon proposed that political appointees replace career civil servants as heads of the bureau's operating divisions; that its functions in program management, coordination, and information be expanded; and that all functions vested by law in the BOB— now to be renamed the Office of Management and Budget—be transferred to the president. The point of this plan, clearly, was to give OMB greater control of the bureaucracy, to make OMB more responsive to the president, and to expand presidential power.[48] Legislators saw Nixon's proposal for what it was. But the institutional issues, even with Congress in the hands of the Democratic Party, were not sufficient to galvanize opposition—especially because Congress actually had to act in order to block the plan. The Senate never even voted on a resolution of disapproval. The House did, but the Nixon forces put together a coalition of Republicans and southern Democrats that prevailed.[49]

In 1960 the BOB had fewer than ten political appointees: the director, the deputy director, three assistant directors, and a handful of personal staff.[50] By 1973, with the Nixon reforms in place, the newly reorganized OMB had twenty political appointees. These appointees extended down to lower levels of the agency, including the examining divisions, which had previously been headed by career employees. The Carter administration added even more layers of appointees, and subsequent presidents have consistently supported these high levels of politicization. Presidents want people in OMB who will do their bidding and thus promote their power.[51]

If Congress had a budgetary moment in the sun, it came in the midst of the Watergate crisis—an episode of presidential excess that, needless to say, raised the specter of the imperial presidency and gave presidential power a very bad name. At least for a while. In the budgetary realm, the symbol of Nixon's imperial misbehavior was that he had "impounded" (refused to spend) certain funds appropriated by Congress, arguing that legislators' spending was profligate and a cause of inflation.[52] Congress responded by passing the Congressional Budget and Impoundment Control Act of 1974, which created a new and more centralized budgetary process within the legislature, and made it more difficult for presidents to impound money.

As a group, members of Congress wanted spending to be cut—they just didn't want the president to choose the cuts. Legislators were unable, however, to control spending on their own. Each member agreed on the need for overall reductions but was reluctant to cut spending in his or her own district or state. As Andrew Rudalevige explains, "it is not surprising that each member of Congress seeks gains for his or her own district and seeks to lower the costs imposed on his or her own constituents. And while those goals make individual sense, when pursued by 535 legislators, they add up to fiscal disaster."[53]

In passing the 1974 budget act, Congress was not only recognizing that excessive presidential power was a problem. It was also recognizing its own collective action problems—and the new law was fully intended as a remedy. The act included three main provisions. First, it created new budget committees in each chamber that would set an overall annual budget ceiling, as well as ceilings for each policy area, in order to limit what the appropriations committees could spend. Second, it established a series of deadlines and procedures to usher each year's budget legislation through Congress. Finally, it created the Congressional Budget Office to provide Congress with its own source of fiscal expertise as a counterbalance to the power of OMB.[54]

This reform has been a colossal failure. Members of Congress still wanted to bring home the bacon to their constituents, and the act provided no mechanism to force them or their committees to stick to the targets set by the budget committees. The budget committees themselves, moreover, could and did change (meaning: increase) the targets throughout the legislative year. Nor did Congress abide by the procedures and deadlines designed to promote speedy, coherent decision making.

These problems became sorely apparent in the 1980s. President Reagan pushed for lower taxes and higher defense spending; Congress sought to protect entitlements and social programs. Deficits ballooned. With its reforms not working, Congress added still other mechanisms to get control over the budget.[55] One device involved automatic spending cuts: if deficits hit certain prespecified levels, cuts would go into effect on all programs not specifically exempted from the process. Another device involved hard spending caps, augmented by "pay as you go" requirements stipulating that all new spending proposals must identify a new source of revenue (or cuts in other programs) to compensate for the new spending. Ultimately, both devices failed. Members of Congress used accounting tricks, program exemptions, and clever scoring to maneuver around their own rules. Having designed these reforms because they knew they couldn't trust themselves, they proved they were right. Even during periods of fiscal surplus, such as the late 1990s, the budget caps were exceeded by close to $60 billion per year.

Congress's most extreme capitulation came in 1996. Controlled by Republicans for the first time in forty years, and thus by conservatives who had long railed against the Democrats' "irresponsibility" in overspending, it passed the Line Item Veto Act. This was, to be sure, at least partly an act of ideology. But it was also rooted in a simple recognition that Congress's collective action problems made it inherently incapable of controlling the budget. What the act did was to give presidents—in this case, a Democratic president, Bill Clinton—the power to single out specific spending or revenue items within a larger bill, and to veto only those items. These vetoes would then prevail unless Congress passed another bill to reinstate the spending. In June 1998, however, the Supreme Court struck down the act as unconstitutional.

But this setback to the presidency was just a blip in the historical timeline. The budget process remains heavily presidential. Year after year, Congress is unable to stick to the targets that its own members have selected. And year after year, it cannot enact appropriations bills on time: in the twenty fiscal years between 1990 and 2009, only twice has Congress passed its funding bills before the new year began. Congress is just not good at exercising its budgetary power—nor at holding on to it—as presidents grasp for more.

Regulation

Appointments and budgets have long been fundamental levers of presidential power. Another is regulatory review, which in recent decades has become a mainstay of the modern presidency and a telling barometer of how much the institutional balance of power has shifted in the president's favor.[56]

The first traces of regulatory review emerged in the early 1970s, when President Nixon—acting unilaterally—instituted the Quality of Life Review program under OMB. His real target was the Environmental Protection Agency (EPA), newly created in 1970, which had been devising antipollution rules that stood to cost industry billions of dollars a year at a time when the national economy—Nixon's main concern—was headed for trouble. The administration required EPA to submit its rules to OMB for prepublication review so that other agencies could comment, economic costs could be analyzed, and pressure could be applied to bring EPA's rules more in line with the president's program.

EPA wasn't Nixon's only target. In the early 1970s, six other regulatory agencies had been created, and twenty-nine new regulatory statutes had been enacted.[57] Nixon wanted to gain control of all this because it affected his entire economic agenda.

Environmental, labor, and other liberal interest groups were not pleased with the president's moves, nor was Congress. The new agencies had been created to engage in aggressive regulation, and Nixon—without any clear statutory authority—was trying to replace their priorities with his. Still, it wasn't clear at this point whether regulatory review was simply a Nixon power grab, which would soon be over, or something bigger.

It turned out to be something bigger, although its ultimate proportions could hardly have been anticipated at the outset. When Gerald Ford became president in 1974, he too faced serious economic problems and expanded Nixon's early system of regulatory review as a means of attacking them. Jimmy Carter's election in 1976 gave Congress and Democratic constituencies hope that EPA and other regulatory agencies would be unleashed, but this was not to be. Carter took even more aggressive action on regulatory review than his Republican predecessors had. In his Executive Order 12044, agencies were told to prepare—for all rules having major economic consequences—"regulatory analyses" that rigorously evaluate their cost-effectiveness. Carter also created a new organizational arrangement, led by OMB and other presidential agencies, for carrying out the reviews. With these developments, it became clear that regulatory review was not merely a Nixon or a Republican device to frustrate liberal ideals. It was a *presidential* device—one that would serve presidential interests regardless of party.

When Ronald Reagan took office in 1981, he pushed regulatory review to unprecedented heights. He began quickly, appointing a Task Force on Regulatory Relief that promptly suspended some two hundred pending regulations and prepared a hit list of existing regulations for review. He followed up with the groundbreaking Executive Order 12291, which brought regulatory agencies under presidential control as never before.[58] The executive order required agencies to submit all proposed rules to OMB's Office of Information and Regulatory Affairs (OIRA) for prepublication review, accompanied by rigorous cost-benefit analyses and evaluations of alternative approaches. In a departure from past practice, OMB now allowed agencies to issue rules only when the benefits exceeded the costs; it also required them to choose among possible rules so as to maximize the net benefits to society as a whole. Moreover, OMB now asserted the right to delay proposed rules indefinitely while review was pending.[59]

Environmental groups, especially, were furious and launched all-out attempts to persuade Congress to break the president's hold on regulatory review. Pressure to do so had been building for more than ten years, as frustration with past presidents escalated demands for a congressional counterattack. But now, with the Reagan agenda so aggressive, these groups were pulling out the stops.

How did Congress respond? It did not take on the president directly—say, through major legislation declaring that Executive Order 12291 was null and void. Instead, its approach was piecemeal, fragmented, and altogether predictable from a constituency-dominated institution: special interest legislation—such as the 1982 amendments to the Endangered Species Act, the 1984 amendments to the Hazardous and Solid Waste Act, and the 1986 Superfund amendments—that, through countless new restrictions, narrowed the EPA's discretion, hobbled it with cumbersome administrative burdens, and, on very specific items, directed the president and the OMB not to interfere. For the most part, legislators and groups attacked the president by burying EPA in more bureaucracy and trying to insulate its decisions from presidential interference.[60]

At the same time, another drama was unfolding over OIRA. This agency was created during the Carter years for other purposes, and only later did Reagan, acting unilaterally, vest it with authority for regulatory review.[61] The problem was, it had to weather the congressional budgetary process every year to get funding and, to make matters worse, its authorization was set to expire in 1983. In principle, then, OIRA was very vulnerable to congressional attack.

What happened? OIRA's opponents were able to block its reauthorization for a few years. But Congress continued to fund OIRA, which continued to carry out its regulatory review activities. Eventually, a compromise was struck. OIRA was reauthorized, but Reagan agreed that its head would henceforth be subject to Senate confirmation and its processes made more public.[62] These were not serious concessions, considering that Congress could have put OIRA out of business. The president held the upper hand. And regulatory review churned on, shaping and delaying regulations and infuriating its opponents.

The Bush years witnessed more of the same. Although the more moderate George H. W. Bush was not as zealous about regulatory review as Reagan, he left the basic structure of Executive Order 12291 in place, and OIRA continued to do its presidential job. Interest groups, meanwhile, continued to nibble away at OIRA through piecemeal congressional action. Environmental groups scored an indirect success (with Bush's assistance) when Congress passed and Bush signed the Clean Air Act of 1990, which buried EPA in more bureaucratic constraints and timetables intended to guide its future behavior.[63] Environmentalists also took direct shots at OIRA, whose authorization was set to run out again. In 1990 legislative opponents agreed to reauthorize OIRA if Bush would accept certain restrictions on its activities, but wrangling within Congress caused the effort to collapse. By default, OIRA wasn't reauthorized.[64] Nonetheless, Bush (and later, Bill Clinton) succeeded in getting it funded.

Legislative opponents did score a big (but temporary) victory: the Senate never confirmed a nominee to head OIRA during George H. W. Bush's administration. But the president simply acted unilaterally, shifting regulatory review from OIRA to the Competitiveness Council, a purely presidential unit headed by Vice President Dan Quayle.[65] The Competitiveness Council, which earlier had been assigned issues ranging from legal reform to job training, dove quickly into regulatory review—with staff assistance from OIRA. For the remainder of the Bush presidency, opponents trained their ire on the council, going after it in the usual ways.[66] But they were never able to deny it funding, they had no influence over its personnel or appointments, and they never passed legislation to challenge its activities.[67]

Bill Clinton retook the White House for the Democrats in 1993 and immediately got rid of the Competitiveness Council, evoking a joyous response from many legislators and interest groups. But Clinton's action was largely symbolic, because he surely did not get rid of regulatory review. Indeed, he fully embraced it as essential to his leadership. During his first year in office, Clinton issued Executive Order 12866, which, in the course of repealing Reagan's Executive Order 12291, imposed a review structure that was very similar to Reagan's, even retaining cost-benefit requirements. The difference was that the new structure was better suited to Clinton's agenda, which was more proregulation than Reagan's. Accordingly, regulatory review was returned to OIRA; environmental, labor, and other such groups were granted greater access to the process; and only the most costly rules were targeted for review.[68]

What made the Clinton years unusual is that, after Congress shifted from Democratic to Republican control in 1995, the president came under pressure from Congress to use his powers of regulatory review more forcefully than he wanted to. With Clinton insisting on using regulatory review as he saw fit, Republicans pushed ahead with bills to impose heavy new restrictions on the regulatory agencies.[69] These failed to become law—because Congress, as usual, was unable to take bold action—and the president ultimately prevailed: another reflection of the presidential advantage.

Republicans in Congress did succeed in enacting the Congressional Review Act of 1996, which made it easier—by streamlining its own procedures—for Congress to overturn proposed regulations, and thus to participate in regulatory review. Yet the review act hasn't worked. The streamlined procedures have been used successfully just once, in 2001, to overturn controversial ergonomics regulations promulgated by the Clinton Labor Department. Even in this case, legislative action was successful only because the newly elected president, George W. Bush, supported the repeal. Congress's problems are always the same: the obstacles to collective action are huge, and the president can veto.

The controversial election of 2000 that sent Bush to the White House also gave the Democrats more seats in Congress, and it restored the politics of regulatory review to familiar footing. Bush kept Clinton's executive order in place, but used Clinton's review structure to take policy in a more conservative direction. On the day of his inauguration, Bush issued an order delaying last-minute Clinton regulations and calling for further review, with the clear intent of derailing those that conflicted with his own agenda. There was a loud reaction from liberal legislators and their interest group allies, who put the spotlight on certain rules with public appeal, such as those regarding the level of arsenic in drinking water. Although Democrats portrayed the new president as probusiness and insensitive to the environment, Bush stuck to his agenda, and his agency heads were expected to keep regulation to a minimum.

Bush's conservative approach was reflected in his nominees to head OIRA. His first nominee, John Graham, was a Harvard University expert on risk analysis who was skeptical of regulation and advocated strict cost-benefit analysis.[70] The liberal Natural Resources Defense Council called Graham "a nightmare choice."[71] In midsummer 2001, despite much conflict, Bush succeeded in getting the Democrat-controlled Senate to confirm Graham—who then served until 2006 and oversaw an aggressive OIRA review process in which large numbers of regulations were sent back to their agencies for modification.[72]

In July 2006, Bush nominated Susan Dudley to replace Graham. Dudley, a former OIRA official under Reagan and George H. W. Bush and a longtime critic of regulation, was strongly opposed by liberals and environmental groups. More than one hundred of these groups opposed her confirmation.[73] By not moving Dudley's nomination forward, the Senate effectively rejected it without ever voting. On January 5, 2007, President Bush appointed Dudley as a senior advisor to the OMB director—a position that did not require Senate confirmation—and in April he gave her a recess appointment to head OIRA. As a recess appointee, Dudley was able to serve until the end of the Bush administration without ever being confirmed. In the end, the president got what he wanted. Congress tried to stop him but failed.

President Bush strengthened his regulatory powers in 2007 by issuing Executive Order 13422.[74] The new order required that every regulatory agency have a regulatory policy review office headed by a presidential appointee. These offices were directed to supervise the development of new rules, as well as to impose new criteria (such as proof of market failure) that increased the threshold for issuing any new rules. Their most significant role, however, was to oversee how agencies use "guidance" documents: that is, informal statements that instruct businesses as to how agency rules will be interpreted and enforced. White House officials and business groups were concerned that agency careerists were using these guidance documents to work around the presidential restrictions they didn't like, and the new regulatory offices were designed to extend presidential control to these informal practices. Congressional critics hit the roof, and in the summer of 2007 the Democratic House voted to prohibit OIRA from using any federal money to enforce Bush's executive order. No action was forthcoming from the Senate, however, and the order remained in effect. So did the new regulatory offices, and the extension of presidential power.[75]

Barack Obama assumed the presidency in January 2009, and so far there has been no indication that he intends to back away from regulatory review. One of Obama's goals, clearly, is to differentiate his leadership from that of George W. Bush—and in the process, to please Democratic constituencies that spent eight years in the cold. Thus it is not surprising that, as part of an avalanche of actions during his first few months in office, Obama reversed Bush's Executive Order 13422 and its intrusion into agency decision making and informal guidance. But this is a small step and, for a Democratic president who favors more regulation, one that is consistent with his own agenda. As for the basic structure of regulatory review, it remains intact: a mainstay of presidential power that Obama will surely maintain and use in the years ahead.

Regulatory review has been an arena of ongoing struggle between the presidency and Congress. But it is a struggle sparked continually by the imperialistic initiatives of presidents, and one that presidents have dominated time and again. Regulatory review is now a routine part of government. Presidents began it, built it up, and have used it regularly to pursue their agendas in the face of interest group and legislative hostility. Congress did not rise up and pass major legislation to stop them, although it had the power to do so. It did not refuse to fund the review agencies, although it had the power to do that, too. Instead, it succeeded only in imposing minor restrictions—while presidents expanded their power relentlessly.

Conclusion

The story of the president, Congress, and the bureaucracy is not entirely a story of presidential triumph. Separation of powers creates a system of government that is distinctly unfriendly to presidents. It fragments authority, multiplies sources of opposition, creates a bureaucracy resistant to central control, and in a host of other ways produces a political setting hostile to any kind of forceful, coherent leadership.

But presidents are strongly motivated to lead and are reluctant to accept a system that is stacked against them. Their strategy has been to modify the architecture of the system to make it more presidential—and it is through this effort that the story becomes brighter for them. For whatever separation of powers does to frustrate their leadership, it also gives them critical advantages over Congress in the politics of institution building and bureaucratic control.

Presidents derive important advantages from their capacity for unilateral action. These involve powers that Congress cannot readily stop them from exercising, and that allow them to shift the status quo on their own, winning by default when Congress fails to react effectively. They also benefit because they are unitary decision makers motivated to protect and promote their own institution, whereas Congress is vulnerable to serious collective action problems and unable to take coherent, forceful action on its own behalf. The combination produces a built-in asymmetry in the president's favor when the two branches struggle for power.

The three case studies in this chapter illustrate how these presidential advantages play out in American politics. In matters of personnel, the budget, and regulatory review, presidents have clearly been aggressive in building their own institutions for controlling the vast government bureaucracy. In contrast, Congress has typically been disorganized, ineffective, and even passive in response. Presidents did not always get their way in these cases, and Congress did not always fail to act. But changes in the institutional balance of power came about because presidents were pushing and shoving to occupy new institutional terrain, and Congress did not have what it took to stop them.

The future promises more of the same. In 2009 Barack Obama became president in the midst of enormous domestic and international challenges: an economic meltdown, ongoing wars in Iraq and Afghanistan, a broken health care system, a frightening deficit, and more. Obama's presidency will be defined, and his legacy ultimately determined, by how successfully he deals with these challenges—and he has no choice but to push for as much discretion and institutional capacity as he can get. He needs these things if he is to exercise forceful, coherent leadership. And he needs them if he is to overcome the impediments that the separation of powers system places in his way. There will be no backing down, no going back. Much as Obama may want to separate himself from George W. Bush—and no doubt he will, in terms of his policy agenda—he needs power. And he will pursue it.

Notes

1. This account relies heavily on Michael Cutrone, *Essays on Presidential Signing Statements*, Ph.D. dissertation, Department of Politics, Princeton University (2008), 2–4.

2. Eric Schmitt, "Senate Moves to Protect Military Prisoners Despite Veto Threat," *New York Times*, October 6, 2005.

3. Ibid.

4. Eric Schmitt, "President Backs McCain Measure on Inmate Abuse," *New York Times*, December 16, 2005.

5. George W. Bush, "Statement on Signing the Department of Defense, Emergency Supplemental Appropriations to Address Hurricanes in the Gulf of Mexico, and Pandemic Influenza Act, 2006," December 30, 2005, retrieved from www.presidency. ucsb.edu/ws/index.php?pid=65259.

6. American Bar Association, "Report of the Task Force on Presidential Signing Statements and the Separation of Powers Doctrine," Honolulu, HI: American Bar Association, 7, www.abanet.org/op/signingstatements. See also Cutrone, *Essays on Presidential Signing Statements*.

7. Terry M. Moe, "The Politicized Presidency," in *The New Direction in American Politics*, ed. John E. Chubb and Paul E. Peterson (Washington, D.C.: Brookings Institution, 1985); and John P. Burke, *The Institutional Presidency* (Baltimore: Johns Hopkins University Press, 1992).

8. For a more fully developed discussion of the logic and substance of the issues we cover in this section, see Terry M. Moe, "The Politics of Bureaucratic Structure," in *Can the Government Govern?* ed. John E. Chubb and Paul E. Peterson (Washington, D.C.: Brookings Institution, 1989); and David E. Lewis, *Presidents and the Politics of Agency Design* (Stanford: Stanford University Press, 2003).

9. For a detailed review, see Terry M. Moe and William G. Howell, "A Theory of Unilateral Action," *Presidential Studies Quarterly* 29(4): 850–871; and William G. Howell, *Power without Persuasion: the Politics of Direct Presidential Action* (Princeton: Princeton University Press, 2003).

10. Richard Pious, *The American Presidency* (New York: Basic Books, 1979), 38.

11. Harold H. Bruff, "Presidential Power and Administrative Rulemaking," *Yale Law Journal* 88 (1979): 451–508; Bruff, "Presidential Management of Agency Rulemaking," *George Washington Law Review* 57 (1989): 533–595; Lloyd N. Cutler, "The Case for Presidential Intervention in Regulatory Rulemaking by the Executive Branch," *Tulane Law Review* 56 (1982): 830–848; and Peter Strauss, "The Place of Agencies in Government: Separation of Powers and the Fourth Branch," *Columbia Law Review* 84 (1984): 573–669.

12. Pious, *American Presidency*.

13. See, for example, Andrew Rudalevige, *The New Imperial Presidency* (Ann Arbor: University of Michigan Press, 2006); and Gordon Silverstein, *Imbalance of Powers: Constitutional Interpretation and the Making of American Foreign Policy* (New York: Oxford University Press, 1997).

14. On how the courts have approached presidential power, and particularly presidential powers of unilateral action, see, for example, Joel L. Fleishman and Arthur H. Aufses, "Law and Orders: The Problem of Presidential Legislation," *Law and Contemporary Problems* 40(3): 1–45; Thomas Cronin and Michael Genovese, *The Paradoxes of the American Presidency* (New York: Oxford University Press, 1998); and Silverstein, *Imbalance of Powers*.

15. Louis Fisher, *The Politics of Shared Power* (Washington, D.C.: CQ Press, 1993); and Strauss, "The Place of Agencies in Government."

16. Craig Volden, "A Formal Model of the Politics of Delegation in a Separation of Powers System," *American Journal of Political Science* 46(2002): 111–133.

17. Eugene Fama and Michael Jensen, "Separation of Ownership and Control," *Journal of Law and Economics* 26 (1983): 301–325.

18. Pious, *American Presidency*; Bruff, "Presidential Power and Administrative Rulemaking"; Bruff, "Presidential Management of Agency Rulemaking"; Strauss, "The Place of Agencies in Government"; and Cutler, "The Case for Presidential Intervention in Regulatory Rulemaking by the Executive Branch."

19. Mancur Olson, *The Logic of Collective Action*, 2nd ed. (Cambridge: Harvard University Press, 1971).

20. Gary Cox and Mathew McCubbins, *Legislative Leviathan* (Berkeley: University of California Press, 1993). See also Gary Cox and Mathew McCubbins, *Setting the Agenda* (New York: Cambridge University Press, 2005).

21. On the relative roles of constituency and party, see, for example, David W. Rohde, *Parties and Leaders in the Postreform House* (Chicago: University of Chicago Press, 1991); J. H. Aldrich, "Political Parties In and Out of Legislatures," in *The Oxford Handbook of Political Institutions*, ed. R. A. W. Rhodes, Sarah A. Binder, and Bert A. Rockman (New York: Oxford University Press, 2006); and Keith Krehbiel, "Where's the Party?" *British Journal of Political Science* 23 (2): 235–266.

22. Hugh Heclo, "The OMB and the Presidency: The Problem of Neutral Competence," *Public Interest* 38 (Winter 1975): 80–98.

23. Richard D. McKelvey, "Intransitivities in Multidimensional Voting: Models and Some Implications for Agenda Control," *Journal of Economic Theory* 12 (June 1976): 472–482.

24. See John Kingdon, *Agendas, Alternatives, and Public Policies* (Boston: Little, Brown, 1984); Paul Light, *The President's Agenda* (Baltimore: Johns Hopkins University Press, 1982).

25. Thomas H. Hammond, Jeffrey S. Hill, and Gary J. Miller, "Presidents, Congress, and the 'Congressional Control of Administration' Hypothesis" (paper presented at the annual meeting of the American Political Science Association, Washington, D.C., 1986).

26. George C. Edwards III, *Presidential Influence in Congress* (San Francisco: W. H. Freeman, 1980); and Stephen J. Wayne, *The Legislative Presidency* (New York: Harper and Row, 1978).

27. Sean M. Theriault, "Patronage, the Pendleton Act, and the Power of the People," *Journal of Politics* 65(1): 50–68; Ronald N. Johnson and Gary D. Libecap, *The Federal Civil Service System and the Problem of Bureaucracy* (Chicago: University of Chicago Press, 1994); and Martin West, "Bargaining with Authority: The Political Origins of Public-Sector Collective Bargaining," manuscript, Brown University (2006).

28. It increased from 603,587 employees to 3,332,356 between 1933 and 1944. Susan B. Carter, Scott Sigmund Gartner, Michael R. Haines, Alan L. Olmstead, Richard Sutch, and Gavin Wright, eds., *Historical Statistics of the United States: Earliest Times to Present, Millennial Edition*, vol. 5 (New York: Cambridge University Press, 2006), 5–127.

29. By the end of the Truman administration, close to 90 percent of all federal civilian employees were governed by the civil service system. David E. Lewis, *The Politics of Presidential Appointments* (Princeton: Princeton University Press, 2008), 20.

30. Lewis, *Politics of Presidential Appointments*, 70.

31. Jerry Kluttz, "The Federal Diary: Whims of Politics Govern Conservation, Gabrielson Charges," *Washington Post*, December 3, 1953, 25.

32. For details of the "Jobs for Republicans" or "Willis Directive," see Jerry Kluttz, "White House Seeks Jobs for GOP Favorites," *Washington Post*, October 27, 1954, 1; and Kluttz, "Ike Defends GOP Plans for Job Hunt," *Washington Post*, October 28, 1954, 1.

33. Judith Havemann, "Top Federal Jobs 'Politicized'," *Washington Post*, August 6, 1987, A1.

34. Paul Blustein, "Commerce Nominee Promises Reforms," *Washington Post*, January 23, 1997, E1.

35. Lewis, *Politics of Presidential Appointments*, chaps. 4–5.

36. National Commission on the Public Service, *Leadership for America: Rebuilding the Public Service*, Washington, D.C. (1989); and National Commission on the Public Service, *Urgent Business for America: Revitalizing the Federal Government for the 21st Century* (Washington, DC: Brookings Institution Press, 2003).

37. Richard Polenberg, *Reorganizing Roosevelt's Government 1936–1939* (Cambridge: Harvard University Press, 1966); and Peri E. Arnold, *Making the Managerial Presidency* (Princeton: Princeton University Press, 1986).

38. Felix A. Nigro, "The Politics of Civil Service Reform," *Southern Review of Public Administration* 20 (1979): 196–239.

39. Patricia W. Ingraham, "The Civil Service Reform Act of 1978: The Design and Legislative History," in *Legislating Bureaucratic Change: The Civil Service Reform Act of 1978*, ed. Patricia W. Ingraham and Carolyn Ban (Albany: State University of New York Press, 1984); and Harlan Lebo, "The Administration's All-Out Effort on Civil Service Reform," *National Journal*, May 27, 1978, 837–838.

40. Nigro, "The Politics of Civil Service Reform." The original design allowed for a little over 9,000 SES employees, but the number has varied somewhat over time and has generally been in the neighborhood of 8,000. Also, of the 800 political appointees, 350 were in newly created positions and 450 were moved into the SES from the old system.

41. Arnold, *Making the Managerial Presidency*; and Ann Cooper, "Carter Plan to Streamline Civil Service Moves Slowly toward Senate, House Votes," *Congressional· Quarterly Weekly Report*, July 15, 1978, 1777–1784.

42. For a good review, see Bradley H. Patterson Jr. and James P. Pfiffner, "The Office of Presidential Personnel," in *The White House World*, ed. M. J. Kumar and T. Sullivan (College Station: Texas A&M University Press, 2003); and Thomas J. Weko, *The Politicizing Presidency: The White House Personnel Office, 1948–1994* (Lawrence: University Press of Kansas, 1995).

43. Lewis, *Politics of Presidential Appointments*, 27–30.

44. Ibid., 24.

45. Ibid., 27.

46. Presidents had much earlier earned a reputation as guardians of the Treasury against extensive spending by Congress. As early as 1909, Congress asked the secretary of the Treasury to estimate revenue for the coming year, determine whether there was likely to be a deficit, and make recommendations for cuts or other sources of revenue to cover the deficits. Fisher, *Politics of Shared Power*, 220–221.

47. Fisher, *Politics of Shared Power*, 222–223.

48. Hugh Heclo, "The OMB and the Presidency"; Moe, "The Politicized Presidency"; and Arnold, *Making the Managerial Presidency*.

49. "Congress Accepts Four Executive Reorganization Plans," *Congressional Quarterly Almanac, 1970* (Washington, D.C.: Congressional Quarterly, 1971), 462–467.

50. See Heclo, "OMB and the Presidency"; and Hugh Heclo, *A Government of Strangers: Executive Politics in Washington* (Washington, D.C.: Brookings Institution Press, 1977), 78–81.

51. See Mike Causey, "Political Aides See Shift," *Washington Post*, May 25, 1977, C2; House Committee on Post Office and Civil Service, *Policy and Supporting Positions* (1960); Senate Committee on Post Office and Civil Service, *Policy and Supporting Positions*. 93rd Congress, 1st sess. (1973).

52. Whether Nixon was correct is contestable. See Fisher, *Politics of Shared Power*, 226–227.

53. Rudalevige, *New Imperial Presidency*, 129.

54. Ibid., 129–130.

55. Ibid., 141–152.

56. The basic history of regulatory review is well known. The following account relies largely on William F. West and Joseph Cooper, "The Rise of Administrative Clearance," in *The Presidency and Public Policy Making*, ed. George C. Edwards III, Steven A. Shull, and Norman C. Thomas (Pittsburgh: University of Pittsburgh Press, 1985); Elizabeth Sanders, "The Presidency and the Bureaucratic State," in *The Presidency and the Political System*, 3rd ed., ed. Michael Nelson (Washington, D.C.: CQ Press, 1990), 409–442; Thomas O. McGarity, *Reinventing Rationality: The Role of Regulatory Analysis in the Federal Bureaucracy* (Cambridge: Cambridge University Press, 1991); and Robert V. Percival, "Checks without Balance: Executive Office Oversight of the Environmental Protection Agency," *Law and Contemporary Problems* 54 (Autumn 1991): 127–204.

57. Percival, "Checks without Balance," 139.

58. To this already stringent set of procedures, Reagan later added Executive Order 12498, which required agencies to submit annually a program outlining all significant regulatory actions planned for the coming year so that OMB would have plenty of time to review them without the pressure of statutory deadlines.

59. Peter M. Benda and Charles H. Levine, "Reagan and the Bureaucracy: The Bequest, the Promise, and the Legacy," in *The Reagan Legacy: Promise and Performance*, ed. Charles O. Jones (Chatham, N.J.: Chatham House, 1988).

60. Percival, "Checks without Balance," 175.

61. Benda and Levine, "Reagan and the Bureaucracy."

62. Ann Cooper, "OMB Regulatory Review," *Congressional Quarterly Almanac*, 1986 (Washington, D.C.: Congressional Quarterly, 1987), 325.

63. Jonathan Rauch, "The Regulatory President," *National Journal*, November 30, 1991, 2902–2906.

64. Kitty Dumas, "Administration Deal Pushes Paperwork Reduction Act," *Congressional Quarterly Weekly Report*, October 27, 1990, 3602; and Janet Hook, "101st Congress Leaves Behind Plenty of Laws, Criticism," *Congressional Quarterly Weekly Report*, November 3, 1990, 3699.

65. Rauch, "The Regulatory President."

66. Kirk Victor, "Quayle's Quiet Coup," *National Journal*, July 6, 1991, 1676–1680.

67. On the failed attempt to deny the council funding, see Susan Kellam, "Social Security Riders Thrown from Senate Treasury Bill," *Congressional Quarterly Weekly Report*, September 12, 1992, 2712–2713; and Kellam, "Conferees Cut $200 Million, Pave Way to Approval," *Congressional Quarterly Weekly Report*, September 26, 1992, 2936.

68. Executive Order 12866, 58 *Federal Register* 51735 (1993). This order also repeated Reagan's Executive Order 12498.

69. See, for example, John H. Cushman Jr., "Republicans Plan Sweeping Barriers to New U.S. Rules," *New York Times*, December 25, 1994, A1.

70. See, for example, Stephen Labaton, "Bush Is Putting Team in Place for a Full-Bore Assault on Regulation," *New York Times*, May 23, 2001; Douglas Jehl, "Regulations Czar Prefers New Path," *New York Times*, March 25, 2001; and Susan E. Dudley, "Bush's Regulatory Record," *Intellectual Ammunition*, July/August 2001, www.heartland.org/ia/julaug01/regulation.htm.

71. Cyril T. Zaneski, "Rule Breakers," *Government Executive Magazine*, January 1, 2002.

72. Cornelius Kerwin, *Rulemaking: How Government Agencies Write Law and Make Policy*, 3rd ed. (Washington, D.C.: CQ Press, 2003), 231.

73. Public Citizen, "The Back Door to Power: Susan Dudley's Sneaky Rise to OIRA Administrator," April 10, 2007, retrieved from www.citizen.org/autosafety/regs/dudley/articles.cfm?ID=16403.

74. Robert Pear, "Bush Directive Increases Sway on Regulation," *New York Times*, January 30, 2007.

75. Jim Abrams, "House Balks at Bush Order for New Powers," *Washington Post*, July 3, 2007.

14 The President and Congress

Matthew J. Dickinson

The renowned presidential scholar Richard Neustadt described the American system of constitutional government as one of "separated institutions sharing powers." One implication of this description is that it is difficult for the president to accomplish much without the support or the acquiescence of Congress. Political parties developed as a bridge between the constitutionally separated branches early in American history. A president could count on the support of most of his fellow partisans in Congress, as well as of some legislators who belonged to the opposition party but who shared the president's views. In recent decades, however, the two parties have become ideologically polarized, which makes it hard for the president to find allies across the partisan divide. Matthew J. Dickinson suggests that even presidents such as Barack Obama, who promised in his campaign for the presidency in 2008 to transcend partisan divisions, have little choice but to govern through their congressional parties.

In his inaugural address as the nation's forty-fourth president, Barack Obama proclaimed "an end to the petty grievances and false promises, the recriminations and worn-out dogmas that for far too long have strangled our politics."[1] Obama's pledge reprised a recurring theme of his successful 2008 presidential campaign: that as president he would work to heal the partisan divisions that so dominated politics during his predecessor George W. Bush's eight years in office. Within days of his inauguration, however, Obama became embroiled in a highly publicized battle between Democrats and Republicans in Congress regarding perhaps the most significant domestic legislation since Franklin Roosevelt's New Deal: an $800 billion package of spending programs and tax reductions intended to stimulate growth in the nation's shrinking economy. Although most Democratic and Republican legislators concurred on the need to pass some version of a stimulus package quickly, they differed about key elements of that package, particularly about the most effective mix of spending increases and tax cuts. Democrats generally pushed for more spending, while Republicans sought greater tax reductions.

Three days after Obama's inauguration, congressional leaders of both parties gathered at the White House to discuss a working draft of the stimulus bill. Republicans seeking to reduce the legislation's price tag pressed Obama to eliminate a provision giving tax credits to individuals who did not pay income taxes. Obama refused and, referring to the recent presidential election, reportedly reminded them, "I won."[2]

That exchange highlighted the partisan division already in place at the start of congressional deliberations on the stimulus package—a division that would only harden during the following two weeks. Five days after the White House meeting, a version of the stimulus bill written predominantly by the Democratic House leadership under Speaker Nancy Pelosi's direction easily passed that chamber by a 244–188 margin—but without a single Republican vote in support. Initially, as the House deliberated, Obama tried to stay above the partisan debate. But when faced with unified Republican opposition in the House and the threat of a Republican filibuster in the Senate, he changed tactics and began stumping on behalf of the Democratic bill in Indiana and Florida, states hit particularly hard by the recession.

As Obama issued veiled criticism of Republican intransigence, debate moved to the Senate, where the Democrats, with a 58–41 advantage, lacked the 60 votes needed to pass the bill on a straight party basis.[3] The balance of power rested with a small group of moderate Democratic and Republican senators who used their leverage to force spending cuts to the House-passed bill. These reductions included almost $40 billion in aid to the states, another $27 billion in a variety of programs designed to help low-income families, and $27 billion in education aid, coupled with increases in tax cuts totaling $76 billion.[4]

There were limits, however, to how far Obama and Senate Democrats could go to meet the moderates' demands, as evidenced by Pelosi's threat to restore the cuts in state aid when the bill went to a House-Senate conference committee. Nonetheless, the changes were not nearly enough to satisfy most Senate Republicans. When the stimulus bill passed the Senate on February 10 by a 61–37 vote, only three Republicans supported it.[5] Differences between the two chambers' versions were quickly ironed out in conference, and the final bill was approved by the House and Senate on February 13 in party-line votes almost identical to those recorded on the original versions. Four days later, Obama signed into law the $789 billion American Reinvestment and Recovery Act. The bill included about $282 billion in tax cuts, with the remaining $507 billion allocated to spending on public works projects for transportation, energy, and technology; increased unemployment benefits; and state aid to meet rising Medicaid costs, among other programs.

In less than a month, Obama and the Democratic congressional leadership had drafted and passed a potentially historic piece of legislation. Although experts debated whether the stimulus package contained the right mix of targeted spending and tax cuts to reverse the economy's downward spiral, most agreed that it was a necessary first step. Democrats saw potential long-term political payoffs in the bill. Depending on its perceived effectiveness, the stimulus package might fundamentally shift public attitudes in favor of a more activist national government and, not incidentally, usher in a lasting period of Democratic control of the presidency and Congress. By these standards, passing the stimulus bill was a major legislative accomplishment for Obama and congressional Democrats.

In light of Obama's declaration of a new bipartisan era, however, the failure to persuade more than three Republican members of Congress to support a bill of such importance is also noteworthy. It suggests that, rather than a new era, the president and Congress may instead be facing the mirror image of the political polarization that characterized much of the previous eight years. During almost six of those years, Republicans controlled the White House and both chambers of Congress, and Democrats often voted along party lines against President Bush's legislative agenda.

Moreover, that period of polarization occurred despite Bush's vow at the start of his presidency to be a "uniter, not a divider." In his 2001 inaugural address Bush, like Obama, stressed a bipartisan theme, saying: "Civility is not a tactic or a sentiment. It is the determined choice of trust over cynicism, of community over chaos. And this commitment, if we keep it, is a way to shared accomplishment."[6] To his credit, Bush worked closely with congressional Democrats during his first term to pass the No Child Left Behind law in 2001 and the 2002 farm subsidy act.[7] But after Republicans increased their majorities in Congress by gaining a total of eleven House and five Senate seats in the 2002 and the 2004 elections, Bush unsuccessfully promoted more divisive positions such as Social Security reform. Eventually the combination of Republican rule; declining support for Bush's handling of major issues, most notably the Iraq war and the relief effort after Hurricane Katrina; and a faltering economy fueled a growing perception that he was a polarizing figure. That perception contributed to the Republicans' loss of Congress in the 2006 midterm elections and to Obama's victory and further Democratic congressional gains in 2008.

When Bush left office, only 34 percent of Americans surveyed approved his performance as president—the third lowest final Gallup poll rating of all the post-FDR presidents. That loss of support, however, masked a deep partisan

Figure 14.1 George W. Bush Job Approval, by Party ID—Recent Trend

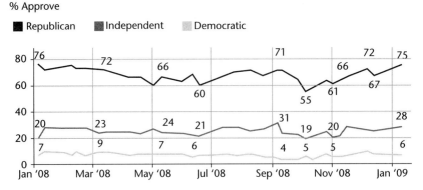

Source: Lydia Saad, "Bush Presidency Closes with 34% Approval, 61% Disapproval," January 14, 2009, www.gallup.com/poll/113770/Bush-Presidency-Closes-34-Approval-61-Disapproval.aspx.

divide in how Americans evaluated Bush's job performance. As Figure 14.1 shows, during Bush's last year as president his approval rating among Republicans hovered in the 70 percent range, but it never went higher than 9 percent among Democrats.

By itself, the debate about Obama's economic stimulus bill did not guarantee a reprise of the polarization that characterized politics during the Bush era. But the fiercely partisan nature of the debate augured poorly for Obama's claim that "the stale political arguments that have consumed us for so long no longer apply."[8] To the extent that the debate and the subsequent near-party-line vote on the bill was an omen that the 111th Congress would continue to divide bitterly along party lines, it raises important questions about the source of that polarization and about presidents' capacity, and willingness, to overcome it.

This chapter addresses those questions. The rise of partisan polarization in Congress, I argue, is traceable to a series of electoral and constituency-related developments dating back at least three decades whose cumulative effect has been to winnow out ideologically moderate members from both the House and the Senate. That process has produced two ideologically cohesive and opposed congressional parties: liberal Democrats and conservative Republicans. It has also reduced presidents' incentive to reach across the political aisle for support in enacting their legislative agenda.

Under the constitutional system of "separated institutions sharing powers," to use Richard Neustadt's apt description, the president and members of Congress are compelled to share the responsibilities of governing. But the Constitution also ensures that they will do so from fundamentally separate vantage points because they have different constituencies, terms of office, and responsibilities. In theory, a shared party affiliation between the president and members of Congress can help to bridge these otherwise distinct institutional perspectives. With control of enough seats in Congress, the president may find it easier to legislate primarily through his party majority, exercising a form of "responsible party government" in which the voters hold both president and party responsible for policy outcomes. As Bush discovered, however, the same conditions that promote party government also encourage the minority party to unite in opposition. That further reduces the incentive for bipartisan action and creates the condition for a more polarized political climate.

The remainder of the chapter develops these initial observations in more detail. I begin by sketching the likely limits on Obama's ability to build bipartisan support for his policies in Congress. I then explain those limits in the context of the fundamental forces shaping presidential-congressional relations, beginning with the constitutional design of the government and the creation and evolution of political parties. Although parties helped to ameliorate some of the centrifugal political tendencies inherent in the American political system during the nation's first century, they never completely bridged the constitution-based separation of the president and Congress. This was partly because congressional and presidential elections did not always move to the same rhythms. Nor did party labels always accurately reflect the ideological leanings of representatives and senators, which meant that a Democratic or Republican president could not always rely on full party support in Congress.

The recent strengthening of ideological differences between the two parties reflects in part a process of partisan sorting, particularly in the South, where during the past two decades most conservative Democrats in Congress either became or, more commonly, were replaced by Republicans. The result is that party labels today more accurately reflect members' ideology. Recent elections have done nothing to halt this trend toward party purification; indeed, the Democrats' gains in the 2006 and 2008 House and Senate elections typically came at the expense of both chambers' more moderate Republican members. By some measures, Congress today is more polarized than it has been since the post–Civil War Reconstruction era.

Under these conditions, Obama is likely to abandon his professed desire to legislate in a bipartisan fashion in favor of a more partisan strategy aimed at mobilizing the Democratic majority. The risk, however, is that he will further divide Congress and alienate moderate members of both parties who can, under some circumstances, play a decisive legislative role despite their diminished numbers. The public, too—particularly the many ideologically centrist voters—may become disenchanted if the polarization that occurred under

Bush continues. Yet any attempt by Obama to cater to the moderates and govern from the center will be opposed by party purists at both ends of the political spectrum. What, then, is his best legislative strategy? I conclude the chapter by exploring the possibilities for presidential influence in Congress during the contemporary era of polarized parties.

Obama and the 111th Congress: The More Things Change...?

Throughout Obama's campaign for the presidency, he pledged repeatedly that if elected he would bring the country together by rejecting the divisive tactics that characterized politics during the Bush era. In May 2007 Obama announced his candidacy standing, as he said, "in the shadow of the Old State Capitol where Lincoln once called on a divided House to stand together...."[9] A little more than a year later, after clinching the Democratic nomination, Obama vowed to run a general election campaign free of polarizing tactics: "What you won't see from this campaign or this party, is a politics that sees our opponents not as competitors to challenge, but enemies to polarize, because we may call ourselves Democrats and Republicans, but we are Americans first."[10] The same bipartisan theme graced his acceptance speech at the Democratic National Convention: "The challenges we face require tough choices, and Democrats as well as Republicans will need to cast off the worn-out ideas and politics of the past.... What has also been lost is our sense of common purpose—our sense of higher purpose. And that's what we have to restore."[11]

Campaigning in part on this pledge, Obama won the election decisively, defeating his Republican opponent John McCain in the popular vote by 53 percent to 46 percent and in the Electoral College by 365–173. Most news organizations interpreted these results as a clear mandate for Obama to bring change to Washington.[12] Exit polls supported this analysis: when voters were asked which candidate-quality mattered the most, their most frequent response (34 percent) was the "ability to bring change." Of those citing change as the preferred quality, 89 percent voted for Obama.[13]

As he took office, Obama enjoyed broad popular support. In the first Gallup Poll after the inauguration, Obama's job approval rating was 68 percent, with only 11 percent disapproving. Even though polling numbers tend to be inflated during this traditional presidential "honeymoon," his approval rating was nonetheless the second highest ever recorded for a modern president this early in the term.[14]

Election results for the House and the Senate promised to give Obama the support he needed on Capitol Hill to fulfill those expectations. Democrats gained twenty-one House seats, increasing their majority over the Republicans to 254–178; they also added seven Senate seats, for a 58–41 majority in that chamber.[15] These gains continued the favorable election trends for Democrats that began in the 2006 midterm elections, when they retook control of both houses for the first time since 1994. Party leaders on both sides of the aisle seemed initially to embrace Obama's bipartisan theme. "The country must be governed from the middle," said House Speaker Nancy Pelosi. "You have to bring people together to reach consensus on solutions that are sustainable and acceptable to the American people." Her Republican counterpart, Minority Leader John Boehner, promised that House Republicans would work with Democrats "[i]f Obama and the Democrats who run Congress choose to keep their promise and govern in a bipartisan way."[16]

But these indicators of broad political and popular support masked a tension that was implicit in Obama's "mandate for change." For most Democrats, the election results signaled more than simply the need to implement a bipartisan spirit of cooperation. Change also meant replacing Bush's policies with Obama's policies, as laid out in his campaign. These included bringing all combat troops home from Iraq within sixteen months; closing the Guantánamo Bay prison; eliminating questionable interrogation practices, including the practice of rendition of "unlawful enemy combatants" captured in the war on terror to nations that use torture; reevaluating the use of military commissions to try suspected terrorists; and working more closely with allies through international forums to restore the United States' standing abroad. Domestically, Obama promised to reform health care, address the burgeoning costs of entitlement programs, and wean the nation from its reliance on foreign oil while pursuing a more "green" environmental policy.

Public dissatisfaction with the economy, however, was the campaign issue to which Obama primarily owed his victory. Fully 63 percent of exit poll respondents cited this as the main influence on their vote, and these voters broke for Obama by 53 percent–44 percent.[17] By the time of Obama's election, the economy had been in recession for almost a year. The primary cause of the downturn was the bursting of the housing bubble that began in 2006. That bubble, in the form of rising home prices, had kept the economy afloat for most of the previous five years. But when it deflated, the suddenly shrinking housing market set off an economic chain reaction, beginning with the collapse of the subprime mortgage industry. That collapse, in turn, threatened the survival of some of the nation's largest investment firms, which had traded in mortgage-backed securities, as well as the companies that insured these securities.

As banks reduced their lending by tightening credit standards, economic activity slowed. Despite the joint effort of the Bush administration and the

Democratic Congress in October 2008 to pass a massive $700 billion bank bailout bill, credit remained tight and the effects of the fiscal meltdown continued to ripple throughout the economy, threatening the survival of key economic sectors, most notably the automotive industries. Facing possible bankruptcy, the presidents of the Big Three American automobile companies went to Capitol Hill to plead for their own bailout package. When a divided Congress refused to pass such legislation, the Bush administration stepped in to divert $17.4 billion of the bank bailout money as loans to General Motors and Chrysler.

It was against this backdrop that President Obama met with leading members of both parties in January 2009 to discuss his stimulus legislation. And it was the congressional debate about the contents of that legislation that revealed the tension inherent in his electoral mandate. Simply put, bipartisanship presumes that Democrats and Republicans can find some common ground on which to form a legislative coalition. But for all his bipartisan rhetoric, Obama was elected by rejecting the "failed policies of the past." The stimulus bill, by focusing debate on the role of government in the economy, inflamed the issue that historically has proved most important in differentiating Republicans from Democrats.

Obama's two goals—bipartisanship and passing the Democratic policy agenda—collided in the debate over the stimulus bill. Although he urged both sides to work together, Obama also resisted Republican entreaties to scale back some of the spending items in the package. Republicans seized on this refusal as evidence that Obama's desire for bipartisanship was all style and no substance. They also complained that congressional Democrats had shut them out of the legislative process, particularly when drafting the stimulus bill in the House. Democrats, in turn, accused Republicans of obstructionism designed to place the blame for a lingering recession entirely on Obama's policies.[18]

The party-line votes on the economic stimulus bill in both houses of Congress ignited a lively debate among politicians and journalists regarding the meaning and importance of bipartisanship. Some members of the Obama administration sought to soften the meaning of "bipartisanship" by claiming that rather than change congressional voting patterns, what Obama really meant to do was to redefine the tone of political discourse. And they suggested that the final bill, despite its lack of Republican support, did incorporate some Republican ideas.[19] Pundits on both sides of the ideological divide weighed in with their own views regarding the virtues of bipartisanship. Those on the Democratic left, particularly bloggers and members of the "netroots" that had campaigned actively for Obama, proclaimed loudly that bipartisanship for its own sake served no useful purpose.[20] They urged Obama to quit trying to reach out to a Republican Party that clearly did not share his values. Many of their conservative counterparts agreed, urging Republicans in Congress not to sacrifice Republican principles, such as a belief in small government and the efficacy of the free market, on the altar of bipartisanship.

But other Democrats argued that despite the policy differences that separated the two parties, it was important that Obama continue to reach a hand across the political aisle so that the public understood it was the Republicans who were rejecting bipartisanship. Some veteran Washington observers pointed out that by making the concessions needed to attract the three Republican votes in the Senate, Obama had passed the stimulus bill—a sign that bipartisanship, even in this limited fashion, worked.[21]

For his part, Obama vowed to continue reaching out to Republicans, arguing that even if the initial results were less than satisfying, such efforts would eventually bear fruit. "All those (efforts) were not designed simply to get some short-term votes," he said in his first televised news conference after the stimulus bill became law. "They were designed to try to build up some trust over time. And I think that as I continue to make these overtures, over time hopefully that will be reciprocated."[22]

The debate over bipartisanship is not new.[23] Its origins date to the creation of the constitutional system and the formation of political parties. Thomas Jefferson's election as president in 1800 marked the first change in party control of that office in history. In Jefferson's inaugural address, he reminded his audience, "We have called by different names brethren of the same principle. We are all Republicans, we are all Federalists." Jefferson's election, however, owed much to voters' rejection of some of his predecessor John Adams's Federalist policies, such as the Alien and Sedition Acts.

Both the presidency and Congress have undergone considerable change since Jefferson's time, as has the role of political parties. However, those changes have not mitigated the tension between presidents' desire to govern in bipartisan fashion while also implementing their own partisan agenda. Indeed, as the next two sections make clear, the increasing polarization of the two parties during recent decades has only exacerbated that tension.

Congress, the President, and Political Parties, 1789–1960

The Constitution sets the basic parameters that govern the president's relationship with Congress. For the two branches to fulfill their constitutional obligations, from legislating to conducting foreign policy to managing the bureaucracy, they must collaborate actively. Consider what is arguably their most significant function: to make laws. Article I, Section 1, specifies that "all legislative Powers herein granted shall be vested in a Congress of the United States" consisting of "a Senate and House of Representatives." Article I, Section 7, establishes much of the president's legislative role: before bills passed by Congress can become law they must be signed by the president or, if vetoed, be passed again by at least two-thirds of the members in each house. Article II, Section 3, adds that the president shall recommend to Congress "such Measures as he shall judge necessary and expedient." Modern presidents have interpreted this phrase as an invitation to submit a legislative program, and legislators have come to expect them to do so. To be sure, proposing legislation is no guarantee that it will be enacted, but doing so provides the president with significant power to set the congressional agenda.[24]

So it goes across the range of the national government's functions. In foreign affairs, Congress declares war, but the president is commander in chief of the armed forces. Presidents appoint ambassadors and negotiate treaties, but only with the Senate's advice and consent. Congress establishes the executive departments and a system of federal trial and appeals courts, but presidents appoint their members, including Supreme Court justices—again with Senate approval. Moreover, Congress establishes and funds all government departments and agencies, as well as determines who controls appointments to them.

Clearly, the Constitution requires Congress and the president to work together if the shared powers of the national government are to be exercised. The Constitution also ensures that the two branches will do so from decidedly different perspectives because the president, the House, and the Senate represent distinct constituencies and serve different terms of office.

To become president, one must win a majority of Electoral College votes, and these are apportioned according to the number of each state's representatives and senators in Congress. Because of the evolution of a winner-take-all voting system, in which the candidate with the most popular votes in a state receives all of its electoral votes, presidential candidates typically hew to the ideological center of the political spectrum.[25] For would-be presidents there is no electoral payoff from attracting a significant minority of a state's popular vote.[26]

Representatives are selected through a single-member, simple-plurality voting system, from electoral districts where constituencies are much smaller and typically more homogeneous than the nation as a whole.[27] Depending on a district's makeup, a candidate for the House might succeed by staking out a relatively extreme ideological position. Moreover, because the entire House is up for election every two years, it tends to be more responsive than the president to prevailing political passions.[28]

Senators act on yet a third set of political imperatives. Although they also are chosen by a simple plurality of the popular vote, their states vary widely in size and diversity of population.[29] Generally speaking, senators represent constituencies that are more populous and heterogeneous than House districts, which reduces the likelihood that senators will be beholden to ideologically extreme viewpoints.[30] In addition, because senators serve for six years, with only one-third of the chamber up for election at a time, the Senate as a whole is unlikely to be as responsive to the political forces that influence presidential or House elections.

In sum, presidents, senators, and representatives come to their shared constitutional tasks with different political needs and goals. This was the Framers' original intent: as Madison explained in *Federalist* no. 51, with power apportioned among the branches in this way, it will be difficult for any branch to abuse its authority.[31] But the Framers also hoped to establish an effective government, and in this respect the original constitutional scheme had several defects.

First, the presidential selection system did not provide the presidency with a strong enough electoral base to resist congressional encroachment. By 1800 presidential nominations were determined by congressional caucuses, each controlled by a single political faction. Moreover, as James Sterling Young documents, the Framers' emphasis on limited government, together with the tendency for each branch to jealously protect its institutional prerogatives, prevented the president and Congress from addressing many national problems during the nation's early years. Citizens, in turn, did not develop a strong attachment to a government that seemed largely ineffectual.[32]

To address these problems in the decade after the Constitution's ratification, the nation's leading politicians gravitated toward a single solution: political parties. The Constitution makes no mention of parties, but their precursors were already evident during George Washington's administration, when debates broke out among his advisers on issues such as the constitutionality of the Neutrality Proclamation and the creation of a central bank. These disputes highlighted the growing ideological divide between those, led by Secretary of the Treasury Alexander Hamilton, who favored a strong presidency and a more powerful national government and those, led by Secretary of State Thomas Jefferson and Rep. James Madison, who sought to limit national authority, particularly presidential authority.

By the Third Congress (1793–1795), voting within both chambers was occurring along clearly discernible party lines, as the two major political factions mobilized support among legislators on important issues. Their efforts spilled into the electoral arena as well. When Washington published his farewell address in 1796, he warned of "the baneful effects of the spirit of party generally."[33] Despite that warning, in 1796 the presidential election to determine Washington's successor showed early evidence of party cleavages among the political elite, and by 1800 the race between Jefferson and Adams for president had become overtly partisan.

Despite the Framers' deep antipathy toward parties, they developed because they performed a number of useful functions. First, by providing the presidency with a popular base of support, parties rescued the office from its dependence on Congress. The process by which the presidency gained an independent electoral base involved several steps. To begin with, the Electoral College was transformed from an independent body that both nominated and elected the president to an instrument of the parties. By 1800 competing slates of presidential electors in each state were pledging before the election to vote as a bloc on behalf of a particular candidate.[34] This change provided the means for parties to aggregate electoral support across state lines behind a single candidate, increasing the possibility that their candidate would win a majority in the Electoral College.

The use of the party ballot fostered the election of a national figure as president; without it, electoral votes would usually have been scattered among a host of local favorites. But to provide the president with a truly independent electoral base, an additional link to the voters was required. This connection was established by the development of mass-based political parties that nominated presidential candidates and mobilized the electorate to support them. The advent of the national convention, first used by a major party in 1832, moved the presidential nominating process out of the hands of the congressional caucus and into the hands of local and state political leaders.

Meanwhile, the growth of mass-based campaigns organized by parties helped create within the citizenry an attachment to the national government. By the 1820s, spurred by the sharper competition for the presidency, popular participation in elections began to rise.[35] In the 1824 presidential election, less than 30 percent of the eligible electorate voted. In 1840, sixteen years and four elections later, turnout jumped to almost 80 percent. The presidency and the national government had become visible and durable parts of the political landscape.

Parties served an additional function: they provided a means to bridge the constitutional gap between president and Congress. If voters' choices in presidential and congressional elections were driven by party allegiances, a single party would likely control both branches after each election. And if candidates elected on the same party ticket shared a similar ideological outlook, presidents could capitalize on these shared preferences to convince Congress to pass their legislative program. Voters could then reasonably hold the party accountable for the policies the government produced. In this way political parties might compensate in part for the centrifugal tendencies inherent in the Constitution.[36]

In truth, throughout the nineteenth century, the promise of "responsible party" government proved greater than the reality. For one thing, parties were loosely knit federations of factions led by state and local chieftains, not unified national bodies organized around a coherent party program. Second, presidents possessed few tools for enforcing party discipline in Congress. They had to share their most potent weapon, political patronage, with members of the legislative branch. And with the rise of the nonpartisan civil service and the decline of patronage-based parties beginning in the late nineteenth century, this tool became less effective as a source of presidential leadership. Third, unified party government could not be taken for granted: even when political parties reached their apex of influence during the sixty-eight years from 1832 to 1900, divided government existed in some form for thirty-two of those years—nearly half the time. Nor did unified party control always translate into congressional support for a president's policies. As noted earlier, presidents, senators, and representatives from the same party respond to different political incentives because of their varying constituencies and terms of office. In short, what the Constitution set apart, the parties only partially put together.

Except for dramatic periods of electoral realignment, when presidential and congressional elections were subject to the same intense political pressures, legislators seldom felt a shared sense of political fate with presidents. Moreover, the ties that bound the two branches began to fray during the first half of the twentieth century, as the services that the parties traditionally provided were undermined gradually by progressive reforms. The advent of the direct primary further weakened party leaders' control over the nomination of political candidates.[37] Ballots that were provided to voters by the parties and cast publicly gave way to the Australian, or secret, ballot, making it harder for party officials to enforce discipline in elections. Civil service reforms, beginning in 1883 with the Pendleton Act, reduced the value of patronage as a source of presidential influence in Congress. Collectively, these developments sent the parties into a slow but inexorable decline that extended throughout the twentieth century. The result was a further unraveling of the weak bonds linking the presidency and Congress.

The Era of Incumbency and Insulation, 1960–1984

In the 1960s political parties sank to their nadir of influence. Congress entered what Morris Fiorina describes as the "era of incumbency and

Figure 14.2 Split-Ticket Voting in Presidential Election Years (1952–2008)

Percent

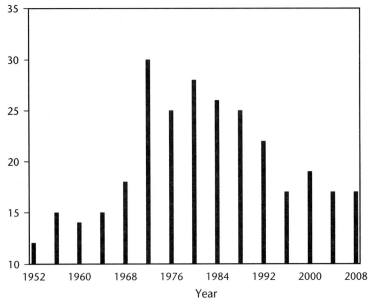

Split Ticket Voting Presidential/Congressional 1952–2008

	'52	'56	'60	'64	'68	'72	'76	'80	'84	'88	'92	'96	'00	'04	'08
Dem. Pres./Dem. Congr.:	39	39	45	59	40	31	42	35	36	40	48	44	43	43	45
Dem. Pres./Rep. Congr.:	2	2	4	9	7	5	9	8	6	7	10	13	10	7	9
Rep. Pres./Dem. Congr.:	10	13	10	6	11	25	16	20	20	18	12	4	9	10	8
Rep. Pres./Rep. Congr.:	49	45	41	26	42	40	34	38	39	34	30	38	39	40	37
	1009	1151	1187	947	776	1293	1280	762	1144	1030	1124	855	814	674	1294

Source: American National Election Studies data.

insulation," in which the outcomes of presidential and congressional elections became less unified.[38] As Figure 14.2 depicts, voting studies revealed a growing tendency for voters to split their ticket between a presidential candidate of one party and a House candidate of the other. At the same time, as Figure 14.3 shows, the number of self-identified independent voters was on the rise. Although scholars dispute how to interpret this development, it suggests at the very least that partisanship was becoming less important to voters.[39]

Electoral reforms and other developments after the 1968 elections further diminished the importance of parties in the presidential nominating process. In 1972, for the first time, a majority of delegates to the presidential nominating conventions were selected in primaries. The primaries weakened the party leaders' traditional role as gatekeepers to nomination. Meanwhile, campaign

Figure 14.3 Self-Identified Independent Voters (1952–2008)

Percent

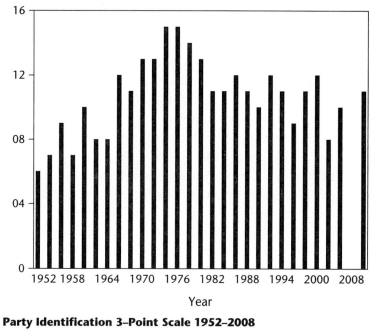

Year

Party Identification 3–Point Scale 1952–2008

	'52	'54	'56	'58	'60	'62	'64	'66	'68	'70	'72	'74	'76	'78	'80	'82	'84	'86	'88	'90	'92	'94	'96	'98	'00	'02	'04	'08
Democrat (incl leaners) :	57	56	50	56	52	54	61	55	55	54	52	52	52	54	52	55	48	51	47	52	50	47	52	51	50	49	49	50
Independent :	6	7	9	7	10	8	8	12	11	13	13	15	15	14	13	11	11	12	11	10	12	11	9	11	12	8	10	11
Republican (incl leaners):	34	33	37	33	36	35	30	32	33	32	34	31	33	30	33	32	39	36	41	36	38	41	38	37	37	43	41	38
Apolitical/Other:	3	4	4	4	2	4	1	1	1	1	1	3	1	3	2	2	2	2	2	1	1	1	2	1	0	0	0	
N	1784	1130	1757	1808	1911	1287	1550	1278	1553	1501	2694	2505	2850	2283	1612	1411	2236	2166	2032	1966	2474	1787	1710	1276	1797	1478	1197	2072

Source: American National Election Studies data.

finance reforms designed to minimize the influence of private money in elections helped to elevate the importance of single-issue interest groups as sources of candidate funding. The public's growing use of radio and television encouraged congressional candidates to take their campaigns directly to the people, with minimal reliance on party organizations. The result was that the candidate-centered campaign replaced the party-mediated campaign.

No longer needing to cater to the party's interests, members of Congress proved particularly adept at putting together their own coalitions to win reelection. The benefits of incumbency for senators and representatives began to rise. The percentage of the popular vote that incumbents gained between their first and second elections to Congress—the "sophomore surge" attributable to incumbency—rose from about two percentage points in the 1950s to seven percentage points in the 1970s. In the same period, the number of marginal congressional races, those in which the winning candidate won with 55 percent or less of the popular vote, declined, signifying a decrease in party competition.[40] The congressional swing ratio, formally defined as the number of seats a party gains in the House for every 1 percent increase in its national popular vote, also declined—another indication that congressional races were less responsive to shifting national political forces than in the past.

According to Fiorina, at least part of this heightened incumbency effect reflected legislators' effective use of casework to bolster their support among their constituents. Because helping people solve their problems with government is a nonpartisan and nonideological service, it also contributed to the voters' sense that parties mattered less than ever.[41] Finally, incumbents proved more adept than challengers at using the new campaign finance regulations to raise money, even though studies showed that money was more crucial to the challenger's chances of electoral success. This further padded the incumbent advantage.

Whatever the explanation for the rise in incumbent reelection rates, Democrats, as the majority party in Congress at the time these changes were occurring, benefited disproportionately, especially in the House. In the forty years from 1954 to 1994 the Democrats never lost control of the House, even though Republicans won six of ten presidential elections and increased their share of the national popular vote in congressional races.[42] The Republicans had better luck in the Senate, winning control of that chamber from 1981 to 1987, but the outcomes of senatorial elections also diverged from the national trends influencing presidential races.

By the mid-1980s, Congress and the presidency appeared more separated from each other than ever. Presidential coattails, never very long in American elections, were diminishing. The proportion of congressional districts carried by a congressional candidate of one party and the presidential candidate of the other jumped from less than 5 percent in 1900 to more than 40 percent in 1984. As a result, presidential landslides no longer guaranteed large gains for the president's party in Congress. Although Richard Nixon was reelected overwhelmingly in 1972, winning 520 electoral votes and 62 percent of the popular vote, the Republicans gained only twelve House seats and lost two in the Senate; the Democrats retained control of both chambers. Similarly, in 1984 Reagan won a landslide reelection with 525 electoral votes and 59 percent of the popular vote, but his party gained only sixteen House seats—not nearly enough to capture control—and lost two in the Senate. Two years later Reagan's party lost its Senate majority as well.

The result of all these changes was an increased occurrence of divided government. From 1947 to 1991 the parties divided control of Congress and the presidency for twenty-four of forty-four years.[43] Without a sense of shared political fate, members of Congress saw little virtue in working closely with the president to address national issues. Critics decried what they saw as a decline in collective responsibility in Washington and the concomitant failure of the political system to address major national concerns, such as the burgeoning budget deficit and the growth in spending on entitlement programs.[44]

For many scholars, the solution to divided government and legislative gridlock was to return to strong political parties. But not everyone agreed that divided government meant gridlock. A study by David Mayhew showed that from 1946 to 1990 the legislative process was no more prone to deadlock under divided government than under unified control.[45] One reason was that neither the Democrats nor the Republicans were an ideologically homogeneous party in the post–World War II era. Conservative Democrats rarely faced serious opposition in elections in the one-party South, which enabled them to accrue enough seniority in Congress to become a potent conservative force within their otherwise liberal party. The Republicans, too, although a mostly conservative party, included a liberal wing of legislators centered in the Northeast.

Party labels, therefore, did not clearly distinguish legislators' ideological preferences. Democratic conservatives and Republican liberals frequently crossed party lines to vote with the opposition, and presidents could cultivate bipartisan coalitions of support. The especially heterogeneous nature of the Democratic Party allowed both Democratic and Republican presidents to mobilize bipartisan coalitions on many issues, which explains Mayhew's finding that Dwight Eisenhower, Richard Nixon, and Ronald Reagan were able to persuade a Congress controlled by Democrats to pass significant legislation. They did so by mobilizing coalitions consisting of a majority of Republicans and the minority conservative wing of the Democratic Party. Alternatively, Lyndon Johnson relied on Republicans to overcome opposition from conservative Democrats to his civil rights legislation.

Even as the scholarly community debated Mayhew's findings, however, changes were under way that threatened to undercut the implications of his research.[46] First, the two parties started shedding their more moderate members as early as 1964. As each became more ideologically cohesive during the next three decades, they also grew more distinct from one another. In the 1970s congressional races became more attuned to national political trends. Although district-level factors were still critical in determining the outcomes of House races, by the 1990s it was no longer true that, in the words of former House Speaker Thomas "Tip" O'Neill Jr., "all politics is local." Congress had entered a new, more partisan era of increasingly nationalized politics.

Congress and the President in the Post–Reform Era: Toward More Responsible Party Government?

Scholars were slow to recognize the changing nature of congressional elections and political parties. With hindsight it is clear that by the mid-1970s the decline of parties had been arrested. Split-ticket voting peaked in 1972, when 30 percent of voters supported a congressional candidate of one party and the presidential candidate of the other. From then on it declined, falling to 17 percent of voters in the 2008 election. Similarly, the percentage of voters labeling themselves "pure" independents—that is, those who do not even lean toward a party—plateaued at 15 percent in 1976. It then declined slowly to 8 percent in 2002, the lowest percentage since 1964, before rising slightly in 2008 to 11 percent. The number of self-identified strong Democrats increased only incrementally from a low of 15 percent in 1972 to 17 percent in 2004, but those identifying themselves as strong Republicans doubled from a low of 8 percent in 1978 to 16 percent in 2004.

At the same time, congressional races became even more responsive to national forces. One can construct a rough measure of the relative importance of national and local forces in House elections by regressing the House district vote on the previous election's House district and presidential vote, and using the coefficients for the presidential vote as a proxy for national political trends.[47] As Figure 14.4 shows, by 1976 the relative influence of national forces in House races in presidential election years had begun to rebound, after declining through the 1960s. Beginning in 2000, national forces proved more important than local influences on House races. The same trend is visible in House midterm elections (see Figure 14.5), with national influences growing stronger during the period 1986–1994 and finally transcending local influences in the 2006 midterm election. Since 2000, then, the relative influence of national forces on House elections has proved greater than during any previous House elections dating back more than half a century.

What explains this turnabout in party influence? Scholars cite several causes that collectively transformed and revitalized the parties and made members of Congress more responsive to national forces. First, the Republicans began making inroads among voters in the once solidly Democratic South, which changed both parties' geographical base. A precipitating event was the Democratic Party's embrace of civil rights under Presidents John Kennedy and Lyndon Johnson, fueled by the surge of liberal Democrats into Congress in the 1958 and 1964 elections. Some conservative southern voters reacted to the 1964 Civil Rights Act and 1965 Voting Rights Act by switching parties, and young voters just entering the electorate were more likely than in the past to become Republicans. In 1964 only

Figure 14.4 Decomposition of Presidential-Year House Elections (Contested Seats Only)

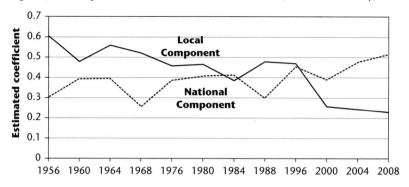

Source: For 2000, 2004, and 2008, author's calculations using data from swingstateproject.com and polidata.us. For previous years, data provided by Arjun Wilkins, Stanford University.

Figure 14.5 Decomposition of Midterm House Election (Contested Seats Only)

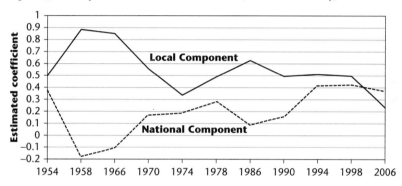

Source: For 1998 and 2006, author's calculations using data from swingstateproject.com and polidata.us. For previous years, data provided by Arjun Wilkins, Stanford University.

17 percent of southern voters called themselves Republicans. Twenty years later the number had increased to 31 percent, and in 2000 it was 37 percent—the same proportion as outside the South. This trend was encouraged by the Republicans' "southern strategy," which was designed to split the Democratic Party by emphasizing the parties' differences on social issues such as school busing, abortion, school prayer, affirmative action, and crime. At the same time, thanks in large part to the Voting Rights Act, African Americans' electoral participation in the South rose, and they voted overwhelmingly Democratic.

But differences on social issues tell only part of the story. Polarization within the electorate was also helped by the Republican Party's adoption of a more libertarian economic platform against the backdrop of an increasingly affluent society. As Americans became wealthier on average, their support for economic redistribution and government-run social programs declined. Upper-income citizens in particular were more likely to identify with the Republican Party and its advocacy of an "ownership" society.[48] In the 2008 presidential election, exit polls indicate that voters earning $100,000 to $200,000 (20 percent of those surveyed) narrowly supported John McCain, although Obama won among the 6 percent of those polled who earned more than $200,000. Among those voting in House races, the partisan effect of income was even more pronounced, with Republican candidates attracting more votes among those with incomes of $100,000 or above, but getting fewer votes from those whose incomes fell below $100,000, with the Republican share of the vote dropping steadily with decreasing income levels.[49]

Population shifts from the East and Midwest to the West and South (that is, from the Rust Belt to the Sun Belt) accentuated these trends.[50] Moderate Republicans in the East found themselves marginalized in a national party whose center was moving to the more conservative southern and Rocky Mountain states. The decennial redistricting process, in which House seats are reapportioned to take account of changes in population, contributed to the partisan restructuring. In particular, the creation of "majority-minority" congressional districts, in which a majority of the eligible voters belong to a racial or an ethnic minority, helped accentuate the party divisions. First established by the Justice Department after Congress amended the Voting Rights Act in 1982, these districts increased minority representation in Congress, nearly all of it Democratic.[51] But they also helped to increase the Republican vote in neighboring districts. The result was further ideological polarization between the two parties: representatives elected in majority-minority districts, particularly African Americans, were typically on the extreme left of the Democratic Party. At the same time, because the surrounding areas were "bleached" of minority voters, adjacent districts became more likely to elect conservative Republicans.

The changing nature of campaign finance also contributed to the parties' transformations. In the early 1970s Congress passed the first of a series of reforms designed to mitigate the influence of big money in politics by providing public funding for presidential races, capping individual contributions to all federal campaigns, and requiring public disclosure of campaign expenses. Decisions by the Supreme Court equating some types of campaign spending with free speech, however, allowed single-issue interest groups, whose views frequently were well outside the ideological center of the electorate, to become an important source of campaign funding.[52] The influx of special interest money and the increased participation of issue activists, particularly in congressional nominating contests, tended to reward more ideologically extreme candidates. Much of this money flowed from groups outside a candidate's state or district. No longer were congressional races local affairs; national political actors now also influenced them.

At the same time, the parties took advantage of campaign regulations that, until Congress passed the 2002 McCain-Feingold act, allowed them to raise unlimited amounts of money for "party-building" exercises. These "soft money" contributions became an important source of campaign funds and helped transform political parties. Instead of the loose federations of locally controlled, vote-mobilizing organizations of the past, parties became synonymous with their national committees, which focused on fund raising and on candidate recruitment and training. These committees became adept at using their resources in ways that maximized their party's seats in Congress, further contributing to the nationalization of congressional elections.

Although the McCain-Feingold act outlawed soft money contributions to parties in national elections, both parties' presidential candidates in 2004 and 2008 benefited from the activities of a network of independent organizations—called 527 groups after the relevant election law subsection in the tax code—which could legally accept such unregulated contributions. These groups acted much like "shadow" parties by spending money on "issue advocacy" campaigns closely linked to particular candidates. In 2008 spending by 527 groups, although down from the amount spent in 2004, totaled almost $258 million. The two major political parties, meanwhile, continued to raise and spend "hard money" (money raised under federal contributions limits) on behalf of their congressional and presidential candidates. In the 2008 election, the Democratic and Republican Parties each funneled almost $1 billion to their candidates through their parties' national, congressional, and senatorial campaign committees.[53]

Evidence on voter turnout suggests that the transformation of the parties affected electoral participation in two somewhat contradictory ways. On the negative side, faced with candidates espousing widely divergent political views, voters were left to choose between extremes or not participate at all. For a growing number of voters the second option seemed for a time to be more palatable. Political scientists began attributing some of the decline in voter turnout in presidential and congressional elections that began after 1964 to public dissatisfaction with the partisan and ideological tone of public debate.[54]

On the positive side, both parties became increasingly effective at spending the money they raised to get out the vote. Although turnout among eligible voters in presidential elections declined steadily to a post-1964 low of 51.7 percent in 1996, it increased in successive elections, reaching 61.7 percent in 2008,

Figure 14.6 Polarization in Congress

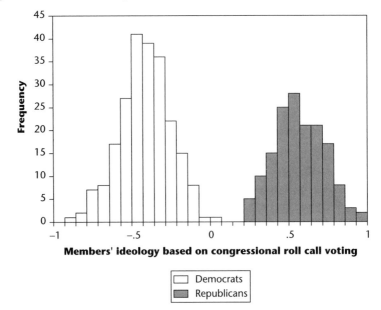

Members' ideology based on congressional roll call voting

Democrats
Republicans

Source: Author's calculations using Poole-Rosenthal data at voteview.com.

the highest turnout rate in forty years. Turnout also went up in the 2006 midterm elections, reaching 40.3 percent, the highest since the 1994 midterm elections and the second highest since 1982.[55]

Even with the increase in turnout, however, voters still often faced a choice in the general election between two ideologically extreme candidates. By one measure, the number of moderates in Congress had declined by 2008 to about 10 percent of the members of each chamber.[56] As Figure 14.6 shows, this left no overlap between congressional Republicans and congressional Democrats on which to construct a bipartisan coalition.

Instead, the reduction in the two parties' moderate wings created the conditions for what David Rohde and John Aldrich call "conditional party government." When political parties in a legislative body are evenly matched and internally unified, Rohde and Aldrich argue, rank-and-file legislators may find it in their electoral interest to strengthen their party's leaders. In the House, institutional reforms pushed primarily by liberal Democrats from 1970 to 1977 helped facilitate strong party leadership. These included a "subcommittee bill of rights" that weakened the power of committee chairs, rule changes that enhanced the Speaker's powers, and a revitalization of the majority-party caucus as a decision-making forum.[57] These reforms granted more power to

Democratic Speakers Tip O'Neill, Jim Wright, and Tom Foley in the 1970s, 1980s, and early 1990s. Their Republican successors, Newt Gingrich and Dennis Hastert, exercised similarly strong leadership after the 1994 Republican congressional takeover.[58]

The GOP's 1994 takeover provided compelling evidence that congressional races were more susceptible to national forces than in the 1960s. Through a combination of population shifts, effective candidate recruitment, a focused agenda, and extensive fund raising, the Republicans led by Gingrich had positioned themselves to capitalize on voter dissatisfaction with the Clinton administration and the Democratic Congress in the 1994 midterm election. In dramatic fashion, they picked up fifty-three House seats and eight Senate seats to take control of both chambers for the first time in forty years. Subsequent events revealed just how partisan Congress had become. Legislators in the Republican-controlled House could not persuade their Senate counterparts to sign on fully to their conservative Contract with America, and in the winter of 1995–1996 partisan wrangling over the federal budget led to several government shutdowns. Congressional Republicans followed this fight with the bitterly partisan impeachment and trial of President Bill Clinton in 1998–1999.

Although George W. Bush's election in 2000 in conjunction with Republican control of the House and Senate muted these overt signs of partisan conflict for a time, conflict reemerged after the Democrats retook both houses of Congress in 2006, most notably in Democratic efforts to link further spending on the Iraq war to a fixed timetable for withdrawing U.S. troops. Bush, using his veto, rebuffed those efforts and actually increased troop levels—the so-called surge. In turn, congressional Democrats quashed Bush's efforts to reform Social Security.

Other data support these highly visible indicators of growing partisan conflict. The difference between Republican and Democratic mean party ideology scores in Congress reached a low from 1968 to 1972, and then climbed steadily thereafter.[59] Party unity scores, a measure of roll call votes in Congress in which a majority of the legislators of one party vote against a majority of the other, also increased, from about 30 percent in both chambers in 1970 to nearly 70 percent in 1995, before dropping to about 53 percent in 2008.[60] The number of individual party votes, defined as the percentage of times the average Democrat or Republican votes with his or her party in roll calls that split the two parties, also increased steadily in this period, from below 60 percent for both parties in 1970 to almost 90 percent in 2008.[61] Since 1968 the importance of party affiliation in explaining roll call voting by legislators has grown stronger.[62] Voting analysis indicates that the 110th Congress was the most polarized since the post–Civil War Reconstruction era, and there is no evidence as yet that the 2008 elections reversed this trend. Clearly, partisan politics now dominates the way Congress conducts business. This development has had profound consequences for presidential leadership of Congress.

Politics, Partisanship, and Presidential Influence in Congress

Under unified government, the development of ideologically distinct, internally cohesive parties and the nationalization of congressional elections can strengthen the president's hand on Capitol Hill. Indeed, this is precisely the rationale behind the notion of responsible party government, a theory of governing most famously espoused in a 1950 report by a committee of political scientists who were seeking to reform the American two-party system.[63] The report was a response to the concern that it was often difficult to differentiate Republicans' views in Congress from Democrats'. On important issues such as civil rights, many Democrats were more conservative than most Republicans. Critics argued that this partisan blurring left voters without any real choice in elections. Moreover, the lack of distinct party alternatives weakened political accountability and undercut presidential leadership by making it difficult to hold either party responsible for enacting—or failing to enact—the president's legislative programs. The cure, according to responsible party advocates, was to develop more clearly differentiated, internally cohesive parties characterized by strong party loyalty and distinct party platforms, preferably within the context of unified government.

By the 1990s, the two parties had evolved along the lines long sought by responsible party advocates. Democrat and Republican legislators were no longer "tweedle-dee and tweedle-dum," as critics had dubbed them four decades earlier. But the extreme partisan polarization that characterized the new party system revealed a dark side to the practice of responsible party government. Debate in Congress became increasingly contentious, as each party closed rank on behalf of its policy objectives and in opposition to the other party's preferences. The more transparent congressional proceedings—a product of sunshine laws that opened committee hearings to the public; the increased use of recorded teller votes, which made public how legislators voted; the introduction of live televised coverage of Congress by C-SPAN; and the increasingly hothouse media environment in which these policy debates played out—exacerbated partisan differences and made political compromise more difficult to achieve. Congress appeared increasingly unable or unwilling to address significant national problems, such as health care and entitlement reform. Legislative productivity, even under unified government, decreased compared to what it had been in less polarized Congresses.[64] In response, the public grew increasingly dissatisfied with both Congress and the president. In Bush's last year in office, his approval ratings hovered in the mid-30-percent range, a drop of almost 60 percentage points from his peak rating shortly after 9/11. Public approval of Congress's job performance fell to 14 percent, the lowest level ever recorded during Gallup's thirty-four-year history of asking the public to evaluate Congress's performance. [65]

Both of Obama's immediate predecessors, Bill Clinton and George W. Bush, entered office preaching the virtues of bipartisanship. But they found it difficult to follow their own sermons. Whipsawed between two ideologically extreme parties, both presidents fell back on their own party's majority in Congress to enact their most important legislation. In Clinton's first year as president, the Democratic-controlled Congress passed his 1993 omnibus deficit reduction bill, which made a significant down payment on reducing the deficit by raising tax rates for high-income earners, increasing the gasoline tax, and raising the tax on corporate incomes above $1 million. The bill barely passed the House by 218–216, without a single Republican vote in favor, and squeaked by in the Senate by a 51–50 vote, again without the support of a single Republican.[66]

The signature domestic initiative of Bush's first year was a ten-year, $1.35 trillion tax cut. Foreshadowing the strategy Obama later employed in passing the stimulus bill, Bush initially supported the larger, $1.65 trillion tax reduction bill that was passed by the Republican-controlled House. Then, to win approval from the Senate, where the Republicans held a one-vote majority, he agreed to reduce the size of the tax cut. The final version of the tax bill passed with unanimous Republican support in both chambers, but with only 12 of 50 Senate Democrats and 28 of 181 House Democrats voting in favor—a coalition only slightly more bipartisan than the one that enacted Clinton's deficit reduction legislation.[67]

These two examples drive home the lesson learned by Obama during the stimulus debate: in an era of polarized parties, the president's need to pass his program usually trumps any desire to legislate in a bipartisan manner. This is particularly true on the economic issues that most clearly divide the two parties.

Nor is it surprising that Bush and Obama adopted similar strategies for passing their major economic legislation. Their choice of tactics was dictated by structural factors that influence how presidents bargain with Congress in this highly partisan era. First, under the Constitution, tax bills must originate in the House, a practice that historically has been extended to spending bills as well. Second, the correlation between House members' roll call votes and the level of support for the president by the voters in their districts has been increasing steadily since 1978.[68] Finally, the House has evolved institutionally in ways that empower the majority party. Thus, under unified government the president's initial policy preference is likely to receive a favorable response in the House. For this reason, both Bush and Obama chose to stake out their economic policy position in that chamber first and then moderate that stance as needed to meet the Senate's sixty-vote requirement for passage of most bills.

To be sure, not all legislation will follow this roadmap even under conditions of unified government with polarized parties. In his study of lawmaking in the post–World War II era, Charles O. Jones shows that patterns of lawmaking vary considerably.[69] In part, this variation reflects differences in the substance of the bills under consideration. As noted earlier, legislation such as the economic stimulus bill is most likely to prompt a deeply partisan process of deliberation. Some other issues cut across the partisan divide, however, and on these it may be possible for presidents to build bipartisan coalitions, as Clinton did with the North American Free Trade Agreement and Bush with the No Child Left Behind law. Republicans supported No Child Left Behind because it instituted mandatory student testing. Democrats favored it because it increased education spending.

If Obama wishes a more bipartisan legislative process, he would do well to focus his agenda on policies that cut across party lines and avoid framing the debate in ways that activate deep-seated party differences. But presidents are not free to exercise these tactics in a political vacuum. This was evident in the congressional deliberations at the start of Obama's presidency regarding a bank bailout bill. Conservative Republicans sought to portray as socialism the Obama administration's plan for the federal government to buy bank assets. The Republican strategy made sense in light of public opinion surveys indicating that, although 54 percent of Americans supported the government's "temporarily taking over major U.S. banks" in order to stabilize them, only 37 percent supported "temporarily nationalizing" banks for the same purpose.[70] When the debate was framed in terms of "nationalizing" banks—which many people view as a codeword for socialism—public support for Obama's policy dropped.

The limited number of issues that have bipartisan appeal, and the difficulty in framing those issues to attract both Republican and Democratic support, is a reminder that a president's influence in Congress is predicated primarily on institutional and political forces that are not amenable to presidential influence. These include the partisan and ideological composition of Congress, and the procedures by which both chambers operate.[71] The Democrats' current majority in Congress places Obama at the head of the legislative table on most issues. But Obama will rarely command the type of leadership authority in Congress suggested by the term *mandate*, despite his reminder to Republicans: "I won."

In view of Obama's decisive electoral victory, however—as well as the increase after the 2008 elections in both chambers' Democratic majorities—Obama may be tempted to respond to legislative opposition by "going public" to promote his agenda.[72] Early signs of this were evident during the stimulus bill debate, when he traveled to Indiana and Florida to mobilize public support for the bill.[73] It is not surprising that Obama's efforts appeared to yield little in the way of concessions by congressional Republicans. Much research by political scientists finds only limited success for presidents who try to augment their legislative influence by mobilizing public support.[74] For that strategy to be effective, four conditions must be met. First, the president must already be in good standing with the public. Second, the public must pay attention to and understand the arguments the president is making. Third, the president's general popularity must be fungible, that is, it must translate into support for the president's stance on specific issues. Finally, opposition members of Congress must not be equally able or willing to mobilize countervailing support among their own constituencies.

In this regard, it is telling that political scientists who try to demonstrate the effectiveness of going public usually cite the same example: Ronald Reagan's first-term success in getting Congress to pass his tax and spending bills.[75] Even in that case, however, there is reason to question whether Reagan's rhetorical appeals carried the day.[76] In short, Obama's postelection popularity is not likely to translate across the board into greater legislative support, particularly since history suggests that his approval ratings will decline from the initial high levels experienced in his first months in office.[77]

Considering the built-in limits on presidential influence in Congress, Obama may be tempted to avoid legislative bargaining altogether by relying instead on so-called unilateral actions—executive orders and directives, administrative rulemaking, and signing statements—to accomplish certain policy objectives. Indeed, one of Obama's first acts as president was to issue executive orders closing the Guantánamo Bay prison within one year, and establishing new rules for interrogating and treating enemy detainees. But critics suggested the effect of these orders was more symbolic than real, since they did not specify how Obama intended to deal with the prisoners currently held at Guantánamo Bay and provided an escape clause for him and future presidents to reinstate harsher detention and interrogation practices if circumstances seemed to warrant them. When in May 2009 Obama sought money to fulfill his goal of closing the Guantánamo prison, congressional Democrats and Republicans refused to fund his request until Obama could provide an alternative plan for relocating those held there.

Moreover, as Bush discovered, because these unilateral directives are typically based on the advice of presidential advisers who do not fully understand the president's vantage point, such orders may work in the long term to lessen a president's influence rather than extend it. In Bush's case, his 2001 executive order establishing military commissions to try enemy combatants was based on legal advice from aides that was later overturned by the Supreme Court.[78] In response, Bush was forced to work with Congress to develop legislation to allow the use of military commissions. Similar difficulties arose with Bush's initial directive authorizing warrantless eavesdropping; again, he was eventually forced to go to Congress for legislation to amend his program. More generally, as Richard Neustadt warned, when it comes to making significant and enduring policy change and protecting the president's sources of power, reliance on executive orders and other acts of "command" are a poor substitute for bargaining with Congress.[79]

With even fewer liberal Republicans and conservative Democrats than in the recent past, the 111th Congress (2009–2011) is likely to be more polarized than its predecessors. For Obama, this means his first two years as president—and likely the two after that—will be spent navigating between the Scylla of majority-party extremism and the Charybdis of legislative gridlock. Rather than building bipartisan coalitions, Obama is likely to rely on the Democratic majority to pass his legislative agenda. The lack of moderate legislators may make it more difficult for Obama to use the prospect of Senate opposition to soften the often ideologically extreme policies backed by the House Democratic caucus. As a consequence, he may be pushed farther left on some issues than he and the public would prefer. If Obama cannot resist pressure from his party's most liberal wing, he risks backing policies that could engender the type of political backlash that hurt the Republican Party in the aftermath of its historic victory in 1994.

Because Republicans can still use procedural rules to block Senate action, however, the potential for gridlock on the legislative program Obama envisions, including health care and entitlement reform, remains high. And it means that despite their dwindling numbers, centrists in both parties may yet hold the balance of power, particularly in the Senate, as they did on the stimulus bill.

Within these broad constraints, however, Obama enjoys several advantages. With his party in control of both chambers, he can be certain that almost every item on his policy agenda will be debated in Congress at least until the 2010 midterm elections. The ability to influence Congress's agenda is a powerful tool because on many issues it allows the president to determine what policy alternatives will come to a vote on Capitol Hill. And he can use the veto to prevent bills he opposes from becoming law. Even the threat of a veto might be enough to swing legislative debate his way. Although Bush did not veto a single bill during his first term, he issued twelve vetoes during his second term, all but one of them occurring when Congress was controlled by the Democratic Party.

In February 2009, in his first address to a joint session of Congress, Obama laid out an ambitious legislative agenda, including health care reform, reducing the country's reliance on imported energy and relying more on "green" technology, rebuilding the nation's transportation infrastructure, and greater investment in education. His ability to make this wish list come true, however, likely depends on whether and to what degree the economy begins to recover. In this regard, Obama's first priority after passing the stimulus bill was to loosen credit by reforming the banking system. Nonetheless, fresh off the stimulus debate, there were already signs of growing resistance in Congress to the administration's plans to buy up "toxic assets" owned by banks at a projected cost of $500 billion. Moreover, the specter of looming budget deficits, which had already reached a record $1.75 trillion in Obama's first budget proposal, threatened to kill any legislation, including health care reform, that would require additional large-scale expenditures.

History indicates that Obama's window of opportunity to be an agent of change may close rapidly. Since FDR's presidency, only George W. Bush saw his party gain seats in Congress during the first midterm election. The average midterm losses for the president's party, dating back to 1954, have been twenty-seven seats in the House and four seats in the Senate. As an additional reminder of the ephemeral nature of his political capital, Obama need look back no further than Bill Clinton's first two years as president, when the fallout from his deficit reduction plan, which raised taxes, and the failure to pass health care reform cost the Democrats control of Congress.

Considering the urgency of the problems Obama faces, and the limited time he has to address them, a purely partisan leadership strategy may be the price he will initially have to pay to govern. Should Obama succeed, working with the Democratic-controlled Congress, in passing much of his ambitious agenda, Democrats may find themselves entrenched in control of the presidency and Congress for the next generation, much as FDR's New Deal coalition dominated American politics well into the 1960s. But four years prior to Obama's election, Republicans, fresh off their own electoral victories in 2004, were dreaming similar dreams. As George W. Bush discovered, a purely partisan leadership strategy can be risky. Should the majority party's policies fail, voter retribution against that party can be strong and swift.

Nonetheless, if the debate over the stimulus bill is an accurate indicator, it appears that Obama may have little choice but to rely on the Democratic

Party's majority to pass his legislative agenda. Although not the action of a "postpartisan" president governing in a new, less polarized era, it may be the only way that the president and Congress can work together. The alternative is to risk not legislating at all—an unacceptable option in a time of war and economic crisis.

Notes

*The chapter benefited from the research assistance of Avery White.

1. Barack Obama, inaugural address, the American Presidency Project, www.presidency.ucsb.edu/ws/index.php?pid=44.

2. Jonathan Weisman, "Obama to GOP: 'I Won,'" Washington Wire, http://blogs.wsj.com/washwire/2009/01/23/obama-to-gop-i-won.

3. Under Senate budget rules, the legislation was subject to a point of order. Democrats needed Republican support to obtain at least sixty votes needed to block a point of order request.

4. Michael Grabell, "The Stimulus Bills: House vs. Senate," ProPublica.com, February 10, 2009, www.propublica.org/special/the-stimulus-bills-house-vs.-senate.

5. Voting in favor were Republican senators Olympia Snowe and Susan Collins, both from Maine, and Arlen Specter from Pennsylvania.

6. George W. Bush, inaugural address, the American Presidency Project, www.presidency.ucsb.edu/ws/index.php?pid=25853.

7. The final version of the No Child Left Behind bill passed by 87–10 in the Senate and by 381–41 in the House. The farm subsidy bill passed the House by a vote of 280–141, and passed the Senate by a vote of 64–35.

8. Obama, inaugural address.

9. "Obama Declares He's Running for President," CNN.com, www.cnn.com/2007/POLITICS/02/10/obama.president/index.html.

10. "Transcript: Obama Democratic Nomination Victory Speech," FoxNews.com, www.foxnews.com/politics/elections/2008/06/03/transcript-obama-democratic-nomination-victory-speech.

11. Obama remarks from *New York Times* transcript, retrieved from www.nytimes.com/2008/08/28/us/politics/28text-obama.html.

12. See, for example, Michael Grunwald "Barack Obama Elected President with Mandate for Change," *Time,* www.time.com/time/politics/article/0,8599,1856560,00.html; Vaughn Ververs "A Mandate for Change," www.cbsnews.com/stories/2008/11/05/politics/main4572553.shtml; and "Obama's Victory Is a Mandate for Change," *Los Angeles Times,* www.latimes.com/news/opinion/editorials/la-ed-election5-2008nov05,0,587735.story.

13. "Local Exit Polls," CNN Election Center 2008, www.cnn.com/ELECTION/2008/results/polls/#val=USP00p6.

14. Only John Kennedy, at 70 percent, received a higher initial approval rating in the Gallup Poll.

15. There are, as of this writing, three House vacancies. Democrats subsequently gained two more Senate seats when Pennsylvania senator Arlen Specter switched parties from Republican to Democrat, and Al Franken was finally declared the winner in the

Minnesota Senate race over incumbent Norm Coleman. All results are from the CNN election web site, www.cnn.com/ELECTION/2008/results/main.results.

16. Shawn Zeller, "2008 Vote Studies: Party Unity—Parties Dig in Deep on a Fractured Hill," *CQ Weekly*, December 15, 2008, www.cqpolitics.com/wmspage.cfm?docID=weekly report-000002997734.

17. "Local Exit Polls," CNN Election Center 2008.

18. Jackie Calmes, "With Stimulus, Partisanship Proves a Worth Foe," *New York Times*, February 7, 2009.

19. Michael Shear, "Obama Aides Cite Bipartisan Success," *Washington Post*, www .washingtonpost.com/wp-dyn/content/article/2009/02/15/AR2009021500472.html.

20. The sentiment is captured by Richard Cohen, "Partisan Realities," *Washington Post*, www.washingtonpost.com/wp-dyn/content/article/2009/02/16/AR2009021601104. html.

21. See, for example, David Broder, "Betting on Bipartisanship," *Washington Post*, www.washingtonpost.com/wp-dyn/content/article/2009/02/18/AR2009021802697.html; and Lou Cannon, "Obama's Bipartisan Mentors: FDR and Reagan," http://100days.blogs. nytimes.com/2009/02/24/obamas-bipartisan-mentors-fdr-and-reagan/?ref=opinion.

22. Zachary Coile, "Obama Shifts Tactics after GOP Outreach Fails," *San Francisco Chronicle*, February 18, 2009, www.sfgate.com/cgi-bin/article.cgi?f=/c/a/2009/02/17/ MN5515ffETU.DTL.

23. See, for example, James Morone, "One Side to Every Story," www.nytimes. com/2009/02/17/opinion/17Morone.html?pagewanted=all*New York Times*, February 16, 2009, A33.

24. See George C. Edwards III and Andrew Barrett, "Presidential Agenda Setting in Congress," in *Polarized Politics*, ed. Jon R. Bond and Richard Fleisher (Washington, D.C.: CQ Press, 2000), 109–133; and Andrew Rudalevige, *Managing the President's Program: Presidential Leadership and Legislative Policy Formulation* (Princeton, N.J.: Princeton University Press, 2002).

25. The exceptions are Maine and Nebraska; in both states it is possible to split electoral votes between candidates, as was the case with Nebraska in 2008, when one of its four electoral votes went to Obama.

26. The classic case is Ross Perot, who received 19 percent of the popular vote in 1992 but did not win a single Electoral College vote.

27. This is not mandated in the Constitution, but it gradually became the norm in the United States and is now based in statute.

28. Since the Twenty-second Amendment was ratified in 1951, presidents can be reelected only once.

29. Senators were not popularly elected until 1914, after ratification of the Seventeenth Amendment.

30. See Gerald C. Wright and Michael Berkman, "Candidates and Policy in U.S. Senatorial Elections," *American Political Science Review* 80 (June 1986): 576–590.

31. James Madison, *Federalist Papers*, no. 51 (Norwalk, Conn.: Easton Press, 1979), 347.

32. James Sterling Young, *The Washington Community, 1800–1828* (New York: Columbia University Press, 1966).

33. George Washington, farewell address, 1796, retrieved from http://avalon.law.yale. edu/18th_century/washing.asp.

34. See Richard McCormick, *The Presidential Game: The Origin of American Presidential Politics* (New York: Oxford University Press, 1984).

35. Ibid.

36. E. E. Schattschneider, *Party Government* (New York: Farrar and Rinehart, 1940).

37. In 1901 Florida became the first state to use a presidential primary.

38. Morris Fiorina, "Epilogue: The Era of Incumbency and Insulation," in *Continuity and Change in House Elections*, ed. David Brady, John Cogan, and Morris Fiorina (Stanford: Stanford University Press, 2000).

39. Some researchers believe scholars misinterpreted survey results and overestimated the actual increase in the number of "true" independent voters. See Bruce E. Keith, David B. Magleby, and Candice J. Nelson (Berkeley and Oxford: University of California Press, 1992); and Jody Baumgartner and Peter L. Francia, *Conventional Wisdom and American Elections* (Lanham, Md.: Rowman and Littlefield, 2007).

40. On the incumbency advantage, see Andrew Gelman and Gary King, "Measuring the Incumbency Advantage without Bias," *American Journal of Political Science* 34 (1990): 1142–1164. On the declining marginals, see David Mayhew, "Congressional Elections: The Case of the Vanishing Marginals," *Polity* 6 (Spring 1973): 295–318.

41. The classic statement of this thesis is Morris Fiorina, *Congress: Keystone of the Washington Establishment*, 2nd ed. (New Haven: Yale University Press, 1989).

42. Republican popular support in congressional elections peaked at 48 percent in 1968 and reached 46 percent in 1980.

43. For a readable overview of the issues, see Morris Fiorina, *Divided Government* (New York: Macmillan, 1992).

44. For example, see Gary Jacobsen, *Politics of Congressional Elections*, 5th ed. (New York: Longman, 2001), 237–270; and Morris Fiorina, "The Presidency and Congress: An Electoral Connection?" in *The Presidency and the Political System*, 5th ed., ed. Michael Nelson (Washington, D.C.: CQ Press, 1988), 431.

45. David Mayhew, *Divided We Govern: Party Control, Lawmaking, and Investigations, 1946–1990* (New Haven: Yale University Press, 1991).

46. Looking at new data through 1997, for instance, Sarah Binder finds that policy gridlock is higher under conditions of divided government. Sarah H. Binder, "Congress, the Executive, and the Production of Public Policy," in *Congress Reconsidered*, 7th ed., ed. Lawrence C. Dodd and Bruce I. Oppenheimer (Washington, D.C.: CQ Press, 2001), 293–314.

47. The figures control for whether an incumbent representative is running. Note that figures are unavailable for the midterm elections immediately after the decennial census because the congressional districts have been redrawn to reflect population shifts. Figures through 1996 based on data provided by Arjun Samuel Wilkins from Stanford University.

48. See Nolan McCarty, Keith Poole, and Howard Rosenthal, *Polarized America* (Cambridge: MIT Press, 2006).

49. "U.S. House Exit Polls," CNN Election Center 2008, retrieved from www.cnn.com/ELECTION/2008/results/polls/#USH00p1.

50. See Bruce Oppenheimer, "Deep Red and Blue Congressional Districts: The Causes and Consequences of Declining Party Competitiveness," in *Congress Reconsidered*, 8th ed., ed. Lawrence C. Dodd and Bruce I. Oppenheimer (Washington, D.C.: CQ Press, 2005), 135–158.

51. Fifteen new black-majority districts and nine new Latino-majority districts were established in 1992.

52. In 1976 the Supreme Court ruled in *Buckley v. Valeo* that campaign finance regulations prohibiting individuals from making campaign expenditures independent from a candidate's campaign violated constitutionally protected free speech.

53. Data based on Federal Elections Commission records as reported on the Open Secrets web site. See www.opensecrets.org/parties/index.php.

54. Regarding declining turnout, see Stephen Ansolabehere and Shanto Iyengar, *Going Negative: How Political Advertising Alienates and Polarizes the American Electorate* (New York: Free Press, 1996); and Morris Fiorina and Theda Skocpol, eds., *Civic Engagement in American Democracy* (Washington, D.C.: Brookings Institution Press, 1999).

55. All turnout data are from Michael McDonald's web site, http://elections.gmu.edu/turnout_materials.html.

56. Based on DW-Nominate scores reported at http://voteview.com/polarized_america.htm. These scores are based on an analysis of congressional voting records dating back to 1789 that indicate the primary issue differentiating liberal, moderate, and conservative members of Congress is their views regarding the role of the government in the economy.

57. See David W. Rohde, *Parties and Leaders in the Post-Reform House* (Chicago: University of Chicago Press, 1991); and John H. Aldrich and David W. Rohde, "Congressional Committees in a Partisan Era," in *Congress Reconsidered*, 8th ed., ed. Dodd and Oppenheimer, 251.

58. Steven S. Smith and Gerald Gamm, "The Dynamics of Party Government in Congress," in *Congress Reconsidered*, 8th ed., ed. Dodd and Oppenheimer, 196.

59. Gary Jacobson, "Party Polarization in National Politics: The Electoral Connection," in *Polarized Politics*, ed. Bond and Fleisher, 13

60. "Frequency of Party Unity Vote Drops," *CQ Weekly*, December 15, 2008, retrieved from www.cq.com/graphics/weekly/2008/12/15/wr20081215-48partisan-unity-freq.pdf.

61. Based on Congressional Quarterly data. See www.cqpolitics.com/wmspage.cfm?docID=weeklyreport-000002997734.

62. Jacobson, "Party Polarization in National Politics," 27.

63. See "Toward a More Responsible Two-Party System: A Report of the Committee on Political Parties," *American Political Science Review* 44:3 (1950), part 2, supplement.

64. For evidence that high levels of party polarization decrease legislative productivity, see Lawrence C. Dodd and Scot Schraufnagel, "Reconsidering Party Polarization and Policy Productivity: A Curvilinear Perspective," in *Congress Reconsidered*, 9th ed., ed. Dodd and Oppenheimer, 393–418.

65. Lydia Saad, "Congressional Approval Hits Record-Low 14%," July 16, 2008, retrieved from www.gallup.com/poll/108856/congressional-approval-hits-recordlow-14.aspx.

66. See "Final Vote Results for Roll Call 406," retrieved from http://clerk.house.gov/evs/1993/roll406.xml; and "U.S. Senate Roll Call Votes 103rd Congress - 1st Session," retrieved from www.senate.gov/legislative/LIS/roll_call_lists/roll_call_vote_cfm.cfm?congress=103&session=1&vote=00247.

67. Ten House Republicans and 29 Democrats did not vote. See "Final Vote Results for Roll Call 149," retrieved from http://clerk.house.gov/evs/2001/roll149.xml; and "A Bill to Provide for Reconciliation Pursuant to Section 104 of the Concurrent Resolution on the Budget for Fiscal Year 2002," www.senate.gov/legislative/LIS/roll_call_lists/roll_call_vote_cfm.cfm?congress=107&session=1&vote=00170.

68. Jacobsen, *The Politics of Congressional Elections,* 253.

69. Jones identifies five distinct patterns of lawmaking: straight partisanship, competitive partisanship, bipartisanship, competitive bipartisanship, and cross-partisanship. Charles O. Jones, *The Presidency in a Separated System*, 2nd ed. (Washington, D.C.: Brookings Institution, 2005), 341–354.

70. Frank Newport, "Americans' Views on Bank Takeovers Appears Fluid," February 24, 2009, retrieved from www.gallup.com/poll/116065/americans-views-bank-takeovers-appear-fluid.aspx.

71. Jones., 355.

72. For a cogent summary of the reasons behind and effectiveness of this strategy, see Samuel Kernell, *Going Public: New Strategies of Presidential Leadership*, 3rd ed. (Washington, D.C.: CQ Press, 1997).

73. See data at the American Presidency Project at www.presidency.ucsb.edu.

74. See, for instance, Jon R. Bond and Richard Fleisher, *The President in the Legislative Arena* (Chicago: University of Chicago Press, 1990); and Brandice Canes-Wrone, *Who Leads Whom? Presidents, Policy and the Public* (Chicago: University of Chicago Press, 2005).

75. For example, Kernell, *Going Public*, 140–167; Theodore Lowi, *The Personal Presidency: Power Invested, Promise Unfulfilled* (Ithaca, N.Y.: Cornell University Press, 1985).

76. Marc Bodnick, "Going Public Reconsidered: Reagan's 1981 Tax and Budget Cuts," *Congress and the Presidency* 17 (Spring 1990): 13–28

77. For further evidence of the limited fungibility of popularity, Obama need only consult his predecessors' experiences. After the September 11, 2001, terrorist attacks, George W. Bush capitalized on his high approval ratings to push a number of war-related initiatives through Congress. But on most of his other legislative proposals that became law, Bush's success came not from public appeals but from bargaining and compromise. And the strategy became increasingly moot as Bush's approval ratings dipped into historically low territory, culminating with the loss of Republican control of both houses in the 2006 midterm elections. Bush's father George H. W. Bush also enjoyed stratospheric popularity ratings when he led a successful international coalition against Iraq, which had invaded neighboring Kuwait, in the Persian Gulf War. But that support dissipated quickly in the economic downturn that followed, and Bush was voted out of office in 1992. His successor, Bill Clinton, enjoyed his highest popularity ratings while being impeached by the Republican-controlled House and acquitted in the Senate.

78. See *Hamdan v. Rumsfeld* (2006).

79. See Richard E. Neustadt, *Presidential Power and the Modern Presidents* (New York: Free Press, 1990), esp. 33–35.

15 The Presidency and the Judiciary[1]

David A. Yalof

Richard Nixon's election as president in 1968 marked a great political divide in American political history. Until then, Americans almost always had elected a "united party government"—that is, they gave the president (at least initially) a Congress controlled by his political party. Nixon's election marked the beginning of an era of "divided government," in which split party control of the presidency and Congress has been much more common. As David A. Yalof shows, divided government, along with several other factors, affected the politics of Supreme Court nominations in enduring ways. Before 1968, for example, most nominees to the Court were chosen from the political arena; since then they have come almost exclusively from the ranks of sitting jurists. Yalof also finds that a Court dominated by justices without extensive political experience has been less willing than high Courts of the past to defer to Congress and the presidency on matters of constitutional and political importance. These divided-government-spawned changes in judicial politics shape judicial politics even when the president's party controls Congress, as George W. Bush's Republicans did when he appointed John Roberts and Samuel Alito to the Supreme Court, and as Barack Obama's Democrats did after his election in 2008.

When Chief Justice John Roberts administered the oath of office to President Barack Obama just after noon on January 20, 2009, the moment must have been a bit awkward for both men.[2] As a freshman senator in 2005, Obama had cast one of the twenty-two votes against the confirmation of Roberts to become the seventeenth chief justice of the United States. Roberts had been the preferred candidate of George W. Bush and social conservatives; his appointment as chief justice promised to consolidate recent conservative gains by the Rehnquist Court on issues such as abortion, religion, equality, and defendants' rights. Just as important, Roberts's relative youth (he was fifty years old at the time of his nomination) offered conservatives the hope of even more gains on these and other issues far into the future. Defending his vote at that time, Senator Obama noted that although Roberts was qualified to serve, he had "far more often used his formidable skills on behalf of the strong in opposition to the weak." Still, the forty-four Senate Democrats split down the middle on Roberts's appointment, and with Republican senators lined up solidly behind him, his confirmation was never in doubt. Now, three-and-a-half years later, Chief Justice Roberts was swearing in a new president who not only had opposed his appointment but also stood poised to nominate justices bent on reversing the conservative tide that Roberts's presence was supposed to advance.

In modern times the Senate often has stood as an obstacle against the appointment of judicial ideologues from both ends of the political spectrum. Yet with nearly sixty Senate Democrats in place at the start of the 111th Congress, the politics of Supreme Court confirmation tilted heavily in favor of Obama's intention to appoint one or more avowed liberals to the high court. The last time a Senate controlled by the president's party formally rejected one of his Supreme Court nominations was in 1930, when Herbert Hoover's nomination of Judge John Parker was defeated by a narrow margin (41–39). The only successful filibuster of a Supreme Court nomination occurred during the fall of a presidential election year against a lame-duck president: Lyndon Johnson's nomination of Abe Fortas to be chief justice was filibustered by Senate Republicans in 1968. Thus the greatest obstacle facing President Obama would be the composition of the Court itself. In the post–World War II period, Democrats have lagged behind Republicans in their relative success at winning presidential elections. From 1945 to 2008, Republicans held the White House for thirty-six years to the Democrats' twenty-eight years. Taking disproportionate advantage of that edge, Republicans during the same period appointed nearly twice as many justices to the Supreme Court, enjoying a margin of eighteen to ten over the Democrats on this score. (See Figure 15.1). The trend from 1968 to 2006 has been even more pronounced, with Republicans appointing thirteen of fifteen justices to the high Court, even though Democrats Bill Clinton and Jimmy Carter held the White House for a combined dozen years during this period.

Included among the Republican presidents' eighteen successful Supreme Court appointments have been the last four chief justices. Naturally, this has contributed to an era of Republican-influenced, mostly conservative leadership of the Court. Even more telling, between 1975 and 2009, no less than seven of the Court's nine justices at any given time owed their seats to Republican presidents. Even allowing for the occasional Republican appointee who strays into the moderate-to-liberal camp, as Justices John Paul Stevens, Harry Blackmun, and David Souter did, it would be difficult to imagine a scenario in which the

Figure 15.1 The White House and Supreme Court Appointments, 1945–2008

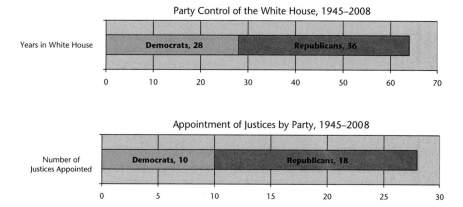

Republican presidents' dominance of the Court's composition would not have produced significant conservative gains in this period. If, as at least one noted scholar has argued, the Rehnquist Court became "the most activist Supreme Court in history,"[3] the direction of that activism was preordained by the Republicans' recent dominance of the Supreme Court nomination process.

The implications of the Republican advantage in the composition of the Court are profound. On average, presidents are able to appoint a new justice approximately once every 2.2 years. The first justice to leave during Obama's presidency was David Souter (at age sixty-nine), who announced his retirement plans on May 1, 2009. Yet Souter's exit (President Obama nominated Sonia Sotomayor as his replacement) offered only limited prospects for a significant transformation of the constitutional landscape, given his propensity to vote with the more liberal justices on most hot-button issues. Meanwhile, the two oldest justices at the time Obama took office were Stevens (eighty-eight years old on inauguration day) and Ruth Bader Ginsburg (seventy-five), perhaps the most liberal justices still serving. Neither one's departure would offer Obama the chance to move the high court in a liberal direction. If anything, Obama's selection of a moderate liberal to replace either justice might actually have the opposite effect, moving the Supreme Court slightly to the right.

What about the prospects of President Obama replacing a conservative justice with a more liberal successor? Of the four most conservative justices on the high Court in early 2009, only Antonin Scalia (seventy-two years old at the time of Obama's inauguration) was nearing the age when justices begin to consider retirement. Meanwhile, Clarence Thomas (sixty), Samuel Alito (fifty-eight), and Roberts (fifty-three) are likely to remain fixtures on the Court long after Obama departs the political scene. In short, because of the long Republican

The Presidency and the Judiciary 437

Figure 15.2 The U.S. Senate and Supreme Court Appointments, 1945–2008

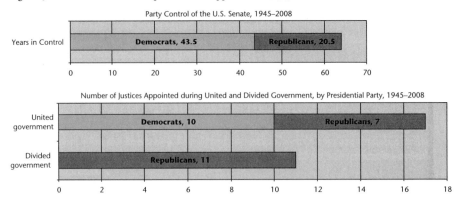

Party Control of the U.S. Senate, 1945–2008

Number of Justices Appointed during United and Divided Government, by Presidential Party, 1945–2008

dominance of Supreme Court appointments, Democrats will have to keep control of the White House at least through 2020 to begin shifting the constitutional landscape in a significantly more liberal direction.

How have Republicans managed to dominate the selection process so thoroughly in an era when party rotation in the White House every four to eight years has been the norm? Although a bulwark against the most controversial nominees, the Senate's role as gatekeeper of the Supreme Court tends to be overestimated, even during periods of divided government. Since 1945, Democrats have controlled the Senate more than twice as often as Republicans (Figure 15.2). In that same period, eleven of the Republican presidents' eighteen Supreme Court appointments were confirmed by a Democratic Senate; and only three times did a Democratic Senate outright reject a Republican president's nominee.[4] Indeed, in the one instance when Senate opposition to a nominee had the effect of transferring control over a nomination from one party's president to the other's (Fortas's failed promotion to chief justice in 1968), it was a Democratic Senate that frustrated a Democratic president's intentions.

The Republicans' disproportionate dominance of the Court's composition is the product of a number of factors:

- **Luck.** One should never underestimate the role that simple luck has played in Republican fortunes. No Supreme Court vacancies occurred during Democratic president Jimmy Carter's one term in office, rendering him the first chief executive since the short-lived Zachary Taylor to suffer that fate. In contrast, Republican George H. W. Bush had two opportunities to name justices during his one term, and Republican Gerald Ford filled a Supreme Court vacancy during his brief two-and-a-half-year tenure as president.

- **Strategic exits.** According to recent scholarship on the subject of Supreme Court retirements,[5] as well as anecdotal reports,[6] since 1980 several justices appointed by Republicans (Potter Stewart, Lewis Powell, Warren Burger, and Sandra Day O'Connor) may have timed their exits strategically so that a Republican president could replace them. By comparison, just one appointee of a Democratic president (Byron White) did the same for a Democratic president in this period.

- **The Republicans' youth movement.** Since the mid-1970s, Republican presidents have perpetuated a youth movement of sorts on the high Court. Gerald Ford's lone appointee, John Paul Stevens, was fifty-five, and President Reagan's first three successful appointees from outside the high Court were all in their early fifties. The four high Court appointments of Presidents George H. W. Bush and George W. Bush averaged 49.5 years of age at the time of their respective nominations, with Clarence Thomas leading the way in this regard, at age forty-three. All the justices appointed by Reagan outlasted Bill Clinton's presidency, and, in all likelihood, nearly all of them will outlast Barack Obama's tenure as well.

Another factor that has increased the predictability of justices' voting patterns is the rise of the career jurist. In the early to mid-twentieth century, Supreme Court justices often were appointed from the ranks of the executive branch, Congress, or the private sector. By contrast, twenty of the twenty-three nominees to the Court between 1968 and 2009 had been sitting jurists at the time they were chosen, including all nine justices still serving in early 2009. (See Table 15.1.) Only two arrived directly from either of the two political branches: Rehnquist, who was an assistant attorney general, and Harriet Miers, who was the White House counsel. (The other, Lewis Powell, was in private practice.) Jurists—especially federal appeals court judges who hear cases similar to those that the justices review routinely—offer the president an opportunity to examine prospective nominees' judicial opinions and philosophy in action. And although some judges' views change over time, the vast majority of conservative judges stay conservative, whereas liberal jurists remain liberal. Certainly judges' views on the matters likely to come before the Supreme Court are easier to assess than are those of executive branch officials, legislators, and private practitioners. In the past century, the list of jurists who genuinely surprised their appointing presidents with judicial views radically different from those they held previously can be reduced to one or two: Blackmun and, perhaps, Souter. Compare that to the list of nonjurists who dramatically defied expectations: Frankfurter, Jackson, Warren, White, and Powell.

Table 15.1 Positions Held by Supreme Court Nominees at the Time of Their Nominations, 1937–2009

Nominee	Year	Appointing President	Position Held Previously
Hugo Black	*1937*	*Roosevelt*	*U.S. senator*
Stanley Reed	*1938*	*Roosevelt*	*U.S. solicitor general*
Felix Frankfurter	1939	Roosevelt	Law professor
William Douglas	*1939*	*Roosevelt*	*SEC chairman*
Frank Murphy	*1940*	*Roosevelt*	*U.S. attorney general*
James Byrnes	*1941*	*Roosevelt*	*U.S. senator*
Harlan Stone (C.J.)	1941	Roosevelt	U.S. Supreme Court associate justice
Robert Jackson	*1941*	*Roosevelt*	*U.S. attorney general*
Wiley Rutledge	1943	Roosevelt	Federal appellate judge
Harold Burton	*1945*	*Truman*	*U.S. senator*
Fred Vinson (C.J.)	*1946*	*Truman*	*U.S. secretary of the Treasury*
Tom Clark	*1949*	*Truman*	*U.S. attorney general*
Sherman Minton	1949	Truman	Federal appellate judge
Earl Warren (C.J.)	*1953*	*Eisenhower*	*Governor of California*
John Harlan	1954	Eisenhower	Federal appellate judge
William Brennan	1956	Eisenhower	N.J. Supreme Court judge
Charles Whittaker	1957	Eisenhower	Federal appellate judge
Potter Stewart	1958	Eisenhower	Federal appellate judge
Byron White	*1962*	*Kennedy*	*Deputy attorney general*
Arthur Goldberg	*1962*	*Kennedy*	*U.S. secretary of labor*
Abe Fortas	1965	Johnson	Private practice, presidential adviser
Thurgood Marshall	*1967*	*Johnson*	*U.S. solicitor general*
Abe Fortas (C.J., withdrew)	1968	Johnson	U.S. Supreme Court associate justice
Homer Thornberry (withdrew)	1968	Johnson	Federal appellate judge
Warren Burger (C.J.)	1969	Nixon	Federal appellate judge
Clement Haynsworth (rejected)	1969	Nixon	Federal appellate judge
G. Harrold Carswell (rejected)	1970	Nixon	Federal appellate judge
Harry Blackmun	1970	Nixon	Federal appellate judge
Lewis Powell	1971	Nixon	Private practice
William Rehnquist	*1971*	*Nixon*	*Assistant attorney general*
John Paul Stevens	1975	Ford	Federal appellate judge
Sandra Day O'Connor	1981	Reagan	Arizona appellate judge
William Rehnquist (C.J.)	1986	Reagan	U.S. Supreme Court associate justice
Antonin Scalia	1986	Reagan	Federal appellate judge
Robert Bork (rejected)	1987	Reagan	Federal appellate judge
Douglas Ginsburg (withdrew)	1987	Reagan	Federal appellate judge
Anthony Kennedy	1987	Reagan	Federal appellate judge
David Souter	1990	Bush I	Federal appellate judge
Clarence Thomas	1991	Bush I	Federal appellate judge
Ruth Bader Ginsburg	1993	Clinton	Federal appellate judge
Stephen Breyer	1994	Clinton	Federal appellate judge
John Roberts (C.J.)	2005	Bush II	Federal appellate judge
Harriet Miers (rejected)	2005	Bush II	*White House counsel*
Samuel Alito	2005	Bush II	Federal appellate judge
Sonia Sotomayor*	2009	Obama	Federal appellate judge

Source: Compiled by the author.
Note: C.J. = chief justice. Nominees who came directly from executive or legislative branches are highlighted in bold italics.
*Senate confirmation vote was pending at the time this book went to press.

Democratic and Republican presidents have contributed equally to the new "norm of federal judicial experience."[7] President Clinton chose two justices with extensive experience on the Court of Appeals. Yet because Republicans have made the lion's share of recent appointments, they have benefited disproportionately from their more predictable nature, eschewing the "crapshoot" of choosing nominees from the political branches, private practice, or even the state courts.

Presidential Campaigns and the Judiciary

Even before presidents take office, they must address critical questions concerning their views on controversial legal precedents and on the way they hope to shape the judiciary. Occasionally during the nineteenth and twentieth centuries, the Supreme Court and related issues figured prominently in campaigns for the presidency.[8] In the 1800 race between President John Adams and Vice President Thomas Jefferson, the latter owed his victory largely to his party's steadfast denunciation of the controversial Alien and Sedition Acts of 1798, which criminalized the act of criticizing government officials. The Federalist Party had supported the legislation, and Adams signed it. The law provided a forum for Federalist judges to rail against Republican editors and publishers at sedition trials. The voters put the judiciary on trial in the election of 1800, and the judiciary lost.

A half-century later, the Supreme Court's decision in *Dred Scott v. Sandford* was used as a whipping boy by the recently formed Republican Party during the election campaign of 1860.[9] The *Dred Scott* decision invalidated the Missouri Compromise of 1820, which had divided U.S. territories into free and slave states. In the process the Court aggressively articulated the theory that slaves were the personal property of their owners. In the 1860 campaign Republican Abraham Lincoln alleged that the timing and substance of *Dred Scott* pointed to a conspiracy by the Democrats to nationalize slavery. According to political scientist Donald Grier Stevenson, the 1860s were the nadir of Supreme Court influence, largely because Lincoln's 1860 victory placed the mostly Democratic Court on the losing side of the presidential election.[10]

During the twentieth and early twenty-first centuries, the Supreme Court was only infrequently a factor in presidential elections. In many ways the Court's low profile in election campaigns stands in marked contrast to the high profile it assumed as a national policymaker. The Court was certainly on Franklin Roosevelt's mind during the 1936 election because the justices had recently stymied the president's New Deal initiatives by invalidating the

National Industrial Recovery Act and the Agricultural Adjustment Act, among other pieces of legislation.[11] Surprisingly, Roosevelt maintained a "studied silence" about the Court during the campaign. As historian William Leuchtenberg points out, Roosevelt enjoyed only a five-point lead in the Gallup poll that summer, and with some other surveys predicting his defeat, "deliberately raising the Court question seemed foolhardy."[12] Later it would appear that Roosevelt had fumbled away the opportunity to create a mandate for the Court-packing plan he unveiled after the election, a bold initiative to expand the number of justices that went down to an embarrassing defeat in 1937. Thus, at one of those rare moments in history when voters were focused on Court-related issues, they were denied a rich debate among the presidential candidates about how they would address the constitutional crisis that was brewing.

The same pattern prevailed in subsequent decades, as the Court and judiciary-related matters provided mostly side stories in presidential elections. Harry Truman, John Kennedy, and Lyndon Johnson barely discussed the Court during their campaigns. Dwight Eisenhower occasionally sought to distinguish his preferred method of judicial selection from that of the Democrats, who he believed awarded judgeships on the basis of patronage and partisanship. Yet Eisenhower rarely highlighted this point in his most important campaign speeches. And when he nominated California governor Earl Warren (to pay back a campaign debt) and circuit court judge John Marshall Harlan (promoted by Ike's close friend and former legal partner Attorney General Herbert Brownell) to the Court, critics barely stirred.

Richard Nixon's campaign for the presidency in 1968 marked the first concerted attempt by a major-party candidate in the twentieth century to place the Supreme Court and its recent rulings squarely before the voters. Blaming the Warren Court and its "pro-felon" decisions such as *Miranda v. Arizona* for the civil unrest that was sweeping the country, Nixon promised that he would appoint only conservative "law and order" judges who would "strictly interpret" the Constitution and not "make law."[13] Nixon's campaign strategy made sense, especially in the South, where resentment against civil rights and other liberal initiatives had spilled over into resentment against the Warren Court. In securing a Republican plurality in the South for the first time in the century-long history of the GOP, Nixon demonstrated that when legal issues were couched in the right electoral rhetoric, they could make a difference.

Although Nixon's 1968 campaign changed the rhetoric of future campaigns, subsequent election outcomes were not affected by Court-related issues to nearly the same degree. Running for reelection in 1972, President Nixon could point to his nomination of four moderate-to-conservative justices as proof of his sincerity. But it was the relative prosperity of the country that propelled Nixon into office for a second term. Eight years later, Ronald Reagan went a step further in his campaign by targeting Supreme Court decisions that were politically divisive, even among Republican voters. Reagan directed his fiercest criticism at *Roe v. Wade*, which created a constitutional right to abortion, observing that the decision was "an abuse of power worse than Watergate."[14] Reagan also decried other controversial rulings banning Bible readings and prayer in the public schools, protecting nonobscene pornography as free expression, approving busing as a means of facilitating racial integration in the schools, and upholding certain affirmative action programs. Reagan even borrowed from Nixon's playbook of a decade earlier, denouncing Supreme Court decisions that protected the rights of the accused.

Reagan's anti-Court rhetoric may have shored up the support of the most socially conservative Republicans, but those voters were certain to vote Republican in any case. Reagan's 1980 and 1984 election victories were due to the state of the country's economy more than anything else. Still, it was telling that Reagan was not punished for such rhetoric by more moderate Republican voters. Democratic presidential nominee Walter Mondale's repeated harping on the conservative leanings of the Supreme Court proved little match for the peace and prosperity the country enjoyed in 1984. And when Massachusetts governor Michael Dukakis hammered Vice President George H. W. Bush on social issues and the future composition of the Court in 1988, his attacks barely registered with the crucial swing voters who had elected Reagan twice and then elected Bush despite his controversial social agenda.

Arkansas governor Bill Clinton's successful effort to bring many of these same swing voters back to the Democratic Party in 1992 was notable for its lack of emphasis on Court-related issues. During President George H. W. Bush's term, the Supreme Court had curtailed abortion rights, first in *Webster v. Reproductive Health Services* (1989) and then in *Planned Parenthood v. Casey* (1992).[15] In these decisions the Court narrowly saved *Roe v. Wade* from its seemingly inevitable demise, while opening the door to more government restrictions. Clinton and the Democrats could have made the Court an issue in the 1992 election but chose instead to focus on the economy.

Perhaps Clinton's advisers had learned something from the Dukakis and Mondale failures. Although Court-related rhetoric is now considered an essential aspect of every presidential campaign, it apparently sways relatively few voters. Since 1968 each presidential candidate has been asked to provide his views on the right to abortion (all Republican candidates have opposed the right; Democrats have supported it), affirmative action (Republicans oppose;

Democrats support with qualifications), and the "philosophy of judging" that the candidate favors (Republicans support "strict interpretation"; Democrats support the notion of a "living Constitution"). How these campaign positions translate into the practice of selecting judges is less certain.

This type of Court-related campaigning has significant implications, however, because in general, all of the winning presidential candidates have kept their promises. The socially conservative Republican presidents, Nixon, Reagan, and Bush, appointed mostly conservative jurists to the Court. President Clinton appointed two moderate-to-liberal jurists to the Court. The one aberration during this period—President Bush's appointment of moderate-to-liberal David Souter to the Court in 1990—is notable because it offered such a clear exception to the rule.

Thus, although presidents are not elected because of their positions on the judiciary, they still attempt to fulfill their campaign promises about judicial appointments. George W. Bush's bold proclamations during both the 2000 and 2004 presidential campaigns that he hoped to appoint more Supreme Court justices in the conservative mold of Antonin Scalia and Clarence Thomas heightened expectations among his most conservative supporters that Bush would shift the high Court further to the right. His appointments of Chief Justice Roberts and Justice Alito clearly satisfied these Republican constituencies. As a presidential candidate, Barack Obama indicated that he hoped to appoint judges who would be "sympathetic enough to those who are on the outside, those who are vulnerable, those who are powerless...." That was the basis of Senator Obama's vote against the John Roberts nomination, and it offers at least some indication of his commitment to nominate more liberal justices to the high Court. Indeed, Obama's first high court nominee, Sonia Sotomayor, fit that description to a tee.

Like a "Bolt of Lightning"? Presidential Appointments to the Federal Judiciary

Selection to any federal court—but especially the Supreme Court—has been likened to the spin of a roulette wheel or a bolt of lightning that can strike anywhere without warning. Harvard law professor Thomas Reed Powell summed it up this way: "The selection of Supreme Court Justices is pretty much a matter of chance."[16] Certainly, the composition of the federal judiciary until recently could have been characterized fairly as a collection of friends and allies of senators from the president's party (lower court judges) and a collection of friends and allies of presidents (Supreme Court justices). Because no one can know very far in advance who will one day become a senator or a president, being in the right place at the right time demands political acumen, expert networking, and even luck. In the case of the

Supreme Court, those nominees whom the president did not personally know were often friends of someone well connected in the administration. Eisenhower's selection of Harlan, a longtime friend of the attorney general, is a case in point.

Today, lower federal court appointments are still often the product of well-honed connections with U.S. senators. Jimmy Carter's short-lived attempt to displace this patronage system with merit-based "nominating commissions" ran into political obstacles and was disbanded quickly by his successor, Ronald Reagan. Subsequent presidents have tried to shape the appointment of some lower court judges, especially at the circuit court level. Certainly considerations of merit and ideology have played a significant role in the elevation of candidates to the courts of appeals since the 1980s. President George W. Bush's aggressive campaign for the confirmation of conservative judicial nominees during his first term rankled Senate Democrats so much that they filibustered ten of his most objectionable nominees, denying them even a vote on their confirmation in 2003 and 2004. President Bush responded by offering two of those filibustered nominees (Charles Pickering and William Pryor) recess appointments to the U.S. Courts of Appeals, effective until the end of the following congressional session. But such divisive tactics should not obscure the larger reality that senators acquiesce to the president's lower court appointments in all but a handful of cases.[17] Patronage, especially with regard to district court judgeships, still plays a central role in determining who will land a coveted appointment to the federal judiciary.[18]

In contrast, the process for identifying and selecting candidates for the Supreme Court has undergone a dramatic transformation. The identification of Supreme Court nominees by presidents originated as a private affair, handled entirely by the president and perhaps a small coterie of his closest advisers. George Washington worked alone after his first inauguration in 1789 to sort through the multitude of written suggestions he received concerning whom he should place on the new Court.[19] Thomas Jefferson consulted with legislators from his party, and Ulysses Grant and Woodrow Wilson sought the advice of cabinet members. Sitting Supreme Court justices have managed to break into this inner circle of advisers on occasion. Most notably, Chief Justice William Howard Taft exerted considerable influence over the Court appointments made by Presidents Warren Harding and Calvin Coolidge during the 1920s. To the extent that the attorney general played a role, it was simply as an adviser, with no special resources to draw on other than his own expertise on Court-related issues. Presidents huddled with the attorney general and any other trusted advisers to toss around the names of potential nominees. Once a short list was identified, little research was conducted other than perhaps to invite comment informally from congressional leaders or officials in the organized bar.

Since the mid-twentieth century, however, a confluence of factors has transformed the political environment that shapes the recruitment of candidates for the Supreme Court. These factors include the following:[20]

1. *Growth and bureaucratization of the Justice Department.* From a modest-sized agency in the late nineteenth century, the Justice Department has grown into a mammoth enterprise, assuming many litigation functions on behalf of the federal government that previously were performed by the individual agencies. Especially significant was the creation of the Office of Legal Counsel (OLC) in the 1930s. The OLC was conceived of as a bureaucratic resource for the attorney general, serving him in his role as legal adviser to the president. In recent years, the heavily politicized OLC has been headed by an assistant attorney general with a staff of about twenty lawyers. During the 1980s and early 1990s Presidents Reagan and Bush relied heavily on the OLC and other Justice Department lawyers to generate lists of candidates for the federal judiciary, including the Supreme Court.

2. *Growth and bureaucratization of the White House staff.* The White House staff underwent a growth spurt of its own, expanding from just thirty-seven employees in the early 1930s to more than nine hundred staffers by the late 1980s.[21] Beginning with President Kennedy, who consulted regularly with White House counsel Theodore Sorenson, presidents have increasingly relied on staff lawyers to assist in vetting prospective judicial candidates and, more recently, as a source of independent legal research.

3. *Growth in the size and influence of the federal judiciary.* Congress's creation of new federal judgeships during the twentieth century has affected the process of judicial recruitment in significant ways. With 866 full-time federal judgeships in existence today, modern presidents enjoy far more opportunities than their predecessors to place their imprint on judicial policymaking. The president may have to fill, on average, as many as forty to fifty vacancies on the federal bench every year. During his two terms as president, George W. Bush successfully appointed 324 federal judges, including sixty-one to the U.S. Courts of Appeals. Moreover, a large number of those judgeships, including all of those on the Court of Appeals for the D.C. Circuit, are unencumbered by typical considerations of senatorial courtesy, the legislative norm that allows senators of the president's party to all but dictate local appointments. These judgeships are readily available as a testing ground for future Supreme Court justices. Federal appellate judges who prove to be ideologically compatible with the president's agenda may find themselves on short lists for elevation to the Supreme Court, either by the president who appointed them or by a later president of the same

party. President Reagan followed this practice, nominating to the Court two judges, Robert Bork and Antonin Scalia, whom he had earlier appointed to the D.C. circuit. President Clinton nominated two jurists to the Court, Ruth Bader Ginsburg and Stephen Breyer, who had been appointed to circuit court judgeships by President Carter more than a decade earlier. Because these prospective justices have already issued multiple rulings from the federal bench, they have fashioned a judicial portfolio that usually makes their behavior on the Supreme Court more predictable.

4. *Divided party government.* Between 1896 and 1946, opposing parties controlled the White House and the Senate during just two sessions of Congress, but since then divided party control has become a more common feature of government. The president has faced a hostile U.S. Senate in sixteen of thirty-three Congresses since World War II, including eight of eleven Congresses convened between 1987 and 2008. Opposition-party control of the Senate confirmation process usually does not spell defeat for Supreme Court nominees, but it does confer significant advantages on those who want to air grievances against a nominee and his or her ideology. By creating witness lists stacked against the nominee, establishing ground rules for hearings that encourage open-ended debate, and delaying hearings until interest group opposition can mobilize, the chair of the Senate Judiciary Committee can score political points against the president and at least increase the odds that the nominee will not be confirmed. If Robert Bork had been tapped for the Supreme Court in 1986, he would have been steered through a committee led by ardent Reagan supporters Strom Thurmond of South Carolina and Orrin Hatch of Utah; instead, nominated a year later, he faced Delaware senator Joseph Biden's Democratic-controlled committee and was rejected.

5. *Increased participation by interest groups, including the organized bar, in the selection process.* Although organized interests occasionally mobilized to defeat Supreme Court nominees in the nineteenth and early twentieth centuries, the level and intensity of interest group participation in the process today is unprecedented. Since World War II, interest groups have extended their influence into the early stages of judicial selection. The American Bar Association has been rating nominees to all federal courts since the early 1950s; negative or even unenthusiastically positive recommendations can damage a nominee substantially, if not derail the nomination altogether. Other groups, such as the Alliance for Justice, People for the American Way, and the Leadership Conference on Civil Rights, have made Supreme Court appointments a high priority for their organizations. During the George W. Bush administration, the Federalist Society, an organization of conservatives

seeking reform of the American legal system, enjoyed unprecedented influence in the judicial selection process. By some accounts, the withdrawal of Harriet Miers's Supreme Court nomination (and the subsequent selection of Samuel Alito in her place) was influenced in part by the actions and commentary of Federalist Society luminaries such as Robert Bork, Randy Barnett, and John Yoo.[22]

6. *Increased media attention before and during Supreme Court confirmation hearings.* In the not-so-distant past, the media's spotlight would fall on a prospective Supreme Court justice only after he or she was officially nominated, and even then the process of confirming the nominee—including the conduct of Senate committee hearings—was mostly an inside-the-beltway diversion. Today the process extends from rumors of a pending vacancy to the final confirmation vote and is a thoroughly public matter. National reporters assigned to cover the Supreme Court provide their readers with updated short lists of the candidates the president is considering. In a nod to this reality, Bill Clinton strategically floated the names of candidates to a hungry media contingent even before he decided on his final selections. This practice of "politics by trial balloon" provided Clinton with advance warning of the opposition he was inviting, but it may have also given the administration's enemies too much influence over the selection process. For example, in 1993 Senator Hatch and Senate minority leader Robert Dole of Kansas torpedoed the prospective Supreme Court nomination of Interior Secretary Bruce Babbitt with their not-so-subtle public hints about Babbitt's lack of judicial experience.[23] President Clinton's failure to commit to Babbitt before he underwent Hatch and Dole's rhetorical assault may have rescued the administration from considerable embarrassment, but it also invited public attacks from critics who might otherwise have feared the wrath of a White House already significantly invested in that one candidate. More recently, President Obama's short list of prospective candidates for David Souter's vacated seat underwent intense scrutiny in the media and elsewhere during the spring of 2009.

7. *Advances in legal research technology.* In 1956 Herbert Brownell sought to investigate the record of a prospective nominee for the Court, New Jersey Supreme Court justice William Brennan. To perform the task Brownell did what any first-year law student would have done at that time: he read the printed New Jersey court reports, skimming Brennan's written opinions. By the 1980s this traditional method of legal research had been replaced by new research programs such as LEXIS/NEXIS and WESTLAW, which allow officials to gather all of a prospective candidate's past judicial opinions, scholarship, and public commentary at the click of a mouse. Justice Department officials can

even construct elaborate word searches to pinpoint the candidate's most controversial statements. Naturally, these advances in research technology are a double-edged sword: media outlets and opposition interest groups are just as likely as the administration to discover negative information about prospective candidates. Eleventh-hour revelations, such as the news that Supreme Court nominee G. Harrold Carswell had given a speech at a Ku Klux Klan rally (which helped to undermine his nomination in 1970), seem much less likely in the computer age. The ease of information gathering may also contribute to a streamlining of the selection process that favors lackluster candidates whose bland inoffensiveness renders them capable of surviving intense scrutiny of their backgrounds. For all the conservative critics' frustrations at some of Justice Souter's rulings, many have forgotten that it was Souter's complete lack of a controversial, substantive record on important legal issues—and thus the difficulty of attacking him—that made his candidacy so appealing to the George H. W. Bush administration.

These seven changes in the political landscape have profoundly influenced the process by which prospective Supreme Court nominees are identified and eventually selected. In recent administrations, high-level political operatives, who did not want to expend all of the president's political capital on a confirmation fight, have battled ardent ideologues hell-bent on transforming the constitutional landscape through the selection of right-thinking Supreme Court justices. Such arguments bring out the worst in both groups: by underselling others' preferences and overselling their own, administration officials corrupt the advice they offer to the president and undermine his unique interests in the process.

The factors that have shaped the political environment for Supreme Court recruitment have tilted the Court toward professional judges whose long records on the bench satisfy the administration's ideologues, but whose lack of political experience and relatively uncontroversial public profiles satisfy even the most cautious members of the president's inner circle. As we shall see, many of these variables came into play during President Reagan's second term, highlighting the modern tendency to produce a Court of judicial "insiders" who are also political "outsiders."

The Reagan Administration and the Modern Era of Judicial Recruitment

During Reagan's first term, conservative lawyers in the Justice Department—determined to alter the constitutional landscape in a conservative direction—were forced to cool their heels and wait. The only Supreme Court vacancy arose when

Potter Stewart informed officials that he intended to retire at the conclusion of the Court's 1980–1981 term, just six months into the Reagan presidency. As a candidate in 1980, Reagan had on more than one occasion professed his desire to name the first woman justice to the Supreme Court, and that promise was still fresh in the public's mind at the time of Stewart's decision. Attorney General William French Smith immediately went to work on a list of prospective candidates that was topped by female jurists, most of whom were more moderate than administration conservatives desired. Smith was the driving force behind the selection of Judge O'Connor of the Arizona Court of Appeals, even though her views on critical issues such as school prayer, affirmative action, and abortion were largely unknown. Nevertheless, on the basis of extensive research gathered by Smith's associates and the recommendations of O'Connor's Stanford Law School network, which included classmate William Rehnquist and Assistant Attorney General William Baxter, among others, O'Connor's name was approved for nomination by the president in July 1981. If the Reagan administration was preparing to fight for a more conservative Court, it did not plan any bold moves in that direction so early in the president's term.

Soon after Reagan secured his landslide reelection in 1984, administration lawyers began preparing in earnest for the next Supreme Court vacancy. Beginning in February 1985, an informal group of Justice Department officials was formed, led by OLC head Charles Cooper and William Bradford Reynolds, the head of the Civil Rights Division. Together these officials reviewed potential nominees on a near-weekly basis. In defining the attributes of the "ideal candidate," the group worked from a list of twelve criteria:[24]

1. "awareness of the importance of strict justiciability and procedural requirements"
2. "refusal to create new constitutional rights for the individual"
3. "deference to states in their spheres"
4. "appropriate deference to agencies"
5. "commitment to strict principles of 'nondiscrimination'"
6. "disposition towards 'less government rather than more'"
7. "recognition that the federal government is one of enumerated powers"
8. "appreciation for the role of the free market in our society"
9. "respect for traditional values"
10. "recognition of the importance of separations of power principles of presidential authority"
11. "legal competence" and
12. "strong leadership on the court/young and vigorous"

In searching for individuals who met these criteria, administration lawyers followed a familiar path. Their attention focused quickly on four appellate court judges whom President Reagan had appointed during his first term: Robert Bork and Antonin Scalia of the D.C. circuit, Patrick Higginbotham of the fifth circuit, and Ralph Winter Jr. of the second circuit. Joining these four on the Justice Department's short list were two earlier Republican appointees to the U.S. Court of Appeals for the Ninth Circuit: J. Clifford Wallace, who was appointed by Nixon in 1972, and Anthony Kennedy, a Ford appointee in 1975. All six jurists were relatively young (Bork at fifty-eight was by far the oldest), and all were strong proponents of conservative principles. None was a politician of the traditional sort: Scalia and Bork had served brief stints in the Justice Department, but the group consisted mainly of academics and jurists. The administration's intense review of their judicial records was comprehensive and even uncovered a few surprises. Kennedy was a stalwart conservative but had strayed occasionally on privacy issues, where his "easy acceptance of privacy rights as something guaranteed by the Constitution" was viewed as "really distressing."[25] Perhaps this was a harbinger of Kennedy's eventual reluctance to overturn *Roe v. Wade* and his willingness to craft opinions championing homosexual rights, first in *Romer v. Evans* (1996)[26] and more recently in *Lawrence v. Texas* (2003).[27]

Scalia and Bork stood out as the most consistently conservative judges in the lot. Scalia, a fifty-year-old Italian American, was described by Justice Department attorneys as "especially creative and successful in transforming the common intuition that 'courts are running the country' into a set of coherent principles about what courts should not do."[28] His opinions on separation of powers and jurisdictional questions were deemed especially brilliant. In addition, a thorough computer search of Scalia's record on the D.C. circuit uncovered not a single opinion in which either the result or the ground of decision seemed problematic from a conservative legal perspective. Bork was more controversial, both because he had obeyed President Nixon's order to fire the Watergate special prosecutor, Archibald Cox, during a stint as solicitor general in 1973 and for his colorful and controversial academic writings decrying landmark Supreme Court rulings that protected the right to abortion and an expanded right of free speech. But as a judicial conservative, Bork had few equals. According to one Justice Department report, Bork's guiding philosophy was that "if the judiciary overrules democratically sanctioned choices by creating rights not found in the constitutional text, it has engaged in an illegitimate—indeed, tyrannical—suppression of self-government."[29]

Most important, Bork and Scalia were considered ideal candidates to survive the partisan sniping that was expected during the Senate confirmation process.

They were circuit court judges who had survived Senate confirmation a few years earlier. And like many other appellate judges, their written opinions tended to disprove outsiders' perceptions of them as sharp ideological extremists. Even Bork's fiercest opponents would later admit that his circuit court opinions were on the whole both "balanced in judgment" and "fair in treatment of the arguments of losing parties and dissenters."[30] In short, these two court of appeals judges represented the administration's greatest hope of placing a true conservative onto the Supreme Court.

Several critical differences between the two candidates ultimately vaulted Scalia ahead of Bork on the Reagan administration's Supreme Court promotion list. First, Scalia was eight years younger than Bork, giving him more staying power on the Court. Second, Scalia carried less pre-judicial baggage than Bork, who was still (perhaps unjustifiably) saddled with the stigma of having fired the Watergate prosecutor. Finally, Scalia would be the first Italian American justice, a fact that officials hoped would provide him with political cover among Senate Democrats.

In late spring 1986, more than a year after the administration's prescreening process began, Chief Justice Warren Burger informed White House officials of his intention to retire. Once Attorney General Edwin Meese began to press for Justice Rehnquist's elevation to chief justice, all eyes turned to Scalia as Rehnquist's replacement. In truth, Rehnquist's appointment carried some baggage of its own: Democrats were eager to revive accusations that he had harassed African American voters in Arizona during the 1960s, a charge that was never proved, and that he had written memos critical of school desegregation when he was a clerk to Justice Robert Jackson in the early 1950s. In discussions with the president, White House chief of staff Donald Regan pointed out that nominating Rehnquist together with Bork might be too difficult a battle to win, even with the help of a Republican-controlled Senate Judiciary Committee. Convinced that Regan was correct, the president on June 17, 1986, announced his selections of Rehnquist to be chief justice and Scalia to be associate justice. Scalia glided to confirmation in the Senate by a 98–0 vote. Rehnquist's confirmation, however, bogged down in debates about his conservative opinions. Although his nomination drew the highest number of negative votes ever cast against a successful nominee for chief justice to that time, Rehnquist was confirmed, 65–33.

Lewis Powell's decision to retire a year later, on June 26, 1987, precipitated another battle, but not within the administration. Bork was the highest ranking candidate remaining from the previous year, and nothing had happened since then to alter the administration's preference. At least one outside factor had changed, however. In January 1987 the Democrats had taken control of the Senate for the first time since 1981, and the Senate Judiciary Committee was now led by Senator Biden, who planned to run for president in 1988. Lawyers in the White House Counsel's Office foresaw some problems for Bork, but they did not argue forcefully against his selection. After all, Biden had stated that he would vote to confirm Bork if he were ever nominated to the Supreme Court. But immediately after the nomination was announced on July 1, liberal interest groups began to mobilize against Bork. His nomination would eventually become a watershed in confirmation politics. Senator Biden exercised the majority party's prerogative to delay confirmation hearings until September, and the long paper trail Bork had left—more as a law professor than as a judge—was dissected by critics in a way that few had anticipated. During his testimony before the Judiciary Committee, Bork's lecture-like academic discourses about a range of constitutional issues began to convince moderate Republican senators, including Arlen Specter of Pennsylvania and John Warner of Virginia, that the bearded jurist lacked compassion for the problems of ordinary people. Few were surprised when, on October 23, the Senate defeated Bork's nomination by a 58–42 vote.

President Reagan turned to two more court of appeals judges in the wake of Bork's rejection: first, Douglas Ginsburg of the D.C. circuit, who quickly withdrew amid allegations that he had used marijuana when a law professor, and then Anthony Kennedy, who was easily confirmed. Thus, all five of the candidates Reagan nominated to the Court were sitting judges on federal or state appeals courts, and in his second term all four were judges on U.S. Courts of Appeals. Although Bork, Scalia, and Ginsburg had logged time working in the Justice Department for Republican administrations, they were, by the time of their nominations, political outsiders in every sense. None represented the type of political insider (senator, attorney general, governor) that had been more commonly tapped for Supreme Court appointments during the early and middle twentieth century (see Table 15.1).

Political scientist Mark Silverstein correctly identified 1968 as a pivotal year in Supreme Court politics, because (1) Abe Fortas's ill-fated nomination to be chief justice became the first of several all-out confirmation battles to be waged in the modern era, and (2) the election of Richard Nixon brought to the White House a chief executive willing to elevate ideology over factors such as personal and party loyalty in his selection of justices.[31] It was not until the early to mid-1980s, however, that the Court underwent its more complete transformation into a bench of outsiders, more isolated from the rough-and-tumble of national politics than most Courts of the past. The post–World War II Court was considered a collection of intellectual giants, including Felix Frankfurter, Hugo Black, Robert Jackson, and William Douglas. Their intellects, however, previously had served presidents and their administrations, whether informally—Frankfurter was one of Roosevelt's private confidantes, and Black was his loyal foot soldier in the Senate—or formally—Jackson was Roosevelt's attorney general, and Douglas was head of the Securities and Exchange Commission. In contrast, the justices appointed since 1968 have enjoyed little, if any, direct interaction with the presidents who appointed them. President George H. W. Bush tapped two federal circuit judges, Clarence Thomas and David Souter, for the Court during his single term in office.[32] President Clinton tried to buck the pattern by seriously considering New York governor Mario Cuomo, Senate majority leader George Mitchell, and Secretary of Education Richard Riley, in addition to Babbitt, for the Supreme Court during his first two years in office. But when political push came to shove in the form of threats of stalled confirmations and the loss of political capital, Clinton also turned to two federal circuit judges, Ginsburg and Breyer. Although these judges were well known in legal circles, they had remained outside the trenches of political warfare for well over a decade. John Roberts and Samuel Alito, the two justices appointed by President George W. Bush, were federal appeals court judges, as well.

"May It Please the Court": Presidential Influence on the Judicial Process

The growth and bureaucratization of the Justice Department have facilitated more than just a thorough vetting of prospective Supreme Court nominees. They have also made possible greater White House involvement in the cases that flow to the Supreme Court, the lower federal courts, and the various state courts. The federal government has long been the most frequent litigant in the federal courts and the Supreme Court; each day countless new lawsuits are filed against federal agencies such as the Department of Health and Human Services and the Department of Defense. Executive branch lawyers settle many such lawsuits, but others go to trial either before an administrative law judge or in a federal court.

Drawing on social scientist Marc Galanter's landmark framework for understanding the systematic features of a legal system, the executive branch is a "repeat player"—that is, a litigating actor engaged in many similar cases over time.[33] Accordingly the federal government enjoys a number of advantages in the litigation process, including expertise, informal relationships with the other actors, a prior "bargaining reputation," and the ability to "play the odds" for advantages that may accrue only in later cases. All of these factors weigh heavily in the government's favor in most forms of litigation.

In recent years the White House has sought to use these advantages to gain through the courts what it could not attain elsewhere, whether because of congressional inertia, concerted interest group opposition, or the president's fears that legislative solutions would redound to the detriment of fellow party members in Congress. Unable to enact conservative modifications to the Voting Rights Act in the early 1990s, for example, the George H. W. Bush administration supported private legal efforts to overturn congressional districts that were drawn to protect certain racial groups. The Clinton administration switched sides and, beginning in 1993, supported upholding many of those same districts. The Justice Department under Clinton also aggressively prosecuted Microsoft Corporation for antitrust violations in the late 1990s and managed to attain a stunning judicial order in 2000 to break up the company, which was subsequently overturned on appeal. George W. Bush, Clinton's successor, encouraged his Justice Department to adopt a less aggressive approach in the Microsoft litigation. Executive branch agencies with litigation expertise may also lend behind-the-scenes assistance in legal cases to which the government is not a direct party. The Clinton administration lent support to private plaintiffs suing tobacco companies and gun manufacturers in the mid- and late 1990s.

The federal government's repeat-player advantage also pays dividends for the White House when it takes an interest in cases before the Supreme Court. The solicitor general, who represents the United States in most such cases, enjoys an especially close relationship with the justices, no matter which party controls the White House. Not surprisingly, the solicitor general's office has enjoyed an extraordinary level of success before the Court, as reflected both in the Court's rulings on cases and, even more dramatically, in the Court's selection of which cases to hear.[34]

Although frequently a petitioner or respondent before the Supreme Court, the solicitor general influences matters more subtly by submitting amicus curiae ("friend of the court") briefs in cases in which the U.S. government is not directly involved but in whose outcome it nonetheless takes an interest. In the 1960s Archibald Cox became the first solicitor general to aggressively involve his office in the filing of amicus briefs. From 1961 to 1965 Cox's office filed an average of seventeen amicus briefs per year, including twenty-eight in 1963 alone.[35] During the 1970s and 1980s the federal government routinely filed amicus briefs in 20 percent to 30 percent of all cases decided by the Court, and sometimes in as many as half.

This high level of amicus filings by the U.S. government, which has held steady in recent years, is driven largely by perceptions that the Supreme Court serves as an important venue for deciding a range of politically significant legal issues. The Reagan administration in particular sought to use the amicus brief as a tool of constitutional change, and it achieved considerable success in this regard under its first solicitor general, Charles Fried.

The solicitor general and the president at times may differ on legal strategy. During the Nixon administration, Solicitor General Erwin Griswold declined to argue for the government before the Supreme Court in two cases involving national security and the military draft. The Carter administration's attorney general, Griffin Bell, engaged in a well-reported feud on the president's behalf with Solicitor General Wade McCree concerning how to handle the controversial affirmative action case *Regents of California v. Bakke* (1978).[36] Still, most solicitors general are chosen in the first place for their compatibility with the president's agenda, and they act accordingly to defend the president's interests.

Presidential Powers and the Supreme Court: Limited Checks and Tenuous Balances

On rare occasions, the president finds himself in the Supreme Court battling over the metes and bounds of his own constitutional and statutory powers. Traditionally the president has enjoyed considerable success in these circumstances. For reasons both practical and political, the Court is poorly situated to control the president through its rulings. Even the members of the Court not appointed by the sitting president understand that the president's status as a nationally elected official and his position at the reins of every executive branch agency make him a formidable foe under any circumstance. President Andrew Jackson famously declined to enforce the Supreme Court's 1832 ruling in *Worcester v. Georgia*, declaring perhaps apocryphally of the chief justice, "John Marshall has made his decision—*now let him enforce it!*"[37] Even some unpopular presidents have considered throwing down the gauntlet. During the Watergate crisis, immediately after the Supreme Court voted 8–0 against President Nixon's claim that he retained an absolute executive privilege to protect White House communications, a politically weak president still weighed the possibility of not complying. According to one report, Nixon openly wondered if to preserve the power of his office he did not have a "constitutional duty" to reject the Court's order.[38]

Faced with this reality, the Supreme Court has traditionally proceeded with caution when considering attempts to curtail presidential authority. In *Marbury v. Madison* (1803), Chief Justice Marshall cleverly established a power of judicial review for the Supreme Court by invalidating a 1789 law that the plaintiff was invoking to secure an overdue judicial commission from the Jefferson adminis-tration.[39] Marshall's fear of noncompliance by Jefferson persuaded him not to order the new administration to deliver the commission. Sixty years later, dur-ing the Civil War, the Supreme Court upheld President Lincoln's seizure of ships in *The Prize Cases* (1863), even though he issued those orders nearly three months before Congress had authorized him to declare that a state of insurrec-tion existed.[40] Although the Supreme Court appeared to show more backbone in *Ex parte Milligan* (1866), when it invalidated Lincoln's suspension of habeas corpus, the Court's ruling was handed down only after the war was over and Lincoln was dead.[41]

Like Congress, the Supreme Court of the early to mid-twentieth century stood little chance of prevailing against a presidency that was increasingly involved in domestic and international politics. In 1936 the Court declared that a president has "plenary and exclusive power . . . as the sole organ of the federal government in the field of international relations."[42] With the conduct of for-eign relations and war lying squarely within the domain of the chief executive, few were surprised either by the Supreme Court's deference to President Roosevelt's internment of Japanese Americans during World War II or by its acquiescence when President Carter terminated a defense treaty without Senate approval nearly a half-century later.

In domestic affairs Supreme Court deference to the president's conduct of the executive branch has prevailed as well, albeit with a few exceptions. In *Myers v. United States* (1926), the Court granted the president unbridled discretion to fire executive officials, a generous reading of presidential power that was undone only partially by its decision a decade later to restrict presidential terminations of independent agency commissioners.[43] President Truman was deeply angered by the Court's 1952 ruling invalidating his administration's seizure of the steel mills to avert a labor strike, but he complied with the Court's order to return the mills to their owners. Yet the Court gave far more to the presidency in *Youngstown Sheet and Tube Co. v. Sawyer* (1952) than it took away.[44] A majority of justices formally accepted the theory that the president enjoys "inherent powers" not expressly stated in the Constitution. The same could be said of *United States v. Nixon* (1974), in which the Court recognized for the first time that presidents have an executive privilege to protect documents and conversa-tions in many circumstances, although not in Nixon's specific case.

In each of these instances, the Supreme Court expanded presidential powers far more than it constricted them. The presidential excesses at issue did not become an excuse to limit future executives who exercised a bit more caution. In contrast, no such limits emerged from *Nixon v. Fitzgerald* (1982), in which the Court narrowly decided that a president is immune from lawsuits concerning any of his official acts. Notably, it was the new arrivals on the Court—Burger, Powell, Rehnquist, Stevens, and O'Connor—who sided with former president Nixon in *Fitzgerald*. Yet in the decades that followed, some of those justices helped to create a majority far more willing to interfere with, rather than defer to, the chief executive.

Two cases in particular exemplify the current Court's willingness to cast away traditional notions of deference to the president in favor of concerns such as "efficiency" and "fairness." Little of value was granted to the president in *Morrison v. Olson* (1988), in which the Court upheld a statute providing for an independent counsel to investigate possible federal criminal violations by high-level executive officials, including the president. Because the specially chosen counsel, although an "executive officer," was deemed an "inferior" officer by the Supreme Court, Congress could constitutionally preclude the president from firing him or her without due cause.[45] As Justice Scalia noted in his passionate dissent, the statute essentially deprived the president of the exclusive control over the exercise of executive power that the Constitution vests in him alone.[46] Scalia, however, joined with a unanimous court in *Clinton v. Jones* (1997) to deny President Clinton's request to delay a civil suit brought against him until after he left office. Writing for the Court, Justice Stevens confidently asserted that "if the past is any indicator, it seems unlikely that a deluge of litigation will ever engulf the presidency."[47] The fact that this lawsuit did engulf the presidency, spawning the Monica Lewinsky investigation, among other matters, simply highlights how unsympathetic the current Court has grown to the plight of modern presidents.

In view of the Court's position in *Morrison v. Olson* and *Clinton v. Jones*, few should have been surprised when it stood up against the executive branch in three recent cases related to detainees in the war on terrorism. In the first case, *Hamdi v. Rumsfeld* (2004), the Court considered whether the U.S. military could indefinitely detain an American citizen who had been arrested while allegedly fighting for the Taliban in Afghanistan in 2001.[48] Although the high Court initially pleased the Bush administration by acknowledging that a detainee could be classified as an "unlawful combatant" with limited rights, six of the nine justices voted to vacate the lower court judgment that Yaser Esam Hamdi could be held without a more "searching review" of the facts underlying his detention. According to Justice O'Connor, "[A] state of war is not a blank check when it comes to the rights of the Nation's citizens." But the Court refused to indicate what sort of legal process Hamdi and the other enemy combatants should receive.

The Bush administration suffered similar defeats in *Hamdan v. Rumsfeld* (2006)[49] and *Boumediene v. Bush* (2008).[50] In *Hamdan*, the Supreme Court held that the military commissions the administration had set up without congressional authorization at Guantánamo Bay, Cuba, violated both the Uniform Code of Military Justice and the Geneva Conventions. In *Boumediene*, the Court ruled that even enemy combatants held at Guantánamo Bay are entitled to the writ of habeas corpus, guaranteeing them a meaningful opportunity to offer evidence that they were being wrongly detained. The Court's majority included just five members in both cases.

In sum, even a conservative court dominated by Republican presidents' appointees proved unwilling to give a Republican president the authority he sought to manage the war on terrorism as he saw fit. In the future, President Obama may not be able to dislodge the Court from its generally conservative moorings through the appointment process. But recent decisions indicate that the Court, even as it is currently constituted, will continue to look skeptically at the exercise of executive power, regardless of which party is exercising that authority. That is good news for Obama and his constituents if they favor a libertarian philosophy of judging. It is bad news, however, if Obama's presidency relies on the continued extension of executive authority to achieve its goals.

Notes

1. Some of the discussion in this chapter is borrowed from my work on Supreme Court appointments, David Yalof, *Pursuit of Justices: Presidential Politics and the Selection of Supreme Court Nominees* (Chicago: University of Chicago Press, 1999, pbk. 2001).

2. Indeed, the awkward moment was rendered even more so by Chief Justice Roberts's failure to state the oath correctly and by the president-elect's willingness to go along with Roberts's failure to follow those dictates. Chief Justice Roberts incorrectly asked the president-elect to repeat, "I will execute the office of President *to* the United States … *faithfully*"; after that false start, Roberts then followed Obama's "execute" with the word "faithfully," which resulted in the incorrect phrase "execute faithfully." Obama repeated Roberts's initial, mistaken prompt, with the word "faithfully" after the "United States." Although many constitutional experts argued that the oath was not technically a necessary precondition for the exercise of presidential power, Chief Justice Roberts administered the oath the next day at the White House out of what White House aides called "an abundance of caution."

3. See Thomas Keck, *The Most Activist Supreme Court in History* (Chicago: University of Chicago Press, 2004).

4. The three rejected nominees were Clement Haynsworth, G. Harrold Carswell, and Robert Bork; Douglas Ginsburg withdrew without a formal vote on the merits.

5. The most notable work on this subject is David M. Atkinson, *Leaving the Bench: Supreme Court Justices at the End* (Lawrence: University Press of Kansas, 1999).

6. See Jess Bravin et al., "Supreme Interests: For Some Justices, The Bush-Gore Case Has a Personal Angle," *Wall Street Journal*, December 12, 2000, A1.

7. Lee Epstein et al., "Circuit Effects: How the Norm of Federal Judicial Experience Biases the U.S. Supreme Court," *University of Pennsylvania Law Review* 157 (2009): 833–880.

8. For a full discussion of the preconditions for such Court-related campaigns, see Donald Grier Stevenson Jr., *Campaigns and the Court: The U.S. Supreme Court in Presidential Elections* (New York: Columbia University Press, 1999).

9. *Dred Scott v. Sandford*, 60 U.S. 393 (1857).

10. Stevenson, *Campaigns and the Court*, 103.

11. See *United States v. Butler*, 297 U.S. 1 (1936); and *Schechter Poultry Corp. v. United States*, 295 U.S. 495 (1935).

12. William Leuchtenberg, *The Supreme Court Reborn: The Constitutional Revolution in the Age of Roosevelt* (New York: Oxford University Press, 1995), 107.

13. *Miranda v. Arizona*, 384 U.S. 436 (1966).

14. *Roe v. Wade*, 410 U.S. 113 (1973); Reagan is quoted in Stevenson, *Campaigns and the Court*, 204.

15. *Webster v. Reproductive Health Services*, 492 U.S. 490 (1989); and *Planned Parenthood v. Casey*, 505 U.S. 833 (1992).

16. Quoted in David M. O'Brien, *Storm Center: The Supreme Court in American Politics*, 8th ed. (New York: Norton, 2008), 35.

17. Although the lower court appointment process was marked by considerable strife during both the 107th and 108th Congresses, by the end of his first term President Bush had still managed to see 204 of his 260 nominees confirmed, with another twenty-four nominees still pending. After securing his reelection in November 2004, the emboldened president promised to renominate twenty of the unconfirmed candidates, including seven of the nominees filibustered by Senate Democrats during his first term. The conflict between President Bush and the Democratic minority in the Senate began to heat up even more during spring 2005, as Senate majority leader Bill Frist, R.-Tenn., threatened to use his party's majority to permanently change Senate rules to prevent future filibusters on judicial nominees (this maneuver was nicknamed by angry Senate Democrats the "nuclear option"). Eventually a compromise was brokered by the so-called Gang of 14—a group of seven Senate Republicans and seven Senate Democrats who were determined to head off the looming crisis. Under the May 2005 agreement, the seven Senate Democrats agreed to allow five of the seven controversial nominees a vote by the entire Senate (all five were confirmed eventually); they further agreed to support future Democratic filibusters on nominees only in "extraordinary circumstances." In return, the seven Senate Republicans agreed to reject the "nuclear option" favored by party leaders.

18. For a fuller discussion of Carter's nominating commissions, as well as the politics of lower court appointments in general, see Sheldon Goldman, *Picking Federal Judges: Lower Court Selection from Roosevelt through Reagan* (New Haven: Yale University Press, 1997).

19. John Anthony Maltese, *The Selling of Supreme Court Nominees* (Baltimore: Johns Hopkins University Press, 1995), 24.

20. The discussion of these factors and of the Reagan administration's practice of selecting Supreme Court nominees is borrowed largely from Yalof, *Pursuit of Justices*.

21. Stephen Hess, *Organizing the Presidency* (Washington, D.C.: Brookings Institution Press, 1988), 5.

22. The leading work on the subject of Federalist Society influence is Steven M. Teles, *The Rise of the Conservative Legal Movement* (Princeton: Princeton University Press, 2008).

23. Richard Berke, "Hatch Assails Idea of Justice Babbitt," *New York Times*, June 9, 1993, A17.

24. These criteria are listed in a memo written by Roger Clegg, a special assistant to the attorney general, defining the attributes of a so-called ideal Supreme Court candidate. Although Clegg's paper has not yet been made available to the public (see Withdrawal Sheet, 6 August 1996, Supreme Court/Rehnquist/Scalia General Selection Scenario [1 of 3] file, Box 14287, Peter Wallison files, Ronald Reagan Presidential Library), its contents may be reconstructed by examining judicial profiles tailored to adhere to the terms of the criteria he discusses. See, for example, Report on Patrick Higginbotham paper, Supreme Court-Rehnquist/Scalia Notebook (2 of 4) file, Peter Wallison files, Ronald Reagan Presidential Library.

25. Memo, Steven Matthews to Special Projects Committee, May 23, 1986, Supreme Court-Rehnquist/Scalia Notebook I (3 of 4) file, OA 14287, Peter Wallison files, Ronald Reagan Presidential Library.

26. 517 U.S. 620 (1996).

27. 539 U.S. 558 (2003).

28. Report on Antonin Scalia, Supreme Court-Scalia (3 of 5) file, Peter Wallison files, Ronald Reagan Presidential Library.

29. Report on Robert Bork, Supreme Court-Rehnquist/Scalia Notebook (1 of 2) file, Peter Wallison files, Ronald Reagan Presidential Library.

30. For example, the American Bar Association's Committee on the Judiciary opposed Bork's candidacy but praised the tone of his circuit court opinions. See Letter, Harold R. Tyler to Joseph Biden, September 21, 1987, reprinted in U.S. Congress, Senate, Committee on the Judiciary, *The Nomination of Robert H. Bork to be Associate Justice of the Supreme Court of the United States*, 100th Cong., 1st sess., September 21, 1987, 1232.

31. Mark Silverstein, *Judicious Choices: The New Politics of Supreme Court Confirmations* (New York: Norton, 1994), 10–12.

32. Thomas had served in the executive branch as an assistant secretary of education and head of the Equal Employment Opportunity Commission during the Reagan administration, but he had limited contact with the president.

33. See Marc Galanter, "Why the 'Haves' Come out Ahead: Speculations on the Limits of Legal Change," *Law and Society Review* 9 (Fall 1974): 95–151.

34. Rebecca Mae Salokar, *The Solicitor General: The Politics of Law* (Philadelphia: Temple University Press, 1992), 106–150.

35. Lincoln Caplan, *Tenth Justice* (New York: Vintage Books, 1987), 197.

36. *Regents of California v. Bakke*, 438 U.S. 265 (1978).

37. *Worcester v. Georgia*, 6 Pet. (31 U.S.) 515 (1832); Jackson quoted in Horace Greeley, *The American Conflict*, vol. 1 (Hartford, Conn.: O. D. Case, 1864), 106 (emphasis in original).

38. Bob Woodward and Carl Bernstein, *The Final Days* (New York: Avon Books, 1976), 300.

39. *Marbury v. Madison*, 1 Cr. (5 U.S.) 137 (1803).

40. *The Prize Cases*, 22 Black (67 U.S.) 635 (1863).

41. *Ex parte Milligan*, 24 Wall. (71 U.S.) 2 (1866).

42. *United States v. Curtiss-Wright Export Corp.*, 299 U.S. 304, 320 (1936).

43. *Myers v. United States*, 272 U.S. 52 (1926). The later case is *Humphrey's Executor v. United States*, 295 U.S. 602 (1935).

44. *Youngstown Sheet and Tube Co. v. Sawyer*, 343 U.S. 579 (1952).

45. According to Article II, Section 2, Clause 2, of the Constitution, "the Congress may by Law vest the Appointment of such inferior Officers, as they think proper, in the President alone, in the Courts of Law, or in the Heads of Departments."

46. *Morrison v. Olson*, 487 U.S. 654, 728 (1988) (Scalia, J., dissenting). (In 1999 Congress discontinued the controversial statute, a political nod to the harsh consequences it had wrought on both political parties since its inception.)

47. *Clinton v. Jones*, 520 U.S. 681, 702 (1997).

48. *Hamdi et al. v. Rumsfeld*, 542 U.S. 507 (2004).

49. *Hamdan v. Rumsfeld*, 548 U.S. 557 (2006).

50. *Boumediene v. Bush*, 128 S. Ct. 2229 (2008).

16 The Presidency and Unilateral Power: A Taxonomy

Andrew Rudalevige

Hemmed in by the Constitution's checks and balances, as well as by the limited powers the document explicitly grants to the executive, presidents are continually tempted to act unilaterally. Doing so promises quick and decisive action and the opportunity to transform their preferences directly into public policy. Thus, throughout American history, but especially since the mid-twentieth century, presidents have interpreted the "executive power" granted them in Article II very broadly, culminating with George W. Bush's expansive claims regarding presidential conduct of the global war on terror. Presidents have been aided in this effort by their status as a unitary actor, by the growth of a massive administrative establishment, and, not least, by the willingness of the other branches to delegate power to them. In this chapter, Andrew Rudalevige provides a brief history and extensive taxonomy of the president's unilateral powers, in war and peace—and explores the real limits, both substantive and normative, of their going it alone.

Toward the start of his 2004 reelection campaign, President George W. Bush addressed a friendly crowd of workers from religious organizations. He touted his creation, by executive order, of the White House Office of Faith-Based and Community Initiatives, and then turned to a second directive ordering that faith-based organizations receive the "equal protection of the laws" in their procurement efforts from federal agencies. He had been trying to achieve this by statute, Bush said, but "got a little frustrated in Washington because I couldn't get the bill passed out of the Congress. They were arguing process." No problem, he added. "Congress wouldn't act, so I signed an executive order. That means I did it on my own."[1]

In the American constitutional system of intertwined institutions, doing things "on my own" is hugely tempting to any president. Acting unilaterally promises quick and decisive action, the chance to short-circuit the tedious "process" in which legislators delight and to directly transform presidential preferences into public policy. As Bill Clinton aide Paul Begala said in 1998, "Stroke of the pen, law of the land. Kind of cool."[2] Cool enough, anyway, for President Clinton to issue 364 executive orders in his eight years as president, for George W. Bush to offer 288 orders in his subsequent eight years, and for Barack Obama to mark his first weeks in office in 2009 with a flurry of his own. Nor, as discussed in detail in this chapter, do executive orders constitute the whole of potential unilateral actions by the president—many other such actions are less visible but reach farther.

How much can the president do on his own? Certainly the president's roles as head of an expansive executive branch, as commander in chief, and, not least, as beneficiary of the grant of the amorphous "executive power" denoted in the Constitution combine to empower presidential unilateralism, especially in times of national emergency. The fact that Congress is a divided body run by collective choices affords presidents inherent advantages: even if they don't get the last say, presidents often get to make the first move, thereby shaping the landscape over which subsequent options range. "The executive, in the exercise of its constitutional powers," Alexander Hamilton observed, "may establish an antecedent state of things, which ought to weigh in the legislative decision."[3]

Yet presidents—who, after all, are by name "presiders" rather than "deciders"—form only one part of a system grounded in checks and balances. Congress is the first branch of government described in the Constitution. As James Madison argued, the executive's powers "must pre-suppose the existence of the laws to be executed," and "to see the laws faithfully executed constitutes the essence of the executive authority."[4] During the ratification debate, defenders of the Constitution did not dispute opponents' contention that "to live by one man's will [becomes] the cause of all men's misery." Instead, they sought to show that the president's will would be hemmed in by institutional checks, not least Congress's power to impeach and remove him from office.[5]

This early debate highlights a recurring dispute in American history: Can presidents act only when the Constitution, or Congress, gives them permission to act? Or can presidents act whenever they have not been forbidden to do so? Or can presidents go even further and disregard "the legislative decision" if they think it is inconsistent with their constitutional duties and the national interest? The answer to these questions has been forged not by scholarship but by history, worked out in practice through interbranch contestation.

The remainder of this chapter traces that practice, cataloging the tools of executive discretion and the scope of their use. The last three decades have witnessed both broad claims of unilateral presidential power, and occasions of congressional backlash against those claims. But on the whole the presidential power to do things "on my own" has expanded. This raises the age-old question of efficiency versus accountability. In a system as large and fragmented as ours, there is real value in clear leadership. On the other hand, presidential leadership is not by definition virtuous, especially if it does violence to constitutional tenets. In 1952 Supreme Court Justice Robert Jackson put it this way:

The claim of inherent and unrestricted presidential powers has long been a persuasive dialectical weapon in political controversy.... [But] with all its defects, delays and inconveniences, men have discovered no technique for long preserving free government except that the Executive be under the law, and that the law be made by parliamentary deliberations.[6]

The Executive Power

In 1926 the journalist H. L. Mencken echoed Madison by observing that "there is no sense of power in merely executing laws." But Mencken took the thought in a rather more cynical direction: "no man would want to be President of the United States in strict accordance with the Constitution."[7]

A quick scan of Article II suggests why. The president is given the ability to grant reprieves and pardons, unchecked.[8] But most of the office's other enumerated powers come with an asterisk of sorts. The president's treaties must be ratified, and his appointments confirmed, by the Senate. The president may propose laws, but Congress must pass them; he may veto bills, but Congress can override him. He may conduct wars, but Congress declares them. The president may "require, in writing," the advice of his department heads, but Congress creates and funds the departments. Very little, it would seem, can be done by the president alone.

On the other hand, the first sentence of Article II declares that "the executive power shall be vested in a President of the United States of America." The "executive power" is nowhere defined. James Wilson, the most persuasive advocate of a strong executive at the Constitutional Convention, assured his colleagues that the only strictly executive powers under the Constitution were to carry out the laws and appoint personnel.[9] Nonetheless, the wording of the vesting clause has suggested to many—and certainly to many presidents—a broader reading.

For one thing, the parallel language pertaining to Congress in Article I includes a qualifier: "all legislative powers *herein granted* shall be vested in a Congress of the United States, which shall consist of a Senate and House of Representatives." Proponents of presidential authority as early as the Washington administration argued that this discrepancy means the executive power goes beyond the brief list of powers noted above. Others link the vesting clause to other clear or implied authorities. Grover Cleveland, for example, argued that the president possesses "a grant of all the power necessary to the performance of his duty in the faithful execution of the laws." Others, including the Supreme Court, have suggested that inherent powers are implied by the president's oath of office to "preserve, protect, and defend the Constitution," or by the title of commander in chief, even in peacetime, especially now that large standing armies have become a permanent part of American governance.[10]

Most presidents have believed that as long as an initiative was not specifically forbidden by the Constitution, "it was" (as Theodore Roosevelt put it) "not only [the President's] right but his duty to do anything that the needs of the Nation required."[11] This logic had special force in times of national emergency, which activated what the seventeenth century English philosopher John Locke called "prerogative"—the power of the executive "to act according to discretion, for the publick good, without the prescription of the Law, and sometimes even against it." Abraham Lincoln argued, in the context of the Civil War, that "measures, otherwise unconstitutional, might become lawful, by becoming indispensable to the preservation of the constitution, through the preservation of the nation." After the September 11, 2001, terrorist attacks, George W. Bush's Justice Department advised him that no statute could "place any limits on the President's determinations as to any terrorist threat, the amount of military force to be used in response, or the method, timing, and nature of the response. These decisions, under our Constitution, are for the President alone to make."[12]

These assertions have hardly gone unchallenged. After the Civil War, the Supreme Court upbraided Lincoln, arguing that any notion that the Constitution could be suspended by some "theory of necessity" was "pernicious" and "false." In 2004 the Court likewise reminded Bush that "a state of war is not a blank check for the President." William Howard Taft, rebutting his one-time mentor, Roosevelt, claimed that "the President can exercise no power which cannot be fairly and reasonably traced to some specific grant of power. . . . There is no undefined residuum of power which he can exercise because it seems to him to be in the public interest."[13]

Presidential power has also ebbed and flowed with political tides. In the 1970s, reacting to the steady growth of the office (and the growth spurt spurred by the Vietnam War and Watergate scandal) into what Arthur Schlesinger Jr. enduringly called the "imperial presidency," legislators pushed back.[14] In a series of enactments, they sought to create a much greater role for Congress in interbranch relations. Even a partial list of laws enacted during that decade gives a sense of the scope of Congress's ambition: the War Powers Resolution, the Intelligence Oversight Act, the Foreign Intelligence Surveillance Act, the Congressional Budget and Impoundment Control Act, the new Freedom of Information Act, and the Independent Counsel Act. In 1980, former president Gerald Ford complained that congressional efforts had been so successful that "[w]e have not an imperial presidency but an imperiled presidency."[15]

Yet the next thirty years would see presidents regain much of the ground they had lost, either by their own initiative or because Congress was unwilling to commit the time and political capital necessary to enforce the rules it had imposed. Presidents retained a solid base of authority grounded in their ability to grab the spotlight and set the public agenda, as well as in the commander-in-chief power and in executive authority over policy implementation through appointments and centralized management. Especially after Ronald Reagan's election in 1980, they refined these tools to enhance their influence over bureaucratic agencies and avoid legislative dictation. Further, Congress let the consultation procedures laid out in law—especially in the War Powers Resolution and Intelligence Oversight Act—be enforced on presidential terms, which is to say, rarely.[16] Even the process of impeaching the president, Congress's ultimate weapon, was exercised in 1998–1999 in the face of such hostile public opinion that it failed, bringing the independent counsel statute down with it as collateral damage. After the September 11 attacks, an array of broad discretionary powers were granted to the president and older ones were reasserted. Thus, Barack Obama took office in 2009 with a full toolkit of unilateral powers, albeit with a Congress newly resentful of the scope of their use.

The Growth of Executive Unilateralism: A Toolkit

How has historical practice equipped presidents for unilateral action? The answer is wide ranging, but in general presidents have engaged in strategies to control bureaucratic behavior and thus influence policy implementation, or they have exercised powers that flow specifically from emergency situations.

Controlling Bureaucratic Behavior

The president's power as chief executive expanded in concert with the growth of the executive establishment. Nearly four million people now work for the executive branch, spread across fifteen cabinet departments and nearly sixty independent agencies.[17] They report to the president but often have conflicting loyalties. Legislative power over their agencies' statutory missions and budgets; the contrast between the long tenure granted to civil servants and the relatively short presidential term; the conflicting demands of relevant interest groups and the national interest—all these mean that the president's preferences are far from automatically enforced upon the permanent government. But controlling bureaucratic behavior is worth the effort, for it means controlling policy.

Presidents have reacted to that challenge in various ways. One tactic has been to centralize functions in a large White House organization that can serve either to ride herd on or simply to evade the wider executive branch. The personal staff available to presidents has grown from a handful of aides under Franklin Roosevelt to about two thousand assistants with substantive duties under Barack Obama. New staff units can be created by each president to reflect personal priorities or societal concerns, from energy (Richard Nixon) to urban affairs (Barack Obama). These aides do not require Senate confirmation and do not suffer from divided loyalties. As Clinton advisor George Stephanopoulos wrote in his memoir, "doing the president's bidding was my reason for being; his favor was my fuel."[18]

The staff gives the president the resources to coordinate, or sometimes compete with, the advice given by bureaucratic actors. Occasionally the temptation to use it even to carry out policy has overtaken presidents' better judgment, as in the Iran-contra scandal that saw National Security Council aides engaged in covert operations and financial chicanery.[19]

From its position astride the annual budget process, the Office of Management and Budget (OMB), in particular, gives the president powerful leverage over bureaucratic behavior. Since 1921 federal law has required a unified executive budget, affording presidents a useful mechanism for managing their agenda. In 1939 Franklin Roosevelt moved OMB's predecessor, the Bureau of the Budget, from the Treasury department to the Executive Office of the President. Over time, OMB has picked up various management functions, as reflected in its current name. George W. Bush's "President's Management Agenda" empowered OMB to develop the Program Assessment Rating Tool, intended to grade the effectiveness of all government programs and link those grades to funding decisions.

Another method for controlling bureaucratic behavior is controlling the people who run the bureaucracy.[20] As the Reagan administration credo had it, "Personnel Is Policy." Presidents pay close attention to those personnel, starting with the 5,200 executive branch political appointments each president gets to make, ranging from the cabinet secretaries all the way to posts deep within the bureaucracy. By appointing personal loyalists throughout the executive branch—even, sometimes, to ostensibly nonpartisan positions such as inspector general and U.S. attorney—presidents have sought, in the words of one recent aide, to "implant their DNA throughout the government." To clone that DNA more widely, they have developed aggressive personnel recruitment and vetting operations. In one controversial case, Justice Department staff under George W. Bush changed the hiring procedures for civil service jobs in order to lock in Republican control of divisions considered insufficiently loyal to the president's priorities.[21] These efforts can be counterproductive. Loyalty that trumps competence can lead to performance in office that reflects badly on the president.

Although high-level appointees must receive Senate confirmation, the sheer size of the federal government means that many appointments have been vested directly in the president. Recent presidents have also rediscovered a useful unilateral tool for circumventing the confirmation process: the "recess appointment," which derives from a provision in Article II that allows presidents to fill vacancies while the Senate is in recess. (These appointees serve until the end of the next Senate session.) Although Congress is in near-continuous session, recess appointments remain a way of installing contested nominees without the Senate's interference. After Reagan was unable to abolish the Legal Services Corporation statutorily, for example, he used recess appointments to name a new board hostile to the agency's mandate. In all, Reagan made nearly 250 recess appointments in eight years, Clinton made nearly 140, and George W. Bush made more than 170—including two federal judges; a key OMB official overseeing regulatory review; and the ambassador to the United Nations, John Bolton.[22] To be sure, recess appointments may provoke a bitter congressional response and thus serve only as a temporary fix. Bolton, for instance, was not confirmed by the Senate when his recess appointment expired and had to vacate his post. When Democrats took control of the Senate in 2007, their leaders refused to allow the Senate to adjourn formally, even during holidays, to prevent further recess appointments.

Controlling Process

One of the president's most important duties is to "faithfully" execute the law. But the vagueness of many congressional enactments means that the specifics of that fidelity are subject to interpretation. In other cases, presidents may believe that part of a statute is unconstitutional and should not be executed. Presidents have therefore sought unilateral influence over the specifics of policy implementation, using devices ranging from the subtle manipulation of the agency rulemaking process to the issuance of direct administrative commands.

Rulemaking and Regulatory Review. For many reasons, including the complexity of contemporary issues and legislative lassitude, Congress often writes statutes that delegate authority to the executive branch to write the rules that transform the law's vague intent into specific governmental action.

The importance of the rulemaking process rose as the federal government grew. By the 1970s, federal regulation reached into most corners of American life. Because the rulemaking process is so complex, the regulations issued by executive agencies serve as a low-salience (even safely soporific) instrument for effecting tangible policy change, sometimes in ways not anticipated by a statute's sponsors.[23] For example, in early 2002 Congress passed the No Child Left Behind education reform act. But how its testing and accountability requirements would affect schools and students was not clear until the Department of Education issued rules governing what kind of tests were required and how state standards for measuring pupil performance would be defined. The department continued to issue revised regulations throughout both terms of the Bush administration, even as the act's reauthorization languished in the 109th and 110th Congresses.[24]

Part of the appeal of the personnel strategy is that it helps ensure that even lower-level appointees are in tune with administration policy preferences when it comes to writing regulations. It is no accident that the Department of Education is one of the most politicized agencies in the federal government.[25] Environmental, workplace safety, and health care policies have also attracted a good deal of recent attention from presidents seeking to shape regulatory outcomes.

One key mechanism for shaping these outcomes more systematically is OMB's process of "central clearance" of regulations. In 1981, after fits and starts in this direction by earlier presidents, Ronald Reagan issued an executive order declaring that "regulatory action shall not be undertaken unless the potential benefits to society for the regulation outweigh the potential costs to society." OMB's Office of Information and Regulatory Affairs (OIRA) was granted authority to recommend that regulations be withdrawn if they did not meet that test. In 1985 another order extended OMB's reach to agency "pre-rulemaking activities" and required OMB to approve an annual regulatory program for each agency. In 2007 George W. Bush added a new layer of control by ordering that a political appointee must approve each agency's regulatory program. Bush also ordered that "significant guidance documents"—that is, advisory opinions that do not reach the formal status of rules—be included within the scope of OIRA review.[26] Others in the White House may also weigh in. Under Bush, the Office of the Vice President was particularly active in this regard.

The process as it has developed is largely off-the-record, since rulemaking power is formally vested directly in agencies, not the president. It is no less effective at shaping outcomes for that. In 2008, for instance, a major potential regulatory change in the government's stance on greenhouse gas emissions was preempted by White House resistance.[27]

Despite intermittent congressional grumbling about the elevation of ideology over expertise, there has been little formal legislative reaction to the regulatory review process, which has remained in place across presidencies of both parties for almost thirty years.

Signing Statements and Item Vetoes. Another means that presidents use to direct policy implementation is the issuance of "signing statements" when they sign bills into law. These statements give the president a chance to comment on various aspects of the new statute, congratulate its sponsors, and pledge future good wishes—but also, more crucially, to influence its judicial interpretation, guide agency rulemaking, and announce how the executive branch will enforce the disputed provisions. Although examples of signing statements can be found as far back as the Monroe administration, Reagan and his successors pioneered a more systematic usage. George W. Bush's use of signing statements to declare certain items within bills unconstitutional attracted considerable attention because of the scale and scope of their issuance. By one count, he issued more statements than all other presidents combined, recording nearly 1,200 objections to parts of more than 170 laws—including 116 separate objections to the Consolidated Appropriations Act of 2005 alone.[28]

Signing statements take a number of tacks. Most commonly, they serve as a means for the president to object to congressional incursions across the border between Articles I and II. In 1999, for instance, Bill Clinton defied a statutory dictate to fill vacancies at the newly created National Nuclear Security Administration with existing Energy Department staff. In 2001 George W. Bush likewise ignored a directive from Congress to submit a bill addressing livestock diseases, saying he would interpret it instead as a suggestion to do so. As a candidate, Barack Obama claimed that "no one doubts that it is appropriate to use signing statements to protect a president's constitutional prerogatives," and he followed through by issuing his first such statement in March 2009.[29]

Obama claimed to be providing "transparency" by making his objections public; Reagan, by contrast, saw signing statements as traction in court cases. A 1986 memo by his aide Samuel Alito (who now sits on the Supreme Court) noted that "our primary objective is to ensure that Presidential signing statements assume their rightful place in the interpretation of legislation." Alito acknowledged the "potential increase of presidential power" these statements entailed and the likely resentment they would stir in Congress. He also asked a key question: "What happens when there is a clear conflict between the congressional and presidential understanding? Whose intent controls?"[30]

Alito offered no answer to this question. But presidents have done so, especially in claims concerning foreign policy. For example, after Reagan issued a national security directive with strict enforcement provisions governing leaks of sensitive information, Congress passed a bill forbidding the administration from enforcing those provisions. Reagan signed the bill but stated in doing so that he would not enforce the ban on enforcement. Since it "impermissibly interfered with my ability to prevent unauthorized disclosures of our most sensitive diplomatic, military, and intelligence activities," Reagan said, "in accordance with my sworn obligation to preserve, protect, and defend the Constitution, [it] will be considered of no force or effect." Other presidents have routinely included similar language in signing statements in order to reject provisions that, as George W. Bush put it, "unconstitutionally constrain my authority regarding the conduct of diplomacy and my authority as Commander-in-Chief."[31] In late 2006, Bush's signing statement to an act regulating atomic energy cooperation between the United States and India claimed that because Congress could not "purpor[t] to establish U.S. policy with respect to various international affairs matters," he would consider the law's ban on the transfer to India of certain nuclear materials to be merely "advisory."[32]

Treating the law as "advisory" aroused particular controversy in late 2005 when Bush asserted that he would construe the Detainee Treatment Act's ban against "cruel, inhuman, or degrading treatment or punishment" of prisoners captured in the war on terror "in a manner consistent with the constitutional authority of the President to supervise the unitary executive branch and as Commander in Chief and consistent with the constitutional limitations on the judicial power."[33] Bush's argument was that congressional regulation of detainee treatment was itself unconstitutional because it overrode the president's authority as commander in chief to conduct the war as he saw fit. Yet whether that power was exclusively executive was far from clear. Others pointed to Congress's Article I power to "make rules for . . . the regulation of the land and naval forces" and "rules concerning capture on land or water."

In any case, signing statements provide a clear example of how presidents claim the right to determine how—and if—laws will be implemented. The language presidents use to assert that claim may be formulaic, but the claim itself is a broad affirmation of the executive power. Still, the practical effect of signing statements on policy implementation is hard to determine. A 2008 report by a congressional auditor found that executive agencies had implemented twenty of twenty-nine selected statutory provisions in accordance with the president's statements, but that courts had placed little reliance on them in parsing the meaning of statutes.[34]

Signing statements are a variant of the line-item veto that most state governors have. Unlike those governors, presidents may not veto specific provisions of legislation. But this has not stopped them from long claiming the right to refuse to spend appropriated funds when, as in Ulysses Grant's declaration, these funds are "of purely private or local interest." At times Congress has given presidents discretionary impoundment power in order to limit expenditures. President Nixon upped the ante by arguing that this was not necessary—that although Congress had the power to appropriate funds, the executive power covered their actual expenditure. "The Constitutional right of the President of the United States to impound funds," he claimed, "is absolutely clear." Nixon's impoundments eventually encompassed about a fifth of the federal government's discretionary spending, aimed largely at programs whose passage he had opposed.[35]

That practice was made illegal by the 1974 Impoundment Control Act and declared unconstitutional in the 1975 case *Train v. City of New York*.[36] Still, the issue of presidential control of spending has never gone away. Times of budget deficit tend to revive pressure for some form of line-item veto, peaking in 1996 when Congress provided the president with "enhanced rescission" power. This allowed the president's vetoes of specific spending or revenue items to go into effect unless Congress passed a bill to reinstate them (a bill that could itself be vetoed). President Clinton used briefly what Senate Appropriations Committee chair Ted Stevens called "the most significant delegation of authority by the Congress to the President since the Constitution was ratified," but the law was declared unconstitutional by the Supreme Court in 1998. When persistent deficits returned in the mid-2000s, George W. Bush again urged legislation providing item veto authority. It passed only in the House, but with budget deficits pushing $1.5 trillion annually as Barack Obama took office, a bipartisan group of senators made similar proposals in the spring of 2009.[37]

Executive Orders. Another instrument for executing the law is the executive order. Recent presidents have issued on average nearly one per week during their terms. Approximately 30,000 have been issued overall since 1789.[38]

Executive orders take various forms and names, including proclamations, national security directives, and presidential decision memoranda.[39] By whatever name, executive orders are presidential directives intended to shape the manner in which the president's powers are carried out by the executive branch. Thus the legal authority of an executive order must derive from either the law or the Constitution.

Executive orders typically make for uninspiring reading. They lay out careful definitions; they set agency priorities and procedures; they organize task forces, reorganize bureaus, and shape decision-making processes. But the dull prose disguises their real power to control military action or to effect new and important policies. The Louisiana Purchase was consummated by an executive order in the form of a proclamation, as was the emancipation of the slaves during the Civil War. Presidents have used executive orders to create everything from Indian reservations to marine sanctuaries and to mold policies ranging from federal procurement to the treatment of suspected terrorists detained at Guantánamo Bay.

A recent trend has been for new presidents to kick off their terms by issuing multiple orders designed to set the symbolic tone for their administration. One of Bill Clinton's first actions in January 1993 was to end a "gag rule" that had, in the Reagan and George H. W. Bush administrations, prohibited abortion counseling and referrals by family planning clinics that received federal funds. George W. Bush reversed Clinton's order in January 2001. Eight years later, Barack Obama restored it. He also issued a flurry of other directives reversing George W. Bush administration policies concerning everything from CIA interrogations to the Environmental Protection Agency's regulatory stance toward greenhouse gas emissions.

As this sequence suggests, executive orders are both powerful and constrained. Although they have the force of law, they can be overturned not only by subsequent administrations but also by congressional action or court ruling. In late 2006, for example, a district court judge overturned George W. Bush's September 2001 executive order naming various groups and individuals as "specially designated global terrorists." The judge objected to the president's claim to "unfettered discretion."[40]

Still, outright negation of an executive order is relatively rare. And in the interim, executive orders can give the president power to mold or remold the policy landscape, thereby shaping Hamilton's "antecedent state of things." Like regulations, executive orders often move under the political radar screen. Unlike regulations, their formulation may legally evade public comment. Although the number of executive orders issued by presidents has dropped since the early 1940s, the number of significant orders has risen dramatically. One exhaustive survey of the executive orders issued between 1936 and 1999 found that the proportion of substantively significant orders tripled from the 1950s to the 1990s. A separate study concluded that the number and scope of substantive orders has risen sharply since the Reagan administration.[41]

Executive orders are supposed to be grounded in statutory or constitutional authority. In practice, they often embody the unintended consequences of congressional delegation. Clinton's 1996 set-aside of millions of acres of Utah land as a national monument, for example, rested on a 1906 statute long forgotten by Congress, but not by presidents. Franklin Roosevelt closed the banks in 1933 under authority granted to Woodrow Wilson in World War I. Even congressional efforts to constrain executive authority sometimes legitimate it. In 1977 Congress passed the International Emergency Economic Powers Act (IEEPA) to limit the use of certain emergency powers. But by providing a statutory process for declaring emergencies as a means of preventing economic transactions with disfavored regimes, Congress legitimized a previously shadowy claim to power—and presidents invoked the act to issue executive orders declaring thirty "national emergencies" between 1979 and 2000. In some cases these orders overrode legislative preferences, as when President Reagan applied IEEPA sanctions against Nicaragua in 1985 as a substitute for those Congress had refused to enact.[42] As Clinton aide Rahm Emanuel put it in 1998, "Sometimes we use [an executive order] in reaction to legislative delay or setbacks. Obviously, you'd rather pass legislation that can do X, but you're willing to make whatever progress you can on an agenda item."[43]

Executive orders are less contentious when clearly grounded in a statute or when they move in areas unaddressed by congressional enactment. Greater controversy occurs when orders seek to elide those enactments or when they rely not on clearly delegated authority but on a broad sense of the executive power. Consider, for instance, the brief and vague justification offered by Harry Truman when he nationalized America's steel mills: it was done "by virtue of the authority vested in me by the Constitution and laws of the United States, and as President of the United States."[44] Federal courts tend to move case-by-case when considering executive orders, but they usually give presidents the benefit of the doubt when Congress has failed to decide an issue over a prolonged period. Practice trumps theory: an early-twentieth-century case suggested that as "government is a practical affair, intended for practical men," courts should presume that "unauthorized acts [by the president] would not have been allowed [by Congress] to be so often repeated as to crystallize into a regular practice."[45]

Presidents, then, may proceed confidently in the absence of congressional disapproval. Even when faced with it, they often choose to act on the assumption that Congress will acquiesce eventually; often, they are right.

Emergency Powers in Peace and War

Crises empower the executive branch. A menacing world enhances the value of centralized leadership's swift decision-making capacity. By the middle of the twentieth century, which was marked by wars cold and hot, the United States had settled into a seemingly perpetual period of crisis. What would have been "emergencies in policy" in the world before World War II, Richard E. Neustadt wrote in 1960, quickly became business as usual—"a way of life."[46] With the threat of nuclear Armageddon, and then international terrorism, as the backdrop, [47] national security became the primary justification for unilateral executive action in the post–World War II era. Such action was often encouraged and empowered by legislative delegation.

Domestic Crisis. Because threats to security do not always come from abroad, presidents may wield emergency powers during periods of economic instability, domestic unrest, or natural disaster. "In the event Congress shall fail to act, and act adequately, I shall accept the responsibility, and I will act," Franklin Roosevelt declared in 1942. "The President has the powers, under the Constitution, and under Congressional acts, to take measures necessary to avert a disaster." Roosevelt was seeking a law authorizing wage and price controls, and he got one. Indeed, although FDR relied heavily on executive initiatives to attack the Great Depression and rally the nation (he issued 654 executive orders in 1933 alone), in most cases he received quick and sometimes retroactive congressional approval.

Subsequent presidents have also received blanket authority from Congress to deal with economic crises. Richard Nixon was able to impose wage and price controls, and take the dollar off the gold standard, in August 1971. The Emergency Economic Stabilization Act of 2008 gave George W. Bush's Treasury department wide discretion in designing a program to disburse $700 billion in funds to prop up the collapsing banking sector. [48] Presidential authority over efforts to help the economy was augmented yet again by the $787 billion American Recovery and Reinvestment Act passed in 2009.

Domestic Unrest and Natural Disaster. Presidential emergency powers include stand-by authority to call out federal troops or take control of state national guards in order to quell domestic unrest or deter violence. Such authority has been used in the United States to put down strikes, protect mail delivery, and impose order during natural disasters and urban riots.

During the nineteenth century, the most common use of presidential police power involved labor unrest. Hoping to prevent violence between strikers and company security forces, presidents often used troops to break strikes. As recently as 1970, President Nixon responded to a postal strike by calling out federal troops to sort and deliver the mail.

In the 1950s and 1960s presidents deployed federal troops or state national guards to keep the peace during efforts to enforce racial desegregation. For example, in 1957 Dwight Eisenhower sent troops to Little Rock, Arkansas, to protect children enrolling in integrated schools from angry mobs. During the late 1960s, when lawless disorder was instead in inner cities or linked to U.S. involvement in Vietnam, soldiers again were used frequently to maintain the peace. More recently, George H. W. Bush sent Marines to help quell the looting triggered by the 1992 acquittal of white Los Angeles police officers accused in the severe beating of Rodney King, an African American suspect.

Presidential emergency powers are also invoked frequently during natural disasters such as hurricanes, floods, or earthquakes. By declaring a local state of emergency, the president sets in motion government machinery that can provide immediate food, shelter, and police protection, as well as longer-term economic aid. Bill Clinton used disaster relief to build political support after the massive floods along the Mississippi River in 1993 and California's Northridge earthquake in 1994. Barely a week after his inauguration, Barack Obama declared states of emergency after winter storms in Arkansas and Kentucky. But such powers can be a double-edged sword. In August 1992, Florida residents complained bitterly about the Bush administration's tardy response to Hurricane Andrew, and Clinton won the state in November. Far worse, after Hurricane Katrina devastated the Gulf Coast and especially the city of New Orleans in 2005, federal officials' slow reaction to, and even apparent denial of, events on the ground—all of it broadcast live to a disbelieving world—prompted widespread anger at the perceived incompetence of George W. Bush's administration.[49] Expectations for presidential action in response to domestic unrest and natural disasters may be inflated (not least by presidential promises), but they are no less real for that.

War Powers. In foreign relations, and most of all in times of war, presidential powers reach their greatest expanse. Since 1789 the United States has entered myriad hostilities of all shapes and sizes, from declared wars to brief "police actions." In each instance, presidents have asserted claims to inherent powers to deal with the threat at hand.[50]

These claims often are based on a broad reading of the executive power. The 1936 Supreme Court decision *U.S. v. Curtiss-Wright*—a text cherished by presidents, but by few scholars of constitutional law—affirmed the "very delicate, plenary, and exclusive power of the President as the sole organ of the federal government in the field of international relations—a power which does not require as a basis for its exercise an act of Congress." When Franklin Roosevelt sought to aid Hitler's enemies, despite legislative efforts to maintain American neutrality, he declared first a "limited" and then (after the fall of France) an "unlimited" state of emergency. Roosevelt also concluded a series of executive agreements making important commitments to foreign governments. Most famously the United States transferred fifty destroyers to Britain in return for eight Caribbean naval bases. The attorney general's opinion justifying the agreement was grounded partly in the "plenary powers of the President as Commander-in-Chief of the Army and Navy and as head of state in its relations with foreign countries."[51]

This formulation stuck. When President Reagan sent Marines to Lebanon in 1982, for instance, he said the troops had been deployed under his "constitutional authority with respect to the conduct of foreign relations and as Commander-in-Chief." Truman never sought congressional approval for the Korean War; and although George H. W. Bush did, for the first Gulf War, he said he did not need to: "I didn't have to get permission from some old goat in the United States Congress to kick Saddam Hussein out of Kuwait." An interesting twist in these cases, as well as in Bill Clinton's air war with Serbia over Kosovo, was the erroneous claim that decisions by international organizations such as the UN and NATO could substitute for congressional action in activating presidential war powers.[52] But on the whole, presidents have resisted admitting to an absolute need for external authorization of any sort in such circumstances; instead they assert, as George W. Bush's Justice Department wrote in 2002, that "the Constitution grants the President unilateral power to take military action to protect the national security interests of the United States. ... This independent authority is *supplemented* by congressional authorization."[53]

Even so, wartime also tends to lead to broad congressional grants of executive authority to prosecute war, both on the military and economic fronts. Woodrow Wilson and Franklin Roosevelt, during World Wars I and II, respectively, received such grants. Congress also authorized the first Gulf War in 1991 and the second in 2003, voting in the latter case to grant largely unfettered autonomy to George W. Bush to renew the fight with Saddam Hussein. In 1964 and 2001, even more expansive discretionary powers were delegated to Presidents Johnson and Bush, respectively, to allow them to respond to outside aggression: the disputed Gulf of Tonkin attacks in Vietnam, and the terrorist attacks on New York and Washington. In September 2001, Congress resolved that "the president has authority under the Constitution to take action to deter and prevent acts of international terrorism against the United States" and authorized "all necessary and appropriate force against those nations, organizations, or persons he determines planned, authorized, committed, or aided the terrorist attacks that occurred on September 11, 2001, or harbored such organizations or persons, in order to prevent any future acts of international terrorism against the United States. . . ." This wide authority—along with $40 billion in discretionary funding also provided by Congress—was used almost immediately to overthrow the Taliban regime in Afghanistan and was critical to justifying far-flung executive action.

Presidents do not always inform Congress about their actions abroad. The use of executive agreements to cut binding deals with foreign leaders is one way they can institute policy change without going through the arduous process of seeking Senate ratification of a treaty. The Case-Zablocki Act of 1972 was supposed to make sure that such agreements were reported to Congress, but enforcement of this requirement has been spotty. President Reagan concluded 3,000 such agreements between 1981 and 1988, compared with only 125 treaties. Agreements outnumbered treaties by more than nine to one under Presidents George H. W. Bush and Clinton. George W. Bush chose an executive agreement rather than a treaty to formalize a long-term arrangement with Iraq about the continued presence of U.S. troops in that country.[54]

Covert action is also largely an executive operation. The CIA and other intelligence organizations have long constituted a "secret arm of the executive, with a secret budget."[55] "Black ops" helped guide the overthrow of governments in Iran, Guatemala, and Laos in the 1950s but failed to do so in Cuba in the 1960s and Nicaragua in the 1980s. Covert operations remain important weapons in the foreign affairs arsenal. CIA agents were among the first to arrive in Afghanistan in 2001 and Iraq in 2003, and "human intelligence" has demonstrated particular value in the battle against terrorism. In the aftermath of the September 11 attacks, the operation of "black sites" in various places around the world, and the practice of "extraordinary rendition," were justified by the same claims about executive power that underlay the dispute about interrogation techniques noted earlier.[56]

Although Congress has sought to require consultation before and notification after intelligence operations, presidents have been reluctant to comply. In part, they suspect correctly that Congress has trouble keeping secrets. Sometimes, however, secrecy is simply a useful means to fend off legislative interference. Confidentiality and accountability coexist uneasily at best, as suggested by an extraordinary handwritten letter from Sen. John Rockefeller, the senior Democratic member of the Senate Select Committee on Intelligence, to Vice President Dick Cheney in 2003. "The activities we discussed raise profound oversight issues," Rockefeller wrote, carefully not mentioning the administration's domestic wiretapping program. "Given the security restrictions associated with this information, and my inability to consult staff or counsel on my own, I feel unable to fully evaluate, much less endorse these activities."[57]

As the subject matter of that example illustrates, covert action can occur at home as well as abroad. During World War II, Franklin Roosevelt directed his attorney general to surveil "persons suspected of subversive activities against the Government of the United States." This policy extended most infamously to FDR's executive order authorizing the detention of more than 100,000 Japanese Americans in internment camps for the duration of the war. During the Vietnam War, Lyndon Johnson and Richard Nixon used the intelligence agencies to investigate Americans and determine whether they posed threats to national security, a program that included interception of mail and phone calls, break-ins, and the use of informers to infiltrate antiwar groups. [58]

George W. Bush's interpretation of the commander-in-chief power was even broader. In October 2001, Bush issued a secret executive order authorizing the National Security Agency to track communications between suspected terrorists abroad and Americans within the United States. This order violated the 1978 Foreign Intelligence Surveillance Act, which generally required a warrant by a special court in order to conduct such surveillance. When the wiretapping program became public in late 2005, the administration argued that the president had both inherent and statutory powers to order such wiretaps as a "fundamental incident" of warfare, "supported by the President's well-recognized inherent constitutional authority as Commander in Chief and sole organ for the Nation in foreign affairs to conduct warrantless surveillance of enemy forces for intelligence purposes to detect and disrupt armed attacks on the United States. The President has the chief responsibility under the Constitution to protect America from attack, and the Constitution gives the President the authority necessary to fulfill that solemn responsibility." By this reasoning, any statute that sought to limit the president's "core exercise of Commander in Chief control" was unconstitutional and did not need to be enforced.[59]

The Bush administration's reasoning in its defense of the wiretapping program extended to a variety of unilateral claims stemming from the commander-in-chief power. Similar language was used to defend the president's power to use military force within the United States and to designate individuals—even U.S. citizens—as "enemy combatants" who could be held indefinitely without charge, removed from normal judicial processes, and tried by military commissions established by presidential decree.[60] The methods used to interrogate those detainees were likewise deemed to be within the commander in chief's sole purview, as made clear by the signing statement to the Detainee Treatment Act. As late as 2007, after the Supreme Court had overturned the administration's military commission system in the *Hamdan* case, Bush issued an executive order establishing that the president's determinations regarding what interrogation procedures were legal "shall be treated as authoritative for all purposes as a matter of United States law, including satisfaction of the international obligations of the United States."[61]

Secrecy and Executive Privilege

A final issue deserves mention: the power to impose a cloak of secrecy over executive branch actions. Checking presidential power requires that other political actors know what the president is doing; the penchants for executive secrecy and for excluding Congress from decision making are linked. Federal law mandates that executive orders and proclamations be published but allows for secret orders to protect the public interest in dealing with military or intelligence matters. Presidents also issue classified executive directives drafted through the National Security Council staffing process. In the mid-1980s, secret directives underlay the policies that devolved into the Iran-contra scandal. In the 1990s, such directives dealt with emerging issues of counterintelligence and cyber-warfare. In the 2000s, they shaped national strategies toward ballistic missile defense and the war on terror.[62] More generally, presidents control classification procedures and intelligence gathering, and the amount of "secret" information has grown enormously. Manipulation of the classification process can shape the information legislators have—or don't have—when making decisions about presidential initiatives.

A related issue is the exercise of "executive privilege," which, when claimed as an offshoot of Article II's "executive power," prevents congressional oversight of—presidents would say, meddling with—administration behavior. Although the phrase dates only to the 1950s, the practice of executive privilege extends back to the Washington administration. From the start, most presidents have claimed the right to determine what, in James Polk's phrase, is "compatible with the public interest to communicate."[63] Later, as the Executive Office of the President grew, claims of privilege expanded to include other links in the advisory chain, based on the model of lawyer-client privilege. Nixon's attorney general, Richard Kleindienst, told a Senate hearing that the president could direct any member of the executive branch to refuse information in response to a congressional request. "Your power to get what the President knows," Kleindienst said, "is in the President's hands."[64]

That argument ran aground on the shoals of Watergate, when a unanimous Supreme Court ruled in the 1974 case of *U.S. v. Nixon* that the president had to release the incriminating tape recordings that subsequently forced his resignation from office. But although Nixon lost that battle, presidents won the war, since the Court also held that some sort of communications "privilege is . . . inextricably rooted in the separation of powers under the Constitution." When "military, diplomatic, or sensitive national security secrets" were at stake, the Court owed the president "great deference." In 1994 a circuit court endorsed a "presidential communications privilege" that, when invoked, made documents "presumptively privileged."[65] The idea was to protect the confidentiality of the advice presidents receive to ensure it would be given freely.

In itself this doctrine is a reasonable offshoot of the separation of powers. But it can be taken too far. The Clinton administration, for example, refused a congressional request for documents dealing with its policy toward Haiti on the grounds that Congress had no power to conduct oversight of foreign affairs. The George W. Bush administration went to the Supreme Court, successfully, to defend the principle of withholding from congressional auditors even basic information about an energy policy task force headed by Vice President Cheney.[66]

Barack Obama began his presidency with memoranda telling executive agencies that he was "committed to creating an unprecedented level of openness in Government" and that "in the face of doubt, openness prevails" in questions involving Freedom of Information Act requests.[67] Experience suggests, however, that in at least some cases the temptations of secrecy will override these good intentions.

"Perfectly Coordinate"

An aide to President John Kennedy once observed, "Everybody believes in democracy—until they get to the White House."[68] Congress is the first branch of government, and it remains the institution with the greatest potential authority over the workings of government. Yet from the other end of Pennsylvania Avenue, Congress's version of democracy seems frustratingly slow and "process"-driven, the challenges of presidential leadership seem immense, and the enumerated powers of the office appear limited. Successful leadership, it has long seemed to presidents, depends on evading congressional constraint by expanding the bounds of executive power.

The result is that presidents have pushed to do things on their own: to define the vague terms of their charter expansively. Sometimes Congress has pushed back, but often it has not. Sometimes it has even helped presidents to get the powers they want. As the federal government grew enormously in size and scope, presidents' administrative authority grew with it. The broad outcome has been an accretion of precedents for unilateral presidential power, despite latent congressional authority and occasional periods of congressional resurgence.

Few would argue that presidents should not enjoy at least some discretionary authority when administering laws and carrying out executive functions. Looking ahead, the key questions concern the scope of that authority and who gets to define it. The theory of the "unitary executive"—that the executive power is indivisible—is fine to the extent that it holds that all of the executive powers under the Constitution are exercised by the president. But problems arise when, as in recent iterations of the theory, it holds further that only the president can determine what those powers are.[69] As Madison wrote in *The Federalist* no. 49, "The several departments being perfectly co-ordinate, . . . none of them . . . can pretend to an exclusive or superior right of settling the boundaries between their respective powers." Much as the president might prefer it, he is not alone in his responsibilities. Nor is the president always right.

One of the president's mandates, then, is to exercise leadership through coalition, not command; by persuasion, not dictate. As heavy reliance on unilateral action becomes the norm, it reinforces itself, potentially undermining democratic accountability. During his first week in office, President Obama reversed many of the policies implemented by the Bush administration executive orders—but he did so by executive order.

Although the presidency still has potent tools readily at hand, presidents may want to rethink their automatic resort to these tools. When the contributions of other political actors are neither desired nor valued, both the quality and legitimacy of the president's decisions are lessened. More pragmatically, as setbacks mount the president may be left out on a lonely limb, without support from others who have a stake in the choices he has made. George W. Bush aide Jack Goldsmith has written eloquently of the irony that results when "the hard power of prerogative" is undermined by the president's failure to "take the softer aspects of power seriously."[70] There are risks not just to the polity, then, but also to presidents, in acting alone.

Notes

1. "President's Remarks at Faith-Based and Community Initiatives Conference," Office of the White House Press Secretary, March 3, 2004; Executive Orders 13199 and 13279.

2. Quoted in James Bennet, "True to Form, Clinton Shifts Energies Back to U.S. Focus," *New York Times*, July 5, 1998.

3. Alexander Hamilton, first letter as "Pacificus," 1793; see the University of Chicago's "Founders' Constitution" site, http://press-pubs.uchicago.edu/founders/print_documents/a2‑2‑2‑3s14.html.

4. James Madison, first letter as "Helvidius," 1793, available at http://press-pubs.uchicago.edu/founders/documents/a2‑2‑2‑3s15.html.

5. "Cato," Letter V, 1787, www.liberty-page.com/foundingdocs/antifedpap/cato/5.html; in response, see especially (if ironically), Hamilton, *Federalist* no. 69.

6. Jackson, concurring opinion to *Youngstown Sheet & Tube v. Sawyer*, 343 U.S. 579 (1952).

7. H. L. Mencken, *Notes on Democracy* (New York: Dissident Books, 2009 [1926]), 139.

8. This power, while unilateral, is substantively different from those discussed in this chapter. However, see Jeffrey Crouch, *The Presidential Pardon Power* (Lawrence: University Press of Kansas, 2009).

9. Indeed, later scholars argued, if the president was vested with vast executive authority, why bother to authorize him to seek written opinions from his department heads? See David Gray Adler and Michael A. Genovese, "Introduction," in *The Presidency and the Law: The Clinton Legacy*, ed. Adler and Genovese (Lawrence: University Press of Kansas, 2002).

10. Grover Cleveland, *The Independence of the Executive* (Princeton: Princeton University Press, 1913), 14–15; in *In re Neagle* (135 U.S. 1 [1890]), the Court agreed that the oath must, "by necessary implication," be read to "invest the President with self-executing powers; that is, powers independent of statute."

11. Theodore Roosevelt, *An Autobiography* (New York: Da Capo Press, 1985), 372.

12. John Locke, "*Second Treatise of Government*," ed. C.B. Macpherson (Indianapolis: Hackett, 1980 [1690]), 84; "Abraham Lincoln to Albert Hodges," April 4, 1864, reprinted in *The President, Congress, and the Constitution*, ed. Christopher H. Pyle and Richard M. Pious (New York: Free Press, 1984), 65; George W. Bush, Office of Legal Counsel opinion of 25 September 2001, www.usdoj.gov/olc/warpowers925.htm. See also Thomas Jefferson's earlier formulation, in which he argued that "to lose our country by a scrupulous adherence to written law, would be to lose the law itself, with life, liberty, property and all those who are enjoying them with us; thus absurdly sacrificing the end to the means." "Jefferson to Colvin, September 10, 1810," reprinted in Pyle and Pious, eds., *President, Congress, and the Constitution*, 62.

13. *Ex parte Milligan*, 71 U.S. (4 Wall.) 2 (1866); *Hamdi v. Rumsfeld*, 542 U.S. 507 (2004); William Howard Taft, *Our Chief Magistrate and His Powers* (1916), in Pyle and Pious, eds., *President, Congress, and the Constitution*, 70–71.

14. Arthur M. Schlesinger Jr., *The Imperial Presidency* (Boston: Houghton Mifflin, 1973); for more detail and a bibliography, see Andrew Rudalevige, *The New Imperial Presidency: Renewing Presidential Power after Watergate* (Ann Arbor: University of Michigan Press, 2005).

15. Gerald Ford interview in *Time*, November 10, 1980, 30.

16. Louis Fisher and David Gray Adler, "The War Powers Resolution: Time to Say Goodbye," *Political Science Quarterly* 113 (Spring 1998): 1–20.

17. This figure includes approximately 700,000 postal employees and 1.4 million military personnel.

18. George Stephanopoulos, *All Too Human: A Political Education* (Boston: Little, Brown, 1999), 210.

19. See John P. Burke, chap. 12, this volume; David E. Lewis, "Staffing Alone: Unilateral Action and the Politicization of the Executive Office of the President," *Presidential Studies Quarterly* 35 (September 2005): 496–514. New staffs can be created by executive order but must attract congressional appropriation to become permanent.

20. David E. Lewis, *The Politics of Presidential Appointments* (Princeton: Princeton University Press, 2008).

21. Reagan aide quoted in Thomas J. Weko, *The Politicizing Presidency: The White House Personnel Office, 1948–1994* (Lawrence: University Press of Kansas, 1994), 89; Bush aide quoted in Mike Allen, "Bush to Change Economic Team," *Washington Post*, November 29, 2004, A1. More generally, see Richard Nathan, *The Administrative*

Presidency (New York: Macmillan, 1983); Alexis Simendinger, "Help Wanted," *National Journal*, December 16, 2006, 26–29; Charlie Savage, *Takeover* (Boston: Little, Brown, 2007), 294Ff.

22. Simendinger, "Help Wanted," 29; Henry B. Hogue and Maureen Bearden, *Recess Appointments Made by President George W. Bush*, Report RL33310 (Washington, D.C.: Congressional Research Service, November 3, 2008).

23. Cornelius Kerwin, *Rulemaking: How Government Agencies Write Law and Make Policy*, 3rd ed. (Washington, D.C.: CQ Press, 2003).

24. See the announcement of October 2008 regulations at www.ed.gov/policy/elsec/ reg/title1/webcasts.html.

25. Lewis, *Politics of Presidential Appointees*, chap. 3.

26. See Executive Orders 12291, 12498, and 13422; Kenneth R. Mayer, *With the Stroke of a Pen: Executive Orders and Presidential Power* (Princeton: Princeton University Press, 2001), 125–134; Cindy Skrzycki, "Tiny OIRA Still Exercises Its Real Influence Invisibly," *Washington Post*, November 11, 2003, E1; William F. West, "The Institutionalization of Regulatory Review: Organizational Stability and Neutral Competence at OIRA," *Presidential Studies Quarterly* 35 (March 2005): 76–93.

27. John Shiffman and John Sullivan, "An Eroding Mission at EPA," *Philadelphia Inquirer*, December 7, 2008, A1.

28. Thanks to Christopher Kelley for this count of signing statement objections as of October 15, 2008, available at www.users.muohio.edu/kelleycs; *Weekly Compilation of Presidential Documents*, December 8, 2004, 2924.

29. Michael Abramowitz, "On Signing Statements, McCain Says 'Never,' Obama and Clinton 'Sometimes,'" *Washington Post*, February 25, 2008, A13; Office of the White House Press Secretary, "Statement by the President," March 11, 2009; Phillip J. Cooper, *By Order of the President: The Use and Abuse of Executive Direct Action* (Lawrence: University Press of Kansas, 2002), 204ff.

30. Samuel A. Alito Jr., to Litigation Strategy Working Group, "Using Presidential Signing Statement to Make Fuller Use of the President's Constitutionally Assigned Role in the Process of Enacting Law," National Archives, RG 60, Files of Stephen Galebach, Accession 060-89-269, Box 6.

31. Cooper, *By Order of the President*; and Phillip J. Cooper, "George W. Bush, Edgar Allan Poe, and the Use and Abuse of the Presidential Signing Statement," *Presidential Studies Quarterly* 35 (September 2005): 515–532. See also Christopher S. Kelley, ed., *Executing the Presidency* (Albany: State University of New York Press, 2006), chap. 4.

32. "President's Statement on H.R. 5682," Office of the White House Press Secretary, December 18, 2006.

33. "President's Statement on Signing of H.R. 2863," Office of the White House Press Secretary, December 30, 2005.

34. *Presidential Signing Statements: Agency Implementation of Selected Provisions of Law*, GAO-08-553T, U.S. Government Accountability Office, March 11, 2008; it is not clear whether GAO's analysis covered a representative sample of such statements. A circuit court once scolded the Reagan administration's effort to avoid parts of a contracting act by saying "this claim of right for the President to declare statutes unconstitutional and to declare his refusal to execute them . . . is dubious at best." See *Ameron, v. U.S. Army Corps of Engineers*, 787 F.2D 875 (3D Cir. 1986). But see also 18 *Opinions of the Office of Legal Counsel* 199 (1994), listing Supreme Court decisions that purportedly condoned signing statements.

35. James Sundquist, *The Decline and Resurgence of Congress* (Washington, D.C.: Brookings Institution, 1981), 202ff; Schlesinger, *Imperial Presidency*, 239.

36. *Train v. City of New York*, 420 U.S. 35 (1975).

37. Rudalevige, *New Imperial Presidency*, 141–149; Peter Baker, "Bush Calls on Senate to Pass Line-Item Veto," *Washington Post*, June 28, 2006, A3; "Unlikely Team Pushes Line-Item Veto Bill," CBS News, March 4, 2009, www.cbsnews.com/stories/2009/03/04/politics/100days/main4842840.shtml.

38. President Obama's order on Detention Policy Options of January 22, 2009, was Executive Order 13493. However, haphazard record-keeping before 1946 likely means that between 15,000 and 50,000 directives were never recorded. In 1946 Congress mandated that the text of all nonclassified executive orders, executive branch announcements, proposals, and regulations be published in the *Federal Register*. See Mayer, *With the Stroke of a Pen*. Executive orders back to 1937 are available online from the National Archives, www.archives.gov/federal-register/executive-orders/disposition.html.

39. The Supreme Court ruled in 1879 that there is no material difference between proclamations and executive orders; nor is there much practical difference between executive orders and the other forms of presidential orders described most comprehensively in Cooper, *By Order of the President*. See also Graham Dodds, "Executive Orders from Nixon to Now," in Kelley, ed., *Executing the Presidency*; William G. Howell, *Power without Persuasion: The Politics of Direct Presidential Action* (Princeton: Princeton University Press, 2003); Mayer, *With the Stroke of a Pen*.

40. Adam Liptak, "Judge Rules 2001 Listing of Terrorists Violated Law," *New York Times*, November 29, 2006, A24; Howell, *Power Without Persuasion*.

41. Mayer, *With the Stroke of a Pen*, 79–87; Howell, *Power without Persuasion*, 83–85; Executive Order 13279.

42. Harold Hongju Koh, *The National Security Constitution: Sharing Power after the Iran-Contra Affair* (New Haven: Yale University Press, 1990), 46–48.

43. Quoted in Alexis Simendinger, "The Paper Wars," *National Journal*, July 25, 1998, 1737.

44. Executive Order 10340.

45. *U.S. v. Midwest Oil*, 236 U.S. 459 (1915).

46. Richard E. Neustadt, *Presidential Power and the Modern Presidents* (New York: Free Press, 1990), 3.

47. See especially Philip Bobbitt, *Terror and Consent* (New York: Knopf, 2008).

48. Nigel Bowles, *Nixon's Business* (College Station: Texas A&M Press, 2005); P.L. 110-343.

49. U.S. House, "A Failure of Initiative: Final Report of the Select Bipartisan Committee to Investigate the Preparation for and Response to Hurricane Katrina" (Washington, D.C.: U.S. Government Printing Office, 2006), http://katrina.house.gov.

50. For a useful review—but also a useful reminder of the conditions under which congressional power might be exercised in such instances—see William G. Howell and Jon C. Pevehouse, *While Dangers Gather: Congressional Checks on Presidential War Powers* (Princeton: Princeton University Press, 2007).

51. See *U.S. v. Curtiss-Wright Export Corp. et al.*, 299 U.S. 304 (1936); Barton J. Bernstein, "The Road to Watergate and Beyond: The Growth and Abuse of Executive Authority since 1940," *Law and Contemporary Problems* 40 (Spring 1976).

52. Louis Fisher, "War Power," in *The American Congress: The Building of Democracy*, ed. Julian E. Zelizer (Boston: Houghton Mifflin, 2004), 696. Note that the War Powers Resolution specifically prohibits the use of treaty obligations as an approval mechanism.

53. Office of Legal Counsel, "Authority of the President under Domestic and International Law to Use Military Force Against Iraq," October 23, 2002 (emphasis added), 1, 7. But see Howell and Pevehouse, *While Dangers Gather*, for an analysis of how presidents anticipate congressional reaction to their own choices.

54. Kiki Caruson, "International Agreement-making and the Executive-Legislative Relationship," *Presidency Research Group Report* 25 (Fall 2002): 21–28; Steven A. Shull, *Policy by Other Means* (College Station: Texas A&M Press, 2006), chap. 6; and Karen DeYoung, "No Need for Lawmakers' Approval of Iraq Pact, U.S. Reasserts," *Washington Post*, March 6, 2008, A18. See Rep. William Delahunt's complaint on the topic, November 19, 2008, www.house.gov/delahunt/delahuntopening1119.pdf.

55. Bernstein, "The Road to Watergate," 81; more generally, see John Prados, *Safe for Democracy: The CIA's Secret Wars* (Chicago: Ivan Dee, 2006).

56. Rudalevige, *New Imperial Presidency*, chap. 7; Jane Mayer, *The Dark Side* (New York: Doubleday, 2008).

57. The letter, dated July 17, 2003, is available at www.talkingpointsmemo.com/docs/rock-cheney1.html. See, more generally, the Intelligence Oversight Act of 1980 and its later amendments.

58. Bernstein, "Road to Watergate," 64; Robert H. Jackson, *That Man: An Insider's Portrait of Franklin D. Roosevelt* (New York: Oxford University Press, 2003), 68–73.

59. U.S. Department of Justice, *Legal Authorities Supporting the Activities of the National Security Agency Described by the President*, January 19, 2006, 1–2, 10–11, 17, 30–31.

60. Office of Legal Counsel (OLC), memorandum re: Applicability of 18 U.S.C. §4001(a) to Military Detention of United States Citizens, June 27, 2002; president's military order of November 13, 2001; and see OLC memorandum re: Authority for Use of Military Force to Combat Terrorist Activities within the United States, October 23, 2001, which was criticized in but not quite rescinded by a subsequent OLC decision of January 15, 2009. These memoranda and opinions are collected at the Justice Department site, www.usdoj.gov/opa/documents/olc-memos.htm.

61. Executive Order 13440, July 2007.

62. George H. W. Bush called these national security directives, Clinton called them presidential decision directives, and George W. Bush called them national security presidential directives. Rep. Lee Hamilton, D-Ind., complained in 1988 that such directives "are revealed to Congress only under irregular, arbitrary, or even accidental circumstances, if at all." See Cooper, *By Order of the President*, 144, 165, 194–195. The Federation of American Scientists has made a game attempt to catalog such orders, www.fas.org/irp/offdocs/direct.htm.

63. Mark J. Rozell, *Executive Privilege*, 2nd rev. ed. (Lawrence: University Press of Kansas, 2002); Louis Fisher, *The Politics of Executive Privilege* (Durham, N.C.: Carolina Academic Press, 2004).

64. Richard Kleindienst, Hearings before the Senate Subcommittee on Intergovernmental Relations, "Executive Privilege, Secrecy in Government, Freedom of Information," 93rd Congress, 1st sess., April 10, 1973.

65. *U.S. v. Nixon*, 418 U.S. 683 (1974); *In re Sealed Case*, 121 F. 3D 729 (D.C. Circuit 1998).

66. Rozell, *Executive Privilege*, 106–107. In the Cheney case, the Supreme Court did not decide the case directly but directed circuit court action: see *In re Cheney* (02-5354), D.C. Circuit 2005; Barton Gellman, *Angler: The Cheney Vice Presidency* (New York: Penguin, 2008).

67. See the memoranda of January 21, 2009, and Executive Order 13489 relating to the Presidential Records Act, www.whitehouse.gov/briefing_room/executive_orders.

68. Quoted in Thomas E. Cronin, "'Everybody Believes in Democracy Until He Gets to the White House,'" *Law and Contemporary Problems* 35 (1970): 573–625.

69. Steven G. Calabresi and Christopher S. Yoo, *The Unitary Executive: Presidential Power from Washington to Bush* (New Haven: Yale University Press, 2008). For a more expansive variant, see John Yoo, *War by Other Means* (New York: Atlantic, 2005); Jess Bravin, "Judge Alito's View of the Presidency: Expansive Powers," *Wall Street Journal,* January 5, 2006, A1.

70. Jack L. Goldsmith, *The Terror Presidency* (New York: Norton, 2007), 215.

17 The Presidency at War: Unchecked Power, Uncertain Leadership

Andrew J. Polsky[1]

The Constitutional Convention was on the verge of voting to grant Congress the power "to make war" when Pierce Butler, a delegate from South Carolina, voiced his concern that Congress might not even be in session when the need arose to respond to foreign invasion. Persuaded, James Madison of Virginia and Elbridge Gerry of Massachusetts moved to substitute "declare war" for "make war," thereby "leaving to the Executive the power to repel sudden attacks." That exception to the general rule of congressional initiative in decisions to go to war has been broadened almost beyond recognition throughout American history, but especially since World War II. "Deployment is destiny," writes Andrew J. Polsky, observing that the president's constitutional authority as commander in chief has always allowed him to order U.S. troops to go anywhere, including places where their presence was all but certain to provoke a war. During most of American history, the armed forces were too small for presidents to make much use of this authority, except when Congress voted to increase the nation's military apparatus in preparation for a war that Congress intended to declare. The massive standing army, navy, and air force since the mid-1940s, however, have given presidents from Harry Truman to Barack Obama the means to exercise the commander in chief's power to deploy forces on a scale that has rendered Congress's war-declaring authority almost meaningless.

When Barack Obama assumed the presidency in January 2009, he inherited a situation that few incoming commanders in chief have faced. Only a handful of his predecessors entered office with a major war on their hands.[2] Obama became responsible for two conflicts involving significant American troop commitments. More than 100,000 American military personnel continued to fight in Iraq, where, despite declining levels of violence, political stability remained in doubt and no clear exit path for the United States presented itself. Meanwhile, in Afghanistan, a resurgent Taliban mounted attacks across a broadening swath of territory and the hold on power of the western-backed regime in Kabul weakened, alarming American and North Atlantic Treaty Organization (NATO) commanders and propelling the conflict once again to the forefront of American foreign policy. As the incoming president weighed several unappealing strategic options,[3] he was confronted with a basic challenge of wartime presidential leadership for which there is no clear solution. In war, the president must use military and other means effectively to achieve American political goals. But although presidents have often led the nation into wars, no one has devised a reliable approach for converting American military power into victory in the larger, more important political sense.

Indeed, the most striking feature of the American presidency at war lies in the gap between the modern president's enormous and effectively unchecked capacity to wage war and the uncertainty of success. From the beginning, the constitutional distribution of authority has invited the president to assert responsibility during national security crises. Add to this the post–World War II expansion of the president's capacity to wage war, in particular the ready availability of a large standing military. More recently, the events of the 1990s and 2000s suggest that a president can deploy substantial military forces on short notice to any location in the world, secure approval from Congress to use those forces even when the available evidence suggests no direct threat to vital American interests, convince the public that military measures are necessary, and act without regard for international diplomatic or military consequences. Nevertheless, a careful historical assessment reveals that effective wartime leadership requires more than enormous military advantages and a political free hand. Presidents have wrestled with different approaches to the challenges of command and often failed to find one that succeeds.

Presidential War Powers in the Constitutional Framework

For more than two centuries, the Constitution has been the constant that has shaped the president's power to make war. The document's ambiguities and silences have invited presidents to expand their capacity to undertake military operations on their own initiative. Although the Constitution is quite clear about how some national security responsibilities are allocated, many situations arise in which "strict construction" cannot define the extent of presidential authority. Political leaders and scholars have argued heatedly about the proper constitutional limits of presidential war powers.

Without question, however, the broader logic of the constitutional system endows presidents with the means to dominate when they think the nation faces a threat to its security. Article II unifies military direction in the hands of the president. The first presidential power listed in the article is to serve as the commander in chief of the nation's armed forces, including state militia called into national service. Having barely survived the inefficiency of legislative direction of military affairs during the war for independence, the Framers chose to make plain that the chain of command leads directly to the president. Interestingly, in a constitutional system otherwise filled with elaborate institutional checks, the president may act as commander in chief without securing approval from any other branch.

Congress is given the power to create and regulate the nation's military capacity, as well as to declare war. Under Article I, it falls upon Congress to establish and finance the nation's armed forces, to call state militia into service to repel foreign attack and put down domestic insurrections, and to impose standards upon the state militia. The article prohibits the use of any army appropriation for longer than two years, a legacy of colonial mistrust of standing armies. In giving Congress the power to declare war, the Framers recognized that such a step should be taken only after careful consideration. As James Madison observed in *The Federalist*, legislative deliberation, by slowing the pace of governmental action until a consensus forms, should prevent passionate and ill-considered decisions. Although Madison did not refer to national security matters in those passages, a deliberative mechanism to weigh the choice between war and peace would be consistent with his approach.

Much about national security authority remains unresolved by the spare provisions of the Constitution. For example, Article IV requires the United States to defend republican government in every state and to repel invasions, but it does not specify which branch is responsible for taking the required measures. The president as commander in chief has the authority to order an immediate military response, but only Congress may call state forces into national service. Nor does the Constitution define "invasion." Could the term be construed to include not just a massive attack across the borders of the United States but also more modest incursions or raids, possibly by irregular forces operating without the approval of any government? Perhaps most important, the Framers understood the difference between armed conflict and a formal state of war. As Joseph Avella points out, they purposefully decided to grant Congress the power to *declare* war, not the power to *make* war.[4] Less certain is what they intended to accomplish by incorporating that distinction into the Constitution.

Constitutional ambiguity has fueled a never-ending political and scholarly debate about the scope of presidential war-making authority. On one side are those such as Avella who contend that the Framers invested the president with broad authority to preserve the national security. In choosing to limit Congress to the power to declare war, they recognized both that securing the nation might require urgent action (not the strong suit of a legislature), and that situations might arise in which an application of force short of war would be appropriate. From this *presidentialist* viewpoint, Congress can restrain president-ordered military operations only by resorting to its explicit constitutional power to withhold funds from the armed forces, thereby compelling the president to bring the troops home.[5] By this reckoning, the 1973 War Powers Resolution, like other legislative efforts to force the president to seek congressional approval for military actions short of war, encroaches improperly upon presidential authority.

The opposing view—that Congress has the authority to make most decisions to employ military force—has been asserted by *congressionalists* such as Louis Fisher. According to this school, the Framers expected Congress to practice vigorous restraint on the president's use of force. Because military action can have far-reaching consequences, the decision to take it ought to be made after the careful deliberation that only a legislative body offers. That presidents have repeatedly employed the military without legislative sanction, Fisher insists, does not legitimize the practice.[6] David Currie offers historical support for the claim that the Framers intended the president to have only limited authority to commit American forces. He notes that the early presidents doubted their constitutional authority to engage in military action without congressional approval.[7]

One early example of presidential war-making has been invoked by presidentialists and congressionalists alike to support their conflicting constitutional interpretations. In 1803 Thomas Jefferson dispatched most of the tiny U.S. Navy to the Mediterranean Sea to do battle with the Barbary pirates, who had attacked a number of American merchant ships. As Avella notes, Jefferson saw no need to secure Congress's approval for his order. His action, Avella maintains, confirms the willingness of the founding generation to countenance presidential use of force.[8] But Currie draws a different conclusion from Jefferson's conduct in the Barbary conflict. When Jefferson sought to explain his action to Congress, he felt it necessary to dissemble by representing the capture of a pirate vessel as a purely defensive action by the navy and noting that the vessel was released because Congress had not yet approved military intervention.[9]

Notwithstanding the intensity of the debate, both presidentialists and congressionalists recognize an enduring reality of the constitutional structure: the president is in a strong position to assert control, perhaps even supremacy, in national security matters. Consider, for example, the Article IV mandate to repel invasions. As commander in chief, the president may define what constitutes an invasion and order a response by any available military forces. Once the United States finds itself engaged in military conflict, political pressures are certain to make Congress's powers less significant. Congress would not deny funds to embattled American forces lest it be accused of failing to support the troops, thus rendering the power of the purse useless as a device to shape policy during a war. Intentionally or not, by creating a unitary executive, the Framers gave the president a decisive edge over Congress in situations involving prompt action.

The combination of unchecked command authority and the ability to act with dispatch has allowed presidents to shape the course of action in national security crises and has reduced Congress to a reactive role. Presidents can manipulate diplomatic and military circumstances by ordering American troops into situations in which hostilities are likely, leaving lawmakers little choice but to acquiesce. After Saddam Hussein's Iraqi forces occupied Kuwait in 1990, George H. W. Bush sent 400,000 U.S. troops to Saudi Arabia and other Middle Eastern countries before asking Congress to approve military action. In 2002, in the same Persian Gulf region, George W. Bush repeated his father's preparatory measures, dispatching troops to nations bordering Iraq before seeking legislative approval. What these presidents did by sending troops into harm's way in order to undermine potential congressional opposition was not new. In 1846, James Polk ordered troops into the disputed Texas border region between the Nueces River (which Polk's predecessors regarded as the true southern border of Texas) and the Rio Grande, hoping thereby to provoke an armed Mexican response and create a cause for war. When the Mexicans obliged by attacking an American cavalry detachment, Polk asked Congress to recognize that a state of war existed, brought on by Mexico's "aggression." Legislative opposition to Polk's expansionist agenda collapsed.[10] Simply put, by controlling the placement of American forces, the president can all but determine when and where the nation will go to war. Deployment is destiny.

Only when a president requires legislative action to prepare for war can Congress neutralize the executive's inherent constitutional advantages. Such a situation arose several times in the years leading up to American involvement in the Second World War. President Franklin Roosevelt wanted Congress to increase military expenditures, authorize an increase in the size of the armed forces, approve the lend-lease program that made it possible for Great Britain to continue fighting Nazi Germany, and institute the first peacetime draft in the nation's history. Congress agreed to all of these requests, but only after much persuasion and sometimes by a slender margin. Amid extreme international tension in August 1941, the House of Representatives agreed by only a single vote to extend the tour of duty for draftees to eighteen months. If the House had not approved the measure, most of the army would have been discharged in October—less than two months before the Japanese attack on Pearl Harbor.[11]

The constitutional system affords but two possible constraints upon presidential dominance in national security matters. First, Congress could deny the president the tools to initiate a major conflict by limiting the size of the nation's standing military forces. Second, presidents could choose to restrain themselves in their exercise of the power to wage war; after all, nothing compels a president to expand the authority of the office in a national security crisis. Unlikely though presidential self-restraint may seem, James Madison offers an example. He reluctantly led the nation into war with Great Britain in 1812. Faithful to the ideal that Congress ought to control legislation, Madison stood by as senators and representatives delayed or weakened measures to prepare the United States for war against a major power and then shirked hard choices about financing the armed forces once the war started.[12] He also declined to assert himself once war began, failing to insist on unity of command for the invasion of Canada or to discipline inept generals.[13] Still, Madison's fidelity to his conception of the Constitution had certain saving graces. The unpopularity of the war, especially in New England, provoked vociferous political dissent and even a refusal by some states to send their militia to participate in operations along the Canadian border. Yet Madison refused to take repressive measures against his political opponents, a precedent to which few of his wartime successors have adhered.

Expanding the President's Capacity to Wage War

Although the Constitution facilitates assertive presidential leadership on matters of national security, until the post–World War II era presidents lacked the resources to wage war without congressional support. The United States maintained a small standing army in peacetime. For every major war through the mid-twentieth century, a suitable military force had to be created from scratch. Substantial armies were established either just months before the shooting started (as in the War of 1812, the Spanish-American War, World War I, and World War II) or, in some cases, after the war began (the Mexican War and the Civil War). In the absence of a declared war, presidents made frequent use of the limited military means at hand, usually to suppress Indian resistance to western expansion, but the modest available forces contained executive bellicosity. In a series of steps beginning in the late nineteenth century, the president's war-making capacity was transformed. Congress first created a permanent fleet, then a large standing army and an air force. Consequently, modern presidents have had at their disposal enormous military resources.

The situation that confronted Abraham Lincoln in 1861 illustrates the obstacles early wartime presidents had to overcome, while also suggesting the potential scope of executive assertiveness. When Lincoln took office, he faced the gravest threat to national survival that any incoming president has encountered: the secession of several southern states, the siege of Fort Sumter, and the looming prospect of civil war. The puny U.S. Army and Navy were in no way equal to the challenge.[14] Congress was not in session when fighting began in April 1861, so Lincoln acted swiftly on his own presumed executive authority to call up the militia, expand the regular army, impose a naval blockade on southern ports, and suspend the right to a writ of habeas corpus in border states. Lincoln acknowledged that the Constitution did not explicitly grant him the power to do most of these things; indeed, Article I placed some of his actions under congressional authority. But he argued forcefully that it made no sense to respect the letter of the Constitution while the entire constitutional framework collapsed.[15] Congress later ratified Lincoln's emergency actions, conferring post hoc legitimacy on them. Yet, even with a broad warrant to act, Lincoln had to turn to his Republican Party to mobilize sufficient military means to defeat the rebellion. No national bureaucratic apparatus existed that could meet this challenge. Instead the president relied on Republican governors to raise the vast majority of Union troops on a volunteer basis.[16]

In the decades after the Civil War, as industrial expansion vaulted the United States to the forefront of the global economy, the inadequacies of the established pattern of responding to national security crises prompted efforts at military reform. These efforts yielded oddly mismatched outcomes. Advocates of army reform, both within and outside the service, pushed to develop stronger mechanisms for centralized control of the army in the event of war. But the reformers were thwarted by opposition from several sources: congressional committees wedded to the status quo, governors who wanted to retain their authority over state militia as a source of patronage, and southerners still resentful of army occupation during Reconstruction and fearful of what a strong national army might mean for civil rights enforcement.[17] Meanwhile, naval reformers, who did not face the same political obstacles, made significant headway in securing political support to modernize the fleet. Congress passed several major battleship construction bills during the early and mid-1890s.

The consequences of the uneven development of the military services were demonstrated vividly during the Spanish-American War. President William

McKinley was a reluctant warrior who preferred a negotiated resolution of the Cuban insurrection against Spanish colonial authority. Pushed into war in 1898, however, he asserted firm control over both military and political developments.[18] The navy quickly crushed two small Spanish fleets, in Manila Bay in the Philippines and near Santiago, Cuba. But even though the conflict had loomed for several years, the army, lacking a general staff, had not prepared a plan for an invasion of Cuba. A hastily formed collection of state militia and army regulars landed at Daiquiri, Cuba, on June 22, 1898, amid such chaos that the few horses embarked on the ships were tossed overboard and forced to swim for land (alas, some instead headed to sea). Only overwhelming force enabled the poorly organized army to prevail. Making use of excellent telephone and telegraph equipment installed in a "war room" in the White House, McKinley remained in close contact with his field commanders. He was thus able to supervise the terms of the truce offered to the Spanish in Santiago and to boost the morale of his officers when disease decimated the American forces.[19]

Although the United States achieved great-power status in the early twentieth century, the presidents who would face world wars still functioned within a traditional constitutional order that depended on legislative action to bring the armed forces to a war footing. Apart from a large, modern navy, the resources at the disposal of a commander in chief remained modest. After war erupted in Europe in 1914, Woodrow Wilson hesitated to prepare the United States to enter the conflict. His reluctance to ask Congress to create a suitable army combined with legislative opposition to intervention to delay American military readiness; as a result, the United States was able to contribute little to the Allied effort even after declaring war in April 1917. Only in the final months of the conflict in 1918 were large numbers of American troops engaged in combat.[20]

Nor was the nation equipped for the unprecedented national economic mobilization required for twentieth-century warfare. Although Congress hurriedly delegated extraordinary authority to the president to control the production and distribution of goods and services in both the military and the civilian economy,[21] very little of the war production was available before the November 1918 armistice. What had been created in a mad rush was then dismantled almost as quickly. Fierce political opposition to Wilson's vision of a new postwar world order centered on a League of Nations, along with public disenchantment with peace terms that fell far short of that vision, contributed to the swift dismantling of the wartime mobilization apparatus.[22] Even the American naval advantage was negated by a postwar treaty that limited the U.S. Navy to parity with Great Britain and left Japan with a potential advantage in the Pacific Ocean.

The cycle of frantic mobilization and equally swift demobilization was repeated a generation later in the Second World War. When Nazi Germany invaded Poland on September 1, 1939, the United States again found itself woefully unprepared. The army stood as the nineteenth largest in the world, ranking just behind that of Portugal.[23] Although President Roosevelt and his military advisers recognized the nation's vulnerability, efforts to modernize and expand the armed forces lagged until America entered the war. Again the nation rushed to build a huge army and to expand the navy so that it could wage war in two oceans. As warfare had become more complex, however, the time needed to train and equip militaries had increased. The United States required two years to mobilize fully, delaying the decisive Allied invasion of Europe until 1944 and thereby prolonging the conflict. Even that sobering experience, joined to the postwar threat posed by a hostile communist superpower, the Soviet Union, did not entirely uproot the old habit of shrinking the military in peacetime. The outbreak of war in Korea in June 1950 caught the army once more at a low level of readiness.

Still, despite these echoes of the past, important changes occurred before the Korean conflict began. The late 1940s marked the birth of a new era, both in American security policy and in presidential war-making capacity. Force reductions after the Second World War were not as severe as those following previous conflicts. More important, the years immediately after the war saw the beginning of the modern national security state through several key developments: the American embrace of collective security through establishment of the United Nations and NATO; passage of the 1948 National Security Act, which created the Department of Defense, the Central Intelligence Agency, and the National Security Council; and the adoption of a broad commitment to resist the spread of communism.[24]

From that time forward, the president as commander in chief has been able to call upon a permanent national security apparatus that can rapidly plan and execute large-scale military deployments. No longer does the president have to await the organizing, equipping, and training of an army before embarking on a military venture. Indeed, the United States has maintained a standing military establishment in peacetime that dwarfs any of the nation's pre-twentieth-century wartime forces. Contrast two interventions that occurred less than a century apart: first, the clumsy, poorly provisioned assault on Cuba in 1898 by some 15,000 men, which taxed U.S. military resources to the limit even though the troops embarked from nearby Tampa; and second, the rapid deployment of more than 400,000 troops and all the paraphernalia of modern warfare to the distant Persian Gulf in 1991. American conventional military capacity is sufficient today to wage major wars in Iraq and Afghanistan without recourse to conscription or mandatory economic mobilization. Scholars debate when the modern presidency began. Plainly, in terms of the president's military capacity, it began in Harry Truman's first term.

The Weakened Constraints on Presidential War Making

As the nation's capacity to wage war has expanded, the constraints on the president's military initiative have weakened. The constitutional checks on the presidency in matters of national security, never strong in the first place, have become largely irrelevant. Political forces that would give a president pause seldom materialize unless a military campaign falters, and even then they cannot compel the president to end a conflict. Thus domestic factors barely inhibit presidents from seeking military solutions to international problems or crises. Nor does the international context—specifically, the lack of a competing superpower with which the United States must reckon—in the post–Cold War era curb a chief executive from employing American military might nearly anywhere on the globe. Self-restraint in the Oval Office seems to be the last remaining inhibition, and it has proven a weak one.

The demise of the classical legal step for going to war and the acceptance of a large permanent military establishment have nullified the main constitutional tools that Congress commands to block presidential war-making. The formal declaration of war has become a constitutional anachronism; the last time the United States formally declared war on an adversary was in 1941, yet since then the nation has found itself in major conflicts in Korea, Vietnam, the Persian Gulf, Iraq, and Afghanistan.[25] To legitimize military intervention, a president can draw upon extraconstitutional legal authority, including the UN Charter and a host of treaties that bind the United States to fight on behalf of other countries. At the same time, because Congress now routinely appropriates funds for the world's most powerful military, massive force is always at the president's immediate disposal.

The War Powers Resolution was intended to restore a measure of congressional control over the use of American armed forces in hostile situations or in actual combat, but the statute has failed to give Congress a real voice when presidents decide to commit troops. To be sure, the Vietnam experience taught presidents that it is unwise to send American forces into a potential major conflict without a clear endorsement by the people's representatives. Despite declining to acknowledge the constitutionality of the War Powers Resolution, chief executives have deemed it prudent to seek Congress's endorsement before commencing large-scale military operations. But they have timed their requests for congressional approval strategically, seeking a vote either just prior to hostilities (the 1991 Gulf War) or on the eve of an election (in late October 2002 to authorize the use of force against Iraq).

Antiwar legislators in 1991 displayed considerable backbone, questioning whether military action should be postponed until economic sanctions and diplomacy had been given every chance to compel Saddam Hussein to withdraw Iraqi troops from Kuwait. The congressional resolution supporting the use of force passed by only a narrow margin.[26] In contrast, during the 2002 debate, fearing that an antiwar vote would be used against them in the midterm election, lawmakers swallowed any doubts about the merits of the Bush administration's case against Hussein. Paradoxically, the War Powers Resolution may have enhanced presidential power to initiate military action by inoculating presidents against one important set of potential critics. Once a member of Congress votes to support the use of force, it becomes politically awkward for that member to second-guess the decision—as John Kerry found during the 2004 presidential campaign when he tried to criticize President Bush for using the authorization that Kerry had voted to give him.

Because the judiciary was never intended to play a major role in decisions of war and peace, the courts have shaped the exercise of presidential war powers only at the margins. The Supreme Court approved Lincoln's exercise of broad prerogative powers during the Civil War, Wilson's suppression of dissent during World War I, and FDR's internment of Japanese Americans during World War II. More recently, responding to President Bush's post-9/11 military and antiterrorist campaigns, the courts have upheld certain due process rights of persons classified by the administration as enemy combatants or suspected terrorists. But these decisions have not addressed the core war-making powers of the chief executive.

In contemplating war or other major military operations, presidents must consider how the public will react. Popular dissent has been a common theme in many American wars, starting with the War of 1812. As a conflict continues and casualties mount without either a victory or an apparent resolution, the political risk to the president increases. The growing unpopularity of the Vietnam War convinced Lyndon Johnson not to face the voters in the 1968 election. George W. Bush enjoyed high public approval during the post-9/11 Afghanistan campaign to topple the Taliban regime and the swift initial triumph in Iraq in 2003. By 2006, however, public disenchantment with the ongoing violence and turmoil in Iraq contributed to the Republicans' loss of Congress in the midterm election. Even military triumph carries no assurance of future political success. Despite victories on the battlefield, several presidents, including James Polk, Woodrow

Wilson, and George H. W. Bush, either went down to defeat or saw their party's candidate for president lose the next election.

Still, political risk has not prevented presidents from engaging the United States in armed conflict. Presidents considering a military campaign never expect it to be long and costly. For a time, the experience of Lyndon Johnson and Richard Nixon in Vietnam had a cautionary effect on their successors. But in the 1980s and 1990s, as the margin of American military superiority over potential adversaries widened and the United States fought brief, effective campaigns with low casualties in Grenada, Panama, Iraq and Kuwait, Bosnia, and Kosovo, it became easier for presidents to conclude that the vast American technological advantage had reduced the political downside of using force. No conflict seemed likely to last long enough for political opposition to coalesce to the extent that it might lead to a strong congressional reaction or defeat at the polls. This assumption held true for George W. Bush in both Afghanistan in 2001 and Iraq in 2003. In both wars, organized resistance by the regime the United States decided to oust collapsed as quickly as American military planners expected, even though every assumption about the ease of meeting the postwar challenges proved mistaken and the conflicts reignited in new and more difficult forms.

Mounting domestic opposition to a war, moreover, has never compelled a president to disengage. In theory Congress could refuse to provide the funding for the military to continue a war, but in practice this has proven politically impossible. As long ago as the Mexican War, President Polk's Whig opponents conceded that Congress "would never refuse to grant anything and everything necessary or proper for the support and succor of our brave troops, placed without any fault of their own, in the heart of a distant country, and struggling with every peril, discomfort and difficulty."[27] What was true then has remained true ever since. Although the Democrats in 2007, fresh from their triumph in the 2006 midterm election, introduced several measures to require the withdrawal of American troops from Iraq by a specified deadline, none passed. Apart from the institutional obstacles to such legislation—including the prospect of a presidential veto and a filibuster rule that requires sixty votes to force a Senate decision—antiwar Democrats could not persuade their peers to assume responsibility for the policy consequences of an American withdrawal on a congressional timetable.[28] Just how impotent Congress is became clear when President Bush decided to increase combat forces in Iraq in late 2006. This troop "surge" proceeded without hindrance from the Democratic majority, which had been elected on an antiwar theme.

It is also unlikely that presidents will be deterred from military action by other international powers. Even when the United States was a minor power and Great Britain ruled the waves, Jefferson sent most of the navy to the Mediterranean. That said, presidents had to know that the use of force might lead to a clash with another major power. For example, during the Civil War, Abraham Lincoln worried that Great Britain and France might grant diplomatic recognition to the Confederacy and then break the Union blockade of southern ports. After World War II, when the United States faced a hostile Soviet Union, presidents had to consider that any large-scale military action in one theater might leave the United States and its allies dangerously vulnerable elsewhere. Presidents also worried that a limited war might become a global conflagration if American military intervention went beyond what the Soviets were prepared to tolerate. The end of the Cold War and the collapse of the Soviet Union in 1991 put an end to such concerns. After the United States became the world's only military superpower, presidents could act without fear of provoking a military response from an adversary capable of defeating American forces. George W. Bush invaded nations that only recently had been either within the Soviet sphere of influence (Afghanistan) or Soviet client states (Iraq), actions his Cold War predecessors would not have contemplated.

In the face of ineffective domestic and international checks on presidential war-making, some policymakers and scholars have revived the idea that presidents should restrain themselves. The use of force can yield poor results and generate political backlash, these voices caution, so presidents considering military action would be wise to subject their decision to rigorous criteria designed to make certain the risks have been weighed carefully and lives will not be wasted.[29] The Framers of the Constitution, of course, scoffed at the notion that those with power can be trusted to check themselves. And in this case, the Framers' fears have been justified fully. Self-applied "tests" of the appropriateness of military action have not prevented presidents from wielding force in situations that involved no direct threat to the United States, including Panama, Bosnia, and Kosovo. For that matter, the exposure of the weak and even patently phony prewar intelligence that was used to justify the invasion of Iraq has shown that presidents and their advisers may interpret (or even invent) intelligence to construe a grave danger to American security when no such menace exists.

Approaches to Wartime Leadership: Delegation versus Active Direction

The renowned German military theorist Carl von Clausewitz famously remarked that war is the extension of diplomacy by other means.[30] As historian James McPherson explains, wartime political leadership requires reconciling the nation's military strategy with its political goals.[31] In the American constitutional system, it is the president who must find the military means to realize larger political ends. Indeed, this is the central task of the commander in chief, and one that recurs in every war. The nature of the strategic leadership challenge, McPherson adds, varies according to the type of conflict and may evolve during the course of a war. Enhancing the military capacity at a president's disposal does not necessarily make it easier to achieve wartime political goals. American military means may be superior on paper to those of any adversary, but they also may be poorly suited to the political challenge presented by a particular conflict.

A president in wartime also operates under a historical constraint. Even though presidents enjoy considerable discretion in how they choose to exercise wartime leadership, they do not begin from scratch but instead inherit a legacy of approaches from their predecessors. This history confronted Barack Obama when he entered the Oval Office in 2009.

With the professionalization of military services since the late nineteenth century, one common model of the relationship between wartime political and military leaders has embraced a separation between the two. Samuel P. Huntington captured the logic of this approach in 1957 when he propounded the theory of "objective control": political leaders should define a nation's political objectives when going to war and provide the means necessary to wage the struggle, while military professionals should decide how best to achieve those objectives when planning combat operations.[32] This division of labor recognized that politicians and soldiers have different talents and areas of expertise and sought to use each to its greatest advantage. Among wartime presidents, Woodrow Wilson stands out clearly as a commander in chief who kept his hands off the field decisions of his senior military commander, General John "Black Jack" Pershing, while remaining in close charge of the political direction of the American war effort.

Reacting against the objective-control school, some strategic theorists counter that political leaders need to be involved in wartime command decisions down to the operational level. If war is an extension of diplomacy, the dissenters' argument runs, then it follows that no separation properly exists between politics and combat. Rather, to make certain that military decisions conform to and help secure political objectives, political leaders must maintain close oversight of their field commanders. Eliot A. Cohen, a leading proponent of the hands-on or "active direction" model, notes that a political leader in wartime must perform a range of tasks—selecting commanders from among unproven generals, managing alliances, restructuring the military, setting operational priorities—that goes well beyond what the objective-control model prescribes.[33]

Great statesmen have often violated the tenets of objective control and succeeded precisely because they involved themselves intimately in all aspects of military decision making. Abraham Lincoln not only established and later modified the Union's goals during the Civil War but also immersed himself in the details of the war effort.[34] Although he once complained, "I am as powerless as any private citizen to shape the military plans of the government,"[35] his exasperation did not stop him from trying to synchronize military offensives against the South in order to capitalize on the Union's greater manpower. Lincoln also goaded his generals into action when their inertia threatened to stall operations, and he replaced commanders who suffered from what he called "the slows."[36]

Recent American experience contains examples of both models of wartime presidential leadership. During the Vietnam War, President Johnson and his senior advisers, notably Secretary of Defense Robert McNamara, intervened directly in certain military decisions in an effort to tie military policy closely to diplomatic initiatives. They did not want battlefield decisions to interfere with their efforts to induce North Vietnam to accept a negotiated settlement without risking a wider war that would draw in the leading communist powers, the Soviet Union and the People's Republic of China.[37] As Johnson and his advisers selected specific bombing targets and ruled others off-limits, military commanders chafed under the White House–imposed restrictions. On the other hand (and much less visibly at the time), when it came to ground operations, the president granted considerable latitude to his generals in the field.[38] Neither Johnson's active control over air operations nor his deference to commanders in their direction of ground combat yielded the results he sought. The Vietnamese communists stubbornly refused to respond to Johnson's carrot-and-stick combination of force and diplomacy. By the time the president decided not to seek reelection in March 1968, he faced diplomatic frustration, military stalemate, and declining public support.

In the wake of the Vietnam fiasco, critics of Johnson's approach concluded that presidents should leave military decisions to military professionals. The military resented what it regarded as excessive political meddling in the conduct of military operations and questioned the judgment of politicians about how to use force effectively. Brushed aside in this reassessment was the failure of American military commanders in Vietnam to articulate a coherent strategy of their own; instead, they seemed to be able to do no more than ask for additional troops.[39] Nevertheless, by the time of the next major American military commitment, the 1991 Gulf War, the objective-control perspective had taken firm hold in both military and senior political circles. George H. W. Bush and his key civilian advisers left most prewar planning to the military and, more important, permitted the American field commander, General Norman Schwarzkopf, to determine when to halt the attacks in Kuwait and to negotiate the terms of the ceasefire that concluded the fighting. The administration expected that the defeat of Iraqi forces would lead to the swift overthrow of Saddam Hussein's regime. As it turned out, however, many of the dictator's best and most loyal troops had survived the fighting, and he used them to brutally suppress Shiite and Kurdish uprisings.[40]

The ambiguous long-term results of the Gulf War produced a divided reaction among American military and foreign policy leaders. To the military, the stunning American triumph on the battlefield demonstrated the wisdom of objective control: warfare is something best left to the experts. To others, notably the foreign policy intellectuals known as neoconservatives, Hussein's survival in power and his ongoing determination to circumvent UN sanctions directed against his regime meant that the military had misread the situation and permitted a major threat to regional and American security to remain in power. This suggested that Bush had granted military commanders too much discretion, ignoring the implication of von Clausewitz's dictum that in war military operations must be subordinated to political ends. Neoconservatives such as Paul Wolfowitz argued throughout the 1990s that political leaders ought to exercise firm control of war policy.[41]

Thus the stage was set for a collision between proponents of the two models of wartime presidential leadership when George W. Bush prepared for wars in Afghanistan in 2001 and Iraq in 2003. Bush surrounded himself with civilian advisers—including Vice President Dick Cheney, Secretary of Defense Donald Rumsfeld, and Deputy Secretary of Defense Wolfowitz—who believed that political leaders needed to keep tight rein on military commanders. Rumsfeld in particular regarded the top military leaders with disdain.[42]

Although these views augured that the president would exercise hands-on direction of any military campaign, George W. Bush viewed himself as a leader in the mold of the modern corporate chief executive officer who sets the broad direction for his organization and then delegates its execution to others. Rather than assert personal control over the military in the manner of a Lincoln, Bush permitted his senior political subordinates to exercise that authority in his name.

What followed represented a new variant on presidential wartime leadership. The delegation of authority to civilian subordinates such as Rumsfeld and Wolfowitz meant that they, rather than the president, controlled military planning and operations. When confrontations between Pentagon civilian leaders and uniformed commanders ensued, the civilians prevailed. Rumsfeld first overruled the military on how best to oust the Taliban regime in Afghanistan, which harbored Osama bin Laden and the al-Qaida leadership. Emboldened by the United States' swift initial victory there in late 2001, Rumsfeld and his aides then insisted on a relatively modest troop commitment for the expected invasion of Iraq.

Some military leaders worried that the troop level would be insufficient for what are termed "Phase IV" or post-combat stability operations. The division between Rumsfeld and the generals became public shortly before the invasion in early 2003 when Army Chief of Staff General Eric Shinseki responded to a question in a congressional hearing by suggesting that as many as 400,000 troops might be needed to secure Iraq against a possible postinvasion insurgency. Shinseki was repudiated by Wolfowitz and shunted off to early retirement.[43] Disputes over military strategy continued in the wake of the invasion when American troops confronted a rising insurgency and casualties mounted. Significantly, in the numerous published accounts of the debates among civilian and military leaders about how to cope with the insurgency, one person is notably absent—the president. At no point did he reclaim control in order to draw together political goals and military efforts.

The failure of American policy in Iraq finally forced President Bush's hand. Rather than increase his own direction of the war, however, he chose instead to make a different kind of delegation. In 2006 a blue-ribbon commission, the Iraq Study Group, recommended that the United States begin a process of scheduled withdrawals while pursuing a face-saving regional political accommodation. Although the president rejected the proposal, he recognized the need to change how American forces were being used. The president endorsed a temporary troop increase (the surge) to make more American forces available for a new operational approach. As advocated by General David Petraeus and several other current and retired senior officers, American soldiers and marines would not merely sweep through Baghdad and other areas embroiled in Shiite-Sunni strife but would remain in place to assure the areas' ongoing physical security.[44] In the president's one Lincoln-like moment in the war, Bush also tapped Petraeus as the new U.S. commander in Iraq, while replacing Rumsfeld at the Pentagon with Robert Gates, a less controversial figure. Bush made clear that force levels in Iraq would be determined by conditions as judged by Petraeus. Having tried to manage the war through political delegation and found that model wanting, the president chose to return to the objective-control model.

When Barack Obama assumed the burdens of a wartime commander in chief in 2009, he inherited a confusing legacy that offers no obvious "right way" to exercise presidential leadership. His predecessors variously tried hands-on direction (Johnson's Vietnam air war), letting the military make operational decisions (George H. W. Bush in the Gulf War), and delegating control to political subordinates (George W. Bush in Afghanistan and Iraq). No method offers a surefire path to success. Of course, it is easy to suggest that the very riskiness of war is a good reason for presidents to avoid choosing military solutions to international security challenges. That may be sound advice for a future confrontation, but Obama inherited two wars that started on Bush's watch.

On balance, the better argument lies with the advocates of hands-on wartime leadership. What troops do on the battlefield necessarily shapes whether a nation's political goals can be realized. For that reason, the commander in chief must assert active control over military operations. More than that, though, a president needs to be sufficiently engaged to recognize when, within existing American military and diplomatic capabilities, wartime political goals need to be adjusted or even abandoned.

President Obama faces just such a challenge in Afghanistan, where his predecessor's vision of a stable democratic government collided with the stubborn realities of ancient tribal animosities, the appeal of Islamic fundamentalism, corruption and opium trafficking, the fragile regime in neighboring Pakistan, conflict between India and Pakistan, and more. Such complexity demands active presidential leadership, not delegation to either political or military subordinates. Within his first weeks in office Obama approved deployment of an additional 17,000 American troops to Afghanistan. More important, recognizing that Afghanistan was becoming "his" war, he ordered a thorough strategic review of all military and political options. As the new president seems to understand, there is no escaping the burden that the Framers placed on the commander in chief.

Notes

1. The author thanks his students at Hunter College for their comments on the previous version of this chapter and Jerry Mileur for the opportunity to present a draft to the 2008 Institute in American Politics and Political Thought for Higher Education Faculty at the University of Massachusetts.

2. The others were Andrew Johnson (the Civil War), Harry Truman (World War II), Dwight Eisenhower (the Korean War), and Richard Nixon (the Vietnam War). In Johnson's case, the Civil War had virtually ended by the time he succeeded Abraham Lincoln, though the challenges of Reconstruction were just beginning.

3. On the choices for Afghanistan as they appeared at the end of 2008, see Michael Crowley, "Obama vs. Osama: Has He Picked the Right War?" *New Republic*, December 24, 2008, 18–21.

4. Joseph R. Avella, "The President, Congress, and Decisions to Employ Military Force," in *The Presidency Then and Now*, ed. Phillip G. Henderson (Lanham, Md.: Rowman and Littlefield, 2000), 51–52.

5. Ibid., 57.

6. Louis Fisher, "Congressional Checks on Military Initiatives," *Political Science Quarterly* 109 (1994–1995): 739–762.

7. David P. Currie, "Rumors of War: Presidential and Congressional War Powers, 1809–1829," *University of Chicago Law Review* 67 (2000): 1–40.

8. Avella, "President, Congress, and Decisions to Employ Military Force," 51.

9. Currie, "Rumors of War," 1–2.

10. John H. Schroeder, *Mr. Polk's War: American Opposition and Dissent, 1846–1848* (Madison: University of Wisconsin Press, 1973), chap. 1.

11. Eric Larrabee, *Commander in Chief: Franklin Delano Roosevelt, His Lieutenants, and Their War* (Annapolis, Md.: Naval Institute Press, 2004), chap. 1; David M. Kennedy, *Freedom from Fear: The American People in Depression and War, 1929–1945* (New York and Oxford: Oxford University Press, 2005), 495–496.

12. J. C. A. Stagg, *Mr. Madison's War: Politics, Diplomacy, and Warfare in the Early American Republic, 1783–1830* (Princeton: Princeton University Press, 1983), chap. 3.

13. Robert Allen Rutland, *The Presidency of James Madison* (Lawrence: University Press of Kansas, 1990), chaps. 6–7.

14. Andrew J. Polsky, "'Mr. Lincoln's Army' Revisited: Partisanship, Institutional Position, and Union Army Command, 1861–1865," *Studies in American Political Development* 16 (2002): 176–207.

15. For Lincoln's justification of his emergency actions, see Abraham Lincoln, "Message to Congress in Special Session," July 4, 1861, in Lincoln, *Selected Speeches and Writings* (New York: Vintage/Library of America, 1992), 300–315.

16. Mark E. Neely Jr., *The Union Divided: Party Conflict in the Civil War North* (Cambridge: Harvard University Press, 2002), chap. 7.

17. Stephen Skowronek, *Building a New American State: The Expansion of National Administrative Capacities, 1877–1920* (Cambridge and New York: Cambridge University Press, 1982), chap. 4.

18. Lewis L. Gould, *The Spanish American War and President McKinley* (Lawrence: University Press of Kansas, 1982), chap. 2.

19. Ibid., chap. 3.

20. Kendrick A. Clements, *The Presidency of Woodrow Wilson* (Lawrence: University Press of Kansas), chap. 8.

21. Marc Allen Eisner, *From Warfare State to Welfare State: World War I, Compensatory State Building, and the Limits of the Modern Order* (University Park: Penn State Press, 2000), chap. 3. For the most part, Wilson exercised his enhanced economic powers hesitantly and ineffectually. Robert H. Ferrell, "Woodrow Wilson: A Misfit in Office?" in Joseph G. Dawson III, ed. *Commanders in Chief: Presidential Leadership in Modern Wars* (Lawrence: University Press of Kansas, 1993), 65–86.

22. Clements, *Presidency of Woodrow Wilson*, chap. 10; Andrew J. Polsky and Olesya Tkacheva, "Legacies versus Politics: Herbert Hoover, Partisan Conflict, and the Symbolic Appeal of Associationalism in the 1920s," *International Journal of Politics, Culture, and Society* 16 (2002): 207–235.

23. Larrabee, *Commander in Chief*, 114.

24. Michael J. Hogan, *A Cross of Iron: Harry S. Truman and the Origins of the National Security State, 1945–1954* (Cambridge: Cambridge University Press, 1998); Aaron L. Friedberg, *In the Shadow of the Garrison State: America's Anti-Statism and Its Cold War Strategy* (Princeton: Princeton University Press, 2000), chap. 2.

25. Robert F. Turner, "The War on Terrorism and the Modern Relevance of the Congressional Power to 'Declare War,'" *Harvard Journal of Law and Public Policy* 25 (Spring 2002): 519–537.

26. Gary R. Hess, *Presidential Decisions for War: Korea, Vietnam, and the Persian Gulf* (Baltimore: Johns Hopkins University Press, 2000), 190–194.

27. "The Whigs and the War," *The American Review* 6 (October 1847): 343, as quoted in Norman Graebner, "Lessons of the Mexican War," *Pacific Historical Review* 47 (August 1978): 325–342.

28. Andrew J. Polsky, "Collective Inaction: Presidents, Congress, and Unpopular Wars," *Extensions* (Spring 2008): 4–8.

29. Avella, "President, Congress, and Decisions to Employ Military Force," 57–67.

30. His statement is sometimes translated differently: war is the extension of *politics* by other means.

31. James M. McPherson, *Abraham Lincoln and the Second American Revolution* (New York: Oxford University Press, 1991), chap. 4.

32. Samuel P. Huntington, *The Soldier and the State* (Cambridge: Harvard University Press, 1957).

33. Eliot A. Cohen, *Supreme Command: Soldiers, Statesmen, and Leadership in Wartime* (New York: Anchor Books/Random House, 2002), chap. 1.

34. Ibid., chap. 2.

35. Geoffrey Perret, *Lincoln's War: The Untold Story of America's Greatest President as Commander in Chief* (New York: Random House, 2004), 340.

36. See James M. McPherson, *Tried by War: Abraham Lincoln as Commander in Chief* (New York: Penguin, 2008).

37. Hess, *Presidential Decisions for War*, chap. 4.

38. Cohen, *Supreme Command*, 175ff.

39. Ibid., 179–181.

40. Ibid., 188–198.

41. Thomas E. Ricks, *Fiasco: The American Military Adventure in Iraq* (New York: Penguin Books, 2006, 2007). Wolfowitz's views were evidently influenced by Eliot Cohen. See *Fiasco*, 15–16.

42. See Dale R. Herspring, *Rumsfeld's Wars: The Arrogance of Power* (Lawrence: University Press of Kansas, 2008).

43. Ricks, *Fiasco*, 96–100.

44. Differences exist over the origins of the surge initiative. For an account that emphasizes the role of military advocates of counterinsurgency (COIN) doctrine, see Thomas E. Ricks, *The Gamble: General David Petraeus and the American Military Adventure in Iraq, 2006–2008* (New York: Penguin Press, 2009). For a different perspective that credits President Bush with a more active role, see Bob Woodward, *The War Within, A Secret White House History, 2006–2008* (New York: Simon and Schuster, 2008). I share Ricks's view that there is little evidence to suggest the president abruptly became the prime architect of U.S. policy in Iraq, despite the urging of people such as Eliot Cohen.

18 The Vice Presidency: Dick Cheney, Joe Biden, and the New Vice Presidency

Joseph A. Pika[1]

Constitutionally, vice presidents have virtually no meaningful powers and responsibilities. Historically, they were almost without informal influence as well. But in recent decades, Joseph A. Pika argues, a new vice presidency has developed: active, influential, and endowed with ample institutional resources to take on new assignments for the president. Hastening this transformation has been the political skill and governing experience of most recent vice presidents, especially Walter Mondale, George H. W. Bush, Al Gore, and Dick Cheney. Cheney, in particular, was so influential and controversial that during the 2008 election campaign, charges of an "imperial vice presidency" were raised. His successor to the office, Joe Biden, declared that he had secured a "commitment" from Barack Obama that he would "get to be in the room" when "every important decision" was made. Will Biden build on the Cheney legacy or reject it?

Moments before Barack Obama took the oath of office on January 20, 2009, Joseph R. Biden Jr. was sworn in as the forty-seventh vice president. Biden assumed an office that for eight years had been the object of controversy regarding the role and influence of Bush administration vice president Dick Cheney. Cheney was described widely as "the most powerful vice president in American history." Some observers even began referring to "the imperial vice presidency," a play on the term made famous by Arthur M. Schlesinger Jr.'s *The Imperial Presidency,* a Vietnam-era history of how presidents had aggrandized power during war. Columnist Jonathan Alter argued that "Cheney has simultaneously expanded the power of the vice presidency and reduced its accountability."[2]

Discussing vice presidential power, let alone its imperial overtones, is a dramatic departure from the vice presidency's status throughout most of American history. The office reached its modern nadir in 1973 when Vice President Spiro Agnew was forced to resign after pleading *nolo contendere* to a Justice Department charge of accepting bribes. Gerald Ford and then Nelson Rockefeller became the nation's first unelected vice presidents under provisions of the Twenty-fifth Amendment, ratified only a few years earlier, in 1967. When President Richard Nixon resigned in 1974, Ford succeeded to the presidency and chose Rockefeller as his vice president. Although Ford dropped him from the Republican ticket in 1976, Rockefeller made the vice presidency a more integral part of the modern presidency rather than an office that was largely disconnected from either the White House or Capitol Hill. Rockefeller and his successor, Walter Mondale, fostered a renaissance in the vice presidency by enlarging the possibilities and influence of an office often ridiculed even by its occupants. Mondale, especially, has been credited with creating the "new vice presidency" that Biden entered by providing it with resources and a new vision.[3]

The foundation laid by Mondale was built on by his successors, George H. W. Bush, Dan Quayle, and Al Gore, who consulted one another about how best to structure the office.[4] By serving for eight years each, Bush and Gore provided stability to several of Mondale's changes. Cheney's eight years, however, have triggered new questions about the job and the newfound influence of its occupants.

Bush, the two-term vice president to Ronald Reagan, played a largely behind-the-scenes role in the administration. For example, it was never really clear whether Bush participated actively in shaping foreign policy, his principal area of policy expertise, and his involvement in the Iran-contra affair remained controversial even in the final days of his own presidency. Dan Quayle, Bush's choice as his running mate in 1988 and 1992, never overcame initial public and media doubts about his capacity for the job. For some, Quayle's elevation to the second-highest office in the land did little to remove doubts about whether the vice presidency had overcome its history as "a resting place for mediocrities."[5]

Gore's performance restored confidence in the office's possibilities. Bill Clinton gave his vice president important assignments and relied on him as a senior adviser on both domestic and foreign policy issues. Gore's early effectiveness earned accolades, and he was described by Warren Christopher, a savvy Washington insider who was then serving as secretary of state, as "the most influential vice president in history."[6] After Clinton's first two years in office, Gore was even described as "easily the biggest success story of the administration."[7] But Gore's Boy Scout image was tarnished badly early in the second term by media charges that he had solicited large donations from wealthy "fat cats" during Clinton's 1996 reelection campaign, earning him within the White House the dubious title of "solicitor-in-chief."[8] Clinton had entrusted Gore with sensitive political and policy assignments, evidence of how the vice president's role remained strong in the post-Agnew era. But playing an integral role in the administration carried a price.

Cheney loomed large during the first six years of the George W. Bush administration, rising to a position of influence that some described as a "deputy president" so trusted by Bush that many important issues were delegated fully to him.[9] Several of Cheney's assignments were controversial—energy policy, environmental policy, counterterrorism, intelligence gathering, tax policy, selection of Supreme Court nominees—and he was more interested in achieving policy results than in finding politically palatable solutions. Worse yet, Cheney refused to court the media. He emerged periodically to issue dire warnings prior to the 2003 invasion of Iraq but remained distant from the working press, often literally so when he relocated to "undisclosed locations" outside Washington in an effort to ensure the continuity of government against possible terrorist attacks. To administration critics, Cheney became a dark and sinister force. Unlike Mondale, Bush, Quayle, and Gore, however, Cheney would never be held accountable by the voters for his actions as vice president. He made clear from the outset that he had no intention of pursuing the presidency after Bush completed his term. He answered only to George W. Bush.

Cheney's performance helped to focus unusual attention on the vice presidency during and after the 2008 elections. Numerous books claimed to detail the bureaucratic strategies used by Cheney and his staff to achieve their goals in foreign and domestic policy. Presidential candidates of both parties routinely decried the "Cheney model" when asked about the role their vice president would play in the next administration. The vice presidential debate between Democrat Joe Biden and the Republican nominee, Alaska governor Sarah Palin, attracted more viewers than any of the three debates between presidential candidates John McCain and Barack Obama, although most of the audience was probably attracted more by the furor that surrounded Palin's nomination than by Cheney's record. Vice President Cheney remained unrepentant during interviews with reporters conducted in the last weeks of the administration, even as his successor publicly denounced his practices in interviews of his own. Thus, media and political elites reached a consensus that the Cheney vice presidency had become too powerful, raising new questions about the position's evolution since Mondale.

The debate inspired by the Cheney vice presidency has important implications. If vice presidents have become integral to the day-to-day workings of the modern presidency, a recurring nightmare of the political system may be ended: a vice president forced to assume the complex and critical responsibilities of the presidency but largely unprepared to do so. This was the situation that confronted Vice President Harry Truman when he succeeded Franklin Roosevelt in April 1945. Roosevelt had served as president since March 1933, guiding the country through the Great Depression and World War II. Truman had been vice president less than three months and had met with the president only ten times before being called upon to replace him. In the decades following Truman's succession, concern about instability at the top of the government was heightened by the ever-present possibility of a nuclear confrontation with the Soviet Union. Although the nuclear danger receded, it was replaced by the threat of terrorist attacks like those directed at New York City and Washington, D.C., on September 11, 2001. "Decapitation" is a strategy aimed at causing chaos by killing a nation's leaders. Fear of decapitation pervaded the Bush administration after 9/11, and the new danger elevated the vice presidency.

Rise of the Vice President as Policy Adviser

What is new about the vice presidency? Both journalists and academics have drawn attention to the expanded policy role played by Rockefeller and Mondale, a set of new responsibilities that supplemented the job's traditional ceremonial and political activities.[10] Before agreeing to serve as vice president, Rockefeller sought an explicit mandate from President Ford to chair the Domestic Council. From this vantage point, Rockefeller expected to direct the administration's domestic policy agenda much as Henry Kissinger had dominated foreign policy making from his position as head of the National Security Council staff. But Rockefeller's influence was thwarted by more conservative members of the White House staff, including Cheney, who served initially as deputy chief of staff under Donald Rumsfeld and then as chief of staff when Rumsfeld left the White House to become secretary of defense. Mondale entered office with an even broader charge and much greater support from the president. From the start, Jimmy Carter made it clear that Mondale would be welcome to weigh in on the full range of issues confronting the White House. Carter also let senior staff members know that he would not tolerate efforts to thwart Mondale's influence.[11] Mondale served as an across-the-board senior adviser to Carter and emerged as a key figure in shaping the administration's annual legislative agenda. He was even allowed to arrive and depart by helicopter from the White House grounds, a privilege reserved previously for the president.

Both Rockefeller and Mondale benefited from having a large and professional staff, ready access to the Oval Office, and presidents who were receptive to their advice and involvement. The vice president's staff grew from twenty aides in 1960 to more than seventy during the Carter presidency.[12] This expansion gave the vice president an independent staff structure that largely paralleled the president's, including specialists in domestic and foreign policy and assistants for scheduling, speechwriting, congressional relations, and press relations. Thus, when Rockefeller and Mondale participated in group meetings or met with the president privately, as they both did at least once per week, they benefited from a substantial amount of analytic support. The same support has remained in place and grown still larger for subsequent vice presidents.

Mondale enjoyed additional advantages. He was the first vice president to have a permanent office in the West Wing of the White House, just down the hall from both the Oval Office and the president's other senior advisors. (Agnew had briefly occupied a White House office but usually worked next door in the Executive Office Building, where Lyndon Johnson had become the first vice president to be given an office instead of working exclusively out of the Senate.) Mondale also had an open invitation to attend any meeting on the president's schedule and was given access to all White House papers, including the most sensitive national security information. Members of the vice president's staff closely coordinated their efforts with those of their presidential counterparts and several were cross-listed as members of the president's staff. The result was an enlarged, more challenging position that brought the vice president clearly within the presidential orbit instead of leaving him where the Constitution placed him, halfway between Congress and the presidency.[13] Mondale's activities went well beyond the job's traditional responsibilities to lobby Congress on the administration's behalf, serve as a spokesman to the general public and politically important interest groups, attend ceremonial functions in the president's stead, and assist the party's candidates for office.

Mondale's experience was a watershed. Previous vice presidents had enjoyed only limited policy responsibilities that were exercised largely through study commissions and interdepartmental committees the president might appoint them to chair. In the long history of the office, only Henry Wallace, vice president to Franklin Roosevelt from 1941 to 1945, wielded substantial authority as head of the Economic Defense Board and the Board of Economic Warfare. Rockefeller's influence in the Ford administration was limited,[14] but Mondale, as a "generalist," moved in to and out of issues as he chose. This approach to the job, combined with his extensive Washington experience, numerous contacts with the Democratic Party's liberal wing, and strong interpersonal skills, enabled Mondale to become a major White House presence. Ultimately, however, Mondale's influence depended on Carter's willingness to redefine the role. As Mondale's vice presidential chief of staff acknowledges, "the importance of the office depended entirely on the degree of empowerment and authority that the president was willing to delegate to its occupant."[15]

The more presidents adhere to precedents established by Carter and Mondale, the more firmly such practices have become part of White House lore and are expected of succeeding administrations. Although subject to reversal by any president at any time, informal norms may begin to force presidents to provide their vice presidents with the resources they need to exercise influence. The Mondale precedents have endured. Like Mondale, Vice President George H. W. Bush enjoyed a West Wing office, had a weekly slot on the president's schedule, received the president's daily briefing on foreign policy, and could attend any meetings he wished.[16] The same held true for Quayle, Gore, and Cheney, and these precedents will constitute a baseline test of Biden's stature. Moreover, an informal mechanism transmitted these precedents from one administration to the next. Mondale learned about the job in several meetings with Rockefeller and Hubert Humphrey, Lyndon Johnson's vice president and one of Mondale's longtime mentors.[17] Bush likewise met with Mondale during the Carter-Reagan transition. Bush mentored Quayle, much younger and far less experienced on the national scene than any recent vice president. Al Gore spoke with Mondale and Quayle about their experiences before assuming office and acknowledged that he had studied accounts of the Bush and Mondale experiences, making a conscious effort to learn from their advice and lessons.

Cheney needed no orientation from predecessors to prepare him for the vice presidency. He had gained firsthand experience in the inner workings of presidential administrations through his service in the Ford White House and later as George H. W. Bush's secretary of defense. He had thought through the relationship between president and vice president in 1980 when he participated in discussions at the Republican National Convention between Ronald Reagan and former president Ford. Reagan explored ways to lure the former president onto a "dream ticket" as his vice presidential running mate by creating a "copresidency," with Ford exercising broad responsibilities over personnel, the federal budget, and foreign policy. (The talks fell apart.) When Dan Quayle visited with Cheney in January 2001 and described what the new vice president might expect, Cheney explained that he had reached "a different understanding" with George W. Bush about what his responsibilities would be. Quayle concluded that Cheney expected to be a "surrogate chief of staff," deeply enmeshed in the White House's day-to-day operations. Knowing of Cheney's involvement in the 1980 discussions, Quayle also wondered whether Cheney aspired to become "deputy president," though he acknowledged that Cheney did not believe the president's responsibilities can be shared with anyone else and did not use the term during their meeting.[18] Nonetheless, from the very beginning of the Bush administration, reporters speculated on the heavy influence that the thoroughly experienced Cheney would wield, perhaps tantamount to a copresidency. Such reports produced a conscious effort by Bush's aides, argues Cheney's official biographer, to keep him out of the public eye, contributing in part to his subsequent image problems.[19]

Regardless of whether Cheney's role as vice president is described as "surrogate chief of staff," "copresident," or "deputy president," the implication is clear: Cheney was an enormously influential member of the Bush administration and is commonly regarded as the most powerful vice president in history. Cheney's successor made it clear that he intended to define his role differently. Biden and Cheney engaged in a postelection media debate about the appropriate role of the vice president. Biden described the role he expected to play during an interview with ABC's George Stephanopoulos. Biden said that he had made his expectations for the position clear during a three-and-a-half-hour meeting when Barack Obama asked him to join the ticket: "I said I want a commitment from you that in every important decision you'll make, every critical decision, economic and political as well as foreign policy, I'll get to be in the room."[20] Biden went on to say that during the transition he had participated in making all of Obama's cabinet and White House staff selections. And he was asked to chair two cabinet task forces, one on the condition of the middle class and the other an assessment of the situation in Iraq. Early in the administration, President Obama also assigned to Vice President Biden the job of monitoring spending under the $787 billion stimulus package designed to save jobs and stimulate economic growth. Biden later headed a team assessing the situation in Iraq and played a leading role in the evaluation of candidates for the Supreme Court vacancy created when Justice David Souter retired.

Although Biden once had suggested that he would follow the model set by Vice President Lyndon Johnson,[21] his later description of the position accords more closely with the Mondale model: avoid long-term policy assignments and serve as a senior adviser to the president on the full range of issues where his judgment would be valued.[22] In fact, Biden and Mondale spoke at the 2008 Democratic National Convention and later during the transition, and Biden acknowledged studying closely the agreement about the vice president's duties that Mondale and Carter had drafted in 1976.[23] In general, Biden said he hoped to restore "balance" to the vice presidential role, a swipe at Cheney, whom he had described during the campaign as "probably the most dangerous vice president we've had in American history." Cheney responded in an interview on *Fox News Sunday*: "if he wants to diminish the office of vice president, that's obviously his call."[24]

Vice Presidential Roles

Students of the presidency customarily examine the major roles associated with the office. A similar approach to the vice presidency reveals how meager its responsibilities are and how recent is their vintage. The president's many roles originate in the Constitution, statutes passed by Congress, and the practices and precedents established by predecessors.[25] The president's constitutional roles include chief diplomat, commander in chief, chief legislator, chief magistrate, and chief administrator, whereas the economic manager and party leader roles are traced to extra-constitutional sources. Although the modern era has seen a proliferation of new tasks assigned for presidents to perform, the executive's constitutional roles have been the basis for a substantial expansion of presidential power. This is especially true in the formulation of foreign and domestic policy, in which presidents have come to take the lead. Vice presidential roles offer a sharp contrast both in significance and origin.

Constitutional Roles

Under the Constitution, vice presidents serve as *heir designate* in the event of vacancy or incapacity in the presidency. They also preside over the Senate, casting a vote only in the event of a tie. Far from serving as the basis for expanded influence, as in the case of the presidency, these constitutional roles have seriously inhibited the development of the job.

John Tyler was the first vice president to assume the presidency following a president's death—William Henry Harrison's—and had to overcome congressional resistance to his assuming the title of president rather than "acting president." Historically, presidents who came to the office by vice presidential succession have been held in lesser regard than their predecessors by the public and historians alike.[26] Serving as vice president during a period of presidential illness also has been difficult. Cabinet members and White House aides often actively communicate their resentment of the person who is most likely to prosper at their mentor's expense. For example, jealousy plagued Vice President Bush in 1981 when Ronald Reagan was shot and again in July 1985 when he underwent surgery for colon cancer.[27] In general, vice presidents, by their mere presence, remind presidents of their own mortality.

Presiding over the Senate has made the vice presidency a "constitutional hybrid," lacking a home in either branch of government.[28] Long excluded from executive branch deliberations, vice presidents also were denied a meaningful legislative role by Senate norms that minimized the presiding officer's discretion in controlling business and debate.[29] Even the frequency of vice presidents casting tie-breaking votes declined as the Senate's membership expanded with the addition of new states. Throughout history, vice presidents have cast 244 tie-breaking votes. John Adams cast twenty-nine tie-breakers and John Calhoun twenty-eight, but only sixty-seven were cast from 1900 to 2008. Of the vice presidents since 1961, Lyndon Johnson cast no tie-breaking votes, Humphrey four, Agnew two, Ford none, Rockefeller none, Mondale one, Bush eight, and Quayle none. Most recently, Gore cast four and Cheney eight, six of them from 2001 to 2003, when the partisan balance between Democrats and Republicans in the Senate was quite narrow.[30] Until the changes introduced by Rockefeller and Mondale, the vice president "dwelt in a constitutional limbo somewhere between the legislative and executive branches," while functioning as a full-time member of neither.[31]

Three constitutional amendments made important changes in the vice presidency. The Twenty-fifth Amendment, ratified in 1967, established procedures for dealing with presidential disabilities and for filling vice presidential vacancies, providing guidelines for the selection of Ford and Rockefeller.[32] The Twelfth Amendment (1804) provided for separate Electoral College balloting for president and vice president in order to avoid a repetition of the electoral confusion of 1800 when Thomas Jefferson and his party's vice presidential nominee, Aaron Burr, received the same number of votes for president, throwing the election into the House of Representatives. (Under the original Constitution, all electoral votes were cast for president with the runner-up becoming vice president.) Most scholars believe this change reduced "the Vice Presidency to an insignificant office sought only by insignificant men."[33] The revised selection process, together with popularly based political parties, ensured that vice presidential nominees would be used to balance tickets, placate party factions, or gain electoral votes from a critical state.[34] Vice presidents literally became "also-rans," party tagalongs of mediocre qualifications and accomplishments rather than the second-most qualified candidates for president, which was arguably the case with John Adams and Thomas Jefferson, the nation's first two vice presidents. These electoral consequences so prominent in American history were largely reversed by the Twenty-second Amendment, ratified in 1951, which limits presidents to two terms in office. By moving successful presidents aside, the amendment encourages second-term vice presidents to seek the presidency, as Nixon, Bush, and Gore did. Cheney broke this pattern when he chose not to run for nomination, and that is likely to be the case with Biden, as well.

Statutory Roles

Vice presidents, unlike presidents, have neither numerous statutory responsibilities nor the influence that goes with them. The greatest potential for influence is found in the vice president's statutory membership on the National Security Council (NSC), a role that Harry Truman sought for his vice president to prevent a recurrence of his own experience.[35] But even here, the vice president's actual involvement hinges on the president's preferred style of making foreign policy, which may or may not include the NSC. John Kennedy, for example, created an *ad hoc* group of advisers to help him resolve the Cuban missile crisis in 1962 that included both NSC and non-NSC members but not Vice President Johnson. Nixon sidestepped the NSC altogether (as well as Vice President Agnew) when deciding to invade Cambodia (1970), reestablish ties with mainland China (1972), and sign the Strategic Arms Limitation Treaty (SALT I) with the Soviet Union (1972). Nor did Reagan use the NSC to advise him on secret negotiations with Iran in 1985–1986.

Practice and Precedent

Practice and precedent have been by far the most important determinants of vice presidential roles. The development of these roles was a twentieth-century phenomenon. Although some roles of the modern president can be traced to precedents established by nineteenth-century and early twentieth century predecessors, harbingers of vice presidential power are few and far between, making the office a distinctly recent product.

John Adams was the only vice president to participate in cabinet meetings until Woodrow Wilson asked Vice President Thomas Marshall to preside over these sessions during the president's lengthy trip abroad to negotiate the peace treaty that concluded World War I. A few presidents relied on their vice presidents for policy advice (notably James Polk, Abraham Lincoln, and William McKinley), but doing so was not routine. As a vice presidential candidate in 1896, Theodore Roosevelt suggested that vice presidents join the cabinet (although he never adopted the practice himself when given the opportunity as president), and both tickets endorsed this idea in the 1920 presidential election. Calvin Coolidge, who was Warren Harding's vice president, regularly attended cabinet meetings, but Charles Dawes, elected on the Republican ticket with Coolidge in 1924, did not. To do so, Dawes argued, would limit the freedom of future presidents to select their advisers. Herbert Hoover reinstituted the practice with his vice president, Charles Curtis, and vice presidents have routinely been included in meetings of the cabinet ever since.[36]

Vice presidents also began to serve as administration representatives to foreign and domestic audiences in the twentieth century. John Nance Garner, who was Franklin Roosevelt's vice president from 1933 to 1941, was the first to travel abroad in an official capacity. Until then, vice presidents were not involved in

Table 18.1 Foreign Trips by Recent Vice Presidents

Vice president	Number of foreign trips	Vice president	Number of foreign trips
Nixon	7	Mondale	14
Johnson	10	Bush	23, 18[a]
Humphrey	12	Quayle	19[b]
Agnew	7	Gore	25, 5[c]
Ford	1	Cheney	2, 9[d]
Rockefeller	6		

Sources: Data covering Nixon through Mondale come from Joel K. Goldstein, *The Modern Vice Presidency*, 159. Reprinted by permission of Princeton University Press. [a]Bush data, separated by term, come from "George Herbert Walker Bush: Chronology," a document issued by the White House. [b]Quayle data come from the former vice president's records. [c]Gore data, separated by term, come from his office and cover travel through August 19, 1997, with later data recreated by the author from public sources. [d]Cheney data, separated by term, are recreated from news releases and speeches posted on http://georgewbush-whitehouse.archives.gov/vicepresident.

international relations, a pattern established by Jefferson when he declined a request from John Adams to visit France as the president's diplomatic representative. Henry Wallace, FDR's second vice president, went on several wartime missions, and recent vice presidents have traveled extensively as roving ambassadors, although often for ceremonial purposes. As Table 18.1 shows, a sudden decline in vice presidents' foreign travel began in 1997. The Clinton administration's political problems at home and Gore's need to prepare his own presidential campaign in 1999 probably account for the decline in his second-term travel. Cheney traveled overseas only twice during his first four years in office, testimony to the pressing nature of his post-9/11 responsibilities at home.

In addition to making ceremonial appearances, modern vice presidents carry explicit political messages to Congress and important interest groups. The origin of these activities is quite recent. Historically, few vice presidents lobbied Congress to support administration proposals. Even more surprisingly, several of them actively conspired with administration opponents to defeat such proposals.[37] FDR saw liaison with Congress as an activity ripe for greater vice presidential activity and dispatched Garner on legislative assignments.[38] Garner, a former Speaker of the House of Representatives, devised the system of weekly presidential conferences with congressional leaders that subsequently became a mainstay of legislative-executive relations. But Garner opposed Roosevelt's proposal to expand the Supreme Court in 1937 and broke with FDR when the president violated the norm of serving only two terms. Garner's successors have varied widely in their efforts as congressional lobbyists, but eleven of the fourteen men who have served as vice president since Garner brought congressional experience to the job, including Mondale, Bush, Quayle, Gore, Cheney, and Biden.

Most vice presidential activities are recent developments that have been firmly translated into public expectations. Today it is inconceivable that a vice president would oppose a president's nominee for an appointed post or openly question administration policy, steps that were not uncommon until the mid-twentieth century. A critical change in the office occurred in 1940, when FDR became the first presidential candidate to demand the right to select his own running mate. Party bosses, who previously controlled nominating conventions, were never concerned about whether the members of a victorious ticket would serve well together as a team after their election. Since 1940, however, presidential nominees have stressed compatibility as an important criterion for vice presidential nominees, opening the door to selecting someone who is expected to be the president's "lieutenant." Both parties allowed the convention delegates to choose running mates in 1948 and the Democrats continued to do so in 1952 and 1956, but since then conventions invariably have followed the presidential nominee's preference. This change created a greater opportunity for vice presidents to become trusted advisers, even though presidential nominees continued to consider traditional concerns about geographic and ideological balance.[39]

John Kerry, the Democratic nominee for president in 2004, reportedly argued that a presidential candidate can select an August, October, or January running mate. An *August* candidate satisfies the demands of the party faithful gathered in the national conventions, energizes a faltering campaign, and perhaps unifies the party if he or she is the second-place finisher in the primaries or the leader of an ideological wing. An *October* candidate will perform well on the campaign trail, thereby serving as a true asset to the ticket in garnering support from critical constituencies in major battleground states. A *January* candidate's main virtue will be to help the president govern. Optimally, one candidate meets multiple goals, but each presidential nominee is likely to face different strategic circumstances. Sarah Palin, for example, proved an asset at the 2008 Republican convention but less so on the campaign trail, partly because of the doubts surrounding her qualifications to serve starting in January. Both George W. Bush and Barack Obama seem to have placed maximum emphasis on selecting a *January* candidate. Cheney and Biden came from two of the nation's smallest states, delivering only three electoral votes each.[40]

An Expanded Political Role

Since World War II, death, assassination, and resignation have thrust vice presidents frequently into the national spotlight. Between 1945 and 1977, three men originally chosen as vice president occupied the presidency nearly half the time: Truman, Johnson, and Ford. Roosevelt and Kennedy died in office, and their successors, Truman and Johnson, were elected to full terms of their own. Nixon's resignation from the presidency in August 1974 led to Ford's brief tenure. The frailty of presidents was underscored further by the medical problems of presidents Dwight Eisenhower, Johnson, and Reagan. Unsuccessful assassination attempts were made on Truman, Ford, and Reagan while they were in office. George H. W. Bush had two health scares; the relatively good health of Presidents Carter, Clinton, and George W. Bush was unusual.

During the same period, vice presidents also became more prominent figures in presidential elections. Nixon, Humphrey, Mondale, Bush, and Gore received their party's presidential nomination, but until Bush's victory in 1988, no incumbent vice president had been elected to the presidency since Martin Van Buren in 1836. Vice presidential candidates also receive more attention during the general election campaign. Repeating the precedent set in 1976, vice presidential debates were televised during each subsequent election cycle except 1980 and gained a record audience in 2008. Vice presidential candidates are also now closely integrated into the national campaign. Clinton and Gore made many joint appearances in 1992 and 1996; Bush and Cheney campaigned more separately in 2000 and 2004; Gore and his running mate, Joe Lieberman, made more joint appearances in 2000 than did Kerry and John Edwards in 2004. McCain and Palin seemed inseparable in 2008; Obama's and Biden's campaigns, although closely coordinated, targeted largely different states.

Cheney as Corporate CEO (Chief Executive Officer)

Dick Cheney enjoyed all the trappings associated with the modern vice presidency: a West Wing office; a large, professional staff integrated with the president's; a private weekly luncheon with the president; access to the White House paper flow and national security briefings; inclusion in all important policymaking meetings; and selective policy assignments in addition to his role as general adviser. Cheney's experience and Washington savvy enabled him to make more of these resources than any previous vice president had been able to do. Bush enhanced the vice president's role substantially by delegating lead responsibility for important policy areas. Cheney's reputation for exercising power during the Bush administration was enormous. Only thorough documentary research will establish the reality of that influence, a task made more difficult by the shroud of secrecy under which Cheney operated. Nor can we rely on insiders' firsthand accounts. Close Bush associates, seeking to honor their boss, have already gone to some lengths to deny that Cheney overshadowed the president in any way.[41]

Journalists concluded quickly that Cheney was "the most influential vice president in history." Similar language, of course, was used for Mondale and Gore, suggesting either that the office has been on a consistent upward trend or that journalists are easily impressed, perhaps influenced by spin issued by the vice presidents' staffs. But considerable evidence indicates that the "special understanding" between Bush and Cheney involved a new definition of the vice president's role: chief executive officer (CEO) to Bush's chairman of the board. Even before Cheney took office in 2001, Dana Milbank of the *Washington Post* anticipated much of what emerged during the next eight years: "Call it Bush-Cheney Inc. Chairman Bush sets the tone, sets goals and signs off on final decisions. CEO Cheney makes it happen."[42]

This transfer of the corporate authority structure to the presidency was especially congenial for two men with extensive corporate experience. Bush had served as CEO of his own oil firm and then as managing partner of the Texas Rangers baseball team before becoming governor of Texas; and Cheney was chairman of the board and CEO of the Halliburton Corporation from 1995 to 2000 before reentering politics. Their styles were also complementary. Bush was notoriously uninterested in details and willing to rely on gut instincts in making decisions, whereas Cheney revealed the career staffer's quintessential drive to master details on the way to making carefully reasoned decisions. Cheney's greatest strength as vice president was also his greatest weakness: "a preference for ends over means, or results over process."[43] In the pressure to advance the war on terror, Cheney's willingness to circumvent colleagues in the administration and ignore Congress reflected this results-oriented approach to advancing the president's agenda.

Much of the current understanding of Cheney's role in the Bush administration relies on journalistic accounts, which provide impressive evidence of the vice president's influence based on Bush's confidence and Cheney's acumen for exercising power in Washington. At times Cheney functioned as the administration's principal decision maker. As Barton Gellman summarizes, "Cheney took the helm—sometimes at Bush's direction, sometimes with his tacit consent, and sometimes without the president's apparent awareness."[44] On other occasions, especially in the second term, Gellman argues that Bush intervened to redirect affairs, particularly as the president's confidence and mastery of issues grew and he recognized that Cheney's uncompromising commitment to fundamental principles was so deep that he often did not weigh the political costs of his actions.[45]

Cheney's Influence

Why did Bush lean so heavily on Cheney? To a large degree, he did so because of Cheney's lack of ambition for higher office. Mondale argued that

Carter could rely on him for objective advice because he had no other institutional loyalties; unlike a cabinet secretary, he would not seek to advance the fortunes of the department he headed. But Mondale and all other modern vice presidents were concerned with their own political fortunes. Not so, Cheney. From the outset, Cheney made it clear that he would not seek to succeed Bush—if for no other reason than his health would not allow it. During his eight years as vice president, Cheney experienced eight health episodes, including a heart attack (his fourth since age thirty-seven), angioplasty, and procedures to insert a stent and implant a defibrillator.[46] But as Gellman observes, "no ambition" is not the same as "no agenda," and Cheney found many ways to advance the policies he embraced and thwart those he opposed.[47]

Cheney established his credentials with Bush during the 2000 campaign, when he headed the search for a Republican vice presidential candidate, emerging as the surprise pick himself. He later oversaw transition planning, launched even before the winner of the election was decided in Florida. Unlike other presidential nominees, Bush did not interview any of the many rumored candidates for vice president, either the Republican governors of major states (John Engler of Michigan, George Pataki of New York, Tom Ridge of Pennsylvania, and Frank Keating of Oklahoma) or prominent Republican senators (John Danforth of Missouri, Bill Frist of Tennessee, Jon Kyl of Arizona, and Chuck Hagel of Nebraska). Cheney conducted the interviews, and he and Bush made the choice together. After election day, the transition was run for several weeks out of the kitchen in Cheney's McLean, Virginia, home, tapping his extensive Washington network to assemble lists of names while others focused on the unfolding developments in Florida. This work allowed Cheney to populate the administration with allies whose ties to the vice president ensured that they would support his preferred policies.

Cheney was in charge on 9/11 when terrorists attacked the World Trade Center and the Pentagon. On that morning, the president was in Florida promoting his education initiative and returned only later in the day after the danger had clearly passed. Cheney presided over meetings in the underground White House bunker, conversing with the president by phone but also taking action when needed. Although both the president and vice president denied it, Cheney, acting on his own, issued the shoot-down order to American fighter pilots to fire on other jetliners if they approached Washington.[48]

Cheney also emerged as the central administration figure in the weeks and months after the attacks, driving the administration's strategy in the war on terror. The tasks were clear: find and defeat the bad guys; assert the president's prerogatives in fashioning a wartime response; and prevent any subsequent attack that might involve chemical, biological, or nuclear weapons. In the face of such a daunting agenda, the administration sought as much discretion as possible to combat Islamic terrorists.[49] Cheney and the Office of the Vice President stood at the center of many controversial decisions. He guided the National Security Agency in creating a domestic surveillance program (officially called the Terrorist Surveillance Program) that monitored Americans' e-mail, telephone, and fax traffic to detect potential al-Qaida agents and collaborators.[50] This program clashed with the protections established by Congress in 1978 against unauthorized wiretapping and consequently was kept secret from all but four members of Congress and from many administration principals, including Condoleezza Rice, the national security advisor.

The vice president's personal schedule reflected his fixation on possible impending attacks and the need to ensure continuity of government so that another surprise attack would not disrupt the federal government's operations. It became a running joke that Cheney was working from an "undisclosed location" outside Washington. Less widely known was that scores of other government managers also were being rotated to locations outside the capital.[51] Cheney's concern with gloomy scenarios and his publicly announced willingness to consider "any means at our disposal, basically, to achieve our objective," led to a new nickname: "Dark Side."[52] The term took on sinister meaning with later revelations that Cheney's office had taken the lead in crafting administration policies for detaining suspected terrorists; trying them in military commissions outside the reach of the established federal, state, and military court systems; and using aggressive interrogation techniques, including some considered around the world to be torture, to secure "actionable intelligence" that would enable U.S. forces to prosecute the war on terror. All gloves were off in this new war, whose legal justification was termed "the New Paradigm."[53] David Addington, Cheney's legal counsel, led the closely held campaign within the administration to redefine presidential powers, aided by cooperative allies, particularly John Yoo in the Office of Legal Counsel in the Justice Department. Cheney and Addington "offered legal certitude at a moment of paramount political and legal confusion."[54]

According to Bob Woodward, Cheney played a major role in selling the president on invading Iraq as the way to change its regime, nourish democracy in the Middle East, and prevent weapons of mass destruction from falling into the hands of terrorists. Secretary of State Colin Powell described Cheney as harboring "an unhealthy fixation" on the link between al-Qaida and Iraqi dictator Saddam Hussein, often losing sight of the uncertainty and ambiguity that surrounded pieces of intelligence as the vice president connected dots that were really unrelated.[55] Cheney simply would not accept the CIA's interpretation, later confirmed by the 9/11 Commission, that there was no connection between Saddam's regime and al-Qaida.[56]

In August 2002 it was Cheney who first publicly raised the specter of Hussein's developing nuclear weapons, and he openly challenged the value of UN-sponsored weapons inspections, the policy preferred by European allies and congressional Democrats. In the case of Iraq, Cheney regarded "the risks of inaction [as] far greater than the risk of action."[57] Moreover, on the eve of the 2003 invasion he publicly predicted great success, telling Tim Russert on NBC's *Meet the Press* that American forces would be greeted as liberators and that large numbers of ground forces would not be needed after military operations halted. In 2005, as American casualties mounted and Iraqi deaths soared, he told CNN interviewer Larry King that the high casualty figures demonstrated that the terrorists were in the "last throes" of the insurgency.[58]

Master of Bureaucratic Politics

September 11 may have cemented Bush's reliance on Cheney, but Bush had already signaled his intent to lean heavily on the vice president. During the early months of the administration, the vice president's portfolio included economic and security policies (the latter included terrorism and intelligence), as well as relations with Congress. Each domain involved Cheney's participation in coordinating meetings. Cheney was the first vice president to regularly attend the Principals Meeting, at which the members of the National Security Council meet without the president. At one point, the vice president explored the possibility of chairing these sessions, but Condoleezza Rice, as national security assistant, retained that assignment.[59] Another indication of Cheney's deep involvement in national security matters was the daily prebriefing he received from the CIA before the same material was presented to the president an hour later.[60]

On economic policy, Cheney attended meetings of the National Economic Council, another White House coordinating group, and also joined the informal weekly White House lunches of the secretaries of commerce, labor, and Treasury; the director of the Office of Management and Budget (OMB); and others. Nor did he shy away from exercising direct authority over budgetary matters. Cheney chaired the administration's Budget Review Board, the body that guided agencies' preparation of annual budget requests and heard appeals from OMB's decisions. Unlike previous administrations, the vice president, not the president, heard and resolved those appeals.[61] In relations with Congress, Cheney became the first vice president to join his party's weekly Senate caucus meetings, serving as an authoritative White House contact. Unlike other vice presidents, he also was given an office on the House side of the Capitol Building to meet with House Republicans.

Cheney's regular attendance in these coordinating meetings reflected his willingness to invest enormous time and energy to sustain relationships with key players in the executive and legislative branches, the kinds of activities usually delegated to members of the vice president's staff. His personal efforts were in addition to the coordination provided by members of the Office of the Vice President staff, who were similarly well-connected with their counterparts in the White House. Lewis "Scooter" Libby's official title made him a presidential as well as a vice presidential aide on national security matters, and Addington worked closely with attorneys in the White House, the Department of Justice, and the Department of Defense on issues of national security law.[62] But Cheney derived important advantages from attending meetings himself. The vice president's status allowed him to steer deliberations in these meetings, even though he usually listened more than he spoke. Unlike other presidential advisers, Cheney had three opportunities to influence policy: in preliminary meetings held to shape options, in the meetings at which options were presented to the president, and in private meetings with the president. These multiple opportunities to exert influence were not lost on other participants in the never-ending game of bureaucratic politics.

Many accounts suggest that Cheney did not feel constrained by the formal procedures established to structure presidential decision making. He was not reluctant to conduct end-runs around other advisers if that is what it took to accomplish his goals. For example, Cheney convinced the president to reverse the nation's position on global warming and to question whether there was sufficient scientific evidence to condemn carbon dioxide emissions. At Cheney's urging (he assumed the lead role as chair of the president's Energy Task Force), Bush reversed his 2000 campaign position on global warming without consulting Secretary of State Colin Powell or Christine Todd Whitman, the head of the Environmental Protection Agency, both of whom were concerned about the likely international repercussions this step would have.[63] Similarly, Cheney overrode Attorney General John Ashcroft's objections to the plan drafted by the Office of the Vice President to process captured enemy combatants and suspected terrorists. When Ashcroft went to the White House to complain about the emerging policy, he was told to meet with Cheney, not Bush. Neither Powell nor Rice was informed that Bush was on the brink of approving the use of military commissions rather than the U.S. courts. Bush made this decision at one of his private lunches with the vice president, and the policy went into effect without following the usual procedures to distribute the plan and secure the approval of interested executive agencies.[64]

Cheney understood bureaucratic politics like no other vice president because he had worked in the Ford White House and as George H. W. Bush's secretary of defense. His staff was equally adept at inside strategy and tactics. This gave Cheney a competitive advantage during the first term. The decline in Cheney's power during the second term can be traced to multiple factors: other administration players had learned to play the game; Libby was forced by scandal to resign, thereby removing a skillful aide; and many of the vice president's original allies, placed in high-ranking positions during the transition, had left their jobs.

Opposition mounted to many of the policies Cheney had been instrumental in establishing. Justice Department officials rebelled against the administration's domestic surveillance program. Only last-minute interventions by several White House aides prevented a mass resignation, which the press would have compared to the Saturday Night Massacre during the Watergate scandal, when the three highest-ranking officials of the Justice Department resigned.[65] The 9/11 Commission scrutinized administration policies and raised questions about its performance on intelligence gathering. A series of Supreme Court decisions held that detainees at Guantánamo Bay were not beyond the reach and protections of American law.[66] Libby resigned after lying about his involvement in a classic Washington maneuver: leaking a story to the press to damage a critic. Although several administration officials had revealed to reporters the identity of a CIA agent, Valerie Plame, the wife of a vocal critic of the administration's invasion of Iraq, only Libby was prosecuted, after lying about his actions to the grand jury.

Although Cheney's influence declined, it was still substantial in Bush's second term. For example, the vice president headed the selection panel that identified candidates for two Supreme Court vacancies in 2005; both John Roberts and Samuel Alito were on Cheney's short list. But Bush did not follow Cheney's advice about Donald Rumsfeld. After resisting pressure that mounted throughout 2006 to remove Rumsfeld as secretary of defense, Bush asked for his resignation when the Republicans suffered a major midterm election defeat in November. Cheney made it known publicly that he disagreed with the president's decision. Independent of Cheney, Bush then reassessed policy in Iraq and adopted the "surge," a rapid increase in U.S. troop strength deployed differently under the leadership of General David Petraeus.

Imperatives of Responsibility

By chance, Cheney was vice president at the time of a major national security crisis. His outlook on the president's powers in foreign policy profoundly influenced the American response to the terrorist attacks. Cheney's views had been shaped by three factors: his service as Ford's White House chief of staff during a period when Congress imposed severe limits on the president's foreign policy powers; his service on the congressional committee that investigated the Iran-contra affair; and his service as secretary of defense during the Persian Gulf War. Combined, these experiences had convinced him that the president's constitutional powers had been eroded severely by Congressional aggrandizement.

Cheney's interpretation was directly counter to the prevailing post-Vietnam consensus, which held that presidents had aggrandized their war powers and in doing so had threatened the constitutional balance with Congress. Cheney frequently pointed to the minority report of the Iran-contra investigating committee (written by Addington) as an expression of his own views.[67] Despite his years in the House of Representatives, Cheney believed that giving Congress a say before an administration launched covert actions or used military force was a formula for government inaction; the consensus building needed to persuade Congress to act meant that problems would go unaddressed.[68] Nor, in Cheney's view, did the administration need to inform Congress of its top-secret tactics in the war on terror. Consequently, the administration limited its briefings to the narrowest possible group in Congress, the chairs and ranking members of the intelligence committees. Based on his expansive interpretation of presidential powers, Cheney had informed Congress in 1991 that President George H. W. Bush had the authority to invade Iraq without a congressional authorization. A decade later, he went still further. Cheney believed that Congress could not prohibit President George W. Bush from using the military on American soil to deter or prevent terrorist attacks, since the homeland had become a battlefield.[69]

Several times during his vice presidency, Cheney said that he and the president hoped to overcome the "unwise" erosion of institutional power that had afflicted the presidency since Watergate and restore the institution to its rightful constitutional status.[70] Moreover, Cheney directly associated efforts to weaken the vice presidency with those that had weakened the presidency, arguing that he, like the president, deserved to enjoy the right of executive privilege. In 2002, when an arm of Congress, the General Accounting Office (renamed the Government Accountability Office in 2004), sought information from Cheney about meetings he had conducted with business executives while fashioning the administration's energy plan, Cheney explained that both he and the president needed "to preserve our ability to get unvarnished advice from anybody we want on any subject," the classic justification for presidential—and now vice presidential—executive privilege.[71] Going further, Bush issued an executive order in March 2003 that for the first time gave the vice president authority to classify and declassify documents throughout the government, a power previously exercised only by the president.[72] No other modern vice president has had such grand goals: to reestablish presidential power and to extend some of those powers to the vice presidency, as well.[73]

As a result of the 9/11 attacks, Bush and Cheney viewed America as not only at war but also under siege, with the next assault imminent. This new conflict, they argued, would be less predictable than any in the nation's past. There was no way to know when or where the enemy would strike, and the potential costs, given the advances in weaponry, would be catastrophic. After 9/11, the White House was dominated by "imperatives of responsibility," a commitment to ensure that such an attack would never happen again. This outlook set off frequent clashes throughout the administration "between fear of another attack, which drives officials into doing whatever they can to prevent it, and the countervailing fear of violating the law, which checks their urge toward prevention."[74]

Cheney used his voice and bureaucratic skills to carve out maximum presidential discretion, a course he justified on the basis of a novel interpretation of presidential authority known as the "unitary executive." In this view, the president's unique responsibility to "preserve, protect and defend the Constitution" differs from the obligation to "support the Constitution" sworn by other federal officials. In emergencies, presidents should not allow adherence to the laws to endanger the nation's safety. Both Lincoln and FDR exercised such powers of presidential prerogative; and Cheney led the effort to justify and further expand Bush's use of prerogative, arguing that such powers rested on an inherent constitutional authority subject to check by neither Congress nor the judiciary.[75]

During a final interview televised on PBS, Cheney carefully avoided the term *mistake* but acknowledged making "miscalculations," such as underestimating the difficulty of getting Iraqis to create a self-governing democracy. But Cheney defended gathering intelligence through "robust" or "enhanced" interrogations, the administration's "terrorist surveillance program," and other counterterrorism efforts that he believed had succeeded in preventing additional 9/11-style attacks on the United States. The threat of terrorism had been paramount in the administration's mind and remained so to the end.[76]

Conclusion

Cheney's greatest legacy for the modern vice presidency will be his all-out campaign to reclaim presidential power. Unlike Lincoln and FDR, Cheney asserted a novel interpretation: prerogative power does not require that the president receive even after-the-fact approval by other branches of government. Nor did Cheney believe that public support was important to sustain. As he told PBS's Jim Lehrer, being "willing to take the political heat" from doing what is right "is more important . . . than being loved."[77] After Bush's 2004 reelection, Cheney would never again appear on a ballot, the foundation of his influence with the president. As Cheney told Lehrer, "my effectiveness for the president has been directly related to the fact that I've not been a candidate—that when I get involved in issues on the White House or on Capitol Hill, it's because I'm representing the president and we're working on his agenda . . .," not worrying about "how I'm going to do in the Iowa caucuses."

Cheney's tenure in office poses a novel question: is it good for the system to have a vice president who is accountable only to the president? Cheney's experience suggests the dangers of such an arrangement. A vice president committed to serving the president's interests to the exclusion of his own is also likely to be committed to maximizing presidential power. Ironically, after so much public concern about Cheney's excessive influence, the American public may have repeated history by electing Vice President Biden, who is unlikely to seek the presidency in 2016 at age 73. Biden could follow a path of total commitment similar to Cheney's or develop a new model for the vice presidency that involves both total commitment and public accountability.

Notes

1. The author thanks Kyle DeRouen for his able research assistance on this project.

2. Jonathan Alter, "The Imperial (Vice) Presidency," *Newsweek*, February 27, 2007, www.opednews.com/maxwrite/linkframe.php?linkid=12322.

3. Joel K. Goldstein, "The Rising Power of the Modern Vice Presidency," *Presidential Studies Quarterly* 38:3 (September 2008): 374–389; Richard Moe, "The Making of the Modern Vice Presidency: A Personal Reflection," *Presidential Studies Quarterly* 38:3 (September 2008): 390–400.

4. For a discussion of these vice presidencies see Joseph A. Pika, "The Vice Presidency: New Opportunities, Old Constraints," in *The Presidency and the Political System*, 6th ed., ed. Michael Nelson (Washington, D.C.: CQ Press, 2000), 533–569.

5. Arthur M. Schlesinger Jr., *The Cycles of American History* (Boston: Houghton Mifflin, 1986), 341.

6. Warren Christopher, as quoted in Elaine Sciolino and Todd S. Purdum, "Al Gore, One Vice President Who Is Eluding the Shadows," *New York Times*, February 19, 1995, A1.

7. Peter J. Boyer, "Gore's Dilemma," *The New Yorker*, November 28, 1994, 104.

8. Bob Woodward, "Gore Was 'Solicitor-in-Chief,'" *Washington Post*, March 2, 1997, A1. Woodward documented that Gore had made fifty-two calls from White House phones, raising about $800,000.

9. Barton Gellman, *Angler: The Cheney Vice Presidency* (New York: Penguin, 2008).

10. Academic attention devoted to the vice presidency flourished in the 1980s. Joel K. Goldstein, *The Modern American Vice Presidency: The Transformation of a Political*

Institution (Princeton: Princeton University Press, 1982), drew a distinction between institutional and political duties performed by vice presidents (134–135). Paul Light, *Vice-Presidential Power: Advice and Influence in the White House* (Baltimore: Johns Hopkins University Press, 1984) divided the job into ceremonial, political, and policy activities (chap. 2). For other general discussions of the vice presidency, see Thomas E. Cronin, "Rethinking the Vice-Presidency," in *Rethinking the Presidency*, ed. Thomas E. Cronin (Boston: Little, Brown, 1982), for a twelve-part job description (326–327); Michael Nelson, *A Heartbeat Away* (New York: Priority Press, 1988); Michael Turner, *The Vice President as Policy Maker: Rockefeller in the Ford White House* (Westport, Conn.: Greenwood, 1982). More recent treatments include Timothy Walch, ed. *At the President's Side: The Vice Presidency in the Twentieth Century* (Columbia: University of Missouri Press, 1997) and the Symposium on the New Vice Presidency published in *Presidential Studies Quarterly* 38:3 (September 2008). In the latter, see especially the essays by Joel K. Goldstein, "The Rising Power of the Modern Vice Presidency," 374–389; and by Richard Moe, "The Making of the Modern Vice Presidency: A Personal Reflection," 390–400. Finally, see Jody C. Baumgartner, *The American Vice Presidency Reconsidered* (Westport, Conn.: Praeger, 2006).

11. Moe, "The Making of the Modern Vice Presidency."

12. Light, *Vice Presidential Power*.

13. The Constitution assigns vice presidents legislative, not executive, responsibilities: to preside over the Senate and cast a tie-breaking vote. Most vice presidents, therefore, operated within the walls of Congress, not as part of the executive branch.

14. For example, he proposed nineteen policy recommendations for the 1976 State of the Union message, but only six were adopted. Turner, *Vice President as Policy Maker*, 85 and 210, n. 91.

15. Moe, "The Making of the Modern Vice Presidency," 392.

16. Light, *Vice Presidential Power*, 265.

17. Letter, Rockefeller to Mondale, December 10, 1976, folder "Transition-Rockefeller (4)," box 22, *Cannon Papers*, Gerald R. Ford Library, Ann Arbor, Michigan.

18. Gellman, *Angler*, 57–60. Also see the four-part series published in the *Washington Post* from June 24, 2007, to June 27, 2007, coauthored by Gellman and Jo Becker. For an account of the 1980 discussions, see Stephen F. Hayes, *Cheney: The Untold Story of America's Most Powerful and Controversial Vice President* (New York: HarperCollins, 2007), 152–155.

19. See Hayes's discussion of Andrea Mitchell's report using this term on the NBC *Nightly News* January 23, 2001. Hayes, *Cheney*, 305.

20. Quoted in Brian Knowlton, "Biden and Cheney Clash on Role of No. 2," *Caucus* the *New York Times* Politics Blog, posted December 21, 2008, http://thecaucus.blogs. nytimes.com/2008/12/21/with-biden-and-cheney-clashing-views-of-a-job.

21. Ryan Lizza, "Biden's Brief," *The New Yorker*, October 20, 2008, 5.

22. Jennifer Parker, "Biden to Chair White House Task Force on Middle Class," http:// abcnews.go.com/ThisWeek/Story?id=6502378&page=1.

23. This story is recounted in Lizza, "Biden's Brief." An eleven-page talking memo had been drafted by Richard Moe, Mondale's chief of staff, and formed the basis for the discussion with Carter as per Moe's discussion in "The Making of the Modern Vice Presidency." The memo can be found at www.mnhs.org/collections/upclose/Mondale-CarterMemo-Scanned.pdf. For a report of transition contacts with Mondale, see Chris Barrish, "Former Vice President Mondale Deems Biden Fit to Follow Trail He Blazed," *News Journal* (Wilmington, Del.), January 10, 2009, A1.

24. Knowlton, "Biden and Cheney Clash."

25. For a discussion and critique of the focus on presidential roles, see David L. Paletz, "Perspectives on the Presidency," in *The Institutionalized Presidency*, ed. Norman Thomas and Hans Baade (Dobbs Ferry, N.Y.: Oceana, 1972).

26. Steven J. Jarding, "Historical Assessments of Succession Presidents," *Extensions* (Carl Albert Congressional Research and Studies Center), Fall 1985, 14–15. Jarding found that "succession presidents cannot overcome the martyred image of their predecessors" and that this judgment endures among historians, 15.

27. See articles in the *New York Times* for July 24, August 16, and September 26, 1985.

28. For the term "constitutional hybrid," see John D. Feerick, *From Falling Hands: The Story of Presidential Succession* (New York: Fordham University Press, 1965), *ix*; and Cronin, "Rethinking the Vice-Presidency," 239.

29. Lyndon Johnson, as noted earlier, was the first vice president to have an office in the presidential compound, in this case in the Old Executive Office Building (now known as the Eisenhower Executive Office Building). With the provision of office space in the West Wing, vice presidents enjoyed three prestigious office locations because they retained space in the Capitol, as well. Cheney was also extended use of an office on the House side, giving him four such locations.

30. Senate Historical Office, table 6-1, "Occasions When Vice Presidents Have Voted to Break Tie Votes in the Senate," www.senate.gov/artandhistory/history/resources/pdf/VPTies.pdf. See the discussion in Baumgartner, chaps. 2, 6. Cheney nearly had the opportunity to make a significant ruling from the chair, announcing that he would approve the so-called nuclear option that Republicans were prepared to use in cutting off Democratic filibusters of judicial nominees. However, a political settlement was reached.

31. Donald Young, *American Roulette: The History and Dilemma of the Vice Presidency* (New York: Viking, 1979), 3–4.

32. The Twenty-fifth Amendment provides that the vice president shall serve as acting president when a presidential disability is declared either by the president or by the vice president supported by a majority of the cabinet. It also provides that a vacancy in the vice presidency can be filled by presidential appointment, with the consent of both houses of Congress.

33. Quote from Young, *American Roulette*, 21.

34. Goldstein, *Modern American Vice Presidency*, 48.

35. Baumgartner, 30.

36. Young, *American Roulette*, 123, 156–157.

37. This was especially true of vice presidents Burr, Calhoun, and Charles Fairbanks.

38. FDR made the suggestion as a vice presidential candidate in 1920 in a popular magazine of the era, *The Saturday Evening Post*, during October 1920. See Feerick, *From Falling Hands*, 182.

39. Baumgartner, *American Vice Presidency Reconsidered*, dates the onset of the "modern" vice presidency to 1960 when both parties' presidential nominees selected their own running mates.

40. Attributed to Kerry by his former press secretary, David Wade. See Ryan Lizza, "Biden's Brief."

41. Michael Abramowitz, "Two Advisers Reflect on Eight Years with Bush; Bolten and Hadley Decry 'Mythologies'," *Washington Post*, January 2, 2009, A1.

42. Dana Milbank, "The Chairman and the CEO," *Washington Post*, December 24, 2000, A1. Also see Baumgartner, *American Vice Presidency Reconsidered*, 133, and Goldstein, "The Rising Power of the Modern Vice Presidency," 384.

43. Milbank, "The Chairman and the CEO."

44. Gellman, *Angler*, 388. On the best sources see n.14 *supra*.

45. Ibid., 325, 375.

46. Ibid., 371.

47. Ibid., 49.

48. Ibid., 118–128.

49. In fact, Attorney General Ashcroft told Jack Goldsmith, his new head of the Office of Legal Counsel in the Department of Justice, that he had promised to give the administration maximum discretion. Jack Goldsmith, *Terror Presidency: Law and Judgment Inside the Bush Administration* (New York: Norton, 2007) 40.

50. Gellman, *Angler*, 139–154.

51. Ibid., 157. The undisclosed locations varied, but a major one was apparently Raven Rock Mountain near the Maryland-Pennsylvania line and just north of Camp David, the presidential retreat. The mountain had been hollowed out during the Cold War to provide a command-and-control center close to the nation's capital. See Steve Goldstein, "'Undisclosed location' disclosed," *Boston Globe*, July 20, 2004, www.boston.com/news/nation/articles/2004/07/20/undisclosed_location_disclosed.

52. Charlie Savage, *Takeover: The Return of the Imperial Presidency and the Subversion of American Democracy* (Boston: Little, Brown, 2007), 154–155.

53. Jane Mayer, *The Dark Side: The Inside Story of How the War on Terror Turned into a War on American Ideals* (New York: Doubleday, 2008), 51.

54. Ibid., 54.

55. Bob Woodward, *Plan of Attack* (New York: Simon and Schuster, 2004), 292, 429.

56. Bob Woodward, *State of Denial* (New York: Simon and Schuster, 2006), 120ff. On the 9/11 Commission's conclusions, see Walter Pincus and Dana Milbank, "Al Qaeda-Hussein Link Is Dismissed," *Washington Post*, June 17, 2004, A1.

57. Bob Woodward, *Bush at War* (New York: Simon and Schuster, 2003), 344. Also see Woodward, *Plan of Attack*, 428–429.

58. Woodward, *State of Denial*, 151, 398.

59. Mayer, *Dark Side*, 53.

60. Gellman, *Angler*, 244.

61. Ibid., 259–261.

62. For an elaboration of Addington's key role in redefining national security law in the areas of surveillance and torture, see Mayer, *Dark Side*.

63. Gellman, *Angler*, 83–91.

64. Ibid., 164–168; Mayer, *Dark Side*, 86.

65. Gellman, *Angler*, 277–326.

66. See the Supreme Court decisions in *Hamdi v. Rumsfeld* (2004), *Rasul v. Bush* (2004), and *Hamdan v. Rumsfeld* (2006).

67. House Select Committee to Investigate Covert Arms Transactions with Iran and Senate Select Committee on Secret Military Assistance to Iran and the Nicaraguan Opposition, S. Rep. No. 216, H. Rep. No. 433, 100:1 (1987).

68. Savage, *Takeover*, 60–61.

69. Ibid., 130-131.

70. See, for example, Cheney's televised interview on ABC's *This Week*, January 27, 2002; Savage, *Takeover*, 75; and Goldsmith, *Terror Presidency*, 232, n.39.

71. Transcript, "The Vice President Appears on ABC's *This Week*," January 27, 2002, www.whitehouse.gov/vicepresident/news-speeches/speeches/vp20020127.html.

72. Savage, *Takeover*, 163.

73. When it suited his purpose, however, Cheney distanced himself from the president. Cheney's initial justification for refusing access for the National Archives to classified information in the Office of the Vice President's possession was that the vice president's legislative duties exempted him from guidelines meant for executive branch agencies. Peter Baker, "Cheney Defiant on Classified Material: Executive Order Ignored Since 2003," *Washington Post*, June 22, 2007, A1; Peter Baker, "White House Defends Cheney's Refusal of Oversight," *Washington Post*, June 23, 2007, A2; Michael Abramowitz, "Cheney Aide Explains Stance on Classified Material," *Washington Post*, June 27, 2007, A5.

74. Goldsmith, *Terror Presidency*, 79, 90.

75. Ibid., 80–90.

76. Transcript, interview of Jim Lehrer with Vice President Cheney, January 14, 2009, *PBS News Hour with Jim Lehrer*, www.pbs.org/newshour/bb/politics/jan-june09/cheney_01-14.html.

77. Ibid.

Index

AARP, 250, 254
Abolitionist movement, 80
Abortion, 443, 474
Abraham, Spencer, 228
Abramoff, Jack, 290*n*1
Abu Ghraib, 231, 367
Adams, John, 73, 150, 168, 409, 441, 517–519
Adams, John Quincy, 75, 77, 168, 169
Adams, Sherman, 60, 343, 352–353
Addington, David, 524, 526, 528
Administrative clearance. *See* Regulatory
    Review
Afghanistan, 134, 229, 479, 489, 504–506
AFL-CIO, 284
African American vote, 193
Agnew, Spiro, 509, 513
Agricultural Adjustment Act (1933), 442
Agricultural Adjustment Administration, 92
Agriculture subsidies, 198
Aid to Families with Dependent Children,
    99, 336*n*71
Albright, Madeleine, 226
Aldrich, John, 422
Alien and Sedition Acts, 75, 150, 409, 441
Alito, Samuel, 437, 444, 448, 454, 471–472, 527
Alliance for Justice, 447
Alliance for Worker Retirement Security, 253
Alter, Jonathan, 509
Amalgamated Clothing Workers of
    America, 274
American Bar Association, 447, 461*n*30
American Civil Liberties Union, 290
American Federation of Labor, 272–274
American League of Lobbyists, 290
American Liberty League, 277–279
American Medical Association, 283
American Recovery and Reinvestment
    Act (2009). *See* Economic stimulus
    bill
Americans with Disabilities Act (1990), 281
Amicus briefs, 455–456
Anderson, Patrick, 352
Anderson, Robert, 174
Anti-Federalists, 9, 70

Anti-Masonic Party, 170
Arctic National Wildlife Refuge, 285
Ashcroft, John, 55, 526, 533*n*49
Aspin, Les, 62
Atwater, Lee, 319, 338*n*92
Automobile industry bailout, 408
Avella, Joseph, 491–492
Axelrod, David, 351, 356

Babbitt, Bruce, 448, 454
Bailey, Douglas, 206
Bailey, Jeremy, 73
Bailey, John, 302
Baker, Howard, 116
Baker, James, 50, 112, 119, 122, 222, 276, 350, 353,
    354, 356
Baltimore Evening Patriot, 85
Bank bailouts, 92, 132, 408, 426, 429, 476
Bank of the United States, 77, 411
Barbary pirates, 492
Barber, James David, 109, 142–163, 165*n*25,
    166*n*42
Barbour, Haley, 286
Barnett, Randy, 448
Barthes, Roland, 212
Baruch, Bernard, 94
Bauer, Gary, 276
Baxter, William, 450
Bay of Pigs invasion, 39, 46, 119, 362
Begala, Paul, 464
Beirut attack, 219
Bell, Griffin, 456
Berlin Wall, 47
Berry, George, 273
Berry, Jeffrey, 282
Best, Judith, 195–196
Biden, Joseph, 61, 134, 161, 201, 447, 453, 509, 511,
    515, 520, 530
Billings, Robert, 276
Binder, Sarah, 432*n*46
Bishop, Maurice, 219
Black, Hugo, 454
Blackmun, Harry, 436
Blackwell, Morton, 275

Blumenthal, Richard, 286
Bob Jones University, 276
Boehner, John, 407
Bolton, John, 469
Bork, Robert, 60–61, 447, 448, 451–453, 461*n*30
Boskin, Michael, 223
Bosnia, 127
Boumediene v. Bush (2008), 459
Bowles, Chester, 94
Boxing, 212
Brady, Nicholas, 223
Brennan, William, 448
Breyer, Stephen, 447, 454
Brinkley, Alan, 274, 311
Brock, William, 307
Broder, David, 179, 188
Brown, Harold, 218
Brown, Michael, 63–64, 232
Brownell, Herbert, 361, 442, 448
Brownlow, Louis, 331*n*17, 343, 363*n*5
Bryan, William Jennings, 177
Bryce, James, 171
Brzezinski, Zbigniew, 67*n*46, 118, 349
Buchanan, James, 174
Buckley v. Valeo (1976), 432*n*52
Budget and Accounting Act (1921), 386
Budget process, 385–389
Budget Review Board, 525
Bumiller, Elisabeth, 230
Bundy, McGeorge, 348
Bureau of the Budget (BOB), 93, 358,
    386–387, 468
Burger, Warren, 439, 452
Burnham, Walter Dean, 223
Burr, Aaron, 517
Busby, Horace, 304
Bush, George H.W., 122, 500
    approval ratings, 49–50, 434*n*77
    as party leader, 296, 310
    as vice president, 309, 510, 514, 516, 521
    economic policy, 124, 223
    environmental policy, 281
    foreign policy, 222–223, 354
    institutional management, 40–41, 44, 350
    judicial nominations, 438, 443–444, 454
    legal actions, 455
    management style, 124–125, 354
    presidential campaigns, 39, 125, 174, 175
    psychological character, 161–162
    public image, 59, 214, 221–224
    regulatory policy, 99, 281–282, 310, 391–392
    relations with Congress, 392–393
    relations with executive branch, 55
    relations with interest groups, 280–282

    use of executive power, 477, 478
    wartime leadership, 493, 503–504
Bush, George W.
    address to special session of Congress
        (2001), 229, 320
    and the "second constitution," 26–27
    and 2008 election, 175, 233, 325
    approval ratings, 48, 49, 228, 403–404, 425,
        434*n*77
    as party leader, 296, 317–325
    "axis of evil" speech, 229
    communications strategy, 237–238, 252–256
    compassionate conservatism, 318, 338*n*85
    conservative policies, 130, 319
    dismissal of U.S. attorneys, 55–56
    education policy, 99, 285, 320, 351
    environmental policy, 286–287, 471, 526
    executive orders, 323, 463–464, 474
    faith-based initiative, 285, 318, 338*n*94, 463
    financial rescue package, 132
    first inaugural address (2001), 403
    frustration with press, 245
    fundraising, 323, 338*n*97
    grassroots mobilization, 339*n*100
    handling of Hurricane Katrina, 63–64, 232,
        324, 477
    identification with U.S. troops, 230–231
    influence of predecessors on, 228–229
    institutional management, 40, 43, 44,
        350–351, 468
    Iraq War, 27, 59, 131–132, 230–231, 321, 324,
        355, 479, 493, 499–501, 504–505
    judicial nominations, 444, 445, 446, 454,
        460*n*17, 527
    legal actions, 455
    limited policy knowledge, 108, 128
    management style, 111, 127–132, 355
    midterm elections, 321–322, 324, 429
    "Mission Accomplished" landing, 40,
        230–231
    on elections, 204
    partial embrace of New Deal, 99–100
    partisan divisions, 401
    presidential campaigns, 157, 182, 186, 193,
        199–200, 202, 204, 523
    psychological character, 162–163
    public image, 36, 37, 48, 59, 214, 228–233
    regulatory policy, 285–287, 393–394, 470
    relations with Congress, 323–324, 393–394,
        403, 423, 425, 434*n*77
    relations with executive branch, 55–56,
        367–368
    relations with interest groups, 266,
        285–287

relationship with Dick Cheney, 510, 514–515, 520, 521–522

Social Security reform, 240, 242, 252–256, 364n20, 423

staffing, 232, 347, 385

State of the Union address (2001), 252

tax cuts, 318, 425

terrorism policies, 69, 229, 324, 350, 367–368, 428, 458–459, 466, 472, 479–480, 529

transition process, 128, 360

troop surge, 132, 500, 505, 508n44, 527

use of executive power, 468–469, 471, 478–480, 482

use of signing statements, 367–368, 471–472

use of veto power, 428

weapons of mass destruction controversy, 131, 140n85

Butler, Pierce, 145, 489

Byrd, Robert, 134

Cabinet government, 53–54, 169

Cabinet secretaries, as presidential candidates, 175–176

Calhoun, John, 517

Califano, Joseph, Jr., 303, 353

Cambodia, 518

Cameron, Simon, 170

Campaign finance, 173, 180, 188

   presidential matching funds, 180–181

   reform efforts, 414–416, 420–421

Cannon, Lou, 217

Cantril, Hadley, 331n21

Card, Andrew, 128, 351, 355, 360

Carlucci, Frank, 120

Carswell, G. Harrold, 449

Carter, Jimmy

   as party leader, 336n64

   energy policy, 24, 117

   foreign policy, 118

   Iran hostage crisis, 67n46, 220, 349

   judicial nominations, 438, 445

   legal actions, 456, 457

   management style, 110, 353

   presidential campaigns, 174

   psychological character, 143, 153

   public image, 36, 47

   regulatory policy, 390

   relations with Congress, 122, 353, 383–384

   relations with executive branch, 56, 382–384, 387

   relationship with Walter Mondale, 512, 523

   Rose Garden strategy, 26

   staffing, 345, 347

Casework, 416

Case-Zablocki Act (1972), 479

Castro, Fidel, 39

Cato (Anti-Federalist writer), 70

Cato Institute, 253

Caucuses, presidential nominating, 181

Ceaser, James, 4

Central Intelligence Agency, 101, 120–121, 362, 479

Chase, Salmon, 85, 170

Cheney, Dick, 128–132, 200, 232, 323, 355, 479, 504, 509–511, 520, 521–530, 534n73

   as CEO, 521–522

   as Ford's chief of staff, 53, 512

   as secretary of defense, 222

   energy policy, 286, 364n20, 482, 526, 528

   experience, 350, 360, 514–515

   influence in Bush administration, 129–130, 511, 522–527

   overseas travel, 519

   relations with Congress, 525–526, 528, 532n30

   tie-breaking votes, 319, 517

   views on executive power, 527–530

Chicago Tribune, 82

Chief of staff, White House, 53, 60, 346

Chile, 216

China, 216, 518

Christian Right movement, 275–277

Christian Voice, 275

Christopher, Warren, 510

Chrysler, 408

Civil Rights Act (1964), 418

Civil Service Commission, 380

Civil service reform, 380–385, 413

Civil War, 78–79, 82–84, 495, 501, 503

Civil War amendments, 88

Clapper, Raymond, 299

Clark, Wesley, 177, 181

Clark, William, 120, 349

Classification procedures, 481, 529

Clausewitz, Carl von, 501, 504

Clay, Henry, 169

Clean Air Act (1970), 378

Clean Air Act Amendments (1990), 281, 391

Clegg, Roger, 461n24

Cleveland, Grover, 71, 466

Clines, Francis X., 220

Clinton, Bill, 178

   and the "second constitution," 25–26

   and 2000 election, 175

   approval ratings, 46, 49–51, 337n82, 434n77

   as party leader, 310–317, 336n64

   as postmodern personality, 224

budget policy, 46, 225–226, 312, 314, 337*n*77, 389, 423, 425
communications strategy, 236–237, 247–251
embrace of free markets, 98–99
entitlement reform, 311, 317
executive orders, 335*n*62, 464, 474–475
fundraising, 316
gays in the military, 61–62, 312, 335*n*62
grasp of policy issues, 126
health care plan, 127, 225, 237, 240, 247–251, 282–285, 313
impeachment, 25–26, 50, 63, 126, 227, 316, 423
institutional management, 40–41
judicial nominations, 441, 443–444, 447, 448, 454
legal actions, 455, 458
Lewinsky scandal, 25–26, 50, 62–63, 126–127, 162, 227–228, 316
management style, 125–127, 359–360
midterm elections, 313–314, 316, 429
presidential campaigns, 181, 182, 186, 199, 226, 315
psychological character, 152–153, 162
public image, 48, 59, 62–63, 179, 213–214, 224–228
regulatory policy, 99, 392–393
relations with Congress, 392–393, 423, 425
relations with executive branch, 382
relations with interest groups, 282–285
relationship with Al Gore, 510
staffing, 360, 385
State of the Union addresses, 38, 248, 315
transition process, 359
use of executive power, 469, 471, 473, 477, 478, 482
welfare reform, 98–99, 315
Clinton, Hillary Rodham, 127, 133–134, 178, 180, 183, 185, 226, 241, 265, 313 326
Clinton v. Jones (1997), 458
Club for Growth, 253
Cohen, Eliot A., 502, 508*n*44
Cohen, Jeffrey, 232
Colbert, Stephen, 232
Cold War, 73, 100, 501
Committee for the Re-Election of the President, 307
Committee on Administrative Management (Brownlow Committee), 343, 363*n*5, 363*n*7, 383
Committee on the Conduct of War, 86
Committee on the Present Danger, 218
Commonwealth Club Address, 89, 90–91, 296
Communications warfare, 246–259

Competitiveness Council, 281–282, 310, 393
Compromise of 1877, 89
Conditional party government, 422
Congress
and president's legislative strategy, 56–58, 378
approval ratings, 425
as board of directors, 374–375
benefits of incumbency, 415–416
budget process, 385–389
collective action problems, 375–380, 382, 395
committees, 19
conflicts with president, 12–13, 369, 373–380, 391–394, 466–467, 482
constituencies, 410–411
institutional reforms, 422, 424
investigations of president, 310
legislative process, 378
majority-minority districts, 420
motivational disadvantage, 379–380
political polarization, 403–406, 423–426
relations with bureaucracy, 370–372, 374, 381–382
relations with president, 401–430
role in presidential nominations, 168–169
structure of, 12, 376, 425–426
war powers, 478–479, 491–492, 498–499
Congressional Black Caucus, 229
Congressional Budget and Impoundment Control Act (1974), 388, 473
Congressional Budget Office, 255, 388
Congressional Government (Wilson), 13
Congressional Review Act (1996), 392
Congress of Industrial Organizations, 273–274
Connecticut Compromise, 202
Conservative coalition, 93
Consolidated Appropriations Act (2005), 470
Constitution, U.S., 1–13
Article II vesting clause, 74, 465–466
branches of government, 10–13
executive power under, 68–69, 372–373, 464–466
invasion clause, 491, 493
nonpartisan presidency, 295
perspective on presidential psychology, 144–145
presidents' relationship with Congress, 409–410
protection of minority interests, 196–197
relationship to Declaration of Independence, 72, 80–81
"second constitution," 1–2, 23
structural changes to, 28*n*1
war powers under, 490–492, 495

Constitutional Convention, 8, 195, 197, 202, 489
Constitutional Government in the United States
    (Wilson), 13
Contract with America, 127, 314, 423
Conventions, national party, 170–171,
    183–187, 188–189, 412
  delegates to, 183–185
  post-convention "bounce," 186
Coolidge, Calvin, 71, 174, 445, 518
Cooper, Charles, 450
Council of Economic Advisers, 115, 343
Council on Competitiveness. *See*
    Competitiveness Council
Council on Women and Girls, 43
Covert action, 479–480
Cox, Archibald, 451, 455
Crittenden, John J., 84
Croly, Herbert, 329, 330*n*13
Cronin, Thomas, 213
C-SPAN, 424
Cuba, 127, 496
Cuban missile crisis, 39–40, 362, 518
Cummings, Homer, 107*n*78, 297
Cunliffe, Marcus, 144
Cuomo, Mario, 454
Currie, David, 492
Curtis, Charles, 518

Dahl, Robert, 192
Daley, William, 382
Danforth, John, 523
Darman, Richard, 217, 223, 354
Daschle, Tom, 361
Dawes, Charles, 518
Dayan, Daniel, 211
Dean, Howard, 178, 180, 190, 326
Deaver, Michael, 238
Debord, Guy, 213
Declaration of Independence, 72, 74, 80–82,
    90–91
Declaration of war, 498
Defense of Marriage Act (1996), 282
de Grazia, Alfred, 41
Deliberation, 18
Demagoguery, 3–6, 21–23
Democratic Leadership Council, 311–313, 318
Democratic National Committee (DNC),
    185, 298, 302, 327–328, 333*n*43, 336*n*64
Democratic National Convention, 298, 305,
    333*n*43
Democratic Party, 77–78, 92–93, 170, 171–172
  alliance with organized labor, 274
  conservative wing of, 417
  embrace of civil rights, 418–419

under Barack Obama, 325–328
under Bill Clinton, 310–317
under Franklin Roosevelt, 298–301
under Lyndon Johnson, 302–306
under Woodrow Wilson, 329*n*4
Democratic theory, 192
Department of Commerce, 382
Department of Defense, 101, 120–121
Department of Education, 470
Department of Homeland Security, 351
Department of Housing and Urban
    Development, 282, 305
Department of Justice, 446, 454
Department of Labor, 287
Deregulation, 99
Derthick, Martha, 95
Detainee Treatment Act (2005), 367–368,
    472, 480
Devroy, Ann, 251
Diem, Ngo Dinh, 54
DiIulio, John, 130
Dionne, E.J., 318
Divided government, 413, 416–417, 447
Dole, Robert, 162, 199, 205, 207, 248, 251,
    315, 448
Domestic Council, 346, 357, 512
Domestic Policy Council, 353
Douglas, Stephen, 80
Douglas, William O., 454
Dowd, Matthew, 339*n*100
Dowd, Maureen, 224, 230
Downie, Leonard, 161
Dred Scott v. Sanford (1857), 80, 441
Drew, Elizabeth, 127
Du Pont family, 277, 279
Dubinsky, David, 273
Dudley, Susan, 393
Dukakis, Michael, 179, 309, 443
Dulles, John Foster, 361
DW-Nominate scores, 433*n*56

Eastwood, Clint, 216
Economic Policy Council, 353
Economic Recovery Tax Act (1981), 276
Economic stimulus bill, 134–135, 401–403, 408,
    476, 515
Edison Electric Institute, 286
Education Task Force, 303
Edwards, George, 25, 210
Edwards, John, 178, 521
Eisenhower, Dwight, 4, 71, 100, 174–175
  approval ratings, 49
  criticism of Kennedy tax cuts, 115
  enforcement of desegregation, 96, 476–477

judicial nominations, 442, 445
management style, 111, 343, 352–353, 361–362
on New Deal, 95
presidential campaigns, 39
psychological character, 153
public perception, 146
relations with executive branch, 381
staffing, 347
Eisenhower, Edgar, 95
Eisenhower, Milton, 361
Elections
congressional, 203, 418
cyclical theory, 155–157
federal oversight of, 203–204
resonance, 157–160
split ticket voting, 414, 418
voter turnout, 412, 421–422
Electoral College, 6, 30*n*15, 146, 168, 192–207,
    412, 517
arguments for and against, 194–205
case for direct election, 205–207
Electoral time, 57
Electric Reliability Coordinating Council, 286
Emancipation Proclamation, 86–87, 474
Emanuel, Rahm, 53, 133, 135, 355–356, 360, 475
Emergency Economic Stabilization Act (2008).
    See Bank bailouts
Emergency powers, 475–477
Employment Act (1946), 343
Endangered Species Act Amendments (1982), 391
Engler, John, 523
Entman, Robert, 212
Environmental organizations, 280
Environmental Protection Agency (EPA),
    96, 112–113, 286–287, 378, 383, 389–391
Equal Rights Amendment, 275
Erickson, Paul, 217
Ethics in Government Act (1978), 310, 337*n*81
"Ex-Com," 362
Executive agreements, 479
Executive branch, 367–395
    organization of, 370–372
Executive Office of the President, 40–44, 93,
    111, 300, 342, 344, 363*n*5, 375
Executive orders, 473–475, 486*n*38
Executive Order 12044 (Carter), 390
Executive Order 12291 (Reagan), 390–392
Executive Order 12498 (Reagan), 399n57
Executive Order 12866 (Clinton), 392
Executive Order 13422 (Bush), 393–394
Executive power, 69, 463–483
Executive privilege, 12, 456–457, 481–482
Executive Reorganization Act (1939), 92–93,
    300–301, 343

Ex parte Milligan (1866), 457
Extraordinary rendition, 479

Facebook, 244
Fahrenheit 9/11, 163
Falwell, Jerry, 275–276
Family Assistance Plan, 58
Farley, James, 170, 298, 333*n*36
"Favorite son," 170
Federal Election Campaign Amendments
    (1974), 180
Federal Farmer (Anti-Federalist writer),
    104*n*7
Federalism, 202–204
Federalist Society, 447–448
Federalist, The, 2–3, 7–9, 16, 21, 68–70, 75, 145,
    411, 483
Fifteenth Amendment, 88
Filibusters, 196
Fillmore, Millard, 174
Financial regulation, 277
Fiorina, Morris, 413, 416
Fisher, Louis, 492
527 groups, 421
Florida, 193
Flowers, Gennifer, 162
Flynn, Edward, 170, 298, 333*n*36
Foley, Tom, 423
Ford, Gerald, 514
    conflicts with Congress, 467
    economic policy, 116
    institutional management, 43, 53, 350
    judicial nominations, 438
    primary campaign, 174, 179
    psychological character, 143
    public image, 38, 45, 213
    regulatory policy, 99, 390
    succession to presidency, 521
    vice presidential appointment, 175, 509–510
Foreign Intelligence Surveillance Act
    (1978), 480
Forest Service, 287
Fortas, Abe, 436, 438, 453
Fort Sumter, 82, 85
Four Freedoms, 91
Fourteenth Amendment, 88
Frankfurter, Felix, 299, 454
Fraser, Donald, 333*n*43
Freedom Council, 275
Fried, Charles, 456
Friedersdorf, Max, 122
Frist, Bill, 460*n*17, 523
From, Al, 337*n*77, 338*n*85
Frost, David, 46

Gabriel, Richard, 219, 221
Galanter, Marc, 454
Galbraith, John Kenneth, 348
Gallup Organization, 51
Galvin, Daniel, 334n50
Gang of 14, 460n17
Garfield, James, 176
Garner, John Nance, 170, 518–519
Garrison, William Lloyd, 80
Gates, Robert, 132, 133, 505
Geithner, Timothy, 133
Gellman, Barton, 522–523
General Accounting Office. *See* Government
    Accountability Office
General Motors, 277, 408
Geneva Conventions, 459
George III, 144
George, Alexander, 150
Gephardt, Dick, 181
Gergen, David, 112, 127, 226
Gerry, Elbridge, 489
Gerson, Michael, 318
Gettysburg Address, 82, 87
GI Bill (1944), 94
Gilmore, James, III, 319
Gingrich, Newt, 127, 225–226, 254, 314–317, 423
Ginsburg, Douglas, 453
Ginsburg, Ruth Bader, 437, 447, 454
Glass-Steagall Act (1933), 99
Goffman, Erving, 214
Goldsmith, Jack, 483, 533n49
Goldwater, Barry, 176, 186
Gonzales, Alberto, 351
Gorbachev, Mikhail, 113, 120, 216
Gore, Al, 157, 162–163, 174–175, 193, 199–200,
    204, 226, 313, 317, 510, 514, 519, 522
Gorsuch (Burford), Anne, 112, 280
Government Accountability Office, 255, 528
Government, objectives of, 11–12
Governors, as presidential candidates,
    176–177
Graham, John, 393
Gramm-Leach-Bliley Financial Services
    Modernization Act (1999), 99
Grant, Ulysses, 342, 445, 473
Great Depression, 90, 154
Great Society, 72, 302–305, 383
Greenstein, Fred, 37, 111, 152–153
Gregg, Judd, 340n113, 361
Grenada, 215, 219–221
Griswold, Erwin, 456
Grossman, Michael, 45
Ground Zero, 229
Groupthink, 117, 354

Gruenther, Alfred, 361
Guantánamo Bay prison, 427, 459, 527
Gulf of Tonkin, 478

Habeas corpus, 83, 86
Hagel, Chuck, 523
Haig, Alexander, 120, 214, 349
Haiti, 127, 482
Hall, Arsenio, 179
Halliburton Corporation, 522
Hamdan v. Rumsfeld (2006), 459, 480
Hamdi v. Rumsfeld (2004), 458
Hamilton, Alexander, 2, 5, 8, 29n3, 68–71, 145,
    411, 464
Hamilton, Lee, 487n62
Handlin, Oscar, 95
Harding, Warren, 171, 176, 342, 445
Hargrove, Erwin, 146, 154
Harkin, Tom, 181
Harlan, John Marshall, 442, 445
Harrison, Benjamin, 176
Harrison, William Henry, 516
"Harry and Louise" ads, 248, 284
Hart, Gary, 161, 180, 181
Hastert, Dennis, 423
Hatch, Orrin, 447, 448
Hatch Act (1939), 331n20
Hazardous and Solid Waste Act Amendments
    (1984), 391
Health Insurance Association of America,
    283–284
Health Security Act, 283–284
Heclo, Hugh, 97, 100
Heineman task force, 334n49
Heller, Walter, 115
Help America Vote Act (2002), 204
Heritage Foundation, 253
Herring, E. Pendleton, 268
Higginbotham, Patrick, 451
Hillman, Sidney, 273–274
Hodges, Albert G., 83
Homeless movement, 279
Homestead Act (1862), 88
Hoover, Herbert, 90, 150, 152, 154, 174, 176, 342,
    436, 518
Hoover Commission, 343, 383
House of Representatives, 14, 410
Housing bubble, 407
Howe, Daniel Walker, 82
Hughes, Karen, 128, 355
Hult, Karen, 356
Humphrey, Hubert, 172, 174–175, 303, 306, 514
Huntington, Samuel P., 502
Hurricane Andrew, 477

Hurricane Katrina, 48, 63–64, 231–232, 324, 477
Hussein, Saddam, 59, 131, 222, 499, 524–525

Image gap, 47
Imagery, 35–40, 44–52, 211
Impeachment, 145–146, 467
Impoundment, 387, 473
Independent commissions, 371
Independent counsels, 310, 316, 337*n*79, 458, 467
Intelligence failure, 117
Intelligence Oversight Act (1980), 467
"Interest group liberalism," 95–97
Interest groups, 264–290, 415
    adversarial breakthrough politics, 277–280
    adversarial politics-as-usual, 282–285
    collaborative breakthrough politics, 272–277
    collaborative politics-as-usual, 280–282,
        285–287
    co-optation of, 274–275, 277, 289
    influence on campaign finance, 420–421
    influence on judicial nominations,
        447–448, 453
    model of presidential relations, 267–272
    relations with Congress and bureaucrats,
        266–267
International Emergency Economic Powers
    Act (1977), 475
International Monetary Fund, 255
Iowa caucuses, 181
Iran-contra scandal, 25, 54, 61, 120–121, 216, 309,
    335*n*55, 349–350, 354, 468, 510, 528
Iraq Study Group, 505
Iraq War, 27, 59, 131–132, 175, 230–231, 321, 324,
    423, 489, 500, 505, 524–525

Jackson, Andrew, 73, 81, 169, 456
    as conservative revolutionary, 77–78, 102
    use of veto, 76
    views on the presidency, 75–76
Jackson, Jesse, 229
Jackson, Robert, 452, 454, 465
Janis, Irving, 119, 354
Jarding, Steven, 532*n*26
Jarrett, Valerie, 347, 351, 356
Jay, John, 2, 145
Jefferson, Thomas, 10, 69–70, 168, 342, 411, 441,
    457, 484*n*12, 517
    as conservative revolutionary, 76–78
    as vice president, 519
    First Inaugural Address, 70, 74, 409
    influence on Lincoln, 81
    judicial nominations, 445
    revenue policies, 76
    Second Inaugural Address, 75

    views on the presidency, 73–75
    wartime leadership, 492, 501
Jeffords, James, 319
Johnson, Andrew, 89, 174, 316
Johnson, Lyndon, 178
    administrative reforms, 334*n*49
    as party leader, 301–306
    as vice president, 513, 515, 518, 521, 532*n*29
    civil rights legislation, 216, 303, 417
    judicial nominations, 436
    management style, 110, 348
    personnel policy, 304–305
    presidential campaign, 186
    psychological character, 147, 150, 152
    public image, 59
    relations with executive branch, 55
    use of task forces, 303–304
    Vietnam War, 110, 150, 154, 175, 478, 480,
        499–500, 503
    withdrawal from re-election, 174, 306, 499
Joint Chiefs of Staff, 62
Jones, Charles O., 426
Jones, James, 133
Jordan, Hamilton, 53, 353
Jordan, Vernon, 316
Judicial review, 456–457
Judiciary. *See also* Supreme Court
    expansion of, 446
    role in institutional conflicts, 373

Kaine, Timothy, 327
Kaiser, Robert, 161
Kansas-Nebraska Act (1854), 80
Karl, Barry, 94
Katz, Elihu, 211
Keating, Frank, 523
Keller, Morton, 103
Kennedy, Anthony, 451, 453
Kennedy, David, 91
Kennedy, Edward, 99, 320
Kennedy, John
    approval ratings, 46
    assassination of, 37, 146–147
    communications strategy, 239
    Cuba policy, 39–40, 362
    judicial nominations, 446
    management style, 361–362
    policymaking process, 119, 518
    public image, 36, 213
    senatorial experience, 176
    staffing, 384
    tax policy, 115–116
    use of public opinion, 24
    Vietnam War, 54

Kentucky Resolutions, 75
Kernell, Samuel, 210–211
Kerry, John, 157, 163, 176, 178, 181, 183, 186, 187,
    202, 231, 499, 520
Keynesian economics, 115
King, Larry, 525
King, Rodney, 477
"King Caucus," 168–169
Kissinger, Henry, 348, 350, 512
Kleindienst, Richard, 481
Koppel, Ted, 186
Korean War, 39, 58–59, 478, 497
Kosovo, 478
Kristol, William, 284
Krock, Arthur, 277
Krugman, Paul, 256
Kumar, Martha, 45
Kyl, Jon, 523

Labor Nonpartisan League, 273
Labor unions, 272–275
Lance, Bert, 214
Landon, Alfred, 278, 343
Lauck, W. Jett, 272
Lawrence v. Texas (2003), 451
Leadership Conference on Civil Rights, 447
League of Nations, 150, 496
Leaks, 60
Lebanon, 478
Legal Services Corporation, 469
Lehrer, Jim, 530
Lemann, Nicholas, 218
Lend-Lease Act (1941), 91
Leuchtenberg, William, 442
Lewinsky, Monica, 25–26, 50–51, 162, 227, 316
Lewis, Anthony, 221
Lewis, John, 272–274
LEXIS/NEXIS, 448
Libby, Lewis "Scooter," 526–527
Liberty League. See American Liberty League
Libya, 215
Lieberman, Joe, 181, 521
Lincoln, Abraham, 69, 71–72, 78–89, 170, 174,
    279, 518
    address to special session of Congress
        (1861), 82, 86
    as conservative revolutionary, 88, 102
    as party leader, 84–86
    assassination of, 89
    criticism of executive power, 79
    First Inaugural Address, 81
    psychological character, 153–154
    slavery and emancipation, 80–82,
        86–89, 441

use of veto power, 88
war measures, 82–84, 457, 466, 495,
    501, 503
Lincoln-Douglas debates, 80
Line Item Veto Act (1996), 389, 473
Lipset, Seymour Martin, 144
Little Rock, 96, 476–477
Lobbyists. See Interest groups
Locke, Gary, 361
Locke, John, 296, 466
Lodge, Henry Cabot, 54, 361
Long, Huey, 170
Lott, Trent, 227
Louisiana Purchase, 69, 74–75, 76, 474
Lowi, Theodore, 96, 213
Lyceum Address, 71, 79

MacArthur, Douglas, 58–59
Macy, John, 304–305, 333n36
Madison, James, 2, 4, 7–8, 10, 30n25, 31n39,
    69, 144, 195–197, 411, 464, 483, 489, 491
    as president, 168–169, 494
Madonna, 224
Magaziner, Ira, 127, 313
Marbury v. Madison (1803), 456
March for Life, 276
Marcus, Ruth, 251
Marshall, John, 10, 456
Marshall, Thomas, 518
Mayhew, David, 417
Maysville Road, 77
McCain, John, 63, 157, 163, 175, 176, 178, 180,
    186–187, 201, 265, 367, 406, 420
McCain-Feingold campaign finance reform
    law (2002), 421
McCarthy, Eugene, 172, 306
McCarthy, Joseph, 4
McClellan, George B., 86, 87
McClellan, Scott, 232
McCree, Wade, 456
McFarlane, Robert, 54, 354
McGovern, George, 142, 176, 181, 186, 333n43
McGovern-Fraser Commission, 172, 305,
    333n43
McKinley, William, 239, 495–496, 518
McKitrick, Eric, 85
McLarty, Thomas "Mack," 126
McNamara, Robert, 503
McPherson, James, 501–502
Media
    and presidential communication efforts,
        236–259
    choice of sources, 250
    coverage of national conventions, 186

coverage of presidential elections, 160–163
coverage of primary season, 179
focus on president, 37–38
"horse race" coverage, 241–242, 251
impact on electoral moods, 156
impact on presidential spectacle, 212–213
influence on judicial nominations, 448
role in shaping presidential image, 45
transition to "new" media, 245
24-hour news cycle, 51–52, 232
Medicare, 99, 285, 302, 314
Meese, Edwin, III, 218, 452
Mencken, H.L., 465
Merit Systems Protection Board, 383
Meusnier, Jean Baptiste, 73
Mexican War, 79, 493, 500
Michel, Robert, 276
Microsoft Corporation, 455
Miers, Harriet, 439, 448
Milbank, Dana, 522
Military
    development of, 493–498
    officers as presidential candidates, 177
    relations with president, 502–506
Military commissions, 83, 428, 526
Military industrial complex, 100
Mine Safety and Health Administration, 287
Minimalist management style, 111–113
Miranda v. Arizona (1966), 442
Missouri Compromise (1820), 80–81, 441
Mitchell, George, 249–250, 281, 454
Moe, Richard, 531*n*23
Moe, Terry, 358
Mondale, Walter, 175, 180, 182, 443, 510, 512–515, 522–523
Monroe, James, 77, 168–169, 368
Montesquieu, Charles de, 15
Moore, Frank, 122
Moore, Michael, 163
Moral Majority, 275–276
Morris, Dick, 26, 51, 226–227
Morrison v. Olson (1988), 458
Morrow, E. Frederic, 347
Moyers, Bill, 305
Murray, Philip, 274
MX missile, 123
Myers v. United States (1926), 457

Nader, Ralph, 193, 207
Napoleon, 75
National American Woman Suffrage
    Organization, 269
National Christian Action Council, 275
National Economic Council, 43, 525

National Federation of Independent
    Businesses (NFIB), 283–284
National Highway Traffic Safety
    Administration, 287
National Industrial Recovery Act, 272, 442
National Labor Relations Act, 92
National Labor Relations Board, 274
National primary, 187
National Recovery Administration, 92
National Republican Congressional
    Committee, 307–308
National Republican Senatorial
    Committee, 307
National Security Act (1947), 101, 302, 343, 497
National Security Agency, 480, 524
National Security Council, 41, 101, 120, 343,
    348–350, 369, 481–482, 518
Natural disasters, 477
Natural Resources Defense Council, 393
Neoconservatives, 131
Neustadt, Richard, 10–11, 109, 146, 362, 404,
    428, 476
Neutrality Proclamation, 69, 411
New Century Alliance for Social Security, 254
New Deal, 24, 27–28, 72, 89–95, 102–103,
    277–279, 296–301, 386
New Deal coalition, 270
New Freedom, 90
New Frontier, 362
New Hampshire primary, 182
New Orleans, 63–64
New Source Review program, 286
Newsweek, 217
New York City draft riots, 83
New York Times, 254–256
Nicaragua, 125
Niles, David, 347
9/11 Commission, 524, 527
Nixon v. Fitzgerald (1982), 457–458
Nixon, Richard
    administrative policy, 306–307, 335*n*54, 346,
        357–358
    as party leader, 306–307
    budget policy, 387–388, 473
    environmental policy, 96
    foreign policy, 518
    judicial nominations, 442–443, 453
    lack of coattails, 416
    legal actions, 456–458
    presidential campaigns, 174–175, 307
    psychological character, 142–143, 147, 150
    public image, 36, 59
    regulatory policy, 389–390
    relations with Congress, 387–388

relations with executive branch, 55
resignation, 43, 521
staffing, 347, 384
use of covert operations, 216, 480
use of executive power, 476
Vietnam War, 500
view of presidential power, 46–47
Watergate, 456, 481
welfare reform, 58
No Child Left Behind Act (2001), 99, 426, 470
Noncareer executive assignments, 305
Noncoordination, 117
Noriega, Manuel, 215, 222, 354
North, Oliver, 54
North American Free Trade Agreement
	(NAFTA), 126, 282, 284, 313, 336n66, 426
North Atlantic Treaty Organization
	(NATO), 490
Northwest Ordinance (1787), 81, 88
Nueces River, 493
Nullification controversy, 75
Nunn, Sam, 62, 335n62
Nussbaum, Bernard, 126

Oath of office, 71
Obama, Barack
	Afghanistan policy, 134
	and role of executive, 103–104, 467
	and the "second constitution," 27–28
	appointments process, 133–134, 360–361
	approval ratings, 134, 406
	as party leader, 325–328
	bank policy, 426, 429
	bipartisan efforts, 405–409
	budget policy, 429
	Democratic National Convention address
		(2004), 132, 406
	economic policy, 407–408
	economic stimulus bill, 134–135, 242,
		290, 328, 401–403, 425
	embrace of Internet, 238–245, 256–257
	ethics rules, 265
	executive orders, 266, 289, 329, 427, 464,
		474, 483
	fundraising, 181, 245, 326
	grassroots political activities, 28, 233,
		243–245, 327–328
	inauguration, 401, 435, 459n2
	institutional management, 43, 53, 351, 395
	judicial nominations, 435–437, 444, 448, 515
	knowledge of public policy, 108
	lack of executive experience, 176, 178
	legislative agenda, 429
	management style, 132–136, 355–356

presidential campaign, 157, 163, 180, 183,
	185–187, 201, 265, 325, 328, 420
public image, 37, 38, 214, 233
regulatory policy, 394
relations with Congress, 134–135, 401–403,
	405–409, 427–430
relations with interest groups, 264–266,
	289–290
relationship with Joe Biden, 515, 520
staffing, 345, 347, 468
transition process, 133, 360
use of "czars," 134, 329
use of executive power, 471, 477, 482
wartime leadership, 489–490, 505–506
"Obama 2.0," 327–328
O'Brien, Larry, 332n30
Occupational Safety and Health
	Administration, 378, 383
O'Connor, Sandra Day, 439, 450, 458
Office of Administration (White House), 42
Office of Economic Opportunity, 55, 348
Office of Faith-Based and Community
	Initiatives, 43, 130, 338n94, 463
Office of Global Communications, 43
Office of Homeland Security, 43, 320, 350–351
Office of Information and Regulatory Affairs
	(OIRA), 390–394, 470
Office of Legal Counsel, 446
Office of Legislative Affairs (White House),
	42, 347
Office of Management and Budget (OMB),
	42–44, 56, 113, 309, 335n54, 358–359, 369,
	387–390, 468, 470
Office of Personnel Management, 383–384
Office of Public Liaison and
	Intergovernmental Affairs (White
	House), 42, 347
Office of Strategic Initiatives, 43, 128, 319
Office of Women's Initiatives and Outreach, 43
Omnibus Budget Reconciliation Act
	(1981), 276
O'Neill, Paul, 128, 130
O'Neill, Tip, 180, 417, 423
Operation Desert Storm, 222–223
Organizational time, 57
Organization of Eastern Caribbean
	States, 219
Organizing for America, 28, 327
Oxford Union, 22

Paletz, David, 212
Palin, Sarah, 183, 186–187, 189, 201, 511, 520
Panama, 125, 222
Panetta, Leon, 127, 356

Parker, John, 436
Parliamentary systems, 189
Party unity scores, 423
Pataki, George, 523
Patronage, 84–85, 413
Paul, Alice, 269
"Pay as you go" rules, 388
Peirce, Neal, 203
Pelosi, Nancy, 402, 407
Pendergast machine, 170
Pendleton Act (1883), 380, 413
People for the American Way, 447
Perot, Ross, 311, 313, 431*n*26
Pershing, John, 502
Persian Gulf War, 49, 124, 222–223, 354, 434*n*77,
    478, 497, 503–504
Personal Responsibility and Work
    Opportunity Reconciliation Act (1996).
    See Welfare reform
Peterson, Mark, 270, 287, 293*n*63
Petraeus, David, 505, 527
Pharmaceutical Research and Manufacturers
    of America (PhRMA), 284
Phillips, Alfred, Jr., 298
Pickering, Charles, 445
Pierce, Franklin, 80, 174
Pious, Richard, 372
Plame, Valerie, 527
Planned Parenthood v. Casey (1992), 443
Plouffe, David, 327
Podesta, John, 360
Poindexter, John, 54, 354
Political parties
    accountability, 413
    decline of influence, 413–417
    development of, 77–78, 411–413
    fundraising, 421
    impact of primaries on, 188
    interest groups and, 270, 415
    polarization of, 404–406, 418–420
    programmatic, 307–308
    relationship with presidency, 295–329
    revitalization of, 418–424
    role in constitutional refoundings, 72
    role in selecting presidential nominees,
        167–190
    third parties, 206–207
Political scientists, 34–35, 64–65
Polk, James K., 79, 174, 481, 493, 499–500, 518
Polls, 51, 179–180
Portney, Kent, 282
Powell, Colin, 128, 131, 176, 222, 335*n*62, 350, 354,
    355, 524, 526
Powell, Lewis, 439, 452

Powell, Thomas Reed, 444
Presidency
    as public spectacle, 210–234
    bureaucratization, 356–357
    candidates for president, 174–178
    centralization of staff, 351–356, 468
    complexity of organization, 344–346
    constitutional roles, 516
    emergency powers, 475–477
    external relations, 346–347
    Founders' perspective of, 1–13
    imagery of, 35–40, 44–52
    independence of, 9–10, 16, 20–21
    institution of, 35, 40–44, 52–58, 296, 341–363
    isolation under Nixon, 307
    permanent war footing, 100–101
    personal influence on institution, 359–363
    politicization of institution, 357–359
    popular mandate, 20, 32*n*51
    primacy of, 213, 369
    public attitudes toward, 23, 146
    relationship with political parties, 295–329
    removal power, 374
    source of authority, 23
    staff conflict, 357
    statutory authority, 375
    stewardship model, 96
    symbolism of, 45, 211
    term of office, 7, 94, 145
    unilateral power of, 372–375, 463–483
    war powers, 477–480, 489–506
Presidential campaigns, 38–39, 199–202
Presidential Character, The (Barber),
    142, 148–155, 157–160
Presidential election of 2000, 193, 317
Presidential Power (Neustadt), 109, 146
President's Council on Sustainable
    Development, 43
President's Critical Infrastructure Protection
    Board, 43
Presidents
    advisers to, 64–65, 214
    agenda-setting power, 378, 428
    as chief executives, 372
    as commanders in chief, 373, 491–494,
        497–498
    as public characters, 213
    budgetary authority, 386–389
    competence and management styles,
        108–136
    conflicts with Congress, 12–13, 373–380, 482
    electoral base, 412
    judicial nominations, 435–459, 460*n*17
    media strategies, 236–259

mistakes of, 58–65
motivational advantage, 379–380
nominating process, 167–190
personnel policy, 380–385
pets, 37
policy formulation, 114–117
policymaking process, 117–121, 348–351
policy promotion, 121–123
psychology of, 142–163
relations with Congress, 56–58, 347, 401–430
relations with executive branch, 55–56, 367–395, 467–469
relations with interest groups, 264–290
relations with Supreme Court, 454–459
responsiveness to public opinion, 210
shifts in public approval, 49–52
use of regulatory review, 389–395, 470–471
use of secrecy, 481–482
wartime leadership, 501–506
Primary elections, 171–173, 182–183, 187–189, 306, 413
Principals Meeting, 525
Privacy and Civil Liberties Oversight Board, 43
Prize Cases (1863), 86, 457
Professional Air Traffic Controllers
    Organization (PATCO), 97, 215
Program Assessment Rating Tool, 468
Progressive Party, 90
Project for the Republican Future, 284
Pryor, William, 445
Public Utility Holding Company Act (1935), 99
Public Works Administration, 92
Publius, 29*n*7
Pulse of Politics, The (Barber), 143, 155–160

al-Qaida, 59, 524
Quality of Life Review, 389
Quayle, Dan, 282, 310, 393, 510, 514
Quirk, Paul, 143

Racicot, Marc, 319
Rakove, Jack, 195
Ramspeck Act (1940), 94, 331*n*19
Rather, Dan, 187
Raven Rock Mountain, 533*n*51
Rayburn, Sam, 331*n*18
Reagan, Ronald
    air traffic controllers strike, 97, 215
    and 1988 election, 174, 309
    and the "second constitution," 24–25
    approval ratings, 49, 221
    arms control negotiations, 113, 120
    as "Great Communicator," 217
    as party leader, 98, 296, 307–310

assassination attempt, 516
budget policy, 24, 112, 358–359
challenge of New Deal order, 97–98
Christian Right and, 275–277
conflict with liberal groups, 279–280
defense policy, 24
executive orders, 309
fundraising, 323
influence on George W. Bush, 228
institutional management, 44, 54
invasion of Grenada, 219–221
Iran-contra scandal, 54, 69–70, 120–121, 216, 309, 518
judicial nominations, 60–61, 443, 445, 447, 449–454
lack of coattails, 416
legal actions, 456, 471–472
legislative strategy, 122–123
management style, 111–113, 353–354
policymaking process, 119–121, 358–359
political mobilization, 244
presidential campaigns, 98, 275, 514
public image, 213–214, 216–221, 399*n*57
regulatory policy, 99, 309–310, 390–391, 470
relations with Congress, 13, 353–354, 391, 427
relations with executive branch, 55–56, 382
tax policy, 24, 98, 115–117, 354
team of advisers, 217–218
use of executive power, 469, 471–472, 478, 479
Realignments, 135, 413
Recess appointments, 469
Reconstruction, 87, 89, 102
Redistricting, 420
Reed, Ralph, 277
Reedy, George, 150
Refoundings, 72
Regan, Donald, 112, 119–120, 353–354, 356, 452
Regents of California v. Bakke (1978), 456
Regulatory review, 56, 389–394, 470–471
Rehnquist, William, 439, 450, 452
Rehnquist Court, 437
Reichley, A. James, 334*n*51
Religious Roundtable, 275
Reno, Janet, 226
Representation, 6–9, 17–21
Republican National Committee (RNC), 307, 319, 322
Republican National Convention, 87, 514
Republican Party, 79, 84–86, 170
    alliance with Christian right, 276–277
    dominance of judicial nominations, 436–439
    economic libertarianism, 419–420
    "southern strategy," 419
    under George W. Bush, 317–325

under Richard Nixon, 306–307
under Ronald Reagan, 307–310
Republican Party (of Jefferson and
    Madison), 77
Republic Steel Corporation, 273
Responsible party government, 405, 413, 424
Reuther, Walter, 274
Reynolds, William Bradford, 450
Rhetorical presidency, 25
Rice, Condoleezza, 128–129, 130, 139n63,
    350–351, 355, 524–526
Rich, Spencer, 251
Richardson, Bill, 361
Ricks, Thomas, 508n44
Ridge, Tom, 523
Ridgway, Matthew, 59
Riley, Richard, 454
Roberts, John, 435, 437, 444, 454, 459n2, 527
Robertson, Pat, 275
Rockefeller, John (Jay), 237, 241, 250, 479
Rockefeller, Nelson, 509–510, 512–513
Rockne, Knute, 217
Roe v. Wade (1973), 443, 451
Rohde, David, 422
Romer v. Evans (1996), 451
Romney, Mitt, 180
Roosevelt, Eleanor, 226
Roosevelt, Franklin
    address to Congress (1936), 278
    administrative reforms, 300–301, 363n5, 381,
        386, 468
    and the "second constitution," 24, 27–28
    approval ratings, 49
    as conservative revolutionary, 94–95, 102
    as party leader, 92–93, 296–301
    civil service reform, 300–301, 331n19
    communications strategy, 239, 299
    conflict with business groups, 277–279
    court packing plan, 92–93, 299, 442, 519
    death of, 511–512
    expansion of executive power, 89–95
    internment of Japanese Americans, 457, 480
    management style, 109–110, 342–343, 352
    New Deal program, 91–94
    organized labor and, 272–275
    presidential campaigns, 91, 93, 191n27, 278
    purge campaign, 92–93, 298–299, 331n14
    relations with Congress, 298
    relations with interest groups, 270
    relationship with vice presidents, 518–520
    staffing, 345, 468
    Supreme Court and, 441–442
    use of executive power, 475–480
    World War II, 69, 91, 94, 477–478, 493, 497

Roosevelt, Theodore, 102, 300, 518
    activism, 35
    leadership style, 28
    New Nationalism speech, 331n16
    on role of executive, 72–73, 90, 466
    Progressive Party candidacy, 311, 330n13
    relations with interest groups, 268
Rose Garden strategy, 26
Rossiter, Clinton, 84
Rostenkowski, Dan, 353–354
Rostow, Walt, 348
Rouse, Peter, 351, 356
Rove, Karl, 128–129, 232, 238, 253, 257, 318–319,
    321, 323, 338n92, 347, 355
Rowe, James, 304, 333n36, 333n41
Rudalevige, Andrew, 388
Rumsfeld, Donald, 53, 128, 131–132, 229, 232, 350,
    355, 504–505, 512, 527
Russert, Tim, 525

Sampling error, 66n26
Sampson, Kyle, 55
Scalia, Antonin, 437, 447, 451–452, 458
Schlesinger, Arthur, Jr., 109, 466, 509
Schlesinger, James, 117
Schmidt, Eric, 243
Schneider, William, 336n69
Schneiders, Greg, 356
Schurz, Carl, 88
Schwarzenegger, Arnold, 322
Schwarzkopf, Norman, 222, 504
Scopes trial, 275
Scowcroft, Brent, 350
Sebelius, Kathleen, 361
Second Bill of Rights, 95, 300, 331n15
Self-reliant management style, 109–111
Senate, 196, 204, 411, 436, 438, 516
Senate Judiciary Committee, 447
Senators, as presidential candidates, 176
Senior Executive Service (SES), 383–384,
    398n39
Separation of powers, 10–13, 14–17, 31n30, 373,
    394–395, 405
September 11 (2001) terrorist attacks, 27, 40, 48,
    59, 229, 320, 355, 478, 523
Serbia, 127, 478
Sesno, Frank, 38
Seventeenth Amendment, 28n1, 431n29
Seward, William H., 84, 85
Shays, Daniel, 4
Shinseki, Eric, 505
Shultz, George, 120, 218, 349
Sidey, Hugh, 143
Sierra Club, 280

Signing statements, 367–368, 471–473, 485*n*34
Silverstein, Mark, 453
Simpson, O.J., 38
Skowronek, Stephen, 71–72, 287, 325
Slavery, 80–82
Small states, 197–198
Smith, Al, 277–278
Smith, Caleb, 170
Smith, William French, 450
Social networking, 243–244
Social Security, 24, 95, 99, 139*n*61
Social Security Act (1935), 91, 92
Soft money, 315–316, 421
Solicitor general, 455
Somalia, 248
Sorenson, Theodore, 446
Souter, David, 436–437, 444, 449, 454, 515
Soviet Union, 47
Spanish-American War, 495–496
Speaker of the House, 422
Specter, Arlen, 453
Spellings, Margaret, 351
Spoils system, 77–78, 380
Staff, presidential, 341–363, 468
Stallone, Sylvester, 216
Stanton, Edwin, 86
Starr, Kenneth, 51, 63, 227, 316
Stassen, Harold, 361
Stein, Herbert, 116
Steinbruner, John, 120
Stephanopoulos, George, 468, 515
Stevens, John Paul, 436–437, 439, 458
Stevens, Ted, 473
Stevenson, Donald Grier, 441
Stewart, Jon, 232
Stewart, Potter, 439, 450
Stiles, Ezra, 145
Stockman, David, 112–113, 214, 217, 358–359
Stokes, Thomas, 299
Strategic Arms Limitation Treaty (SALT I), 518
Strategic competence, 114–123
Strategic Defense Initiative ("Star Wars"),
    24, 120
Summers, Lawrence, 133, 351
Sununu, John, 60, 338*n*92, 354, 356
Superdelegates, 184–185
Superfund amendments (1986), 391
Supply-side economics, 116
Supreme Court, 12, 86, 96, 435–459, 466, 481,
    486*n*39, 499
    campaign politics of, 441–444
    career background of justices, 439–441, 453
    conflicts with presidency, 456–459
    process for selecting nominees, 444–449

Republican influence on, 436–439
    rulings on detainees, 458–459
Swanson, Claude, 170
Swift Boat Veterans for Truth, 163

Taft, Robert, 95
Taft, William Howard, 71, 176, 298,
    445, 466
Taliban, 489
Taney, Roger, 80
Task Force on Regulatory Relief, 309, 390
Tax Reform Act (1986), 24, 117, 123, 354
Taylor, Zachary, 174, 438
Television, 201–202, 212
Tenet, George, 131
Terrorist Surveillance Program. *See*
    Wiretapping
Texas Rangers, 522
Thanksgiving Proclamation, 71
Third New Deal, 92
"Third way," 316
Thirteenth Amendment, 87–88
Thomas, Clarence, 437, 439, 454, 461*n*32
Thomason, Harry, 26
Thurmond, Strom, 207, 447
Tiananmen Square massacre, 216
Time magazine, 142–143, 221
Train v. City of New York (1975), 473
Truman, Harry, 52, 55, 266
    firing of General MacArthur, 58–59
    health care plan, 282–283
    national security policy, 101, 301–302, 498, 518
    public image, 36
    seizure of steel mills, 457, 475
    staffing, 347, 384
    succession to presidency, 511–512, 521
    use of executive power, 478
    withdrawal from re-election, 174
Tsongas, Paul, 182
Tulis, Jeffrey, 70, 145, 153–154
Twelfth Amendment, 28*n*1, 517
Twentieth Amendment, 28*n*1
Twenty-fifth Amendment, 175, 510, 517, 532*n*32
Twenty-second Amendment, 28*n*1, 94,
    431*n*28, 517
Tyler, John, 174, 516
Tyranny of the majority, 6

Uniform Code of Military Justice, 459
Unitary executive, 70–71, 323, 483, 529
United Mine Workers, 272–273
United Nations (UN) Charter, 498
Unit rule, 170, 172
USA Freedom Corps, 43

USS *Abraham Lincoln*, 40, 230–231
U.S. v. Nixon (1974), 457, 481
U.S. v. Curtiss-Wright (1936), 477

Van Buren, Martin, 77, 170, 175, 521
Vance, Cyrus, 67n46, 118, 349
Van Riper, Paul, 301
Veterans' benefits, 99
Veto power, 76, 102, 428–429
Vice presidents, 509–530
  as policy advisers, 512–515
  as potential successors, 520–521
  as presidential candidates, 175
  constitutional roles, 516–517, 531n13
  development of increased influence, 518–521
  selection of, 520
  staffing, 512–513
  statutory roles, 517–518
  tie-breaking votes, 517
Vietnam, South, 54
Vietnam War, 110, 171, 305, 478, 480,
  499–500, 503
Voting Rights Act (1965), 418–420, 455
Voting Technology Project (Caltech/MIT), 203

Wade-Davis bill (1864), 87, 88
Wagner, Robert, 273
Wagner Act (1935), 273
Walker, Jack, 293n63
Wallace, George, 207
Wallace, Henry, 93, 513, 519
Wallace, J. Clifford, 451
Warner, John, 453
War of 1812, 169, 494, 499
War on Poverty, 55
War on Terrorism, 73, 320–321, 324, 523–524
War Powers Resolution (1973), 467, 486n52,
  492, 498–499
Warren, Earl, 442
Warren, Rick, 257
Warren Court, 442
Washington, George, 69–71, 73, 144–145, 168,
  411, 445
  Farewell Address (1796), 412
Washington Post, 251, 255, 256
Watergate, 143, 150, 387, 456, 481
Watson, Marvin, 302, 303
Watt, James, 13, 280
Wayne, Stephen, 213
Weber, Max, 144
Webster, Daniel, 20
Webster v. Reproductive Health Services
  (1989), 443
Weinberger, Caspar, 113, 120, 218

Welfare reform, 58, 99–100, 282, 315
WESTLAW, 448
Weyrich, Paul, 276
Whig theory of government, 111
Whiskey Rebellion, 76
White, Byron, 439
White House Legislative Strategy Group, 119
White House Press Office, 42
White House Transition Project, 34
Whitewater, 240, 248
Whitman, Christine Todd, 286, 526
Wilderness Society, 280
Will, George, 134
Williams, Walter, 354
Willkie, Wendell, 171, 274
Wills, Garry, 24
Wilson, Graham, 289
Wilson, James, 10, 196–197, 465
Wilson, Woodrow, 178, 499–500, 518
  activism, 35
  as party leader, 329, 329n4
  judicial nominations, 445
  "Newtonian" and "Darwinian"
    government, 15
  on demagoguery and leadership, 21–23
  on role of executive, 90, 330n13
  political theory of, 2, 13–21, 297–298
  psychological character, 150
  relations with interest groups, 268–269
  theory of "interpretation," 18, 20–21
  view of Congress, 16–17, 19, 32n42
  view of Constitution, 14
  wartime leadership, 94, 478, 496, 502,
    507n21
Winner-take-all system, 192–193
Winter, Ralph, Jr., 451
Wiretapping, 76, 480, 524, 527
Wolfe, Christopher, 14
Wolfowitz, Paul, 131, 504–505
Women's suffrage movement, 269
Woodward, Bob, 524
Worcester v. Georgia (1832), 456
Works Progress Administration, 106n59
World Trade Center, 40
World War I, 268, 496
World War II, 91, 100, 497
Wrestling, professional, 212
Wright, Jim, 423

Yoo, John, 448, 524
Young, James Sterling, 71, 411
Youngstown Sheet and Tube Co. v. Sawyer
  (1952), 457
YouTube, 241–242